HISTORY OF
EAST AFRICA

HISTORY OF
EAST AFRICA

Edited by
VINCENT HARLOW
and
E. M. CHILVER
assisted by
ALISON SMITH

With an Introduction by
MARGERY PERHAM

VOLUME II

OXFORD
AT THE CLARENDON PRESS

Oxford University Press, Ely House, London W. 1

OXFORD LONDON GLASGOW NEW YORK
TORONTO MELBOURNE WELLINGTON CAPE TOWN
IBADAN NAIROBI DAR ES SALAAM LUSAKA ADDIS ABABA
KUALA LUMPUR SINGAPORE JAKARTA HONG KONG TOKYO
DELHI BOMBAY CALCUTTA MADRAS KARACHI

ISBN 0 19 822713 2

First published 1965
Reprinted 1968, 1976

Printed in Great Britain by
Lowe & Brydone Printers Limited, Thetford, Norfolk

PREFATORY NOTE

THE first of the three volumes of this History of East Africa, edited by Professor Roland Oliver and Dr. Gervase Mathew, was published in 1963. Readers of that volume will recall that the project (first mooted at an East African Governors' Conference in 1952) was planned on the initiative of the then governments of Tanganyika and Uganda and of the Colonial Science Research Council. Subsequently the Council obtained the consent of the Secretary of State for the Colonies to the use of Colonial Development and Welfare funds for the preparation of an history of East Africa which could be used in the East African universities and by students of African and imperial history elsewhere. This somewhat unusual use of funds was approved in the belief that aid to the emergent nations of East Africa which would make a contribution to the development of their own historical research and teaching could be ranked with aid of a more obviously practical nature. In making the arrangements for the editing and preparation of the History, the Secretary of State gave the editors complete control over the contents and choice of contributors and delegated the administration of the project to the University of Oxford Institute of Commonwealth Studies and Makerere University College. Contributors to the volume have had neither more nor less access to the public records of the United Kingdom or in East Africa than other scholars working in the same field.

Given the present stage of East African studies, there are inevitable gaps in this volume, to be filled in as locally based research expands. The most serious is the absence of a special chapter within the main body of the volume on the development of tenurial policy in East Africa, and in particular in Kenya. The editors, after much consideration, concluded that this subject, for long a highly controversial one, could not be adequately treated until monographs based on original research had been published. One such monograph has now been completed by Dr. Keith Sorrenson, who worked extensively on the papers of the Kenya Lands Office under the auspices of the East African

School of History and Archaeology. The editors also hope that
some of the scholarly work of the African Studies Branch in the
Colonial Office will be published. Meanwhile a brief survey by
Dr. Sorrenson of the legislative history of land tenure in Kenya
has been included in an Appendix as an aid to students making
their first approach to the topic. Those seeking to pursue it
further are referred to the lists of published material on the subject prepared by the African Studies Branch of the Colonial
Office, and particularly to the *Bibliography of Land Tenure in the
Colonies* (London, H.M.S.O., 1950). Details of these and other
relevant works will be found in the bibliography of this volume.

All the first and several of the second drafts of the chapters in
this volume had been received when its editor, Professor Vincent Harlow, died suddenly in November 1961. Inevitably the
work lacks the final editorial polish which he would have given
it. Besides editing this volume he had been, with Dr. Kenneth
Ingham, Dr. Gervase Mathew, Professor Roland Oliver, and
Miss Margery Perham, one of the animators of the whole
project. The final preparation of this volume for the press was
undertaken in the Oxford University Institute of Commonwealth Studies with Miss Perham's advice.

His successors would like to thank Dr. R. E. Robinson, Dr.
L. W. Hollingsworth, Dr. J. H. M. Beattie, Dr. Audrey Richards,
Mr. H. B. Thomas, and Professor Wilfred Whiteley for their
help at various stages; Miss Anne Brewin, Mrs. B. Clifton, Mrs.
C. Newbury, Mrs. M. Carr, Mr. J. Redfearn, and Miss M.
Potter for their work on the bibliography, index, and maps;
Mr. Bernard Cheeseman, Librarian of the combined Colonial
Office and Commonwealth Relations Office Library, for his
valuable help to contributors; the Colonial Office Research
Department (subsequently that of the Department of Technical
Co-operation and of the Ministry of Overseas Development) for
their ready understanding of the consequences of academic
freedom; and the staff of the Oxford Institute of Commonwealth
Studies, and especially its Librarian, for their co-operation and
encouragement throughout. They are grateful to the authorities
of Makerere University College for permission to base Map 9 on
an original drawn by Mr. J. K. Mbazira of the East African
Institute of Social Research; and to Her Majesty's Stationery

Office for permission to use the maps contained in *The East Africa Royal Commission 1953–1955 Report* as the basis for Map 8. Mr. C. Wrigley, who was a Leverhulme Research Fellow of the Institute of Commonwealth Studies at London University from 1954 to 1959, wishes to acknowledge his indebtedness to the Leverhulme Trust and to the Institute for making possible the studies on which Chapter V is based.

The spelling of African tribal names, &c., as in the first volume, follows—with a few exceptions in deference to more familiar forms—the practice of the International African Institute. Bantu prefixes of tribal names have been omitted.

CONTENTS

LIST OF ABBREVIATIONS

C.O.C.P.	Colonial Office Confidential Print
E.A. Agricultural Journal	*East African Agricultural Journal*
E.A. Standard	*East African Standard*
Eng. Hist. Rev.	*English Historical Review*
E.S.A.	Entebbe Secretariat Archives
F.O.C.P.	Foreign Office Confidential Print
H.C.	House of Commons
H.L.	House of Lords
J. Af. History	*Journal of African History*
M.P.A.	Mombasa Provincial Archives
P.P.	Parliamentary Papers
S.M.P.	Secretariat Minute Papers
Uganda J.	*Uganda Journal*
Z.R.A.	Zanzibar Residency Archives

LIST OF MAPS

INTRODUCTION

MARGERY PERHAM

T HE first volume of this series took the record of the East African territories as far back as archaeology, ethnology, and tribal tradition has hitherto been able to take it, and brought it up through the history of the nineteenth century to the time when European rule was imposed. The older students of the African record will be aware, as they read this and other contemporary works, that the present generation of historians are regarding the continent from a new angle. As the editors of Volume I say in their introduction, they have rejected a standpoint from which Africa was regarded as having no history but that of its European occupation, and instead are writing a history of Africa and not only that of its invaders.

The most practical reason for this change of viewpoint is that, through the recent and co-operative researches of a number of students from different disciplines, light is now playing over what was for long regarded as the almost impenetrable darkness of Africa's past. With this new possibility has come a new need in that very suddenly, in the last few years, most of tropical Africa has become independent of Europe. This has occurred at much the same time as a numerous western-educated minority has become fully literate in English or French and has become deeply interested in Africa's past as a basis for Africa's future. The political and the intellectual developments are, of course, closely connected. A third, less easily definable factor has influenced the Africans' attitude. Their presumed lack of any known history was formerly regarded as being one of the results of the innate inferiority of the Negro race, and the general concept of the darkness of the continent, and the darkness of the skins of its inhabitants, was extended to the condition of their minds. In a natural reaction against this attitude Africans, even more than other peoples who have achieved their independence from alien rule, desire to see their history re-written, or rather, for the first time fully written. They rightly see this history as part of the basis of their self-respect and self-identification, both as a race and also as members of the new nations which are struggling to find internal unity and external status.

The editors of the first volume, aware of all this, recognize that the time is coming when the majority of those who read this history will be East Africans. In their introduction they write that these readers may come to regard 'the colonial period in retrospect as an episode, albeit a most important episode, in the history of their own countries'. Even in that period the Africans were, they say, primarily interested in what colonial policy has done to *them*.[1]

I have referred to the editorial views expressed in the first volume for two reasons. Firstly, as it will be possible to buy separately each of the volumes which form this *History*, there may be readers who, greatly to their own loss, will take up this second volume without having read the first. But at least they can be informed here of a basic concept with which this work was begun. Secondly, they may not realize that this intention to view African history from Africa has influenced the plan of the present volume in that its chapters deal with events in each territory taken separately, and not with the general politics and problems of the colonial powers or the organization through which they exercised their rule. The emphasis was planned to be upon the effects of European government and influence upon the peoples and their reactions. It has not been easy to carry out this intention because the evidence for African reactions in this period is fragmentary. The vast bulk of the records of the period covered in this volume, always increasing with the years, was written by white men for white men mainly about the actions of white men; the ideas, the policies, the laws, the administrative, economic, and social measures which these men imposed, and to which black and, indeed, brown men—Arabs and Asians—in varying degrees, responded. For most of the period covered by this book Africans, outside the exceptional state of Buganda, wrote little that has found its way into print and said little that is recorded elsewhere than in the files of government, especially of local government. For the most part, during the first ten or twenty years after annexation, they carried on their tribal existence much as before; and as European influence and

[1] See vol. i of this *History*, introduction, p. i.

government increasingly and unevenly impinged upon their lives, the effects must be judged largely by evidence of their actions, or lack of action, as described in this book. Some studies were made of tribal life, but few of these before the middle 1930's dealt with the effects of European influence on that life. It may still be possible to supplement the evidence by recording verbally the ideas of Africans of middle age, but the chance to do this for the oldest generation, who felt the earlier impact of the European entry, is rapidly passing.

This volume and the following one cover the period of European rule from the 1890's to about 1960, roughly seventy years. This volume ends with the conclusion of the second world war in 1945. The period it covers falls into two parts. The first, up to the end of the first world war, is the period of exploration developing into full occupation, of the imposition from above, in somewhat tentative and experimental form, of the basis for unified administrations and economies. The second period, from the end of the first world war to 1945, is one of more purposeful and comprehensive action by the colonial governments. Although it saw increasingly strong economic and educational influences from the outside world, these still came mainly through the ruling nation. During both parts of this period, after a few early and usually very local acts of resistance and rebellion in all the territories, the African peoples were outwardly acquiescent and politically passive and, as the natural complement of this, the governments were essentially authoritarian. The year 1945, with which this volume ends, is a significant date because the war had deep political effects, not only upon Africa but, even more, upon the world which was now impinging upon Africa. The fifteen years which followed 1945 are marked by the growth at an increasing, if territorially uneven pace, of that African political consciousness and assertion which were to lead in the early 1960's to the wholly new era of independence.

It will be seen from this review of the span of the *History* that, in spite of the editorial policy, it has been necessary to devote two out of three volumes to the colonial period. As the independent African nations make their own histories the years of the colonial period will shrink to their increasingly small

proportion of the whole. But their historical significance can hardly
diminish. The East African coast had been open to contacts from
the outer world from the earliest days in which ships began to
emerge from the Red Sea or the Persian Gulf, or find their way
across the Indian Ocean. But the direct contacts for the peoples
of eastern and central Africa who lived behind the coast, before
those brought by the Europeans, had been those of the Arabs,
brief, local, and, through the hunt for slaves and ivory, largely
destructive. European occupation was, therefore, by far the most
important single event which up to that time had befallen the
peoples of the eastern interior. It opened their long-secluded
regions to a far more rapid and ordered relationship with the
rest of the world, and especially with Europe, than any diffused
and unorganized contacts could have achieved. On the mainland the occupying powers enclosed the many disparate tribes
within three large new areas of centralized administration.
They built the costly railways and roads which alone could
break down the isolation of life and alleviate its poverty by
linking the tribal to the new territorial and world economies,
and they fostered the introduction of powerful new ideas, both
religious and political. For the Africans there was certainly a
price to pay. This cost is more difficult to assess than the obvious
gains from all these powerfully imposed changes. It has to be
reckoned in terms of social dislocation and individual humilia-
tion as the virtues of tribal life were impaired or destroyed by
those who could not, at the time, understand the material upon
which they were working with such powerful hands. Perhaps it
is only with our recent experience of the force of African assertion and rejection of European power that we can measure the
depth of the long-unseen social and psychological injuries which
accompanied its obvious benefits. Some intimate evidence of the
nature of these injuries comes from West Africa in the story
appropriately entitled *Things Fall Apart*.[1]

All the chapters in this book deal with the four territories
separately. The most useful contribution that can be made in a
general introduction is therefore to look at the region as a whole
and try to answer two questions. How far did any general

---

[1] Chinua Achebe, *Things Fall Apart* (London, 1958).

policy lie behind the activities described in the chapters? By what means was it enacted? Clearly, within the limits of an introduction, these large inquiries can be handled only in the most general terms. But at least we can remind ourselves that though the metropolitan side of the colonial scene has been, in the main, excluded from the body of this work, it was from here in this period that nearly all that was done in East Africa drew its ultimate origin and sanction. To shorten and simplify the theme I shall have little to say on the relatively brief existence of German East Africa. Zanzibar, too, is somewhat peripheral to Britain's mainland responsibilities, as Dr. Flint's chapter clearly shows, by virtue of its small size, its island position, its full accessibility to Asian and, later, to European contacts, and its entrenched Arab sultanate and ruling class. True, as we can learn from the preceding volume, its power and influence had been extended over the African coast and had reached, however tenuously, far into the interior, but with European influence the links were largely cut.

The nature of a given colonial administration is derived from the character of three elements brought into conjunction, that of the physical setting, of the subject people and of the ruling power. So much has been said in Volume I of the first two that the briefest reminder will suffice here. We were shown that East Africa, before European occupation, was no more a geographical than it was a political entity. Geographically it is an area of dramatic contrasts, a region of vast rifts, huge massifs, and high single mountains, with a wealth of great lakes but few rivers, especially navigable ones. Its large range of altitudes produces variations in rainfall and temperature and this results in surfaces equally various in their covering of grass, bush, forest, swamp, desert sand, and even snow. Within each of the single areas into which the region was divided most of these contrasting conditions can be found, particularly in Kenya. For the newly arrived rulers the physical aspect of East Africa might be scenically attractive, but it presented difficulties of preliminary access and of later development. For all its beauties and its fertile areas—particularly in the lacustrine west—East Africa is a very poor region. This was the first impression made upon the British public by the reports of the travellers who forced their way inland from the coast, especially in the future

Kenya. Indeed, even after some sixty years of European-controlled development, the highly qualified observers who formed the East Africa Royal Commission of 1953–5 could report that 'one of the most vivid impressions which we have formed as a result of our enquiry is the fundamental poverty which prevails in the East African territories'.[1] They described the physical setting as 'a harsh environment' and a 'discouraging background',[2] almost empty of minerals, and pointed out that in 1955, even when the considerable contributions of the immigrant groups were included, 'the per capita net product is among the lowest of all the territories in Africa south of the Sahara for which there is adequate data'.[3]

Turning to the peoples inhabiting this area, which is more than three times the size of France, we find a population which is estimated today to number some 25 million. These tribes show wide differences of custom—some belong to the Bantu language group: others have been classified as Nilotic or Nilo-Hamitic. There is a tendency, by no means universal or unchangeable, for the two latter groups to inhabit the drier lands, to be more pastoral than agricultural and, therefore, less dense in their distribution and less closely affected by European influences, official and unofficial. Tribal distinctions remain a divisive force and have played a large part in the grouping of parties during the movement towards independence in Kenya. The divisions among the Africans and the isolation and poverty of most of them, compared to the peoples of the West Africa coastlands, made them easier to dominate but less easy to administer.

The first need of the new European governments, as it was of the chartered companies which laid some patchy and inadequate foundations for the national administrations, was for advance agents possessing initiative, physical endurance, and courage. These qualities, in face of the early conditions, could easily harden into ruthlessness, a deterioration which was more marked in the German than in the British sphere. In immense and still largely unexplored regions, without roads or railways, or later with a single line and a few seasonal tracks, the first generation of administrative officers had to find their way into

[1] *Report of the East Africa Royal Commission, 1953–1955*, Cmd. 9475 (1955), p. 40.
[2] Ibid., p. 10.
[3] Ibid., p. 28.

and around their new districts on foot, or, sometimes, on bicycle, following the winding paths trodden by the bare feet of the local villagers, their supplies carried on the backs of a score or so of porters, generally unwilling recruits for an unpopular service. Even in the early 1930's, when I first travelled over much of East Africa and when the Ford lorry had revolutionized district touring, there were still considerable parts of East Africa which could be reached only on foot and where the periodic advent of a white official was an event which caused excitement and some apprehension.

The physical character of East Africa may thus be counted a deterrent to the rapid imposition by the new rulers of a uniform system of administration. The human situation reinforced these physical obstacles. The explorers, the missionaries, and the two companies had undertaken the preliminary work of penetration and occupation. But, as more than one chapter of the first volume shows, there remained much to be done before a really effective contact could be made with the new subjects. Language presented an initial barrier. True, Swahili had spread from the coast up the routes traced by the Arabs in what was now German East Africa, but it was as yet very far from being a lingua franca and was even less widely known in Uganda and in Kenya away from the coast. Behind the initial language barrier lay further obstacles. The large number of tribes meant a great variety of custom and of differences in the degree and kind of tribal organization. In his list of East Africa's 101 tribes Mr. Huntingford writes that 45 of these had no chiefs, 47 had district chiefs, and only 9 had central chiefs.[1] In German East Africa and in Uganda there was the whole range of variety from the very small-scale cellular structure of clans held together by the simplest of gerontocratic authority, through intermediate groups of larger size and of more complex organization, to those societies on the west of Lake Victoria, among which Buganda was pre-eminent, which Europeans could call kingdoms. In Kenya the human pattern was less variegated, but perhaps even more intractable to the first British officials, in that there were no larger units, and—with the single rather dubious exception of Mumia—no chiefs. With nothing above the small lineage groups, with their by no means simple diffusion of

[1] See vol. i of this *History*, p. 91.

functions, there was no authority of the kind which elsewhere could provide ready-made executive intermediaries between the new government and the people.

In these circumstances, and remembering that the new rulers believed they had both the need and the right to make a rapid enforcement of their authority, it is perhaps surprising that there was so little overt resistance to its imposition. The most notable incidents of defiance were in German East Africa among the Hehe group and the tribes which joined in the Maji-Maji rebellion. The severe methods of repression employed by the Germans, and directed in the same period against the Hereros of South-West Africa, gave them a notably bad reputation as colonial rulers; but the scandals also led to great concern in Germany and to a period of reform which was interrupted in 1914 by war. On the British side the authors of the relevant chapters in this book rightly draw attention not only to the trouble with Bunyoro and the prolonged contumacy of the Nandi, but also to the fairly widespread use of small, so-called punitive expeditions which marked the extension of British authority in Kenya and Uganda, and which are too often taken for granted in the record. In Zanzibar British annexation came as a culmination of long and close contact. Its main benefit was to the large slave population which was now able to graduate into freedom. As with the Nigerian emirates, and in contrast with the more integrated states of Ashanti or Basutoland, the Zanzibar rulers had no solid population to support them in defiance of the white intruders, and two acts of resistance, in 1895 and 1896, were put down easily, the second with the indiscriminate punishment of a naval bombardment.[1]

There was nothing uniform about the incidents of East African resistance. More work could be done to analyse the impulses behind them, as there is always much to be learned from the few overt acts of native protest. Even without deeper analysis it is possible to distinguish the initial and almost reflex reaction of free clans against a new and alien control from the larger and more organized resistance of chiefs such as Kabarega and Mwanga. It is to be noted that the serious Maji-Maji rebellion was carried out by Africans after they had had some years of experience of white man's rule. The British were to

[1] See Chapter XIII, pp. 645–6, below.

have no comparable experience in East Africa until the Kikuyu outbreak of the 1950's.

It is important to remember the gradualism enforced upon European governments in this first period of their rule by these physical and human conditions. There is today a large output of books about contemporary Africa, many of them written in a very natural reaction against the past complacencies of imperialism. But there are few detailed studies of the first two or three decades of the European period, especially of administration, which is always harder to record and to understand than the central constitutional and political themes. One result of this concentration is that the whole period of colonial rule over the interior lands of tropical Africa is assumed to be all of one texture. The ruling powers are therefore accused of deliberate delay or culpable lethargy in not making an earlier and more vigorous start with the services which are now seen to be those most needed for the rapid building of African nation-states; a culmination which was not, of course, even envisaged in the first decades of colonial rule. There is no doubt that even by the standards of the time, and not those of eager nationalists looking backward, the British and the German governments were slow to estimate the size and character of their task, especially in terms of human relationships and social needs. It is not easy to find any generally acceptable standards, whether administrative or moral, to apply to the first stages of colonial rule. It is probable, however, that the more severe contemporary charges on this account will assume more realistic proportions when the conditions of at least the first years of the period of European rule are closely studied. This is an aspect to which I must return later.

With this brief reminder of the physical and human situation which helped to determine the character of European government, especially at the outset of its rule, and which is fully examined in Volume I, we must turn our attention more towards Europe, focusing it upon the ideas and methods of the colonial power. This is a history of East Africa, but of East Africa under European, mainly British, colonial rule. An undue concentration on the African scene might give the impression that we are observing the action of outstretched hands, while those parts of the body which contain the head and heart directing those hands remain in obscurity.

It has been rightly remarked that the nations whose competition over the partition of Africa seemed to bring them at times almost to the edge of war showed for many years strangely little interest in their new possessions once they had been acquired.[1] The partition occurred at a time of great international tension due to an intensification of the historic Anglo-French rivalry and to the sudden thrust of Germany into the rank of a great power. In the diplomatic struggle the colonies for the most part had been little more than counters in an international game in which the real stakes were national strategic interests, prestige, and security. This lack of any conscious ready-made British plan for making use of the East African acquisition was the result of the mixed and largely negative motives which converged to impel British cabinets—for both political parties were successively involved—along the road to annexation. They were urged not to allow the slave trade to continue, not to allow Buganda to fall back into the chaos of civil war, and, hence, not to sacrifice the brave missionary effort in that remote kingdom. There was a period of hesitation and, within Gladstone's last and Rosebery's first Ministry, of dissension. The new, or renewed, imperial impulse could be detected in the campaign for the retention of Uganda, and it was certainly present in Rosebery, under whom the decisive move was made. But the archives reveal the important part played by another negative motive which arose from the strategic interest created for Britain by the cutting of the Suez Canal. This was the desire not to allow any other power to gain control over the headwaters of Egypt's Nile or over that part of the East African littoral which gave access to it and flanked the route to India.[2]

None of these motives gave British governments any very clear lead as to how to deal with East Africa. The contrast with West Africa in this matter is illuminating. It is true that Britain had there the same negative impulse to suppress the slave trade,

[1] R. Oliver and J. D. Fage, *A Short History of Africa* (Harmondsworth, 1962), p. 196.

[2] For discussions of the Uganda issue and the motives for retention, see R. E. Robinson and J. Gallagher, *Africa and the Victorians* (London, 1961), ch. xi; and M. Perham, *Lugard*, vol. i, *The Years of Adventure, 1858–1898* (London, 1956), chs. xx, xxi.

which had once been the main attraction for her of that coast, and had felt the same spur of international competition in annexation. But during some centuries she had gained a knowledge of the coast, and had already in the 1890's a thriving two-way trade with sophisticated native traders which deeper occupation of the fertile coastlands would certainly increase. By contrast, eastern Africa was a largely unknown and certainly a commercially unpromising asset, the grudgingly adopted black baby of Tenniel's famous cartoon.

A policy, however, had to be made, or at least developed, for dealing with the new protectorates. The question arises as to how colonial policy is made in Britain. How, indeed, is any national policy made? There is a tendency in the mind of the public and, perhaps sometimes even in that of historians, to regard policy as being planned by governments and then carried out continuously for a period of years. In so far as, in the broadest sense, this is true of Britain's domestic affairs, it arises from certain basic characteristics of the nation and from the long-term needs which politicians must try to meet. Thus the shifting projects by which needs are met by ministers, themselves shifting at intervals in party and frequently in composition, can be shown to have a deeper, if often almost unconscious, purpose and direction. But this is not true of colonial policy, least of all in that early experimental stage which filled most of the years covered in this volume.

To appreciate this it is necessary to compare the making and execution of policy in Britain with the comparable process in the colonies. According to the theory of our democratic system in Britain, and to a large extent in practice, the ultimate initiative and control of policy lies with the British people acting indirectly through the medium of parliamentary elections. The popular impulse is carried to the House of Commons by the members and communicated through the majority to the Prime Minister and his Cabinet, who express the national will in their general conduct of affairs and through legislation. Individual ministers as heads of departments, acting through their staffs of civil servants, form the medium through which legislation and administration comes back to act upon the nation, which can, in theory, and in a rough and ready way in practice, pass judgement in the next general election.

I have referred to what will be well known to readers in order to emphasize the contrast between home and colonial politics. For in the sphere of colonial affairs, especially in earlier years, this theory was doubly at odds with practice. The circular action of national opinion into government and of government back again upon the nation was broken. Something more like a linear movement of opinion and action took its place, beginning in Britain and ending in the colonies.

The British electorate was not capable of providing the source of policy even to the limited extent that it could do so in home affairs. It was little qualified to understand the needs of the colonial peoples. There were in this period not only some hundreds of millions of Indians but also about 70 million colonial subjects in some forty territories; and these were situated in every hemisphere and covered a wide spectrum both of type and size. It may be true, as the Germans often pointed out, that in India and elsewhere Britain had gained an experience of imperial responsibility which the Germans had lacked. But tropical Africa presented novel problems of government. It contained the largest group of comparable British dependencies, but there were important contrasts between these, and there was much about them in the early years of this century which was still obscure. Outside an informed minority, made up of groups moved by different interests, humanitarian, scientific, or commercial, there was unavoidably an ignorance that was near to indifference, and this situation inevitably found some reflection in the House of Commons. The Lords generally had a small number of experts in this field, but the experience of these senior men sometimes belonged to yesterday rather than today. Few M.P.s in the first quarter of this century had personal knowledge of the colonies. Their political reputation and their electoral fate did not depend upon the contributions they made to colonial issues. During most of the period under review there were few general debates in the Commons on colonial affairs. There would be a wide-ranging, inconclusive discussion of colonial affairs in the House, sitting in Committee of Supply, when the colonial estimates were debated. To attract parliamentary and public attention colonies needed to provide some crisis, some outbreak of disorder or become entangled in some issue of foreign relations. In East Africa it was Kenya which, owing to the deep conflict of principles raised by the recurrent controversies over the interests and ambitions of the white settlers, attracted most debates. Here, it is true, a long-existing chord of opinion was struck. The conflict between the rights of native people and British colonists had begun, for the British Empire, in the North American states and had become an important issue of policy in South Africa and New Zealand. But this issue did not begin to create widespread interest in its East African form until the early 1920's. Even then it was easier for humanitarians to urge what ought not to be done than to provide positive guidance.

If the electorate could not easily originate a colonial policy, neither, of course, could it register the effects of policy expressed in administration. Nor, during most of this period, was this possible for the colonial peoples, especially in East Africa. The British people were governing unrepresented subjects: democracy was here acting as an autocracy. These subjects, moreover, were far away from the policy-making centre and until towards the end of our period, most of them had neither the political experience nor the machinery which would have allowed them to express their views. Political silence during our period in East Africa was not, however, wholly unbroken. This volume will record some of the lively dialogue on both economic and political issues which could be heard in Buganda, while from the 1920's the Kikuyu were beginning to feel their way towards political organization in order to voice their discontents. But whereas in West Africa there had been first some nominated and, by 1925 in the Gold Coast (now Ghana), a minority of elected members in the colonial legislative councils, it was not until 1944 that the first African member was nominated to the Kenya Legislative Council, an event followed the next year by the first nominations in Tanganyika and Uganda.

The result of this lack both of colonial assertion and of parliamentary and public knowledge of the affairs of his department was to leave the Colonial Secretary with an initiative much wider than that of other ministers. But even he could not steadily encompass in his mind the immense range of affairs for which he was responsible. It must be remembered, moreover, that until 1925 the affairs of the old settled dominions as well as those of the colonies were all under the Colonial Office, though

from 1907 there had been a Dominions Department in the
Office. It was not until 1925 that the Dominions Office hived off
as a new department and for a few years it remained under one
Secretary of State. It might have been thought, in view of the
peculiar difficulties of the Colonial Secretary, that prime ministers would have selected for the post men of the highest ability
and ensured for them the maximum possible continuity of office.
Yet we find that in the thirty-six years before 1945 the office
changed hands twenty-two times. It was held by some men of
high merit and devotion to their task, among whom Mr. Amery
was perhaps the most outstanding; but none, after Joseph
Chamberlain's tenure from 1895 to 1903, rivalled him in
ability, in political status in the Cabinet, or in the number of his
years in office. There were times in our period, and again after
it, when the post was clearly used as a stop-gap. In the later part
of our period, however, colonial secretaries made increasing use
of travel to gain first-hand impressions of their problems. Mr.
Amery, himself a great traveller, left on record an impressive
account of the problems that faced him both from the colonies
and the Commonwealth.[1]

The special difficulties of integrating colonial affairs into the
ordinary mechanism of political action threw an unusual responsibility on the permanent officials of the Colonial Office.
During the period in which the colonial secretaryship changed
hands twenty-two times, the shifting ministers would be confronted by a permanent under-secretary whose office had been
held by only eight tenants.[2] Under the Permanent Secretary
was a body of officials (including all ranks) increasing in number from 125 in 1909 to 187 in 1919 and 431 in 1925.[3] Most of
the senior officials spent their working lives accumulating knowledge of at least those sections of colonial affairs which belonged
to their part of the Office. But, high-minded and intelligent
though these senior officials might be, they were not the men
to popularize colonial issues outside their own department by
promoting publicity and information. They were, moreover, a

[1] L. S. Amery, *My Political Life*, vol. ii (London, 1953), chs. xiii, xiv, xv.
[2] C. Parkinson, *The Colonial Office from Within, 1909–1945* (London, 1947), p. 17.
This book by the man who was Permanent Under-Secretary from 1937 to 1942
gives an interesting picture of the growth of the Colonial Office during the first
half of this century.
[3] *Cambridge History of the British Empire*, iii (Cambridge, 1959), 762.

body imbued with a very strong tradition which had been built up very largely in the atmosphere of the anti-slavery movement of the early nineteenth century and under the influence of their greatest permanent Colonial Under-Secretary, Sir James Stephen, who held the post from 1836 to 1847. It is probable that a liberal and humanitarian secretary of state would find more ready co-operation from his staff than one who was more ready to subordinate native interests to economic or political considerations.

The difficulty experienced by all colonial secretaries but those few who possessed outstanding knowledge, devotion and energy, in mentally encompassing the immense range of their responsibilities, put the officials of their department, in their turn, into an abnormal position. Their position was unusual to begin with in that they did not *administer* the colonies in the sense in which, for example, the Home Office administered Britain. Colonial secretaries often pointed this out when pressed for detailed answers to parliamentary questions. Each colony had its own administration, at which we must look in a moment. It is true that governors sometimes grumbled that the Office *was* interfering in administration, and the provisions relating to finance and appointments in the Colonial Regulations did provide for something rather closer to administration than control. But the more serious question was whether the staff of the Colonial Office invaded the policy-making sphere forbidden to them by the theory of the constitution. They had certainly been accused of this earlier by the so-called Colonial Reformers of the 1830's who cruelly attacked Sir James Stephen as 'Mr. Over-Secretary Stephen', and they ridiculed as 'Mr. Mother Country' the insignificant anonymous officials who, they asserted, wielded the real power over the colonies.

In our period it is easier to raise this issue than to answer it. The archives of the period which are open to inspection certainly show for the African colonies that the officials wielded great influence and that they developed settled ways of dealing with certain issues from which most colonial secretaries would find it hard to depart. Yet in this they were doing no more than fill up that part of the vacuum in policy-making created by the peculiar position of colonial affairs in British public life. There was a time early in the nineteenth century when a colonial secretary might attempt personally to authorize all but the most unimportant communications which left his department. His growing responsibilities in this century can be indicated by the increase in the number of dispatches during our period. In 1909 there were 107,044 and in 1939, 300,841.[1] For telegrams the figure of 2,536 for 1907 had risen to 17,237 in 1915.[2] While many of these telegrams dealt with minor routine matters at the bottom and only a few with major issues of policy at the top, there must have been a vast intermediate range of communications of great importance to the recipient colony, of which the Secretary of State, over whose signature every missive was sent, could not even have been aware. And telegrams often impinged more effectively upon a governor's activities than dispatches.

Fortunately, in handling its growing responsibilities, the Office did not remain a small or insulated department. The accelerating rate in the increase of staff was largely due to the immense growth in the demands of Africa. This growth was due mainly to three parallel developments. The first was an increasing grasp both at home and abroad of the real nature of tropical and especially of African needs and problems. The second was the growth of scientific and other knowledge in Britain applicable to these problems. Thirdly, there was an expanding concept of the functions of the state which accelerated the processes of bringing this growing knowledge to bear upon the newly understood needs. The effects upon the Colonial Office of this complex development can be only briefly indicated here.

One result was the need for much more effective contact between the Colonial Office and other departments of state, and an inter-connecting system of inter-departmental committees was developed. The structure of the Office itself was changed. The original and enduring basis of its organization was found in the geographical departments. These dealt solely and comprehensively with all the affairs of a given region. In 1935, to take a middle year of our period, there were seven of these. One, the East Africa Department, was concerned with Kenya, Uganda, and Zanzibar, while the Tanganyika Department included Nyasaland, Northern Rhodesia, and, rather surprisingly,

---

[1] Parkinson, op. cit., p. 53.
[2] *Cambridge History of the British Empire*, iii. 764.

Somaliland. The years of our period saw a great growth in the number of the general departments. In 1925 there was only one which dealt with all the miscellaneous affairs that could not be attached to one region. By 1945 the General Department had expanded to include a number of strange new activities, including social services, labour, education, public relations, research, and, to deal with the increasing number of colonial students in Britain, welfare. A large and important economic and financial division had developed with departments for commercial relations and supplies, finance and development, and production. To deal with the promotion, control, recruitment, and training of the immensely increased numbers of the Colonial Service, a personnel division with four departments had been developed.

The addition of the general to the geographical departments marked an immense change in the size and the nature of the duties of the Office. It also represented in an acute form the almost insoluble administrative problem of correlating the particular with the general, the regional with the functional. The geographical departments were the real core of the Office in that they dealt with the transactions arising from the political and administrative relationship between colony and metropolis.[1] The general departments dealt with the colonial aspect of what were universal problems. As such they could be effective only in so far as they were in a vital relationship with the sources of current metropolitan thought and action in these spheres. The Office therefore built up a series of advisory committees and scientific bureaux, beginning with medicine in 1909. Others were added, almost year by year. In 1923 an Advisory Committee on Native Education in Tropical Africa was set up with a very distinguished initial membership. In 1928 this committee was renewed and given the whole colonial empire for its field. The number of committees and advisory bodies gradually extended until by 1946 there were eighteen of them. Through these the Office drew upon the experience of the nation in all the increasing aspects of life in the colonies which it added to its responsibilities. It was a two-way traffic of ideas, since service on the committees, as I can testify from experience upon two of them, educated the members in the realities of colonial

[1] C. Jeffries, *The Colonial Office* (London, 1956), pp. 45 sqq.

problems, and thus spread knowledge of the colonial empire widely in the professional worlds of the ruling nation.

With advisory committees there was also an expansion of advisers on the colonial staff. These had no executive duties and spent much of their time touring the colonies, communicating advice, new ideas, and encouragement from Britain, and bringing back information, requests, and, perhaps, complaints.

The picture would not be complete if behind the first circle of committees and advisers we did not visualize a still larger outer ring of semi-official bodies more or less linked with the Colonial Office and dealing with nursing, tropical medicine, mycology, entomology, forestry, botany, cotton-growing, currency, civil aviation, and many other technical questions. Behind these bodies and institutions was a still further group of more un-official, or even wholly voluntary bodies, such as the Royal Botanic Gardens at Kew, the Royal Empire Society, the Royal African Society, the International African Institute, the Victoria League, and a number of offices dealing with the affairs of individual colonies. With all these the Office would have many official and unofficial links. Thus, even beyond the range of the advisory committees, an ever-increasing body of knowledge in Britain was being brought to bear upon the problems of the colonies. When the writers in this book refer to the measures taken to deal with the enemies that wage war in the tropics against the health of men, animals, and plants, or to those employed to foster new production, this expert back-room work in Britain, ever expanding in scope and deepening in grasp, should be remembered.

The single, over-worked figure of the Colonial Secretary might therefore be visualized in his famous room in the old Colonial Office, looking out towards his forty scattered territories and their 60 to 70 million inhabitants. He would be flanked by his parliamentary and permanent under-secretaries and behind them, fanning outwards in a widening pattern according to their degree of responsibility, the Colonial Office staff, committees, and other institutions which have been mentioned here.

From this Office the connecting line of control and policy reached out to each colony, on the other side of the water, where we should picture another single figure, facing towards him, the colonial Governor; and behind him would fan out his staff, large or small, but always growing, through which he in turn conducted his administration. To follow up the links between Britain and East Africa it is therefore necessary at this stage to cross the ocean, all the 15,000 sea-miles that lay between London and East Africa. In the years before the telegraph radiated from colonial headquarters, and later before it was thought proper to make constant use of this luxury, and long before an air mail cut almost straight across the sky, it was sea-miles which counted in dividing colony from metropolis.

The Governor was an official of greater autonomy in the British than in any other modern colonial empire. There were several reasons for this. One was the inheritance from the American colonial period with its necessarily large delegation to governors who were then the inaccessible, indeed, almost the only direct representatives of the Crown. In this last tradition lay another reason for the Governor's stature. In our period the Crown acted, of course, only upon the advice of ministers and yet, by the drawing of his powers from the old prerogative instruments of his Commission and Royal instructions, by his absolute prerogative of mercy, by the ceremonious etiquette which emphasized his high eminence in a colonial society, some of the mystique of delegated royalty clung to the Governor.

The actual range of power wielded by the man who came to East Africa varied according to time and place even within our period. The Crown Colony system provided him with an Executive Council formed of senior officials. Its proceedings were confidential but only a very weak governor was likely to depend upon such a body for guidance in the larger political and administrative issues. The addition of elected unofficials to the Executive Council in Kenya was a major change and one difficult to justify on strict constitutional grounds. The legislative councils in Tanganyika and Uganda were very anaemic institutions in our period, Kenya being the exception as Chapter VI abundantly illustrates. It is true that, in the economic field, where governors were seldom highly qualified, they had to pay attention to the wishes of those who could bring to their poor territories much-needed capital and enterprise. But there was one sphere in which, even in Kenya, the Governor at this time had almost unfettered initiative and control. While he was strictly bound by the Colonial Regulations in the handling of financial matters and in the ordering of the Colonial Service, his instructions left open to him that wide field of administration which most affected the African population.

This situation, which accounts for both positive and negative results of administration in East Africa, and, of course, elsewhere, and especially for the discontinuity of policy in the central sphere of government, demands some further probing. The vacuum which the Governor filled resulted not only from the passivity of most of the peoples annexed to the empire but also from the fact that in this period the Colonial Office rarely promulgated general principles about the form for the structure of that part of government which chiefly affected the native population. This inactivity was due, especially in early years, to the unavoidable ignorance of the officials in Downing Street and their valid sense of the great variety of colonial conditions. But as time went on and knowledge accumulated there was still little sign in this sphere of any guidance to governors. A newly appointed Governor of Uganda told me that, after making a first review of the difficulties inherent in the treaty status of Buganda, he wrote to the Colonial Office asking for advice and precedents in dealing with similar situations. He never received an answer. It has often been remarked about governors, or, indeed, by them, that while they could not write off more than a few pounds of a clerk's defalcation, or dismiss an unsatisfactory junior officer still on probation, they could initiate very large changes in the administrative structure of their colony according to their own principles—or prejudices. One reason is that, for all the development of general departments in the Colonial Office, there was never one that dealt with central issues of administration. This is, perhaps, understandable. This was too vital and confidential a matter for an unofficial committee. But there was not, on an official basis, anything approaching a general staff to work out guiding principles in the sphere of government in order to provide some degree of common purpose, and common principles, even within a region of at least comparable situations such as West or East Africa. It was partly for this reason that from time to time the project of a special department to deal with tropical Africa was put forward.

Responsibility in developing the sphere of African administration, which lay outside the central structure of government, therefore rested firmly with the Governor. It is an interesting question whether this absence of central guidance here is to be regretted. The permanent officials, especially in the all-important years preceding the second world war, would have found it difficult, even if they had been organized for this purpose, to give directions which, while related to existing realities, were also just ahead of them in constructive purpose. It is characteristic of British public life to decentralize, to take great trouble in selecting the right men and then to trust them. This practice could certainly be seen in an advanced form in the relations between governors and the Colonial Office. Thus a Lugard and a Guggisberg were free to guide territories into a direction chosen very largely by themselves. Sir Edward Grigg—though here there was a closer alliance with the Secretary of State— almost succeeded in changing the course of Kenya's development. A Cameron, whom one of his closest associates called 'a human bombshell', could force through his own all-embracing plan of indirect administration with the urgent fervour of a revivalist. But he could also sadly reflect that 'it would have been not at all impossible for my successor, if he had been so minded, gradually to have overthrown all the foundations on which the Native Administrative system in the Territory had been built'. His conclusion was that the weakness of the Colonial Office lay 'in the lack of constructive thinking where large issues are involved: . . . even, I might say, lack of consistent policy in some instances'.[1] But he did not go on to speculate what would have happened if the 'constructive thinking' of the Colonial Office had not found itself able to accept his own masterful plans.

The conclusion must be that for such a task, certainly up to the end of the 1930's, only the 'men on the spot' could have had the necessary equipment both of local knowledge and of local authority. But this is not to say that the Office, or rather its political masters, could not have done more to lay down some general principles within which that man could work, nor that in certain other matters, about which the Office was much better qualified to advise, it could not have imposed more continuity within a territory and, even more, uniformity between

[1] D. Cameron, *My Tanganyika Service and Some Nigeria* (London, 1939), pp. 255–6.

B

neighbouring territories. This question will arise again when Kenya is discussed.

The focal position of the Governor was revealed as much by the mistaken or negative results when inadequate or even too brief appointments were made, as in the impress made by the stronger characters. The Governor combined in his person the roles of social leader, Prime Minister, head of the Civil Service, and for this period, Speaker of the Legislative Council. It must also be remembered that the Governor, whose tenure, at best, was likely to be five years, and who generally came to a territory from outside, had to spend some twelve to eighteen months getting to know both his new responsibilities and his staff, while in his last year he might feel it improper to take much initiative. These conditions must be recalled when evidences of hesitation or inconsistency are recorded in these chapters. It may be said that British governments were sometimes misguided in appointing, and over-indulgent in handling, their representatives, but some of the difficulties were inherent in the administration of distant and, at first, obscure regions, and also, at this early stage of Africa's administration, in finding experienced men for governorships.

In this book it is interesting to remark the record of the governors of Kenya and to speculate whether the appointment of men of stronger character and more confident principles of administration might not have moulded the character of the colony in its plastic years. It had been Lugard's great ambition in the last years of the nineteenth century to return to the then East Africa Protectorate as its earliest Governor. If, with his vigorous notions of justice and his great strength of character and confidence, he, instead of Sir Charles Eliot, had moulded the future Kenya, its history might have been very different. Such speculations are, however, unprofitable except to draw attention to the importance of the governors.

Next to the Governor came the Chief, sometimes called the Colonial, Secretary, the head officer of government. Through his hands passed all the major affairs of administration on their way to and from the Governor. He was flanked by two all-important officials, the Treasurer, in charge of the finances, and the Attorney-General, the legal adviser to the Government. There would be, in the later part of this period, between twelve to fifteen departments, each under its official head, dealing with the main branches of government, public works; railways and harbours; land; posts and telegraphs; customs; mining and audit; and the social service activities of education, health, agriculture, veterinary service, and forests. Standing in a position of special independence from the Governor, in reflection of the British tradition of the independence of the judiciary, was the Chief Justice, assisted by other judges and magistrates for those cases which, because of their character and importance, or the involvement of non-natives, were not justiciable in the native courts.

This official hierarchy was for the most part, except when the senior officials were on tour, concentrated at the headquarters of government. The East African territories were divided into provinces and the provinces into districts. In 1946 Kenya had four provinces and three extra-provincial districts, and Uganda had three provinces, while Tanganyika had eight. In general administrative control of each province was the provincial commissioner, while under him were the district commissioners (or district officers), in charge of the three or four districts into which each province was divided. In each district there would be a very varying number of 'native administrations', chiefdoms or councils of elders, or native courts. It was here that the district commissioner made the ultimate and all-important contact with the people.

The three East African territories followed somewhat different practices with regard to the head of native affairs. The question was whether there should be something like a specialist in this sphere, who would preside over what was the main, though not the only, duty of the provincial and district authorities, that of administering the African population. In Tanganyika Sir Philip Mitchell held this post under Sir Donald Cameron, but it was later left vacant. Uganda, with its sharply contrasting situations in this field, had no such officer. The Provincial Commissioner for Buganda, however, had a very special and difficult responsibility in that kingdom. In Kenya, from 1918, there was an official called the Chief Native Commissioner, and the controversial nature of his duties sometimes put him in a very difficult position and led to the exact extent of his powers being questioned by the settlers. The underlying issue about such posts was whether it was possible to separate 'native' from other affairs in a territory overwhelmingly African in population. There were dangers both in differentiating them and in leaving them without an influential official who could tour the territory, encourage and co-ordinate his provincial officers and give something like expert advice at the centre. As with the governorship it is tempting to speculate what might have happened if, in the list of chief native commissioners of our period there had been one or two very strong and able men. While it is true that the differences in the political situation in the two territories accounted for much, yet personalities played their part. A commissioner who was prepared to resign over a clear issue of native policy and thus appeal indirectly to British public opinion in this field might have prevented at least some of the surrenders in our period to European pressures.

It must, however, be admitted that in most positions, though colonial officials could carry on efficient work in their own defined spheres, they could do little to compensate for the weakness or wrong-headedness of a governor. Occasionally, as occurs in these pages, especially with regard to the issue of plantation versus peasant agriculture in Uganda,[1] the name of a senior official of long standing and devotion to his principles is remembered for influencing major policy. But only the Governor could give the whole service a sense of unity and direction within the framework of a high ultimate purpose.

In most of our period the officers of the so-called technical services, though these services were rapidly growing in size and importance, were still regarded as of different, indeed, inferior status to the administrative officers and very much under the control of the latter in their work in province and district. Certainly the quality of colonial rule at this time depended mainly on the day-by-day relationship of the administrative officials in stations or sub-stations, where some of these might remain isolated from all contact with other Europeans for many months of the year. It was, indeed, a condition of the colonial official's career that it was passed, except for his periodical leave, in exile from his own country and yet all the time he must be drawing upon the intellectual and moral resources of that country, sustained by his own faith in its mission and in the value of his own service.

[1] See Chapter IX, pp. 477–80, below.

When Britain undertook the administration of great blocks
of the East African interior she had, of course, no ready-made
corps of officials to export for this work. A few seasoned men
could be taken over from the British East Africa Company.
But the increasing number specially recruited were inexperienced and their numbers were at first absurdly inadequate in
relation to their task. From early in the century it was realized
how much depended upon recruiting the best human material
that could be found, but it was not until the inter-war years
that thorough reorganization and reform in this sphere could
be carried through. There is no space here to do more than
refer to what was a most intricate and difficult task.[1]

It can be said, in summary, that a three-sided policy was
pursued. Firstly, the aim was followed of recruiting what was
regarded as the very best available material. In the administrative service especially, the desired type was the product of the
public school and the older universities, a young man with a
sense of discipline and service, all-round, athletic, and enterprising rather than highly intellectual. This type was desirable
in the technical services also, but these tended to have a different
background and here the first object was to raise the professional
qualifications. The second objective was to bring greater unity
into a service which fell into seventeen branches. This was imperative in order to foster prestige and co-operation in the
service and to facilitate posting and promotion. Unity was only
partly possible because of the great variety of the conditions and
especially of the revenues which, in most territories, were coming
increasingly under local control or at least criticism. (In East
Africa, in our period, this last condition was provided mainly
in Kenya.) Thirdly, there were great reforms in training,
especially for the administrative service, entailing an academic
year's course for cadets at Oxford, Cambridge, or London.
The most important single document dealing with these changes
is the report of the authoritative Warren Fisher Committee of
1929–30.[2] There is also a very readable and subjective account
of his work by Sir Ralph Furse who from 1919 to 1948 was the

[1] A full description of this can be found in C. Jeffries, *The Colonial Empire and its Civil Service* (Cambridge, 1938).
[2] *Report of a Committee on the System of Appointment in the Colonial Office and the Colonial Service*, Cmd. 3554 (1930).

man behind the scenes, tirelessly pursuing his own ideal of a *corps d'élite* for the colonies.[1]

It is generally admitted, even by critics of some aspects of British colonial policy, that the men of the Colonial Administrative Service were, on the whole, courageous, humane, incorruptible, and industrious. These were, perhaps, at the time the most necessary qualities in what had to be, to some extent, a uniform type. Doubtless in addition to this basic character the ideal officer should also have been intellectual, liberal, imaginative, and, perhaps, a little more tentative in dealing with still obscure peoples and situations. These, however, were not the qualities easily found or, when found, retained among the thousands selected for what was still for many of them frontier work through much of this period. As an eminent civil servant has pointed out, if there was a proportion of men who were unsuitable for the service, the responsibility for retaining them lay mainly with the Colonial Office, which went so far in protecting the individual officer that it was almost impossible to drop the young misfit or even to offer the dispirited senior an early retirement. The defence would have been that this price was worth paying in order to give the service as a whole a sense of freedom and dignity.

We might pause a moment here to ask whether we are any nearer an answer to our question as to how British colonial policy was devised and executed during our period. It would seem that no simple answer can be given. In summarizing what has been said, colonial policy might be compared with a river. Its spring and its general direction were governed by the character of the ruling country. But, as it flowed through time, tributaries of varying volume and character would flow into it, from Parliament, from the Cabinet and the Colonial Secretary and his officials, from the Governor and his staff, and from various more or less organized sectional groups and interests in Britain and across the sea. Except in Kenya and Buganda, influence on policy from the local inhabitants was still very slight. The proportion of influence from these sources would differ from time to time and from place to place and the

[1] R. Furse, *Aucuparius: recollections of a recruiting officer* (London, 1962). See also R. Heussler, *Yesterday's Rulers* (London, 1963).

records will not always be full enough to provide very close estimates.

If what has been said of the complex convergence of forces which have shaped colonial policy is accepted, no very clear-cut product will be expected from them. The study of contemporary domestic affairs generally teaches how little any conscious and continuous purposes govern politicians and this must clearly be more true of activities projected overseas, especially in the earlier years of African colonial rule. Yet the character of Britain, particularly as developed in public life, undoubtedly set certain limits to the possible. This was partly because her administrative agents were chosen to represent what was regarded as the highest ethos of the nation. The control acted as a further safeguard in that if any distant events suggested that there had been some divergence from the national norm on the part of British agents, or even if some readjustment seemed to be necessary in order to bring colonial policy up to the standards— the developing standards—of Britain, then an attempt might be made to reassert the national principles.

The most effective of these reassertions were generally when, through the rather rare debates in parliament or perhaps, even more, through commissions of inquiry representing unofficial opinion, colonial events or policies were subjected to scrutiny. A number of such inquiries are mentioned in this volume, the supreme example being the Joint Select Committee of both Houses of Parliament on Closer Union in East Africa. Periodic committees or commissions could provide useful stocktaking upon this or that aspect of East African affairs and make proposals for reform, though these were not always fully accepted or carried out. But they could not, even when they tried, reform the whole wide field of administration which, in any case, would almost certainly have assumed its general form before it was subject to external examination.

We are therefore still obliged to speculate, in spite of all that has been said of the many sources of British policy, as to where the early governors of East Africa turned, however unconsciously, for their models or at least their principles, as they took up their task of administration. Had the experience of some two to three hundred years of diverse responsibilities for non-European peoples left a deposit of precedents in the minds of what could still at the turn of the nineteenth century be called a ruling class? There had been the long experience in India, for half a century one of direct imperial rule. The idea of a general, all-purpose British official in charge of a district had its roots in Company days under Hastings and Cornwallis. John Lawrence and others had built up a revered tradition of the humane, masterful British agent, relying more upon his national and personal sense of justice and humanity than upon regulations, touring beneficently among the millions of his charges. There were more precise lessons. There was the horror of a corruption which had darkened the record of the Company and even spread its taint into Britain. There were other important lessons, negative as well as positive, to be learned about the handling of land tenure and criminal and civil laws. One of East Africa's most direct borrowings was the Indian Penal Code.

Yet not only did Britain's Indian administration take shape during a very different climate of opinion in Britain, but India presented a very different surface to the grasp of the foreign administrator. Its vast population were the heirs of ancient civilization and practised religions of the book shared by hundreds of millions. They had been under a central government, however inefficient to western eyes, with developed industries, established laws and a native bureaucracy ready to work under British control. The peoples of India well understood the meaning of conquest, and, in spite of conflicts and discontents, could appreciate the significance of the Queen's peace and provide a kind of co-operation with European power unknown in the early years of British Africa except in a few, mainly Muslim, areas.

It would therefore seem, though the subject would repay further study, that except in many subtle ways hard to identify, Britain's long experience in India, and indeed in Asia, had surprisingly little direct influence upon the forms of administration developed in tropical Africa. Lord Lugard, whose early military service overseas had been in India, pointed out that although India's widespread and ancient civilization differentiated its problems from those of most other tropical regions in the Empire, these could have profited much from India's experience in local government, early industrialization, transport, and research. He regretted the defects in Britain's departmental system which prevented India's invaluable lessons being readily accessible to other tropical dependencies.[1] It was not until Lord Hailey, following long service and high office in India, devoted his powerful mind and tireless energy to the study of Africa that a deliberate attempt was made to apply the lessons of Asia to the problems of Africa.[2] Lord Hailey's position was such that he exercised a strong direct influence in colonial circles in addition to that radiated by his massive writings. But it was not until towards the end of our period that his intervention was felt, and that was late in the history of British Africa.

To what other experience but that of India could the British turn for precedents to guide them in handling East Africa? They had been dealing with African tribes in the south of the continent from soon after their conquest of the Cape in the Napoleonic wars. Rule over southern Africa had been extended during the whole of the nineteenth century, but it could hardly be said that by the end of it Britain had worked out any developed or conscious system of African administration. The task had been undertaken in piecemeal and somewhat half-hearted fashion and had been interrupted by conflicts with Boers and with Africans, and, at least on all the more peripheral areas, had been dominated by the desire to reduce trouble, expense, and therefore responsibility to the minimum. Moreover, much of the work had been done by men who belonged to South Africa and who stayed there, men such as Sir Andries Stockenstron and the Shepstones. It was true that even after the Union of 1910 Britain still retained a fragmented responsibility for administration in the three High Commission territories, but she pursued this in the rather half-committed tradition of the nineteenth century until, in the 1930's, the stimulus of a new model was deliberately imported from tropical Africa.

By a process of elimination we come to ask how far experience in British West Africa influenced policy on the eastern side. Britain had, after all, established footholds on the west coast more than two centuries before her nationals started annexation in eastern or, indeed, in central Africa, and some of these foot-

[1] F. D. Lugard, *The Dual Mandate in British Tropical Africa* (London, 1922), pp. 46–47.
[2] Lord Hailey, *An African Survey* (London, 1938); *Native Administration in the British African Territories* (five parts, London, 1950–3); *An African Survey* (revised, London, 1956).

holds had been formally taken over by the 1820's. But, except in Sierra Leone, a fascinating but exceptional humanitarian experiment, relations with the Africans remained for long more diplomatic or economic than administrative, and it was not until much the same time as on the eastern side that the whole of the interior had been occupied. The long association on the coast and the gradual penetration first of British influence and then of control over the southern regions of the Gold Coast and the future Nigeria had given the British administration a tentative, almost permissive, character. It is true, of course, that the sudden advance into the interior from the coastal annexation resembled the simultaneous advance in East Africa but, except where the masterful Lugard occupied Northern Nigeria and imposed his own system upon it, the advance into the interior was largely conditioned by the experience and relationships long established on the coast. The contrast in conditions and in policy was greater because in the Gold Coast and in Yoruba-land, British agents had been confronted by chieftainships strong both by indigenous development and by long contacts, from a basis of independence, with the European traders and missionaries. In East Africa, when allowance is made for the special character and position of Buganda, there were few political units of any comparable size, and they stood deep in the hinterland and far from external influences except the relatively recent penetration of the Arab caravans.

It would seem, therefore, that in East Africa administration was built up at first with swift empiricism and very largely in isolation from other experience. The Colonial Office, as we have seen, was qualified neither by organization nor by tradition to devise and impose the forms of what was soon to be called 'native administration'. The authors in this volume draw a picture of an advance in which methods were dictated by the primary needs of a new government to impose order, to get some sort of economy started in order to raise a revenue, and to obtain labour to work upon the roads and railways without which the other primary purposes could not be carried very far. It is mathematically obvious that one of the few dozen early officials could make effective personal contact only with a few score or perhaps hundreds of the tens of thousands of tribesmen in the area. The new authority had quickly to make use of every grade of African authority, from the rulers of the lacustrine region in their hierarchical courts, through chiefs of diminishing status, down to the Swahili and Arab *akidas* employed by the Germans and the appointed headmen of Kenya.

How much of this was 'indirect rule'? Much has been written upon this subject and there are many references to it in this book. I do not propose to go very far over ground well-trodden by many writers and which I have traversed more than once myself. But it seems important at the outset of this volume to clear away some general misunderstandings which quite frequently arise upon this subject. The improvizations to which I have just referred, except those applied to Kenya 'chiefs' or headmen and the German *akidas*, could be described as 'indirect' in a sense in which all over the Empire, whether in North America, in Malaya, or in Fiji, and especially in the early stages of rule, British agents had taken the obvious course imposed upon them of activating native societies through the ready-made machinery of existing authority. Such expedients employed, at least at a preliminary stage, by many other conquerors, hardly deserved to be regarded as a system. But, in fact, for reasons perhaps peculiar to the British social and political traditions, our agents found this method as congenial to themselves as it was cheap and convenient. They therefore tended in many places, whether in Malaya, Oyo, Ashanti, Basutoland, Barotseland, or Buganda, to retain it, indeed to develop it further.

Upon this widespread, variegated, somewhat empirical base, penetrating and over-laying it in various degrees, there flowed a more refined administrative stratum. Its source can be traced to Lugard's dealings with the large and populous region of Northern Nigeria in the first few years of the century. His system of indirect rule was so strikingly successful in practice, and its principles and techniques so thoroughly worked out on paper, that the name coined for it earned the dignity of capital letters, a usage the continuance of which would certainly clarify subsequent discussions of the subject. Lugard had worked out the fundamentals of his system by the time he left Nigeria for a few years in 1907, and he bequeathed to the Colonial Office a school of administrators if anything almost too deeply and blindly impressed by the merits of the system. Indeed, though with incomplete success, he tried to modify it himself when he returned as Governor-General in 1912. The influence of Indirect Rule reached its height only in the inter-war period, as the men trained under Lugard rose to governorships and his classic book *The Dual Mandate* and his other writings and speeches spread his ideas. The new model reached the East African territories in different ways and with different results. Sir Donald Cameron brought it direct from Nigeria and imposed it upon his predecessor's more tentative but compatible foundations with all the clarity and thoroughness of his powerful nature. I was working in Tanganyika at the time and saw much of Cameron; and he denied, or at least minimized, his debt to Lugard's precedents and reproved me for writing of his Nigerian model. This attitude is expressed in the book, already cited, which so perfectly expresses his confident, highly independent mind. Yet it must be clear to any student of these affairs how much, in spite of some important and deliberate deviations, Cameron's plans were derived from the Nigerian system within which he had spent the greater part of his working life.

The new version of Indirect Rule reached Uganda more incompletely. True, Lugard had made a treaty with the Kabaka and had declared, in the book which described this event, his faith in working through existing African authority.[1] But East Africa was not to be the scene of his administrative actions. The most conscious influence in the direction of Indirect Rule came through Sir Philip Mitchell who, though he had not served in West Africa, was a highly alert and intelligent observer of colonial affairs and, indeed, of public affairs in general. As Cameron's most energetic Secretary for Native Affairs he had been his chief agent in imposing the new order. He found the Buganda system was certainly indirect, but it proved itself recalcitrant to the later principles of Indirect Rule. Sir Harry Johnston's Uganda Agreement of 1900 had exercised a crystallizing effect upon Buganda's already strongly founded government. Although Sir William Gowers, one of Lugard's early Northern Nigeria Residents, had been Governor from 1925 to 1932, and though Mitchell tried to modify the Buganda system by applying some of the experience he had gained in Tanganyika, little impression was made.

[1] F. D. Lugard, *The Rise of our East African Empire* (2 vols., Edinburgh, 1893), ii. 651.

Two of the central ideas of Lugard's system were the unquestioned sovereignty of the British Government, unfettered by treaties, and the active and complete articulation of its authority with that of the indigenous unit, recognized and defined as a 'native administration'. But this articulation never fully took place in Buganda: the native government, protected by the Uganda Agreement of 1900, maintained, as it were, a hard core of independence within its own sphere, while the Protectorate Government operated above or around it, unable to modernize or liberalize the kabakaship or the *lukiko* (advisory council). This conflict of authority and ideas in the dominant African state of the Protectorate was more or less latent during the long minority of Daudi Chwa, but it led ultimately to the temporary exile of the present Kabaka and has remained unresolved to complicate the process of emancipation and to draw a large question mark over the course of Uganda as an independent state.

To Kenya neither pre- nor post-Lugard concepts of Indirect Rule were applicable. Although Sir Percy Girouard, Lugard's successor in Northern Nigeria, came to Kenya full of enthusiasm for the system he had inherited, he found his new Protectorate sterile ground for any administrative transplanting. In his chapter upon Kenya, Mr. Bennett describes the evolution of the Executive and Legislative councils in an almost continuous atmosphere of political controversy about the amount and the kind of representation upon these bodies which should be allowed to the immigrant groups. Under the control of the administrative officers the Africans in their native reserves had their own different institutions: chiefs, headmen, tribal police, and courts composed of elders. In 1924, borrowing a model from Fiji, nominated Local Native Councils were set up in the districts and given minor powers to deliberate, to handle small local revenues, and to pass by-laws.[1] Like the other institutions of African administration, these councils were, by Indirect Rule standards, wholly artificial. However, in the circumstances of Kenya, with its lack of easily adaptable African institutions, and with the example, one might almost say the provocation, of European politics close at hand, these councils offered some training and some expression at least to the more sophisticated

[1] *Laws of Kenya* (1926), cap. 129, section 8.

tribes. Sir Philip Mitchell, who came to govern Kenya in the last year of our period, was inclined to this view though his heart was in Indirect Rule.[1] The story of the development of these councils, with that of the evolution of 'native administration' into local government, will be taken up in the next volume.

While still on the question of native administration it should be remarked that criticisms of the indirect methods are generally aimed at its later stages. It should not be forgotten that during the first twenty to thirty years of this century it made possible a surprisingly effective co-operation between the African tribes and an exiguous British staff. There is evidence in this volume of the immense range of work, especially in Tanganyika and Uganda, carried out by the chiefs, not only in their day-to-day administrative and judicial work, but in developing African production, and especially in maintaining it during the critical period of the second world war. Some of the faults of the system may have been due to the excessive demands made upon it, especially for activities quite alien to African experience. Absorbed in their task and working in some isolation from the world, the colonial authorities were slow to realize that it was impossible for European power, on the one hand, to maintain indigenous institutions and, on the other, to change the whole pre-European environment which those institutions had been evolved to meet. The ideal would have been an adjustment, related to changing needs and to tribal development, by which African administrations could have been shifted gradually on to a more efficient and representative basis. Admittedly, this process is much easier in a retrospective opinion than it could have been in contemporary action. It must also be remembered that today the African policies of our period are nearly always judged according to their efficacy in preparing the way to independence; whereas the earlier administrations were working, against great obstacles, for much more limited and immediate objectives of maintaining law and order and initiating a modest social betterment. The difficulty in judging their achievement is the greater since not only were the conditions without precedent in history but even in the contemporary Africa it is not easy to find, as standards of judgement, examples of more successful administration where the conditions were closely

[1] P. Mitchell, *African Afterthoughts* (London, 1954), pp. 134-5.

comparable. It is possible to observe that the most effective adjustments were where a tribe as a whole had been sufficiently affected by the new forces to be ready at once to retain and adapt their own form of government. In East Africa, in different ways, this is true of the Chagga and the Ganda. But in each case they were helped by favourable conditions, both in their own history and economy, and in the circumstances of their contact with European power.

This book includes some economic sections. When an attempt is made to reconstruct the main features of colonial policy at this period in terms of current political ideas and in face of physical and administrative difficulties, the economic material, like the missing pieces of a jig-saw puzzle, completes the picture. If the first need of a colonial government was to impose the new order, the second was to find a revenue to pay for the basic costs of government. The economical features of the indirect method of rule were its first attraction, however many other advantages it was later seen to possess. The native authorities could even collect the first modest taxes. Any increase in revenue depended upon investment, mainly in basic communications. Joseph Chamberlain had been prophetic in seeing colonial power in terms of economic investment, but the South African war distracted him from the development of the colonial estates and parliament and public were slow to face the costs of such development. As can be learned from Volume I even the cost of annexing East Africa was grudged, while the money for the railway that was the life-line to Uganda had to be obtained by Lord Salisbury from parliament almost by trickery and then in the form of a loan. At much the same time the House of Commons greeted the acquisition of Northern Nigeria with a long grumbling debate about the £865,000 it had to pay the Royal Niger Company for this immense and populous new acquisition. The convenient view had long been held that it was a test of the soundness of a colony that it should be self-supporting at the earliest possible date. Something of the Victorian idea of the morality of solvency and of the hard work by which it was achieved had been extended into the sphere of colonial policy. So, too, perhaps, had the idea of class: there were lower as well as upper and middle classes among nations. The later theory of the Dual Mandate emphasized that the advantages of the colonial nexus should be, and indeed, were, mutual. There was a long ideological way to go before the rich nations would admit an obligation to help the poor with little or no expectation of economic or even political return.

To Britain in the early years of its occupation the most striking feature of East Africa was its economic unattractiveness. As we have seen, even after sixty years of European rule and development the most vivid impression received by the members of the East Africa Royal Commission of 1953–5 was of its 'fundamental poverty'. In the 1890's, especially in contrast with the satisfactorily solvent coastal dependencies on the western side, East Africa seemed an exacting acquisition. Only Zanzibar, with its cloves and its transit trade, promised solvency. A few figures will speak for themselves. In 1900 the revenue of Kenya was £64,000, the expenditure £193,000; the comparable figures for Uganda were £82,000 and £252,000. In the same year the imports of Kenya and Uganda were valued at £450,000 worth and their exports at £71,000.[1] Kenya remained dependent upon the British Treasury up to 1912 and was in the red again in some subsequent years. Between 1895 and 1913, in addition to the cost of the railway, parliamentary grants from Britain totalled £2,843,000. Uganda had a closely parallel financial history up to that time. German East Africa proved even more costly to the Germans, demanding some £10,000,000 between 1910 and 1914.[2] In considering these figures it must be remembered that in Britain during this period Treasury control was still a stern reality. The Colonial Office might seldom be called to account by British public opinion but in the all-important region of finance, which for the colonies meant development, it was closely controlled by the Treasury. The end of the nineteenth century saw a great rise in national expenditure and the Treasury officials were determined to enforce economy where public opinion hardly operated to defy them. The new colonies were obvious victims for economy.[3] Even secretaries of state complained openly of their subjection to this restrictive tyranny. The masterful Amery could complain of the Treasury as 'a surly

[1] A. Pim, *The Financial and Economic History of the African Tropical Territories* (Oxford, 1940), pp. 225, 227.
[2] Ibid., pp. 186 sqq.   [3] *Cambridge History of the British Empire*, iii. 751.

watchdog, grudgingly criticising and holding up all expenditure even when it had already received Cabinet sanction'.[1]

The early conduct of East African affairs must therefore be studied with the understanding that, if the first aim of a new European government was to maintain order, the second and more difficult was to raise a revenue and that many other theoretically desirable aims had to wait upon this second imperative. The early colonial governors, had they then been versed in communist theories, would have bitterly regretted that the Hobson–Lenin concept of economic imperialism, with its basis in the deep design of the financiers to transfer their capital from Britain to the new empire which had been annexed for their exploitation, was so far from the truth. It has been estimated that out of £35,171,000 of external capital invested in Kenya and Uganda up to 1934, more than £27,000,000 came from an unwilling British Government. This figure, it is true, does not include an estimated total of some £28,000,000 invested over the years by individual settlers in developing their farms.[2] But this is hardly the kind of metropolitan exploitation of which Lenin was thinking; and, of course, a great deal of this last investment was lost in experimentation and through the failures of pioneering efforts.

Such facts and figures go far to explain why economic development and the much-needed social services which it could have nourished seem to make such a slow start in these territories. Some will question whether a heavier injection of capital might not have quickened the slow initial pace. But they must reckon with the nature of the country, the unreadiness of the people, and the inexperience of the new rulers. The notorious ground-nut scheme of a much later date contains some retrospective evidence upon this subject. When these difficulties are weighed in the light of Mr. Wrigley's description of Kenya early in the century, and when we add the evidence of contemporary British policy, it is not difficult to see why ministers at home and governors abroad supported white settlement. The Europeans, brought in to fill an economic vacuum, provided economic and political stimulus, but also started a controversy which made Kenya steal the limelight on the East African stage.

---

[1] Amery, *My Political Life*, ii. 358.
[2] Royal Institute of International Affairs, *The Colonial Problem* (London, 1937), pp. 276, 284.

Since there are some who, looking back over Kenya's history from the standpoint of the 1960's, may regard this central theme as one of tragedy, it is important to remember the economic vacuum which the European presence came to fill. In the next volume the political and economic record of a Kenya dominated by the thrust of the settlers' energies will be carried to the latest possible date; and a further chapter will deal with the whole story of the complex interterritorial relationships, both planned and achieved, which were bound up with the white colonists' domination of Kenya.

It should be remembered when making any assessment of the achievements and shortcomings of this period that colonial governments not only started the development race under heavy handicap: they found even after they had made a start that it was an obstacle race in which they were engaged. Among the major obstacles were two world wars and two slumps which had the gravity of crises. War, with its abrupt exigencies, meant the diversion not only of resources but also of many of the already inadequate staffs, with a loss of slowly built contact with the people and an over-reliance upon native authorities. It also meant difficult changes in the economy, and a drain on the African manhood for porters or soldiers, and a lowering of the already low standards of health. Slumps meant the reduction of staff, and the abrupt loss of revenue, so that governments could hardly meet the heavy fixed charges for salaries, pensions, and the service of debts, and were obliged to reduce, or even to cancel, the more elastic items for the social services. In Tanganyika, of course, the first world war meant much more: the displacement of much of the population, its reduction by famine and disease and the destruction of many of the fixed assets built up by the Germans during their brief possession. It would be difficult to choose in the fifty years covered by this volume any period which could be regarded as one of normal colonial rule: only, perhaps, the years just before the 1930 slump and following the recovery from it, soon to be overshadowed by the approach of war in 1939.

It is these considerations which give a special importance to the bringing together of political and economic material in this book. In the third volume one of its three sections will be devoted to economic questions and this, with the addition of fuller statistical data, will throw much retrospective light over the economic aspects discussed in this book.

Those who have read the first volume will have visualized with its help a great block of Africa with a lack of clear natural boundaries and also of human divisions except for the shifting spheres of its hundred tribes. They may, therefore, as they reach the end of this volume reflect with surprise that the territories into which this block was so arbitrarily trisected by European power seem already, both politically and economically, to have acquired distinct characters. This differentiation is the more remarkable since, except for Tanganyika's brief preliminary period of German rule, the whole region was under the administration of one power. It might, therefore, be well for the reader to begin the chapters of this book with certain questions in mind. How far were these ultimate distinctions due to deep differences in the original human and physical character of the three parts which colonial rule discovered and developed? How far did they result from the high degree of administrative autonomy allowed by the British system? How far did they take shape in the different circumstances of the original occupation? This last is a question which is surely of special relevance to Uganda where Britain's entrance into the region by way of Buganda had lasting consequences. In Tanganyika, did the Germans leave some deep, though obscure mark upon this immense territory, or was its special character as a state formed by Sir Donald Cameron and by the mandated status which he welcomed? For Kenya there can be no doubt that the dominant influence was provided by white settlement, one which by positive economic and by negative political influence deeply affected its two neighbours, and within its own boundaries evoked the deep African reaction which, for want of an exact word, we call nationalism. It is this development which, I have suggested, makes the watershed between the periods covered by this volume and the next, between the record of colonial power acting for seventy years almost without restraints, except those imposed by itself or by the difficulties of the task, and the developments of the last seventeen years, in which we have seen the effects of this power in an African demand, unforeseen in its suddenness and strength, for immediate and complete independence.

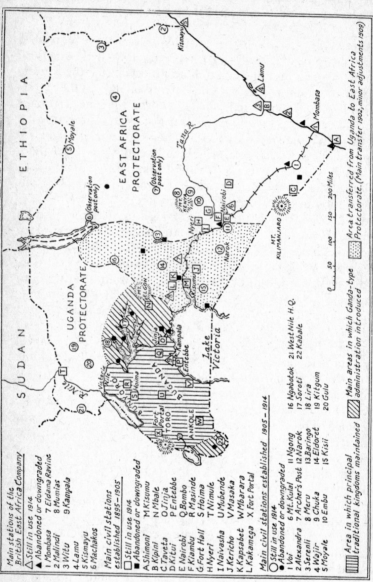

MAP I. BRITISH EAST AFRICAN PROTECTORATES: the extension of civil administration, to 1914.
(Compiled mainly from annual administrative reports)

Main stations of the
British East Africa Company
△ Still in use 1914.
▲ Abandoned or downgraded
1 Mombasa   7 Eldama Ravine
2 Malindi   8 Mumias
3 Witu   9 Kampala
4 Lamu
5 Kismayu
6 Machakos

Main civil stations
established 1895–1905
☐ Still in use 1914.
■ Abandoned or downgraded
A Shimoni   M Kisumu
B Kipini   N Mbale
C Taveta   O Jinja
D Kitui   P Entebbe
E Nairobi   Q Bombo
F Kiambu   R Masinde
G Fort Hall   S Hoima
H Nyeri   T Nimule
I Naivasha   U Mubende
J Kericho   V Masaka
K Kapsabet   W Mbarara
L Kakamega   X Fort Portal

Main civil stations established 1905–1914
○ Still in use 1914.
● Abandoned or downgraded
1 Voi   11 Ngong   16 Ngabotok   21 West Nile H.Q.
2 Alexandra   12 Narok   17 Soroti   22 Kabale
3 Serenli   13 Baringo   18 Lira
4 Wajir   14 Eldoret   19 Kitgum
5 Moyale   15 Kisii   20 Gulu
6 Mt. Kulal
7 Archer's Post
8 Meru
9 Chuka
10 Embu

▨ Area in which principal
traditional kingdoms maintained

▧ Main areas in which Ganda-type
administration introduced

⬚ Area transferred from Uganda to East Africa
Protectorate. (Main transfer 1902, minor adjustments 1909)

I

BRITISH EAST AFRICA: THE ESTABLISHMENT OF BRITISH RULE 1895–1912

D. A. LOW

THE Masai were the hinge of Kenya. Their marauding skills had made them the most ubiquitous of the peoples between Lake Victoria and the sea, lords of the plains and open plateaux between Mount Kilimanjaro and Lake Nakuru, and the dominant anxiety of every intruder from the east. Although they had never established any political control over their Bantu and Nilo-Hamite neighbours, they had everywhere confined them to the land which lay enclosed within the available natural defence works of forest and steep hillside; they continued to raid them for cattle, moreover, until the last years of the nineteenth century.[1] Nevertheless, for all their reputation as fierce warriors, the Masai proved to be far more tolerant of movement by alien travellers across their homeland than most of their neighbours, chiefly because, as a by-product of their military pre-eminence, they were more confident of their ability to control it. As alien interests therefore increased, so trade routes through Masailand extended. Throughout the nineteenth century, however, the Masai remained their unquestioned arbiters.

Yet by the end of the century they were not the power they had been; and at least one competent observer postulated that the day could soon come when they would have to fall back before the advancing hordes of their neighbours[2] who, nurtured

---

[1] See, for example, the report by Ainsworth on the progress of the Ukamba Province, in *Reports relating to the Administration of the East Africa Protectorate*, P.P. Africa no. 6, Cd. 2740 (1906). (Hereinafter 'Ainsworth's *Report*'.)

[2] Ainsworth to Crauford, 20 Nov. 1896, Mombasa Provincial Archives (hereinafter 'M.P.A.') Sub-Commissioner, Ukamba, In, 1896–1900,

in the fertile fastnesses to which they had been confined, had armed themselves not only with the weapons but with many of the institutions so successfully employed by the Masai. Discipline was the key to the success of the Masai. It was chiefly, however, the discipline of individual warriors and individual warbands; it never embraced a tribal-wide fighting force. In addition, during much of the nineteenth century, the Masai found themselves distracted by a long series of civil wars between different Masai-speaking sub-tribes and by a succession of lethal infections, sometimes animal, sometimes human.[1] Never, moreover, did they suffer a greater combination of afflictions than in the last decade of the nineteenth century.

There was, to begin with, a further civil war. In 1890 their most renowned *laibon*, Mbatian, had died. Two of his sons, Sendeyo and Lenana, thereafter fought for the succession to his unrivalled ritualistic powers (the authority of a *laibon* being more prophetic than political), and a number of Masai sub-tribes lined up in support of the one against the other.[2] This heralded for the Masai a new species of civil war. Hitherto they had known conflict between two probably quite distinct groups of Masai-speaking sub-tribes;[3] but now some of the formerly victorious core fought for the first time amongst themselves. At the outset Sendeyo's faction, which comprised (in the main) the south-western sub-tribes around the Loita plains, fought the more successfully. By 1893 the Loita themselves had inflicted a major defeat upon the Kaputie and Matapatu (two of the northern sub-tribes who bore allegiance to Lenana) in the area south-east of Kikuyu;[4] but in the following year Lenana, who one way and another had a very much larger following, dispatched a major raid against Sendeyo and his supporters in retaliation.[5] Two years later there was talk of a *rapprochement* between the brothers,[6] which was probably prompted both by the tribal-wide circumcision ceremonies which were then due, and by Sendeyo's desire for assistance against the Germans

---

[1] See ch. ix in vol. i of this *History*.
[2] A. C. Hollis, *The Masai: their language and folklore* (Oxford, 1905), pp. 328–9.
[3] See ch. ix in vol. i of this *History*.   [4] Ainsworth's *Report*.
[5] Hall to Pigott, 22 Oct. 1894, Zanzibar Residency Archives (hereinafter 'Z.R.A.') D7.
[6] Ainsworth to Crauford, 17 Oct. 1896, Foreign Office Confidential Print (hereinafter 'F.O.C.P.') 6913; Ainsworth to Hardinge, 15, 23 Apr. 1897, Z.R.A. D11.

upon Mount Kilimanjaro with whom he was in conflict.[1] The truce, however, if truce there was, was only short-lived. Lenana declined to assist Sendeyo against the Germans,[2] and during each of the three years from 1898 to 1900 launched at least one major expedition against the sub-tribes supporting his brother.[3] Sendeyo attempted to retaliate;[4] but, bludgeoned by Lenana, by the Kissongo (one of the Masai sub-tribes enkraaled near Kilimanjaro),[5] and by the Germans,[6] he failed to maintain his earlier promise. In 1902 he threw in his hand, renounced his ambitions, and agreed to settle in obscurity not far from Lenana's headquarters near Ngong.[7] At no time were the Masai organized to fight as a single tribal army, but such bitter internecine warfare served to aggravate their disunity during a most critical period.

It would be a mistake, however, to picture their civil strife at this time simply as a fraternal struggle, since much of its substance lay in a conflict for cattle.[8] For in the early 1890's rinderpest had swept through the herds of the Masai on its way across the African continent.[9] Cattle, more than any other possession, were both the livelihood and the ambition of the Masai. Any epizootic visitation making inroads upon their herds constituted a grievous calamity. The instinctive reaction of the Masai was to seek to make good their losses at the expense either of their neighbours or of their fellows. Here very often lay the kernel of their internecine combat. But such were the ravages of their contagions that this time[10] swift recovery

[1] Ainsworth to Hardinge, 15 Apr. 1897, Z.R.A. D11; 15 May 1897, Z.R.A. D14.

[2] Hardinge to Salisbury, 18 Nov. 1897, F.O.C.P. 7024; ibid., 19 Aug. 1898, F.O.C.P. 7090.

[3] Hardinge to Salisbury, 18 Nov. 1898, and enclosures, F.O.C.P. 7159; Ainsworth to Crauford, 5 Oct. 1899, M.P.A., 1899 Commissioner, Ukamba, In; Ainsworth to Ternan, 26 Nov. 1900, F.O.C.P. 7690.

[4] Ainsworth to Crauford, 13 June 1899, F.O.C.P. 7402.

[5] Ainsworth to Hardinge, 14 Dec. 1898, Z.R.A. D25.

[6] Hardinge to Salisbury, 19 July 1898, F.O.C.P. 7090.

[7] Jackson to Lansdowne, 8 July 1902, and enclosures, F.O.C.P. 7954; Ainsworth's Report.

[8] See, for example, S. L. and H. Hinde, The Last of the Masai (London, 1901), pp. 5–9.

[9] R. W. M. Mettam, 'A short history of rinderpest with special reference to Africa', Uganda J. v. i (1937), 22–26; Ainsworth's Report.

[10] Although it seemed as if the Masai might escape a further outbreak in the later 1890's, it struck them in 1899: Ainsworth to Hardinge, 18 June 1898, F.O.C.P. 7090; Ainsworth to Crauford, 15 Nov. 1899, M.P.A., 1899, Commissioner, Ukamba, In.

proved to be out of the question because their difficulties were simultaneously multiplied. Pleuro-pneumonia followed hard upon the heels of rinderpest,[1] and on top of both came two very serious outbreaks of smallpox, killing many of the Masai themselves.[2] Throughout the decade they reeled under a succession of galling blows.

These afflictions, and others too, struck some of their neighbours as well. During the 1890's rinderpest and pleuro-pneumonia spread through the herds of the Kamba and the Kikuyu,[3] while locusts denuded both their cattle pastures and their standing crops.[4] In addition, particularly during the latter part of the 1890's, smallpox attacked the Kikuyu with particular virulence, especially in the more recently occupied southern tip of Kiambu;[5] while throughout most of the three years from 1897 to 1899 a harrowing famine racked both them and their neighbours, particularly the Kamba to the eastward.[6] These disasters do not seem to have afflicted the peoples upon the western side of the Rift Valley. Here the Nandi had recently become the most formidable people of the area. Relieved, some years earlier, of pressure from the Masai, they had now embarked on extensive raiding against their neighbours. With a *laibon*-like figure in their *orkoiyot* to give direction to their energies, they raided with impunity to most points of the compass, and cast a disdainful eye over their less adventurous neighbours.[7] Around 1890 their close kin the Kipsigis adopted an *orkoiyot* too, and thus armed themselves for similar proceedings.[8]

---

[1] Ainsworth to Hardinge, 17 Jan. 1898, Z.R.A. D18.

[2] Kenya Land Commission (Carter Commission), *Evidence and Memoranda*, Col. no. 91, (1934), i. 167, 502–3, 596.

[3] Ibid., p. 698, Hardinge to Salisbury, 15 Apr. 1898, and enclosures, F.O.C.P. 7077; Hardinge to Salisbury, 22 Feb. 1899, and enclosures, F.O.C.P. 7401.

[4] Ainsworth to Pigott, 24 July 1894, F.O.C.P. 6661; Whitehead to Hardinge, 1 Feb. 1899, Z.R.A. D26.

[5] Kenya Land Commission, *Evidence*, i. 696–7.

[6] Whitehead to Bradbridge, 4 Nov. 1898, Z.R.A. D24; Ainsworth to Crauford, 19 Apr. 1899; Traill to Crauford, 6 Nov. 1899, M.P.A., 1899, Commissioner, Ukamba, In; Ainsworth to Hardinge, 28 Dec. 1899, Z.R.A. E10. A useful summary is in R. R. Kuczynski, *Demographic Survey of the British Colonial Empire* (London, 1949), ii. 195–9.

[7] G. W. B. Huntingford, *Nandi Work and Culture* (H.M.S.O., London, 1950), p. 13; Hobley to Berkeley, 12 July 1898, Entebbe Secretariat Archives (hereinafter 'E.S.A.') A4/11.

[8] G. W. B. Huntingford, *The Nandi of Kenya: tribal control in a pastoral society* (London, 1953), p. 39.

It was of singular importance in the determination of events on the line between Mombasa and the Kavirondo Gulf during the critical decade about the turn of the century that while on the one hand the Kamba, the Kikuyu, and even the Masai were demoralized and pre-occupied, farther west the Nandi and their like were buoyant and eagle-eyed.

The islamized coastline

Upon the coast there took place in 1895 a change of régime. The Imperial British East Africa Company surrendered its charter, and the British Foreign Office found it necessary to determine what authority was to assume responsibility in the British sphere of East Africa for the area which the Company was abandoning. Already in the previous year an imperial protectorate had been declared over Buganda; but the British Commissioner there was so busily pre-occupied with the urgent problems of a nascent protectorate 800 miles from the coast that he could scarcely be made responsible for the coast and its immediate hinterland as well, any more than an administrator at the coast could hope to exercise effective control in the far interior.[1] Because of this prior inland commitment, the British sphere in East Africa, unlike the German (where there was nothing comparable to the up-country British involvement in Buganda), became divided between two separate administrations.[2]

The immediate problem in 1895 which was left to the Foreign Office to resolve was the relationship between the coastline, its immediate hinterland, and Zanzibar. A decision upon the issue in this form could not be avoided, for by the Anglo-German Agreement of 1886 the authority of the Sultan of Zanzibar to a depth of 10 miles along the East African coastline had secured international recognition. Although the Germans had (by the terms of the Anglo-German Agreement of 1890) purchased outright the sultan's rights in the strip adjoining their sphere, there had been no corresponding purchase by the British. Between 1888 and 1895, indeed, the I.B.E.A. Company had

[1] Report of Committee on Administration of East Africa, 17 Apr. 1894, F.O.C.P. 6489.
[2] It was for this reason that there eventually emerged in the northern half of East Africa the two separate territories of Kenya and Uganda.

been lessees of the sultan for the strip along the Mombasa coastline, while with their impending withdrawal the Sultan was assuming that he would now recover control over his undoubted inheritance. But despite the protests of Hardinge, the British Consul-General in Zanzibar, and others, the British Foreign Office decreed otherwise. Although the sultan's nomnal suzerainty was maintained, the Foreign Office decided to take over itself the lease of the coastal strip which the Company was relinquishing, and (to the chagrin of the sultan and his friends) to assume sole responsibility for its administration.[1] For all practical purposes the 'Sultan's coast' thus became incorporated in the new British East Africa Protectorate which was proclaimed on 1 July 1895.[2]

Ironically, however, the new Protectorate was at first managed from Zanzibar. In order to avoid additional expense Hardinge combined the post of British Commissioner of the E.A.P. (as it was familiarly called) with that of British Consul-General in Zanzibar; and the senior British officials in Zanzibar, including Lloyd Mathews, the Sultan's First Minister, were formed into an East Africa Protectorate Council to advise and assist him.[3] A number of government departments were organized, and most of the employees of the now defunct Company were taken into the Protectorate's service. From the security of his vantage point in Zanzibar, Hardinge was able to cast an olympian eye over his new domain in a manner which was never possible for any of the early British Commissioners in Uganda; at the outset, in 1895, five years before there was any similar attempt for Uganda, he divided his new Protectorate into a number of administrative provinces and districts (with sub-commissioners and district officers respectively at their head).[4] Three of Hardinge's four provinces—Seyyidie, Tanaland, and Jubaland—stood along the coastline, where one single Coast Region stands today.[5] This, however,

[1] See ch. xi in vol. i of this *History*, and Chapter XIII below.

[2] Hardinge to Salisbury, 2 July 1895, F.O.C.P. 6761; *London Gazette*, 15 June 1895. Until 1902 the East Africa Protectorate only extended inland up to the eastern wall of the Rift Valley.

[3] Minute Book of the East Africa Protectorate Council, item 313, Zanzibar Museum.

[4] Hardinge to Kimberley, 25 Feb. 1895, F.O.C.P. 6693; Hardinge to Salisbury, 6 July 1895, F.O.C.P. 6761.

[5] The fourth province, comprising most of the hinterland between Mombasa and

was a precise reflection of realities. For, at the outset, the East
Africa Protectorate was first and foremost a British protectorate
over the islamized coastline.

Yet it was not until the defeat by the British of the Mazrui
that their control over Seyyidie and Tanaland was successfully
consolidated. Amongst the numerous Arab tribes of the Mombasa coastline, the Mazrui had long held a primary position;
for a century, however, and more, they had been at odds with
the Albusaidi dynasty of Oman and Zanzibar, who maintained
a form of suzerainty over them. When the I.B.E.A. Company
leased the dominion of the Mombasa coastline from the Sultan,
the Mazrui leader, Mbarak bin Rashid, who in the past had
periodically sought to cast off the Sultan's authority, welcomed
their advent as putting an end to the overlordship of his traditional foe. He was even led to believe that he himself was now
at last to be lord of the coast in his place. It gradually became
clear, however, that it was the British and not the Mazrui who
were to supersede the Albusaidi as masters of the coastline.

This issue was eventually put to the test about the time of the
Company's withdrawal. In February 1895 the Mazrui shaikh-
dom of Takaungu, north of Mombasa, had fallen vacant. The
British thereupon managed to instal a candidate named Rashid
bin Salim, who seemed likely to prove amenable to their wishes;
but a quarrel soon broke out between Shaikh Rashid and a
younger Mbarak bin Rashid 'the legal heir according to Moslem
law'.[1] When Hardinge, in June 1895, called upon young
Mbarak to desist, an accidental shot precipitated an open conflict, into which, much against his inclinations, the elderly
Mbarak bin Rashid, the effective leader of the Mazrui, soon
found himself drawn. Since he would not deliver up the young
Mbarak, who had gone to seek refuge with him, Hardinge
rejected the elder Mbarak's successive attempts at a general
reconciliation; drove him from his stronghold at Mwele; and
made it plain that for the British there could be 'no question as
to our being the masters'.[2] Yet despite Hardinge's initial success,
for several months Mbarak effectively raised the country-side

the Rift Valley, was named Ukamba. The Jubaland Province was ceded to Italy
in 1925, as part of her reward for supporting the Allied cause in the first world war.
    [1] As Hardinge himself averred. Memorandum by A. Hardinge respecting
the Mazrui chiefs, encl. 1 in Hardinge to Salisbury, 26 Aug. 1895, F.O.C.P. 6761.
    [2] Hardinge to Salisbury, 26 Aug. 1895, F.O.C.P. 6761.

against him, pinned down his forces, and burnt several coastal
towns; and it was not until the arrival in March 1896 of a
regiment from India (for which Hardinge had found it necessary
to send) that Mbarak and his followers eventually succumbed.
They fled across the German border, surrendered to the German
Governor, von Wissmann, and were granted political asylum.

This Mazrui war overshadowed the first months of the
nascent Protectorate.[1] A collision between British pretensions
and Arab susceptibilities could not have been delayed very
much longer.[2] It was exceedingly fortunate, however, for the
British that the struggle for power arose as it did out of a
succession dispute which was largely the family concern of the
Mazrui leaders rather than from amid the widespread resentment of many other coastal Arabs at Britain's anti-slavery policy,
and in particular against the refuge which British missionaries
provided for runaway slaves. Had the clash arisen upon these
issues, the crisis for the British could have been several times
worse; the coastal Arabs might very well have united against
them. In the event, however, the British never lost their foothold
in Mombasa; and the force which they proved themselves capable of fielding against the Mazrui served to cow the whole
coastline. Henceforward the authority of the British passed here
virtually unchallenged. As heirs to both the Albusaidi and the
Mazrui, they took possession of the political order along the
coast, and proceeded to transform the quasi-diplomatic agents
of the sultan—the *liwalis* and their subordinates—into the
administrative and judicial agents of British authority, even
where this ran counter to the interests of the indigenous institutions, both of the Arab tribes along the coast and of the Bantu
immediately adjoining.[3] All in all, the British had secured a
firm foothold from which to develop their Protectorate.

---

[1] In addition to the papers in the Zanzibar, Mombasa, and British Foreign
Office Archives (F.O.C.P.'s and F.O. 2), see A. H. Hardinge, *A Diplomatist in the
East* (London, 1928), pp. 155–86, and H. Moyse-Bartlett, *The King's African Rifles*
(Aldershot, 1956), pp. 106–11. Shihabuddin Chiraghdin's Makerere College Arts
Research Prize Essay of 1953–4, on 'Sheikh Mbaruk bin Rashid bin Salim bin
Hemed al-Mazrui', has also been especially helpful.

[2] Similar collisions had already occurred upon Lake Nyasa, upon Lake Victoria,
and upon the coast adjoining the German sphere in East Africa in 1888. The Nyasa
clash continued undecided until 1895, by which time there had been a parallel
conflict between the Arabs and the Belgian administration upon the upper Congo.

[3] e.g. *Report on the East Africa Protectorate, 1903—4*, Cd. 2331 (1905); H. E.

There was no comparably decisive occurrence in the early years upon the Juba river to the north. By 1895, when the Company's rule gave way to the Protectorate, a semblance of overlordship had been established by the British over the Herti Somali around Kismayu, and in the following year a chief of the Ogaden Somali farther inland went through a form of submission, which was confirmed after his death in 1897 by his son and successor. The British accordingly imagined that their claims to authority hereabouts were being accepted: but the Ogaden showed no disposition to desist from their traditional raiding—their unceasing struggle for pasture and water. As a result, by 1898 news of their continued depredations upon neighbouring peoples (which culminated in an assault upon a British outpost at Yonte) moved the British to dispatch a military force to 'punish' them. Launched in April 1898, this only succeeded, however, in inflicting a significant defeat upon the Ogaden in the following August; but the Ogaden then sued for peace, and were made to pay a fine of 500 head of cattle. For the next two years the Ogaden and their neighbours, in part because they were perturbed about Ethiopian advances towards their inland flank, presented to the British a conciliatory face. But when Jenner, the British Sub-Commissioner for Jubaland, proceeded in 1900 to take an imperious line about some Ogaden raids upon a small riverain people, a group of Ogaden chiefs plotted his murder. This they accomplished in November. In revenge the British unleashed a second Ogaden expedition early in 1901, consisting this time of about 1,500 men under the command of the Acting Commissioner, Colonel Ternan.[1] A severe encounter occurred in February of that year in which about 150 Somalis were killed and wounded. Ternan's expedition, however, failed to inflict a decisive defeat upon the elusive, nomadic Ogaden. In the years that followed the British denied them access to some of their water-holes and placed obstacles in the way of their trade with the coast; but they made no preparations for a further invasion, and the Ogaden remained virtually unmolested. Their overthrow was not for the

Lambert, 'The Arab community of Mombasa', unpublished typescript, Jan. 1957. Cf. Hardinge, op. cit., p. 155. Gazetted Nyika and Giryama headmen were first appointed, it seems, only in 1908. *Report on the E.A.P., 1908–9*, Cd. 4964–9 (1910).
[1] It was the largest expedition which the E.A.P. Government ever launched.

time being a salient British objective. The only significant
British interest at this time ran not north-westwards from
Kismayu, but north-westwards from Mombasa.[1]

The road to Uganda

The number of alien intruders into the areas inland from
Mombasa which pivoted on Mount Kenya was growing
steadily as the nineteenth century died away. Most of them were
traders who were going farther and farther north-west in search
primarily of ivory.[2] In three distinct ways, however, the trading
pattern in the 1890's was displaying novel features. In the first
place the coastal traders, anxious to avoid the prying eyes of
British agents along the southern edge of Kamba country, made
much greater use than before of the road to the coast through
Kitui Kamba, the control of which the Kamba had by now
completely lost.[3] Secondly, while the total number of trading
caravans grew substantially, their aggregate size declined considerably; the typical trader no longer participated in a large
caravan several hundred strong; he was now a small trader with
a few followers only.[4] And thirdly, to the Arab and coastal
traders were now added Asian traders and even several Europeans.[5] These were the only aliens of whom most Africans in the
interior were at all conscious. There was certainly little or no
suspicion that this commercial penetration was about to be
overtaken by the greatest political transformation which the
hinterland had ever experienced. Such opaqueness of vision was
primarily due to the absence amongst the essentially stateless
societies of the interior of any conception of prescriptive political
dominion. Among the peoples east of the Mau escarpment this
lack of prescience was gravely aggravated at the turn of the
century by their preoccupation, as we have seen, with famine,
disease, and civil war.

[1] Again there is evidence on these events in Z.R.A., M.P.A., and F.O. papers.
See also Moyse-Bartlett, *K.A.R.*, pp. 111–20; Hardinge, op. cit., pp. 140–1, 216–21;
and T. S. Thomas, *Jubaland and the Northern Frontier District* (Nairobi, 1917),
pp. 24 sqq.
[2] See, for example, Dundas, 'The destruction of elephants by the Hill Suk', File
on 'Chebleng, Nilo and Hill Tribes', D.C.'s Office, Tambach.
[3] Ainsworth to Hardinge, 15 Nov. 1895, Z.R.A. E3.
[4] Ainsworth to Hardinge, 21 Dec. 1895, Z.R.A. E5.
[5] e.g. Dick, West, Boyes, Gibbons.

But there was, in any event, little about the first ten years of imperial penetration in the interior to warn them of its pro-clivities. It was at once very restricted and bedecked in a garb exciting little comment. This was chiefly due to the limited significance which before 1900 attached to this region in the minds of both the I.B.E.A. Company and the British Foreign Office. To them the Kenyan interior was simply the road to Uganda. The route, moreover, along which British agents plied was the one which had become most frequented by the traders in the mid-1880's. From Mombasa, past the Teita hills, it ran through Machakos to the southern edge of Kiambu; thence north-west to Lake Baringo, across the Uasin Gishu plateau to Mumia's in Kavirondo, and so on to Buganda. Along this route the Company had posted agents at Ndi, at Machakos and Dagoretti (at both of which it had built forts), and at Mumia's.[1] There was for a time a very wide gap between the last two; it was here, therefore, during 1894 that a new post was built at Eldama Ravine north of Lake Nakuru on the western side of the Rift Valley.[2] These posts were without doubt a substantial advance upon anything hitherto established in this region by the coastmen; they were the first palpable signs of the greater ingenuity of the white men. But all of them were primarily supply and resting points. The Africans who first associated with them were chiefly employed as food collectors and caravan porters. The posts, therefore, bore all the marks of being purely commercial agencies. Such appearances were, of course, de-ceptive. Although each post had been established by a British company, that company's main interest had been political. As agent of the British Crown it had claimed dominion over the whole region, and in the minds of most British agents on the spot they themselves were the district officials, and their forts were the district headquarters, first of a chartered company, and then of an undoubted British protectorate—even where their effective jurisdiction ceased at their perimeter fence. If these were, on several accounts, presumptuous claims, they were nevertheless seminal. For such British officials unhesitatingly believed that

---

[1] See ch. xi in vol. i of this *History*. Dagoretti Fort was replaced by Fort Smith in 1891.

[2] Wilson to O. C. Ravine, 10 Oct. 1894, (Copy) E.S.A. A2/3. This obviated, too, the circuit north to Lake Baringo.

their ultimate task was to spread British rule.[1] Such an idea was barely comprehensible to many of their African neighbours.

First contacts between the British and the Masai

The one people who might seriously have frustrated British ambitions in the interior were the Masai. Lording it, as they did, over the open country across which every British enterprise had to pass on its way from one British post to the next, it lay in their power to have obstructed British operations by sudden descents upon isolated outposts or vulnerable caravans, since they could always be sure of retreating with an ample margin of safety to the wide expanses that only they themselves knew intimately. No one, however, realized this better than the British, who in consequence, during the early years of their occupation (when the number of troops at their disposal was extremely limited)[2] and more especially while the Uganda Railway was being built, were generally most careful to avoid any conflict with the Masai, since they correctly surmised that a premature collision with them could scarcely breed any but evil consequences for themselves. The peaceful penetration of Masailand, therefore, became the order of the day. As Ainsworth the Sub-Commissioner, Ukamba Province, put it in 1899:

A policy of gradually bringing these people [the Masai] under our complete control is better than one of using absolute force at once. The latter alternative cannot be effectual while the large tracts of territory to the north and north-east remain open to them, and this gradual policy will undoubtedly during the time that the Uganda Railway is building, be one more compatible to our own interests as well.[3]

In saying this he was only echoing almost every other British official who pondered the topic.[4]

This policy of caution proved to be supremely successful. It required from the British patience and discrimination. They had to reconcile themselves to the idea that it would be futile

---

[1] See, for example, the diaries and letters of Francis Hall, *passim*, Rhodes House, Oxford, MSS. Afr., S54–62.

[2] See ch. xi in vol. i of this *History*.

[3] Ainsworth to Crauford, 13 June 1899, F.O.C.P. 7402.

[4] e.g. Hardinge to Salisbury, 18 Nov. 1897, F.O.C.P. 7024; Hall to Hill, 22 Aug. 1898, F.O. 2/165; Ternan to Lansdowne, 4 Dec. 1900, and enclosures, F.O.C.P. 7690.

to attempt to restrain Masai raids into areas where British jurisdiction was non-existent. But such necessities were accepted with good grace;[1] and dividends followed. The Masai, of course, scarcely realized that British officials were aiming at establishing British rule over them. Moreover, as we have seen, they themselves were heavily preoccupied not only with their own raids, but more particularly at this time with their epidemic lesions and their civil war. The latter, it so happened, reached its peak at the time which was most critical for the British— during the years when the Uganda Railway was stretching out across the northern part of Masailand.[2] But in any event, since the British, unlike the Germans, were careful to do nothing provocative, the Masai saw no cause in their presence for concern. They looked exactly like the travellers and traders with whom the Masai had become familiar. Their forts all lay in the no-man's-lands which ran under the lee of non-Masai peoples away from the main Masai grazing areas. They showed no disposition to make serious inroads upon Masai-occupied territory; and they possessed no cattle to excite Masai cupidity.

It was generally assumed, however, by the British that a conflict with the Masai could not be avoided for ever.[3] Yet, with one bare exception, avoided it was, chiefly because besides these negative elements in the relationship between the British and the Masai there were in the early years positive elements as well. These began with the refuge which Francis Hall of Fort Smith[4] gave from 1893 onwards to the remnants of the Kaputie and Matapatu Masai who had been denuded of their cattle by disease and by the Loita Masai, and denied adequate sustenance by their unfriendly Kikuyu neighbours. Hall helped them to turn their hands to agriculture and organized a settlement for them which was eventually located at Ngong.[5] Such succour served at a critical moment to recommend British administrators both to the great Masai *laibon* Lenana and to the Masai of his following to which the fugitives belonged.

The really vital incident, however, was the Kedong massacre

---

[1] Hardinge to Salisbury, 18 Nov. 1897, F.O.C.P. 7024.
[2] See Chapter V, pp. 209–10 below.
[3] e.g. Hardinge to Salisbury, 2 Nov. 1897, F.O.C.P. 7032.
[4] Hall was at first a company, and then a protectorate official.
[5] Hall to Pigott, 13 Feb. 1894, F.O.C.P. 6557; Gilkison to Pigott, 25 Oct. 1895, Z.R.A. E2.

of November 1895. A caravan of Kikuyu was returning from
Eldama Ravine when a fracas with some neighbouring Masai
suddenly blew up into a major clash in which the Masai killed
nearly 650 Kikuyu and Swahili porters. On hearing the news
a Scots trader named Andrew Dick, who was camped nearby,
set forth with two French travellers to attack the Masai, and
shot about 100 of them dead before he himself was killed.
A British official named Gilkison thereupon organized a further
force to attack the Masai, but only to find they had fled. Other
British officials in the area very soon realized, however, that
they had no adequate force with which to pursue the Masai;
while the Masai for their part were so dismayed at the ability of
three white men to shoot down 100 of their warriors in a single
encounter that they immediately sought for peace. There
followed an investigation of the whole incident by British
officials in close accord with Lenana and his associates, which
laid the blame for the original massacre very squarely upon the
Kikuyu and Swahili porters. It seems that this whole affair
profoundly impressed both Lenana and his Masai, at once with
the military ability of the white man and with the magnanimity
of British officials who for their part had thus successfully turned
a really awkward corner.[1]

Certainly from these beginnings good relations between the
British and Lenana's Masai advanced unchecked. Friendly
visits between Lenana and British officials occurred more and
more frequently.[2] Lenana's Masai procured British assistance
in first fending off and then curbing the rinderpest outbreak of
the later 1890's,[3] and numbers of their warriors found profitable
employment as auxiliaries in British expeditions against other
peoples.[4] An official report to the E.A.P. Government was later
to complain that 'no punitive expedition has ever been undertaken against the Masai'; an omission, it said, which subsequently enabled the Masai to eschew British pressures for

[1] There are a number of accounts of the Kedong massacre, e.g. Pordage's
'Report re Masai' 18 Dec. 1895, E.S.A. A4/4, and F. H. Goldsmith, *John Ainsworth,
Pioneer Kenya Administrator, 1864–1946* (London, 1955), pp. 26–31.
[2] e.g. Hardinge to Salisbury, 18 Nov. 1897, F.O.C.P. 7024; Ainsworth to
Crauford, 18 May 1899, F.O.C.P. 7401.
[3] Minutes 29 Aug. 1898, E.A.P. Council, Zanzibar Museum, item 313; Ainsworth to Crauford, 15 Nov. 1899, M.P.A. 1899, Commissioner, Ukamba, In.
[4] e.g. Moyse-Bartlett, *K.A.R.*, pp. 87–89.

change.[1] But this was the price which the British paid for the unhindered establishment of their first few stations in the interior, and the unhampered completion of a firmly anchored line of communications—first the Sclater road[2] and then the Uganda Railway[3]—which served as the backbone for their protectorate, athwart the domain of the one people in the region whose hostility they had most cause to fear. To the British it was a triumphant conclusion. It rested, to a very considerable extent, upon the close accord they had attained with Lenana, the important Masai *laibon* who, to the great advantage of the British, had simultaneously emerged triumphant from his protracted civil war with his brother and thus held sway over the great majority of the northern Masai sub-tribes.

The preliminary extension of British dominion

Although it could plainly not be said that the Masai were now under British administration, the absence of any conflict with them, which could so easily have undermined the uncertain British footholds in the interior, allowed British officials to proceed contemporaneously, and without interruption from the rear, with the very preliminary extension of their self-conceived dominion over the Masai's neighbours. This process contrasted in several ways with the parallel story in Uganda. It had, to begin with, no one starting-point; it issued forth simultaneously from each of the E.A.P. road stations on the way to Uganda. Because, moreover, the peoples of the E.A.P. (unlike the peoples of the Uganda kingdoms)[4] had hardly any extensive political authorities for the British to capture, British authority was rarely established at a single blow over any considerable area. It could only be imposed piecemeal. The full story of its imposition is therefore compounded of numerous petty incidents, most of which were marked (in contrast with British dealings with the Masai) by a show of force, if not indeed by its actual use.[5]

[1] G. R. Sandford, *An Administrative and Political History of the Masai Reserve* (London, 1919), p. 1.
[2] Built by Captain Sclater, it completed the so-called Mackinnon Road, which the Company had begun from Mombasa, and reached the shores of Lake Victoria in 1896: several letters from Sclater to Hill are in F.O. 2/114 and 115.
[3] See Chapter V below.   [4] See Chapter II below.
[5] Hall to Ainsworth, 15 Apr. 1899, M.P.A., 1899, Commissioner, Ukamba, In.

Nevertheless, the whole process developed at the outset very slowly. Ndi station (about 100 miles inland from Mombasa) the Protectorate had inherited from the Company; from here British authority was gradually extended into the surrounding Teita hills with the help of a number of small punitive expeditions.[1] From Machakos farther north-west Ainsworth, a company and then a protectorate man, had by 1900 spread British overlordship into most of the modern Machakos District. Between 1894 and 1897 his achievement was punctuated by four important punitive expeditions and the establishment of two police outposts.[2] Further petty expeditions also brought some of the area around Fort Smith, in southern Kiambu, Kikuyu, under British overrule[3] (although British officers here were so preoccupied with the Masai and with organizing food caravans for Uganda—especially after the outbreak of the Sudanese mutiny in 1897—that they scarcely had time to extend their influence very far beyond the immediate vicinity of their station). But in all three districts it was generally possible for the British to obtain the support of one small section of tribesmen against another. In each of them successive groups of Africans began to adhere to British officials as traditionally they would have done to any successful leader;[4] while in all three, British purposes were aided considerably by the ravages of famine and disease in the last years of the nineteenth century. So long as these raged, any kind of concerted opposition to British control was out of the question. By the time they had abated the British were firmly installed at three or four key points in the Mombasa hinterland—at Machakos and Fort Smith in particular.

To the westward the region extending from the Rift Valley to Lake Victoria was until 1902 part of the Uganda Protectorate. But here, in Kavirondo upon the north-west corner of the lake, a parallel story was being simultaneously enacted. A protectorate official had been posted in 1894 to Mumia's, the

---

[1] e.g. Weaver to Ainsworth, 25 Mar. 1898, Z.R.A. D19; Teita District Record Book, vol. IA, D.C.'s Office, Wundanyi. By 1909 the E.A.P. Annual Report was averring that 'the Teita can be reckoned among the most obedient and peaceful natives in the Protectorate' (*Report on the E.A.P., 1908–9*, Cd. 4964–9).

[2] Ainsworth to Pigott, 16 Mar. 1894, F.O.C.P. 6557; Ainsworth to Hardinge, 8 Mar. 1897, Z.R.A. D11.

[3] Gilkison to Pigott, 25 Oct. 1895, Z.R.A. E2.

[4] e.g. Hall to Pigott, 16 Apr. 1894, F.O.C.P. 6557.

traders' entrepôt, to maintain a supply post on the road to Uganda;[1] Mumia himself was thereupon glad to transform his former association with the coastal traders into an alliance with the British. Soon afterwards there was a clear instance of the manner in which such an establishment became the starting-point for the extension of British dominion into the surrounding area. In December 1894 the Bugusu,[2] a neighbouring people, attacked a British mail party; and when an attempt was made to force them to disgorge their captured rifles they resisted.[3] As a result in 1895 two punitive expeditions were sent against them,[4] whose success formed the basis for the initial over-awing of both the Bugusu and their neighbours in the region round about. In three formative journeys immediately after-wards, one northwards, one south-eastwards, and one due south from Mumia's,[5] C. W. Hobley[6] extended his personal influence —sometimes by direct attack, sometimes by playing one small section off against another—over most of the Luhya peoples and over some of the Luo clans on the northern shore of the Kavirondo Gulf. As a result by 1900 he could say with some justice, 'I know every chief [sic] from Elgon to Kitoto's and they know me'.[7]

But Hobley's very success aggravated the major problem confronting the British in this eastern part of Uganda, for he was casting his mantle over many of the peoples whom the Nandi on their plateau between Lake Victoria and the Rift Valley had in the preceding years come to look upon as their own legitimate prey. In 1895 the Nandi murdered a British trader named West[8]—a typical Nandi exploit, since they had long made it their practice to rid themselves of all alien in-truders. They then proceeded to attack some passing British caravans—in both instances revealing how much they differed

---

[1] Colvile to Spire, 19 May, 15 July, 1894, Spire Papers.
[2] The Bugusu were called by the British at the time the Ketosh.
[3] See half a dozen letters from Spire, E.S.A. A2/3.
[4] Grant to Jackson, 16 Jan. 1895, E.S.A. A4/1; Berkeley to Kimberley, 4 Sept. 1895, and enclosures, F.O. 2/93.
[5] Hobley to Berkeley, 8 Jan. 1896, E.S.A. A4/4; 22 Sept. 1896, E.S.A. A4/5; 13 Nov. 1896, E.S.A. A4/6.
[6] The second protectorate official posted to Kavirondo.
[7] Hobley to Johnston, 9 Mar., 1900, E.S.A. A4/26. C. W. Hobley, *Kenya from Chartered Company to Crown Colony* (London, 1929), ch. v.
[8] Jackson to Kimberley, 3 Aug. 1895, F.O. 2/93.

in their attitudes from the Masai. But unlike the Masai, the
Nandi lived in a compact area, and the British felt none of
that necessity for caution towards them which they displayed
towards the Masai. Accordingly, in 1895 a full-scale British
military expedition was launched against them. But it was
in no sense decisive; for it was during this period that the
prowess of the Nandi stood at its zenith, and their pervasive
self-confidence remained firmly invulnerable. Two years later,
indeed, F. J. Jackson[1] became so perturbed at the incipient
hostility of the Nandi and their Nilo-Hamite confrères on the
west side of the Rift Valley that he called for a further expedition to be launched in that year not only against the Nandi
but against the Keyo and the Tuken to their north-east as well.[2]
But this too failed to be decisive. Still cock-a-hoop with their
recent ebullient hegemony, the Nandi maintained their opposition to any *détente* with the British for several years longer.

In reality, therefore, a *tour d'horizon* in 1900 emphasizes that
outside Ainsworth's Machakos District, and parts of Hobley's
northern Kavirondo, British authority was still by 1900 a very
peripheral phenomenon to most of the Kenyan peoples. Projects for new British stations had abounded. Ngong, Naivasha,
and Taveta had been opened (to maintain contact with the
Masai)[3] and a Nandi station too;[4] but the only significant new
departure had been the opening of Kitui station in 1897[5]—a
move which reflected the one constant interest of the Victorian
Foreign Office in Africa; they had accepted Hardinge's dictum
that Kitui was a slave-trade centre which needed to be controlled.[6] None of these new stations, however, enjoyed very much
local influence. To the British, moreover, the Mombasa hinterland was still essentially the road to Uganda, and as late as 1899

---

[1] In 1895 he had been placed in charge of the Mau District which was based on
the station at Eldama Ravine.

[2] A summary account of all these expeditions (on which there is a good deal of
detailed information in F.O. 2/93, 113, 133, and in E.S.A.) will be found in Moyse-
Bartlett, *K.A.R.*, pp. 64–69.

[3] In 1895, 1896, and 1897 respectively. Gilkison to Pigott, 25 Oct. 1895, Z.R.A.
E2; Berkeley to Salisbury, 11 Feb. 1896, F.O. 2/113; Taubman to Hardinge,
8 May 1897, Z.R.A. D11.

[4] In its first five years it had no less than twelve changes in the officer commanding. Jackson to Johnston, 20 Nov. 1900, E.S.A. A8/1.

[5] Ainsworth to Hardinge, 29 Dec. 1897, F.O.C.P. 7024.

[6] Hardinge to Salisbury, 11 June 1896, F.O.C.P. 6861.

the Foreign Office continued to deny permission for further British stations amongst the Kikuyu to the north of Fort Smith.[1]
Nevertheless, the first steps had now been taken towards extending British control over the interior. The danger of Masai
opposition had been largely circumvented. The Sclater road
had by now been stretched from Mombasa to Lake Victoria,
in the wake of which the Uganda Railway was slowly but surely
advancing; and in three or four marginal areas British officials
had shown themselves capable of penetrating where the Masai
had invariably stopped short.

Policy and administration in the interior: the prime decisions

It was upon these slender, but critically important foundations, that the trunnions of the future Kenya now came to be
laid. In 1901 the Uganda Railway reached the shores of Lake
Victoria. As a result the British enclaves which studded the
route between Mombasa and Kavirondo were firmly linked
together. And with this, British attention was directed towards
the E.A.P.'s hinterland as never before. There appeared to be
little prospect of development along the torrid coastline. It
began to seem obvious that the future now lay in the temperate
uplands lying inland. Accordingly, in 1900, Sir Charles Eliot,
the new British Commissioner, devolved his responsibilities for
Zanzibar upon the British Consul there and henceforth devoted
all his energies to rough-hewing the destinies of the interior.[2]
Three years before, in 1897, his predecessor, Sir Arthur
Hardinge, had brought the Sultan of Zanzibar up the railway
line towards the Athi river for a meeting with some Masai,
Kamba, and Kikuyu 'chiefs'.[3] But this proved to be the last
occasion upon which there was any suggestion that the Kenyan
uplands might in any sense become an appanage of Zanzibar.
Ten years later, indeed, in 1907, after a sojourn since the turn
of the century at Mombasa, the capital of the E.A.P. was
eventually transferred to Nairobi,[4] and thereafter the Protectorate ceased altogether to hinge upon the islamized coastline. It

---

[1] Salisbury to Hardinge, 15 Apr. 1899, F.O.C.P. 7400.
[2] C. Eliot, *The East Africa Protectorate* (London, 1905); L. W. Hollingsworth,
Zanzibar under the Foreign Office (London, 1953), p. 168; and see Chapter XIII
below.
[3] Hardinge, *A Diplomatist in the East*, pp. 153–4.
[4] *Official Gazette of the East Africa and Uganda Protectorates*, 15 May 1907.

now pivoted not upon the Arab town of Mombasa—nor indeed about any indigenous centre at all—but upon an exotic railway town planted at the edge of Francis Hall's enclave between the Masai and Kikuyu—a point of some psychological moment since *inter alia* it comported with nothing which was significantly African in origin.

Earlier, in 1902, Uganda's former Eastern Province[1] had been transferred to become the Kisumu and Naivasha provinces of the E.A.P. This ensured that British Masailand lay in future within only one British protectorate; that the original Uganda Railway became the responsibility of only one administration (paradoxically the E.A.P.'s); and that the E.A.P. now became solely responsible for all the extensive upland areas—some hilly, forested, and populated; some open, flat, and practically deserted—which lay between the sea and the eastern shores of Lake Victoria. At the same time Sir Harry Johnston's[2] proposal to federate the Uganda and British East Africa protectorates under a single high commissioner (with headquarters upon the Mau plateau) was curtly dismissed in the Foreign Office;[3] henceforward they went their own distinctive ways—more especially because Uganda lost, by the transfer of its Eastern Province, all of its former 'highland' areas.

Owing to the Mazrui war the Uganda Railway had had an even later start than had finally been determined upon in London; work upon the line had begun amid difficult circumstances at Mombasa in December 1895, and as the tracks struck inland there had been further interruptions—from lions, for instance, near the Tsavo;[4] but in 1899 the last flat open space was reached before the climb up through southern Kiambu. Here in the following year the main workshops were transferred from Mombasa (so as to be nearer the workings on the second

---

[1] Also a small part of its former Central Province, and a bite out of its Rudolf Province.

[2] Johnston was Special Commissioner for the Uganda Protectorate 1899–1901.

[3] H. B. Thomas, 'A federal capital for Eastern Africa—some early proposals', *Uganda J.* ii. 3 (1935), 247–9; K. Ingham, 'Uganda's old Eastern Province: the transfer to East Africa Protectorate in 1902', ibid. xxi. 1 (1957), 41–46; A. T. Matson, 'Uganda's old Eastern Province and East Africa's federal capital', ibid. xxii. 1 (1958), 43–53; G. Bennett, 'The eastern boundary of Uganda in 1902', ibid. xxiii. 1 (1959), 69–72.

[4] The classic stories are to be found in J. H. Patterson, *The Man-eaters of Tsavo* (London, 1910).

and more difficult part of the line through the highlands), and
the foundations were unwittingly laid for the future city of
Nairobi. Serious engineering obstacles were meantime being
overcome upon both scarps of the Rift Valley. After climbing
the Mau summit at 8,500 feet the railway eventually continued
down the Nyando Valley, south of Nandi;[1] and the first locomo-
tive ran through to Kisumu on the Kavirondo Gulf in December
1901. The last of the 580 miles of line was finally opened to
traffic in September 1904. The whole had cost the British taxpayer about £5½ million.[2]

Already some traffic had begun to offer, but the serious losses
incurred in the running of the railway during its first few years
so greatly increased the already unwelcome cost to the British
Treasury of administering the Protectorate, that the Protectorate Government was urgently obliged to seek ways and
means of making both the Protectorate and the railway pay.
Since British administrative control over the Africans of Kenya
was, at the time when the railway was being built, very limited,
Indian coolies had been introduced as construction labourers
instead.[3] Thereafter there was some possibility of Indian migrants
being entrusted with the country's future development.[4]
But all such suggestions soon gave way to a more fashionable
proposal. Even at the turn of the century British control over
the surrounding African population remained so tenuous that
there was little possibility of prompt economic development
coming from them;[5] and the obvious alternative, to any late
Victorian Britisher, wherever physical conditions (as in the
Kenyan uplands) allowed, was to seek the sovereign economic
remedy in extensive white settlement. Had not white settlement
—in the Americas, in Australasia—constituted one of the most
notable achievements of the white race throughout the preceding century? In an age of European expansion was it not
wrong to lock up potentially productive lands? To these questions there could be only one reply, and the result was that by

---

[1] The original plan had been to take the railway north of Nandi.

[2] M. F. Hill, *Permanent Way*, vol. i, *The Story of the Kenya and Uganda Railway*
(Nairobi, 1950), pt. ii.

[3] Ibid., pp. 147 sqq.

[4] e.g. Eliot to Lansdowne, 5 Jan. 1902, F.O.C.P. 7946; 25 Apr. 1902, F.O.C.P.
7953.

[5] e.g. *Report on the E.A.P., 1903–4*, Cd. 2331 (1905).

1902 the E.A.P. was committed to a policy of introducing white
settlers as a means of establishing its economic prosperity and
wiping away its continuing indebtedness to the British Treasury.
At the time this critical decision was taken, very little of modern
Kenya was under British control, and white settlement as
the deliberate policy of a protectorate government with few
resources, few troops, and no mandate to ignore the interests
of large numbers of Africans, was a practicable possibility only
because, as we have seen, just a few areas upon the periphery
of Masailand were by 1902 under effective British control. As a
result the first lands to be alienated were located in the border-
lands between the former domains of the Masai and their Kikuyu and Kamba neighbours (between Machakos and Nairobi)
and in those areas around Fort Smith where the Kikuyu population had recently been decimated by famine and disease, and
where Hall and his colleagues had spent the past decade
establishing British supremacy.[1]

No one was more responsible for carrying through the introduction of white settlement than Sir Charles Eliot, but in 1904,
following a dispute with the Foreign Office over the disposal
of some ex-Masai lands to a London syndicate, he suddenly
resigned his post.[2] His successor, Sir Donald Stewart, died
a year later. Sir James Hayes Sadler, who then succeeded,
became in 1907, following the transfer in 1905 of responsibility
for the Protectorate's affairs in London from the Foreign Office
to the Colonial Office, its first Governor. He was widely felt,
however, to be weak and ineffective, and in 1909 was removed
to the governorship of the Windward Islands.[3] Thereupon Sir
Percy Girouard, Lugard's successor in Northern Nigeria, was
promoted to his place. He had served in Egypt and South Africa
as well, and probably had a broader conspectus of African

---

[1] On the origins of white settlement there is a considerable literature, see Hill,
op. cit., pt. iii; E. Huxley, *White Man's Country: Lord Delamere and the making of
Kenya* (London, 1935), vol. i. Dr. Robert A. Remole has most kindly allowed access
to his valuable Harvard Ph.D. thesis (1959), *White Settlers, or the Foundation of
European Agricultural Settlement in Kenya*: he is not, of course, responsible for the
conclusions reached here. A further account will be found in Chapters V and VI
below.

[2] *Correspondence Relating to the Resignation of Sir Charles Eliot and to the Concession to
the East Africa Syndicate*, Cd. 2099 (1904).

[3] e.g. Minute by R. Popham Lobb on Sadler to Crewe, 1 Apr. 1908, C.O.
533/43; Huxley, op. cit., pp. 236–7.

conditions than any other governor of his day. But his term, like Eliot's, was cut short in 1912 by yet another contretemps over some Masai lands with his official superiors in London.[1]

It was this succession of chief executives which built up the Protectorate's permanent administration. In 1902 the East Africa Order in Council, which remained the Protectorate's basic law, was promulgated, and thereafter a mass of legal enactments established the necessary legal and administrative superstructure. By 1903 bureaucracy had proliferated; there were already fifteen distinct government departments.[2] Municipalities, too, were being set up—in Nairobi in 1901 and in Kisumu in 1904;[3] while various arrangements were made to provide the Protectorate with a larger military force. At one time fourteen companies of the King's African Rifles were stationed within its borders.[4] These were required, more especially, to assist with the extension of British overlordship over most of the Bantu, Nilotic, and Nilo-Hamitic peoples lying within the Protectorate's boundaries, which, side by side with the introduction of European settlers, had now become the other main preoccupation of the Protectorate Government. Because both the agents of the British Company and thereafter the first Protectorate officials had adhered so closely to the route to the interior which the coastal traders were using in the mid-1880's (which, because of the hostility of the Kamba, the Kikuyu, and the Nandi, had skirted their domains), the main centres of African population in the E.A.P. had hitherto lain outside the aegis of British authority. Immediately upon the turn of the century, however, it was decided that with the promulgation of a hut tax[5] it should be possible to make every extension of British authority into a heavily populated area pay before long for itself. As Eliot himself put it in 1903: 'The introduction of an efficient administration is likely to produce a very large increase of revenue.'[6] The two areas he had parti-

[1] Ibid., p. 269.
[2] Hill, op. cit., p. 253.
[3] Notices in the *Official Gazette of the Uganda and East Africa Protectorates*, 1 Dec. 1901 and Feb. 1904.
[4] Moyse-Bartlett, *K.A.R.*, p. 137.
[5] Hut Tax Regulations were first issued in October 1901.
[6] Eliot to Lansdowne, 26 Nov. 1903, F.O.C.P. 8290. See also Eliot's letters of 18 June 1901, F.O.C.P. 7867; 19 Nov. 1902, F.O.C.P. 8040.

cularly in mind were the so-called Kenya and Kisumu Provinces,[1] the most heavily populated areas in the country. Their
conquest was in the main accomplished by 1908.

British expansion into Kenya Province

Kenya Province, as the British defined it at this time, comprised the areas surrounding Mount Kenya. Southward of its
peaks the Kikuyu peoples had since 1890 grown accustomed to
the European fort at the southern edge of their country. The
area around Fort Smith and Nairobi had become subordinated to a Kikuyu named Kinyanjui, who had originally
been a caravan headman for the British but had now been
elevated by them to be the local chief.[2] Farther north, however,
there was no foreign political intrusion until in 1898 a European
trader named John Boyes entered the country over the Aberdare
range from the west in search of food for railway survey parties
and Uganda caravans, and all unknowingly laid the foundations
for British rule in central Kikuyuland. For Boyes very soon
established a close trading alliance with a prominent Kikuyu
named Karuri of Metume. Side by side they fought those who
would not co-operate with them, and by battening upon the
lethargy which had overtaken the Kikuyu as a result of the
famine and smallpox which was plaguing their country at this
time, carved out for themselves a sphere of influence in Metume
and Karura. Riding high upon the crest of a sudden renown,
Boyes successfully made contact too with Wangombe of Gaki,
another prominent Kikuyu to the north-west. In 1900 this part
of his career, however, was abruptly curtailed when he was
arrested by British officials on a charge of 'dacoity'.[3] But by
that time the decision had been taken to establish a second
British fort in Kikuyuland, for which Francis Hall had selected
a site at Mbirri.[4] Upon his death it was renamed in 1901 Fort
Hall; and in the main its establishment proved capable of peace-

---

[1] *Report by H.M.'s Commissioner on the East Africa Protectorate, June 1903*, Cd. 1626
(1903).
[2] Ukamba Province Quarterly Report, Oct.–Dec. 1909.
[3] For a no-doubt-embellished account see C. W. L. Bulpett (ed.), *John Boyes,
King of the Wa-Kikuyu* (London, 1911). For his later career see J. Boyes, *The Company of Adventurers* (London, 1928).
[4] Hardinge to Salisbury, 11 June 1900, and enclosures, F.O.C.P. 7675.

ful accomplishment, for, unlike the next two stations in the
Mount Kenya area, it did not require official punitive expeditions to pave its way, primarily because Karuri's appetite had
been so whetted by his alliance with Boyes that upon the latter's
removal he was ready to throw in his lot and that of his followers
with the officials who took Boyes' place.[1] Although Fort Hall
stood a mere 50 miles north of Nairobi, it was the first British
station in the E.A.P.'s hinterland (with the rather particular
exception of Kitui) which was not founded either to hold the
Masai in check or to keep the Uganda road open. Its establishment gave birth to a new era.

There ensued, late in 1902, the foundation of the third and
most northern of the British forts in Kikuyuland at Nyeri,[2]
following the massacre of an Indian trading caravan and the
official punitive expedition sent to avenge it. Here Boyes's
activities once more bore fruit, for the closest ally of the new
British fort was his old acquaintance Wangombe of Gaki.[3]
Hostility towards the British, however, was by now mounting on
the east; in particular the Iraini Kikuyu and their Embu allies
had begun to make periodic attacks upon those Kikuyu who
had submitted to British jurisdiction. Here was a typical
situation to confound an imperial power; for if the British
could not protect those who had acknowledged their overlordship the likelihood was that they would forfeit their allegiance.[4]
It took three successive military expeditions to overthrow the
hostile combination. Early in 1904 a force was launched against
both the Iraini and the Embu;[5] a second followed in mid-1905;[6]
and a third (this time more particularly against the Embu)

---

[1] *Report on the E.A.P., 1903*, Cd. 1626. There followed, however, a series of minor
operations against a few remaining pockets of resistance during which several
defiant villages were destroyed by British-led troops, one in return for a peculiarly
gruesome killing of a European—when every Kikuyu man and woman was shot
down or bayoneted. R. Meinertzhagen, *Kenya Diary, 1902–1906* (Edinburgh, 1957),
pp. 51–52, also pp. 39–41, 50; W. S. and K. Routledge, *With a Prehistoric People:
the Akikuyu of British East Africa* (London, 1910), pp. x–xi.

[2] Meinertzhagen, op. cit., pp. 60 sqq. *Report on the E.A.P., 1903*, Cd. 1626.

[3] *Report on the E.A.P., 1903–4*, Cd. 2331 (1905).

[4] e.g. Hinde, 'Report on the Embo question . . .', enclosure in Sadler to Elgin,
1 Aug. 1906, C.O. 533/16.

[5] Meinertzhagen, op. cit., pp. 136, sqq. Eliot to Lansdowne, 4 May 1904, and
enclosures, F.O.C.P. 8356.

[6] Stewart to Lyttelton, 14 Aug. 1905, Colonial Office Confidential Print (hereinafter C.O.C.P.), African no. 771.

a year later. Only then was the opposition overthrown and an
Embu station founded in 1906.[1]

These expeditions, however, proved to be the crucial encounters for the whole Mount Kenya region. It seems almost
certain, for instance, that the British were able to establish a
station in 1908 at Meru to its north-eastward, effortlessly and
peacefully, because several prominent Meru had taken note of
these events and had decided in consequence to follow in the
footsteps of Karuri and Wangombe rather than of the Iraini
and the Embu.[2] Only the Tharaka, to the eastward of Mount
Kenya, held out for a little longer, but they soon submitted
before the punitive measures of a small British military patrol
in September 1910;[3] and three years later the last British post
in this area, half-way between Embu and Meru, was established
amongst the Chuka without opposition.[4] The key to the maintenance of the British position in these hilly, wooded and
populated districts lay in the end in the construction of roads.
In a striking manner these became the arteries of the King's
peace, carrying police and officials about their administrative
business, but also allowing an entirely novel ebb and flow across
the ridges into which for many social and political purposes the
country had hitherto been divided.[5] *Pax Britannica* had come
to Mount Kenya.

British expansion into Kisumu Province

In the main, however, the *pax* was not so much the fruit of
peaceful and carefully prepared extensions of British administration as of a series of small punitive expeditions by British-led
troops and auxiliaries. This was especially so in the Kisumu
Province between the Rift Valley and Lake Victoria; and just
as the process by which British overlordship was asserted in the
Kenya Province reached its climax in Embu in 1905–6, so there
was a similar climax in the Kisumu Province in those very same
years in the fifth and final British expedition against the hitherto
irrepressible Nandi. Kisumu itself had been founded in 1899

[1] Sadler to Elgin, 1 Aug., 31 Aug. 1906 and enclosures, C.O. 533/16.
[2] Sadler to Elgin, 5 Mar. 1908, and enclosure, C.O. 533/42.
[3] Moyse-Bartlett, *K.A.R.*, p. 206.
[4] D. R. Crampton, 'Early history of Chuka and Mwimbe', unpublished memo.,
D.C.'s Office, Embu; Chuka Political Records, vol. ii.
[5] e.g. *Report on the E.A.P., 1903–4*, Cd. 2331. Routledge, op. cit., p. xi.

as the future terminus of the Uganda Railway and as the port
from which shipping—canoes, dhows, and steamers—set forth
for Uganda's headquarters at Entebbe.[1] Already in 1899 the
land route to Uganda through Mumia's was being superseded
by this new water route—and with a typical result. In October
1899 a group of Luo upon the northern lip of the Kavirondo
Gulf attacked a British canoe party; in retaliation a small British
expedition was sent against them and the ensuing depredations
persuaded most of the Luo clans upon the northern shore of
the gulf to submit to British authority.[2] A similar fate overtook
the Nyanguori, a borderline Nilo-Hamite people immediately
to the north of Kisumu, in 1900.[3]

The major obstacle to the successful assertion of British
authority in this lakeward area lay, however (as it had from the
outset), in the hostility of the Nandi. Hobley, the local British sub-
commissioner, recognized that they would probably continue
to resist any sustained British intrusion to the last: and in the
middle of 1900 Nandi attacks upon British parties in the Nyando
Valley (where the railway was being laid) eventually precipitated the third open conflict between them. Hobley himself
felt strongly that this time the Nandi should be crushed once
and for all;[4] but Sir Harry Johnston and Sir Clement Hill
insisted that it was more important to keep the British route
with the coast clear and allow the Uganda Railway to be
completed without further ado.[5] The decisive encounter was
accordingly postponed, and at the end of 1900, after an inconclusive campaign, peace was patched up.[6]

For the time being Hobley and his colleagues concentrated
instead upon the extension of their rule over the immediately
surrounding areas, and in 1903 opened three new administrative stations. The first at Kakamega amongst the eastern Luhya,
immediately west of the Nandi, was designed to supplement the
otherwise meagre control exercised over them from Mumia's

[1] Ternan to Salisbury, 6 July 1899, F.O. 2/203.
[2] e.g. Johnston to Salisbury, 5 and 26 Feb. 1900, and enclosures, F.O. 2/297.
[3] Hobley, 'Report on Wanyanguori expedition', Apr. 1900, E.S.A. A4/28.
[4] Hobley, 'Report on the Nandi rising of 1900', 24 Aug. 1900, F.O. 2/556.
[5] Johnston to Jackson, 7 Oct. 1900, E.S.A. A9/1; Hill to Salisbury, 27 Oct. 1900, F.O. 2/556. Hill was head of the F.O. African Protectorates Department and was visiting East Africa.
[6] Hobley to Johnston, 1 Jan. 1901, E.S.A. A18/1.

farther westwards. The establishment of the second, at Kericho among the Kipsigis (the most closely related of the Nandi's neighbours in the region south of the railway and the Nyando Valley), was a somewhat delicate proceeding since the Kipsigis were at this time no less predatory in their habits and no less jealous of outside intervention than the Nandi; but a *modus vivendi* was established with one important section of them, and the hostility of the remainder, and more particularly of their *orkoiyot*, seems for the time being to have been successfully contained. The third station opened in this year stood at Karungu amongst the southern Luo on the shore of Lake Victoria southwards of Kisumu. The British hoped that its preliminary contacts with the Gusii, a Bantu people living immediately inland, might lead to a peaceful advance into their country as well.[1] All these proceedings, however, proved in the event to be contemporaneous with yet another outbreak of fighting between the British and the Nandi. This time it was the Nandi Kamelilo (inhabitants of the Tinderet hills close to the railway) who, having indulged in frequent 'tip-and-run' raids upon isolated parties upon the railway line, had provoked the fourth of the British Nandi expeditions.[2] This like its predecessors scoured the country-side, but the assumption, which the British made upon its termination, that the Nandi would probably now turn docile,[3] proved to be seriously mistaken.

But before any further conclusions were tried, the arm of British power had swung south into the territory of the more important of the unsubdued peoples immediately to the north of the German border. Here, early in 1905, the Sotik raided the Masai to their eastward. The British thereupon assumed responsibility for exacting penance, and in June 1905 launched an expedition against the Sotik, which, with the assistance of the neighbouring Buret people, soon drove them into submission.[4] Three months later a somewhat similar attack over to the westward by the still unsubdued Gusii against some of their Jaluo neighbours, who had now passed under British control, led to the dispatch of a further British expedition which in a

---

[1] e.g. *Report on the E.A.P., 1903*, Cd. 1626; *Report on the E.A.P., 1903–4*, Cd. 2331.
[2] Eliot to Lansdowne, 18 May 1903, F.O.C.P. 8177; 24 June 1903, and enclosures, F.O.C.P. 8192.   [3] *Report on the E.A.P., 1903–4*, Cd. 2331.
[4] Stewart to Lyttelton, 8 June, 16 Sept. 1905, and enclosures, C.O.C.P. African no. 771.

short campaign killed nearly 400 Gusii tribesmen.[1] Neither of
these expeditions, however, was quickly followed by the establishment of any further British stations because in that same
September 1905 the British were yet again organizing a military
expedition against the Nandi.

There had once more been a succession of Nandi raids. The
Nandi, in other words, still acknowledged no check to their
local hegemony. But this the British had now finally decided to
apply.[2] Accordingly the fifth and largest of the British Nandi
expeditions began operations in October 1905; and this time,
at the very outset, during an encounter at which peace was to
have been discussed, the senior Nandi *orkoiyot* was killed. His
death immediately demoralized the Nandi most profoundly,
for by it they lost at a critical moment the ritual leadership
which had been so vital an element in their latter-day successes.
In the fighting which followed there were several sharp encounters; but with 600 of their warriors killed by the end of
November, the Nandi eventually agreed to withdraw into a
reserve away from the railway—the Kamilelo abandoning in
particular the Tinderet hills. This retreat proved to be the end
for the Nandi of their ten years' open resistance to British
intrusion. It was the end, too, of any substantial opposition to
the establishment of British authority in their self-styled Kisumu
Province. For if the British could overthrow the Nandi, they
could obviously make short shrift of those round about who had
themselves been the victims of Nandi hegemony.[3]

There were in fact only two further British expeditions of any
note in this lakeward area. Both of them took place in 1908.
The first attacked the northern Bugusu, the northernmost of
the Luhya peoples, some of whom had in the past twelve years
deliberately slipped north to escape the bounds of British
dominion. They were quickly routed and forced to submit.[4]
The other followed the spearing of the first British officer
stationed in Kisii.[5] After twenty Gusii warriors had been killed,

[1] Sadler to Elgin, 2 Aug. 1906 and enclosure, C.O. 533/16; Lobb's minute on
Sadler to Crewe, 1 Apr. 1908, C.O. 533/43.
[2] Jackson to Lyttleton, 26 Sept. 1905, tel., C.O.C.P. African no. 771.
[3] Meinertzhagen, op. cit., pp. 221 sqq.; C.O. 534/3 *passim*; C.O.C.P. African
no. 771, *passim*; Nandi Political Record Book, D.C.'s Office, Kapsabet.
[4] Jackson to Crewe, 20 Oct. 1908, and enclosure, C.O. 533/47.
[5] Northcote to his father, 13 Jan. 1908, C.O. 533/41.

the Gusii sued for peace; but over 200 more of them were killed in subsequent fighting. This time there was a highly critical inquiry into the whole affair in the Colonial Office,[1] and, as a result, in 1910 detailed instructions were issued to all district officials for a much more careful approach to any further operations. In the Kisumu Province, however, they were too late. Its overall submission was already complete.

The Northern Frontier District and Jubaland

There remained, however, a very large area, three times the size of the already dominated protectorate, to the north and north-east of the Kisumu and Kenya provinces, which was still unsubdued. This was peopled in the main by widely dispersed nomadic tribes—Pokot, Samburu, Turkana, Rendile, Boran, and Somali. In 1900, after an abortive attempt to establish an administrative post in the Ribo hills, a British station was built near the shores of Lake Baringo, from which British administrators sought during the succeeding decade to bring the Tuken in the neighbouring hills, and the Keyo and Marakwet peoples who lived upon the scarp of the Rift Valley to the westward, under their jurisdiction. In 1908 a further British post was opened in the Kerio Valley so as to establish friendly contact with the Pokot who throughout this period were subject to raids from the Turkana to the north. After a first British expedition had been sent against the Turkana, the Kerio post was moved in 1910 to Ngabotok, so as to be in closer contact with them; and in 1912 a second (though indecisive) conflict with the Turkana took place. Ever since the 1880's the major concern of most of the peoples in this northern region—certainly of the Turkana, the Samburu, the Rendile, and to some extent the Boran—had lain in the advance from the north of Ethiopian ivory and cattle raiders, who were now armed with guns. In 1907, after some protracted negotiations, an Anglo-Ethiopian agreement was reached about a boundary line, and in that year the British organized a rather amateur frontier patrol with headquarters at Moyale. Its inability, however, to protect the northern tribes against Ethio-

---

[1] There are about 200 pages in the Colonial Office archives dealing with this whole affair: Sadler to Elgin, 1 Apr. 1908, and minutes, sqq. C.O. 533/43. See also C.O. 533/41 and 533/42.

pian raids led two years later to the establishment by the British of their Northern Frontier District with additional stations at Archer's Post, at Marsabit, and, from 1910, at Mount Kulal.[1]

It was in 1910, too, that the British adopted a similarly 'forward' policy in their Jubaland Province eastwards towards the sea. Although there had been some minor attempts to extend British authority over the southern Somalis in the years following the Ogaden expedition of 1901, effective British control had in reality remained confined to the coastline. The Somalis, however, were obviously still bent, as they had been for centuries past, upon advancing southwards.[2] In 1909 a number of them reached the River Tana. Shortly afterwards Sir Percy Girouard decided that they must be prevented from encroaching any farther upon the grazing grounds and water-supplies of their southern neighbours, and in 1910 ordered a station to be opened at Serenli so as to begin the process of bringing them under British control. Two years later a further British post was opened at Wajir to safeguard the neighbouring wells for the local Boran.[3] But by 1912 all the decisive occurrences in this northern and north-eastern region—the major British expeditions against the Turkana, the Somali, and the Ethiopian raiders—still lay in the future. British rule was still largely confined to the more populated southern regions of the Protectorate.

Force and Peace

Enough has been said to indicate that it was force and military prowess which in the main effected the critical submissions to British authority of the peoples of this region. There were some attempts at the peaceful extension of British overlordship. In a number of places alliances were forged with prominent individuals whose allegiance was thereafter carefully nurtured. In particular in the Kavirondo area Hobley took great pains to try and establish his personal authority by establishing first his personal influence. But even he did not hesitate to employ his maxim gun whenever there were signs of oppo-

[1] T. S. Thomas, *Jubaland*, chs. iii–v; Moyse-Bartlett, *K.A.R.*, pp. 209–14.

[2] See I. M. Lewis, 'The Somali conquest of the Horn of Africa', *Journal of African History*, l (1960), 213–30.

[3] T. S. Thomas, *Jubaland*, pp. 38–48; Moyse-Bartlett, *K.A.R.*, pp. 215–21.

sition. To British officials their 'punitive' expeditions were, of course, justified both by the depredations of 'offending' Africans, and by the necessity to inflict a 'severe lesson' to procure the final pacification of a recalcitrant area; and it was, of course, their firm belief that as servants of the British empire it was their mission to bring peace and order to lawless regions—a mission which they assuredly fulfilled. But there was in addition a strong tendency in the E.A.P.—which was encouraged, no doubt, by the frequently dangerous isolation of British officials —to resort to arms without considering possible alternatives; to inflict 'punishment' on a scale out of all proportion to any 'offence' which had been committed, and to treat as rebellion actions by Africans which, in truth, were only the expression of a natural instinct to preserve their own freedom and be rid of obstinate and unwelcome intruders.[1] Any map which outlined the operational theatres of the many small British military expeditions during the first fifteen years of British rule in the Kenyan uplands would exhibit few interstices. Within them, proximity to the scene of one or other expedition generally sufficed to create a readiness to submit amongst those who were not directly assaulted. And for all the exiguousness of these expeditions in European terms they were often vastly greater, more lethal demonstrations of force than any which the defeated tribes had experienced from any quarter in the past, since they almost invariably took the form of a wholly unequal conflict between guns upon the British side and spears upon the African.

Yet at the same time the end result of these expeditions was equally beyond the experience of most of these tribes. In the first place, unlike the Masai, the Nandi, the Sotik or the Gusii,

[1] This is not hindsight: see the exhaustive Minute upon the Kisii expedition of 1908 by R. Popham Lobb (a Northern Nigeria official temporarily posted to the Colonial Office) on Sadler to Crewe, 1 Apr. 1908, C.O. 533/43, '. . . The operations did not cease until 38 natives had been killed or wounded, many villages burnt, and livestock to the estimated value of £2,400 seized, in respect of each one of the six murders [Lobb's own emphasis] actual or attempted, of which members of the tribe had been guilty. . . . As a matter of fact, as opposed to legal fiction, there was no such thing as a revolt. Like any other people, European or otherwise, under similar circumstances, the Kisii rose up to prevent the forcible intrusion of strangers to whom they had never submitted.' See also Girouard, 'Interim report on British East Africa', in Girouard to Crewe, 13 Nov. 1909, C.O. 533/63.

who, whenever they raided, invariably retreated to their home-
lands with their loot shortly afterwards, the British were apt to
follow up a successful expedition by setting about the establishment of a continuing overlordship over those they had defeated.
Unlike the Masai and other African depredators in this area,
moreover, the British did not generally repeat their destructive
assaults after an initial success, unless it proved to have been
indecisive, or unless for some specific reason they felt themselves
especially provoked. On the contrary, they made it their prime
business to put a stop to all such raids—raids which most
Africans had hitherto looked upon as part of the immutable
order of nature. So successful were the British in the enforcement
of this policy that they effected a profound and far-reaching
revolution. Before long the Kikuyu were cutting back their
forest fringe because this traditional first line of defence was
rapidly becoming anachronistic; they began for the first time
to travel long distances unarmed; their menfolk abandoned
their hill-top sentry posts, and they ceased to barricade their
homesteads.[1] The Kamba, moreover, presently dared as never
before to move out of their hilly sanctums on to the open plains
beyond.[2] Amongst the eastern Luhya the Bugusu gradually
learnt that it was no longer necessary to maintain the high mud
walls which had been such a notable feature of their settlements
in the past and discovered that it was now safe to scatter un-
defended homesteads across the open country-side.[3] No-man's-
lands were apparently no longer required either.[4] Boundary
disputes between Luo clans were now determined not by the
clash of spear and shield, but by the arbitration of a British
district officer.[5] In Kikuyu country, as we have seen, and in
Kamba country and in the Kisumu Province, a network of
roads and bridges began to be built. New local markets were
opened up. Townships were laid out and some efforts were
made by administrative officers to develop African agriculture.[6]

[1] e.g. *Report on the E.A.P. 1903–4*, Cd. 2331; Routledge, *The Akikuyu*, pp. 7, 329.
[2] Hobley, 'Report of journey to Mumorii', enclosure in Sadler to Crewe,
18 Mar. 1908, C.O. 533/42.
[3] G. Wagner, *The Bantu of North Kavirondo*, i (London, 1949), 12–13.
[4] P. Mayer, 'The lineage principle in Gusii society', International African
Institute, *Memorandum xxiv* (1949), p. 3.
[5] Kisumu Political Record Book, vol. i.
[6] See, for example, Goldsmith, *Ainsworth*, ch. vi.

A quarter of a century later an Embu chief, who came before the Carter Commission of 1932 to seek redress for a number of deeply felt grievances, nevertheless let drop a gratuitous appreciation: 'We are grateful to Government', he said, 'for having established peace.'[1] He was echoed by others.[2] There were many, no doubt, young as well as old, who still yearned for the legendary excitements of yore.[3] But the grateful and the grumblers alike were agreed that a great change had occurred. A *pax* had come to the Kenyan uplands. It redounded, of course, to the benefit of the British Administration; for British overlordship was in large part acquiesced in because it guaranteed the peace which many Africans regarded as so considerable an advance upon their former conditions of life; and for those who had any doubts about its desirability there was always the uncomfortable awareness that the cost of resisting the Europeans was really very great. British military power had proved itself formidable, and so soon as the British had established their administration, they generally controlled the most efficient mechanism for enforcing authority which the country was to know for many years to come. A revolution had been accomplished; nothing was ever to be quite the same again.

The Masai moves

The effects of this revolution are nowhere better demonstrated than in the contemporary behaviour of the Masai. Both of the two current preoccupations of the British—the settlement of Europeans and the conquest of Africans—bore upon them directly. Between 1904 and 1913 a fair proportion of the Masai were moved about from one grazing ground to another, mainly in order to make way for British settlers. Such movements were, no doubt, less unpalatable to the Masai than they would have been to any of their agricultural neighbours. Even so it is at first sight astonishing that the lordly Masai (now no longer

---

[1] Kenya Land Commission, *Evidence*, i. 89.

[2] See, for example, the not untypical remarks recorded by Beech in the midst of a long list of complaints: 'We thoroughly appreciate the protection which we have obtained from Government, and the peace wherein we now live . . .', Beech's memorandum on 'The Kikuyu point of view', 12 Dec. 1912, Dagoretti Political Record Book, 1908–12, vol. i, D.C.'s Office, Kiambu.

[3] See, for example, G. Lindblom, *The Akamba in British East Africa*, 2nd edn. (Uppsala, 1920), p. 205.

distracted by disease and civil war) should have proved so malleable. They were, of course, greatly influenced by their senior *laibon* Lenana, who, while enjoying British support for his 'traditionally imprecise' pre-eminence, placed his confidence in British administrators. But there can be no doubt, too, that the fairly extensive participation by the Masai in the British conquest of neighbouring peoples had pointed its own moral. The British were obviously not to be resisted with impunity. They had shown themselves capable of penetrating where the Masai had only harried the fringes. They had freed themselves in consequence from dependence upon Masai forbearance. They had now, with Masai assistance indeed, outstripped the Masai as the chief arbiters of the Kenyan uplands. In 1903 the mere presence of a British force deployed to check a Masai raid upon some of their neighbours sufficed to halt them.[1] By 1912 the foremost Masai opponent of British policy confessed that the Governor 'had power to punish him'[2]—clear recognition, it would seem, of a dexterous (though by the British quite unpremeditated) checkmate.

A major problem for the British was in consequence to know what to do with the Masai. 'Their customs', Eliot wrote, 'may be interesting to anthropologists, but morally and economically they seem to be all bad.'[3] In particular he saw no reason why their relatively small numbers should monopolize so much of the land which ran alongside the expensively unremunerative railway. In his view much of the adjoining area should be made available for white settlement; this, in British circles, was widely agreed.[4] All the same Eliot was strongly opposed to the removal of the Masai into reserves, because he believed that proximity to Europeans might wean them away from their traditional pursuits. But upon this he was successfully opposed both by those who feared a clash between isolated settlers and encircling Masai, and by those who believed the Masai should be allowed a greater liberty.[5] Upon Eliot's resignation,

[1] Eliot to Lansdowne, 10 Oct. 1903, F.O.C.P. 8290.

[2] Account of meeting at Nakuru, 5 Dec. 1912, enclosed in Belfield to Harcourt, 17 Dec. 1912, C.O.C.P. African no. 1001.

[3] Memorandum by Sir Charles Eliot on 'Native rights in the Naivasha Province', 7 Sept. 1903; Sandford, *Masai Reserve*, ch. iii.

[4] e.g. Hobley to Lansdowne, 22 July 1904, F.O.C.P. 8357.

[5] e.g. Ainsworth's *Report*; Lansdowne to Stewart, 21 Oct. 1904, F.O.C.P. 8382.

Sir Donald Stewart accordingly concluded with Lenana and his associates the Masai Agreement of 1904, by which the Masai undertook to move into two reserves, one south of Ngong and the railway, the other to the northward upon the Laikipia plateau, both areas to be reserved to the Masai 'so long as the Masai as a race shall exist'; all of the intervening areas beside the railway being then made available for white settlement.[1]

The 1904 Agreement, however, proved to be only a temporary expedient. It was tolerated by the Masai only because they were not in fact obliged to confine themselves to the reserves it had defined.[2] And it was not strictly adhered to by the Government. The agreement's provision for a half-mile-wide roadway linking the two reserves was never honoured, and in 1908 all movement between the two reserves was prohibited lest 'disease-ridden' Masai cattle should infect the settlers' herds. As early as 1908, it seems, some administrators were in consequence beginning to wish for some rather tidier arrangements, and it was not long before their purposes coincided with a rising desire amongst the settlers for an opportunity to appropriate the broad expanses of the Laikipia plateau. The idea began to be mooted for the removal of the northern Masai to a single extended southern reserve south of the railway.

This operation was eventually accomplished by 1913: but not before an unbelievably tortuous saga had played itself out. In December 1908 a possible extension immediately west of the existing southern reserve was favourably reported upon by two British officials. In January 1909 Lenana expressed his agreement with the suggestion that the northern Masai should remove themselves thither, since he, and many other Masai, were becoming gravely perturbed at their growing division as a result of the 1904 Agreement into two distinct halves. Legalishu, however, the northerners' spokesman, was non-committal, and Girouard ordered another investigation before proceeding further. Two senior officials who were sent to inspect the new area declared it would first require a substantial improvement

---

[1] Stewart to Lansdowne, 5 Sept. 1904, and enclosures, F.O.C.P. 8382.
[2] Because of the rapid increase of their herds upon the long fallow pastures of the Laikipia plateau, the northern reserve was in any event more than once extended in the years which immediately followed.

in its water-supply. But because increasingly the northerners were now acting without regard to his authority, Lenana early in 1910 pressed Girouard to execute the move without more ado. In February 1910 at a formal meeting between the Government and the Masai, the northern leaders were prevailed upon to agree, and the move to the south began shortly afterwards. But in April 1910 it was abruptly halted upon the orders of the Colonial Secretary in London,[1] who insisted that the northern reserve should be maintained until the 1904 Agreement had been formally replaced by another agreement comparable in status. A further meeting between Girouard, Lenana, Legalishu, and their associates discussed the position in May, and it was then agreed that the northerners should inspect the southern extension themselves. In August, however, their representatives advised against its occupation. But in March 1911 Lenana died at Ngong, and his deathbed wish that the northerners should move to the south was skilfully exploited, with the result that eventually on 4 April 1911 the second Masai Agreement was signed. By it the northerners undertook to abandon Laikipia for an enlarged southern reserve: the Colonial Office was assuaged, and the move recommenced in June. Owing, however, to the quite inadequate arrangements for the movement of the northerners' stock, utter confusion ensued. Ainsworth was called in from Kisumu to take charge and ordered all those who could to return to Laikipia. It was then reported that the southern reserve was already fully stocked. But there was still an unoccupied area farther westwards of the recent extension, and the Colonial Office agreed that this should be added to the enlarged southern reserve and that the northerners should be moved there if after further inspection they were satisfied with it. In February 1912 Legalishu and his associates, after visiting the area, once more pronounced themselves opposed to the move. The Colonial Secretary, however, directed that the move should nevertheless be carried out. Thereupon the northern Masai, with some unofficial European prompting, appealed to the Protectorate High Court against eviction from Laikipia and procured a temporary injunction: but the case was eventually dismissed as being beyond a protectorate court's jurisdiction, and by April 1913 the move

[1] The Earl of Crewe in Asquith's first Ministry.

was completed. Laikipia was then thrown open to white settlement.[1]

Once again Masai affairs profoundly affected the destinies of Kenya. In the first place the creation of reserves for the Masai set the pattern for the demarcation of reserves for all of their neighbours—although unlike the Masai none of them had their boundaries guaranteed by an agreement. There was to be no deliberate intermingling of African tribes and European settlers. They were each (in theory) to have their own separate regions. The Kenya patchwork of 'settled areas' and 'native reserves' was thereby laid down.[2] Secondly, although the moves of the Masai had thrown open a large area to white settlement, they had at the same time done grave damage to the long-term ambitions of the settlers. For Eliot's and Girouard's resignations (both of which followed disputes over the disposal of Masai lands) and the later interminable muddles quickened the lynx-eyed suspicions of liberal and humanitarian elements in Britain that the interests of the European settlers in Kenya were being allowed an unwarrantably free rein. Whereas in Central Africa the butt of such critics was not the ambitions of the settlers, but the pursuits of the British South Africa Company, in Kenya they henceforth concentrated their gaze upon the settlers directly.[3]

Stateless societies and colonial administration

In the meantime, following the assertion of British supremacy in the E.A.P., British officials had turned their attention towards the exercise of administrative control over the African areas

[1] C.O.C.P. African no. 1001. The classic account is in Sandford, *Masai Reserve*, ch. iii. The series F.O. 2 and C.O. 533 contain numerous items referring to the Masai. See also *East Africa Protectorate, Correspondence relating to the Masai, July 1911*, Cd. 5584 (1911) and *East Africa Protectorate, Judgment of the High Court in the Case brought by the Masai Tribe against the Attorney-General of the East Africa Protectorate and others, dated 26th May, 1913*, Cd. 6939 (1913).

[2] Lansdowne to Stewart, 21 Oct. 1904, F.O.C.P. 8382; *Official Gazette of the Uganda and East Africa Protectorates*, 1 July 1906.

[3] This was not the least of the reasons why the settlers in Kenya, unlike the settlers in Southern Rhodesia, failed a decade or so later to procure responsible government for themselves, and with it control of all the territory's internal affairs. cf. J. H. Harris, *The Chartered Millions; Rhodesia and the challenge to the British Commonwealth* (London, 1920) with N. Leys, *Kenya* (London, 1924) and W. McGregor Ross, *Kenya from Within: a short political history* (London, 1927), both of which quote the Masai story at length.

of the Protectorate. In many parts and for several years this was most rudimentary. As the E.A.P. Government, for instance, soon realized, the successive moves of the Masai were no evidence that the Masai were now subject to British administrative control. Unlike almost all the other peoples of southern Kenya, they were not producing labourers in any quantity for European farms[1] and public works: they were scarcely even paying tax.[2]

In all the peripheral parts of the Protectorate the position was essentially analogous. Consider, for example, the situation in Kitui District, which to the British comprised the northern half of Kamba country. Its total area was about 20,000 square miles, or perhaps two-thirds the size of England. The local population was sparse and scattered; they yielded no allegiance to any central authority which the British might have controlled; and in the early years there were rarely more than three British officials stationed amongst them. From at least 1909 onwards these officials used to submit reports to their superiors in Machakos and Nairobi on the trade, crime, and administration of Kitui. To suggest, however, that Kitui was under British administration was plainly spurious. Obviously the Kitui Kamba only felt the pressure of British administration very partially. The activities of the British officials living amongst them were still no more than an excrescence upon the complex nature of their traditional tribal life.[3]

Even so, British officials in such peripheral areas sometimes indulged in considerable make-believe about the character of their operations. According to official reports from Baringo District (where in the first decade of the twentieth century district headquarters stood upon the Baringo lakeshore, several days' journey from the main centres of the district's population),

[1] Cf. Sandford, *Masai Reserve*, pp. 1–27.
[2] Hobley, *Kenya*, p. 159.
[3] Ukamba Province Reports, D.C.'s Office, Machakos; Kitui District Reports, D.C.'s Office, Kitui. e.g. 'It is in fact now far from possible to give any appreciable effect to many laws and administration is therefore not as good as the law makes it possible to be. This condition is of course keenly felt in large Districts and is proof that the administration of vast numbers of natives by a few Europeans is no longer possible. The mass, however inferior it may be, must be reckoned with. It is thought that the awe in which natives stand of the government is often overrated. By passive resistance they obtain their own way while they pretend to be only anxious to do as they are told'; Kitui Annual Report, 1912–13. C. C. F. Dundas, *African Crossroads* (London, 1955), chs. ii and iii, records memories of early administration in Kitui.

British administrators used to perambulate periodically amongst the Keyo, Marakwet, and Pokot peoples, upon the westward escarpment of the Rift Valley, collecting hut taxes in accordance with the E.A.P.'s Hut Tax Regulations of 1901. There was, however, very little specie hereabouts; and in the early years district officials never made any systematic enumeration of huts to form the basis of their tax assessment. They satisfied themselves instead with a bulk collection of goats, sheep, and cattle, which the local populace seem to have paid as a kind of 'danegeld' to make the British go away and leave them once again to their customary devices.[1] Generally having made a fairly handsome collection, the British quite willingly departed, and for most of another year left the escarpment peoples virtually unmolested. They drove their accumulated stock to district headquarters at Baringo, where the garrison subsisted upon it until the meat-supply became exhausted; the next annual tax collection then became due, and an expedition set out for the hills once again. To call this a 'tax collection' was pretentious in the extreme. Although the British usually preferred to make a peaceful approach in the first instance, it was really not very different in effect from the predatory raiding of the Masai.[2]

None the less, such misconceptions about the precise operation of British administration were never really very harmful. It was otherwise, however, with another illusion which seriously befogged the upper echelons of the E.A.P.'s administration during the early years—the idea that at any rate some of its African peoples had traditionally had chiefs. This was fostered in the main by the original close association between the British and some of the formerly prominent figures in the country, such as the Masai *laibon* Lenana. Cordial relations with men who had been locally prominent prior to the imperial advent were, of course, of singular importance to an invading imperial power. In the E.A.P. itself one has only to contrast the relatively smooth flow of British relations with the Masai and their protracted difficulties with the Nandi. Unlike the senior Masai *laibon* the senior Nandi *orkoiyot* remained persistently hostile towards them, and his attitude determined the

---

[1] Dundas, op. cit., p. 34.
[2] File marked 'Chebleng, Ndo and Hill Tribes', D.C.'s Office, Tambach.

demeanour of his whole tribe. It was much the same with the Kipsigis *orkoiyots*. Although they never stirred their tribespeople to battle with the British, they never openly co-operated with them. Instead they made it their business to embarrass the Administration along the by-ways it could not control until the point was reached in 1914 when the E.A.P. Government decided that the Kipsigis would never come under effective administrative authority until the *orkoiyots* had been removed. Accordingly in that year three of them were deported.[1]

There were, nevertheless, several such previously influential figures who for one reason or another were prepared to co-operate with the British. Imperial rule, as the British understood it, always needed to have under its hand a native administrative infrastructure of some kind, and the British always preferred to make use of a pre-existing structure of authority wherever this existed. Since Lenana and his like were obviously influential, the British presumed they enjoyed traditional political authority. It proved to be but a short step from this to calling them African 'chiefs' and employing them as administrative assistants.[2] The truth was, however, that none of the leading figures in the E.A.P. (friendly or hostile), with the exception of Mumia of the Wanga, had traditionally wielded anything more than a very indirect political authority. Elsewhere (in large areas of India and Malaya, for instance, in southern Uganda, in Northern Nigeria, in large parts of the Rhodesias) the British in extending their dominion were able either to supersede a pre-existing polity or bring it under their control. But in the E.A.P. there were virtually no pre-existing political authorities which they could either effectively supersede or effectively subjugate. There was hardly anyone who was traditionally entitled to political

[1] 'Memorandum on the Lumbwa Laibons' (Kipsigis *orkoiyots*), by Provincial Commissioner, Nyanza Province, 1930, Nairobi Secretariat Library. There was, of course, an issue of considerable consequence here. For if imperial authority was to be successfully consolidated, those who had formerly been influential had either to be brought under imperial domination or removed from the pathway of imperial control. No imperial power seeking to establish its hold over a newly acquired domain could easily tolerate any local rivals to its mastery. If such formerly prominent individuals were ready (if only tacitly) to acknowledge British over-lordship, there was every chance that a niche would be found for them in the new superstructure of imperial authority which was being established; if not, then they would almost certainly go the way of the Nandi and Kipsigis *orkoiyots*.

[2] For an early example, see Hardinge to Salisbury, 11 June 1896, F.O.C.P. 6861.

obedience.[1] Accordingly the major task in the post-conquest
era which devolved upon the E.A.P.'s administrators was to try
and create in almost virgin territory a political order which
might be looked to by Africans as having legitimate authority
over them—in short, to establish an embryonic state where
previously there had only been stateless societies.

There were no insoluble problems at the centre. Nairobi, as
we have seen, was soon overflowing with government departments. As early as 1907 it even boasted a Legislative Council.
Every provincial and district administrator, however, was confronted by the real problems constantly. As early as 1896 Sir
Arthur Hardinge had sensed some of their difficulties when he
endorsed Ainsworth's grant of British support to a few Kamba,
who commanded a little very local influence, in order that they
might act 'as our native representatives in a larger area than
that of their own immediate districts, which would serve as the
centre and the starting point of their sphere of influence'.[2]
Fourteen years later Sir Percy Girouard recognized that 'many
of the tribes in East Africa . . . have no Chiefs of recognised
authority'. However, these difficulties were in the event considerably aggravated because no commissioner or governor, nor
any of their senior advisers, could ever at the same time divest
himself entirely of the notion (in Girouard's words) of 'administering the people through their chiefs'.[3] In struggling to cope
with their inherently difficult task of fashioning a native administration, district administrators were hobbled throughout by
a persistent ambiguity in high-level thinking.

Their difficulties, as it chanced, were made very much worse
because in the establishment of the E.A.P.'s up-country administration no existing native administrative structure was used
as a prototype. There was no Buganda at the core of the
Protectorate to fashion official thinking. There were no officials
with anything more than a fleeting acquaintance with British

[1] See, for example, Ainsworth's *Report*. Upon this and the following topics there
are political records and district reports in the Bantu, Nilotic, and Nilo-Hamitic
regions of modern Kenya in the D.C.s' Offices at Wundanyi, Machakos, Kitui,
Kiambu, Nyeri, Embu, Meru, Kapsabet, Nakuru, Eldoret, Kakamega, Kisumu,
and Kisii: some papers will be found elsewhere too, e.g. at Tambach.

[2] Hardinge to Salisbury, 11 June 1896, F.O.C.P. 6861.

[3] East Africa Protectorate, *Memoranda for Provincial and District Commissioners*
(Nairobi, 1910), p. 5.

administration in, say, India or South Africa. When the early
E.A.P. administrators first buckled to their task, 'indirect rule'
had barely been formulated.[1] There were, of course, the coastal
provinces with their adaptation, as we have seen, of the sultan's
hierarchy of agents. Nothing, however, illustrates better the
shift at the turn of the century of the country's centre of gravity
from the coast to the interior than the subsequent complete
failure to employ the coastal administration as the model for the
interior.[2] Had there existed an administrative system amongst
the Masai, or had it been possible to transform their traditional
structure of ritual and military authority into an effective
administrative instrument, they might very well have provided
the Kenyan uplands with the necessary prototype, since they
were the one people whose sterling qualities many British
officials genuinely admired. The British dubbed the faithful
Lenana in his later years 'Paramount Chief'. He was, however,
nothing of the kind, as the British very soon discovered. He
commanded no administrative machine; he was not a chief,
but a *laibon* or ritual expert.[3] During the opening decade of the
new century the title of paramount chief was in like manner
fastened upon a number of other prominent individuals whose
allegiance the British had secured—upon Kinyanjui, Karuri,
and Wangombe, for instance, among the Kikuyu.[4] It proved
quite impossible, however, to transform any of them into an
Oni of Ife, a Citimukulu of the Bemba, or a Kabaka of Buganda,
for none of them could claim a traditionally derived authority
for any administrative orders which they gave. It is hardly

[1] This is not, of course, to say that its application here would have been any more
successful than, for instance, in Eastern Nigeria.

[2] The Germans in German East Africa, as they thrust out their administrative
infrastructure, used Arabs and Swahilis as subordinate *akidas* and *jumbes*; and in
1899, when Lenana was first placed upon a British payroll, it was proposed that
he should 'practically perform the duties of Liwali', Ainsworth to Ternan, 26 Nov.
1900, in Ternan to Lansdowne 4 Dec. 1900, F.O.C.P. 7690. But German East
Africa was always based upon its coastal towns. Unlike British East Africa, which
had no coastmen's settlements in its interior (beyond Taveta), it had, too, a pool
of Arabs and Swahilis up-country, who could be transformed from traders' agents
into administrative subordinates. The E.A.P.'s most influential officials, Ainsworth,
Hobley and Jackson, moreover, had no experience of the working of the coastal
administration.

[3] See, for example, Sandford, *Masai Reserve*, p. 2.

[4] For an interesting review of the original system, see report of *baraza* addressed
by Acting Governor Wade in 1933, Political Record Book, North Kavirondo
District, vol. ii, D.C.'s Office, Kakamega.

surprising, therefore, that the 'paramount chief' idea soon proved itself abortive, and was before long abandoned.

Chiefs, headmen, and elders

It was against this singularly discouraging background that the E.A.P.'s native administration groped its way into existence. It made what use it could of two sources of capital. In the first place, by enrolling in its service men who had in some sense at all events been formerly influential, it ensured that at any rate some of its African personnel possessed some kind of authority, even if this was, as with the *laibon*, little more than a priestly or prophetic authority, or with the Kikuyu *athamaki*, based solely upon their personal prowess.[1] This set, indeed, a pattern; for the idea of trying to make contact with men of local prestige thereby gained currency in the E.A.P. with the result that at the start British authority was conferred not just upon 'paramount chiefs', but upon lesser men too (as, for instance, by Ainsworth in Ukamba) with perhaps little more than a very circumscribed influence; such men provided the British with at least something which approximated to a 'native' administration. Yet even with their appointment there remained places, often important places, where such people either did not exist, were not to be found, or were not prepared to cooperate. It was when they were faced with these lacunae that the British turned to their only remaining expedient and transformed some of their former mercenary associates—some of them caravan headmen, some of them Masai military aides—into administrative chiefs and headmen. In British eyes the E.A.P.'s hinterland had originally been, as we have seen, the road to Uganda. Porters had accordingly been enlisted from amongst neighbouring peoples to collect foodstuffs and carry loads. The most enterprising of them had learnt European ways, had learnt to command, and in due course had been promoted caravan headmen; they were wholly the creatures of the British and so were generally loyal to them. In similar ways a number of Masai warriors had become closely associated with British officials during punitive expeditions in which they had

[1] In war, trade, arbitration, debate, witchcraft, 'diplomacy', etc., *athamaki* were leaders. H. E. Lambert, *Kikuyu Social and Political Institutions* (London, 1956), pp. 100 sqq.; Routledge, *The Akikuyu*, pp. 206–7.

participated as auxiliaries. Because many of these men spoke a
vernacular and also learnt the Swahili *lingua franca* which the
British used, they were well equipped to communicate decrees
to their own people, or to people whose language was akin
to their own. They were, therefore, an obvious group to fall
back upon to provide additional native administrators wherever
these were in short supply.[1] Two streams accordingly emerged
in the early days to form the hierarchy of chiefs and headmen in
the E.A.P.—prominent local individuals and men schooled
in mercenary service with the British. Their official appointments were at first made under the E.A.P. Village Headmen
Ordinance of 1902—a typically olympian and typically wrong-
headed E.A.P. production; for hardly one of the appointees
was in any sense a village headman; and while they were prescribed legal responsibilities, they were granted no legal powers.[2]

The whole system which was harnessed to this ordinance was
soon, however, running into difficulties. It suffered, to begin
with, from two perversions which corresponded to the two main
strands upon which its membership was founded. First, in
seeking to appoint administrative headmen in every corner of
their districts, British officials all too frequently picked out men
as locally prominent who were nothing of the kind. It might be
that a man had successfully ingratiated himself with some
British official and had successfully exaggerated his own importance. Sometimes, however, men of no local consequence
were foisted upon a British official by a popular gathering
because those who were locally influential were anxious to
remain in the background lest they be caught in the meshes
of British supremacy. In either event the headmen gazetted

---

[1] Some of them also came to hold the very important, but ungazetted, office of
interpreter. Two sets of examples of the conjunction of prominent individuals and
mercenary associates (in both instances caravan headmen) may be cited from
amongst the paramount chiefs. The paramount chief around Fort Hall was
Karuri, Boyes's old companion and one of the pre-European *athamaki*: in Kiambu
the paramount chief was Kinyanjui, perhaps the most famous of the caravan headmen promoted to a chieftainship. Among the Nandi, after their final defeat, there
was one paramount chief for north Nandi, Kibellas, the Nandi *orkoiyot*, and another
for south Nandi, Arap Cheno, a Kakipoch, who was a Swahili-speaking trading
agent from neighbouring Kitoto's. Several Masai became chiefs in Nandi.
Mr. A. T. Matson has kindly made available this and much other useful information. See also Machakos District Political Record Book, vol. i (pt. i), under
'Chiefs and Headmen', *passim*.

[2] *Official Gazette*, 1 Nov. 1902.

soon proved to be useless: they possessed little experience of
British requirements and no local influence. The second aberration followed upon the licence which the system allowed to
headmen and their followers to harry the country-side. It was
an abuse to which both Masai mercenaries and those nurtured
in the caravan business (where customary restraints had, of
course, little influence) were especially prone and, at its worst,
an avaricious headman, excited by novel vistas of opulence,
would employ his band of *askaris*[1] to harvest himself a fortune.[2]
The basic problem, however, was not so much the noxious
distortions from which the system suffered, as the completely
alien ethos of the imposed system of political authority itself.
The difficulty, as Ainsworth put it in 1905,[3] was 'to get the
natives, as a whole, to recognize any one individual member of
their tribe as a person of authority over them'.

The only people in the E.A.P. amongst whom traditionally
the leading figures had been endowed with political authority
were the Wanga. They were, furthermore, unique in the E.A.P.
in that their traditional authority was joined to a long-standing
connexion first with the coastal traders and then with the
British, so that they combined in themselves the two strands
which elsewhere amongst the E.A.P.'s African chiefs were found
in separation. They were uniquely qualified, in short, to serve
the E.A.P. as subordinate administrators. It is not altogether
surprising, therefore, that upon the conclusion of the last,
'Ketosh', expedition in northern Kavirondo in 1908, Archer,
the district commissioner, should have placed half a dozen and
more of Mumia's kinsmen and followers as headmen over
neighbouring locations which from his point of view had proved
themselves refractory,[4] nor that in 1909 Mumia should have
joined the ranks of the paramount chiefs, to hold the title longer

---

[1] Armed men, such as the British and Germans employed to guard their forts
and caravans.
[2] So profitable did such appointments become that it was not unknown for men
with no pretensions at all to British support to flaunt scribbled pieces of paper
(which were incomprehensible to illiterates) as commissions from the British to
lord it over others. There is an admirable discussion of the whole question in the
'Historical' section of the Machakos District Political Record Book, vol. i (pt. i),
D.C.'s Office, Machakos.
[3] Ainsworth's *Report*.
[4] Political Record Book, North Kavirondo District, vol. ii, D.C.'s Office,
Kakamega.

than any of the rest of them.[1] Had this area still been part of Uganda one can readily imagine Uganda officials seeking to transform Mumia into a 'kabaka' and Wanga hegemony into a 'kingdom' on the Buganda model. Wanga, however, was part of the E.A.P. Moreover, it soon became apparent that Wanga political authority only functioned smoothly in Wanga itself, and that the appointment of Wanga headmen over non-Wanga peoples was just as alien an imposition as the appointment of administrative headmen everywhere else in the Protectorate.[2]

Archer's measures, however, were a pointer to the search upon which several British district officers had now embarked for a much more articulated system of native administration than that originally adopted. By 1908–9 a number of them had become convinced that the situation was seriously awry. Abuses were rife; numerous headmen were broken reeds; senior headmen often had difficulty in controlling their subordinates: above all there was little or no contact by the Administration with any institution to which the people themselves gave their ungrudging allegiance.[3] In 1909 the new Governor, Sir Percy Girouard, went a step further and expatiated at some length to the Colonial Office on the 'utter absence of any defined policy',[4] and in 1910 issued an official memorandum[5] outlining his own directions on policy. Apart, however, from expressing his own personal abhorrence of direct rule, he made little contribution to the resolution of the basic issues at stake. It seems to have been Hobley, by now Provincial Commissioner at Nairobi, who formulated the only notable proposal. He suggested that the most promising way to resolve the current defects in the native administration would be to recognize and employ the councils of tribal elders which in most areas had traditionally arbitrated in disputes.[6] This suggestion was quickly seized upon. Already in 1907 the E.A.P. had promulgated a Courts Ordinance, which gave powers to headmen to hear petty cases. Before long it was

[1] North Kavirondo Quarterly Report, Oct.–Dec. 1909, ibid., vol. i.

[2] There are about ten typescript memoranda on 'Wanga domination' in the Nairobi Secretariat Library.

[3] See, for example, Machakos District Political Record Book, vol. i (pt. i), under 'Historical'.

[4] Girouard's 'Interim report on British East Africa', enclosure in Girouard to Crewe, 13 Nov. 1909, C.O. 533/63.

[5] *Memoranda for Provincial and District Commissioners* (Nairobi, 1910).

[6] Hobley, *Kenya*, p. 160.

agreed that these judicial powers should be exercised by councils of elders, and the new policy was eventually given legal form in the Native Tribunal Rules of 1911.

The official employment of councils of elders was hailed with enthusiasm by district officers in all parts of the Protectorate.[1] They felt that at last they had unearthed a popular instrument of native government. Encouraged by Hobley's own example, a number of them devoted themselves to studies of native law and custom so that they might co-operate more closely with the new councils.[2] Special buildings were erected for the councils' meetings; the councils themselves were empowered to appoint their own messengers; upon their establishment the lowliest headmen were in some places summarily dismissed; everywhere the remaining chiefs and headmen were enjoined to co-operate closely with them; and in places it was even proposed that the councils should add administrative duties to their initial judicial functions.[3]

But in the upshot they were no real solution to the basic dilemma. To begin with, a traditional gathering of elders to arbitrate in a dispute was essentially *ad hoc*. To formalize it, to establish a permanent amalgamated council for a relatively large area (as was very often done), was to establish an institution as untraditional as chieftainship itself.[4] There was never any suggestion, moreover, that the senior chiefs and headmen could be dispensed with. Taxes had to be collected, labour recruited, roads kept clear, and miscreants apprehended. It was unlikely that the councils of elders would ever adequately fulfil any of these functions, for they were all, almost by definition, conservative and out of sympathy with the Administration's con-

[1] e.g. Machakos District Political Record Book, vol. i (pt. ii), D.C.'s Office, Machakos; Kikuyu District Quarterly Report, 31 Dec. 1910, D.C.'s Office, Kiambu; South Kavirondo Annual Report, 1910–11, D.C.'s Office, Kisii. Dr. Malcolm Ruel kindly made available his notes on this and other Kisii reports.

[2] These issued in an impressive array of articles by E.A.P. officials in the contemporary anthropological journals, e.g. C. Dundas, 'The organization and laws of some Bantu tribes in East Africa', *Journal of the Royal Anthropological Institute*, xlv (1915), 234–306: see also bibliography in J. Middleton, *The Kikuyu and Kamba of Kenya* (London, 1953).

[3] e.g. Machakos District Political Record Book, vol. i (pt. ii); Ukamba Province Annual Report, 1911–12, D.C.'s Office, Machakos. Kikuyu District Annual Report, 1911–12, D.C.'s Office, Kiambu.

[4] C. Dundas, 'Handing-over report', 1 Dec. 1912, D.C.'s Office, Kiambu.

temporary interests.[1] The continued existence of the chiefs was thereby ensured, and this in numerous ways militated against the advance of the councils to a pre-eminent position.[2] The very important Native Authority Ordinance of 1912, for instance, allowed for a council of elders to be appointed 'collective headman', but its main effect was to strengthen the hand of the single gazetted headman by granting him for the first time a substantial number of legal powers. Nevertheless, the somewhat hazy reforms of 1910–11 had one important residual effect: African courts in Kenya were henceforth presided over, not by chiefs, but by select groups of elders.[3] But the hope that, as one district officer put it, the E.A.P. might 'establish a system of government that is suitable to our own interests and in accordance with the ideas of the people', proved in the end to be vain.[4]

Girouard in his 'Memoranda' of 1910 insisted that 'the wishes of the people' should be ascertained before a chief or headman was appointed, and in several ways this directive had a considerable influence upon subsequent E.A.P. practice: shortly afterwards it permitted the virtual election of several Luo headmen.[5] It probably underscored the practice whereby headmen generally confined their service to the location of which they themselves were members; and it eventually killed the dominion of the Wanga over their neighbours.[6] But for the rest the chieftainship system, though shorn of its judicial functions, remained as before, an alien imposition, largely unsupported and largely unrestrained by traditional sanctions.[7] With the institution of more frequent touring by British officials the worst abuses of the first decade of the twentieth century were curbed, and over the years the chiefs certainly became an increasingly efficient instrument in British hands: the African hut and poll tax, for which they became responsible, rose, for

---

[1] e.g. Kisii Quarterly Report, Sept. 1912, D.C.'s Office, Kisii.
[2] See, for example, Kinyanjui's interference with Kikuyu 'Kiamas', Dagoretti Annual and Handing over report, 1912–13, D.C.'s Office, Kiambu; Kitui District Annual Report, 1910–11, D.C.'s Office, Kitui.
[3] A. Phillips, *Report on Native Tribunals* (Nairobi, 1945).
[4] Machakos District Political Record Book, vol. i (pt. i), under 'Historical'.
[5] Kisumu Political Record Book, vol. vii, *passim*, D.C.'s Office, Kisumu.
[6] 'Memo. on the Wanga in North Kavirondo', 23 June 1930, Nairobi Secretariat Library.
[7] See C. Cagnolo, trans. V. M. Pick, *The Akikuyu. Their Customs, Traditions and Folklore* (Nyeri, 1933), p. 24.

instance, in Machakos District from 8,668 rupees in 1901–2 to
168,042 rupees in 1912–13, and in North Kavirondo District
from 26,000 rupees in 1901–2 to 356,000 rupees in 1912–13.[1]
Before long, too, it became difficult to think of an African
reserve without its administrative chiefs. But in Kenya they
never enjoyed a status which was in any significant manner
independent of British authority. The E.A.P. Administration,
having twice failed to incorporate indigenous institutions in its
administrative structure, seemingly became sceptical of the
whole idea. Henceforth Kenya's chiefs took their cue solely
from that other tradition of mercenary service as initiated by
the caravan headmen[2] and the Masai military associates.

The Kenyan complex

As a consequence Kenya's chiefs were never accorded widespread popular support. Yet they would in any event have had
difficulty in winning popular approval, because during the
early formative years they were not only tax collectors and
general administrators, but labour recruiters too. In Kiambu
District, for instance, Kinyanjui's henchmen were freely called
his 'press gang';[3] and they recruited not just for the Government and the railway, but for private employers as well. The
Administration's control over the more populous areas became,
in short, the handmaid of the policy of white settlement. Here
was the central factor in the Kenyan complex as it emerged in
the post-conquest era.

Once again the tap-root of the situation stretched back to the
Masai, since it was their lands which the settlers primarily
occupied. It remains true, of course, that the areas alienated to
Europeans were not confined to Masai territory. In a considerable number of places, portions of peripheral areas indubitably
occupied previously by the Masai's neighbours were transferred
to European hands simultaneously. Indeed, almost all the
peoples between Lake Victoria and the sea could soon join

---

[1] Machakos District Political Record Book, vol. i (pt. i), Machakos District
Annual Report, 1912–13, D.C.'s Office, Machakos; Political Record Book, North
Kavirondo District, vol. i, D.C.'s Office, Kakamega.

[2] Although 'Indirect Rule' was introduced into most of the other British territories in Africa, it was never adopted in Kenya.

[3] Tate to Ainsworth, 15 May 1905, Dagoretti Letter Book, May 1905–Mar.
1911; Dagoretti Political Record Book, 1908–12, under 15 Feb. 1909.

with their neighbours in pointing to some portion of their
ancestral lands which had fallen under European occupation:
it became the major grievance they all held in common.[1]
Nevertheless, a glance at the map will show that the main areas
which the settlers occupied—the Kaputie plains, Donyo Sabuk,
the central Rift Valley, the Mau, Laikipia and Uasin Gishu
plateaux—were all formerly occupied by the Masai. It was indeed just because the settlers in the main replaced the Masai—
sole lords in the past of the region's wide open spaces—that
the European areas came to consist of such extensive, uninter-
rupted stretches of country; and it was because, moreover, so
many Masai subtribes had latterly been decimated by disease
and civil war that such broad expanses of country were so open
to the rapid large-scale alienation to Europeans which took
place during the first decade and a half of the twentieth century.

The alienation was swift and extensive too because the E.A.P.
Government was particularly anxious to attract a well-endowed,
self-sufficient type of settler, who would contribute substantially
to the country's economic development, and would not be a
burden upon its limited resources when faced with any financial
setback. A *sine qua non* of such a policy was the alienation of perhaps 1,000 acres of agricultural land, or upwards of 5,000 acres
of pasture, to each European applicant.[2] Such areas, however,
could hardly be adequately worked by a single European
settler and his family. If the settlement policy, therefore, was
to fructify as planned, African labourers were required as well.
But almost by definition large parts of the areas thrown open
to European settlement contained no local African population.
If, therefore, African labourers were to be procured, it was
necessary to extract them from the populated African reserves
which lay outside the settled areas.

Here was the point at which the different ingredients that
went to the making of the E.A.P. became conjoined. For since

---

[1] Many of them were profoundly dismayed, moreover, when upon the shrinkage
of the Masai and the advent of *pax Britannica* (when for the first time they could
pasture their cattle beyond the confines of their fastnesses in safety) they found their
way barred by the settlement of European farmers backed by the European
Government. It is hardly surprising that they should henceforth have heaped upon
the Europeans the animus they had formerly reserved for the Masai. The whole
subject was discussed by the Carter Commission. Kenya Land Commission,
Evidence and Memoranda.

[2] Remole, *White Settlers*, chs. iii, iv.

European settlement took place mainly in former Masai territory, its spread ran parallel to the introduction of British rule over the main areas of African population, with the consequence that the settlers' growing demands for labour followed hard upon the extension of the Administration's control over the African areas of the Protectorate.[1] These areas, as we have seen, had been invaded by the Administration on the principle that through the institution of taxation they could shortly be made to pay for themselves. The means, however, by which their African population was to procure the necessary cash were not at the outset determined; tax collection throughout the E.A.P. (as in Baringo District) might have had to be in kind. But when the critical period arrived in the Kenya and Kisumu Provinces, the settlers' demands for labourers dovetailed exactly with the Administration's desire for a cash revenue; by encouraging Africans to work for wages for the settlers, the Administration could ensure that their new subjects had the opportunity to procure sufficient cash with which to pay their taxes. Accordingly there was no interlude during which the Administration might have been forced to seek the economic development of the populated African areas *per se* as the solution to their revenue problem: and in consequence, too, the Administration's commitment to the spread of white settlement was irremediably confirmed. It was not, of course, unusual for the economic development of a colonial territory to be concentrated in a few selected areas while the rest were drawn upon as suppliers of labour;[2] but in Kenya these privileged areas were not so much (as elsewhere) those which were most central, most fertile, or nearest the best communications. They were, one and all, the scattered settled areas, the African reserves being made almost without exception the providers of labour, even where they were exceptionally fertile or ran adjacent to the Uganda Railway.[3]

---

[1] *Report on the E.A.P., 1903–4*, Cd. 2331.

[2] See, for example, P. G. Powesland, *Economic Policy and Labour: a Study in Uganda's Economic History*, East African Studies no. 10 (Kampala, 1957), esp. ch. iii.

[3] Cf. 'If some of the expenditure which has been incurred by the Agricultural Dept. on behalf of European Settlers had been spent in the interests of Kikuyu and Kavirondo, it is likely that a speedy return would have resulted. At present the natives are performing the manual labour which enables the latter to grow the best produce for the market without any resultant advantage to the actual workers

At the same time the divorce between the settled areas and the African reserves, which followed upon the settlers' concentration upon Masailand and its environs, had further important consequences. For if African labourers were to be recruited to work upon settlers' farms, then the greater part of them had to be uprooted from their own homesteads; there could be no question of more than a small minority of them returning to their tribal lands and the bosom of their families when their daily tasks were done. A system of migrant labour internal to Kenya accordingly developed. It was the cause of much social and political disturbance. It was argued for the settlers that the E.A.P.'s Africans must be prepared to pay for the boon of the Administration's peace, and that it was in their own interests to learn the dignity of labour.[1] Numbers of them, as it happened, were anxious to seek their fortunes by working for wages, and it was a commonplace that a sympathetic employer had little difficulty in procuring labourers to work for him. Yet there were certainly some Africans remaining idle in the reserves; they were enjoying the first flush of relief from the previous necessity for a constant *qui vive*. They, and others like them, were understandably reluctant to go far afield to labour.[2] Pressure of a variety of kinds, however, was employed to force them out to work for the settlers. Obviously there were abuses in such proceedings;[3] and it is plain that the Kikuyu of Kiambu

from the money sunk by the British Taxpayer' (Kikuyu District Annual Report, 1907–8); 'The native reserve offers possibilities of development which compare favourably with the richest reserves in the country and were it possible for an officer to devote his whole time to it a volume of trade would be brought to the Thika tramway and Uganda Railway, which would add largely to the revenue' (ibid., 1910–11, D.C.'s Office, Kiambu); 'In the E.A.P., of all Protectorates, the presence of a European population of bona fide settlers and the desire to develop its rich natural resources greatly increases the risk of improper pressure being brought to bear on the natives in order to fit them into the vacant place in the economic system, which requires their immediate cooperation. It leads to questionable methods of inducing them to work, and to undue haste in screwing Hut Tax out of them' (Minute by Lobb, 8 Mar. 1909, upon Sadler to Elgin 1 Apr. 1908, C.O. 533/43).

[1] There is a useful summary of the arguments employed in Huxley, *White Man's Country*, i. 222–3.

[2] Meru District Annual Report, 1912–13, D.C.'s Office, Meru; Routledge, *The Akikuyu*, p. 330.

[3] e.g. Kiambu Minute Book, 1905–10, *passim*, D.C.'s Office, Kiambu; Memorandum by Hollis, 8 Apr. 1908, enclosure in Sadler to Crewe, 8 Apr. 1908, C.O. 533/43; Minutes of Chief's *baraza*, 23 Dec. 1911, Political Record Book, vol. i, D.C.'s Office. Kisumu; Routledge, op. cit., p. 332.

District, who were already profoundly discontented at the sinister combination—to them—of the loss of some of their lands, the imposition of an alien régime, and the exaction of tax,[1] were deeply angered, too, by the impressment of their menfolk into labouring for the settlers.[2]

One might have expected the Christian missionaries here and elsewhere to provide an ameliorating influence. Most of the missionaries, however, had come to the E.A.P. not in advance, but in the wake of many of the administrators and settlers. They were not, therefore, in a position at first to pose as experts upon tribal life, or as champions of a differently construed social and political order. Moreover the missionaries in the E.A.P. did not win converts very quickly and they were even sometimes involved themselves in land disputes with Africans. In addition, on the Protestant side their impact was weakened by their division into a considerable number of different sects.[3] In 1913 at an important conference at Kikuyu most of the Protestant churches met together to sketch out a plan for a united church that should overcome the divisions which so patently weakened their witness; but because at its conclusion the two Anglican bishops who were present administered communion to the non-Anglicans who attended, there were loud protests from Anglo-Catholics in the Church of England, led by the redoubtable Bishop of Zanzibar, Frank Weston, who arraigned the 'Kikuyu bishops' upon a charge of heresy. The furore which followed killed the embryonic united church.[4] However, it did not kill the concept of a Protestant alliance, and in the years to come this became a power in the land, more especially through its education programme. Schools, indeed, became the chief instrument through which the missions made their greatest impact upon the Kenyan scene;[5] for they offered an outlet to

---

[1] e.g. memorandum by Beech on 'The Kikuyu point of view', 12 Dec. 1912, Dagoretti Political Record Book, 1908–12, vol. i, D.C.'s Office, Kiambu; Ukamba Province Annual Report, 1911–12, D.C.'s Office, Machakos.

[2] e.g. Tate to Ainsworth, 24 July 1905, Dagoretti Letter Book May 1905–Mar. 1911, D.C.'s Office, Kiambu.

[3] K. S. Latourette, A History of the Expansion of Christianity (7 vols, London, 1938–45), v. 410–12.

[4] R. Oliver, The Missionary Factor in East Africa (London, 1952), pp. 222–30 and the authorities there cited.

[5] The important C.M.S. School at Maseno, for instance, was opened in 1905, Political Record Book, vol. i, D.C.'s Office, Kisumu, under 'Missions'.

energetic Africans other than the cul-de-sac of labour employment. Even before the first world war there was as a result
some discussion about the place of the educated convert in
Kenyan society (he fitted none of the current concepts of the
reserves and the settled areas as the twin props of the Kenyan
system);[1] and in time, education in Christian primary and
secondary schools was to be one of the two or three most important catalysts of a new Kenyan order. But between 1902 and
1912 the labour nexus binding the Administration to the settlers
reigned supreme. (It was, therefore, ironic that it was not as
it transpired the products of European farms which first removed the operating deficits upon the Uganda Railway—which
had been such a powerful influence in inaugurating the policy
of settlement—but expanding trade in the surrounding regions,
and more particularly the growth of the African peasant-grown
cotton crop in Uganda.[2])

In 1904, in issuing instructions to Sir Donald Stewart, the
Foreign Office declared: 'It is only by a most careful insistence
on the protection of native rights that His Majesty's Government can justify their presence in East Africa.'[3] Three years later
there were some doubts in the E.A.P. Administration itself about
the security of those interests, and the new Secretary for Native
Affairs was given two assistants to scrutinize the handling of
African labourers.[4] In 1909 when Girouard, like Johnston
before him, proposed the federation of the Uganda and East
Africa Protectorates, the plan was rejected in the Colonial
Office lest the Africans of Uganda should become subject to
'the disturbing white influences of the E.A.P.'[5] Girouard
himself appears to have thought that it would be possible to
advance the interests of the European settlers and to defend
the interests of the African population at one and the same

[1] Memorandum by Provincial Commissioner, Nyanza (Ainsworth), on the
question of the position of native converts in the Reserves, 22 Apr. 1912, D.C.'s
Office Kisumu; 'Précis of meeting held at Kyambu Station', 25 and 26 Apr. 1912,
Dagoretti Political Record Book, 1908–12, vol. i, D.C.'s Office, Kiambu.

[2] S. Playne (ed.), *East Africa (British): its history, people, commerce, industries, and
resources* (Woking, 1908–9), p. 223.

[3] Lansdowne to Stewart, 8 July 1904, F.O.C.P. 8357.

[4] Jackson to Provincial Commissioner, Mombasa, 18 Nov. 1907, M.P.A. Inward
H.M. Commr. 1907.

[5] Minute by Fiddes of the Colonial Office on Girouard to Crewe, 13 Nov. 1909,
C.O. 533/63. This was an important dispatch with important enclosures.

time.[1] But the crude essentials of the Kenyan scene were nearer those depicted in an official E.A.P. Report published in 1919. In discussing the policies which the Administration pursued in the more populated regions of the Protectorate in the post-conquest era, this declared:

These policies, established and maintained for the most part by the senior administrative officers in each Province, have undoubtedly not been uniform, but they have to a large extent achieved the result which is noticed in the majority of the native administered areas today, of developing the native inhabitants of the Province into useful agricultural labourers fit for residential work on European farms and available for duty on works of public utility.[2]

By the time of the first world war the E.A.P. lay in fee to a vision, at once narrow and contorted, in which European settlers predominated and Africans were simply the labouring proletariat.

[1] Cf. ibid., and Wray to Baylis, 10 Dec. 1910, C.M.S. Archives G3 A5/018 1910(b) quoting a speech of Girouard's on board ship: 'As Governor of this Colony it shall be my policy to put the native claim first. After that, that of the European who has been invited into this country.'
[2] Sandford, *Masai Reserve*.

II

UGANDA: THE ESTABLISHMENT OF
THE PROTECTORATE
1894–1919

D. A. LOW

UPON the headwaters of the Nile, between 1894 and 1919, the Uganda Protectorate was created. It is generally suggested that the partition divided Africa. The greater, if paradoxical, truth is that it set on foot the coalescence of tribally diverse peoples into embryonic nation states, and thus opened the way to the emergence of African nations as constituent parts of a wider world. Upon the headwaters of the Nile this major historical process was launched, all unwittingly, by a tiny British colonial government of less than twenty officials.[1] Established by 1894 upon the north-west shore of Lake Victoria, they had already begun to extend their authority eastwards over Busoga, and westwards into Toro and Bunyoro. The exact boundaries of the future Uganda were not to be fully determined for another twenty years,[2] and it was to be over a quarter of a century before the Protectorate Government's writ ran to every corner.[3] Slow as the process was, however, it brought to all the peoples who were to comprise the future population of Uganda major political changes. Thanks to the exigencies of European diplomacy, these peoples consisted in the main of two very different cultural groups, the southern Nilotes in the north and the northern interlacustrine Bantu in the south—the former organized politically upon segmentary principles, the latter comprising a number of African kingdoms of widely varying

---

[1] In 1895, a year later, the number was only twenty-one. R. A. Snoxall and J. M. Gray, 'The Uganda staff list for 1895', *Uganda J.* i. 1 (1934), 61–63. They still only numbered about fifty in 1919 for a protectorate of over 4 million people.

[2] H. B. Thomas and A. E. Spencer, *A History of Uganda Land and Surveys* (Entebbe, 1938), ch. x. The (Lake) Rudolf Province was transferred to Kenya in 1926.

[3] By 1919 Karamoja District was still not regularly administered.

sizes.[1] By 1919 these had all been reconstituted politically into a single edifice of provinces, districts, counties, and in some instances sub-county and village units too, subject to the overall authority of an autocratically empowered governor of a British colonial protectorate. Much that was most intimate and immediate to the lives of its African population persisted along traditional lines, but there was no denying that the pattern of their former existence had suffered substantial inroads, and that a wholly new superstructure of power had been established.

First and foremost the history of this region during these years was the history of a frontier—one more frontier between peoples who differed, for the time being, quite radically in their technological and organizational skills. Their history was once epitomized by Lord Salisbury, British Prime Minister for much of the last fourteen years of the nineteenth century, with a bluntness peculiarly Victorian, but (allowing for changing fashions in the overtones of words) with an appositeness difficult to question: 'I know by experience', he declared, 'that a great civilized nation in contact with barbarism is always obliged to advance'.[2] By the late nineteenth century, for all the relative indifference of the British Foreign Office—with its eyes, for instance, fixed upon the strategic importance of the Nile Valley, rather than upon the problems of administration in Uganda—this crude reality had become for British officials in the outposts of Empire an occasion for the display not merely of a fervid creative energy, but of a profound moral earnestness. So self-assured had British imperial thinking now become that the initial assumption of every British administrator faced with a new colonial domain was that his purposes were demonstrably right. He belonged to a people whose representatives had struck out lines of communication, curbed parochial anarchies, and established settled governments in numberless reaches of the globe. In consequence he and his companions believed, often with some passion, in their mission as servants of the seemingly inspired British empire to bring peace, prosperity and justice to less fortunate peoples. That they brought all three to Uganda is

[1] For these distinctions see M. Fortes and E. E. Evans-Pritchard, eds., *African Political Systems* (London, 1940), p. 5.

[2] Quoted in Waddington to Ribot, 23 Dec. 1891, *Documents diplomatiques françaises*, 1st series, ix, no. 113, p. 176, quoted by A. J. P. Taylor 'British policy in Morocco, 1886–1902', *Eng. Hist. Rev.* lxvi (1951), 352.

patent. *Pax Britannica* was no figment. Its benefactions were in high demand. It made possible the creation of twentieth-century Uganda.

Yet wherever the gulf in technological and organizational skills was substantial, as it was here, British governments and British administrators believed, too, that at the point of political encounter they themselves were ordained to dispose and to rule. Upon the headwaters of the Nile the appearance of this doctrine in the 1890's was wholly new. In the years before 1890 British visitors to the region had always acknowledged the political authority of the African polities they encountered. British officials now postulated the paramount legitimacy of their own authority,[1] and it was this change which for well over half a century was to make the basic difference from all that had gone before. In justification of the new presumption of the paramount legitimacy of their own authority British officials could point to the Anglo-German Agreement of 1890, which had placed Uganda within the British sphere of influence;[2] to three successive notices in the *London Gazette*, which defined the southern regions of the Uganda Protectorate;[3] to the Foreign Jurisdiction Acts of the British Parliament; to the Africa Order in Council of 1889; in due course to the Uganda Order in Council of 1902; and to a number of agreements with African chiefs. By the standards of Lord Salisbury's own generation Uganda had thus become a British protectorate: it therefore seemed obvious to British officials that within its bounds British authority should be accepted by its African population.

Yet to the questions 'who, or what, was Uganda being protected from?' there was no satisfactory answer; and the truth was that in the initial stages most of the legal demands were largely irrelevant. For the prime practical issue in the establishment of the Protectorate was not, as the British too readily assumed, one of law and right, but one of force and power. Consider, for instance, the commonplace remarks of Sir Hesketh Bell, the first British Governor of Uganda, writing in his diary

[1] e.g. Jackson to Macallister, 6 Sept. 1900, Entebbe Secretariat Archives (hereinafter 'E.S.A.') A21/1: 'The mere fact that Dr. Donaldson Smith did not encounter a British official in the country lying between Rudolf and the Nile does not remove that part of the country from the control of the Uganda Protectorate.'

[2] See ch. x in vol. i of this *History*.

[3] *London Gazette*, 19 June 1894, 15 June 1895, 3 July 1896.

for 1909 about some Gisu of Mount Elgon on the eastern edge of the country:

I am sending [he wrote] two companies of King's African Rifles to make them [the Bagisu] realize that they must come into line with the rest of the Protectorate. . . . Hardly a year passes without the need of punishing some of these wild tribes for the slaying of unarmed and peaceful traders, and nothing but a show of force will induce them to mend their ways.[1]

But what business of Bell's was it (the Gisu by their actions appeared in effect to ask) if they did slay peaceful traders? They had never acknowledged any British authority over their actions. They were not parties to the Anglo-German Agreement of 1890 or to any other agreement either. They had never heard of acts of parliament, or orders in council. There was, indeed, no legitimate reason, which the Gisu could have found intelligible, to suggest why they should have accepted British rule without protest. The British claim to rule over them was wholly uni-lateral. But for these Gisu, as for so many others, the issue was soon settled, not by any answers to the questions that might be posed, but by a few fusillades from the King's African Rifles.[2] What was more, although the ostensible reasons for such British actions might be to put an end to the sporadic violence in which African peoples indulged, and the establishment of a beneficent administration, there can be little doubt that on this occasion, as indeed upon others, the violence of Africans, and often some-thing that was simply the expression of a readily understandable African desire to be left alone, was only expunged by an even greater immediate violence on the part of the British. No doubt it remains true that for the most part the British preferred the broad instrument of power to the blunt implement of force. But the issue here cannot be baulked either. It was once very appo-sitely stated by an Acholi headman when speaking about his own people: 'The Acholi', he said, 'will not obey their chiefs or the Government unless they are afraid, the other Acholi obey

---

[1] H. H. J. Bell, *Glimpses of a Governor's Life* (London, 1946), p. 128; cf. Bell to Elgin, 18 Mar. 1907, and enclosures, C.O. 536/12.

[2] The purpose, it will be noted, as Bell averred, was not only to ensure that the Gisu should 'mend their ways', but that they should 'come into line with the rest of the Protectorate'. The offence prompting the first objective provided the occasion and justification for the second.

the Government now because they are afraid, our people are bad because they don't think the Government will quarrel with them'.[1] One element, therefore, in the process which shaped the political history of Uganda in these years was conquest.

But the cardinal consideration about substantial parts of Uganda was that this was not the only ingredient. For whilst there was little consciousness amongst Africans that they were confronting the agents of a powerful imperial nation, there was no continuing desire on the part of the British to rely upon force alone. Time and again in the peculiarly propitious circumstances of the interlacustrine Bantu kingdoms there was a search, both by British officials and by influential Africans, for a political relationship which could be mutually advantageous. This was difficult to achieve where there were no chiefs, and it was rare for any lasting association to be established between British officials and a ruler or chief who had been paramount before their arrival. But it was common in Uganda for political alliances to be formed by the British with Africans who, though very often new-comers to political power, were, none the less, legitimate holders of traditional offices, and were able with British support to control their own indigenous political orders. These alliances quickened in many areas the administrative structures that came to be established, and ensured that the essentials of the indigenous order became fully incorporated in the new administrative superstructure of imperial authority.

The British and Uganda

By 1894 only a fraction of modern Uganda had felt the presence of European control. Having determined to establish a protectorate, the British Government at first deliberately elected to confine its overrule to Buganda.[2] Even here its activities were at first strictly limited. A British Commissioner was appointed. Several subordinates were engaged. Four military officers were seconded to command the mercenary force of Sudanese and Swahili troops—inherited from the outgoing Imperial British

---

[1] Quoted in Northern Province Annual Report, 1911–12.
[2] Minute by Kimberley, 18 May 1894, Foreign Office Confidential Print (hereinafter 'F.O.C.P.') 6557. Report of Committee on the Administration of East Africa (1894), F.O.C.P. 6489.

East Africa Company[1]—which was the main bulwark of the British position; and the Uganda Administration was permitted to draw £50,000 a year from the British Treasury together with a small capital sum.[2] For the rest the Protectorate presented an essay in myopia. Nothing in the nature of a policy for its future was even considered.[3]

Even so, it is possible to discern two distinct interests which the British initially possessed in this region. In the first place they had determined to maintain in Buganda the authority they had established there over its warring factions.[4] Secondly, the Foreign Office in Britain, which at first had charge of the Protectorate's administration in London, was interested in procuring a foothold in the Upper Nile Valley from which, whenever it might be necessary, they could watch French and Congo advances from the west.[5] Beyond these there were no engrossing British interests, and these two alone determined the arena of British activity between 1894 and 1909. They had, however, important corollaries, whose significance only became gradually apparent. For if these British interests were to be maintained, the lines of communication upon which they depended had to be kept open and the surrounding areas kept free from hostile opponents. What was more, in the eyes of British officials on the spot, the whole area was 'red on the map', so that their presence for whatever reason at any point within it was evidence in their eyes of the actuality of British overlordship.

It was primarily such unspoken assumptions as these which led to the rapid extension of British colonial authority over the kingdoms of Uganda during the first five years of the Protectorate's existence. This accomplishment was very largely the work of individual district officers living very often exposed and alone in tiny scattered outposts. It owed very little to any orders from the British Commissioner in Uganda, and almost nothing

[1] For the events in East Africa leading up to the establishment of the Protectorate, see ch. xi in vol. i of this *History*.

[2] With this a road was built from Mombasa to Lake Victoria to facilitate the passage of supplies. In the years that followed, however, these were never regularly forthcoming.

[3] The lack of any coherent purpose soon became aggravated by the ravages of sickness amongst its commissioners and acting commissioners; in the five years between 1895–9 there were no less than eight changes of command.

[4] See ch. xi in vol. i of this *History*.

[5] Cf. memorandum by Anderson, 13 Sept. 1892, F.O. 84/2258.

to the Foreign Office in London. It involved small-scale political and military actions suited to the precise political realities of the immediate vicinity. For all the relative cultural homogeneity of the interlacustrine Bantu kingdoms these realities when approached at close quarters differed quite considerably. Most district officials confronted by their complex and often fluid intricacies handled them with remarkable perspicacity, and once they had mastered them, set about establishing a workable structure of administration.

For the exercise of British authority in Uganda the European personnel of the administrative hierarchy subject to the British Governor, his Chief Secretary, and the heads of the different central government departments, never spread below the district commissioner[1] and his assistants. Beneath them there was always a purely African infrastructure; and for the whole of this quarter of a century (and for most of another too) reliance was placed almost entirely, not upon elders, nor upon councils of non-officials, nor upon mere government employees but upon hierarchies of African chiefs. To this position the British were led not only by their own predilections, but more especially by their formative experience in the pivotal kingdom of Buganda. Here was developed during these years that cluster of governmental institutions which was in due course to be characteristic of the whole of Uganda: the tribal government (headed in this and three or four other instances by an African ruler) with three senior chiefs holding key positions at the apex; the triple tier of appointed non-hereditary territorial chiefs; the purely native council, or *lukiko*, of chiefs; and the conciliar courts, of chiefs again. There was never, as it happened, any official formulation here of government policy. What one sees instead is the application of an effectual and quite particular rule of thumb. Its rough outlines were worked out in Buganda within two years of the establishment of the imperial Protectorate.

Buganda, 1894–7

In Buganda by 1894 British supremacy had been widely ·accepted for two years past. In accordance with British edicts political power within the kingdom was now partitioned between its three minority religious parties. The Protestants

[1] Or 'collector', as, following British practice in India, he was at first called.

occupied the premier position.[1] They held a majority of the important chieftainships, and their dynamic leader, Apolo Kagwa, was senior *katikiro* (chief minister). But the Roman Catholics, no less than the Protestants, now adhered to the settlement which the British had forged. Though defeated in 1892 they now controlled large parts of south-western Buganda, and their forceful leader, Stanilas Mugwanya, occupied a specially created second *katikiro*ship. Although the Muslims were less well placed,[2] their 'loyal' remnant retained one county chieftainship, and their nominal head, Prince Mbogo, was accorded an honoured position when he returned from temporary exile at the coast.[3] In addition Kabaka Mwanga, despite his previous hostility to Christians, Muslims, and British alike, remained Kabaka; shorn, to be sure, of much of his powers, but not as yet of his royal status. Each party in the kingdom held office on terms traditionally legitimate. Each was dependent, however, upon the British for the position which it held. Each was ready, therefore, to accord the British Administration its support. A plateau of political stability had thus been reached; the internal division of power along these lines was to remain substantially unaltered for at least three generations to come. The British in consequence were now seemingly assured of a firm base for their Protectorate.

Even so, in 1894 the whole position was still singularly novel. The traditional form of this proud native state was being maintained, but its internal political alignments had only just been completely revolutionized, and it was now subject as never before to the authority of an alien power. A decided step away from the uncertain stagnation that ensued upon the conclusion of its protracted internal struggle for power was plainly required. So early in 1895 the country was propelled into a fresh train of activity by George Wilson, the British official newly placed in charge of Buganda. No man played a more important part in the history of the nascent Protectorate. He immediately set about the fashioning of a regular native administration. His first characteristic step was to establish a 'native *baraza*', or council,

---

[1] Thanks to their association in 1892 with Captain Lugard of the Imperial British East Africa Company. See ch. xi in vol. i of this *History*.

[2] Their party having been trounced by the British for rebellion in 1893.

[3] He was one of the chief negotiators of the subsequent Uganda Agreement, 1900.

for the determination of the kingdom's affairs.[1] Traditionally the Kabaka had long held audiences of his chiefs at which issues affecting the country were discussed and decided. Wilson now determined to formalize such discussions under his own personal direction; he was careful, however, to ensure that much of the actual discussion as well as the eventual decisions were those of the Kabaka and the leading chiefs rather than his own. Wilson wrought better than he knew. Before very long the *baraza*, or *lukiko*, as the Ganda termed it in their own language, was being accepted as the major forum of the tribe, and was drawing up laws in true parliamentary style after three successive readings![2] A little later Wilson helped to establish a fixed hierarchy of chiefs' courts, topped by a court for 'first class cases' composed of the two *katikiros* and the senior Muslim chief.[3] By 1896 questions of land tenure were being considered, and although the British Commissioner laid down the main principles which should determine its character, he took it for granted that any necessary administration would be entrusted to the native authorities.[4] Step by step the political energies of this vigorous people were thus channelled into the intricacies of peaceful administration and away from their formerly debilitating internecine struggles.

Not all of Wilson's innovations survived,[5] but they set a pattern which was to be followed first in Buganda and then throughout the rest of the Protectorate; the form of Wilson's *baraza*, for instance—native chiefs sitting in council exercising legislative and eventually judicial power—provided the model for the most important of all governmental institutions in Uganda for nearly sixty years to come.[6] But it was Wilson's whole approach in Buganda during 1895–6 which was of even greater importance; for he adumbrated the main lines which the British Administration was to follow throughout the Uganda Protectorate as it grew. He laid his hands upon the native polity

[1] Wilson to Jackson, 10 Feb. 1895, E.S.A. A4/1. Wilson to Johnson, 16 Oct 1900, E.S.A. A12/1.

[2] See Berkeley to Salisbury, 26 Jan. 1897, F.O. 2/133.

[3] Wilson to Jackson, 3 July 1895, E.S.A. A4/2.

[4] Berkeley to Salisbury, 26 Jan. 1897, F.O. 2/133.

[5] The Executive Council, formed in January 1896, seems to have lapsed soon afterwards.

[6] For Wilson's own account ten years later, see Wilson to Elgin, 6 Feb. 1906, C.O. 536/5.

and made it the instrument of British colonial rule. He and his successors neither confined themselves to externals nor conducted the native administration themselves. Their regular practice was to direct the native administration not so much in details but in the principles of modern government as they understood them.[1] This, in the hands of British officials, who had no anxiety to destroy the indigenous political order but had not yet heard of the doctrine of Indirect Rule, involved the progressive reform of the traditional native government along anglicized lines, with such variations as were deemed to be consonant with African conditions. This process was not completed for many years to come, but proved to be practicable in the early years in its breeding ground in Buganda, because of the close political, and in some respects cultural, links between the British and the native chiefs in power. The essence of Wilson's machinery of government was well described in the subsequent Uganda Agreement of 1900 as 'loyal cooperation' between the Kabaka, chiefs, and people of Buganda and the British Administration in the organization and administration of the kingdom. During 1895 and 1896 this co-operation was closer than ever before, or since.[2] It remained the ideal which British administrators in Uganda always set before themselves and before those subject to their authority.

Busoga, Bunyoro, Toro, 1894–7

Whilst these very important administrative foundations were being laid in Buganda, the authority of protectorate officials was beginning to be extended contemporaneously on the east and on the west. East of the Nile a succession of British officers[3] had been posted in Busoga since 1891, their prime task being to keep open the line of communications for the British with the coast. Few British officials, however, were ready to confine their energies to such mundane duties. Yet in seeking, as they soon did, to extend their authority over the neighbouring people,

---

[1] 'Government by safari'—the practice by which British officers regularly toured their districts to inspect the work of chiefs—did not begin until after 1900.

[2] For a striking example see Wilson to Berkeley, 1 Feb. 1896, E.S.A. A4/4: 'The King formally requested me to beg on his behalf your assistance in framing rules regulating the etiquette to be observed in the court of the King on the presentation to him of European and other visitors, and on state occasions.'

[3] Originally of the Imperial British East Africa Company.

they were immediately confronted by the claims of the Ganda to exercise dominion over the Soga—claims based upon the hegemony which Buganda had exercised over quite a number of the Soga kingdoms in the past. Faced with these claims British commissioners in Uganda at first attempted to create an administrative partnership over Busoga with the Ganda;[1] but because the Ganda would not put an end to their long-standing practice of raiding in Busoga, Grant—the British official actually posted in Busoga—took it upon himself during 1894 and 1895 to replace completely the dominion claimed by the Ganda over Busoga by his own. In doing this he imitated the former policy of the kabakas of Buganda themselves, and intervened in the internal politics of the small, weak, and frequently divided Soga kingdoms so as to assert his own authority over them. If a Soga ruler refused to accept Grant's authority there was rarely much difficulty, with the help of a few Sudanese or Swahili troops, in replacing him by one of his brothers.[2] Grant's new course took a little time to complete because it was necessary before his authority could be generally accepted that it should be acknowledged not in one key position alone, as in the monolithic kingdom of Buganda, but in each of the most substantial dozen or so of the Soga kingdoms. But his overall success was only a matter of time, for he soon proved to be the most formidable patron and pursuer whom the Soga now knew.[3] In 1895 the seal was set upon his proceedings by Berkeley, the newly arrived British Commissioner, who on 12 December 1895 procured the signatures of the Kabaka and chiefs of Buganda to the so-called Uganda–Usoga Agreement of 1895,[4] by which the Ganda renounced to the British all claims to any authority over Busoga in return for the whole of a regularized tribute from the Soga kingdoms.[5] It is noteworthy that it was not until after this agreement had been concluded that the news reached Uganda that the Foreign Office had decided to incorporate Busoga in the

[1] e.g. Macdonald to Grant, 30 Sept. 1893, E.S.A. A3/1.

[2] All sons of a previous ruler being in Soga kingdoms equally legitimate as successors.

[3] It is impossible to list a meaningful selection of references for this paragraph, but see, for example, E.S.A. A2/2, letters from Grant *passim*.

[4] An agreement between the British and the Ganda about Busoga to which the Soga were not in fact parties. Berkeley to Salisbury, 8 Dec. 1895, and enclosures, F.O. 2/93.

[5] This was abolished by Article 2 of the Uganda Agreement, 1900.

British Protectorate.[1] The extension of British authority did not always, therefore, wait upon legal enactments in London. In Busoga it emanated from the belief of British officials in the legitimacy of British intervention within a British sphere of influence, wherever a British officer might be posted (more especially where there seemed a mission of humanity to be fulfilled), even when his prime duty was merely to keep open a line of communications. It flowed, too, from the ability of the British to manipulate local political realities to their own political advantage.

In turning their attention at the same time westwards to Bunyoro, British officials were faced with a situation which was as different from that in Busoga as it was from that in Buganda. Unlike Busoga, Bunyoro was one monolithic kingdom. Unlike Buganda, it contained no elements within it with whom the British could hope at the outset to reach a peaceful political settlement. As it happened, upon this one occasion, the British intrusion derived from a Foreign Office dispatch. In August 1893 Colvile, Berkeley's predecessor as substantive Commissioner of the Protectorate, was ordered to send a reconnaissance to Lake Albert and the White Nile flowing north to ascertain whether any French or Belgian agents had reached the Nile Valley from the west.[2] It seemed that the only road to take ran through Bunyoro. But ever since the days of Sir Samuel Baker, Bunyoro had been reckoned by the British to be implacably hostile.[3] Such a view was now regularly reinforced by the partisan accusations of the Ganda. So in December 1893 Colvile decided upon an armed invasion of Bunyoro. His force successfully reached the Lake Albert shore, and an emissary was dispatched northwards to discover whether any other white men had been recently heard of in the region. There was nothing to report. But in order to hold the route between the Buganda border and Lake Albert, Colvile built four forts athwart Bunyoro and left a British officer in charge with instructions to pacify the country.[4]

Obviously, however, Kabarega, the ruler (Mukama) of

---

[1] Berkeley to Grant, 9 Dec. 1895, E.S.A. A5/1.
[2] Rosebery to Portal, 10 Aug. 1893, F.O.C.P. 6490.
[3] See ch. ix in vol. i of this *History*.
[4] Colvile to Thruston, no date, E.S.A. A3/2. H. E. Colvile, *The Land of the Nile Springs* (London, 1895), chs. vi–xvii.

Bunyoro, and his people, whose independence was thus threatened, but whose unity stood firm, could not meekly accept these alien garrisons in their midst.[1] It was not long, therefore, before the Nyoro were harassing the garrisons under British command. The British promptly retaliated, and there followed several years of desultory but harrowing warfare. In a series of encounters during 1894 the Nyoro were each time heavily defeated, and for the first time in his life Kabarega had to flee from his kingdom, northwards across the Nile.[2] His subsequent attempts to sue for peace were all frustrated, partly by the unauthorized raiding of some of his chiefs, partly by the hostile animadversions of the Ganda, and partly by the acute suspicions of the British.[3] Once in 1895 he successfully repelled a British assault.[4] But he was never able to take the military offensive himself. In consequence by 1896 some Nyoro were beginning to accept the conquest of their country as a *fait accompli*, and were seeking to establish some *modus vivendi* with the British.[5] But Kabarega, embittered by the rebuffs which he himself had suffered, had in the meanwhile turned adamantly hostile, and to the embarrassment of the British was soon successfully frustrating their endeavours to bring a settled order to Bunyoro by dispatching emissaries along the byways they could not control to threaten and destroy any traitors to his cause. It was made very clear that in an interlacustrine Bantu kingdom it was not possible for the British to establish civil control successfully unless there was an alliance with elements whose authority was recognized in traditional terms by its ordinary populace as legitimate. For the time being the British position in Bunyoro was nothing more than a military occupation.[6]

One undoubted consequence of Kabarega's expulsion, however, was the complete dismantling of Bunyoro's recent

[1] They had, after all, been established by the British with the assistance of Bunyoro's greatest enemy, Buganda.

[2] e.g. Thruston to Jackson, 26 Dec. 1894, F.O. 2/72.

[3] e.g. Cunningham to Ashburnham and Dunning, 9 Feb. 1895, E.S.A. A4/1; Jackson to Kimberley, 8 Feb. 1895, F.O. 2/92.

[4] Jackson to Kimberley, 15 Mar. 1895, and enclosures, F.O. 2/93.

[5] e.g. Cunningham to Jackson, 10 July 1895, E.S.A. A4/2.

[6] e.g. Thruston to Ternan, 30 June 1897, E.S.A. A4/8. Now that the Conservatives were back in office in Britain, and objections to the expansion of Empire were no longer publicly pressed, this was regularized in British law by the gazetting of the westward extension of the Protectorate, *London Gazette*, 3 July 1896.

reconquest of Toro. Here there was no necessity for a military occupation, since in Toro the British were faced at the outset with a political situation which was exceptionally favourable— and which was once more notably different from that in any of the other interlacustrine kingdoms. For they found themselves able to win the Toro to their side by restoring the independence of Toro from Bunyoro and by setting up a Toro native confederacy under a restored Toro Mukama. Once before, Lugard, in 1891, had sought to reinstate Kasagama, the exiled ruler, on the throne of his forebears, but the attempt had been undermined by Portal's subsequent withdrawal of the Sudanese garrisons from the area.[1] Colvile now decided, however, upon a second restoration, together with the creation of a confederacy under Kasagama's rule of several surrounding areas; his purpose being to provide a bulwark in the south against Nyoro recovery, and a political structure under British control for British domination of the country.[2] Although at the time Toro was not part of the British Protectorate, a treaty with Kasagama was signed on the Commissioner's behalf on 3 March 1894. This established the Toro Confederacy in return for a payment by Kasagama of a regular tribute in ivory to the British.[3] The Confederacy proved at first to be a most fragile conglomeration. Its core consisted of the original kingdom of Toro, where Kasagama's restoration was warmly welcomed: but to it were added the formerly independent kingdom of Kitagwenda; the Mwenge, Kyaka, and Nyakabimba areas, whose chiefs had never been subject to Toro rulers in the past; and Busongora, which had only accepted Toro rule formerly after being worsted in battle. It was only, indeed, with active British support that Kasagama's Confederacy held together.[4] Kasagama, however, never properly fulfilled at this time the British conception of how a subordinate native ruler should behave. There were many occasions of dispute,[5] and by 1896 the British were even considering whether they should not depose Kasagama altogether, and either replace

---

[1] See ch. xi in vol. i of this *History*.
[2] e.g. Colvile to Owen, 18 Feb. 1894, E.S.A. A3/2.
[3] Owen to Colvile, 8 Mar. 1894, E.S.A. A2/2.
[4] e.g. Colvile to Wilson, 19 Aug. 1894, E.S.A. A4/1.
[5] Some concerning Kasagama's 'illegal' trade with Swahili and other merchants from German East Africa: some arising from his attitude as ruler, and as a Protestant convert, to the growth of a Roman Catholic party in his country.

him by some other potentate, or govern the country by direct British control.[1]

There was a further possibility, too. In 1896 the formerly independent ruler of the tiny kingdom of Koki, upon the south-western borders of Buganda, who had previously paid tribute to the Kabaka, was incorporated in the Kingdom of Buganda by the Koki Agreement of that year as a county chief of Buganda with his erstwhile domain as one of the *sazas* (counties) of Buganda. On the very day that the Koki Agreement was signed, Commissioner Berkeley (despite the protests of the British officer in Bunyoro) made public the agreement of the Foreign Office to the promise in 1894 of his predecessor Colvile,[2] that large portions of Bunyoro should be transferred to Buganda as a reward for Ganda help in the war against Kabarega.[3] Checked by the Anglo-German Agreement of 1890 from further expansion southwards down the western shore of Lake Victoria, and by the Uganda–Usoga Agreement from expansion to the east, Buganda thus expanded westwards and northwards instead; whilst as a result of British intervention and British hostility Bunyoro lost not merely, as we have seen, her recent reconquest of Toro, but substantial portions of her homeland which had never been excised before. Buganda's alliance with the British had thus led to the mutilation of her old rival and to an unprecedented expansion of her own territory. There was a very real possibility that this westward expansion of Ganda dominion might have gone even further, for in 1896 it looked to the British like a convenient administrative device. The structure of government which the British had now established in Buganda seemed under George Wilson to be functioning admirably; by contrast, though Toro and Bunyoro had both now become by their separate routes subject to British authority, their civil administrations were convulsed by uncertainties. So Berkeley proposed, and the Foreign Office agreed, that in due course the whole of these two western kingdoms, as well as Ankole to the south-west (which was still unoccupied), should be incorporated in Buganda, just as Koki and large parts of Bunyoro had already been.[4]

---

[1] e.g. Sitwell to Berkeley, 30 June 1896, E.S.A. A4/5.

[2] E.S.A. 'Interviews' Book, 9 Apr. 1894.

[3] Berkeley to Salisbury, two dispatches, 19 Nov. 1896, F.O. 2/112.

[4] e.g. Berkeley to Salisbury, 18 Dec. 1895, and minutes, F.O. 2/95; Berkeley to Salisbury, 14 May 1896, F.O. 2/112; Bertie to Berkeley, 8 Aug. 1896, F.O. 2/111.

Rebellion and mutiny, 1897–9

During 1897 all such plans were cast awry. On 6 July Kabaka Mwanga fled from his capital to raise a rebellion against the régime established by the British in his kingdom.[1] During the three previous years he had come to acquiesce in the political impotence which it had brought him, but he had obviously determined to submit no longer. Only a few months previously he had been publicly humiliated by the British for 'illegally' trafficking in ivory.[2] It was apparently a threat by the two Christian *katikiros* to denounce him for some further 'misdemeanour' which precipitated his flight.[3] He was not, as it happened, the only Ganda to have fallen foul of the new dispensation—in Church as well as State. There were other men of some consequence, who through a continued partiality for alcohol, for hemp-smoking, or a multiplicity of wives—symptoms very often of a much deeper revolt—had clashed with the new régime too. They came from within both Christian parties, so that the newly discontented cut across the former divisions. In the Roman Catholic *mujasi* (traditional commander of the Kabaka's field forces) they had found themselves a leader, and in Buddu in south-western Buganda, which had been almost completely neglected by the British, since it did not lie astride the road to Kampala and the Upper Nile Valley, they discovered a cockpit for recusancy.[4] To Buddu, therefore, Mwanga fled, and its populace immediately rose behind him.[5]

Yet in the capital not a finger was raised in his support.[6] Apart from any question of their personal estrangement from the Kabaka, the two Christian *katikiros* evidently concluded that there was more to be gained by maintaining the alliance with the British than from any desperate attempt to cast it aside. For unlike the Kabaka and his excommunicated lieutenants, who had lost power with the establishment of British control, the Christian leaders had all gained power. In consequence, throughout the series of crises which followed, they and

---

[1] Ternan to Salisbury, 9 July 1897, F.O. 2/133.
[2] Ternan to Salisbury, 25 Jan. 1897, F.O. 2/133.
[3] Nsambya Mission Diary, 16 July 1897.
[4] Streicher to Wilson, 3 May 1897, E.S.A. A4/8; Ternan to Salisbury, 23 June 1897, F.O. 2/133.
[5] e.g. Forster to Wilson, 10 July 1897, E.S.A. A4/8.
[6] Wilson to Ternan, 6 July 1897, E.S.A. A4/8.

the Muslim leaders in the capital stood firmly by the British
connexion. And in the country, their influence predominated.
Of the dozen or so counties into which Buganda was divided,
Buddu alone joined the revolt.[1] Unlike the people of Buddu, the
western and northern Ganda had only lately witnessed the toll
inflicted upon their Nyoro neighbours and had learnt the cost
of open hostility to the British. The bulk of the Ganda were
therefore soon in the field attacking their own Kabaka at the
side of the British; and following his double defeat in the confines of Buddu and his consequent flight to German East Africa,
they joined in acknowledging his infant son, Daudi Chwa, as
Kabaka in his stead, Kagwa, Mugwanya, and Kisingiri (a
senior Protestant chief) being appointed his regents.[2]

Mwanga's revolt was never militarily formidable. Yet for
two and a half years it persisted hydra-headed. Seven expedi-
tions were dispatched against his elusive field commander,
Gabrieli Kintu, but Kintu was never apprehended, and it
was not until mid-1899, with the establishment of a Ganda
Protestant chief in Kabula, the Ankole district bordering
Buddu, that British control was effectively extended to
Buganda's south-westernmost corner.[3]

One of the consequences of Mwanga's rebellion was the extension of British authority to Ankole. As in the days of the
Christian exiles in 1888, Ankole had once more become the
refuge for those opposed to the prevailing régime in Buganda. If
the British position in Buganda was to be firmly secured, such
possibilities of asylum had to be precluded. The reception
accorded to the British in Ankole, however, was not so much
determined by Ankole's involvement in the fighting in Buganda
as by the outcome of a recent Nyankole succession war. From
this one candidate for the Ankole throne, young Kahaya, had
emerged triumphant. But rivalry persisted between two older
members of the royal house, Igumira and Kahitsi, and Kahaya's
young *nganzi* (his later chief minister), Mbaguta, for the dominant influence over him. Upon the advent of the first British
officer these three vied with each other for British support. There

[1] e.g. Wilson to Hill, 16 Sept. 1897, F.O. 2/133.
[2] Ternan to Salisbury, 20, 23, 29 July, 14 Aug. 1897, E.S.A. A2/133.
[3] There is much detailed information on these events in E.S.A. for the years
1897–9, e.g. Ternan to Wilson, 10 Sept. 1899, E.S.A. A5/7.

was no question of the British being opposed. From the outset they were freely acknowledged as the arch-disposers of political power. By eventually settling the dispute in Mbaguta's favour and banishing his two rivals, the British deprived the conservative elements in the country of their leaders and secured the support of the foremost of the younger generation.[1] British control was thus fairly effortlessly established. It is a mistake to imagine that Africans always looked upon European empire-builders as agents of some horrid Leviathan. More frequently they judged them by the amount of support which they seemed likely to give towards the attainment of purely local and often personal ambitions.

It was not until the end of 1898, however, that a British official actually established himself in Ankole.[2] This delay was one of the consequences of the major crisis which had in the meanwhile threatened the very existence of the British Protectorate. This had been precipitated at the end of September 1897 by the refusal of nos. 4, 7, and 9 Companies of the Sudanese troops to obey orders to advance north from Eldama Ravine (on the west side of the Rift Valley in what is now Kenya). Fatally exacerbated by a burst of fire as they withdrew towards the neighbouring station, they turned to ransack the British post in Nandi country. Then, marching west through Kavirondo and Busoga, they gained control of the British fort at Luba's, close to the outflow of the Nile from Lake Victoria, and sent messages to their countrymen in arms summoning them to join in their mutiny.[3] It is still a marvel that none of their appeals bore fruit, for the Sudanese companies, scattered in a dozen or more stations across the breadth of the Protectorate, had serious and genuine grievances. Their pay (in lengths of cloth), for instance, was less than that of a coastal porter, and owing to the perennial collapse in the Protectorate's supply arrangements was generally months in arrears. However, only the three mutinous companies had had the fatal extra burdens laid upon them. They had

---

[1] Once again it is impossible to give a meaningful selection of references, but see, for example, Tighe to Wilson, 16 Sept. 1898, E.S.A. A27/17, and Racey to Johnston, 28 Sept. 1900, E.S.A. A15/1.

[2] Macallister to Berkeley, 1 Jan. 1899, E.S.A. A4/15.

[3] The best single source on the Sudanese mutiny is Berkeley to Salisbury, 30 May 1898, and its important enclosures, F.O. 2/155.

fought in Bunyoro; they were then sent east against the Nandi and the Tugen of the Rift Valley. Brought back to suppress Kabaka Mwanga's revolt, they were then ordered east again to the far edge of Nandi country with instructions to escort Major Macdonald on a secret expedition[1] to an undisclosed destination in the southern Sudan. The order that each soldier was to take with him only one camp follower pitched them into mutiny.

For the tiny handful of British administrators in the Protectorate the position was immediately exceedingly serious. Within Uganda they were dependent upon two bulwarks; the political support of the Ganda and the military backing of the Sudanese. The first had only recently required some buttressing. Now the second looked like collapsing. Macdonald and Jackson,[2] at first with a motley crowd of Swahilis, but later with a substantial Ganda army, managed to confine the mutineers to Luba's fort; but in revenge the mutineers put to death the three British officers whom they had incarcerated within. At this point reconciliation became impossible.

There quickly ensued a struggle for the loyalty of the remaining companies in the west. Those in Kampala were quietly disarmed. Those in Buddu, Toro, and Bunyoro were kept true to the British connexion through five agonizing months by three isolated British officers exhibiting some remarkable achievements in personal leadership. But in December 1897 the crisis reached a perilous climax when Mwanga erupted with his followers in Buddu once more, and Macdonald with a Ganda force had to move down south-westwards to trounce him; for the mutineers took the opportunity to escape from Luba's fort and launch out north-westwards in an attempt to force the hands of the Sudanese companies in Bunyoro. It was only with Ganda help in a lightning campaign in north-western Buganda that the Sudanese were defeated, and with the arrival at the very last moment of the first reinforcement of Indian troops from Mombasa, which Macdonald dispatched to disarm the Sudanese companies in Bunyoro, that the mutineers' most ambitious plans were frustrated. Their remnants withdrew north of the Nile.

These Indian troops were the forerunners of an important

---

[1] This was part of the preliminaries to the looming European crisis over Fashoda.
[2] For a short time Acting Commissioner.

Indian contingent that together with some Swahili reinforcements from the neighbouring British East Africa Protectorate,
and some reconstituted companies of Swahilis and Sudanese,[1]
set out to pursue Gabrieli and his followers in the south-west,
and the mutineers whenever they recrossed the Nile in the
north. There were numerous encounters, and in places in the
west, more particularly in Bunyoro, the country-side was laid
waste by the depredations of both sides. In August 1898 the
mutineers were seriously defeated at Mruli on the Nile,[2] and
four months later Kabaka Mwanga escaped northwards to join
hands with his hereditary foe, Kabarega; but in April 1899 the
two rulers were captured and deported, first to Kismayu, and
then to the Seychelles.

By that time the British position of dominance in the northern
interlacustrine kingdoms had been saved, partly through the
ability to judge when to stay calm and when to move swiftly;
partly because in the end the three original companies alone
mutinied; partly because substantial non-Sudanese reinforcements were steadily moved up from the coast; and also because
the Ganda Christian leaders had taken the field and provided
thousands of porters not merely against their own Kabaka, but
against the mutineers as well. Had they been at all hesitant in
their support of the British, the British position might very well
have collapsed. The point was not lost on Kagwa, the senior
katikiro and regent. Hitherto the Ganda had always been the
junior partner in the alliance which their leaders had established
with the British. Now the British had had to turn to them as
their chief support during a critical period. Henceforth Kagwa
felt free to insist on the claims of the Ganda to be treated
deferentially.[3] At the same time he and his associates seem to
have taken note of the dangers to their own position with their
own people by their mute acceptance of the British alliance and
British injunctions. As a result, and with considerable daring,[4]

---

[1] These were sifted out from amongst those who had remained loyal to the
British.

[2] The last of them were not rounded up until 1901.

[3] In an illuminating comment on Kagwa in 1899 George Wilson said he doubted
'not his loyalty, for he's as sound as they are made, but his personal ambitions.
He's a bit afraid of my local knowledge or I think he'd make a bid for the chief
seat'; Wilson to Lugard, 22 Mar. 1899, Lugard Papers.

[4] For a people prone to acknowledge, in Dr. Maquet's phrase, the 'premise of
inequality', but encouraged perhaps by the missionaries' notions of human equality.

the standard was raised for Buganda's claims to distinctive privileges and a distinctive autonomy.[1]

Nor was this the only repercussion of the crisis. The military force at the disposal of the British Commissioner was substantially reorganized.[2] Pending the arrival at the Lake Victoria shore in 1901 of the railway from Mombasa,[3] an official transport service was formed. In London the British Treasury was reluctantly obliged to furnish a larger grant-in-aid;[4] and because there was so much criticism in the press and in parliament of the Government's handling of Uganda's affairs[5] the Foreign Office ultimately decided to dispatch a special commissioner to make an extensive report on the Protectorate, and set it upon a surer course for the future. Sir Harry Johnston was eventually appointed in mid-1899.[6]

Johnston's settlement, 1900-2

Johnston had had more experience of African administration than anyone else in the service of the Foreign Office.[7] His mission marked the point at which all conceptions of a limited protectorate were brushed aside, and in their place there emerged the outline of a protectorate which extended to its modern boundaries, and which fashioned a multiplicity of public policies. While Johnston was in Uganda the Foreign Office drew up the Uganda Order in Council of 1902 which was to remain the Protectorate's basic law.[8] He himself divided the area covered by the Uganda Protectorate into provinces and

[1] e.g. Buganda Regents to Johnston, 3 Jan. 1900, E.S.A. A6/8. 'Questions and protests of the Uganda chiefs re land tax', 16 Jan. 1900, E.S.A. Secretariat Minute Paper (hereinafter 'S.M.P.') C450.

[2] Its Sudanese component was reduced, and for a time an Indian contingent was added.

[3] This virtually solved the supply problems of the Protectorate.

[4] It rose from £50,000 for each of the three years between 1894 and 1897 to nearly £400,000 for 1899. It did not drop to £50,000 again until two years before its abolition in 1915. H. B. Thomas and R. Scott, *Uganda* (Oxford, 1935), p. 504. F.O. correspondence with Treasury during 1899, F.O. 2/252.

[5] *Hansard*, 4th ser., H. of C., liv. 504-45, 3 Mar. 1898. *The Times*, 24 Nov. 1897, 23 Jan. 1899.

[6] Salisbury to Johnston, 1 July 1899, F.O. 2/200.

[7] Vice-Consul, Cameroons, 1885; Acting Consul, Niger Coast Protectorate, 1887; Consul, Mozambique, 1888; Commissioner, British Central Africa Protectorate, 1891; Consul-General, Tunis, 1897. See R. Oliver, *Sir Harry Johnston and the Scramble for Africa* (London, 1957).

[8] See F.O. 2/549, 663.

E

districts,[1] while his two reports dealt in outline with almost every imaginable governmental concern of the time.[2] Upon his arrival in Uganda the security of the British position at the core of the Protectorate had been substantially restored. His prime task, as impressed upon him by his superiors in the Foreign Office, was to set the Protectorate's finances in order so that it should now begin to pay its own way.[3] This led him to propose the institution of a hut tax payable to the British Administration[4] for whose collection he looked to the appointment of native chiefs whom British officials, he said, should 'back . . . up in ruling their fellow countrymen'.[5] At the same time he drafted a land settlement scheme which, whilst endeavouring to be generous to Africans, sought to bring into the Government's own hands all unoccupied land as 'one of the assets of the Uganda Protectorate'.[6] These plans provided the groundwork for the important agreements he concluded in Uganda during 1900.

His preliminary negotiations with the regents and senior chiefs in Buganda almost precipitated disaster.[7] His determination to secure native chiefs as British tax-collectors seemed to the Ganda like a blatant attempt to undermine their tribal government. After all the assistance which the Christian parties had rendered, this seeming apostasy was angrily denounced. Johnston, however, had merely been maladroit. He had no intention of ignoring Ganda institutions. But because of the furore he had caused there emerged, not some regulations about land and taxation as he originally proposed, but the Uganda Agreement of 1900. By this British authority over Buganda was confirmed. Buganda was declared to be but one province of the larger Uganda Protectorate; and the Ganda undertook to pay to the

---

[1] Johnston to Salisbury, 25 May 1900, F.O. 2/666.

[2] With administration, with economic development, with land policy, with communications, with public health, among others. *Preliminary Report by Her Majesty's Special Commissioner on the Protectorate of Uganda*, Africa no. 6, Cd. 256 (1900); *Report by Her Majesty's Special Commissioner on the Protectorate of Uganda*, Africa no. 7, Cd. 671 (1901).

[3] e.g. Salisbury to Johnston, 1 July 1899, F.O. 2/200.

[4] Johnston to Salisbury, 24 Dec. 1899, F.O. 2/204.

[5] Johnston to Martin, 5 Jan. 1900, E.S.A. A5/9.

[6] Johnston to Salisbury, 13 Oct. 1899, F.O. 2/204.

[7] This whole episode and its aftermath is discussed at length in D. A. Low and R. C. Pratt, *Buganda and British Overrule, 1900–1955* (London, 1960), pt. i: 'The making and implementation of the Uganda Agreement 1900'.

British Administration a hut tax of 3 rupees to be collected by their own chiefs, the ministers and the county chiefs being paid for their services. At the same time the doubling of Buganda's area (which had taken place at the hands of the British during the previous decade) and the increase in the number of its *sazas* from the pre-European ten to the later twenty was confirmed. And the Ganda system of government was upheld. It was, however, at the same time further refashioned along the lines already adumbrated by George Wilson. The Kabaka was to be called 'His Highness', and upon his majority was to exercise 'direct rule' over his people; but henceforward with the assistance of three ministers—the traditional *katikiro* (shorn of his judicial functions), a newly established chief justice, and a newly created treasurer (the new trio corresponding to the already existing three-member regency, which was thus reorientated). The Lukiko, moreover, was now formally constituted both as the tribal legislature and as a final court of appeal.[1] This marked a further stage in the post-traditional evolution of Buganda's constitution, and constituted a considerable invasion of the Kabaka's traditional autocracy.

From the agreement there also emerged a revolutionary system of land tenure for Buganda, the dominant feature of which lay in its grant of freehold titles to the Kabaka and chiefs. Traditionally the appointed chiefs of Buganda had never owned lands.[2] They had exercised jurisdiction at the Kabaka's pleasure over those who chose to live upon it under them. Johnston had no difficulty in securing the agreement of the Ganda leaders to his expropriation of about half the kingdom's area as Crown Land, but he encountered vehement protests when he proposed that land should only be granted to a few senior chiefs, and that the remainder of the cultivated land should be held by its occupants as tenants of a statutory Board of Trustees; for this would have made many peasants independent of chiefly overlords and deprived many chiefs of their jurisdictions, which seemed to the Ganda hierarchy like yet another onslaught upon their tribal polity. The Board of Trustees was therefore expunged, and the

---

[1] Its membership was fixed for the first time at 60 notables, 6 additional persons nominated by the Kabaka, 20 county chiefs, and the 3 ministers.

[2] There are many accounts of land tenure in Buganda. See Uganda Protectorate, *Bibliography of Land Tenure* (Entebbe, 1957), pp. 1–6.

remainder of the land was then parcelled out in square miles (*mailos*) to the Kabaka, his family, the ministers, the county chiefs, and 1,000 minor chiefs. The revolutionary innovation—that because this settlement was framed in European terms they were to hold their land by individual tenure—seems at the time scarcely to have been noticed.

Although many retained the land they had previously held, the new settlement precipitated numerous migrations of population, since those in power were frequently able to choose new estates in especially favourable areas. For a year or two the country was seriously disturbed. And the whole position was soon substantially aggravated by the simultaneous discontent of the minor chiefs. Most of these had been called upon to collect tax, but none of them were paid, like the county chiefs, for their services; and since there were certainly more than the 1,000 minor chiefs mentioned in the agreement, it looked as if large numbers of them would be excluded from the land allotment as well. Two decisions were therefore taken by the Ganda leaders in which the British acquiesced, not because they saw any threat to the security of their position, but because they realized that if they were to sustain a fruitful co-operation with the Ganda, it was not enough to enjoy the support of the upper echelons of the chiefly hierarchy alone; they were also dependent, like the senior chiefs themselves, upon the goodwill of numerous subordinates. The number of original recipients of *mailo* land was therefore increased to nearly 4,000; and *mailo* owners were empowered to impose annual rents of 2 rupees for each hut on their land. By these means the minor chiefs were won to the support of the definitive settlement with the British that was marked by the agreement, and in consequence the British were now assured for many years to come, not merely of an impregnable base in Buganda for their Protectorate, but of a constructive association with the whole of the powerful Ganda hierarchy. Since these transactions revealed the support which the chiefs could look to from the British, their position with their own peasantry was at the same time immeasurably strengthened.[1]

---

[1] In the second decade of the twentieth century this impression was reinforced by the increases in rents which the British sanctioned as more money began to circulate. P. G. Powesland, *Economic Policy and Labour*, East African Studies no. 10 (Kampala, 1957), p. 22.

Against this formidable coalition popular discontent during the next twenty years[1] scarcely dared to raise its head.

With the implementation of the 1900 Agreement the Christian parties and their Muslim allies had their earlier hegemony confirmed. Taken together they were still a minority in the kingdom, but they dominated its political scene and monopolized its native government. Every member of the reconstituted Lukiko belonged to one or other religious party. No pagan gained more than a minor allotment of land under the agreement. Henceforward between the religious parties themselves there was to be little movement from one to the other. Ten years previously brothers had still chosen to belong to different parties:[2] but families now began to adhere as a whole to one party or the other. A revolutionary period was drawing to a close, and a new rigidity was beginning to overlay Ganda society.

It was not only in Buganda that the years 1900 and 1901 constituted a watershed. They saw important changes in the western kingdoms too. At the beginning of May 1900 Johnston turned westwards to Toro. Here on 26 June he made the Toro Agreement of 1900. It was a shorter, simpler document than the Uganda Agreement, more in accord with his original mental prototype. It instituted hut and gun taxes, and procured for the Crown all the uncultivated land.[3] Its real significance, however, lay very much deeper. For at a blow it removed the threats that had overhung both the institutions and even the independence of Toro, and in two corresponding respects signalized important departures for all the western kingdoms. Because Kasagama had found nothing alluring in Mwanga's revolt or the Sudanese mutiny he had remained loyal to his European benefactors throughout their successive ordeals. At a time when the British were in mortal conflict with the two other paramount rulers in Uganda with whom they had had contact, Kasagama's steadfastness, following so close upon his earlier contentiousness,

[1] Over the compulsory movement of population from sleeping-sickness areas; against the cotton-crop regulations; over the expropriation of clan burial grounds; over the imposition of compulsory labour for private as well as public purposes, &c.

[2] e.g. Ansorge to Colvile, 16 Nov. 1894, E.S.A. A2/3.

[3] Johnston to Salisbury, 25 Aug. 1900, F.O. 2/299. Sadler to F.O., 25 Apr. 1902, F.O.C.P. 7953.

preserved in the minds of British officials the reputation of African monarchy as a workable accessory of imperial authority.[1] This was of singular importance to the British for, as one British officer had divined, in these kingdoms 'the people through force of habit, love for the person, or the prestige of his office, naturally submit to the orders of their Prince. The Prince himself through the instinct of self-preservation if through nothing else, usually willingly obeys the orders of his Protector.'[2] Now with the signing of the Toro Agreement, the future of monarchy in the west, and certainly Kasagama's own position, became assured, and with it the ready acceptance there of British over-rule. At the same time Kasagama's loyalty won British support for the perpetuation of his confederacy. The Toro Agreement, therefore, not only confirmed Toro's independence from Bunyoro but killed the idea, previously entertained by Berkeley and later by Wilson and by certain Ganda,[3] of some form of organic connexion between Buganda and her still unincorporated neighbours. Henceforward the kingdoms in the west, and indeed following in their footsteps the whole of the rest of the Protectorate, were to remain quite independent of her. For half a century to come the sole constitutional bonds linking the different kingdoms and districts of Uganda together were to lie in their common subordination to the same Protectorate Government.

In August 1900 Johnston visited Ankole, but he quickly decided that it was insufficiently prepared to carry out a formal agreement; and it was not until the ruler (the Mugabe) and some of his chiefs had visited Buganda to see its reformed native government in operation that an Ankole Agreement was eventually concluded in August 1901.[4] In the intervening year, however, modern Ankole had been created. Its core consisted of the Mugabe's original but significantly smaller kingdom. In the rulerships to its westward and northward British officers had at first seemed anxious to substitute British for Nyankole

---

[1] e.g. Sitwell to Wilson, 20 Nov. 1897, E.S.A. A4/9; Bagge to Ternan, 20 Aug., 22 Sept. 1899, E.S.A. A4/20.

[2] Thruston to Ternan, 30 June 1897, E.S.A. A4/8.

[3] e.g. Wilson to Berkeley, 8 Feb. 1899, and enclosures, Buganda Residency Archives.

[4] Jackson to Lansdowne, 31 Oct. 1901, and enclosures, F.O.C.P. 7868. See also E.S.A. A 15/1.

influence, much as they had substituted British for Ganda influence in Busoga. But there were no funds for a further British post hereabouts, so that when, at the end of 1900, the chiefs of Bunyaruguru to the north-west asked if they might pay court to the Mugabe Kahaya, the alternative process of subjugating the neighbouring areas to Ankole—and by this means to the British—was set on foot instead. It was not accomplished without friction. The ruler of Igara committed suicide; the ruler of Kajara fled across the German border; the ruler of Buhweju was shot in battle; and the ruler of Rujumbura persistently, and in the end successfully, refused to acknowledge Kahaya's overlordship. But the policy of incorporation naturally enjoyed the strong support of the Nyankole leaders, and in the end came to be accepted by their neighbours since many of them had in the past acknowledged the primacy of Ankole, if not perhaps its actual authority. In this manner with British assistance the original Ankole doubled its area within nine months, and by the Ankole Agreement of 1901 the neighbouring rulerships were turned into counties of the Mugabe's kingdom. Out of the congeries of rulerships southwards from Bunyoro the British had thus by 1901 created the two new polities of the Toro Confederacy and 'greater' Ankole.

Johnston never visited Bunyoro; and because it was deemed a conquered country there was no Bunyoro Agreement until 1933. But during the first years of the twentieth century George Wilson, who was placed in charge of the kingdom in 1900, set about the reconstruction of its traditional native government.[1] The key proved to be the installation of a new, but traditionally legitimate, native ruler.[2] As some had forecast, this restoration of Bunyoro's monarchy, following so hard upon the acute demoralization which had overtaken its peoples during six years of devastating war, did much to revive their self-confidence.

[1] e.g. Wilson to Johnston, 6 Sept. 1900, E.S.A. A12/1.

[2] Since 1896 several British officers had called for such an appointment in Kabarega's place, but the idea had had its opponents too. There were, in fact, no less than seven changes of British policy upon this point before 1900; and in 1902 one of Kabarega's sons who was eventually appointed was replaced by another, Duhaga. At first the new ruler was given a regency, but it was abolished in 1904, and he then reigned undisturbed till his death twenty years later. See, for example, Sadler to Lansdowne, 12 Sept. 1902, F.O.C.P. 8040; *General Report on the Uganda Protectorate for the Year ending March 31, 1904*, Africa no. 12, Cd. 2250 (1904); Unyoro Annual Report, 1903-4.

Kabarega lived on till 1923, but upon his relegation to permanent exile his people soon recognized the mantle of royal
authority which the British had placed upon his son Duhaga;
and before very long the most important of Kabarega's surviving chiefs were accepting office under the new régime.

Thus by 1901 a working settlement had been reached between the British and all the kingdom areas of Uganda. The
initiative in British administrative policy still lay in each individual district officer's own hands. The most thoughtful of
them all echoed George Wilson's view that the right way to
begin was 'by the Administration strengthening the authority of
the king with his people whilst at the same time acquiring by
political conduct on the part of its representatives a controlling
influence over the king.'[1]

And upon this base they had already begun the construction
of Uganda's own particular form of colonial government. It was
based upon the model in Buganda, which comprised the traditional structure of government there, as amended by Wilson
and by Johnston, and as circumscribed by and articulated with
the British claim to be the overruling power. There were already
signs (in, for instance, the Toro and Ankole Agreements) of its
successful export to surrounding areas.

Crises in the western kingdoms, 1900–7

Even so the smooth tenor of events in Toro, Ankole, and
Bunyoro was profoundly disturbed during the first decade of the
new century by a long-remembered occurrence in each one of
them. In the first place, from 1900 to 1906 there was continual
agitation in Toro for the amendment of the Toro Agreement.[2]
Presumably because Johnston had been anxious to avoid a
repetition of his protracted negotiations in Buganda, he had
made the Mukama and his chiefs sign the Toro Agreement of
1900 after the briefest negotiation. He had made some provision
in subsequent addenda for the claims to tax exemption and land
by some of the Toro hierarchy, but the whole proceedings were
keenly resented, and there remained several outstanding objections which continued to rankle. Considering that the Nyankole
looked upon the procurement of an agreement like the Toro

---

[1] Wilson to Ternan, 8 Feb. 1899, E.S.A. A4/16.
[2] E.S.A./S.M.P. R125 contains all the most important papers on this episode.

Agreement as the height of their ambitions, it is at first sight surprising that that same agreement should have been so execrated by the Toro. Yet there was one crucial difference between the two agreements. The Ankole Agreement made Ankole and its neighbours one united kingdom, but the Toro Agreement retained the original conception of Toro as no more than a confederacy. In practice some of the chiefs of non-Toro areas were perfunctory in their allegiance to Kasagama.[1] In one respect—as County Chief of Toro proper—he himself was no more than *primus inter pares*; while his own senior chiefs with responsibilities equal to, and in the case of his *katikiro* greater than, those of the non-Toro chiefs, were neither granted the same status nor allowed the same emoluments.[2] From 1901 onwards the British acknowledged the need for some readjustment, but Kasagama and his supporters had to wait until 1906 before Sir Hesketh Bell made the changes they desired. The prime effect of the formal memorandum which Bell signed on 13 July 1906[3] was to turn the Toro Confederacy into the Toro Kingdom, now at last fully comparable—except in the size and sophistication of Buganda—with each of its three immediate neighbours.

In the previous year the Ankole Agreement had been suspended. On 19 May 1905 Galt, the acting Provincial Commissioner, was speared to death by an assailant whose identity and motives have never been properly established. In two successive investigations, however, George Wilson pinned the blame on a conspiracy of Nyankole chiefs against the British,[4] and upon his recommendation the Ankole Agreement was suspended, heavy fines in cattle were imposed upon the Mugabe, the *nganzi*, and the senior chiefs, and the three counties around the scene of the crime had their hut tax doubled.[5] But it proved to be a completely isolated incident and, thanks to the appeals of some British officers in the region, the punishment meted out, though resented, was not nearly as arbitrary and promiscuous as the

[1] e.g. Toro Monthly Report, Jan. 1905. E.S.A. A14/2.
[2] e.g. Galt to Wilson, 1 May 1905, E.S.A. A14/2.
[3] E.S.A./S.M.P. R125.
[4] It is possible that the crime was part of a Nyankole plot to discredit Mbaguta, the *nganzi*, who had personally profited so enormously from the advent of the British. For the latest account see H. F. Morris, 'The murder of H. St. G. Galt', *Uganda J.* xxiv (1960), 1–15.
[5] Sadler to Elgin, 29 May 1905, C.O. 536/1; 6 June 1905, 24 Aug. 1905, and enclosures, C.O. 566/2; Ankole Monthly Reports, May, June 1905, E.S.A. A14/2.

Nyankole had at first feared.[1] Clearly one of the keys to the success of the British in having their authority accepted lay in their care not to provoke their subjects into violent opposition.

But in thinking, as Wilson did, that Galt's murder was symptomatic of a wider-ranging opposition, he appeared two years later to have his worst fears confirmed by a crisis in Bunyoro. In 1901, in a not unsuccessful attempt to direct Nyoro administration along the lines he had laid down in Ganda, Wilson himself had brought into Bunyoro Jemusi Miti, a Ganda chief, who proved to be but the first of a number of Ganda appointed to Bunyoro posts in the years immediately following.[2] The Nyoro resented this invasion,[3] and their hostility was aggravated by the recent loss to Buganda of large parts of their kingdom.[4] During 1905 and 1906 two successive district commissioners were sympathetic to the idea that the Ganda chiefs should be withdrawn, but before this had led to any result, the Nyoro in 1907 had terrorized the Ganda chiefs in their country into retreating upon district headquarters at Hoima, Nyoro sub-chiefs assuming their places. George Wilson, who happened to be acting Commissioner of the Protectorate at the time, promptly ordered the reinstatement of the Ganda. But the Nyoro refused. Whereupon Wilson marched with a column of troops from Entebbe to Hoima in the expectation that he had a rebellion to suppress.[5]

But the point about *ekya nyangire abaganda*[6] was precisely that the Nyoro did not resort to violence. Here, indeed, lies the real key to the importance of each of these three occurrences in the western kingdoms. For they exemplified the extent to which circumstances in the kingdom areas had changed. In the 1890's the emotions which each incident let loose would almost certainly have provoked one side or the other to violent attack. But

[1] In 1912 their agreement was restored.

[2] By 1905 the British were employing Ganda administrators in many other parts of the Protectorate, too, and they had been introduced as chiefs by Mbaguta into some of the newly annexed areas of Ankole, where they were hardly more popular than in Bunyoro: e.g. Knowles to Wilson, 1 Feb. 1906, E.S.A. A14/3. It was in eastern and northern Uganda, however, that they were principally employed. See below.

[3] Wilson declared that they envied the Ganda their efficiency.

[4] This, as it happened, contained the tombs of most of their kings.

[5] Wilson to Elgin, 25 June 1907, and numerous enclosures, C.O. 536/13.

[6] 'The time of refusing the Baganda', as the Nyoro have called it.

in the years following the suppression of Mwanga's rebellion and the Sudanese mutiny, and in the wake of the settlements forged by Johnston and his associates, there was no further disposition upon the part of the peoples who had now had a decade and more of contact with British officials to challenge their authority with violence. At the same time the British for their part no longer felt the necessity to swing the cudgel to uphold their authority in the Uganda kingdoms. Like Johnston in negotiating the 1900 Agreement with the Ganda, they were even prepared to reach some accommodation where feelings had been deeply aroused. Following the Nyoro affair of 1907, for instance, although over fifty Nyoro chiefs were temporarily deported, the British refrained from physical reprisals, and shortly afterwards declared that no more Ganda chiefs would be appointed in their country.[1] The strength of the legends enshrouding each incident is heir to the relief which attended the avoidance of fatal crises and the attainment of palatable conclusions; but the essential fact was that in the interlacustrine kingdoms the force of argument was superseding the arbitrament of armed assault. Overrule by tacit consent had been firmly installed at the core of the Protectorate.

Kakunguru's 'empire'

As if to mark this stabilization the responsibility in London for the oversight of Uganda's affairs was transferred from the Foreign Office to the Colonial Office in 1905, and in 1907 its Commissioner became a Governor.[2] Yet the extent of this stabilization at the centre of the Protectorate was really not grasped immediately, and despite Johnston's division of the whole Protectorate in 1900 into provinces and districts, the area of protectorate rule continued in the main for the whole of the first decade of the twentieth century to be confined to the interlacustrine kingdoms and circumscribed by the original considerations of 1894. The gradual extension of British authority westwards of the original Ankole in 1904–8 was no more than the rounding off of the British position in Ankole District. In 1898–9 British posts had been established in Acholi, Madi, and

[1] Masindi Annual Report, 1909–10.
[2] There was no Executive or Legislative Council until after 1920.

Bari country north of Lake Albert,[1] but these were no more than
the relics of Colonel Martyr's expedition down the Nile at the
time of the Fashoda crisis.[2] They were confined to the Nile
Valley. They never led to any very effective British control over
the surrounding peoples,[3] and in 1906 Sir Hesketh Bell deliberately decided against the extension of British authority into the
heart of the surrounding country.[4] Although the Protectorate's
finances had improved (thanks to the reduction in the costs of
transport following the arrival of the Uganda Railway at the
Lake Victoria shore and to the collection of hut taxes), a shortage of funds aggravated the continuing doubts about security at
the centre of the Protectorate, and together these precluded for
the time being any deliberate expansion of the Protectorate's
control.

Only one new area, indeed—stretching from Lake Kyoga,
north-eastwards of Buganda, to Mount Elgon on the far eastern
edge of the Protectorate—was brought under British authority
in the ten years before 1909, and in origin this owed nothing to
British initiative. The achievement belonged primarily to Semei
Kakunguru, Apolo Kagwa's chief rival for the Protestant
leadership in Buganda, who in the mid-1890's had been placed
in charge of the northern part of Buganda's conquests from
Bunyoro[5] where he gained a unique experience in subduing non-
Ganda peoples to Ganda authority. This experience he put to
remarkable use. Since it proved impossible for him and Kagwa
to coexist in the same state, Kakunguru was looking by 1898 for
new pastures. The possibility in that year that he might go to
Busoga was baulked by Grant, so in 1899 he seized the opportunity afforded by a British commission to round up rebels and
mutineers to carve out a wholly new dominion for himself upon
the far side of Lake Kyoga. He had already built an outpost

---

[1] Here in 1904 George Wilson established councils of local petty 'chiefs' as the
instruments of British overlordship. Wilson to Fowler, 22 Nov. 1904, E.S.A. A8/3;
Bari District Annual Report, 1904–5; Nimule District Annual Report, 1904–5.

[2] W. L. Langer, *The Diplomacy of Imperialism*, 2nd edn. (New York, 1951),
p. 543 (map).

[3] See Bari, Nimule, and Wadelai Districts and Nile Province reports for these
years, *passim*

[4] Bell to Elgin, 13 Sept. 1906, C.O. 536/7.

[5] For Kakunguru's career see H. B. Thomas, '*Capax Imperii*—The story of Semei
Kakunguru', *Uganda J.* vi. 3 (1939), 125–36. See also A. D. Roberts, 'The Sub-
Imperialism of the Baganda', *J. Af. History* iii. 3 (1962), 435–50.

upon its northern shore in 1896. He now established his authority over the local Kumam, and dispatched warbands to conquer the Teso to the east. With the ending of warfare in the inter-lacustrine kingdoms many Ganda were soon flocking to his banner in the confidence that they would be rewarded with land, cattle, and an adventurous career. By 1900 he had extended his operations south-westwards to Budaka, and when at the end of that year Johnston met him near the slopes of Mount Elgon and airily dubbed him 'Kabaka of Bukedi', Kakunguru adopted the title with alacrity. As might be expec-ted his campaigning hereabouts met with little opposition. The peoples eastward of Mount Elgon had very different political institutions from those of the interlacustrine kingdoms. Their stateless societies had no centralized political authorities to organize their resistance. Nor, by contrast with Kakunguru's followers, were they well supplied with guns:

> The pattern of occupation was everywhere the same; first an armed expedition would be made from an established fort to a new area; the pretexts were often obscure, sometimes a request from a warring faction or sometimes a threat of attack by local inhabi-tants; after skirmishes or pitched battles a new fort would be estab-lished and a garrison of armed Baganda installed.[1]

By such means Kakunguru had within three years subjugated an area of about 10,000 square miles. He then went on to show how the essentials of Ganda administration could be efficiently applied to the control of peoples who had no centralized political institutions themselves, for he was soon dividing his conquests into five administrative counties subject to his own appointees as chiefs—local labour being summoned to build a network of roads and a series of walled forts.

The British, however, soon began to have doubts about the propriety of many of Kakunguru's actions,[2] and in 1901 an administrative officer was ordered to take over his headquarters at Budaka.[3] This proved to be a hazardous undertaking, but Kakunguru eventually withdrew northwards to Mbale near the slopes of Mount Elgon. Since the turn of the century this had been an important centre for the route which Greek and

---

[1] J. C. D. Lawrance, *The Iteso* (London, 1957), p. 18.
[2] Jackson to Lansdowne, 14 July 1911, E.S.A./S.M.P. 519/1909.
[3] On this and subsequent events see E.S.A. A10/2, 3 and A11/1, 2.

Swahili traders were taking to the ivory areas farther north.[1] In
1903 it was decided that it should become the seat of the British
officer in the region. But by this move the British found themselves face to face with a problem quite novel for the Uganda
Protectorate. The neighbouring Gisu seemed to have no powerful chiefs through whom they might be controlled. At the same
time, while the British officer at Mbale was frequently single-
handed, the Gisu were extremely populous. It was now that
Kakunguru's success in establishing his authority in the region
proved to be of such very great importance, for it pointed the
way to a means of extending British authority in the region, and
it was not long before Boyle, the Provincial Commissioner, had
decided to take over the local Ganda administration as established by Kakunguru and make it the instrument of British
authority; Kakunguru himself (instead this time of being ejected
once again) becoming, under the British, *saza* chief of the Mbale
area.[2] At the same time Boyle made one important structural
change in Kakunguru's system. Instead of Kakunguru's appointees being made chiefs themselves, Boyle arranged that they
should become advisers, or 'Agents' as they were called, to local
chiefs, who were to be picked out from amongst the most
prominent local individuals.[3] The aim, in other words, was not
to entrench Ganda hegemony but to build up once more, as in
the western kingdoms, a local administrative structure on the
Ganda model.

This policy of employing Ganda Agents proved to be extra-
ordinarily successful. As successful conquerors, the prestige of
the Ganda ran high with the Gisu and their neighbours. Under
the British the Ganda themselves continued for some years to
enjoy power and position; and since they were extremely well
versed in the essentials of native administration, they were
gradually able to train up local clan heads and others to act as
administrative chiefs. By 1907 Mbale District had been sub-

---

[1] e.g. Sadler to Lansdowne, 2 Dec. 1903 and enclosures, F.O.C.P. 8345, and
Eastern Province Annual Report, 1910–11.

[2] Eastern Province Annual Report, 1903–4; Sadler to Lansdowne, 27 Feb.
1904, F.O.C.P. 8349; *General Report on the Uganda Protectorate for the Year ending
March 31, 1904*, Africa no. 12, Cd. 2250 (1904).

[3] The change was accepted by Kakunguru because his power of appointment
was retained. Boyle to Sadler, 7 May 1904, E.S.A. A10/3; Watson to Boyle, 3 Nov.
1904; Boyle to Wilson, 27 Feb. 1905, E.S.A. A10/4.

divided into twelve sub-districts, and the Ganda Agents had been graded in three ranks on a British payroll.[1] Boyle and his assistants by this means successfully purloined Kakunguru's 'empire', and with Ganda help pressed forward with the establishment of a native administration on the Buganda model in an area which had never known anything like it before.

Chiefs, courts, and land policy

The sequestration of Kakunguru's authority was completed by his transfer to Busoga. Here British control had for some years been established over all the rulers whose authority was locally recognized as legitimate. However, with relatively few exceptions they had failed to fulfil the governmental tasks which the British laid upon them.[2] At first an attempt was made to deal with their subordinates directly,[3] but this met with only a limited success, and Boyle, the Provincial Commissioner, eventually decided instead to employ Kakunguru's talents to construct a really effective native administration. In 1906 he appointed him President of the Busoga Lukiko. Immediately Kakunguru set about the creation of a Ganda-type organization. Busoga District was subdivided into seven sazas, and where necessary Ganda were introduced as advisers to traditional rulers.[4]

As this Busoga story suggested, it was not sufficient for the British after the turn of the century to exercise control over traditional rulers, for the demands which they were now making of a native administration were expanding considerably. In addition to the mere maintenance of peace and the payment of a general tribute, they now required the collection of taxes from each individual peasant; they wanted labour recruited, malefactors apprehended, roads built, and courts held. For these purposes control over the ruler was inadequate, not only because he might be personally incompetent, but, more generally, because he could not be expected to carry out all the details of

[1] Uganda. Report by the Governor on a Tour through the Eastern Province, Colonial Reports, Miscellaneous, no. 57, Cd. 4524 (1909); Central (Eastern) Province Annual Report, 1906–7.

[2] General Report on the Uganda Protectorate for the Year ending March 31, 1904, Cd. 2250.

[3] Eastern Province Annual Report, 1903–4.

[4] Report ... on a Tour through the Eastern Province, Cd. 4524; Central (Eastern) Province Annual Report, 1906–7; Busoga Monthly Report, Aug. 1907.

government himself. It was necessary to employ an infrastructure of administrative chiefs as well.

All interlacustrine Bantu rulers had had their administrative subordinates, but the evolution of general administrators with prescribed jurisdictions, who were neither heads of clans, nor of royal blood, but primarily lay appointees, had not always proceeded very far. In basing themselves on Buganda, however, the British were fortunate in having under their hand in the Ganda *bakungu* chiefs the chieftainship system which approximated most closely to their requirements. It was this system—of appointed county chiefs and their subordinates—which as a matter of broad administrative practice was now exported, not only to Busoga and Bugisu, but to the rest of the Protectorate as well, together with the office of *katikiro*, or head of the general administration, and the Lukiko, or council of administrative chiefs.

The export programme was somewhat haphazard. In Toro the Ganda system, which in large part was novel there, had been introduced with Kasagama's restoration as early as 1891 because the chief architect of his return, Yafeti Byakweyamba, had himself been a chief in Buganda and understood the system from personal experience.[1] But it was not until ten years later that Wilson and Jemusi Miti began the establishment of *sazas* in Bunyoro.[2] There were similar variations in the pace at which *katikiros* and *lukikos* were established. Although the unbroken succession of Toro *katikiros* dates from 1891, the Nyoro succession dates only from 1916,[3] while in Ankole the *nganzi*, who had merely been the ruler's favourite military adviser, only gradually approximated in the person of Mbaguta to a *katikiro*-type figure, after a protracted struggle with Mugabe Kahaya, who resented this invasion of his traditional control over his kingdom.[4] Kahaya granted Mbaguta a 'ministerial' salary only in 1917,[5] though the Toro *katikiro* had had one since 1906,[6] and Kagwa in Buganda since 1900.[7]

As these variations illustrate, there continued to be little or

[1] Margery Perham and Mary Bull, *The Diaries of Lord Lugard*, ii (London, 1959), 201.   [2] e.g. Wilson to Sadler, 30 July 1905, C.O. 536/2.

[3] Northern Province Monthly Report, Dec. 1916; Annual Report, 1916–17.

[4] There are many incidental indications of this, e.g. Wilson to Knowles, 20 Feb. 1906, E.S.A. A14/3.

[5] Western Province Monthly Report, Feb. 1917.

[6] Under Bell's memorandum of 13 July 1906, see p. 85 above.

[7] Under the Uganda Agreement, 1900.

no central direction of administrative policy in Uganda at this time. There was never in fact any administrators' manual such as Lugard produced for Northern Nigeria, or Girouard for the East Africa Protectorate; and there was no Uganda Native Authority Ordinance until 1919. Amongst African administrators Uganda's administration had an excellent reputation; but the secret lay not in any attempt to find and apply a legal or theoretical formula, but in the care which was taken by individual officials to manipulate the political forces which confronted them locally, and then apply the auspicious Buganda working model.

The simultaneous and systematic application of protectorate-wide policies was in fact a rare exception. There was some homogeneity, however, in the establishment of native courts.[1] Lukiko and *saza* chiefs' courts were given legal form in the four major kingdoms almost simultaneously.[2] In 1905 a Protectorate Courts Ordinance regularized the holding in each district of a British Native Court presided over by British officials;[3] and in January 1909 Sir Hesketh Bell issued a formative Buganda Native Courts Proclamation in conjunction with the regents and Lukiko of Buganda, which set on foot a further important development within the Buganda administrative structure, and launched the protectorate-wide establishment of subordinate chiefs' courts.[4] Hitherto the many subordinates of a *saza* chief had not been formally categorized; nor had the counties been systematically subdivided. But by Bell's proclamation the senior subordinates—henceforward to be called *gombolola*[5] chiefs— were given powers to hold recognized local courts, and in the years that followed they, the *saza* chiefs and the British administrators in Buganda, were busily demarcating *gombolola* boundaries, choosing *gombolola* headquarters, and supervising the building of *gombolola* court houses.[6] By a Protectorate Native

[1] A Protectorate High Court was established by the Uganda Order in Council of 1902.

[2] By the Uganda, Toro, and Ankole Agreements of 1900–1 and the Bunyoro Native Courts Ordinance of 1905.

[3] Sadler to Elgin, 16 Aug. 1905, C.O. 536/2.

[4] Bell to Elgin, 21 Jan. 1909, C.O. 536/25.

[5] Or 'sub-county'. *Gombolola* was the fire at the Kabaka's court before which judicial decisions were made.

[6] In 1909 *saza* tax registers were subdivided out and placed in the hands of *gombolola* chiefs; by 1916 *gombolola* chiefs were being paid salaries. Buganda Annual and Monthly Reports, *passim*.

Courts Ordinance of August 1909 provision was made for the extension of this system to the rest of the Protectorate, and here again there was—exceptionally—a virtually simultaneous growth in all the interlacustrine kingdoms.[1] In each of them from 1909 onwards *gombololas*—the sub-county divisions, the chiefs, and their courts—were being formally established.[2]

There was an attempt in the meanwhile to introduce some uniformity in the land tenure systems. In 1906 a committee under Mr. Justice Morris Carter was appointed to make an inquiry; but its sole outcome was the Buganda Land Law of 1908 giving some further precision to the freehold character of *mailo* land.[3] So in 1911 a further committee was appointed, again under Morris Carter. The conclusions of its first three reports were, first, that while Africans should remain undisturbed on the land they occupied, and while there should be room for further expansion, the bulk of the land should pass to the Crown and be available for non-African development;[4] secondly, that the land which Africans would continue to hold should be recognized to be land controlled by chiefs;[5] but that thirdly, and in contrast to the position in Buganda, the bulk of the chiefs' land should become not their own private property but the official estates of their chieftaincies. The first two of these recommendations were vigorously challenged by Simpson, the Director of Agriculture, and Spire, the Provincial Commissioner of the Eastern Province;[6] but in 1915 they were overruled by the Governor, Sir Frederick Jackson; only, however, to be in effect upheld in 1916 by the decision of Bonar Law, the Colonial Secretary in London. In accordance with current Colonial Office policy he brusquely declared that he was 'not satisfied that the Committee's scheme [was] in the best interests either

[1] Uganda Protectorate, Annual Reports, 1909–10, 1912–13, 1913–14.
[2] e.g. Kampala Annual Report, 1910–11; Buganda Annual Report, 1911–12, 1913–14; Ankole Annual Report, 1911–12.
[3] Uganda Protectorate Annual Report, 1908–9.
[4] The belief was prevalent among the majority of European administrators in Uganda at this time that economic development would come primarily from European endeavour.
[5] Thus far in accordance with the position in Buganda, except that far greater alienation was contemplated than in Buganda.
[6] For the influence of these two officials, and for a discussion of the general issue of African as against European development, see also Chapter VIII, pp. 423–30, and Chapter IX, pp. 477–83, below.

of the peasants or of development'. The attempt, therefore, to establish a uniform system of land tenure for the interlacustrine area was cut short, and once again events were left to take their course district by district.[1]

To a greater extent than was often realized, the imposition of protectorate models, whether simultaneously or over a period, was apt to have unforeseen repercussions. These tended to differ, moreover, from area to area, even where, as in the inter-lacustrine kingdoms, there appeared to be a substantial cultural homogeneity. Consider, for example, the elaboration of the tiered array of administrative chiefs. It is plain that even in Buganda it was not a wholly indigenous product. The *gombolola* chiefs date from 1909. Nor should it be forgotten that in pre-1900 Buganda the administrative *bakungu* chiefs were not the only hierarchy that pervaded the country. There had been a parallel estate of military chiefs headed by the *mujasi* and his naval equivalent the *gabunga*, as well as numerous personal agents of the Kabaka. At the turn of the century the personnel of these two quite distinct categories were amalgamated with the administrative hierarchy,[2] more particularly, in the case of the first of them, because the cessation of tribal warfare made their former functions redundant, and in case of the second, because during a critical period the Kabaka was a minor. The merger, if silently conducted, nevertheless constituted a considerable revolution.[3]

Similar amalgamations occurred in the three western kingdoms; but here they involved rather greater changes than in Buganda since in the west the formation of distinctly administrative hierarchies had not in the past proceeded so far. In Ankole, for instance, most of those appointed administrative chiefs were no more than leaders of warbands, and, as British administrators found, it was exceedingly difficult for such men to accommodate themselves to the new régime.[4] Indeed, but for the

[1] C. C. Wrigley, *Crops and Wealth in Uganda*, East African Studies no. 12 (Kampala, 1959), pp. 27–28, 31–32. The Ganda formula continued to provide, if only negatively, the starting point for much of the thinking about the problem.

[2] In 1900, for instance, the *mujasis* and the *gabungas* became *saza* chiefs.

[3] Low and Pratt, *Buganda*, pp. 137–8.

[4] e.g. Ankole Monthly Report, Sept. 1909; Ankole Annual Report, 1911–12; Western Province Annual Report, 1912–13; Western Province Monthly Report, Dec. 1913.

nganzi, Mbaguta, himself originally the leader of a warband,[1] the establishment of the administrative hierarchy would have proceeded even more hesitantly than it did.

In western Ankole, in Koki, in parts of Toro, and in most of Busoga, the necessary transmutation challenged some rather different principles. Here it was not a case of fitting a ruler's subordinates into a more or less new structure; it was the rulers themselves who were appointed administrative chiefs.[2] In Busoga, indeed, there were many rulers who because their ruler-ships were so small became no more than *gombolola* chiefs or even less. Not for them the pomp of European-recognized monarchy, but the routine of detailed administration. But all such men had this advantage over the Ganda chiefs, that at least their authority in traditional terms was within their own areas com-prehensive; whereas in Buganda a pre-European administrative chief's area had been riddled with enclaves over which he had no control, since this was vested in chiefs of rival hierarchies. Part of the revolutionary process of these years in Buganda lay, in fact, in the extension for the first time of the administrative chief's control over most of those who lived within the boun-daries of his chieftainship.[3]

In Ankole the corresponding issue here differed once again. The Hima warband leaders had in the past led their followers about large areas of country in accordance with the grazing requirements of their cattle. Their only connexion with the up-lands where the Iru agriculturalists lived was for the purpose of procuring beer, utensils and food. But after 1900 those Hima chosen as administrative chiefs were given circumscribed juris-dictions within which they were expected to exercise administra-tive control not only over their own warbands, but over those of others as well, and over the Iru who had never been 'adminis-tered' by Hima leaders before.[4] For the many individuals

---

[1] But one in which—such is the play of the fortuitous—there were many Ganda exiles who taught him their ways.

[2] The ruler of Buhweju in Ankole, for instance, became *saza* chief of Buhweju; the ruler of Bulamogi in Busoga became *saza* chief of Bulamogi, &c.

[3] Such a change was facilitated both by the *saza* chief's responsibility for the collection of tax from all within his boundaries, and by his control over the distri-bution of *mailo* land under the 1900 Agreement; even so, the Kabaka's private estates and their tenants continued outside his purview.

[4] The late Dr. Derrick Stenning kindly provided evidence on these matters. He was not, of course, responsible for the interpretation given here.

immediately concerned with each of these complex situations, the problems resulting were not only frequently novel, but exceedingly bewildering too.

Points of tension

The traditional antecedents of each type of administrative chief soon became reflected in the differing nature of the congenital frictions that existed in their relationship with the British. It was one of the characteristics of the régime established in these lacustrine kingdoms that the critical points at which the indigenous and the alien political entities touched were fairly high above the heads of the ordinary peasantry. But these critical points existed even so; there could never be a perfect union into a single structure of government. In Buganda, for instance, it was never quite clear whether the *saza* and *gombolola* chiefs were primarily the administrative subordinates of the British or the traditional appointees of the Kabaka.[1] In Busoga the question was rather, were the chiefs primarily civil servants or primarily rulers?[2] It was with an eye to overcoming this particular problem in Busoga that the British Administration encouraged the Church Missionary Society to open a boarding school for sons of chiefs; and it was, in consequence, temporarily resolved after about 1912 by the appointment to Soga chieftaincies of men of royal blood who had undergone some mission education.[3]

But over and above these issues that arose from the very nature of the readjustments—the revolutions indeed—which were being effected, there were particular variations in the relationships between these Uganda kingdoms and their British overlords as well. It must suffice, however, to notice just two series of them.

In many ways during this period the Ganda chiefs were the pride and joy of the British Administration. The Buganda Annual

---

[1] An uncertainty which led to much anxious concern first in 1900, and again in 1914, over the question whether the *saza* chiefs were primarily responsible to British district officers, or to the Lukiko.

[2] As we have seen it was the original failure to resolve this difficulty in Busoga which had led to the appointment of Kakunguru. For a discussion of this question see L. A. Fallers, 'The predicament of the modern African chief: an instance from Uganda', *American Anthropologist*, lvii. 2 (1955), 290–305.

[3] Eastern Province Annual Reports, 1918–19, 1919–20.

Reports for these years contain glowing recitals of county chiefs' merits.[1] There were, of course, excellent reasons why these Ganda chiefs should have fulfilled with such distinction the roles the British laid upon them. They were unusually literate, and being for the most part baptized Christians they were relatively pro-European in sympathy. They were at the same time holders of traditional offices and the assured leaders of powerful political factions. Unlike their predecessors they were no longer distracted by the arbitrary whim of the Kabaka; nor by rival hierarchies of chiefs; nor by frequent transfers.[2] Most of them, moreover, had had their personal qualities tested and tempered during the successive crises of the 1890's. British confidence in them was, indeed, substantially justified. During the 1914-18 period, for instance, Kagwa and his associates carried through a further set of reforms in the Buganda administration at a time when they had been in office for more than a quarter of a century. One of these provided the tailpiece to the previous establishment of *gombololas*. In 1916 the formalization of the third and lowest category of Ganda chiefs, the *miruka* or village chiefs, was begun.[3] The remaining developments were set on foot by the coming of age in August 1914 of the young Kabaka, Daudi Chwa.[4] In July 1916 steps were taken to reorganize his palace and reform his finances.[5] At the same time with the ending of the regency the ministers concentrated as never before on their purely ministerial duties.[6] In October 1916, with the help of a Ganda committee, Kagwa the *katikiro* began the re-

---

[1] e.g. Buganda Annual Report, 1910-11, 1912-13, 1916-17. Three were dismissed in 1905 for various misdemeanours, but for at least another decade the only one to be seriously criticized was Kamuswaga of Koki: Buganda Monthly Reports, June 1911, Mar. 1914, Mar. 1916.

[2] Many of them held the same chieftainship for nearly a quarter of a century.

[3] Buganda Monthly Reports, Apr. 1916, Nov. 1916, Annual Report, 1916-17.

[4] Buganda Monthly Report, Aug. 1914, Annual Report, 1914-15.

[5] Buganda Monthly Report, Aug. 1916, Annual Report, 1916-17. Although the Kabaka became 'native ruler', owing to the long regency during the evolvement of the main outlines of the reformed Ganda administration, no major administrative responsibilities had been left to him to perform. It is not without significance that of all the important institutions of Ganda government, the kabakaship alone was not exported—except in a diluted form to Busoga, where an elected *kyabazinga* (paramount chief) was first installed in 1917. Whatever the exponential importance of the kabakaship, it was not essential to the working of the Ganda administration, as successive regencies have confirmed.

[6] Uganda Protectorate Annual Report, 1914-15, Buganda Annual Reports, 1914-15, 1916-17, 1917-18; Buganda Monthly Reports, Sept., Nov. 1916.

organization of the kingdom's central administrative bureau-cracy; in November, Mugwanya the *omulamuzi* (chief justice) opened discussions with the Chief Justice of the Protectorate, which led to a more elaborate Buganda Courts Proclamation; and in 1917 the Treasurer, having selected some new clerks, took the significant step of opening a banking account for his funds. These measures comprised the fourth distinct set of administrative reforms since 1894 which these men had under-taken at the instance of the British.

And yet it is possible to discern throughout the first two decades of the twentieth century their steady determination to maintain against the British a measure of autonomy for their kingdom. We have noticed the origins of this at the time of the Sudanese mutiny. The evidence thereafter is necessarily scrappy, but powerful. In 1899 George Wilson, while acknowledging the *katikiro*'s loyalty, noted his independent spirit too.[1] In 1900, when Johnston opened the negotiations which led to the agree-ment, the Ganda vigorously protested once they felt that he was intent upon undermining their whole tribal polity. In 1905 on an occasion when some Ganda court fines were erroneously paid to the British Administration, Kagwa promptly declared that he would seek their recovery.[2] Five years later he and his colleagues actually employed a British solicitor to assert the Lukiko's claims under the 1900 Agreement to unfettered control over the distribution of *mailo* land.[3] In 1911 Kagwa himself deliberately insulted a young British officer who had been de-tailed to lecture him and his associates on native administration.[4] And in 1914 he vigorously complained to the British Administra-tion of their failure to uphold the Lukiko 'as the Final Native Court and Headquarters of the Native Government of Buganda'.[5]

In the resolution of these incidents a compromise was gener-ally effected. In 1900 the elaborate agreement was drawn up. From the altercation in 1910 there emerged the Buganda Agree-

---

[1] See p. 76 footnote 1 above.   [2] Lukiko Minute Book, 12 June 1905.
[3] E.S.A./S.M.P. 1468 contains papers on this episode.
[4] J. R. P. Postlethwaite, *I look back* (London, 1947), pp. 82–83.
[5] Kagwa and Kisingiri to Cooper, 26 Feb. 1914. Copy in Protectorate Agent's Archives, Masaka. Throughout these years the regent ministers always corresponded with the British Administration in a highly formal manner, each of their letters being signed by all three of them.

ment (Allotment and Survey) of 1913, which, while imposing a time limit on the Lukiko's right to distribute *mailo* land, upheld its unfettered right to act on its own in the meanwhile. The 1914 complaints were followed by two attempts by the Provincial Commissioner in Buganda, in 1916 and 1917, to set out his administrative practice. He declared, *inter alia*, 'Buganda is different from other Provinces in that although divided into 4 districts for the convenience of administrative routine, it is necessary to treat it as one large area for the purposes of administrative policy'.[1] And he summed up his administrative policy as 'executive power as much as possible in the hands of the Native Government under the control and advice of the British Administration'.[2] This may seem a platitudinous declaration. It was little more, no doubt, than a précis of the 1900 Agreement, and merely repeated the sense of George Wilson's dictum in 1907 that nothing must be done 'to encroach upon the native powers of self-legislation, powers which are valued beyond general belief by the natives [of Buganda] as a nation'.[3] But if the British were generally accommodating, Kagwa always succeeded in insisting upon the claims of the Ganda to stand somewhat apart from their British protectors, and by 1919, thanks in the main to him, the tradition by which Buganda's claim to a real measure of autonomy was acknowledged seemed to be fairly firmly established.

Such friction as existed between the British and the Ganda was never at this time unrelieved, and it was always characterized by this positive element within it. In Toro, however, a rather different tradition—of almost continuous and certainly very purposeless friction between the British and its chiefs—was being evolved contemporaneously. At first sight this seems somewhat surprising, for of all the western peoples the Toro owed most to the intervention of the British. Had not the British reestablished their kingdom? But upon further reflection considerations accumulate to suggest why relations in Toro continually failed to be harmonious. Before 1897, as we have seen, there was considerable friction between the Mukama and

[1] Cooper to District Commissioner, Masaka, 6 July 1917, Protectorate Agent's Archives, Masaka.
[2] Buganda Annual Report, 1917–18; cf. ibid., 1916–17.
[3] Memorandum by Wilson, 8 July 1907, E.S.A./S.M.P. C119/1906.

the British; on a famous occasion in 1895 the British officer in charge had actually flogged the Mukama and his *katikiro*.[1] In 1900 Johnston forced the much disliked agreement upon Kasagama and his chiefs.[2] Though some amends were subsequently made, it took six years to procure them; and the British Administration continued to monopolize the local (and lucrative) salt deposits. Then in 1911 the British agreed that the Mboga area on the south-west of Lake Albert should pass to the Congo (although it had recently been one of the counties of Toro),[3] while placing Bwamba country on the west side of the Ruwenzori mountains (which was at the same time acknowledged to be within British territory) under their own direct charge, although it had only recently had a Toro *saza* chief.[4] From the British point of view the Toro chiefs were no doubt often unsatisfactory, but this was partly because they had had no Kagwa, no Kakunguru, no Mbaguta, no Miti to give them a lead. Yafeti Byakweyamba, the original factotum in Toro, had committed suicide in 1897 after a personal quarrel with Kasagama, and it may be that since Kasagama played a very much larger part in the early years than any other ruler in Uganda, the emergence of a dominant commoner in Toro was made more difficult. It may be too that the whole position was aggravated by Toro's geographical isolation.[5] The British interest in the Nile Valley had brought relatively good communications to Busoga, Buganda, and Bunyoro. After 1914 Ankole's position as a front line district in the Anglo-German war in East Africa stimulated road-building there, and placed the native administration on its mettle;[6] but both these developments passed Toro by. It remained at the end of 200 miles of very indifferent road from Kampala.

There were further circumstances peculiar to Toro too. About 1910–11 it became the highway for a flourishing ivory trade in the Congo. Against some of the activities involved, in which

[1] *Namasole* of Toro to Berkeley 31 Oct. 1895, E.S.A. A5/1; Tucker to Berkeley, 27 Nov. 1895, A6/1.

[2] Maddox to Wilson, 3 Sept. 1904, E.S.A./S.M.P. R125.

[3] In accordance with an Anglo-Belgian boundary commission's recommendations, Toro Annual Report, 1910–11.

[4] Toro Monthly Report, August 1911; Toro Annual Report, 1911–12.

[5] One provincial commissioner was aware of this: Western Province Monthly Report, Oct. 1912.

[6] Western Province Annual Reports, 1915–16, 1916–17, 1919–20.

certain Toro chiefs participated, the British made vigorous objection. Then in 1912, for some reason unrecorded, a British officer conducted a close investigation of Toro chiefs' impositions on their peasantry, which were almost certainly no worse than those elsewhere, but which added to their evil reputation.[1] There was, in addition, continuing friction about land. Some Toro chiefs had been promised *mailo* land under the Toro Agreement, but despite periodic appeals, it was not actually allotted until twenty years later. During this time many subordinate chiefs, who were definitely excluded, became as angry about their position as the minor chiefs in Buganda had been.[2] Similar discontent might, perhaps, have been expected from other interlacustrine kingdoms which were similarly treated: but amongst the pastoral Nyankole possession of particular areas was not so important as to the agricultural Toro; in Bunyoro there was no agreement, so that no one enjoyed definite commitments, there were in consequence few internal jealousies, and, as it happened, the Mukama took steps to grant land on his own authority to all whom he considered eligible to hold it;[3] while in Busoga one of Kakunguru's major reforms was to split each chieftainship (without troubling himself about the 'legal' position) into a chief's personal estate on the one hand and his official estate on the other; in Toro no such working arrangements seem to have been evolved.

The cumulative effect of these numerous adversities and discontents soon became mirrored in the regular disparagement of Toro chiefs by British officers;[4] in the two depositions of the *katikiro* of Toro, first, sometime before 1910, and again in 1915;[5] in the stern warning issued by Sir Frederick Jackson in 1912 that unless the Toro chiefs proved themselves more co-operative they would all be replaced by Ganda;[6] and in the contrast in 1918 between the Provincial Commissioner's commendation of the Ankole chiefs for their energy, and his criticism of the Toro

---

[1] Toro Annual Report, 1911-12.

[2] In Buganda, however, the minor chiefs had subsequently been assuaged; not so in Toro. *Enquiry into the Grievances of the Mukama and Chiefs of Toro* (Entebbe, 1927).

[3] *Enquiry into Land Tenure and the Kibanja System in Bunyoro 1931* (Entebbe, 1932), paras. 104 sqq.

[4] e.g. Western Province Annual Report, 1913-14, 1916-17.

[5] Toro Annual Report, 1909-10; Western Province Monthly Report, Feb. 1915.

[6] A threat which led to an immediate, but temporary response. Western Province Monthly Reports, Feb., Mar. 1912.

chiefs for their dilatory tax collection.[1] A tradition of friction was becoming established.

What these particulars emphasize is that political conflicts between colonial powers and African peoples have not necessarily been the fruit of later nationalist stimuli alone. They have often been the long-standing concomitant of imperial authority as well.

However, in the meanwhile, from 1909 onwards the area of effective Protectorate authority had begun to be extended for the first time beyond the bounds of the interlacustrine kingdoms and Kakunguru's 'empire'. This was not the result of any carefully considered policy. In the south-west it sprang from a suddenly contrived diplomatic counterplot. When it became clear that the Uganda–Congo Boundary Commission of 1907–8 might place Mount Mufumbiro (which according to the Anglo-German Agreement of 1890 stood within British territory) within the boundary of the Congo, orders were issued from London for the dispatch of an armed British force—the Kivu Mission—to claim possession. In a miniature 'Fashoda' it encountered a rival Belgian expedition; but hostilities were avoided, and in a subsequent settlement the British secured a substantial part of the Mufumbiro complex.[2] They were now confronted by its somewhat unusual political particularities. The most important of these concerned the *nyabingi* spirit possession cult, which amongst the local Kiga exercised a powerful hold.[3] By 1909 this was dominated by Muhumusa, a widow of a former ruler of Rwanda in German East Africa, who upon his death in 1894 had fled to Kiga country and established herself as the *nyabingi*, so as to enlist a disciplined following with which to seize the Rwanda throne for her son. In 1910 her long-planned offensive was thwarted by the Germans; whereupon she tried to carve out an alternative kingdom amongst the Kiga. But this brought her into conflict with the British, and for the ensuing decade there was constant fighting between the adherents of the

[1] Western Province Monthly Report, Sept. 1918.
[2] e.g. J. M. Coote, 'The Kivu mission, 1909–10', *Uganda J.* xx. 2 (1956), 105–12.
[3] M. M. Edel, *The Chiga of Western Uganda* (New York, 1957), esp. ch. vii; M. J. Bessell, 'Nyabingi', *Uganda J.* vi. 2 (1938), 73–86; J. E. T. Philipps, 'The Nabingi: an anti-European secret society in Africa, in British Ruanda, Ndorwa, and the Congo (Kivu)', *Congo*, i. 3 (1928), 310–21.

nyabingi and the local British garrison.[1] Muhumusa herself was captured in 1911, but it was not until the death in battle in 1919 of her most redoubtable follower, Ndochiberi,[2] that the influence of the *nyabingi* began to decline. Meantime the British had imported Ganda Agents, and out of a number of disparate elements were creating yet another native administration on the Buganda model.[3] Kigezi District, as it was called, included Rujumbura (whose ruler had refused to join Ankole), all the Kiga (who had no rulers), and a slice of Rwanda, which the Anglo-German-Belgian boundary commission of 1911 had found to lie within British territory. The authority of the British came in due course to be accepted in the district, not because they had suppressed any pre-existing polity, but because they had shown themselves more potent than the *nyabingi*.

The year 1909 saw, too, the beginnings of important steps forward in the north-east of the Protectorate.[4] Sub-stations were opened at Kumi amongst the Teso, and at Palango on the western edge of Lango country.[5] In 1910 there followed a station at Gulu, farther into Acholi than ever before; a second Acholi post at Kitgum away to the north-east in 1912; and in 1914 a station at Arua in West Nile.[6] It was not till 1918, however, that the British administration of Teso and Lango reached the Moroto river.[7] This expansion was made possible both because the flourishing peasant grown cotton crop in Buganda and the south-east was putting some money into the Protectorate's coffers, and because the assurance of stability at the core of the Protectorate had now released troops and police for its periphery. The advance came, however, not from the long-standing British posts upon the Nile, but across the marches of Kakunguru's 'empire'. Rulers and chiefs with whom political alliances might be made were traditionally almost unknown in this area. Little allowance, however, was made for the radically different

---

[1] Detailed information is scattered through Western Province Monthly and Annual Reports for the period.

[2] Western Province Annual Report, 1919–20.

[3] Western Province Monthly and Annual Reports, 1912–19, *passim*.

[4] Boyle to Crewe, 4 Jan. 1910, and enclosures, C.O. 536/32.

[5] Lango Annual Report, 1910–11.

[6] Northern Province Annual Reports, 1912–13, 1914–15.

[7] Eastern Province Annual Report, 1917–18. Karamoja District on its farther bank, despite periodic visits by troops and administrators, remained in its pristine state throughout.

political realities of these mainly stateless societies, and in these northern areas the British advance was emblazoned almost everywhere by 'punitive' operations. During the first decade of administration in Lango, for example, there was only one year for which 'punitive' actions were not reported; and much the same could be told of Bukedi, Bugisu, and Teso, most of Acholi, and most of West Nile.[1] In 1911 the Provincial Commissioner, Eastern Province, declared: 'Summary, rigorous and decisive action is necessary when dealing with these wild tribes and our prestige . . . is likely to be much increased by . . . prompt punishment of these offenders on the spot'.[2]

Even so, each area had its own distinctive occurrences. Under the aegis of Ganda Agents cotton was introduced in Teso and in parts of Lango hand in hand with British domination. For a people who had only recently undergone one agricultural revolution, a second posed few problems.[3] Teso and its environs were, moreover, unique at this time in having a wide-ranging network of excellent communications: to a system of dugout canoes plying through widely ramifying swamps, there had just been added Kakunguru's roads.[4] As a result swift inclusion in a new economy of unimagined prosperity muted the harsher sensations of alien conquest.[5]

Amongst the Kumam to the west on the Lake Kyoga edge of Teso and Lango there had since 1902 been a lesser Kakunguru in Kazana. When in 1907 the British built a fort at Bululu, Kazana placed his control over the neighbouring Kumam at their disposal;[6] and from here, and from Palango farther north, they advanced two years later into Lango. Ganda Agents were at first commissioned to assist them, and step by step they cut into the interior.[7] Suddenly, however, in 1911, the new Governor, Sir Frederick Jackson, condemned both the Agents and the policy which employed them. Between January 1910

---

[1] See Northern and Eastern Province Annual and Monthly Reports, *passim*.

[2] Minute on Lango Monthly Report, Dec. 1910.

[3] See ch. ix, p. 327, in vol. i of this *History*.

[4] e.g. Eastern Province Annual Report, 1909–10.

[5] e.g. Kumi Annual Report, 1909–10; Mbale Monthly Reports, Feb., Mar. 1911; Eastern Province Annual Report, 1911–12.

[6] Wilson to Elgin, 16 July 1907, and enclosures, C.O. 536/14; K. Ingham, 'British administration in Lango District', *Uganda J.* xix. 2 (1955), 156–68.

[7] e.g. Lango Annual Reports, 1909–10, 1911–12; Monthly Reports, 1910, 1911, *passim*; E.S.A./S.M.P. 519/1909, *passim*.

and July 1911 there had been in Lango, Teso, and Bukedi Districts, he recounted, no less than '109 conflicts between Baganda Agents and their followers and the local natives, in which 5 Agents and 10 followers have been killed, 6 Agents and 11 followers wounded, and 174 natives killed and wounded, and 2185 rounds of ammunition expended'.[1] His attempt to abolish the system outright was resisted, however, by the Provincial Commissioner, Eastern Province,[2] and he himself came to acquiesce in its retention for a time.[3] As one official had put it, 'To effectively occupy and administer a district whose population consists of untamed savages, such as those in Lango, they must be dealt with in a special way, more especially as their so-called chiefs consist of village headmen, who have little or no control over them'.[4] But from 1911 onwards it was the policy of the Uganda Administration to withdraw Ganda Agents as soon as it seemed possible.

When the British advanced into Acholi in the north-central part of the Protectorate two novel problems faced them. In the first place the Acholi had experienced alien governments before —Baker's, Gordon's, Emin's, a British expedition in 1901,[5] and a British post at Keyo in 1907—but none of these foreign intrusions had endured; so that to the Acholi the establishment of a British post at Gulu was no occasion for serious concern. It was necessary, therefore, to persuade the Acholi that this time the British had come to stay.[6] The scepticism of the Acholi made them reluctant, however, to waste much effort in opposing the British, so that by the time they discovered their mistake, serious opposition was no longer feasible. This feeling that alien intrusions were essentially temporary had latterly led the Acholi to welcome the influx of traders selling arms, first from Mbale

[1] Jackson to Lansdowne, 14 July 1911, E.S.A./S.M.P. 519/1909.
[2] Spire to District Commissioners, Eastern Province, 22 Aug. 1911, ibid.
[3] Jackson to Colonial Secretary, 18 June 1912, ibid.
[4] District Commissioner, Hoima, to Chief Secretary, 5 Nov. 1910, ibid.
[5] Jackson to Lansdowne, 23 Dec. 1901, and enclosures, F.O.C.P. 7946; Sadler to Lansdowne, 8 July 1902, and enclosures, F.O.C.P. 7954.
[6] e.g. Nimule Monthly Report, Nov. 1910; Northern Province Monthly Report, Oct. 1911; Eastern Province Monthly Report, Mar. 1914. They had known Khartoum traders and Mahdist dervishes too. Such was the exodus of British officers upon the outbreak of war in 1914, indeed, that it looked as if the foreigners were going once again. Northern Province Monthly Report, Sept. 1914; cf. Eastern Province Monthly Report, Oct. 1914.

and then from Abyssinia; guns becoming their chief insurance against the evil uncertainties which followed in the wake of abortive régimes.[1] The British in consequence found the Acholi better armed than any other Uganda people they encountered.[2] So it was necessary, too, to secure their disarmament and prevent their rearmament.[3] In southern Acholi the climax occurred in 1912 when the British successfully stormed the Guruguru mountain stronghold of the Lamogi Acholi following their refusal to disgorge their guns.[4] In northern Acholi a patrol of the King's African Rifles was permanently occupied from 1911 onwards in clearing the frontier of Abyssinian gun-runners;[5] it successfully overawed the local Acholi as well.

Ganda Agents were only spasmodically employed in these two Acholi districts.[6] But as elsewhere a Ganda-type administration was introduced all the same. Here in Acholi the first important step was the creation of a Central Native Council—in Gulu in 1914—which consisted of the most prominent Acholi, wielding both judicial and executive powers.[7] County and sub-county chiefs were then established from the top downwards, many lesser individuals who at first were employed being gradually eased out.[8] There was no central council in Teso till 1916;[9] nor in Lango or at Mbale till 1919.[10] Here it was the county chieftainships which were established first, counties being etched out

---

[1] Nimule Monthly Report, Dec. 1910; Northern Province Monthly Report, May 1911; Northern Province Annual Report, 1911–12.

[2] e.g. Gulu Annual Report, 1910–11.

[3] e.g. Northern Province Monthly Report, Aug. 1911, Feb. 1912, Mar., Oct. 1913.

[4] Northern Province Monthly Reports, Jan.–Mar. 1912, Annual Report, 1911–12; A. D. Adimola, 'The Lamogi Rebellion 1911–12', *Uganda J.* xviii. 2 (1954), 166–77. Two other incidents in southern Acholi also contributed to the success of the British. In Oct. 1911 Awich of Payera, a prominent Acholi *rwot* (chief) was deported (he had been deported for a short time once before, but this time he was kept away for eight years): and in July 1914 four Acholi murderers of a chief who had co-operated with the British were publicly hanged at Gulu. Northern Province Monthly Reports, Oct. 1911 sqq.; Northern Province Monthly Reports, Feb.–June 1914.

[5] Northern Province Monthly and Annual Reports, 1911–19, *passim*.

[6] e.g. Northern Province Annual Report, 1914–15.

[7] Ibid.; Northern Province Monthly Report, July 1914.

[8] e.g. Northern Province Annual Reports, 1915–16, 1917–18; Northern Province Monthly Report, Mar. 1916, July, Aug. 1918.

[9] Eastern Province Annual Report, 1916–17.

[10] Eastern Province Monthly Report, Oct. 1919; Annual Report, 1919–20.

in all three districts by 1912.[1] Sometimes such chieftainships were held directly by Ganda, sometimes by prominent locals with Ganda Agents as advisers. In Teso and Lango a beginning was often made by creating local *lukikos*, sometimes below the county level, and local chiefs were appointed only later.[2] But there were also three Lango—Okelobong, Odora, and Arum—who were appointed chiefs over considerable areas from the outset.[3] By contrast there were no Teso who became county chiefs till 1919. The model, however, whatever the starting-point, was always Kagwa's Buganda, although in these chieftainless societies the system rarely functioned as smoothly as in the kingdom areas; for in origin it was wholly alien, so that indigenous chiefs found it difficult to wield much power.[4] But just because it was based upon the Buganda model, and had almost everywhere been introduced by Ganda Agents, it was more able to stand apart from the colonial administration than most other governmentally imposed systems of chiefs. It contained, even for chieftainless peoples, the germs of an autonomous tribal government.

The penultimate district to be brought under British administration was West Nile.[5] It contained in miniature most of the varying circumstances encountered elsewhere, besides some problems peculiar to itself. Until the death of King Leopold of the Belgians in 1909, the area west of the Nile—the Lado enclave—was administered by the Congo.[6] It then passed under the British Administration in the Sudan. But in 1912 the southern half—henceforth to be called 'West Nile'—was transferred to Uganda in exchange for the Bari-Lotuka area to the north-east.[7] As in Acholi the local people—Alur, Madi, Lugbara, and Kakwa—looked at first with some disdain upon yet

[1] Eastern Province Monthly Report, Aug. 1912; Annual Report, 1912–13.
[2] Eastern Province Monthly Report, Mar. 1912; Annual Reports, 1911–12, 1913–14.
[3] e.g. Lango Annual Report, 1910–11.
[4] e.g. Eastern Province Monthly Report, Mar. 1914; Kumi Annual Report, 1909–10; Northern Province and Eastern Province Annual Reports, 1916–17.
[5] Karamoja was the last. J. P. Barber, 'The Karamoja District of Uganda: a pastoral people under colonial rule', *J. Af. History*, iii. 1 (1962), 111–24.
[6] In accordance with the Anglo-Congo Agreement of 1894.
[7] Northern Province Monthly Report, Feb. 1912, Annual Reports, 1912–13, 1913–14. For this process see A. W. Southall, *Alur Society* (Cambridge, 1956), pp. 280–93.

another alien régime claiming their allegiance.[1] But Weather-
head, the first district commissioner, went resolutely to work.
Among the Alur there were chiefs. He successfully supported
one candidate to the riverain chiefdom of Ragem against his
rival; and the Ukuru Alur in the highlands soon accepted his
authority because their chief feared lest otherwise he might be
deposed. But the Madi, and more especially the Lugbara, who
had no chiefs, only submitted (like the Lango) after considerable
'punishment'.[2] Here for administrative purposes Agents were
employed at first; but amongst the Alur the most important
traditional chiefs were installed as county chiefs from the outset.[3]
Here, and amongst the Lugbara, councils were formed[4]—upon
the Buganda model once again. West Nile's most distinctive
problem, however, was being illustrated meanwhile by Weather-
head's rigorous abstention from the shooting of elephants.[5]
For before his authority could be readily accepted he had to
distinguish his purposes as sharply as possible from those of the
swarm of European elephant hunters which had roamed over
the region throughout the decade before his arrival.[6]

Here as elsewhere pioneer administrators had to fit their
actions to purely local conditions. They enjoyed, of course, substantial advantages. In the main they had at their disposal
weapons and forces that were overwhelmingly more powerful
than anything which was locally available against them. They
possessed a strong belief in their personal destiny to rule. The
range of their material possessions and their self-confidence in
confronting social and catastrophic natural phenomena made
them appear at this time to the peoples of their districts like
something more than ordinary mortals. By 1919 their piecemeal endeavours had brought the whole of the Uganda Protectorate (except the district of Karamoja in the far north-east)
under British authority. There was still no formal guide to the

---

[1] e.g. Northern Province Annual Report, 1914–15.
[2] e.g. Northern Province Monthly Report, Apr., May 1915, Annual Report,
1915–16. In 1917 much of West Nile became embroiled in an Allah water
cult which (like the *nyabingi*) turned against the British; for his complicity, Chief
Amulla of Ukuru was deported. Northern Province Monthly Reports, Mar. and
Nov. 1917, Annual Report, 1917–18.
[3] The lesser ones were found lower places within the chiefly hierarchy.
[4] e.g. Northern Province Monthly Report, Sept. 1918.
[5] Northern Province Annual Report, 1914–15.
[6] e.g. Northern Province Monthly Report, Sept. 1911.

administrative practice, but one way and another almost all district officers had turned to the reformed Buganda model for inspiration. Uganda, in fact, was fast becoming a congeries of 'little Bugandas'—which was to give its African population, in course of time, both opportunities and problems.

Famines and disease

Yet to many Africans it was not the somewhat remote political happenings of these years which were their major occurrences, but the very considerable physical disasters which overtook the peoples of Uganda during the Protectorate's first quarter of a century.[1] First there was famine, the result not of overpopulation but primarily of drought. In the wake of the Sudanese mutiny famine struck Bunyoro; and it was subsequently believed that about 40,000 died of a simultaneous famine in Busoga. Ten years later, in 1908, there was a further famine in Busoga, in which it was estimated that about 10,000 perished.[2] In 1918–19 there was a third major famine, this time not confined to Busoga, in which over 100,000 were said to have died in Bukedi District alone.[3] The British could do little to arrest the first of these scourges. Energetic steps were taken by George Wilson to meet the second,[4] while in 1918–19 the whole administrative machine was for several months preoccupied by its anti-famine measures.[5] Though colonial administrators might not rank as rain-makers[6] there can be no doubt that they helped with increasing success to mitigate the ravages of famine; but equally that it was not until after 1919 that (largely as a result of greatly improved communications) they were able to master its full lethal propensities.[7] But henceforth in marginal areas

[1] It is difficult—almost impossible indeed—to ascertain with any precision the extent of such disasters in the past.

[2] The estimates were necessarily little better than guesses. *Correspondence relating to Famine in the Busoga District of Uganda*, Cd. 4358 (1908).

[3] Budama lost perhaps a quarter of its population. Eastern Province Monthly Report, June 1919, Annual Report, 1919–20.

[4] 800 tons of food in 12-ounce portions per person per day were distributed at 400 distributing centres throughout Busoga at the cost of a supplementary grant of £10,000, *Famine in Busoga*, Cd. 4358.

[5] e.g. Eastern Province Annual Report, 1918–19; Eastern Province Monthly Report, May 1918, Apr. 1919.

[6] Often the most important attribute hereabouts of leading men in the past: e.g. Bari Monthly Report, July 1910.

[7] There was a very critical leader in *The Uganda Herald*, 18 Apr. 1919.

provision against famine became one of their administrative priorities.

Disease, however, was an even greater killer: in the first place, of animals. The great rinderpest epidemic had swept south by the late 1890's; but the disease reappeared in Karamoja in 1911, and between here and the Nile destroyed, so it was said, between 70 per cent. and 90 per cent. of the cattle of the northern areas.[1] It then appeared sporadically through Buganda and the Eastern Province[2] until it burst forth with great virulence in Buganda and Western Province in 1918–19, killing at least 75,000 head in Ankole alone.[3]

Of human diseases smallpox and plague appear to have been endemic.[4] But then, in 1917, cerebro-spinal meningitis hit the country,[5] followed in 1918–19 by the worldwide epidemic of Spanish 'flu which, taking the Protectorate as a whole, claimed perhaps 25,000 victims.[6] The Government as yet had little to offer towards the abatement of these onslaughts; but henceforward the control of contagious diseases was placed in the forefront of their thinking about medical problems.

They had already attacked two diseases, of which one had proved to be the biggest scourge of all. Sleeping sickness was first diagnosed in 1901 by the doctors J. H. and A. (later Sir Albert) Cook of the Church Missionary Society. Whence it came is still a matter for speculation; but by 1902 deaths from sleeping sickness were being numbered in Buganda and Busoga in tens of thousands, and it was spreading to marginal areas elsewhere. The Government made a prompt approach to the Royal Society, which quickly dispatched a party of research workers to Uganda; and in April 1903 Colonel Bruce, who had come with a second party, announced that the sleeping sickness trypanosome was borne by a species of tsetse fly which clung to the lake-shores and waterways. Yet despite this discovery, and the devotion of missionaries and others to the stricken, it

---

[1] Northern Province Monthly Report, Apr. 1911.

[2] e.g. Eastern Province Monthly Report, Oct. 1913.

[3] Western Province Annual Report, 1919–20. The year 1919 also saw some 40 per cent. of the cattle of Karamoja carried away by pleuro-pneumonia.

[4] There were over 3,000 recorded deaths from plague in each of the years 1911–13, Uganda Protectorate Annual Report, 1913–14.

[5] Monthly and Annual Reports for all provinces, 1917–18, passim.

[6] In Eastern Province, where about 10,000 died, the contemporaneous famine exacerbated the prevailing misery. Eastern Province Annual Report, 1918–19.

was estimated by 1906 that the total mortality had exceeded 200,000. Energetic as ever, Sir Hesketh Bell, who had recently arrived, now decided[1] upon the drastic expedient of clearing the population from the Lake Victoria shore, and any other infested waterways, to a depth of two miles. Thanks to the ready co-operation of the Ganda chiefs (who now revealed the enormous power which they held over their people) the whole operation was completed without untoward incident. With this the peak of the epidemic was passed.[2] In its course it had destroyed many of the rulerships of southern Busoga and denuded the previously heavily populated Sese and Buvuma islands in Lake Victoria. Even a generally very cautious investigator has estimated that by the end it had carried away one-tenth of the Protectorate's total population.[3] It is difficult to doubt that the proportion would have been substantially higher but for the discoveries of the scientists and the energy of Bell and the Ganda chiefs.[4]

The second disease to be faced was syphilis. Here again it was the Drs. Cook who drew attention to its prevalence, and an official report in 1907 announced that an epidemic existed. Once more the Government showed itself prepared (to the extent which its resources allowed) to apply western remedial skills to Uganda's ills. A considerable anti-venereal campaign was quickly instituted,[5] and this proved to be the beginning of the Government's provision for social services[6]—one of the

---

[1] On the advice of his Principal Medical Officer, Dr. Hodges.

[2] Though whether on account of this is still subject to controversy. Towards the end of the following decade preliminary steps were taken to allow some people to filter back to cleared areas, but several important, and fertile, areas remained closed to reoccupation for many years to come. Sesse Tours Book, New Series, Protectorate Agent's Archives, Masaka.

[3] R. R. Kuczynski, *Demographic Survey of the British Colonial Empire*, ii (London, 1949), 320.

[4] *Uganda. Report on the Measures adopted for the Suppression of Sleeping Sickness in Uganda*, Colonial Reports, Miscellaneous, no. 65, Cd. 4990 (1909); *Uganda Protectorate. A History of Sleeping Sickness and Reclamation in Uganda* (Entebbe, 1927).

[5] The latest view, however, is that the prevailing syphilis was not venereal but congenital; that there was no epidemic, but that endemic syphilis was longstanding; and that its prevalence was due to a widespread traditional custom of crude immunization. But with increasing contact with the outside world, venereal strains were, none the less, spreading, and in any event even the incidence of endemic syphilis was frequently serious. J. N. P. Davies, 'Syphilis in Uganda', *Bulletin of the World Health Organization*, xv. 1041 sqq.

[6] The Venereal Diseases Hospital at Mulago, Kampala, developed into the major government hospital in the country.

first fruits of the law and order they had established, without which no such provision would have been practicable. The main complaint of Africans was that such social services were not more widely supplied.

Education and the Christian missions

Governmental provision for medical services remained unmatched until well after 1919 by any corresponding governmental provision for education. For all that, the development of western education was a major occurrence of these years. It was almost wholly, however, the preserve of the missionary societies, which long since had made the ability to read and write the criterion of a genuine desire for baptism. In 1895 the Church Missionary Society[1] took the further step of forming bush schools.[2] Staffed by catechists and pupil teachers, these spread to many parts of the Protectorate. Their education, however, tended to be not only rudimentary, but markedly literary; yet attached as they very often were to the local village church, such schools enjoyed considerable local support. In Buganda they became the symbol of the peasantry's lively desire to seek on its own terms a share in the wider advantages which the white man was bringing. After 1900 three or four boarding schools with greater educational opportunities were founded by the missions for the more important and more promising children from all parts of the country. These promptly replaced the households of rulers and great chiefs as the educational centres for the African *élite*. Though their educational horizons were still relatively narrow, they nevertheless reflected the genuine desire of the missions both to equip some Africans for the larger demands of a rapidly changing environment, and to give of the best that they knew. The foundations were thus laid for the largest western-educated element in eastern and central Africa. And there were two unbudgeted consequences. Owing to the paucity of constitutional links between different parts of the country, in the years to come the bond of a common *alma mater*

[1] On this and further aspects of the missionary story see especially J. V. Taylor, *The Growth of the Church in Buganda* (London, 1958), chs. 3 and 4, and the authorities there cited: also R. Oliver, *The Missionary Factor in East Africa* (London, 1952), chs. iv and v, *passim*.

[2] On the model of the local 'synagogi' first developed by Arthur Fisher in western Buganda.

assumed for many of its chiefs and rulers an unusual importance; and because there were more places in Anglican than in Roman Catholic boarding schools at this time there were to be, for at least the next two generations to come, larger numbers of Protestants than Roman Catholics in Uganda's African *élite*.

This spread of schools was primarily a by-product of the contemporaneous spread of Christianity to almost every part of the Protectorate. Thanks to the often heroic efforts of as remarkable a band of missionaries as the history of missions has known, a mass movement during these years made Uganda (in so far as it adhered to any world religion) a Christian country. There remained everywhere a deep stratum of adherence to older religious practices and older religious beliefs; but charms, shrines, and traditional priestly orders were destroyed, and the formal adherence to Christianity of the African *élite* became extensive.[1] This growth flowed in the first place from the capture in 1890 by the early Christian converts of the Ganda political order.[2] Christianity became thereafter the handmaiden of the spread of Ganda influence into the rest of the Protectorate.[3] For at a time when the Uganda world was obviously undergoing considerable change, the evidence strongly suggested that success in the new era was somehow linked with adherence to Christianity. Such considerations brought many to the missions with requests for baptism and instruction in reading and writing —requests which the missions met not only with enthusiasm, but with some misgivings too; regular catechismal classes were organized, and minimum periods, measured in years, were prescribed for pre-baptismal instruction.[4] One of the reasons, however, for the rapid spread of Christianity at this time lay in the

[1] Christianity, it has often been appositely remarked, became, if not in law certainly in practice, the established religion of Uganda.

[2] D. A. Low, *Religion and Society in Buganda, 1875–1900*, East African Studies no. 8 (1956), pp. 9 sqq.

[3] Ganda Agents built churches near their own houses: e.g. *Uganda Notes*, Mar. 1913.

[4] Vernacular literature was also produced. In George Pilkington the C.M.S. had a most able linguist, who before his death in the mutiny in 1897 had translated the whole Bible into Luganda. Others made translations into the western languages. But Luganda became, partly because of the spread of Ganda Agents, but also because of Pilkington's Bible, the official language of Church and State for most of eastern and northern Uganda. C. F. Harford-Battersby, *Pilkington of Uganda* (London, 1898).

seizure by the missions of the unique opportunity with which the advent of *pax Britannica* presented them; for upon the morrow of its attainment, there was for a short but critical period everywhere, no other preoccupation—no economic one for instance—to compete for people's time and inquisitiveness with the instruction that was offered in Christianity.[1]

Although the Roman Catholics and the Anglicans reproduced in the rest of the Protectorate the deep duality which they had already created in Buganda, they were the only two Christian churches to come to the country; there was no proliferation of Protestant sects. In 1894 the Roman Catholic White Fathers, who were working westwards from Kampala, were joined by some Mill Hill Fathers,[2] who worked eastwards; while in 1911 a third order, the Verona Fathers, moved into northern Uganda. Meanwhile the whole endeavour on the Protestant side was in the hands of the C.M.S., so that there were in Uganda only episcopal churches, which accorded well with the hierarchical predilections of the interlacustrine peoples. At first, indeed, Church and State closely approximated. Some Ganda chiefs were amongst the first Anglicans to be ordained, and both churches relied heavily upon the example and support of Ganda chiefs and Agents. After 1900 Church and State began to separate out;[3] but for many years they persisted side by side[4] as the main organizations overlying much of African life. In 1911 the census[5] claimed one in every three Ganda to be a Christian, with one in every eight in the rest of the Protectorate, where in many areas Christian teaching was only just beginning. Of these the higher proportion declared themselves to be Roman Catholics—a fairly correct reflection of the adherence of the mass as distinct from the educated crust.

It is naturally invidious to assess the quality of Uganda's

[1] e.g. Eastern Province Annual Report, 1917–18.

[2] A substantially English order, which was introduced to overlay the dichotomy between Roman Catholic priests who were French, and Anglican missionaries who were British. H. P. Gale, *Uganda and the Mill Hill Fathers* (London, 1959).

[3] e.g. although Hamu Mukasa who became county chief Sekibobo of Kyagwe in 1905 had earlier been one of the foremost Protestant preachers, he was never ordained. One of his predecessors, Nikodemo Sebwato, who died in 1895, had been both Sekibobo and an ordained Protestant deacon.

[4] Anglican rural deaneries, for instance, coinciding in Buganda with *saza* chiefs' counties.

[5] Not, to be sure, a very accurate one.

Christianity at this time. Much of it, as the missionaries were the
first to affirm, proved to be largely nominal. There can be little
doubt, however, that it established in many African minds
an ideal of conduct, particularly in family questions, which if
honoured in the breach, was none the less honoured. There
was certainly no turning back, even amongst the most disillusioned with the new era, to traditional cults. This was illustrated by the separatist movement called the *abamalaki*,[1] which
broke away from the Anglican Church in 1914.[2] It was in no
sense atavistic. It rejected European control, but its chief
attraction lay in its provision of baptism without the preparation
demanded by the missions. It is doubtful, however, whether the
abamalaki, for all the fervour of heterodoxy, represented the most
lively faith of this period. This was still the preserve of ortho-
doxy. As early as 1893 a 'mission' within the Anglican Church
had led to the dispatch, at the charge of the Ganda Christian
community, of no less than 260 new Ganda evangelists to eighty-
five outstations of which twenty were beyond the borders of
Buganda. Some of these men could have enjoyed greater
affluence in secular callings; many of them had to face considerable hazards; and some of them attained, by any calculation, a remarkable degree of personal holiness. They reached
their apogee in Apolo Kivebulaya, 'the apostle to the pygmies',
who has remained—and on the latest evidence not without
cause[3]—an inspiration to succeeding generations. He, and many
of his contemporaries, served the Anglican Church for a quarter
of a century and more. Less is known about the spread of Roman
Catholicism, but in numbers Catholic European missionaries
and their Ganda catechists even exceeded the Protestants.

This spread raised problems of church order.[4] The most note-

---

[1] After its foremost preacher Malaki Masajjakawa. It called itself 'The Society
of the One Almighty God'.

[2] Its two most prominent figures were Joswa Kate, the most important clan-head
in Buganda and also an important county chief, and Semei Kakunguru, who in
1913 had been removed from his position as President of the Busoga Lukiko. Kate
had long criticized the lack of faith of the Mission as exemplified in the missionaries'
dependence upon doctors. Kakunguru was sore at his successive relegations. F. B.
Welbourn, 'Abamalaki in Buganda, 1914–1919', *Uganda J.* xxi. 2 (1957), 150–61;
Buganda Monthly Reports, Jan. 1915.

[3] Mrs. Anne Luck of Makerere College has made an excellent collection of
Kivebulaya's diaries which she kindly allowed to be seen.

[4] These were simpler for the Roman Catholics, since they were merely founding

worthy policy which the Roman Catholics adopted early on was
to insist that though Africans should be ordained to the priesthood, they should have a theological education fully comparable
with that of Roman Catholic priests the world over. As a result
in the whole region around Lake Victoria only two Africans
were ordained to the Roman Catholic priesthood before 1914.[1]
By contrast Bishop Tucker of the C.M.S.[2] early ordained
several men who, apart from completing a modest course of
elementary instruction, were chiefly notable for their Christian
character and their acknowledged position as leaders of their
own people. He ordained six Ganda deacons in 1893; three
priests in 1896: and by 1914 there were thirty-three African
priests in the Anglican diocese. These men were an invaluable
addition to its staff. They gave the Anglican Church in its formative years an African leadership as distinguished in its day as
any in the country's secular life; and together with the spread of
evangelists, from whom they were drawn, provided the warranty
both for the handing over by the C.M.S. missionaries after 1905
of their pastoral responsibilities to Africans, and for the constitution, drawn up by Tucker, under which the Anglican Church
in Uganda was to be governed by a Synod to which Africans
from all evangelized parts of the country were to send representatives, and in which European missionaries were to participate
on equal terms with their African converts. Its promulgation in
these terms was long opposed by the missionary body, and
in 1909, when it was finally enacted, a separate missionary
committee was retained; but henceforward through the Synod
Africans were able to play a major part in the government of the
Anglican Church, and the Anglican Synod became the only
constituted body in Uganda which successfully cut across the
tribal boundaries that in the political order were such barriers
to countrywide African endeavour.[3] It is scarcely surprising
that it very often reflected many of the secular as well as spiritual
yearnings which permeated the country in an age of transformation.

a further branch of their worldwide Church, than for the Anglicans who were
founding an essentially new Church, though in communion with others of its kind.

[1] The dividends, however, were reaped later.

[2] See his admirable autobiography, A. R. Tucker, *Eighteen Years in Uganda and
East Africa* (2 vols., London, 1908).

[3] e.g. *Uganda Notes*, Jan. 1919.

An African country

The importance of Christianity for Uganda in this period was not, therefore, confined to the religious changes which it brought. It provided, too, the catalyst that set loose the wider ambitions which were overtaking its peoples. These now expanded within the framework established by the Protectorate Government. Towards their attainment it was the Ganda who during this period led the way forward. For all their pride in their own past, in their own institutions, and in their own abilities, these people knew none of the contemporary conservatism of, for example, the Masai. By 1919 they had sustained, in the guise of Christian teaching and Christian example, and through a fruitful encounter with a liberal imperialism, a deep penetration of mind and emotions by the West. Aided, no doubt, by the psychological flexibility which had begun to characterize Ganda society even before the European arrival, and by the political success within their intensely political society of its most daringly progressive elements, their reaction to the alien elixir had been notably positive. It would be false to press too far the analogy with the Japanese, which some contemporary observers advanced, for the Ganda achievement fell substantially short of the Japanese; but the comparison contained this element of truth—that the pressures for the transformation of the country were now coming very largely from Africans themselves. During the first decade of the twentieth century those who observed with Sir Hesketh Bell that Uganda was 'emphatically a black man's country' were nearer the truth than most of them imagined. For though the journey might be into waters charted by Europeans, Africans stood now at the helm. What was more, the voyagers were not just the educated *élite*, but the whole of tribal society. The *évolués* were not *déracinés*. They were precisely those men who as chiefs enjoyed power upon terms traditionally legitimate, and were the accepted leaders of their people. It was they who eagerly grasped the new benefits in religious teaching, in administration, in economic development, in education, and in the attack upon disease, which the white man held out, even when they were careful to see that the transformation of their tribal society took place, not in complete subservience to European directions, but in accord with their own *mores*.[1] Here, in

[1] As Kagwa's policy after 1897–8 signalized.

short, was a deeply proud and profoundly self-conscious tribal people who were, nevertheless, generating their own process of change into a modern society.[1]

Their resilient spirit had already communicated itself to the surrounding areas, partly because Christian missionaries, Ganda catechists, and others had taken the Christian catalyst abroad; partly because George Wilson, Semei Kakunguru, and their followers had introduced the refashioned Ganda system of government into most of the rest of the country; partly because the economic development of peasant agriculture, which first occurred in Buganda, was now spreading to other parts of the Protectorate; but above all because the spectacle of Buganda's remarkably fruitful response to the first onslaught of western ideas and agencies was, in an age of Ganda Agents and catechists, brought close to people's eyes elsewhere.

There were a number of Europeans who appreciated the bent of African endeavours: 'Much of the civilised aspect of the Kingdom of Uganda [Sir Harry Johnston declared] is due . . . to the desire of the existing Chiefs to bring their country into harmony with European ideas and developments'.[2] The zeal displayed by the missions in the creation of schools indicated that they were fully seized of at least one objective of African aspirations; and though he spoke no Luganda, Bishop Tucker in formulating his ecclesiastical policy, which was remarkable for its day, sensed others; while similar impulses were felt in the political sphere by Wilson and his like, and in the economic by Spire, the Provincial Commissioner of the Eastern Province, and Simpson, the Director of Agriculture.

But such comprehension did not always stand unchallenged. Johnston, for instance (and he was echoed by others), thought some of the claims of the Ganda were 'peevish nonsense'. The C.M.S. missionaries long opposed Bishop Tucker's Synod. Morris Carter's Land Committee regularly rejected Spire's con-

---

[1] The possibility that stagnation might supervene was obviated by the removal by the British of the generation of chiefs with whom they had originally allied. This took place all over the Protectorate from about 1916 onwards. Their replacement by a new generation of new men, who wherever possible were the products of the new western education, ensured that, for the time being at any rate, there would be no check to the changes being made: e.g. Northern Province Monthly Report, Oct. 1918; Buganda Annual Report, 1918–19.

[2] Johnston's *Preliminary Report*, Cd. 256.

tention that economic development could be expected from peasant agriculture; while the Protectorate Government's Development Commission of 1919, composed of European commercial men and some government officials, formally rebuked Simpson for his lack of sympathy towards European plantations. Both before and immediately after the first world war, indeed, a serious, if oblique, challenge to the 'African' character of the country appeared with the influence exerted on the Government by the small European commercial community.[1] Bonar Law's decision about land in 1916 had checked but not, as it transpired, ended the pro-planter régime. Its demise only came later. And it was then to leave[2] one significant orphan child—a central Legislative Council composed upon its unofficial side entirely of non-African commercial members. This was not merely out of accord with developments upon every other plane in Uganda. For thirty years it never made contact at any level of reality with African life and African endeavour.[3] Nevertheless, by 1919 Africans in Uganda had good reason to feel confident that despite the entanglements of novel experiences and the overarching of imperial authority, they could at once maintain their own distinctive ethos and advance their own eventful progress. The price of liberty, however, as, tutored by Apolo Kagwa, the Ganda understood very well, was always eternal vigilance.

[1] They dominated this 1919 Commission, for example, which, as the C.M.S. *Uganda Notes* complained in Jan. 1920, contained no missionaries—those confidants of Africans in their dealings with the Protectorate Government, who ten and twenty years before had always participated in important governmental discussions.

[2] In addition to Uganda's one English newspaper, *The Uganda Herald*.

[3] See Chapter IX below.

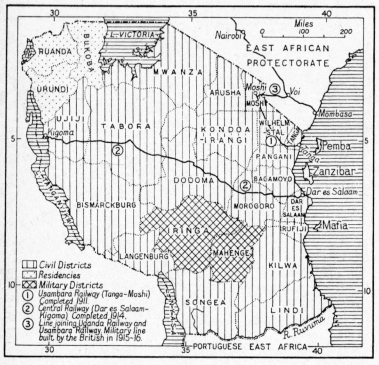

MAP 2. GERMAN EAST AFRICA IN 1914

III

(I) GERMAN EAST AFRICA
1884–1918

W. O. HENDERSON

Carl Peters and the German East Africa Company, 1884–90

EAST AFRICA was no promising field for colonization in the 1880's. The Arabs held much of the coast from Mogadishu to Cape Delgado. The effective authority of the Sultan of Zanzibar was confined to the ports, the hinterland of Bagamoyo and Kilwa Kivinje, and some slave trading and commercial posts in the interior. Zanzibar was the main centre of trade for East Africa. Here European, Indian, and American firms exchanged manufactured goods for ivory or other products from the mainland.

In the interior, the south was the home of Bantu tribes engaged in subsistence farming. Some retained their independence, but others were harassed or conquered by Ngoni invaders from the south. To the north lived the warlike Masai, the Gallas, and the Somalis, who raised cattle. The Swahili, whose language was widely known along the trade routes of East Africa, were settled on the coast. The population was unevenly distributed. Large districts in the centre and west—covering 200,000 square miles—were virtually unfit for human settlement owing to periodic droughts. East Africa was ravaged by tribal wars and by the depredations of the Ngoni and the Arab slave traders. The lot of many of the native inhabitants was indescribably wretched. They lived in terror of the slave-raiders; they suffered from malaria, smallpox, typhus, sleeping sickness, and other diseases; their cattle were victims of the tsetse fly and of rinderpest; their fields were stripped by locusts. Slave-raiding and epidemics increased recourse to witchcraft.

This inhospitable region was coveted in the 1880's by both British and German imperialists for a variety of reasons. Men experienced in Indian affairs wanted Britain to secure a foothold on the East African mainland. Sir John Kirk (the British Consul at Zanzibar) gained the Sultan's confidence. He hoped to exercise an indirect influence on the interior through the Arab authorities. A reformed Arab administration might prevent European powers from partitioning the region, yet maintain an open door for European commerce. British explorers and missionaries were active on the mainland, while William Mackinnon established a regular steamship service between Zanzibar and Aden. There were also Germans who looked to East Africa as a possible field of colonial expansion. In 1849 William O'Swald of Hamburg had established a warehouse in Zanzibar, and by 1871 German firms had secured nearly a quarter of the island's trade. Explorers (Wilhelm Peters and von der Decken) and missionaries (Rebmann and Krapf)[1] had visited the interior. Richard Brenner and Otto Kersten had agitated in favour of German colonization in East Africa.[2]

The movement in favour of establishing German overseas possessions received a powerful impetus by the founding of the German Colonial Union (*Deutscher Kolonialverein*) and the Society for German Colonization (*Gesellschaft für deutsche Kolonisation*) in the early 1880's. The former was a propaganda society, but the latter aimed at founding a colony, and in September 1884 it sent an expedition to East Africa for this purpose. Three young adventurers, Carl Peters, Jühlke, and Count Pfeil, signed treaties with native chiefs whose territories lay in the hinterland between Pangani and Kingani. Thus the society gained nominal control over an area of some 60,000 square miles.[3] Although Lüderitz's establishment at Angra

---

[1] The Lutherans Rebmann and Krapf, however, were in the service of an English missionary body—the Church Missionary Society—and were not concerned with European political expansion. See R. Oliver, *The Missionary Factor in East Africa* (London, 1952).

[2] For German interests in East Africa from the 1840's onwards see the first volume (1885) of the *Kolonial-Politische Korrespondenz* (organ of the German East Africa Company and the Society for German Colonization); B. Kurtze, *Die Deutsch-Ostafrikanische Gesellschaft* (Jena, 1913), pp. 17–39; E. Hieke, *Zur Geschichte des deutschen Handels mit Ostafrika, das hamburgische Handelshaus Wm. O'Swald & Co.*, vol. i, *1831–1870* (Hamburg, 1939); and P. E. Schramm, *Deutschland und Übersee* (Berlin, 1950).

[3] For Carl Peters's expedition of 1884 see his own account in C. Peters, *Die Gründung von Deutsch-Ostafrika* (Berlin, 1906). The treaties with the chiefs are printed in C. Peters, *Das deutsch-ostafrikanische Schutzgebiet* (Munich, 1895), appendix; J. Wagner, *Deutsch-Ostafrika . . .*, 2nd edn. (Munich 1895), pp. 1–9, and Kurtze, op. cit., pp. 178–86.

Pequeña (in South-west Africa) had received Imperial protection in April 1884, Bismarck had told Carl Peters in
November that he could not expect similar protection if he
tried to establish a colony in East Africa. But when Peters
returned in February 1885 the Society for German Colonization did receive a charter in respect of its newly acquired
possessions.

There has been much controversy concerning Bismarck's
change of policy with regard to colonies. For twenty years, in
public and in private, Bismarck had declared his opposition
to the acquisition of overseas territories. He argued that in the
field of diplomacy Germany derived great advantages from
being a purely continental state with no overseas commitments.
He feared that a colonial empire would be expensive to maintain, and that its acquisition might lead to demands for the
building of a large navy and might involve Germany in disputes
with Britain. Nevertheless, in 1884 and 1885 Bismarck changed
his mind and secured for Germany substantial territories in
West Africa, East Africa, and the Pacific. It has been suggested
that Bismarck had always favoured colonial expansion but had
cunningly concealed his true views. It has been argued that
he was forced by the pressure of public opinion to embark
unwillingly upon a policy of colonial expansion. Another suggestion is that the establishment of colonies was an incidental by-
product of the brief Franco-German *entente* of 1884–5. Bismarck,
it is said, secured colonies to try to convince France that he
was really determined to pursue an anti-British policy. None
of these explanations is very convincing. It seems most likely
that Bismarck changed his mind over colonies because circumstances were changing. Germany was rapidly becoming a highly
industrialized state, and it seemed prudent to secure territories
which might in future provide her with additional raw materials
and new markets for manufactured goods. Moreover, if Bismarck had remained inactive in the 1880's, the last opportunity
of acquiring a German colonial empire would have disappeared.
The final scramble for territories in Africa and the South Seas
had begun, and there was obviously no time to be lost if
Germany were to have a share of the spoils.

The charter granted to the Society for German Colonization
in 1885 declared that certain districts lying to the west of the

possessions of the Sultan of Zanzibar and not under the authority of any other state were placed under Imperial protection. Bismarck's definition of Imperial protection was as follows:

'The German Empire cannot carry on a system of colonisation like France's. It cannot send out warships to conquer overseas lands, that is, it will not take the initiative; but it will protect the German merchant even in the land which he acquires. Germany will do what England has always done—establish chartered companies, so that the responsibility rests with them.'[1]

The Society for German Colonization was granted sovereign rights in the territory which it had acquired as well as the actual ownership of land and the authority to dispense justice. The only condition imposed upon the society was the obligation to remain a German organization. But no provision was made concerning the organization of the private society, which claimed wide powers over a huge tract of East Africa. No obligation to refrain from establishing a trade monopoly and no duties regarding the construction of public works were imposed. No provision was made concerning the prohibition of slavery or the sale of liquor and fire-arms to the natives.[2]

The Sultan protested that these territories belonged to him and sent troops to enforce his claims, but a German naval demonstration off Zanzibar in August 1885 forced him to recognize the rights acquired by the Germans. By a treaty of 20 December 1885, Germany secured privileges at Dar es Salaam and Pangani and also the right to send certain goods duty-free through the coastal strip to the interior.

Meanwhile efforts were being made to extend British influence in East Africa. In 1884 Harry Johnston persuaded chiefs in the Mount Kilimanjaro region to accept British protection should the Sultan renounce his suzerainty there. These agreements were private arrangements between Johnston and the chiefs, though the British Foreign Office subsequently made use of them to support British claims in the area. Carl Peters thereupon pursued an aggressive policy of rapid land-grabbing to

[1] Quoted by M. E. Townsend, *Origins of Modern German Colonialism, 1871–1885* (New York, 1921), p. 180.

[2] For English translations of the charter see E. Hertslet, *The Map of Africa by Treaty* (edn. of 1894), p. 303, and R. Coupland, *The Exploitation of East Africa, 1856–1890* (London, 1939), p. 405.

forestall foreign rivals, and by 1886 he was claiming territories which would have formed an empire stretching from the Upper Nile to the Limpopo.[1]

The British and German governments—embarrassed by these empire-building ventures of their nationals—agreed in the autumn of 1886 that a line drawn from the mouth of the 'River Umba or Wanga' to Lake Jipe and from there round the northern slopes of Mount Kilimanjaro to the Victoria Nyanza should divide their spheres of influence. Agreement was also reached on the territories to be recognized as belonging to the Sultan of Zanzibar. The division of the hinterland, however, was incomplete, and the future of Witu (an enclave in the British sphere) was still obscure.[2] In December 1886 Germany and Portugal agreed that the River Ruvuma should divide their territories. Although his more grandiose plans had failed, Carl Peters had secured for the Reich a large East African colony.

He now tried to turn paper claims into realities. The Hamburg firms in Zanzibar—who had resented his interference with their mainland trade—agreed to handle his commercial transactions on a commission basis. The Arabs, however, refused to give the Germans access to the interior as envisaged in the agreement of 1885. It proved difficult to set up an organization in Germany to supervise the territory acquired by Peters and his associates. In February 1885 the Society for German Colonization appointed five 'directors' to supervise the territory, and it was these 'directors' who later set up the German East African Company, which was incorporated in 1887–8. Carl Peters thought that he could dominate the Company provided that it remained in the hands of a large number of small shareholders. But insufficient funds were raised in this way. In the summer of 1885 the banker Karl von der Heydt and the industrialist Friedrich Krupp became shareholders. Later, encouraged by an investment of 500,000 marks on the part of the official Overseas Trading Corporation (*Seehandlung*), other capitalists

---

[1] For the expeditions sent out by Carl Peters in 1885–6, see J. Graf von Pfeil, *Zur Erwerbung von Deutsch-Ostafrika* (Berlin, 1907), pp. 162–79 and R. Schmidt, *Geschichte des Araberaufstandes in Ostafrika* (Frankfurt a/M, 1892), pp. 6–14.

[2] See the exchange of Notes between Great Britain and Germany (29 Oct.– 1 Nov. 1886) and between Great Britain and Zanzibar in Hertslet, op. cit. ii. 615–21, 754–9.

took up enough shares to gain financial control of the Company. They did not, however, provide enough money to exploit the resources of the colony.

In 1885-7 the Company established ten stations which were both plantations and trading-posts. After visiting them in 1887 Count Pfeil reported that they had been costly failures. Nearly all of them were abandoned during the Arab revolt. At the posts the Company tried to deal in native products, but made little headway against well-established traders such as the Indian firm of Sewa Hadji and the Irish merchant Stokes. A few private plantations were started in the 1880's, such as the East Africa Plantation Company, the Mrima Company, and the German East Africa *Seehandlung*. The colony's commerce was still undeveloped, and in the eighteen months from 18 August 1888 to 18 February 1890 its exports were valued at only 2,900,000 marks.[1]

Peters realized that to exploit the colony's resources the Company must secure control over the coast. In 1887 he signed a treaty with Said Barghash, but since it was not ratified he severed his connexion with the Company. In 1888 the German Consul-General at Zanzibar and Said Khalifa (Barghash's successor) agreed that the Company should collect customs dues on the coast, mine minerals, regulate commerce, and improve communications.[2] In August 1888 the Company's agents began to collect import duties and raised its flag, which closely resembled the German one, over certain coastal towns. Spasmodic outbreaks of violence developed into a widespread Arab revolt led by Abushiri. Some of the natives rallied round the Swahili leader Bwana Heri to resist the Germans. Since the insurgents outnumbered the Sultan's forces and the Company's *askari*, the future of the territory hung in the balance.

The causes of the Arab revolt were not far to seek. The British and German representatives of the two companies were establishing themselves on the coast, and it was clear that the position of the Arabs was seriously threatened. They feared that the Europeans would end the slave trade on the mainland as

[1] K. Most, *Die wirtschaftliche Entwicklung Deutsch-Ostafrikas, 1885 — 1905* (Berlin, 1906).

[2] The agreement of 1888 between Germany and Zanzibar is printed by Kurtze, op. cit., pp. 183-7.

they had ended it in Zanzibar. The disappearance of the slave trade would lead to the virtual collapse of the existing economy of the region. To make matters worse, the ivory trade of the Arabs was now being threatened by European competitors. For years the Arabs had controlled the east coast of Africa and the main trade routes of the interior. Now both their political authority and their economic position appeared to be in danger. The murder of a German ivory trader—a representative of the Hamburg firm of Meyer—in Tabora in 1886 showed that the Arabs feared the competition of white traders as well as the political designs of European powers.

Bismarck faced a difficult situation. If territory under Imperial protection were abandoned, Germany's prestige would suffer. Yet the Reichstag might hesitate to vote funds to restore law and order, since Bismarck had stated repeatedly that trading companies—and not the German taxpayer—would finance colonial developments. By claiming that the armed intervention of the Reich was necessary to suppress slavery Bismarck achieved two objects—he secured both a grant from the Reichstag and the naval co-operation of Great Britain.

The experienced African explorer Captain Hermann Wissmann was appointed Reich Commissioner. He recruited 600 Sudanese in Cairo, 350 Zulus in Mozambique, and 50 Somalis in Aden. The Sudanese were experienced soldiers who had fought in the Egyptian army against the Mahdi. A small detachment of *askari*, recruited by the Company in Dar es Salaam and Bagamoyo, were incorporated in Wissmann's force. These native troops, who were commanded by German officers, were supported from time to time by landing parties of marines. Early in May 1889 Wissmann assembled his forces at Bagamoyo and in the following months he gained control over the coast. Abushiri fled into the interior, but his power was broken when Wissmann established a fort at Mpwapwa. Abushiri was betrayed to the Germans in December 1889 and was publicly hanged.[1] Bwana Heri, who was treated as an independent native chief and not as a rebel, came to terms with the Germans. Wissmann now turned his attention to the south.

[1] An eye-witness account of Abushiri's capture and execution is given by A. Becker, *Aus Deutsch-Ostafrikas Sturm- und Drangperiode* (Halle, 1911), 1–21.

Troops landed at Kilwa Kisiwani and soon seized Kilwa Kivinje and Lindi (May 1890). Early in 1891 Wissmann reported that the rebellion had been completely suppressed.

Meanwhile Peters, still dreaming of bringing vast new African territories under German rule, had set off on his travels again. He turned his attention to the Egyptian province of Equatoria. Emin Pasha, the Governor of the province, had survived the Mahdi's rising and had appealed to Britain for help. A committee, led by Sir William Mackinnon, raised funds to send Stanley to rescue the last of Gordon's lieutenants. Leopold II persuaded Stanley to approach Equatoria through the Congo. Leopold II—and Mackinnon also to some extent—had designs upon the province, which seemed to be falling from Egypt's grasp. But Emin Pasha was a German Jew—his real name was Schnitzer—and Peters hoped to persuade him to hand Equatoria over to Germany. So a rival relief committee was organized, and Wissmann was asked to lead an expedition to Equatoria while Peters was to follow with a second party to set up posts on the route. These plans were changed when the Arabs revolted and Wissmann became Reich Commissioner. Bismarck needed British help to suppress the Arabs. He avoided disputes with Britain concerning lands north of the River Tana and tried to dissuade Carl Peters from leaving for Africa.[1]

Peters would not give up his schemes. He slipped through the Anglo-German blockade in the spring of 1889 and marched up the Tana Valley. On the borders of Equatoria he learned that Stanley had found Emin Pasha and that Mwanga (Kabaka of Buganda) was appealing for British aid against his enemies. Since Peters could not rescue Emin Pasha he rescued Mwanga instead, and Mwanga placed Buganda under German protection.[2]

When Peters reached Mpwapwa on his return journey in 1890 he met Emin Pasha, who was leading an official expedition to the interior to persuade the Arab traders that the abolition

---

[1] For the Arab rising see *Further Correspondence respecting Germany and Zanzibar*, no. 1 of 1889 (C. 5822); R. Schmidt, op. cit.; G. von Maerker, 'Kriegführung in Ostafrika' (supplement to the *Militärwochenblatt*, 1894, no. 6, pp. 149–77); M. Prager, *Die Wissmann-Expedition* (Leipzig, 1896); and an article by R. von Spalding in the *Deutsches Kolonial Lexikon*, ed. H. Schnee (3 vols., Leipzig, 1920), i. 68–71.

[2] The abortive treaty with Mwanga was printed by Carl Peters in *Die Gründung von Deutsch-Ostafrika*, p. 261.

of the slave trade need not mean the end of their legitimate commerce. Emin Pasha, Langheld, and Stuhlmann proceeded from Mpwapwa to Tabora, where a treaty was signed with the local Arabs on 1 August 1890. The Arabs accepted German suzerainty and were granted the right to choose their own *wali* or local governor; Say bin Said was elected to this post. The Arabs agreed that if a German station were established at Tabora the *wali* would be subordinate to the official in charge of the station. Emin Pasha also checked the influence of the Nyamwezi chief Siki, who was trying to dominate the tribes formerly ruled by Mirambo.[1] Siki was forced to give up two cannon in his possession and to pay an indemnity in ivory.

By September 1890 Emin Pasha's expedition had reached the Victoria Nyanza, where Langheld established stations at Bukoba and Mwanza.[2] Ignoring an order to return to the coast, Emin Pasha tried to cross the continent to the Cameroons. In October 1892 he was murdered at the instigation of Arab slave traders in the Congo.

Meanwhile Peters reached the coast in July 1890 and was disgusted to learn that the German Government had relinquished its claims to Uganda and Witu.[3] Two treaties between Britain and Germany had recently been signed. The first (14 June 1890) partitioned the territories on the mainland over which the Sultan of Zanzibar had hitherto claimed to exercise authority. The second (1 July) settled Anglo-German spheres of influence which excluded Germany from the Upper Nile and established a British protectorate over Zanzibar and Pemba. Britain gave up Heligoland to Germany and promised to use her influence with the Sultan of Zanzibar to induce him to renounce his sovereignty over the East African coast in return for financial compensation.[4]

The acquisition of the coast, the settlement of spheres of influence, and the suppression of the Arab revolt paved the

---

[1] For Mirambo's career see ch. viii in vol. i of this *History*, pp. 279–80, 290–1.
[2] For this expedition see W. Langheld, *Zwanzig Jahre in den deutschen Kolonien* (Berlin, 1909), and F. Stuhlmann, *Mit Emin Pascha ins Herz von Afrika* (Berlin, 1894).
[3] For Carl Peters's expedition of 1889–90 see C. Peters, *Die deutsche Emin-Pascha-Expedition* (Leipzig, 1891) and *Die Gründung von Deutsch-Ostafrika*, pp. 235–63.
[4] See R. C. Beazley, 'Das deutsche Kolonialreich, Gross-Britannien und die Verträge von 1890' in the *Berliner Monatshefte*, May 1931, pp. 444–59; M. Sell, *Das deutsch-englische Abkommen von 1890* (Bonn, 1926); and G. Jantzen, *Ostafrika in der deutsch-englischen Politik, 1884–1890* (Hamburg, 1934).

way for an agreement between the Reich and the Company on the future organization of the colony (20 November 1890). The Company gave up its administrative functions and became a purely commercial undertaking. It paid compensation to the Sultan of Zanzibar for renouncing his sovereignty over the coast and it agreed to maintain the colony's harbours. The Company received many privileges—the first right to public land and to railway concessions, the right to set up a bank of issue, and to mint coins. The Company was authorized to raise a loan and to receive at least 600,000 marks a year from the customs revenue to provide for interest and amortization. The attempt to rule the colony through the Company had failed, and the Reich now accepted responsibility for the future administration of East Africa.[1]

The pacification of the colony, 1890–1906[2]

Wissmann had hoped to become the first Governor of the new colony. But Caprivi, Bismarck's successor as Chancellor, was not in favour of such an appointment, since Wissmann had left the colony's finances in a chaotic condition. Julius von Soden became the first Governor (1891). Wissmann, however, returned to East Africa in 1891 with an expedition to launch steamers on Lakes Victoria and Tanganyika. Funds had been raised by an anti-slavery lottery, and the expedition aimed at suppressing the slave trade in the Lakes region. It proved impossible to carry out the original plan in full and instead the steamer (the *Hermann Wissmann*) was taken up the Zambezi and Shire to Lake Nyasa (1893). Wissmann established a station at Langenburg and subdued the Nyika and other local tribes. Subsequently the 80-ton *Hedwig Wissmann* was launched on Lake Tanganyika (1901).

In the early 1890's Governors Soden and Schele constructed the framework of an administrative machine for German East Africa. At its head was the Governor, who enforced the laws (*Gesetze*), Imperial edicts (*Verordungen*), and Chancellor's instructions (*Verordnungen*) in the colony. He had the power to issue

[1] The Agreement of 1890 between the Reich and the German East Africa Company is printed by Kurtze, op. cit., appendix 8, pp. 193–6, and by E. Plumon, *La Colonie allemande de l'Afrique orientale* . . . (Rennes, 1905), pp. 95–96.

[2] For military operations in German East Africa in 1892–5 see H. von Bülow, *Deutschlands Kolonien und Kolonialkriege* (Leipzig, 1900), pp. 71–148.

local decrees. If the posts of Governor of the territory and Commander of the Defence Force were held by different persons it was the Governor who decided when the whole (or any part) of the Defence Force should be used. In German eyes it was most unusual to give a civilian official virtually unlimited authority over military forces. At first the forces at the Governor's disposal were very small. The troops formerly under Wissmann's command were divided into a defence force and a police force. In September 1893 the former was composed of 1,600 and the latter of 200 Africans. The two forces together had 163 white commissioned and non-commissioned officers.[1] The Sudanese still formed the nucleus of the Defence Force, but the Zulu soldiers had nearly all left the German service on the expiry of their contracts in 1892 and had been replaced by *askari* recruited in the colony.

The civil administration at Dar es Salaam was gradually organized in separate departments. Rudolf von Bennigsen[2] was head of the Finance Department from 1893 to 1899. He realized that a new colony needed public works and welfare services. The revenue from the customs and from funds voted by the Reichstag was inadequate. Death duties (introduced in November 1893) provided little revenue and it was not until November 1897 that an African hut tax was first levied. Bennigsen habitually exceeded the estimates and argued that money had to be spent on projects which could not be foreseen when the budget was drawn up. In the 1890's the Finance Department was the most important in the Administration and it handled many problems of a general nature. In the early years of the twentieth century, however, the department fell into the hands of professional accountants who rigidly kept within the estimates.

Dr. Franz Stuhlmann was in charge of the Department of Surveying and Agriculture, set up in 1893. He encouraged the collection of information concerning the topography of the colony, and his map of German East Africa (scale 1:300,000) was superior to those of neighbouring territories. Sir Charles

---

[1] These figures are given by von Maerker, 'Kriegführung in Ostafrika', loc. cit., pp. 149–77. See also E. Nigmann, *Geschichte der Kaiserlichen Schutztruppe für Deutsch-Ostafrika* (Berlin, 1911).

[2] For Bennigsen—son of a well-known Liberal statesman—see the *Deutsches Kolonial Lexikon*, i. 163–4.

Eliot stated that when he was Commissioner for the British East Africa Protectorate he 'habitually consulted a German map which took some account of the districts on our side of the boundary and nourished myself so to speak on the crumbs which fell from the Teutonic table. They were better than any repast which our own cartographers could provide.'[1] A Department of Justice (under Eschke), a Medical Department (under Dr. Becker), and a Public Works Department (under Wiskow) were also set up in the early 1890's.

Important public works were undertaken—buildings for the administration, forts, harbours, lighthouses, roads, and bridges—but railway development was slow. Dar es Salaam, a small native settlement in 1890, was described fifteen years later as 'the best built town on the coast'. 'It was laid out with a lavish disregard for cost, and its wide tranquil streets bordered with flowering trees, its parks and gardens, its comfortable residences, its magnificent hospital, and other buildings give it somewhat the appearance of a German *Kurort* transferred to the tropics.'[2] Even in the early days of the colony particular attention was paid to the development of scientific institutions. Dr. Stuhlmann established the botanic gardens at Dar es Salaam, the experimental plantation at Kwai, and the biological-agricultural Institute at Amani. Some twenty stations made regular meteorological observations. All this was achieved with very meagre financial resources. For the financial year 1891–2 expenditure was estimated at 3,409,000 marks and revenue at 1,458,000 marks, leaving 1,951,000 marks to be met by a government grant. It was not until 1895–6 that provision was made for a substantially increased outlay (32,327,000 marks) and a substantially increased Government subsidy (26,111,400 marks).

In the interior, German authority was generally established in three stages. In a number of areas treaties had been signed with local chiefs and German influence depended upon the extent to which the chiefs fulfilled their obligations. In so far as the very limited military resources of the Governor permitted, punitive expeditions were sent against recalcitrant chiefs. The second stage in the establishment of German authority was to set up military posts on caravan routes, at centres of maritime

[1] C. Eliot, *The East Africa Protectorate* (London, 1905), p. 257.
[2] Ibid., p. 252.

trade, at places from which European merchants and missionaries already exercised some influence, and at the headquarters of agents of the Sultan of Zanzibar or of local chiefs. The third stage in the evolution of colonial administration was for the military government to be replaced by that of civilian district officers who exercised both executive and judicial functions. A number of senior civilian officials had formerly served in the Defence Force. In some places a system of local native administration which was already in existence in the 1880's was retained. Officials (*akidas*) of Arab or Swahili extraction had limited powers over groups of villages which they sometimes shared with influential headmen (*jumbes*). The German authorities realized that these officials were sometimes unreliable. But the high cost of employing German officials in relatively subordinate posts in local administration—even if suitably qualified Germans could have been found—made the appointment of indigenous officials inevitable.[1] In 1891 four administrative districts were established on the coast and by 1903 the colony had been divided into twelve civil and sixteen military districts.[2]

Those who thought that the collapse of the Arab revolt heralded a general African submission soon received a rude awakening. In June 1891 Emil von Zelewski, the commander of the Defence Force, set out with three companies on a punitive expedition against the Hehe, who were persistently raiding neighbouring tribes. On 16 August his force was ambushed at Lula-Rugaro and virtually annihilated. Ten Europeans (including von Zelewski) and some 300 *askari* fell in action. Only four Europeans and sixty *askari* survived. The Hehe captured three cannon and 300 rifles. This reverse seriously weakened the military strength of the Germans and was a grave blow to their prestige. Governor Soden tried to overawe the indigenous peoples by establishing armed posts in the interior even at the cost of weakening his hold over the coastal districts. In the Kilimanjaro region—where Carl Peters (now a Reich Commissioner in the Colonial Service) was trying to establish German authority—an expedition against the Chagga chief

[1] G. A. Graf von Götzen, *Deutsch-Ostafrika im Aufstand, 1905–6* (Berlin, 1909), p. 35.
[2] For the administrative structure of German East Africa in 1914 see map, p. 122.

Meli was repulsed near Moshi in June 1892 and two officers, Bülow and Wolfrun, were killed. In the Tabora District, Emin Pasha's treaty with the Arabs had not brought permanent peace. The Nyamwezi leader Siki harassed the caravan route through Tabora and attempts to defeat him were unsuccessful.

E. Wolf's alarmist reports in the *Berliner Tageblatt* concerning the failure to establish law and order in East Africa caused serious concern in Germany. In the autumn of 1892 Colonel von Schele, the new Commander of the Defence Force, restored order in both the Tabora and Kilimanjaro districts. In January 1893 Lieutenant Prince routed the Nyamwezi, and Siki, their chief, was killed. In August Schele defeated Meli and ended the disorders in the Kilimanjaro region. In September 1893 Schele became Governor of the colony and soon sent several expeditions to deal with hostile tribes. The notorious Bwana Heri was dealt with in the spring of 1894. Then in October Schele inflicted a severe defeat upon Mkwawa, the leader of the Hehe. While this force was in the interior there was trouble on the coast, for Hasan bin Omari made a surprise attack on Kilwa. His forces penetrated into the town but were eventually driven off.

When Schele returned to Germany in January 1895 Prince Hohenlohe—the new Chancellor of the Reich—recommended Wissmann's appointment as Governor. During his brief term of office Wissmann continued the work of his predecessors in suppressing tribes which resisted German rule. Lieutenant-Colonel von Trotha, Commander of the Defence Force, led a punitive expedition against Hasan bin Omari, captured him, and seized his correspondence. Evidence from the correspondence showed that certain native officials and Indian merchants in Kilwa had secretly aided Hasan bin Omari when he had attacked the town. Eight death sentences were passed on the rebels and the inhabitants of Kilwa had to pay a collective fine of 20,000 rupees. On the other hand, no military action was taken against the Arab Shaikh Mbarak, who had led the Mazrui in their rebellion in British East Africa.[1] When Mbarak sought refuge in German territory he was allowed to settle near Dar es Salaam with a thousand of his followers.

Wissmann returned to Germany in the summer of 1896.

---

[1] See Chapter I, pp. 7-8, above.

His successor, Colonel Eduard von Liebert, had to deal with disturbances both in the north and the south of the territory. In August 1896 Captain Prince established a new military station at Iringa (in the Hehe country), where Mkwawa was still waging guerrilla warfare. A series of operations in 1897–8 broke the power of the Hehe. Mkwawa took to the bush and committed suicide. The Germans decapitated his corpse, and the skull was said to have been sent to Berlin.[1] Meanwhile Captain Johannes's expedition avenged the murder of two missionaries in the Kilimanjaro region (Meru Mountain) and punished the Masai for stealing cattle. In the summer of 1897 a punitive expedition was sent to the Ngoni country in the Lindi hinterland. The ruthless manner in which district officers enforced the collection of a new hut tax—in districts where the inhabitants were already short of food owing to drought and the ravages of locusts—led to fresh unrest in 1899. By 1900 ugly rumours reached Germany concerning the brutal treatment of the indigenous peoples. In the Kilimanjaro region three chiefs and sixteen subordinate leaders were executed. It was alleged that 2,000 Africans had been killed in resisting the collection of the hut tax.[2] The Government bowed to the storm and Governor Liebert was recalled in March 1901.

He was succeeded by Count Adolf von Götzen, who had made extensive explorations in central Africa. He was both Governor of the Colony and Commander of its Defence Force. Götzen held office between March 1901 and April 1906. He pursued a more liberal native policy and tried to collect taxes without resorting to violence. It seemed as if he had allayed African fears, and the first five years of his term of office were a period of peace.

It came as a shock to the Germans when a serious revolt broke out in the south of the colony in the summer of 1905.[3]

---

[1] The skull was subsequently located at Bremen, and was returned to the Hehe in 1954.

[2] See Dr. Hans Wagener's pamphlet, *Falsche Propheten. Gouverneur von Liebert und seine Presse* (Charlottenburg, 1900).

[3] For the Maji-Maji rising see Margaret Bates's introduction to Abdul Karim bin Jamaliddini, *Utenzi wa Vita vya Maji-Maji*, Supplement to the *East African Swahili Committee Journal* (Arusha, 1957); von Götzen, *Deutsch-Ostafrika im Aufstand 1905–6* (Berlin, 1909); W. Methner, *Unter drei Gouverneuren, 16 Jahre Dienst in den deutschen Tropen* (Breslau, 1938); and A. Prüsse, *Zwanzig Jahre Ansiedler in Deutsch-Ostafrika* (Stuttgart, 1929). I thank Dr. Bates for letting me see the typescript of her essay

This was by far the gravest threat to their authority since the Arab rising. The rebellion had several unusual features. It was a concerted rising by several tribes, whose leaders kept their plans secret until the last moment. The rebels belonged to tribes which had hitherto given the Germans little trouble.[1] Captain Moritz Merker, who had served in the colony for many years, interrogated a number of rebel prisoners and came to the conclusion that the rising had been planned for at least a year in advance. Governor von Götzen accepted this analysis of the situation and regarded the rebellion as 'a rising of the Bantu negroes against intruders of any other race'.[2] Yet neighbouring warlike tribes such as the Hehe remained passive although they had only recently been fighting the Germans. Critics of the German colonial administration argued that the revolt was due to resentment against forced labour and the hut tax and to the harsh treatment of the native inhabitants by the Germans and by minor Swahili and Arab officials. But if this were the correct explanation it is surprising that the northern and central parts of the territory were not affected by the rising.[3]

An important factor in the situation was the continued attempt of the Germans to control a large colony with too few officials. This led to the delegation of wide powers to Swahili and Arab *jumbes* and *akidas* and gave ample scope for the abuse of authority. It was not so much the existence of a hut tax or forced labour which caused discontent as the way in which local officials collected the tax and set the natives to work.

The most serious aspect of the affair was the fanaticism of the rebels, who believed that magic water dispensed by a great medicine man made them immune from death by gunfire. Shouting '*Maji-Maji*'—'Water! Water!'—they faced a hail of bullets without flinching. The *Maji-Maji* cult may have been

on the Maji-Maji rising, which describes the rebellion at greater length than her historical introduction to *Utenzi wa Vita vya Maji-Maji* (1957). The area affected by the rebellion—a region the size of Prussia—lay to the south of a line running from Dar es Salaam to Morogoro, Iringa, and Alt Langenburg.

[1] According to the Governor the following tribes took part in the rebellion: Ngoni, Bunga, Mwera, Sagara, Zaramo, Matumbi, Kitchi, Ikemba, and Bena. A number of the leaders were members of the Pogoro tribe.

[2] Von Götzen, op. cit., p. 47.

[3] An official German commission of inquiry enumerated seventeen reasons for the rising, but many of the grievances which were listed applied equally well to regions which remained loyal to the Germans.

invented by the leaders of the rebellion, but belief in the magic properties of the medicine man's water probably developed independently of the rising, and the insurgents took advantage of the situation to whip up the fanaticism of their followers.

In July 1905 disturbances broke out in the district of Kilwa. At Kibata in the Matumbi hills the natives refused to perform compulsory labour and besieged the house of the local *akida*. The telegraph line from Kilwa to Dar es Salaam was cut on 28 July. Sergeant Hoenicke marched to Kibata with thirty-eight men to restore law and order. He found that the *akida* had fled, that a number of Arabs had been killed, and that the natives were still resisting the authorities. On his march back to Kilwa Sergeant Hoenicke's small force was attacked at Samanga. The Germans beat off the attack and killed twenty-seven rebels. On the following day Hoenicke was joined by Captain Moritz Merker's column of seventy *askari* from Dar es Salaam, which had failed to save a planter named Hopfer from being murdered by the rebels. Major Kurt Johannes, the senior military officer in the territory, now left Dar es Salaam with 112 men to quell what still appeared to be a minor rising. At Kibata he accepted the surrender of the villagers and fined them. At Mohoro he seized two 'witch-doctors' who were regarded as the ringleaders of the rising. These men were hanged. One of them, named Kinjikitire Ngwale, had the title of 'Bokero', and he boasted that the rebellion had already spread to Mahenge and Kilosa.

He proved to be right. At Upogoro discontent was fomented by Ngwale's brother-in-law, a witch-doctor named Ngameya. In the middle of August his followers attacked Europeans, Swahilis, and Arabs in the village of Madaba. At the same time there were risings in the Liwale district.[1] The small government station at Liwale was seized by rebels led by the elephant hunter Mpanda. The place was of some importance at this time, since it was a halt on the caravan route from Kilwa to Songea and Lake Nyasa. Two Germans (Sergeant Faupel and the rubber planter Aimer), several *askari*, and many villagers were killed. A column going to the relief of Liwale was wiped out by the rebel *jumbe* Kinjalla and his wife (the notorious 'Jumbess' Mkanomire). When another relief column reached

[1] i.e. the present Nachingwea.

Liwale some weeks later, it was found that the entire settlement had been destroyed.

In September 1905 the Catholic Bishop Cassian Spiss and his party were murdered by the rebels. Accompanied by two lay brothers and by two sisters of the Benedictine Order, Bishop Spiss was travelling from Kilwa, on the Songea caravan route, to the mission station at Peramiho. Deserted by his porters, the bishop and his party pushed on to Liwale, where they were surrounded by the rebels and killed. The tragic events at Liwale brought home to the German public the gravity of the situation in East Africa.[1]

The authorities on the spot now feared that the rising might spread over the whole of German East Africa. In the Lindi district mining properties were destroyed and several mission stations were attacked. In the Uluguru and Kilosa regions a witch-doctor (*Hongo*)[2] sacked the town of Kilosa, but was unable to capture the government station. His men proceeded to attack Morogoro, but were decisively defeated by the Germans before they could reach their objective. In the Dar es Salaam District the mission station at Maneromango was burned to the ground and caravans from Morogoro and Kilosa were attacked. By the end of August the glare of crops fired by the rebels could be seen at Dar es Salaam. The capital itself appeared to be threatened, and 200 Europeans were hastily enrolled in a militia to defend the city.

The Defence Force and police force were small. Governor von Götzen stated that the two forces together could muster only 1,044 men in the disaffected districts and only 1,316 men in other parts of the territory. Moreover, the Defence Force detachments were scattered over the whole of the colony, so that at first only emergency measures could be taken to deal with the rising. It has been seen that at the beginning of the rebellion the prompt action of the veteran Major Johannes saved Samanga from attack. Similarly, at Iringa Captain Ernst Nigmann enlisted some retired Sudanese *askari* who had been settled in the district after completing their term of service in the Defence Force. He held the Ngoni in check with the small

---

[1] See R. M. Bell, 'The Maji-Maji rebellion in the Liwale District', *Tanganyika Notes and Records*, xxviii (1950), 38–57.

[2] *Hongo* is the title of a superior witch-doctor.

forces at his disposal. On 20 September 1905 Nigmann successfully relieved Lieutenant von Hassel, who (with only sixty
askari) had been besieged for three weeks by some 4,000 rebels
at Mahenge. Reinforcements were sent to military posts which
were threatened by the rebels and efforts were made to rescue
settlers, traders, missionaries, and other Europeans who lived
in isolated places. Landing parties from the *Bussard*, ably led
by Lieutenant Hans Paasche,[1] co-operated with the military
authorities on the coast. In August 1905, for example, he
defeated a thousand rebels near Utete. Only when the Defence
Force had been expanded (by men hastily recruited in Somaliland and New Guinea) and when the small cruisers *Thetis* and
Seeadler reached German East Africa could law and order be
restored.

Fortunately for the Germans the tribes in the districts of
Langenburg and Iringa did not join the rebels. The Hehe, who
had long defied the Germans in the past, showed no inclination
to take up arms again. And in the heart of the rebel country
there were local sultans who remained loyal to the Germans
and sent auxiliary troops to help put down the rising. By the
end of 1905 the Germans were regaining command of the
situation. Their troops held a crescent line some 250 miles in
length. This line was gradually contracted, and the rebels
were contained in an area which continually diminished in
size. Moreover, the Germans held the line of the Ruvuma river
and tried to stop the rebels from escaping into the Portuguese
colony of Mozambique. The Germans burned down the villages
inhabited by the rebels and destroyed their crops. This forced
the insurgents to lead a nomadic life in the bush.

By the spring of 1906 the fighting was over except in the
Songea District, where the rising continued until 1907. The
rebels were defeated in the field and could not continue
the struggle because the Germans destroyed their villages and
crops. It was often hunger which forced the insurgents to lay
down their arms. The rebels suffered heavy casualties. Their
fields were neglected and many of their cattle were lost. Professor Fraas, who visited East Africa in 1907, wrote: 'The
district between Lindi and the River Mbemkuru is now sparsely

---

[1] See Hans Paasche, *Im Morgenlicht. Kriegs- und Jagderlebnisse in Ostafrika*
(Neudamm, 1907).

G

populated, but the many deserted and overgrown settlements which we passed in many hours of marching showed that before the rising of 1905 the region had been cultivated and had supported many natives.'[1] For some years the prosperity of other parts of the colony masked the depressed condition of the south.

An official report of 1907 summarized the measures taken to re-establish the shattered economy of the districts affected by the rebellion.

A great many of the natives who survived the fighting and the famine succumbed to various diseases because their physical condition had deteriorated so much. There was an epidemic of worm diseases which were carried by native labourers to districts formerly free from these illnesses. Badly nourished mothers had no milk for their babies so that in some districts the infant mortality reached alarming heights. In short in the early months of this year (1907) the disaffected districts presented an indescribably tragic scene.

Once the rising had been suppressed the senior officials of the Administration were faced with heavy duties. What had been destroyed by war had to be built up again. An exhausted population, bleeding from a hundred wounds, had to be encouraged to undertake the task of reconstruction. In many districts the sultans and *jumbes* who were formerly in charge of local affairs were no longer available and new appointments had to be made. Natives who had fled from their homes had, if possible, to be brought back and persuaded to rebuild their villages and till their fields again.[2]

The authorities supplied food and seeds to districts threatened with famine. When new crops were harvested the authorities purchased some of the food and stored it so as to prevent speculators from taking unfair advantage of the prevailing shortage. Doctors were sent to those areas where smallpox was prevalent and many people were vaccinated.

Since it took over twenty years to pacify German East Africa, the economic development of the colony was retarded. The Government, the Reichstag, and private capitalists hesitated to invest money in a territory with so uncertain a future. Improved communications were essential before the resources of the colony could be exploited. On 3 July 1890 the first regular steamship service between Germany and her new colony was inaugurated

---

[1] Quoted by Graf von Götzen, op. cit., p. 166.   [2] Ibid., pp. 233–4.

wheɪɪ the *Reichstag* (2,300 tons) sailed from Hamburg. In the same year the Dar es Salaam–Zanzibar cable was opened. Then the ports were linked by telegraph. By 1904 there were telegraph lines in the interior from Tanga to Korogwe and from Dar es Salaam to Tabora and Mwanza. In 1902–3 Cecil Rhodes's Transcontinental Telegraph Company built a telegraph from Abercorn on the Northern Rhodesian border to Ujiji on Lake Tanganyika. In the 1890's postal agencies were set up on the coast and at several military stations in the hinterland. Bridges, ferries, and rest houses were provided on important caravan routes. At some points reliable *askari* were settled on small-holdings which supplied food to travellers. But very few maca-damized roads were constructed.[1]

The colony urgently needed a network of railways. The benefits to be derived from railway construction were illustrated by the way in which the Uganda Railway (built by the British in 1896–1901) promoted the expansion of the Victoria Nyanza and Usambara regions of German East Africa.[2] But the Germans were slow to follow Britain's example. They took twelve years to build the 129 km. Usambara Railway from Tanga to Korogwe and Mombo. It was begun in June 1893, but was not completed until February 1905. Nothing came of plans to join the coast with the great lakes until 1904, when a company was established to build the Dar es Salaam–Moro-goro line (209 km.).[3] When Dr. Hermann Paasche (Vice-President of the Reichstag) visited East Africa in 1905, he reported that, despite the rising in the southern part of the colony, the construction of the railway—begun in February of that year—was making excellent progress.[4]

When the colony was first established, its internal trade was limited by inadequate communications, while external com-

---

[1] For the economic development of German East Africa between 1885 and 1905 see Most, *Die wirtschaftliche Entwicklung Deutsch-Ostafrikas, 1885—1905.*

[2] After visiting the Victoria Nyanza in 1905 Governor von Götzen wrote: 'I saw the beneficial influence which the British Uganda Railway was beginning to have on the Lake, and in association with my local officials, I was able to make arrange-ments for us to draw every possible commercial and military advantage from this factor' (von Götzen, op. cit., p. 2).

[3] F. Baltzer, *Die Kolonialbahnen* (Berlin, 1916), pt. ii, A 1, pp. 35–60.

[4] H. Paasche, *Deutsch-Ostafrika* (Berlin, 1906), pp. 79–82. Dr. Hermann Paasche was the father of the Lieutenant Paasche who was serving in the *Bussard* at the time of the Maji-Maji revolt.

merce was restricted both by this factor and by the lack of suitable exports. Internal trade was confined to barter. External commerce (after the prohibition of the slave trade) consisted largely in the exchange of European goods for ivory and a few other local products. This trade was largely in Indian and Arab hands. Eleven years after Carl Peters's first expedition, ivory still accounted for rather over two-fifths of the territory's exports. By 1904, however, Africans were growing copra (856,409 marks), sesame (374,026 marks), and cotton (123,892 marks) for export, while the most important plantation products were sisal (571,739 marks) and coffee (523,618 marks). In the same year timber and rubber exports were together valued at 2,308,000 marks. The first attempts to grow tobacco, cotton, and rubber on plantations met with little success. The establishment of the Amani Biological-Agricultural Institute (in Usambara) in 1902 was a turning-point in the economic development of the colony.[1] Systematic research in tropical agriculture led to the successful production of sisal and cotton. In 1905 there were 180 white planters and farmers in the colony. It was difficult to recruit African labour to work in plantations. The labour force was depleted by wars and thousands of men were employed as porters. Sometimes compulsory labour was enforced. In Usambara local officials introduced the 'Wilhelmstal system'—by which Africans had to work for one month in every four either on a plantation, of their own choice, or on public works. Certain tribes, however, were exempt from this obligation.

Despite the slow pacification of the colony and the difficulties encountered in promoting its economic expansion, something was done for African welfare. Efforts were made to improve the standard of farming. Agricultural experts, trained in Germany at the Witzenhausen Colonial College, tried to persuade the Africans to use ploughs instead of hoes. They distributed seeds in the villages in the hope of extending the range of crops grown on native farms. In 1902 in the District of Dar es Salaam every *jumbe* was ordered to lay out a common field in his

---

[1] The Amani Institute soon became a 'tropical scientific institute superior to anything in the British colonies and protectorates and comparable with Pusa in India or the Dutch establishment at Buitenzorg in Java' (*Report of the East Africa Commission*, Cmd. 2387 (1925), p. 86).

village, and all the male inhabitants not in European employment had to work in this field twenty-four days in the year. The
total area of these village plantations was 1,200 hectares at the
end of 1905.

The missionaries played an important part in promoting
native welfare and education. English Protestant missionaries
had been first in the field—the Universities Mission for Central
Africa (Usambara 1860), the Church Missionary Society (1876),
and the London Missionary Society (1879). The first German
Protestant Society began its work in 1887. But it was the
Catholics who were the most active. The Fathers of the Holy
Ghost had established a missionary station at Bagamoyo in
1869, and the French Cardinal Lavigerie had sent the 'White
Fathers' to work in the region of the great lakes in 1878.

A start was made in the provision of educational facilities.
On the coast the Muslims had their own 'Koran schools' in
which pupils were taught to read and write Swahili in Arabic
characters. The Administration realized that some Africans
would have to become proficient both in Swahili (in Latin
characters) and in arithmetic so that they could become clerks
in local government offices, on the railways, and on plantations.
Herr Barth took charge of a new school at Tanga in 1893 and
three years later he had ninety-four pupils. In outlying districts
he established junior schools in charge of African teachers. In
1903 there were 8 government schools (5 white and 16 native
teachers and 1,142 pupils), 12 schools run by the local authorities (1 white master, 18 native teachers, and 417 pupils) and
15 missionary schools.

Many Germans were disappointed at the slow progress of
their East African colony in the five years of company rule and
in the first sixteen years of Reich administration. Reasons for
this somewhat tardy development are not far to seek. The
influence of the Sultan of Zanzibar on the coast and the presence
of many warlike tribes in the interior made it necessary to
undertake military operations against the Arabs, the Hehe, and
other opponents of German rule. The Maji-Maji rising showed
that even in 1906 the natives in a third of the territory were
still prepared to fight their white overlords. It was many years
before the evil effects of the slave trade were eradicated. Moreover, the territory was not favoured by nature, since large tracts

suffered from drought and both Africans and their cattle were infected by tropical diseases.

In addition, the Germans made mistakes. At first some of the officials treated Africans cruelly. The founder of the colony set the worst possible example in this respect. In 1896 the Socialist deputy August Bebel told the Reichstag that Carl Peters had been guilty of great cruelty when he was Reich Commissioner in the Kilimanjaro region in 1891–2. It was said that he had ordered the hanging of a native servant called Mabruk for petty theft. Influential friends had long shielded Peters from such attacks, but now the charges could not be ignored. Peters appeared before a disciplinary court, which decided that the case against him in the matter of Mabruk had been proved. He was also found guilty of dereliction of duty on various occasions and of 'conduct unworthy of his official position'. Carl Peters was dismissed from the Colonial Service and deprived of his title and pension. The court of appeal confirmed the sentence and ordered Peters to pay the costs of the hearings.[1]

The case of Carl Peters was only one of many colonial scandals that caused public concern in Germany. The Maji-Maji rising in East Africa, following so soon upon the revolts of the Bondel-swarts and Herero in South-West Africa, suggested that there was something fundamentally wrong in Germany's administration of her overseas possessions. Colonial policy was a leading issue at the Reichstag general election of January 1907. The (Catholic) Centre party—hitherto a supporter of Chancellor Bülow's right wing bloc in the Reichstag—joined the Socialists in criticizing colonial scandals. Since the Socialists lost thirty-eight seats Bülow claimed a victory at the elections. But he could not ignore the fact that the Centre had gained five seats and that there was a widespread demand for a reform in colonial administration.[2] The paradoxical result of this election was that (to a great extent) the colonial policy advocated by the opposition was the one subsequently followed by the Government.

[1] For the judgements see *Die Urteile der Disziplinargerichte gegen Dr. Carl Peters*, (1907). For a defence of Carl Peters see W. von Kardorff, *Bebel oder Peters. Die Amtstätigkeit des Kaiserlichen Kommissars Dr. Carl Peters am Kilimanjaro 1891 – 2* (Berlin, 1907). In 1907 the Kaiser allowed Peters to resume the use of his title (Reich Commissioner) and in 1914 restored his pension.

[2] See G. D. Crothers, *The German Elections of 1907* (Columbia, New York, 1941).

The era of reform, 1907–14

The year 1906 was a turning-point in the history of German East Africa. In the early years of German rule progress was slow owing to the hostility of native tribes, lack of funds, and faults in administration. But the period 1907–14 was a peaceful era of reform and economic expansion. The colonies were now controlled by a Ministry of State. Dr. Bernhard Dernburg, the last Director of the Colonial Section of the Foreign Office, became the first Colonial Minister.[1] He opposed the ruthless exploitation of the material and human resources of overseas territories for the benefit of a few Europeans.[2] He cautiously approached the principles of the 'Dual Mandate'—based upon the idea that 'Europe is in Africa for the mutual benefit of her industrial classes and of the native races in their progress to a higher plane'.[3] Dernburg secured increased colonial grants from the Reichstag, persuaded capitalists to invest money in the overseas possessions, and gave every encouragement to such important organizations as the Hamburg Colonial Institute and the Hamburg Institute of Tropical Medicine.

What Dr. Dernburg preached in Germany, Rechenberg practised in East Africa. Rechenberg (1906–12) was a different type of governor from his predecessors, who had been professional soldiers. He was a Catholic aristocrat of autocratic temperament but progressive views. An extremely able administrator, he knew the colony well, since he had served there as a judge (1893) and had also been German Consul in Zanzibar (1896–1900). He had mastered the Swahili language. Rechenberg believed that the interests of the native inhabitants should not be subordinated to those of the white settlers. He strongly opposed the indiscriminate use of the whip and insisted that corporal punishment should be inflicted only by due process of law. Rechenberg promoted the extension of native health and

---

[1] Dr. Dernburg was a banker who had acquired the nickname of 'the Sanitary Officer' because of his skill in putting on their feet companies which were in financial difficulties.

[2] See B. Dernburg in *Die deutschen Kapitalinteressen in den deutschen Schutzgebieten (ohne Kiaochau). Grösse, Stand und Rentabilität* (Berlin, 1906) and *Die finanzielle Entwicklung der deutschen Schutzgebiete (ohne Kiaochau)* (Berlin, 1906); also *Koloniale Erziehung* (Berlin, 1907); *Koloniale Finanzprobleme* (Berlin, 1907); *Koloniale Lehrjahre* (Stuttgart, 1907); and *Zielpunkte des deutschen Kolonialwesens* (Berlin, 1907).

[3] F. D. Lugard, *The Dual Mandate in British Tropical Africa* (Edinburgh, 1922), p. 617.

education services and fostered scientific advance in tropical
agriculture to benefit native cultivators.

Rechenberg faced opposition from planters, who regarded
his native policy as a diabolical attempt to put them out of
business. He made no effort to placate those who disagreed
with him. His haughty bearing and sarcastic tongue made him
many enemies. He has been described as a 'passionate hater'.
The ruthlessness with which he pursued those who stood in
his way may be illustrated from his dealings with the local
press. He tried to cripple the *Deutsche Ost-Afrikanische Zeitung*
of Dar es Salaam by withdrawing all official advertisements
and announcements. He put the *Usambara Post* out of business
for a time by forbidding the government school at Tanga to
print it.[1]

The issue between Rechenberg and the settlers was whether
the territory should develop as a 'commercial' or a 'plantation'
colony. When Rechenberg first served in German East Africa
it had been a 'commercial' colony and had exported native
products. This type of colonial economy was favoured not only
by Rechenberg but by men like Dernburg (the Colonial
Minister) and Walther Rathenau (who visited the territory in
1907). They believed that the natives—and also the old-
established German trading and shipping firms—would benefit
more from a 'commercial' than from a 'plantation' economy.
Their objection to a 'plantation' colony was that European
estates would attract native workers to districts far from their
homes and that consequently the existing tribal organization
would be disrupted. They feared that a black proletariat would
develop as a new depressed social class on the plantations.
Rechenberg proposed to raise the standard of living of the
Africans, to maintain their economic independence, and to
preserve their tribal structure by encouraging them to grow on
their own lands products suitable for the European market.
They would benefit from such a policy and the Reich would
gain increased supplies of tropical products.[2] Moreover, if the

---

[1] For Rechenberg's dealings with the press see H. Pfeiffer, *Bwana Gazetti. Als
Journalist in Ostafrika* (Berlin, 1933), and D. Redeker, *Journalismus in Deutsch-
Ostafrika* (Frankfurt A/M, 1933).

[2] For this point of view see Walther Rathenau, 'Erwägungen über die Erschliessung des Deutsch-Ostafrikanischen Schutzgebietes' (memorandum of 15 Nov. 1907
to Dr. Dernburg) in W. Rathenau, *Reflexionen* (1909), pp. 143–98.

Africans became more prosperous they would purchase more goods made by German firms.

Rechenberg's critics argued that his policy failed to take into account the changes which had occurred in the colony since the 1890's. In Usambara several plantations had now been established. More would be set up when the northern railway was extended to Moshi. White settlers were making permanent homes for themselves in East Africa. Paul Rohrbach and others who favoured the development of a 'plantation' colony argued that the Reich required territories in which Germans could settle permanently under their own flag. A purely 'commercial' colony could not meet this need. They considered that native labour should be made available so that more European estates could be established and new immigrants could be attracted. Rohrbach argued that Africans should be made to work either by direct compulsion, by levying a poll-tax, or by increasing the hut tax.[1]

The controversy came to a head on the question of native labour. There was an acute shortage of labour in the territory at this time. The sending of prisoners taken in the Maji-Maji rising to the coastal towns and to the Usambara plantations did not long satisfy the insatiable demand for labour. Indian merchants sought porters to transport their goods; planters needed labourers on their estates; contractors could not build railways, harbours and other public works without native labour. Employers wanted to expand the labour force by compelling or persuading Africans to seek employment on plantations or public works. Governor Rechenberg tried to prevent this by refusing to levy a poll-tax or to extend the 'Wilhelmstal system' of forced labour. Consequently there was severe competition between employers for the services of available workers. Yet Rechenberg himself wanted to secure native labour for public works sponsored by the Administration. One unfortunate result of this situation was the emergence of a black market in labour. Unscrupulous agents used dubious methods to persuade Africans to sign labour contracts. Some of the Governor's critics alleged that Rechenberg's strict enforcement of the labour

[1] For this point of view see Paul Rohrbach, *Deutsche Kolonialwirtschaft: kulturpolitische Grundsätze für die Rassen- und Missionsfragen*, Berlin (1909) and Rohrbach's articles in the *Preussische Jahrbücher*, vol. cxxxv (1909), 'Ostafrikanische Studien', pt. i, pp. 82–107; pt. ii, pp. 276–317.

laws actually encouraged the rise of a new 'slave trade'. The number of native wage-earners increased from 70,000 in 1909–10 to 172,000 in 1912–13.[1]

There were also complaints of alleged short-sighted parsimony on the part of the Administration in Rechenberg's day. The closing of a school for European children at Dar es Salaam, for example, led to many protests. Rechenberg thought that the school was too small to justify further expenditure of public money on it. His opponents argued that German officials, professional men, and merchants in the capital of the colony had a right to expect the Administration to maintain a school for white children. In 1908 the Reichstag budget commission recommended the reopening of the school. In 1914 there were forty pupils in attendance.

A more serious controversy arose over the future of the Defence Force. Without consulting its commander the Governor suggested to the Colonial Office that there should be a reduction in the size of the Defence Force which would have involved cutting the number of white officers from 131 to 104. There was a storm of protest in the colony at this ill-advised effort to save a little money. The Europeans had vivid memories of the Maji-Maji rising, when the military and police forces had, at first, been far too small to cope with the emergency and when the flames from burning villages and crops could be seen from Dar es Salaam. Rechenberg lost the support of the officers of the Defence Force who had been almost his only friends among the Germans living in the colony. When the matter was raised in the Reichstag Dernburg bowed to the storm and stated that no reduction in the size of the Defence Force would be made. On the outbreak of the first world war Germany's enemies declared that the Reich had long contemplated aggression in Africa and had militarized the natives for that purpose. In fact only a few years before the war there had been attempts to cut down the size of the Defence Force not only in East Africa but in South-west Africa as well. This can hardly be regarded as the action of a potential aggressor.[2]

[1] These figures are taken from the official annual reports of the German Colonial Office. Each report covered a period of twelve months running from April in one year to April in the next year.

[2] The official British military history of the campaigns in German East Africa between 1914 and 1918 points out that in neighbouring British territories 'a similar

Other aspects of the Administration's native policy aroused less controversy. The missionary societies were encouraged to expand their educational work and the Government itself opened some new schools.[1] In 1911 the Catholic and Protestant missions were each responsible for the elementary education of 30,000 pupils, the Administration had 3,500 pupils in its elementary schools, while 2,500 were receiving a more advanced education in senior or trade schools. By 1914 the Administration was able to conduct much of its correspondence with village headmen in Swahili. A British official stated in 1921 that, owing to education they had received from the Germans, 'the degree of usefulness to the administration of the natives of Tanganyika Territory is in advance of that which we have been accustomed to associate with British African protectorates'.[2] The work of the missionaries in other fields was expanding. In 1909 the Catholics ran sixty-seven stations in the colony and claimed to have made nearly 39,000 converts. Protestant missionaries, with seventy-three stations, had over 11,000 converts.[3] Missionaries and the Administration shared in the task of improving the deplorably low standard of native health. Vaccination against smallpox was carried out on a large scale. One of the greatest achievements of the Germans in the field of tropical medicine was Dr. Koch's discovery of a remedy (*atoxyl*) for sleeping sickness which helped to check this scourge of East Africa.

It was left to Heinrich Schnee, who became Governor in July 1912, to effect a real improvement in the relations between the Administration and the settlers. His success was due partly to the fact that the controversy concerning East Africa's future had lost some of its former significance. Recent expansion in the number of plantations and white settlers had made it obvious that although the territory might for a long time be

tendency was marked by a reduction of military expenditure, which resulted in the disbandment of one of the four battalions of the King's African Rifles'. C. Hordern, *Military Operations: East Africa*, i (London, 1941), 9.

[1] R. H. Harris, 'Education in East Africa: the German system outlined', in the *Empire Review*, xx. 117 (1910), 185–90, and Martin Schlunk, *Das Schulwesen in den deutschen Schutzgebieten* (Hamburg, 1914).

[2] Quoted by R. L. Buell, *The Native Problem in Africa* (2 vols., London, 1928), i. 478.

[3] See Carl Mirbt, *Mission und Kolonialpolitik in den deutschen Schutzgebieten* (Tübingen, 1910), pp. 68–70.

mainly a commercial colony there were, nevertheless, regions in the healthier parts of the territory where permanent European estates had come to stay. The problem now was to reconcile the legitimate aspirations of the white settlers with an enlightened native policy. Governor Schnee accepted the fact that in Usambara and some other districts a plantation economy was in existence, but he was not, on that account, prepared to reverse Rechenberg's policy of protecting the traditional African tribal life. But he was much more tactful than his predecessor in carrying out measures which were inevitably still regarded with misgivings by the white settlers. He introduced a radical reform of the recruitment of native labour. Private recruiting was restricted and most labour contracts were now handled by public officials. In 1913 it was estimated that about 172,000 Africans were employed as wage-earners by Europeans, Indians, and Arabs. The largest groups were plantation workers (80,000), porters (20,000), employees of railway contractors and railway companies (21,000), employees of commercial firms (10,000), domestic servants (9,000), and *askari* serving in the Defence Force and the police (6,000). It may be added that Dr. Schnee recognized that the white settlers should have some say on how the colony was run. In the summer of 1913 he told the Advisory Council that in future half of its twenty members would be elected by white voters.

Despite labour difficulties, there was a considerable development of European plantations in the colony between 1906 and 1914. A sharp rise in rubber prices after 1905 encouraged white settlers to establish plantations of *manihot* rubber in the Tanga and Morogoro districts, and by 1910 some 250 rubber estates had been established. Rubber exports in 1911 were valued at 4,700,000 marks, of which three-quarters came from the plantations while one-quarter was collected by the natives. When the boom reached its climax in 1910 the owners of several large German plantations shrewdly sold their estates at high prices to English companies.[1] Overproduction in south-east Asia led to a collapse of the world price of rubber, and by 1913 it was

---

[1] The English companies were the East African Rubber Plantations Co. Ltd. (1909); Manihot Rubber Plantations Ltd., Muhesa Rubber Plantations Ltd., Mombo Rubber Plantation Ltd., Lew Rubber Estates Ltd., Kamna Rubber Estates Ltd., and Kigulu Rubber Estates Ltd.

clear that virtually all the rubber plantations in the colony were doomed.[1]

The production of sisal hemp—exports were valued at 4,500,000 marks in 1911—was equally important. By 1910 there were fifty-four sisal plantations in German East Africa. The larger producers included the *Sisal-Agaven-Gesellschaft* of Düsseldorf and the *Deutsche Agaven Gesellschaft* of Berlin.[2] This eventually became a great staple crop. Great efforts were made to extend the cultivation of cotton, particularly in the valley of the Rufiji river, but only a modest measure of success was attained. Experimental stations were established both by the Colonial Economic Committee and by the Administration. In 1910 there were seventeen cotton plantations in the colony, but exports in 1912 amounted to only 1,844 tons, valued at 2,000,000 marks.[3] The production of coffee—the most important plantation crop in the Usambara District in the 1890's —declined in the early twentieth century. The number of trees in that region sank from 6,500,000 in 1900 to 4,700,000 in 1907. Coffee culture survived only on small plantations and as a secondary crop on some of the bigger estates. By 1913 three-quarters of the coffee exported was grown by Africans in the Bukoba District. Native farmers in the coastal regions were responsible for the bulk of the colony's exports of copra (dried coco-nut kernels), which were valued at 1,600,000 marks (1912). The natives of the Mwanza District produced three-quarters of the ground-nuts which were exported. The nuts were sent to Mombasa by the Uganda Railway.

In million marks

	1906	1907	1908	1909	1910	1911	1912
Imports	25·2	23·8	25·8	33·9	38·7	45·9	50·3
Exports	11·0	12·5	10·9	13·1	20·8	22·4	31·4
	36·2	36·3	37·7	47·0	59·5	68·3	81·7

[1] Albrecht Zimmermann, *Der Manihot-Kautschuk* (Jena, 1913). See also G. F. Sayers (ed.), *The Handbook of Tanganyika* (London, 1930), p. 216.

[2] W. F. Bruck, *Die Sisalkultur in Deutsch-Ostafrika* (Berlin, 1913).

[3] K. Supf, *Deutsche Kolonial-Baumwolle . . . 1900 — 8* (Berlin, 1909); M. Schanz, *Cotton Growing in German Colonies* (Manchester, 1910); Albrecht Zimmermann, *Anleitung zur Baumwollkultur in den deutschen Kolonien*, 2nd edn. (1910); and the official report, *Die Baumwollfrage* (Veröffentlichungen des Reichskolonialamtes, no. i, Jena, 1911), pp. 115–19.

The table on page 153 shows how the trade of German East Africa expanded between 1906 and 1912.[1]

Improved communications fostered the economic development of the colony. The tempo of railway construction increased after 1906. A short 45 km. extension of the Usambara Railway from Mombo to Buiko was opened in July 1909. After Lindequist (Under-Secretary for the Colonies) had visited Usambara and reported favourably on its prospects as a region for white settlement the Reichstag agreed to pay for the further extension of this railway (1910). The line was continued to New Moshi at the foot of Mount Kilimanjaro and was opened to traffic in February 1912. The length of the whole railway was 352 km. A short narrow-gauge branch line from Tengeni to Sigi provided a useful link between the Usambara Railway and the Amani Institute. Built by the Sigi Export Company, it was later acquired by the German Timber Company. When Dernburg opened the Dar es Salaam–Morogoro section of the Central Railway in 1907 he announced that the line would be extended to Tabora. This section was opened by the Governor on 27 July 1912. The final section to Kigoma, near Ujiji on Lake Tanganyika, was completed in March 1914. The length of the Central Railway was 1,252 km. Plans to hold an exhibition at Dar es Salaam to celebrate the completion of this great enterprise had to be abandoned when war broke out in August 1914.[2]

The economic progress achieved by 1914 owed much to direct government support and encouragement. Of the two railways one was built and owned by the State, though operated by a private company, and the other would not have been constructed had the State not come forward with a guarantee of interest on its shares and the grant of substantial land concessions. The existence of a regular steamship service between Germany and her East African colony was assured by an annual government subsidy of £67,000 to the German East Africa shipping line. The growth of Dar es Salaam owed far more to the Administration than to private enterprise. The great public buildings and the new harbour had been con-

[1] Article on German East Africa by Hans Sache in P. Leutwein (ed.), *Dreissig Jahre deutsche Kolonialpolitik* (Berlin, 1914), p. 98.

[2] F. Baltzer, *Die Kolonialbahnen*, pp. 35–56.

structed by the State and the increase in the volume of trade passing through the port was due largely to considerable imports for the use of the civil administration and the military authorities. The planters were assisted by the world-famous Amani Institute on which the Government spent £10,000 a year. The production of cotton was fostered by a State guaranteed price and by the work of three government cotton institutes. The Administration was a large employer of native labour—*askari* in the Defence Force and police, minor posts in local government, and porters on the caravan routes.

In 1914 only thirty years had passed since Carl Peters had first set foot in East Africa. In that short period what had once seemed to be a singularly unpromising field for colonial expansion had been turned into a flourishing territory. A land which in the early 1880's had suffered seriously from the curse of the slave trade and had been rent by continual tribal wars was now a peaceful colony with an expanding economy. Considerable success had attended the efforts of the Germans to build up again the economy of the southern part of the territory, which had suffered severely from the effects of the Maji-Maji rising of 1905. In 1913 the white population amounted to 5,336, of whom 4,107 were Germans. There were 882 planters and settlers. Striking progress had been made in the study of tropical agriculture and tropical medicine. The Administration had learned much from the mistakes of the past and was fully aware of its responsibilities towards the country's native inhabitants.

The campaign in German East Africa, 1914–18[1]

The outbreak of war in 1914 brought to an end the peaceful evolution of German East Africa. The British navy com-

---

[1] For the East Africa campaign see Hordern, op. cit., vol. i, *1914–16*; F. Brett Young, *Marching on Tanga: with General Smuts in East Africa* (London, 1919) [new edn. 1938]; J. H. V. Crowe, *General Smuts' Campaign in East Africa* (London, 1918); C. P. Fendall, *The East African Force 1915–1919* (1921); W. Arning, *Vier Jahre Weltkrieg in Ostafrika* (Hanover, 1919); L. Deppe, *Mit Lettow-Vorbeck durch Afrika* (Berlin, 1919); H. Schnee, *Deutsch-Ostafrika im Weltkriege* (Leipzig, 1919); P. von Lettow-Vorbeck, *My Reminiscences of East Africa* (London, 1920); and C. J. Thornhill, *Taking Tanganyika* (London, 1937). For the naval operations see J. S. Corbett, *Naval Operations* (London, 1920–31), ii. 236–9 and iii. 63–67; E. Keble Chatterton, *The 'Königsberg' Adventure* (London, 1932); and Max Looff, *Kreuzerfahrt und Buschkampf. Mit S. M. S. Königsberg in Deutsch-Ostafrika* (Berlin, 1929).

manded the seas and the colony was cut off from Germany. No reinforcements or supplies could reach the territory. Lettow-Vorbeck, the Commander of the small Defence Force, appreciated that it would be impossible to stop the British and their allies from overrunning the territory if they wished to do so. He saw that his policy must be to conduct the military operations in such a way as to keep as many enemy troops engaged in German East Africa for as long a period as possible. Colonial campaigns were 'side-shows' which hardly affected the main struggle in Europe. The Allied forces that Lettow-Vorbeck kept occupied in East Africa could not be used on the Western front. Lettow-Vorbeck achieved his aim. He claimed that 130 generals and 300,000 men were used against him. British casualties alone amounted to 967 officers and 17,650 other ranks. In a single action—the battle of Mahina (October 1917)—there were 2,700 British casualties.

Lettow-Vorbeck commanded a Defence Force of some 2,000 *askari* led by 260 German commissioned and non-commissioned officers. As a reserve he drew upon the police force (2,000 men) and the 3,000 German residents and visitors in the colony. He soon took the offensive on the Kilimanjaro front by seizing Taveta and raiding the Uganda Railway. The British, fearing that Mombasa itself might be in danger, counter-attacked by sending an Anglo-Indian expedition of 8,000 men to make an assault by sea on the port of Tanga. Lettow-Vorbeck ambushed the invaders and decisively defeated them (November 1914). In 1915 the British and their allies made elaborate preparations to mount a great offensive against German East Africa and overwhelm Lettow-Vorbeck by sheer weight of numbers. A railway line was built from Voi (on the Uganda Railway) to Taveta to facilitate the movement of men and supplies. Lettow-Vorbeck prepared to meet the offensive by improving the lines of communication from the Central Railway to the Kilimanjaro front. On the Morogoro–Mombo–Korogwe route alone at least 8,000 native porters were continuously employed.

In March 1916 General Smuts, appointed to the command of the British forces in East Africa, launched his offensive. His first objective was to drive the enemy out of the Usambara plantation region, to seize the Usambara Railway and the port of Tanga, and so to remove all danger of a German attack on

British East Africa. His second objective was to advance southwards, to capture the Central Railway, and to cut the German
communications between Dar es Salaam and the interior.

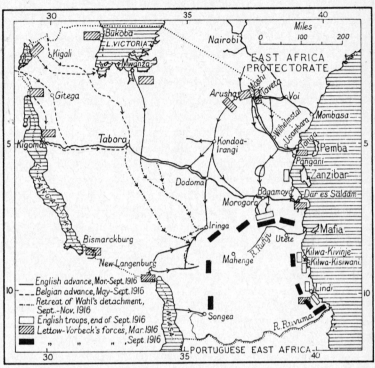

MAP 3. THE CONQUEST OF GERMAN EAST AFRICA

Smuts broke through the Latema–Reata Pass and seized New
Moshi—the terminus of the Usambara Railway—on 13 March.
He then advanced along the railway and the River Ruvu
(Pangani) and drove the Germans out of the principal area of
white settlement in German East Africa. His troops seized the
Usambara plantations and so dealt a severe blow to the economy
of the colony. Meanwhile van Deventer's mounted division had
captured Kondoa Irangi at the end of April. Smuts then took
Handeni and threatened to cut the Central Railway at Moro-
goro. Lettow-Vorbeck took up a position in the forests of the
Nguru mountains. Smuts and Brits resumed the offensive in

August and tried to encircle Lettow-Vorbeck's troops at Kanga, but the Germans slipped out of the net and retired on Morogoro. Once more Smuts tried to encircle his elusive foe and once more Lettow-Vorbeck escaped to a new position, this time on the River Ruvu (Kingani), which held for the remainder of 1916. In the autumn the British seized all the most important parts of the colony, while a Belgian force captured Tabora and so completed the Allied control of the Central Railway.

By his offensive of 1916 Smuts had established control over 85 per cent. of the territory and 90 per cent. of the native population. The capital, the coast, and the great lakes were all in Allied hands. The Germans had lost the ports, the railways, and the main plantations. They were confined to the southern part of the territory which only ten years previously had been the scene of the Maji-Maji rising. It was an inhospitable, unhealthy, and thinly populated region where food and porters were difficult to find. Yet Lettow-Vorbeck, still accompanied by Governor Schnee, was able to hold out in the winter of 1916–17. In 1917, however, the Germans were cleared out of the last corner of the colony. They fought rearguard actions with great skill, but they were far too weak to prevent the steady advance of their enemies.

Lettow-Vorbeck refused to surrender, for he was determined to pursue his policy of keeping as many enemy troops in the field as possible. During nearly the whole of the year 1917 he held on tenaciously to the last corner of the colony and fought rearguard actions with great determination. One of these battles, the four-day action at Mahina in the middle of October, has been described as 'one of the biggest engagements ever fought on African soil from the point of view of casualties on both sides'. 'The British lost 2,700 casualties out of a total strength of 4,900 infantry employed.'[1] At the end of November 1917, however, Lettow-Vorbeck had to leave German territory. He crossed the River Ruvuma and invaded Mozambique with a force of 278 Europeans, 16,000 *askari*, and 4,000 porters. He remained in the Portuguese colony for ten months, living on the territory and supplementing his diminishing stock of arms and ammunition with loot seized from the Portuguese. Then he returned to German East Africa, and finally invaded Northern

[1] W. D. Downes, *With the Nigerians in German East Africa* (London, 1919), p. 226.

Rhodesia, where news of the armistice of 11 November 1918 at last brought the campaign to an end. Friend and foe recognized in Lettow-Vorbeck a master of bush warfare.

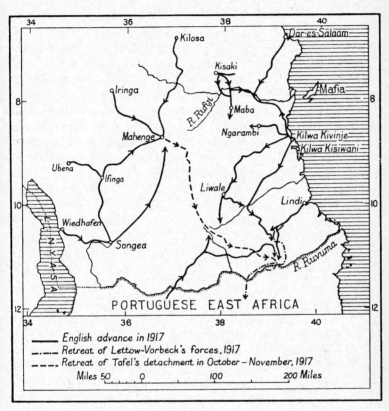

MAP 4. THE CONQUEST OF GERMAN EAST AFRICA: THE CAMPAIGN OF 1917

A factor which contributed to the prolonged resistance of the Germans in East Africa was the unexpected resilience of the colony during the war. It might have been anticipated that a territory which had been under European control for only thirty years and had therefore not had sufficient time to develop industries of its own could not long survive if it were cut off completely from the mother country. Blockaded by sea and virtually surrounded by hostile British and Belgian territories,

German East Africa was left entirely to its own resources in 1914. Yet until the opening of Smuts's offensive in the spring of 1916, the normal activities of the civilian administration functioned smoothly, and, in addition, the exceptional measures necessary to defend the territory were successfully carried out.

The civil and military authorities in German East Africa showed great resourcefulness in solving the numerous problems with which they were faced on the outbreak of war.[1] They had to provide food, clothing, arms, and medical supplies for the troops while still leaving the civilian population (white and black) sufficient supplies for their needs. In August 1914 there were unusually large stocks of European foods and other supplies in Dar es Salaam in readiness for an exhibition which had been planned to celebrate the opening of the Central Railway. It was found that except in the district of Lindi there were adequate surpluses of corn and cattle which could be purchased from the natives and sent to the troops. It was not easy to send supplies from the Central Railway to the troops stationed in the Kilimanjaro region, since no railways or roads were available. Nearly all the supplies had to be carried by porters from Tabora to Mwanza, from Dodoma to New Moshi, and from Morogoro to Korogwe. On the Korogwe route alone 8,000 porters were regularly employed. A narrow-gauge trolley line was constructed between Handeni and Mombo, and this speeded up the transit of goods from the Central Railway to the Usambara Railway. Owing to the failure of the harvest in the northern districts in 1915, the troops on the Kilimanjaro front faced a shortage of food early in 1916. Some 20,000 additional porters were hastily recruited. About 2,000 died, as they were not supplied with sufficient blankets.

The provisioning of the European population also raised serious problems, since no food could now be imported from Europe or from India. In districts served by the Central Railway, wheat, potatoes, and coffee were grown on plantations in place of crops usually grown for export. Considerable ingenuity was shown in producing in the colony manufactured goods and medical supplies normally imported from Europe.

[1] See W. O. Henderson, 'The war economy of German East Africa, 1914–1917', *Economic History Review*, xiii (1943), 104–10.

Quinine was made at the Amani Institute and at Mpwapwa. Cloth, for garments and bandages, was woven by hand. Footwear was made by native artisans. Dye-stuffs were made from native barks. In the first eighteen months of the war the Amani Agricultural Research Institute

prepared for use from its own products 16 varieties of foodstuffs and liquors, 11 varieties of spices, 12 varieties of medicines and medicaments, 5 varieties of rubber products, 2 of soap, oils and candles, 3 of materials used in making boats, and 10 miscellaneous substances. Many of these were prepared in comparatively large quantities, e.g. 15,200 bottles of whisky and other alcoholic liquors, 10,252 lb. of chocolate and cocoa, 2,652 parcels of toothpowder, 10,000 pieces of soap, 300 bottles of castor oil etc.[1]

The long drawn-out conflict inflicted serious damage on the colony. German settlers left their plantations to join the Defence Force. Those who survived the campaign became prisoners of war and were eventually expelled from the territory. During the war years many of their estates fell into decay. Large numbers of Africans were conscripted by both sides to act as porters, and their fields were neglected. The output of staple crops declined. Owing to the blockade, overseas trade came to an end.

German officials were interned, and the smooth functioning of the civil administration gave way to the makeshift arrangements of Allied military control. The work of the German missionaries was seriously hampered and eventually they had to leave the territory. The native labour force was depleted and scattered. Communications were disrupted and internal commerce was disorganized. Scientific and welfare services virtually came to an end.

In some districts there was a sharp decline in population. The fall in the Lindi District has been ascribed to a decline in the birth-rate due to the increase in venereal diseases. In the districts of Dodoma and Kondoa-Irangi the decline was due to a famine in 1919.[2]

---

[1] *Report of the East Africa Commission*, Cmd. 2387 (1925), p. 86.
[2] *Report on the 1921 Census of the Native Population of the Tanganyika Territory* (Dar es Salaam, 1921). The report states that the *total* population of the territory was the same in 1921 as it had been in 1913.

Seven years after the end of the first world war the East Africa Commission reported that 'the task of restoring the wreckage of war has now been largely completed, but in such matters as education, medical work and scientific research the pre-war standard has not yet been reached'.[1]

[1] *Report of the East Africa Commission*, Cmd. 2387, p. 127.

IV

(II) GERMAN EAST AFRICA
CHANGES IN AFRICAN LIFE UNDER GERMAN ADMINISTRATION
1892–1914

O. F. RAUM

Checks on instability

SOME of the peoples whom the first European visitors met in East Africa were conglomerations of clans. Already in the fifteenth century Vasco da Gama described the islamized Swahili as tribeless and chiefless. The Zaramo had the tradition of two leading clans, the Shomvi at the coast and the Pazi in the hills. In the interior the Iramba (Nilyamba) were made up of matrilineal clans forming separate territorial units and for that reason without a common political head. Later some of these people claimed to have had rulers in the past, but presumably this was a political projection because under European occupation the lack of a chief proved to be a handicap. Even the prevailing evolutionary school of anthropology tended to stigmatize chiefless peoples as retarded. Their scientific rehabilitation was due to the functional anthropologists of the 1930's who discovered that the organization of joint activities and the maintenance of 'public order' was possible without chiefs. The chiefless Digo, for instance, had evolved a council to take care of 'civil and criminal' cases. Membership in the council was purchased by the payment of fees in kind, the larger the fee the higher the rank, of which eight were distinguished. The council affixed taboo marks to coco-palms to prevent the theft of nuts. If their judgement, arrived at in secret session, was not accepted by the litigants, a fight between the two parties was allowed on the payment of a fee.

[The author wishes to acknowledge, besides the works cited in the footnotes and bibliography, his debt to unpublished memoranda kindly supplied to him by the Rev. O. Gemuseus, Dr. Th. Gunzert, Pater Ignotus, the Rev. E. Ittameier, Pater O. Meers, H. Mostertz and the Rev. F. Wärthl.]

Most East African peoples possessed a political superstructure over the kinship organization. The factor making for political concentration was not consciousness of cultural or linguistic unity but individual leadership. The unification of clans was sometimes brought about by a stranger, who as arbiter in local quarrels enjoyed certain advantages, by successful war leaders, or smiths, formidable as weapon-makers. The magical control of rain-makers, the religious nimbus of the priest, likewise predestined them for tribal leadership. A leader's helpers, once power had been won, tended to act as checks upon the authority won for him. His foremost supporters, his kin whether patrilineal or matrilineal, insisted on sharing the top position and controlling the chief's action in it when ascendancy over other clans had been achieved. A similar development took place when a leader's contemporaries had assisted him to power. They were determined to be heard in decisions affecting peace and war and to share in the booty taken in raids. The elders formed the third constitutional prop to and check upon a successful tribal head. They represented the clans or genealogical units, and the districts or territorial divisions.

The process of the formation of tribes was rarely a peaceful one. Force was also necessary to maintain the tribe against competitors. Much of the history of East Africa in the nineteenth century is a story of internecine struggles between rival chiefdoms within larger linguistic-cultural units, as the cases of the Nyamwezi, Chagga, Gogo, and others show. The rise of even more powerful supra-tribal units, such as the Ngoni kingdoms or Mirambo's 'empire', was accelerated by the sale of slaves and ivory for guns and powder. These mushroom kingdoms often broke up upon the death of their founder. Their subject groups resumed their independent existence, returned to a former allegiance, or formed new associations.

Military victory did not always result in the incorporation of the defeated. The predatory economy of the Masai made them harvest the stock of their neighbours at intervals, but they left them unmolested otherwise. Among agricultural tribes the usual aim was to subject neighbours to tributary status. The necessary political control was often achieved by appointing rivals of the defeated chief from among his own brothers or cousins within the succession. Where the conquered area was large a complex territorial organization was needed: the Hehe appointed district headmen, 'governors' of frontier areas, and garrison commanders. In situations where the exploitation of the enemy's manpower seemed desirable, war aims might include the extermination of the leadership of the enemy (as happened in the sanguinary struggles between Hehe and Ngoni), the destruction of his economic resources (e.g. the cutting down of banana groves among the Chagga), and the crippling of his military potential (by the slaughter of his warriors as in the wars between Sangu and Nyika). Where wars resulted in the incorporation by the victors of population groups, cultural enclaves were created without difficulty. Political control set up structural relations which—given the close relationship of Bantu languages and cultures—tended to bring about cultural and linguistic assimilation.

'Aping' of powerful war-like tribes by their weaker neighbours had two motives: it protected the imitators against molestation and helped in terrorizing unsuspecting neighbours. The Sangu were imitators of the Hehe, and the Hehe in turn had learned a lot from the Ngoni. With the external trappings some of the ideas and spirit of the imitated passed over to their imitators. The neighbours of the Masai adopted their age-set system, military vocabulary, and, to some extent, their fighting *élan*. The direction of assimilation was not always from the weaker to the more powerful, as the example of the adoption of Bantu speech by the Hamitic Tusi shows. The cultural conservatism ascribed to the Africans in the twentieth century did not exist in the nineteenth. They were characterized by a decided cultural lability. Under the existing conditions of instability the association between social structure and economic system proved to be particularly loose. After the rinderpest had decimated their herds some nomadic Masai turned hunters like their congeners, the Ndorobo, before them. Masai married to Bantu women did not consider it beneath their dignity to settle with their peasant in-laws. A few Masai even became traders, taking ivory on donkeys to the coast. Large contingents of Masai, outnumbering the local people, settled on the early mission stations. Some of the first Christians were from this tribe, which a decade later resisted the teaching of both Muhammad and Christ. Adaptive ability was not restricted to the Nilo-Hamites. Some

Ngoni and Hehe sections did not take up war; some Tusi owned
no herds and had become agriculturalists.

The comparative weakness of the tribal structure at the time
of the arrival of the Europeans was accentuated by three factors
—Islam, slavery, and porterage. Their joint effect was to take a
large proportion of Africans out of their clan and tribal context,
to place them in unfamiliar environments, and thus to strengthen
an individualizing tendency which was absent in the home
society. For this reason the first colonial agents found ready
collaboration in the tribes affected.

Islam had been active as a detribalizing force at the coast
since the ninth century. Through intermarriage of Arabs with
the indigenous population the Swahili people had been formed.
A Swahili proper was born of Swahili parents, read and wrote
Arabic, knew Arabic literature and law, attended the mosque,
and observed the Islamic fasts. Arab influence had changed
some Bantu kinship systems from matriliny to patriliny in
descent, inheritance, and succession. It had introduced a money
economy, promoted the cultivation of cash crops (e.g. coco-nut
and mango), and with it individual land tenure. Even the traditional division of labour was modified: at the coast agriculture
falls to the lot of the man. The absorptive power of Islam was
shown in the large number of 'acculturated' Swahili, i.e.
persons born of inland parents who had adopted the external
signs of Swahili culture: *kanzu* and fez, Swahili speech, the
knowledge of a few lines of the Koran, and circumcision. Of the
16,000 inhabitants of Dar es Salaam in 1903, three-quarters
were tribesmen from the interior. The attractions of the town
exposed them to external arabization.

The persuasiveness of Islam derived from a unique mixture of
tolerance and snobbishness. The islamized natives retained their
'superstitions'. The ethical demands of Islam fitted easily into
the kinship morality of the Africans, since polygyny was permitted. On the other hand, the Swahili certainly made his pagan
brethren feel the abysmal difference between him and them. He
alone claimed to possess *ustarabu*, the genteel manners and
values of Arab civilization. The pagan tribesmen were con-
temptible *washenzi*, 'uncouth, raw natives' or 'persons still under
tribal bondage', while the Swahili were *wangwana*, freemen, i.e.

not responsible to chiefs. The pressure of assimilation was felt not only at the coast but at all population centres which sprang up or expanded under the colonial régime. The *askari* garrison at Bukoba demanded to be circumcised *en bloc* because the arabized prostitutes would not cohabit with them. The most striking illustration of the weakness of tribal cohesion was the fact that although slave raids were organized by Arabs, the most capable of the kidnapped men were easily persuaded to join the ranks of the slavers and soon surpassed them in inhumanity. It must be noted that the reason why Islam was not propagated consistently in the interior was that a person who had become a Muslim could not, according to the *sharia*, be made a slave.

In the 1890's Islam was especially successful around Tanga and Lindi, where the depredations of Masai and Ngoni invasions had worked havoc with the social structure. In 1912, 21,680 Muslims were counted in the Dar es Salaam District, 13·4 per cent. of the population of 161,000. The total for the whole territory was given as 300,000. Missionary estimates were higher. Van der Burgt reckoned one million.[1]

The second detribalizing institution was slavery. In the subsistence economy of the Bantu a mild form of domestic slavery existed; slaves were kept to satisfy the cultural value of status expressed in the number of human dependants. In the cash economy of the Arabs slavery was stricter: they were kept for profit, but the state of unfreedom was circumscribed by the *sharia*. The state of slavery was commonly inherited, but since born slaves did not meet the demand, their number was replenished by capture through private slave-raiding or public war. Economic or debt slavery occurred in several forms; either through the pawning of dependants or for murder, theft, adultery, and witchcraft. The sale of children was customary during famine. A person could sell himself because he desired protection.

A slave lost the protection of his chief and his clan. The owner possessed the right of sale over his slaves, although this was not absolute, for under African law debt slaves were not disposed of. A slave was subject not to the chief but to his master as to

---

[1] *Jahresbericht über die Entwicklung der deutschen Schutzgebiete, 1912—13*; J. M. M. van der Burgt, 'Die Entvölkerung von Unyamwesi', *Koloniale Rundschau*, 1913–14; M. Klamroth, *Der Islam in Ostafrika* (Berlin, 1912).

liability for damage and representation in court. Slaves could not marry without the consent of their masters, and no bride-wealth or dowry was given unless the husband of a slave was a freeman, when the master, not the woman's kinship group, claimed the proceeds. Slaves, according to the *sharia*, could own no property, nor could they inherit it. The customary law was milder: they owned what they acquired; a slave could even own a slave in turn. Under the subsistence economy inland a slave received his food, clothes, and shelter; under cash economy at the coast some pocket money in addition. Slaves with their own household were either plantation workers whose wages consisted of a share of the crops, or semi-independent craftsmen and servants who paid a levy to their masters.

The effect of slavery on tribal structure is difficult to assess. A report for 1900, when government action had encouraged the release of a certain proportion of slaves, estimated that at the coast a fifth of the total population were slaves. The districts with high percentages were those with coco-nut and sugar plantations belonging to Arabs and Indians and where well-to-do Swahili also owned slaves. In Tabora, with its many Arab and Swahili residents, 67 per cent. of the population of the town (35,000) and district (100,000) were slaves.[1] The slave population of the coast drew from almost all tribes of the interior, but Yao, Nyamwezi, and Manyema (from the Congo) were pre-dominant. Of the inland tribes, the nomadic Nilo-Hamites had very few slaves. Only a few of the peaceful agricultural tribes had slavery, in the mild form of debt slavery. The martial tribes, such as Ngoni, Hehe, and Nyamwezi (under Mirambo), owned slaves recruited by raids upon their neighbours. Among the Hehe about 10 per cent. of the total population were at one time slaves.

Among the people who were levered out of the kinship group and tribe the caravan porters were the most picturesque. Cara-vans recruited their porters mainly from three peoples—Swahili, Nyamwezi, and Sukuma. The coastal porters were either free-men or slaves, and both put on airs over the robust inlanders whom they did not equal in either culture or courage. The Nyamwezi spent six months of the year at home. In April, having helped their women to till the fields, they moved off.

[1] See F. Weidner, *Die Haussklaverei in Ostafrika* (Jena, 1915), p. 50.

Some were engaged at Tabora to carry ivory to the coast for low wages and bad food. The majority marched to Bagamoyo carrying hoes for the purchase of victuals on the way. There Indian recruiters hired them out to Arab and white caravan-owners going inland. Nyamwezi porters did not serve beyond Tabora. From this town to Mwanza on Lake Victoria and Ujiji on Lake Tanganyika Sukuma were engaged, a people who had taken up porterage only in the late 1880's and were at first considered unsuitable. With them only young men went, and while with the Nyamwezi porterage was a long-standing tradition involving pride, skill, and adventure, the Sukuma appear to have taken up the work primarily as a means to earn a livelihood.

The leaders of the porters, the *wanyampara*, were self-made men of great physical strength endowed with moral stamina and a sense of justice. Famous leaders spent their best years on the caravan paths, passing from one expedition to another. Among the porters a shallow kind of specialization developed: there were cooks, tent boys, carriers, personal servants; selected men were trained as *askaris*. The caravan personnel formed a community of its own with its own interests and 'culture', expressed, for instance, in songs and stories. The women accompanying the porters were of very mixed origin. As soon as they left their tribes they gave up leather and bark-cloth to adopt the Swahili *kanga*, ear-ornaments, and way of dressing the hair. They also gave up the inland virtues of diligence and humility and the tribal ideal of child-bearing. In caravan marriages no bride-wealth or in-law obligations existed. Because of this, and the disproportion between men and women, the marriages were short-lived. Adultery, misconduct, and fights about women were common. The distinction between a temporary caravan wife and the permanent *bibi ya kitabu*, 'the registered wife', was sharp.

In another significant respect the Nyamwezi porter became detribalized. He learned to live in two economies—the subsistence economy which he helped each year to initiate by his physical labour and the wage economy on the march. For carrying a load from the coast to Tabora he received wages in kind to the value of 8–10 dollars. But his budgeting did not provide for savings for the journey home. He had to hire, jointly with two companions, a carrier for his wages in commodities. And the bulk of these were consumed in fertile Gogoland, where caravans were often held up for weeks and the Nyamwezi porters traditionally spent their wages in riotous living.

In 1890 the numbers of porters away from home were estimated to be a quarter of the male population of Unyamwezi. In 1892 100,000 porters arrived at Bagamoyo and departures reached the same figure. As the caravan trade declined, the numbers engaged fell rapidly. The porters from the interior who had become acquainted with Swahili culture, Islamic religion, and the first signs of European occupation, must have come back as 'sophisticated' men to their tribes, a source of annoyance to their chiefs, unless they brought guns, and of discomfort to their tribal wives.

The weakness of the indigenous political set-up was not the result of outside influences alone. Inter-tribal wars, bloody succession conflicts, and the disruptive effect of witchcraft trials revealed certain inherent defects in it. These showed up quickly when, in the shape of the colonial power, a new master arrived on the scene who brought with him his own law. Many of the first Europeans failed to realize that the Africans had their own law and their own courts. Their experience was, rather, that many Africans appealed to them to act as arbiters in cases where they were dissatisfied with their own legal institutions. The arbiters chosen were in many instances missionaries, but soldiers, explorers, and even farmers were approached. This urge for arbitration was not due to the need for new norms in a new situation. The cases which were submitted usually concerned a man's tutelary power over a woman, including woman inheritance and levirate, contested cases of bridewealth and divorce, quarrels of commoners with chiefs, and conflicts between chiefs. This list indicates either that the principles of tribal law were not yet crystallized or that they were often violated. Moreover, the presence of an extra-tribal authority produced a tendency to escape the obligations of tribal law. The demand for arbitration gradually receded as a result of the recognition of chiefly courts and the establishment of district courts.

By entering into regular relations with an African chief the Germans gave recognition to his position. This helped to stabilize the tribal set-up. Chiefs entered upon the negotiations with their own traditional techniques of diplomacy. Treaties of friendship were cemented by blood-pacts. Chiefs offered the blood-pact to the white new-comers, as the Chagga chief Mandara did to Jühlke.[1] By presenting a daughter in marriage an alliance could be secured. Kiwanga, the Bena chief, offered a small child to Captain Prince to mark his acceptance of German sovereignty. The traditional ritual of submission included the sending of an embassy to the victor. Many African chiefs sent such embassies to the Germans and were told to accept the German flag, to appear in person at headquarters, and to obey the orders issued there. No negotiations were considered valid without the ritual exchange of gifts. In offering and accepting these, delays frequently occurred to carry out contests of rank or to neutralize the magic of the negotiators. Chiefs meeting Europeans for the first time would chew protective medicines or wear amulets, or use 'mouths', or go-betweens. Many chiefs were represented by a double at their first encounter with the Europeans. Such diplomatic finesse was not employed without personal grace. Chief Shangali of Machame was praised for being always polite and friendly. The Hehe chief Mkwawa's diplomacy was a skilful play with alternatives. He sent a delegation to offer peace to the Germans while negotiating with his neighbours for an alliance should the discussions break down.

With regard to the treaties ceding sovereignty to the *Gesellschaft für Deutsche Colonisation* it would be underestimating the intelligence of the chiefs to suggest that they did not know what their purpose was. Tributary dependence, after all, was a recognized political relationship in East Africa. Chiefs may not have been acquainted with the technicalities of concluding treaties of this nature, but they knew the importance of documents. The Arabs had introduced transfer of landed property by letter; in 1899 the chief Merere, in remote Usangu, produced a box with several documents, and a number of chiefs maintained Arab 'secretaries'. The power of chiefs to conclude binding agreements other than cession treaties was repeatedly exercised in the 1890's. Siki, the Nyamwezi chief of Unyanyembe, concluded an armistice with the commander of Tabora. The re-settlement of Merere II and the installation of Mwaryego as paramount of the Safwa followed upon a verbal agreement

[1] K. Jühlke, *Die Erwerbung des Kilimandscharo-Gebietes* (Köln, 1886), pp. 25–30.

between the commander at Tukuyu and the assembled chiefs in December 1899.

A further step in solidifying tribal structure was the acknowledgement of a chiefly succession. In pre-European times the death of a chief often precipitated a period of uncertainty and violence. The colonial Administration naturally considered a fight between rival heirs or an interregnum as undesirable. It had to make up its mind and support one of the candidates. In doing so it added a new factor to those—legitimacy, suitability, and popularity of the candidate—which had previously decided a succession, and it tended to suppress a factor which in the past had been decisive—skill in disposing of rivals. In the circumstances the views of the Administration and the views of the tribe might not always agree. Naturally the Administration would draw upon itself the enmity of a claimant who under 'tribal' conditions could hope to secure a chiefdom but who had no chance in the presence of a government which applied loyalty to itself as a criterion of equal value to legitimacy and suitability. On the other hand, justifiable opposition to a chiefly candidate had little opportunity to express itself effectively if he had the support of the Administration. Even where, as happened in the majority of cases, no government intervention took place, the law of succession was bound to move in the direction of patriliny (and away from matriliny), since the law of the colonial power favoured it.

In certain instances the Administration came to the conclusion that in the interest of the colonial order a particular tribal structure should be completely rearranged. Thus, because of the strong attachment shown by the Hehe to their 'dynasty', the following (temporary) settlement was devised after Mkwawa's death: his close relatives were exiled to the coast; some of his agnates in the direct line of succession were trained for government service; the 'governors' and chiefs of the districts were declared 'independent', that is directly responsible to the station commander. In anticipation of a conflict between the Administration and a chief, his rivals might try to gain the favour of the Germans by flattery or sycophancy. Such unhealthy rivalry is illustrated in the Ukerewe troubles of 1896, after which Chief Lukongo was replaced by his nephew, who for some time had shown extraordinary submissiveness to the *boma*.

associated with the school. To raise the standard of achievement feeder schools were established in the district and a training department and craft departments were added. Schooling was made compulsory for boys at Tanga in 1899. Missions were concerned about supplying Christian clerks to the Government, since they felt that the Muhammadan clerks helped to spread Islam in the interior. But they were not in a position to offer many trained men, since the rapid expansion of their own work created requirements for teachers, evangelists, catechists, and priests, which had priority. The manifold activities which missions initiated to make life meaningful to their adherents necessitated the training of nurses, printers, and welfare workers.

The African response to the education efforts of missions and Administration is reflected in the following figures: in 1900 Protestant missions had 900 pupils at school, the Roman Catholic missions 5,000. The three government schools at Tanga, Dar es Salaam, and Bagamoyo catered for 1,600 pupils, making a grand total of 7,500. In 1914, 6,100 pupils were described as enrolled in government schools and 155,287 in mission schools.[1]

The education of the African is closely related to the adoption of the vernaculars as literary media and their development as means of communication adequate for modern conditions. Missionaries at first translated the sacred books of the Bible, catechisms, and hymn books. Their next task was to construct primers and collect material for readers. In 1900 this range of

---

[1] The statistics for attendance in mission schools do not bear too close scrutiny, for they were worked out without agreed definition of terms like 'attendance', 'school', and 'pupil'. On educational development, see C. Mirbt, *Mission und Kolonialpolitik in den deutschen Schutzgebieten* (Tübingen, 1910); A. M. Adams, *Aus der deutsch-ostafrikanischen Mission* (Berlin, 1898); *Im Dienst des Kreuzes* (Augsburg, 1899); *Lindi und sein Hinterland* (Berlin, 1903); R. Axenfeld, *Küste und Inland* (Berlin, 1912); T. Bachmann, *Ambilishiye, Lebensbild eines ostafrikanischen Evangelisten* (Herrnhut, 1936); P. Fleisch, *Hundert Jahre lutherischer Mission* (Leipzig, 1936); B. Guttmann, *Gemeindeaufbau aus dem Evangelium* (Leipzig, 1925); S. Knak, *Vom Nil zur Tafelbaai* (Berlin, 1934); F. Rauscher, *Die Mitarbeit der einheimischen Laien am Apostolat in der Mission der weissen Väter* (Münster, 1952); F. S. Schäppi, *Die katholischen Missionsschulen in Deutsch-Ostafrika* (Zürich, 1937); M. Schlunk, *Das Schulwesen in den deutschen Schutzgebieten* (Hamburg, 1914); A. J. Schmidlin, *Die katholischen Missionen in den deutschen Schutzgebieten* (Hamburg, 1914); T. Schneider, *Auf dem Missionspfad in Deutsch-Ostafrika* (Münster, 1899); K. von Schwartz, *Mission und Kolonisation in ihrem gegenseitigen Verhältnis* (Leipzig, 1908); and others.

literature was available in print in Sambaa, Zaramo, Bondei, Chagga, and Gogo, not to mention Swahili, which could further boast a number of general knowledge books. How rapidly the interest in reading grew can be seen from the fact that in 1910 11,000 copies of the Barazani series of booklets in Swahili on religious and general knowledge topics were sold.

The Universities Mission to Central Africa had been the first in the field with a monthly, *Habari za Mwezi*, which was printed by Africans at Magila. The German Protestant missions published *Pwani na Bara*; the Roman Catholic monthly was *Rafiki yangu*, and government teachers started *Kiongozi*. That these monthlies catered for a growing taste for reading matter is reflected in the increase in the number of subscribers: *Pwani na Bara* had 700 subscribers in 1908 and 2,000 in 1914. The mission-sponsored publications helped to unite an emerging Christian *élite* in common interests. Together with *Kiongozi* they provided East Africans for the first time in history with a means of communication intelligible over the whole territory and evoking contributions from far and wide. *Kiongozi* contained the following sections: News, General Knowledge, Entertainment, Poetry, Letters to the Editor, and Announcements. Only this last section had contributions by whites. Every month there were a great number of contributions which could not be used for lack of space. The prose articles printed had a strong personal touch; their autobiographical nature afforded an insight into African thinking.

'The civilized habit of letter-writing', which the African had contracted, contributed considerably to the 673,000 letters carried in the territory in 1900, an increase of about 100,000 over the previous year. Travel by rail had acquired a similar popularity, as is proved by the increase in travellers on the Usambara Railway between 1905, when 112,000 were carried, and 1908, when the figure was 200,000.[1] The African showed his adaptability in the rapidity with which he took to urban life. After the Abushiri rising in 1888–9 Dar es Salaam had only 350 inhabitants. In 1891 Governor Soden raised it to be the capital. In 1896 its population had increased to 13,000, of whom approximately 1,000 were Asiatics. In 1905 the population of

---

[1] *Jahresbericht über ... die deutschen Schutzgebieten, 1900–1* and *1909–10*, under 'Postal Services and Transport'.

the larger towns of the territory was: Tabora 37,000, Dar es Salaam 24,000, Ujiji 14,000, Tanga 5,600, Bagamoyo 4,900, Kilwa 4,400, Lindi 3,500, Pangani 3,200, Iringa 2,500, making a total of not quite 100,000. Government buildings, offices, hotels, churches, barracks, warehouses, and stores had been erected in Dar es Salaam. Africans thronged the streets; they lived in Swahili-style houses in the native quarters.

A typical inhabitant of the new towns was 'the boy', a personal servant to a white. A good 'boy' considered himself a living instrument of his master. He mysteriously participated in his master's rank: the boy of a higher official was respected by the servant of a lower official. Every 'boy' on taking service 'got married', using the story as a pretext to obtain a loan of money. Later he had to attend the funeral of a close relative (to enjoy a short leave). 'Boys' studied their masters closely and adjusted themselves to their idiosyncrasies. If treated with justice and kindness a 'boy's' loyalty grew until he completely identified his interests with those of his master. When war broke out in 1914, 'boys' accompanied their masters to their troop units and some died beside them in battle. 'Boys', navvies, plantation workers and porters, masons, carpenters and smiths, teachers, evangelists and catechists—these were the pioneers who laid down the foundations on which their children and grandchildren are erecting the edifice of a new civilization. For in the early colonial system a few *avant-courier* groups function like a lever upon the inert mass of their compatriots.

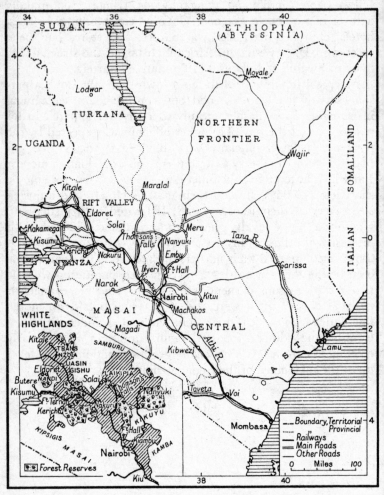

MAP 5. KENYA: ADMINISTRATION AND COMMUNICATIONS 1938–9

V

KENYA: THE PATTERNS OF ECONOMIC LIFE
1902–45

C. C. WRIGLEY

1902–7

ALTHOUGH it came into being in 1895 the career of the East Africa Protectorate, later to be called Kenya, may be said to have had its real beginning in April 1902, when its boundaries were advanced, at the expense of Uganda, from the Rift Valley to Mount Elgon and the eastern shores of Lake Victoria. The backbone of the Protectorate, in its new form, was, oddly enough, the Uganda Railway, which had been opened for public traffic three months earlier. It was this single pair of steel rails that gave the country its unity and its possibilities of economic growth.

The railway, financed by the Imperial Government and built under the supervision of a Foreign Office committee, had set out in 1896 from the ancient Afro-Arab seaport of Mombasa. Crossing the narrow channel which separates Mombasa island from the mainland of Africa, it moved into the interior on a line a little north of west. For some twenty-five miles it ran past coconut plantations and the gardens of the Nyika tribes, but then it plunged into the great belt of waterless thorn-scrub which had been so sore a trial to travellers on foot. At mile 98 it came to Voi, on the edge of the fertile oasis formed by the Teita hills. From here, turning away from Mount Kilimanjaro, which would have been its first objective if it had not become German territory, it ran north-westwards through the continuing wilderness, where man-eating lions made a famous havoc among the Indian labourers.[1] At Kibwezi it came to the first settlements of the Kamba tribe, where Scottish missionaries were already

---

[1] See J. H. Patterson, *The Man-eaters of Tsavo* (London, 1910).

at work, and from there on it kept the hill country of the Kamba on its right, while on its left were the dry grassy plains over which a few Masai herdsmen drove their cattle and their sheep. It was slowly gaining height, and at a point near Kiu it crossed the 5,000-foot contour, which was to be taken as the lower limit of the area in which Europeans could live in full health and work with full efficiency. After some 250 miles it came at last to the stream which the Masai called Enkare Nairobi, or Caldbeck. Here it paused, for the most difficult stage of its journey lay ahead, and here the engineers made their main up-country stores and workshops, around which, by 1899, the nucleus of a future city was already visible to the discerning eye.[1] From Nairobi the railway climbed laboriously to the heights of Limuru, then fell, as abruptly as a railway can fall, into the Rift Valley, along which it meandered, westward and northward, past lakes Naivasha, Elmenteita, and Nakuru, looking for a way of escape. Just north of Nakuru, almost on the equator, a practicable route up the western scarp was found. So here it turned due west, climbed to the cold summit of Mau, and then began its tortuous descent through the hills lightly peopled by the Nandi and Kipsigis tribes. Eventually it reached the plain country of the Luo, then grouped with the Bantu-speaking tribes under the name of Kavirondo, and came to rest at Kisumu on the easternmost gulf of Lake Victoria. Even here its objective was not really attained, but steamers and dhows now took over, plying across the lake to the kingdom of Buganda or Uganda, which gave the line its name.[2]

The railway's objective was Uganda. But its construction also made possible the economic development of the intervening lands. The costs of porter transport were such that hitherto no commodity except ivory had been or could have been exported from any part of Kenya other than the narrow coastal belt. But with freights from Nairobi now ranging from £1. 4s. to £2. 2s. per ton other forms of trade had clearly become feasible. Moreover, the development of these lands had now become not only possible but also necessary. The British tax-

[1] Hardinge to Salisbury, 24 Feb. 1899, Foreign Office Confidential Print (hereinafter 'F.O.C.P.'), 7401.

[2] See V. C. R. Ford, *The Trade of Lake Victoria*, East African Studies no. 3 (Kampala, 1955).

payers and their representatives might, though reluctantly, subsidize the administration of dependent territories, but railways were expected to pay their way. This was none the less true because the real reasons for the construction of this particular line had been administrative and strategic, because it had also been represented as a mortal blow to the slave trade, or because the economic return was expected to be broadly commercial rather than narrowly financial. Parliament might forgo, as in fact it had to, interest on the £5½ million capital outlay which it had provided. It might even postpone to an indefinite future the repayment of the principal, from which liability Kenya was finally absolved in 1933. But it would certainly resent being called on to meet operating losses. And in its first two years the railway did suffer heavy losses, which augmented the already large sums which Britain was contributing to the administration of the two protectorates. Clearly, traffic would somehow have to be created; and it was the East African Administration, which was actually in charge of the railway, that was made to feel the primary responsibility for creating it.

The prospects did not appear particularly bright. By far the simplest method of producing a rapid growth of incomes in a new country is, of course, the exploitation of mineral deposits, but this method, it seemed clear, was not applicable here. In 1902–3 a survey conducted by a group of London and Johannesburg entrepreneurs calling themselves the East Africa Syndicate confirmed the earlier impression that minerals of any consequence did not exist; the only important discovery was a vast deposit of sodium carbonate at Lake Magadi in the steppes near the German border.[1] In the main, therefore, it was evident that the development of an export trade would have to depend on agricultural production. Now from this point of view also the greater part of the Protectorate had to be excluded from consideration, since it was a barren waste in which the rainfall permitted nothing more than a very extensive type of pastoralism. There were only two areas which afforded promise. In the south-east there were the coastal low-

[1] Report by Major Burnham (1903), in *Correspondence relating to the Resignation of Sir Charles Eliot and to the Concession to the East African Syndicate*, Cd. 2099 (1904), pp. 47–53.

lands, with their equatorial maritime climate. This belt, how-ever, was very narrow, and it was a mediocre specimen of its type. Much more extensive and of much higher potential value was the area in the west of the country which comprised a small tract of relatively low-lying land around the north-eastern corner of Lake Victoria and the larger tract of mountainous land later known as the Kenya Highlands. Here were some 40,000 square miles of fertile upland, an H-shaped area formed by the twin flanks of the Rift Valley, with a connecting belt in the centre, where the valley itself rose above the 5,000-foot contour and the 30-inch isohyet. It was on this western area, and particularly on the highlands, which were clearly capable of producing largely and in large variety, that attention was now mainly focused. Hitherto the highlands had figured chiefly as an engineering problem, but now that the railway had been driven through them they began to be seen as the principal source of the country's future solvency and prosperity.

But if there was to be agricultural production for export there still remained two related questions: what kind of agri-culture was to be practised, and how was it to be organized? Relevant to both questions was what appeared to be, after the scarcity of minerals, the salient feature of the whole situation—namely, the scarcity of men. Even in some of the more fertile areas the population was notably sparse. In the central Rift Valley there were only a few groups of Masai herdsmen, loosely occupying a vast area with their wandering flocks and herds. The whole of the western section of the highlands was very lightly peopled, and parts of it, notably the Uasin Gishu plateau north of the railway line, were practically uninhabited. Only two areas were at all densely occupied. There were the numerous Kavirondo tribes of the lake basin, and there were the Kikuyu and allied peoples of the eastern highlands, whose settlements stretched northwards from Nairobi to the slopes of Mount Kenya. The numbers of the Kikuyu, however, had been greatly reduced by famine and small-pox during the previous decade,[1] and in particular their occupation of the southern area, in the neighbourhood of the railway, had become rather tenuous. Their northern settlements had not yet been thoroughly

---

[1] See L. S. B. Leakey, *Mau Mau and the Kikuyu* (London, 1952), p. 9, and Chapter I above.

investigated, and in consequence the scarcity of people in the Protectorate as a whole was believed to be considerably greater than it actually was.[1] It was this partial misapprehension that helped Sir Charles Eliot, who arrived as Commissioner in 1901, and others to think of the country as another New Zealand, 'a white man's country in which native questions [would] present but little interest'.[2]

Even so, the population was undoubtedly small—probably not much more than 2 million all told in a country which contained some 75,000 square miles of readily habitable land. And besides being few in numbers the natives were from the relevant points of view conspicuously inept. They had been but little influenced by the currents of trade which had been animating most other parts of East Africa during the previous half-century, and had barely begun to acquire a taste for cotton cloth and other imported manufacturers. None of the Kenya tribes had rulers comparable with the forward-looking aristocracy of Buganda, which was able in some degree to communicate European ideas and aspirations to the mass of the people;[3] most of them, indeed, had no rulers or aristocracies at all. Pastoral peoples whose sole thought was the increase of the herds, cultivating peoples who left most of the labour of cultivation to their womenfolk and were often unfamiliar even with the iron hoe— these were not likely to respond quickly or effectively to the kind of economic opportunity now theoretically open to them.

It was thus natural to infer both that there was ample room for immigrants and that without immigrants there could be little hope of a rapid growth of production and trade. The system of 'native production', whereby an export trade is built up from the surplus product of large numbers of indigenous peasants, each working independently on his own subsistence holding, was as yet virtually untried anywhere in tropical Africa (for the palm-oil of the west coast, being derived from a more or less naturally growing forest tree, was hardly an agricultural product in the full meaning of the term); its results

[1] In the text of his book *The East Africa Protectorate* (London, 1905), p. 128, Sir Charles Eliot put the Kikuyu population at 200,000–300,000, but added in a footnote that the latest inquiries indicated it to be not far short of a million.

[2] Ibid., p. 302.

[3] See C. C. Wrigley, 'Buganda: an outline economic history', *Economic History Review*, new ser. x (1957), 60–80.

in India and the West Indies had not been particularly impressive; and the East Africa Protectorate did not appear to be a propitious field for the experiment. A variant on this theme, the introduction of Indian peasant colonists, was, indeed, seriously considered, partly as a method conveying 'object-lessons' in industriousness and agricultural technique to the native population; and a beginning was actually made with its application, in the settlement of a few former railway-builders in the Kibos area, on the plain east of Kisumu. Later, for political reasons, the settlement of Indians on the land was disfavoured, and in the highland zone was in effect prohibited, but it is doubtful whether in any event much could have come of it. The mass movement of a poor peasantry, especially under the stringent conditions on which the Government of India insisted, would have required organization and finance on a scale far beyond the resources of the early Protectorate. In fact, by 1928 there were only forty-eight Indian farmers in the western lowlands, and most of these were not peasants in the ordinary sense but sugar-planters, with an average of 200 acres under cultivation, grouped round a central factory.[1] That the country suffered economic loss by setting narrow limits to the action of Indian agricultural entrepreneurs is beyond serious dispute, but this does not affect the point that small family holdings, whether African or Indian, did not appear to be a suitable basis, from an economic point of view, for development in the early years of the century.

Everything then pointed to European-directed agriculture, and thus to European immigration and to European rights in land. It should be emphasized that although Eliot and Lord Delamere, the greatest of Kenya's pioneer settlers, gave a powerful impetus to the process of white settlement, the idea was in no way a new one. Most of the travellers who had trudged over the Highlands to Uganda in the 1890's, whether they were administrators, soldiers, or missionaries, had noted in passing that the country, given means of communication, appeared to be admirably suited to this purpose.[2] The

---

[1] Kenya Annual Agricultural Census, 1929.

[2] See, for instance, F. D. Lugard, *The Rise of our East African Empire* (2 vols., Edinburgh, 1893), i. 415 sqq.; G. Portal, *The British Mission to Uganda in 1893*, ed. Rennell Rodd (London, 1894), p. 76; Letter from Tucker, 9 Nov. 1892, F.O.C.P. 6454.

Foreign Office, for several years before 1902, had taken settlement for granted, and had busied itself with working out the legal and financial terms on which it might take place.[1] Even Sir Harry Johnston, who regarded East Africa as a field, in the main, for Indian and African enterprise, envisaged the planting of a British farming colony in a limited area of the empty western section of the Highlands, round which he drew a red ring on his map.[2]

European-directed agriculture, however, might mean one of two distinct things. There was the traditional tropical plantation, in which European capital and managerial skill were combined with large quantities of indigenous or other unskilled labour for the production of high-value tropical crops. And there was the farming system of the temperate colonies, with British settlers practising, in more spacious lands, the stock-breeding and cereal-growing with which they were familiar at home. The implications of these two systems were manifestly very different. In the one case, the immigrant entrepreneurs would ideally be scattered—'inter-penetrated', as Eliot put it— among the native settlements, taking up but little of their land but drawing heavily upon their labour. In the other, large blocks of land would have to be set aside for the colonists, but in the remaining areas the native populations would be left undisturbed, since, in theory, their services would not be required and their presence in the country (like that of the Maori in New Zealand) would be irrelevant to the main theme. Underlying this distinction there were the two concepts between which Kenya could never bring itself to choose: the concept of the settlers as an aristocracy with supervisory and directive functions, set over the native population by virtue of their superior resources and superior skills, and the concept of the settlers as a distinct community, living with separate institutions in a separate territory.

One main reason for this continuing ambiguity was the fact that in Kenya both types of agriculture were ecologically feasible and attractive. The Highlands appeared to be a small

[1] See Crown Agents to Foreign Office, 21 Apr. 1896, and Foreign Office to Colonial Office, 30 June 1896, in F.O.C.P. 6849; Memorandum by Hardinge, 9 Oct. 1896, in F.O.C.P. 6913; Hardinge to Salisbury, 9 July 1897, in F.O.C.P. 7018; and Gray to Foreign Office, 21 June 1899, in F.O.C.P. 7401.

[2] H. H. Johnston, *The Uganda Protectorate* (2 vols., London, 1902), i. 248.

replica of such temperate colonies as Canada or New Zealand, though exceptionally endowed with rich volcanic soil and two growing seasons in the year. On the other hand, not only the coastal and Lake Victoria lowlands but also the lower parts of the highland zone were clearly capable of producing a wide variety of tropical and sub-tropical crops; in particular, the areas between 4,500 and 6,000 feet were ideally suited to the cultivation of high-grade coffee. For more than one reason, however, the emphasis was at first laid on English-style farming. In the first place, this was the kind of activity that was indicated by the state of the world market. At the turn of the century, and for some years after, tropical plantation agriculture was nearly everywhere at a low ebb. Coffee in particular, which had commanded very high prices in the early 1890's, was now suffering from a large excess of production,[1] and the German investors south of the border, who had invested heavily in this crop, were passing through very trying times. Cotton, it is true, was booming, but cotton, under African conditions, is not a crop which has ever been able to bear the overhead costs of direct European management. On the other hand, this was also a period of immense expansion on the Canadian prairies and the Australian outback, and it seemed obvious that wherever sheep could be grazed and wheat grown, these were the activities on which personal and national fortunes could most rapidly be founded. It is not surprising, therefore, that the East African Syndicate decided to put most of its money into sheep-farming and the settlement of farming colonists, for which purpose it was granted 500 square miles in the Rift Valley in 1903.

On the whole, however, the type of investor known collectively as 'the City' showed little interest in East Africa at this time, or indeed for a long time to come—except, to his misfortune, during the rubber boom of 1908-12. In the first years of the century there was nothing to attract big money to these untried, barely administered, and not especially promising lands. The men who were drawn to the Protectorate in this early period were in fact rarely capitalists of the ordinary type. Broadly speaking they fell into two categories. First there were

[1] V. D. Wickizer, *The World Coffee Economy* (Stanford, 1943), p. 240. Eliot (op. cit., p. 168) was discouraging about the economic prospects of coffee in East Africa.

the roving adventurers, with little or no means, who had begun to trickle into the country in the 1890's, trading in ivory, driving ox-wagons ahead of the railway, running hotels, and occasionally growing fruit and vegetables for the officials and the railway-builders. By 1902 there were several scores of such people in the Highlands, and during the next three years they were largely reinforced by similar restless spirits who at Eliot's invitation came from Natal to try their luck in a new land. (The eighty Boer families who were settled on the Uasin Gishu in 1908 were a later and rather special addition to this class.) Secondly, there were members of the English and Anglo-Irish nobility and gentry. To these people, impoverished by the fall in land rents and bored with the life of a country gentleman or a peace-time cavalry officer, the East African highlands offered the possibility of gain, the certainty of action and adventure. Sun and space, mountain scenery and lions were and long remained Kenya's most important assets, and among the European settlers there were always many whose object was not so much to make money as to spend it on congenial occupations in a delightful land. It was chiefly the presence of such resident tourists that enabled the country for sixty years to maintain a consistently enormous adverse balance of trade and a not certainly known but undoubtedly large adverse balance of payments on income account.

Settlers of the first class lacked the capital necessary for plantation agriculture: those of the second class sometimes had the capital but generally lacked the inclination. There were exceptions; the businesslike Lord Cranworth, for example, put his money from the start into sisal,[1] one of the few plantation crops of which the market value was then rising. But for the most part the gentlemen-settlers preferred the types of agriculture to which they were accustomed—the breeding of sheep and cattle and the growing of wheat. It is significant that although Lord Delamere (who was, of course, very much more than a 'resident tourist') noted in 1903 that coffee grew well and could be profitable, it was not until after the first world war, and then without much enthusiasm, that he added to his multifarious enterprises a stake in what had already for many years been one of the most lucrative of the agricultural industries

[1] Lord Cranworth, *Kenya Chronicles* (London, 1939), p. 18.

of Kenya.[1] The connotations of coffee-growing did not accord with his own tastes or with his ideal of a British colony of settlement. The economic foundations of such colonies were wool and wheat, and it was therefore to wool and wheat that he and other like-minded entrepreneurs devoted their main efforts, in which they persisted despite much discouragement and loss.

The East African Highlands were not really as suited to wheat-growing or to sheep-farming as they at first appeared. They might be cool but they were, nevertheless, equatorial, and, in the absence of a winter, insects and viruses throve as they could never do in a truly temperate region. The wheat fields sown by Delamere and others were repeatedly devastated by the diseases known as 'rust', which brought their owners close to ruin. Long years of experimental breeding were required before wheat could be sown with any secure expectation of a reasonable harvest, and even then the victory was not complete or permanent. And even when the struggle was going relatively well the average yield was not high; from 1921 to 1930 it averaged 9 bushels to the acre, as against 11 in Australia and 14 in the United States.[2] The early experiments with wool-bearing sheep were even more disastrous, for the animals imported from Britain and Australia sickened and died with depressing regularity. The East African Syndicate never made a success of this industry, but individual settlers such as Delamere and the Hon. Galbraith Cole persevered and eventually met with some reward. Crossing with native ewes produced a type of sheep which combined a good commercial fleece with resistance to disease, and on the drier lands such as the Laikipia plateau (from which the Masai were removed in 1912)[3] the flocks throve and multiplied. But the area of suitable land was not large, and wool has never made more than a minor contribution to the export trade. The development of cattle-breeding was made similarly difficult by a multitude of epizootic and enzootic diseases, of which the most destructive was east coast fever; and the strict preventive quarantines were a handicap

[1] E. Huxley, *White Man's Country: Lord Delamere and the making of Kenya* (2 vols., London, 1935), i. 109; ii. 172.

[2] Calculated from Kenya Annual Agricultural Censuses, and *World Wheat Statistics* (1955).

[3] See Chapter I, pp. 36–38, above.

hardly less serious—some maintained that it was more serious—
than the disease itself.

In sum, early experience tended to show that, although
English-style farming operations could be conducted in the
Highlands, it was not in this type of production that Kenya
possessed what a new country must possess if it is to prosper—
namely, a distinct comparative advantage over other, better-
equipped competitors. In the production of coffee, on the other
hand, it did possess a very distinct advantage. Parts of the East
African Highlands provide just that subtle combination of soil
and climate which brings forth the finest qualities of coffee,
and beans labelled 'Nairobi' or 'Kenya' have always commanded prices at or very near the top of the London market
scale. But, for the reasons given, little attention was paid to
coffee in the first years of the country's history. Some trees were
planted near Nairobi by the Holy Ghost Fathers in 1899, and
they were followed by a few lay farmers; but for several years
the scale of planting was very small and the output scarcely
found its way beyond the domestic market. In 1904 Messrs.
Rutherfoord and Swift planted sisal on the fringe of the Kikuyu
country, and in this venture they were followed a year or two
later by Lord Cranworth and his associates. Rutherfoord and
Swift belonged to the type of settler who was to become the
backbone of European agriculture in Kenya—middle-class
citizens with some capital behind them, who nevertheless acted
as their own managers. But for some time they were rare
specimens of their type.

The Protectorate was founded on the premiss of mass colonization by small working farmers of European stock. Though
a few very large grants were made in the first years, the basis
of the Government's land policy was the 640-acre or even 160-
acre homestead of North American tradition—and in the context of pioneer stock and arable farming these were very small
units. But for the small man, the colonist with slender financial
resources, the conditions of East African life in the early years
of the century were exceedingly difficult. He could not usually
plant coffee, still less sisal, which required a heavy outlay with
no immediate return. Nor could he embark on sheep-farming
or wheat-growing, which, in the beginning at least, had clearly
to be conducted on the grand scale, as Delamere conducted

them, or not at all. The only type of agriculture that was open
to him was small-scale market-gardening; and while a few men
could make a living by selling potatoes and milk and apricots
to the citizens of Nairobi and maize to the employers of African
labour, the local market was far too small to sustain any considerable number of producers. Moreover, such products could
perfectly well be supplied by farmers whose expectations were
much more modest than those of Europeans. Indian competition was successfully excluded, but that of Africans could not
be evaded, and before long the potato and similar markets
passed into the hands of Swahili and Kikuyu growers. Again,
in a normal colony of settlement it was assumed that the
pioneers would live for a time at subsistence level and would
sustain themselves in part by wage-labour, but here neither
assumption held good.

The settlers could not live at subsistence level, for that would
be to blur the vital distinction between white and black; and
the presence of wealthy individuals set up a standard of consumption to which every European had to try to conform.
(Private, and, by contagion, public extravagance has always
been a conspicuous feature of Kenyan life.) And with black
labour in the neighbourhood it was both economically difficult
and socially shocking for a white man to work with his hands
for hire. On the contrary, he was expected to be, from the start,
an employer of native labour,[1] even though there were so few
advantages of scale in the type of agriculture that he was
conducting that he could not afford to pay wages which equalled
the opportunity cost to the native worker. Hence the angry
complaints of labour shortage and the angry demands for
measures of compulsion which reached their climax in the
tumult of March 1908.[2] By this time it had become clear that
East Africa was really no place for the small European farmer.
Nor was it a place for the small European trader or the artisan,
for in these fields white men were in direct competition with
Indians, who provided similar services at much lower cost.

---

[1] Cf. the bitter complaint of a settler who, owing to the labour shortage, had
been reduced to 'planting and hoeing after the manner of a native woman',
Correspondence relating to Affairs in East Africa, Cd. 4122 (1908). This does not mean
that all or most settlers disdained manual labour. But they did not expect to have
to work alone.

[2] See Chapter VI, pp. 279-80 below.

There were, of course, exceptions. A few small settlers managed in course of time to build up coffee plantations or otherwise make good, and in the 1950's there were flourishing businesses bearing the names of British storekeepers and craftsmen who worked in East Africa in the first decade of the century. But such individual instances did not alter the fact that by 1908 the project of mass colonization had foundered in a welter of economic and social contradictions, though its phantom was to haunt the country for a long time to come.

1908-14

By 1908, indeed, a general crisis had clearly arisen in the affairs of the Protectorate. In the year ending in March 1909 revenue still fell short of expenditure by £166,000. Exports were valued at a mere £157,000, and by far the greater part consisted of 'natural' products such as ivory, beeswax, and hides and skins, which offered little prospect of expansion, and of copra from the long-established plantations of the maritime belt. In general, however, the old coastal economy was now far sunk in the decay characteristic of systems formerly based on slave labour; the once-flourishing export of grain to Arabia had dwindled almost to nothing. And to offset this decline there was, after six years of effort, little sign of progress in the Highlands. The production of wheat and wool had suffered severe setbacks and its future was entirely uncertain; coffee production was insignificant; no sisal plantation was yet in bearing. The inflow of capital had almost ceased and the original investors were near the end of their resources.

The emphasis placed on settlement and European farming had never been regarded as inconsistent with whatever development of 'native production' might be found feasible; and at the beginning of the Colonial Office era—responsibility for the Protectorate was transferred from the Foreign Office to the Colonial Office in 1905—there were signs that the emphasis might be about to be reversed. One of the first acts of the new authority was to send an emissary, Major (later Sir Humphrey) Leggett, to investigate the economic prospects of the Protectorate. Leggett had served with the Poor Whites Commission in South Africa, and this experience had given him a deep distrust of small-scale colonial agriculture. His report, rendered in 1906, was strongly in favour of highly capitalized plantation agriculture, on the one hand, and of African peasant farming, on the other.[1] The crop chiefly in view, for both systems, was cotton, which was exceptionally dear at this time and was already being grown with some success in Buganda. In 1906 there came into being the British East Africa Corporation, deriving most of its finance from the British Cotton Growing Association, which had been founded in 1902 with the object of reducing Lancashire's dependence on American supplies, but receiving also a small Imperial subvention for experimental work. Leggett himself took charge of the corporation's operations, which were to include the erection of a ginnery at Kisumu and the distribution of cotton-seed to Kavirondo peasants.

Seeing that at this time most of the European settlers were on the verge of bankruptcy and that the Government would plainly have been relieved to see the back of them, it is not unlikely that if this experiment had been successful the history of Kenya would have taken a very different turn. But the experiment failed.[2] Cotton was introduced simultaneously in 1907 in the Nyanza Province of Kenya and the adjoining Eastern Province of Uganda,[3] but in the 1912–13 season the output from the latter area was roughly 6,000 tons of seed-cotton and from the former 166 tons. It is not easy to find an entirely satisfactory explanation for this remarkable contrast, for the populations of the two provinces were of comparable size, the natural conditions were broadly similar, and official pressure does not seem to have been appreciably stronger in one Protectorate than in the other. Something must no doubt be attributed to the presence in eastern Uganda of forceful Ganda chiefs and 'Agents', who in large measure shared European ideas about the virtues of industry and productivity. Something may also be attributed to marginal differences of climate. Certainly the yield from the crop sown in 1908 was very poor in Kenya, so that at a crucial stage growers received a severe discouragement—aggravated by the low prices paid in that period of international depression. The most obvious difference between

---

[1] Joint Committee on Closer Union in East Africa, *Minutes of Evidence*, H.C. No. 156 (1931), vol. iii, evidence of Sir Humphrey Leggett.

[2] This story is told by H. Fearn in his study, *An African Economy. A study of the economic development of the Nyanza Province of Kenya, 1903–1953* (London, 1961).

[3] For the Uganda story see Chapter VIII below.

the two areas, however, was the much stronger demand for wage-labour on the Kenya side of the border; and it seems at least possible that in so far as they wanted to, or were obliged to earn a money income at all, the peoples of the Nyanza Province found it on balance more lucrative or congenial to work for hire than to exert themselves in the cultivation of an unfamiliar and inedible crop. (Though they could not be induced to grow cotton, they did supply substantial surpluses of foodstuffs such as simsim, ground-nuts, and maize.) It might be supposed that the choice was not in reality a free one, since the demand for wage-labour, as we shall see, was presented to Africans at this time in somewhat pressing terms. In this respect, however, conditions in the Nyanza Province, under the régime of its 'pro-native' Commissioner, John Ainsworth, were exceptional, approximating to those which prevailed generally in East Africa in the 1920's: men were not allowed to remain idle, but they could please themselves whether they worked for employers or on their own account.[1]

Meanwhile the disappointment over cotton was being offset by advances in other sectors of the economy. By 1911 the fortunes of the country were clearly on the mend. Capital was flowing in again, revenues were expanding, and exports were at last visibly increasing. The motive power behind this new surge of development was, chiefly, the great expansion of British overseas investment which had begun about 1905 and which reached unprecedented levels in the years from 1910 to 1913.[2] From about 1910 the East Africa Protectorate began to be influenced by this fertilizing tide, for by that time it offered, or seemed to offer, prospects of profit. The reasons for this were also mainly external—the upswing of the trade cycle, and more particularly a dramatic increase in the value of certain primary products. The London price of rubber rose from 3s. 8d. a lb. in 1908 to 12s. in 1912. A few plantations had been started in East Africa as early as 1907, but in 1910–11 big money was attracted to their development. As a result, the focus of interest shifted temporarily back from the Highlands to the coastal

[1] See *Report of the Native Labour Commission, 1912–13* (Nairobi, 1913), vol. iii, *Minutes of Evidence.*

[2] See A. K. Cairncross, *Home and Foreign Investment, 1870–1913* (Cambridge, 1953).

belt. The shift was temporary, for the rubber prospects were in fact quite illusory. By 1913 not only had the boom collapsed, long before most of the plantations had been tapped, but it had been shown that no part of East Africa was particularly well suited to the growth of any rubber-yielding tree. Of far more permanent significance was the concurrent investment in the planting of ˌcoffee in the Highlands. In 1910 the world price of coffee, after a long period of depression, began to rise steeply, and the few acres which had been hopefully planted north of Nairobi suddenly became valuable assets. Considerable numbers of fresh investors were drawn into this industry—not, in this case, great London financiers but upper-class and middle-class settlers who for the first time could see a way to combine the pleasures of life in East Africa with a reasonable prospect of profit. The requirements of coffee production went far to determine the future economic and social structure of the country. A coffee planter is not a colonist in the 'white dominion' sense of the term, supporting himself mainly by the labour of his own hands, but neither is he usually an employee of a large expatriate company. He combines the economic role of a substantial capitalist and employer of labour with the social outlook of a farming settler, and this combination is the key to a great part of Kenya's subsequent history.

But if the coffee planter was to be one main type of European settler he was not to be the only type. About the time that the Protectorate was discovering coffee it was also discovering maize, a crop which could be grown by farmers without the resources for plantation agriculture and in parts of the Highlands outside the very limited areas which were suitable for coffee. The high world price of maize, coupled with governmental aid in the form of special reductions in railway rates, was at this time affording a measure of relief to the struggling farmers of South Africa; and in this as in many other matters the Protectorate followed the South African lead. The assistance which the Government could offer in the matter of lower railway rates was very moderate. It was, nevertheless, the first breach in the policy, which had been the cause of much local complaint, of putting the financial interests of the railway before the interests of producers, and it was sufficient to make the export of maize just feasible. In a more important sense, however, the growth of the maize industry was a by-product of the general growth of the economy, and especially of the plantation industries, for it was the feeding of African labour that provided the maize-growers with their most lucrative market.

Altogether, the years immediately preceding the first world war were years of rapid economic advance. Farmers were at last making profits; profits generated further investment; and investment generated further increases in income. A period of sustained growth appeared to have begun. By 1912–13 the Protectorate was not only solvent, but its prospects were thought to warrant the provision of Imperial loans for the further development of communications. Two branch railways were being built, one to Lake Magadi—capital for the exploitation of the soda deposits had at last been found—and one from Nairobi north-eastwards to Thika, through the coffee and sisal plantations on the edge of the Kikuyu country. There was a steady influx of new settlers, and most of them were men of some substance. Their expenditure added rapidly to the prosperity and the numbers of the shopkeepers, dealers, estate agents, builders, and professional men who were constructing and operating the mechanisms of an exchange economy. By 1914 Nairobi had begun to grow out of the frontier township stage. Nakuru in the Rift Valley, Eldoret, the centre of the Afrikaner farming community on the Uasin Gishu plateau, and the railway terminus Kisumu were becoming sizeable market towns, and clusters of shops were springing up at a number of other places in the European areas of the Highlands and around the administrative headquarters in the African reserves. This business community was a very mixed one. Scotsmen were naturally prominent, but it included members of many European nations and even a few Englishmen as well. The white population as a whole, however, was surpassed in numbers and probably in aggregate wealth by the Indians. The nucleus of Indian families long resident on the East African coast had been greatly swollen by fresh immigrants, and both groups had moved rapidly into the interior to exploit the opportunities created by the railway and the British Administration, operating the railway, filling the clerical cadres, and developing trade, not only around the railway stations but also among the remotest native settlements.[1] Their shrewdness, industry, thrift, and family cohesiveness stood these traders in excellent stead, and whereas most of them remained in a small way of business a few, such as A. M. Jeevanjee, first Indian member of the Legislative Council, rose to affluence and fame.

In the growing prosperity of this period the African population shared to some degree. The widening of the market brought about by the huge reduction in the costs of transport, by the provision of law and order and the enterprise of alien merchants, together with the investment of capital in the establishment of new crops and new methods of production, had raised the marginal value of their labour from zero to a level which, though still very low, made it easy for most of them to earn money incomes considerably in excess of the taxation imposed on them. It is true that this money income was of dubious real utility. A very large part of it was converted into livestock, which was desired both for its own sake and as a means to earlier and more frequent marriage; and since the supply of livestock was not very elastic and the supply of women was completely inelastic, the new wealth was largely dissipated in inflation.[2] Nor were they yet receiving any medical or educational services, except such as the missions were able to provide, or any appreciable assistance in the improvement of agricultural technique. But there was, at least, no war and no famine, and various new amenities such as cloth and household goods were gradually becoming common. In these years nothing that the Government or private employers could do was able to prevent a steady rise in wages, the standard rate being 3 rupees (4s.) in 1909 and 5 rupees in 1912. Wage-labour, moreover, was by no means the only source of income now open to Africans. One of the most frequent and indignant complaints of employers at this time was the ease with which, it was alleged, the people could earn money as independent producers,[3]

---

[1] One of the most persistent of East African legends is that the Asian community of Kenya and Uganda is mainly descended from the low-class coolies who were brought in to build the railway. In fact, according to the official history of the railway the number of indentured labourers who stayed on in East Africa was only 6,724 (M. F. Hill, *Permanent Way*, vol. i. *The Story of the Kenya and Uganda Railway* (Nairobi, 1950), p. 240). They were nearly all Punjabis, and the modern Asian population of Kenya and Uganda, numbering 136,000 in 1948, stems mainly from the merchant and upper peasant classes of Gujerat, Kathiawar, and Cutch.

[2] Native Labour Commission, 1913, vol. iii, *Evidence, passim*.   [3] Ibid.

and these complaints seem to have been not without substance. Of the 13,945 tons of maize carried by the railway in 1913–14, 8,895 tons were loaded at Kisumu and Kibos,[1] and must have been almost entirely the product of Kavirondo farmers, who also grew the whole of the simsim crop, which added more to the value of exports in 1911–12 and 1912–13 than any other commodity. Up to the first world war, in fact, 'native production' was contributing much more than settler agriculture to the wealth of the country. It was already clear that with the maturing of the coffee and sisal plantations this situation would soon be altered, but there was nothing yet to show that both types of production would not continue to expand or that the future would lie exclusively with European agriculture.

The coexistence of the two systems, however, was already producing friction, which expressed itself in competition for land and for labour. To understand the land question we must go back to the beginning of the century. At this time the problem presented itself as a conflict between the undoubted right of the native peoples, who had been taken (in theory by their own consent) under British protection, to remain in possession of their lands, and the necessity of economic development, which was assumed to entail the introduction of European farmers, and therefore of European rights in land. In principle, the solution was clear. Native occupation would be respected, while unoccupied land would be at the disposal of the Crown and available for allocation to immigrants. 'Native occupation', however, could be construed in two different ways. It could be construed narrowly, so that any land not actually in use was regarded as alienable. Or it could be held that each tribe was the owner of a territory, defined by a line drawn through its outermost settlements, so that only land falling outside any such territory could be assigned to colonists. On the whole, the Foreign Office leant at first towards the second interpretation, which was the easier to accept in that a fair proportion of the Highlands consisted of no-man's-lands to which no tribe could assert an effective claim. Before long, however, there were crucial departures from this policy. The claims of development were held to require that Europeans should have the use of land in the immediate vicinity of the

[1] Annual Report of the Department of Agriculture for 1913–14.

railway, even when such land was indisputably tribal territory. Thus in 1903 large grants were made around Lake Naivasha in the central Rift Valley regardless of the claims of the Masai, and in the following year the settlers arriving from South Africa and elsewhere were hastily assigned farms to the north of Nairobi, some of which clearly fell within the boundaries of the Kikuyu tribe. In these cases, indeed, there was some violation of the principle of native occupation even in its narrower construction. For a certain number of Kikuyu, probably of the order of 5,000 persons, were displaced, with compensation at the rate of 2 rupees an acre, from land which was theirs by virtue of beneficial occupation as well as of the more nebulous right of tribal ownership,[1] and the Masai were actually deprived of what were said to be their 'best and most favoured grazing lands'[2] and removed *en bloc* to more remote areas.

It is safe to say that the Commissioner of the day, Sir Charles Eliot, did not accept either the necessity or the virtue of preserving African rights in land at all. Unlike many British administrators, he saw nothing in African barbarism that he could admire. The sooner it was ended, in his view, the better for everyone; and the role which he would have assigned to Africans was that of a proletarian stratum of a civilized society, of which—though of this he was not very sanguine—they might ultimately become full and equal members.[3] But a thorough-going application of this policy was not judged feasible either. Eliot himself conceded that it might be necessary to make an exception for the supposedly formidable Masai, who were allotted new reserved territories at a safe distance from the settlers in the railway zone; and in the Kikuyu country a line was drawn beyond which white settlement was not permitted. Although, as was afterwards established,[4] the frontiers of Kikuyu country had not been fully respected, the great majority of the tribe were left in possession of their lands.[5] On the whole,

---

[1] *Report of the Kenya Land Commission* (Morris Carter Commission), Cmd. 4556 (1934), p. 101. About 3,000 continued to live on alienated land.

[2] Memo by Jackson, 22 Feb. 1904, in *Correspondence relating to the Resignation of Sir Charles Eliot*, Cd. 2099 (1904), pp. 6–7.

[3] Eliot to Lansdowne, 9 Apr. 1904, ibid., pp. 26–28.

[4] See p. 259 below.

[5] It is, of course, quite untrue that the Africans were relegated to the least desirable parts of the country, as has been alleged from time to time. The great majority continued to occupy lands of higher natural productivity than the average

the principles of segregation and reservation prevailed. But, except in the case of the Masai, who in 1904 and again in 1911 received a firm guarantee against further disturbance, and of the Nandi, who were given a similar though less formal pledge in 1907,[1] there was as yet nothing fixed or final about the native reserves. They were simply areas in which it had been decided that for the time being immigrants would not be allowed to acquire rights in land. Conversely, there were as yet no areas of the Protectorate from which Africans were excluded. It needs to be emphasized that in the first decade of the century the area of land to which the Kikuyu and other agricultural tribes had access was not reduced but very largely increased. For they were now able to colonize large areas in and around the Rift Valley from which the fear of the Masai had previously debarred them.[2] It is true that in such areas they were living on European property and were therefore liable to the exaction of rent in cash or kind or labour. But since land, as such, was not at this time a scarce factor, and the scarcity of labour was acute, the landowners' exactions could not be very onerous. (It was not until the 1920's, when economic conditions had changed, that land grievances became at all acute.) Moreover, there is good reason to believe that, having become in any case a subject people, Africans often actually preferred to place themselves under an individual European overlord, where they were safe from government *corvées* and from the oppressive behaviour of government-appointed chiefs and headmen.

The real economic and social problem in the pre-war period was not land but labour. If the Highlands had become a true farming colony, with an economy based on wool or even on wheat, little difficulty would have arisen. But the development of labour-intensive plantation agriculture, together with railway and road construction and an influx of wealthy sportsmen in need of *safari* porters, created a demand which far outran the voluntary supply. The natural result should have been a rise in the price of labour, which, as we have seen, did in fact occur to some extent. Employers, however, were unanimous in

of the White Highlands. See *East Africa Royal Commission 1953-1955 Report*, Cmd. 9475 (1955), especially Map 4.

[1] Carter Commission *Report*, p. 274.

[2] For an excellent account of this colonization, cast in the form of fiction, see E. Huxley, *Red Strangers* (London, 1939).

believing that higher wages did not and would not bring about an increase in the total amount of work done; and it is almost certainly true that the required result could have been achieved only by an increase in costs so steep as to put a large proportion of the settlers out of business. For the conditions of labour supply were peculiar. The crux, of course, was that, unlike the working classes of Europe, the native peoples of East Africa were in possession of the means of subsistence. A money income was a luxury rather than a necessity, so that their bargaining position was a very strong one. In the very first years of European contact, labour had been forthcoming with gratifying promptness, for both the work itself and the consumer goods with which it was rewarded had had the attraction of novelty. But the supply curve thereafter rose very steeply, for few young men could see the point of engaging in regular menial toil, for which there was no precedent in their customary way of life, for the sake of accumulating additional consumer goods. Leisure preference, in other words, was extremely high.

If the supply could not easily be increased, the demand, according to the laws of the market, should have been reduced. But this was a conclusion which could not readily be accepted either by the poorer settlers, for whom defeat on this issue would have meant utter disaster, or by the Government, which, for fiscal if no other reasons, was eager for rapid development. It was thus almost inevitable that efforts should have been made to alter the conditions of supply. One obvious method would have been to suppress African commercial agriculture. So far, however, opinion was generally against this; some of the settlers themselves spoke contemptuously of the 'craven fear of native competition'.[1] On the other hand, by 1912 they were with one voice demanding a reduction of the native reserves[2]— not because the land was urgently coveted for its own sake (most settlers already had more land than they were able to digest) but because more Africans would then be obliged to earn their subsistence by paid labour. Against this demand, however, the Government stood firm.

One potent instrument that the Government did wield was the instrument of taxation. A hut tax of 2 rupees was imposed

---

[1] *The Leader of British East Africa*, 24 July 1909.
[2] Native Labour Commission, 1913, *Evidence, passim.*

in 1901, partly for revenue but also with the object of making work to some extent a necessity. This was later raised to 3 rupees and an equivalent poll-tax was levied in order to catch the youths who did not qualify as householders. Beyond this, however, the authorities did not feel justified in going, at a time when the taxation of Europeans was extremely light, and the amount of labour compelled by this means remained relatively small. There remained the most obvious solution of the problem: the reinforcement of economic pressures and incentives by pressures of a more direct kind. From the beginning the Government had found itself unable to meet its own needs for porters and road-makers without resorting to informal measures of conscription; and the private employers, who for the most part assumed that as members of the ruling race they had a right to the services of the subject peoples, were not slow to demand that labour should be supplied to them by similar methods, to be paid at the 'standard' rates. For some time the authorities seem to have had few qualms about complying with this request. In 1908, however, the Liberal Government declared that forced labour could not be tolerated within the British empire and the edict went forth that conscription for private employers must cease. The resultant situation was confused and unsatisfactory. Though officials could no longer order natives to enter employment they were not debarred from encouraging them to do so, and the distinction between command and persuasion was, in the circumstances, a very fine one, which individual administrators drew in widely different ways according to their personal sympathies.[1] Thus the settlers could not be sure of their labour supply, but neither could the Africans be sure of their freedom.

One main easement of the labour difficulty was afforded by the voluntary efflux of Kikuyu into other parts of the Highlands. European farmers soon discovered that they could always get labour in return for cultivation and more especially grazing rights, which were in increasing demand owing to the growing wealth of the Kikuyu and other tribes in livestock. Thus there arose the 'resident labour' or 'squatter' system, whereby Africans settled with their families on European farms, living

[1] For an illuminating account of labour recruitment c. 1913 see Baron Blixen-Finecke, *African Hunter*, trans. F. H. Lyon (London, 1937), pp. 18 sqq.

for the most part their customary life but undertaking to work for the landowner either at call or for a stipulated proportion of the year. In this way farmers and planters assured themselves of the vital nucleus of a labour force, though the majority of their workers continued to be engaged on monthly contracts. The pattern which thus emerged was a rather curious one. Most of the African population continued to live in autonomous tribal societies, their ancient way of life modified only by the cessation of warfare, the sale of surplus crops, and the exodus of young men to work for hire during one or several months in the year. But a large and growing number, especially of the Kikuyu, were living in a form of villeinage under European seigneurs. Meanwhile the pastoral and primarily pastoral peoples such as the Masai, Nandi, Kipsigis, and Kamba, remained for most purposes outside the new system altogether.

Economic and social facts are extremely resistant to the influence of laws and policies. Given the British conquest and the admission of immigrants with immeasurably greater wealth and competence, no action of Government could have prevented the native peoples from being relegated to a subordinate position in the economic system. On the other hand, given the amplitude of the land in relation to population and capital, no legal or administrative dispositions could turn them into a proletariat. They were bound to retain the use of land—and it was the use, not the ownership, that vitally concerned them.

Life in the East Africa Protectorate in 1914 was in many ways rough and hard. There was as yet little alleviation of the immemorial poverty of the African peoples. In return for peace and a measure of justice, a new burden of labour had been imposed upon them. The housing and feeding of the workers were usually bad and sometimes atrocious, the discipline often harsh. But against all this there were the beginnings of economic growth and the sure prospect of further growth to come. Moreover, the pattern of the future was not yet determined; institutions had not assumed a rigid form.

1914–21

Then came the great disaster, the war that marred so much throughout the world. To the peoples of the Protectorate this conflict brought great suffering and loss of life, both directly through the rigours of the East African campaign and indirectly through the influenza and other epidemics which it brought in its train. The growth of population faltered and in some areas was probably reversed. The development of European farms, and of the economy in general, suffered a severe setback owing to the absence of a large proportion of the white males, the shortage of labour, and the constriction of the export trade, especially in coffee. Yet the check was clearly only a temporary one, and by 1917 plans for further expansion were being framed. Thinking at this time was inevitably conducted in an atmosphere of war economics. It was assumed that in the future as in the embattled present a high degree of imperial self-sufficiency would be the paramount objective, and that East Africa therefore could and should produce all that it was physically capable of producing, regardless of such mundane considerations as comparative cost. Thus the policy-planners of the war and immediate post-war years—who were to all intents and purposes the political leaders of the European settlers[1]—faced the future in a mood of sublime confidence. They drew railway lines across the map of Africa with wild abandon.[2] In 1920, having acquired colonial status and the protection of the Colonial Stocks Act, they caused a loan of £5 million—more than $2\frac{1}{2}$ times the current annual revenue—to be raised in London at 6 per cent., using part of it to repay earlier Treasury loans which had been granted at $3\frac{1}{2}$ per cent. And they produced a scheme for the immediate doubling of the white farming population.[3] About a thousand additional farms were to be demarcated and offered to ex-servicemen on very easy terms. Most of these were largish units of up to 5,000 acres, designed for ex-officers with a capital of at least £2,000. But, still pursuing the ghost of colonization, and in face of much competent advice, the planners insisted on including homesteads of 160–200 acres in the scheme, for the benefit of the 'small man'. To the Home Government this project had obvious attractions. What better, or cheaper, way could there be of providing 'homes for heroes' than by giving them stretches of virgin land

---

[1] See Chapter VI, pp. 288–91, below.
[2] *Final Report of the Economic Commission* (Nairobi, 1919).
[3] *Report of the Commission on Land Settlement* (Nairobi, 1919).

in the delightful uplands of East Africa? The 'Soldier Settlement Scheme' was therefore put into effect in 1919.

For a short time after the armistice the premisses of expansion seemed to have been well founded. Until the summer of 1920 the world prices of most of Kenya's exports ruled extremely high. There was, however, one very large fly in this ointment. At the beginning of their careers, since a large part of their trade was with India and a still larger part of it was conducted by Indian merchants, the East African territories had adopted a rupee currency. In 1905 a fixed ratio of 15 rupees to the gold sovereign had been established, but in 1914, with the abandonment of the gold standard in Britain, this peg was removed. In the monetary convulsions at the end of the war the rupee appreciated sharply, rising from its normal value of 1s. 4d. to 2s. 10d. at the beginning of 1920. Producers were thus getting less than half the number of rupees that they would otherwise have got for the goods which they sold in London. Imports were correspondingly cheaper, but the heavy debts which nearly all the farmers had contracted to the banks and other financiers in Nairobi remained at their former level in rupees. Costs of production were almost equally difficult to cut, for money wages were conventionally rigid. By March 1920 the situation had become so serious that it was decided to fix the East African rupee at 2s. (special measures being taken to prevent its export to India) and, as soon as possible, to introduce a sterling currency based on the florin coin. This was a compromise between the interests of creditors and debtors, which nevertheless left the farmers saddled with a 50 per cent. increase in the real burden of their indebtedness; and there was great bitterness among them when the Indian rupee promptly fell back almost to its original level, but the Colonial Secretary refused to reconsider the florin conversion.[1]

So far, the loss on the exchange had been approximately balanced by the rise in the sterling value of exports. But meanwhile the world commodity boom had collapsed. Kenya coffee, which had been fetching about £150 a ton in London in the

---

[1] There are numerous accounts of this episode. See especially W. McGregor Ross, *Kenya from Within* (London, 1927); Cranworth, *Kenya Chronicles*; L. S. Amery, *My Political Life* (2 vols., London, 1953), ii. 188–9. For its effects in the Uganda Protectorate, see Chapter VIII below.

early months of 1920, was worth only about £60 a year later. Sisal fell from a peak of £96 to £12. 10s. a ton. The worst disaster of all, however, was suffered by those who were growing, or had been preparing to grow, flax. It was largely on this crop, which had appeared to fill the long-felt need for a high-value commodity capable of being produced without very heavy capital outlay in those parts of the Highlands that were unsuited to coffee, that the plans for the rapid expansion of settlement had been based. Immediately after the war the flax market was in a very abnormal state, owing to the disappearance of Russian supplies, but the price fall was as dramatic as its previous rise, and many hopes were thereby buried. Unlike those of coffee and sisal, the price of flax never again recovered sufficiently to make export from Kenya practicable.

By 1921 not only had the more grandiose expectations of progress been dissipated, but most of the European producers were faced with ruin and the Government with a fiscal crisis. By stringent economy disaster was averted, and by 1923 a revival of world prosperity was making the country's economic prospects reasonably bright. Meanwhile steps had been taken to place the farming economy of the Highlands on a new and more secure footing. The Economic and Financial Committee set up in 1922 decided that the first object must be 'to foster and develop, by every possible means and with the least possible delay, an export trade in some easily produced local bulk commodity for which there was a steady and virtually unlimited demand in the markets of the world'—that was to say, of maize.[1] The trouble with a commodity which is easily produced is, of course, that its price is likely to be low and the margin of profit on its production small. Even though Kenya had a slight advantage in yield over most other producing countries, the export of maize in any quantity was made possible only by the reduction of railway rates to the bare level of operating costs. With this assistance, maize did provide a living to the less highly capitalized of the European farmers. As a result, large areas of the Highlands, especially in the Rift Valley and the newly settled country of the Trans-Nzoia in the north-west, were devoted to a virtual monoculture of this simple crop.

[1] *Final Reports of the Economic and Financial Committee, 1922–3* (Bowring Committee) (Nairobi, 1922–3). See Chapter VI below.

Maize, then, provided one prop of the agricultural economy which took shape in the Highlands in the early 1920's. The flourishing plantations of coffee and sisal continued to provide another. And a third was erected by the Tariff Amendment Ordinance of 1923. By this time the cultivation of wheat and the raising of cattle had become technically feasible, but the costs of production were such that neither wheat nor dairy products could compete even on the East African market with the output of other countries. To overcome this difficulty, it was now decided to secure the local market for local producers, thus keeping them in business and allowing them time to become competitive—eventually, it was hoped, even on the export market. The new legislation provided for duties of 5 sh. per 100 lb. on imported wheat, 6 sh. per 100 lb. on wheat flour (a local flour mill had been established in 1908 and was in grave difficulties), 1 sh. per lb. on butter and cheese and 80 cents per lb. on bacon and ham, in addition to similar imposts on timber, sugar, ghee, tea, and beer. These duties were intended to make a contribution to revenue, but protectionist motives were also openly avowed. The demand for such protection had, indeed, been put forward by the Economic Commission of 1919, one of whose more remarkable contributions to economic thought was the proposition that the usual arguments against dear food did not apply to East Africa, which did not contain a consuming class. With protection, English-style stock and arable farming, the ideal of the majority of settlers, at last became possible in the Highlands of Kenya.

As a result of these measures, both the growers of maize and the producers of wheat and dairy produce came to enjoy what was in effect a subsidy at the expense of the remainder of the community. The Government had accepted (as the Government of Uganda was to accept later in a different context) the doctrine that people who contributed capital and enterprise to the country must not be allowed to fail. Prima facie these subsidies offended against the fundamental principle that the resources of a poor country should be devoted to those forms of production in which it has a comparative advantage, rather than to the exploitation of a small internal market. On the other hand, it could be argued that the measures which enabled settlers to make a living out of wheat and maize and butter attracted and retained capital which might otherwise have been lost to Kenya, and that the expenditure of this capital had beneficial effects which were unconnected with the direct return. If the railway lost money on the transport of maize, it gained perhaps as much from the return carriage of the maize-growers' imports. It was even arguable that, since its overhead costs were inflexible, it was better that the railway should carry maize at operating cost than that the trains should run empty or not at all. And the 'infant industry' argument was so far valid that there was in time built up a technically proficient system of agriculture, and especially of animal husbandry, which, in the long run, when the internal market had expanded, would be of great value to the country. For the continuous cultivation of maize, on the other hand, there was little to be said from an agronomic point of view. The whole question is too complex to be discussed adequately within the compass of this chapter, and must be left there. In one respect, however, an undeniably unfortunate precedent had been set. Political rather than economic forces were being allowed to determine the structure of production. The first steps had been taken towards the construction of the artificial framework of legislative control by which large areas of the agricultural economy were to be supported after the second world war.

In other ways, too, the political predominance of the European community during and immediately after the first world war made its impress on the pattern of the economy. The Natives Registration Ordinance, enacted in 1915 and strictly enforced from 1918 onwards, introduced serious imperfections into the labour market to the advantage of the employers; and the process was carried a stage further by the 'Northey circulars' of 1919.[1] Intended to resolve the ambiguities which for the past decade had surrounded the functions of officials with regard to the recruitment of labour, these circulars leant heavily in the direction of compulsion. It was made clear that the duty of officers 'in charge of what are termed labour-supplying districts' was 'to induce an augmentation of the supply of labour for the various farms and plantations in the protectorate'. This time the authorities had over-reached themselves. The missionary and humanitarian interests, aware of the

---

[1] See Chapter VI, pp. (292–3), below.

K

implications of these innocent-seeming words, went into action in London, and a storm was generated of which the reverberations were long to be heard in the land. The circulars were withdrawn; the Chief Native Commissioner, John Ainsworth, whose immediate responsibility they were, resigned; and in 1921 a dispatch from Winston Churchill, who had newly succeeded Milner as Colonial Secretary, laid it down that administrators were to take no further part in labour recruitment except for public works and services of an urgent nature, and then not without reference to the Secretary of State.[1] By this time, as a matter of fact, the worst of the labour crisis was over. As the European farming economy was reconstructed on a more modest scale than had been envisaged in 1919, as growing prosperity made somewhat higher wages possible (by 1924 12–14 sh. a month was the normal rate for agricultural workers), and as a gradually strengthening desire for consumer goods made Africans more willing to engage themselves, a natural balance between demand and supply began to be established.

At the close of the war, however, another and more important measure passed without comment. By 1914, as we have seen, large numbers of Africans were living in European seigneuries. The usual consideration paid for cultivation and grazing rights was service, but it was not necessarily or exclusively service. Sometimes it was a contribution in kind, and occasionally but increasingly it was a money rent. Even before the war, however, opinion was building up among the general body of white farmers against the absentee owners who engaged in what was stigmatized as 'kaffir farming'. The reason was, of course, that an increase in tenant farming had the same effect as an extension of the reserves: it reduced the pressure on Africans to seek wage-employment. In 1918 the employers had their way. The Resident Natives Ordinance of that year decreed that no consideration other than labour should be exacted or accepted, and that no African should live on European land unless he had contracted to work for the proprietor for 180 days in the year. It would be difficult to exaggerate the importance of this measure, which did more than any other act of government to determine the future structure of agrarian

[1] *Despatch . . . relating to Native Labour*, Cmd. 1509 (1921).

society in Kenya. Villeinage—family subsistence agriculture modified by the rendering of work to a superior in exchange for land and protection—is well suited to a society in a rudimentary stage of development. As conditions become more settled the lines of possible evolution are various. It may give way to large-scale estate farming with full-time paid labour, or to tenant-farming, or, if the landowners have become functionless, to peasant proprietorship. Here, however, the two latter possibilities were excluded in advance. In the future, as in the present, Africans were to be allowed to live outside the reserves only as villeins or as labourers. A long step had been taken towards the division of the country into two sections with permanently differing economic and social systems.

1922–8

Having once recovered from the disasters of 1920–2 the economy of Kenya began to make steady progress on most fronts. Ordinary revenue doubled in seven years, rising from £1·64 million in 1922 to £2·41 million in 1925 and £3·33 million in 1929. Provision could now be made for more than the bare needs of administration. Expenditure on public works, for instance, increased from £206,000 in 1922 to £520,000 in 1929. During this period, moreover, the Colony and the Kenya and Uganda Railways and Harbours Administration between them received Imperial loans amounting to £8½ million, which, together with the £5 million which had been raised in 1920, made it possible to strengthen and enlarge the rudimentary existing system of transport. Deep-water berths were constructed at Mombasa, and the railway network was greatly extended. The first objective was to extend the main line into Uganda. In order to satisfy the long-standing need of the European farmers in the north-western highlands for some better link with their markets than a usually water-logged cart-track, the extension was taken, not from Kisumu but from Nakuru, by way of Eldoret. Meanwhile the Thika branch line was extended across Kikuyu-land to the European farming centres of Nyeri and Nanyuki, west of Mount Kenya, and other branches were built to Thompson's Falls and Solai in the Rift Valley, to Kitale in the Trans-Nzoia, and from Kisumu to Butere in the Kavirondo country. By the end of the decade there were few places, either in the European farming areas or in the more populous native reserves, that lay more than 30 miles from a railway station. And those 30 miles were being made much less formidable than hitherto by gradually improving roads and by the advent of the motor-lorry, the most important addition to East Africa's technical equipment since the construction of the original railway.

Meanwhile, with improving finances, and under the able direction of Sir Christian Felling, the general efficiency of the railway system was being greatly improved. In its early days, as we have seen, the paramount objective had been a formal balancing of its accounts, even at the expense of high rates and the sacrifice of improvements and even of proper maintenance. Just after the first world war, this policy had been carried farther, and the railway had been used as an instrument of taxation by the Kenya Government—greatly to the disgust of Uganda. From 1922 onwards all this was changed. The railways and harbours were placed under an autonomous administration, jointly controlled by the Kenya and Uganda governments; large amounts of fresh capital were pumped into them; and they were charged with providing the cheapest possible service that was consistent with proper financial discipline and with the building up of adequate funds for renewals and betterment.[1]

The commercial apparatus of the country was also becoming more complex and efficient. Before the war, only two substantial European organizations had served the commercial needs of British East Africa: the firm of Smith Mackenzie, which had deep roots in nineteenth-century Zanzibar and had had intimate links with the ill-fated Imperial British East Africa Company; and the British East Africa Corporation, which had soon added a variety of mercantile functions to its specific interests in cotton. During the 1920's, however, a number of large firms engaged in oriental and Australasian trade, such as Dalgetys, Mitchell Cotts, and Leslie & Anderson, came to regard East Africa, and Kenya in particular, as worthy of their attention, so that skilled commercial and financial services were now more readily available to producers.

These developments in communications and commerce,

---

[1] For the development of the railway system, see Hill, *Permanent Way*, vol. i, ch. xiv, especially pp. 435 sqq.

and the consequent reduction in the costs of transport and marketing, were both cause and symptom of rapid progress in production. Between 1923 and 1929 the prices of most agricultural products were fairly stable, and high enough to make production reasonably profitable. European agriculture was now on a much firmer footing, and its expansion was steady. True, nothing more was heard of the small farmer whose advent had been hoped for at the end of the war. Practically all the homestead units which had been included in the Soldier Settlement Scheme passed into the hands of existing landowners at the earliest legal moment, and the number of acres per occupier fell only very slightly between 1920 and 1928, from about 2,700 to 2,450 acres. The White Highlands remained a land of large farms, and outside the coffee-growing areas, where units of about 500 acres were normal, a land of very large farms. Much of it was semi-arid pastoral country, and even where crops were grown the return per acre was so low that the costs of European ownership and management could not have been covered otherwise than by large units. But the number of occupiers was growing. Most of the ex-officers who were allotted land in 1919 eventually made good—though only after the easy terms of purchase had been made easier still; and they were reinforced by a steady stream of new immigrants: regular officers smitten by the Geddes axe, upper-class and middle-class youths in search of open air and adventure, here and there a genuine yeoman type, and a sprinkling of wealthy rentiers. (Kenya became, in an off-beat way, fashionable, a kind of African Bermuda.) In 1923 there had been 1,183 European occupiers of land, by 1924 there were 1,715. Thereafter the curve of settlement flattened, and it was not until 1929 that it climbed just over the 2,000 mark,[1] which was to be its virtual peak for many years to come.

Life for the working settler was still precarious and hard. But it was also enormous fun. The worst of the pioneering struggles were over, yet there was still a sense of boundless opportunity and freedom. Every year there were more acres under the plough and more cattle on the pastures, and still the empty untamed land stretched out to the far horizon.

---

[1] Kenya Agricultural Censuses, 1923, 1924, 1929. These figures, of course, exclude the settlers' families.

For the majority of the European farmers the staple crop in these years was maize. The expansion of this form of agriculture was remarkable, the output of the European farms rising from 339,000 200-lb. bags in 1922 to 1,089,000 bags in 1928. Even more impressive, though on a smaller scale, was the increase in the production of wheat, which, with an assured market and relative freedom from rust, rose from 28,000 to 174,000 bags in the same period. Crops of lesser importance included barley, oats, and the quick-growing black wattle tree, the bark of which contained a tanning substance that commanded high prices in these years. Even in 1928, however, only about one-eighth of the occupied area of the Highlands was under cultivation of any kind. In terms of area, stock-farming was easily predominant, and here too there was notable growth. The number of woolled sheep, for instance, increased between 1922 and 1928 from 110,000 to 176,000, and there was also a considerable expansion of dairy farming, which had been practised in a small way as early as 1901 but which became a serious proposition only after the advent of protection. The increase in the number of cows was slight, but their marketable product, thanks to the tariff and the establishment of co-operative creameries, was greatly augmented. In 1922 there were sold off European farms 242,000 gallons of milk, 237,000 lb. of butter, and 65,000 lb. of cheese. In 1928 the figures were 422,000, 325,000, and 131,000.[1]

The real foundation of the country's economy, however, was still, and increasingly, plantation agriculture, the vitality of which was demonstrated by the comparative ease with which, unaided by any kind of subvention, it rode the economic crisis at the beginning of the 1920's. The average output of coffee in the years 1920–2 was 3,500 tons, and that of sisal 5,300 tons. In 1927–9 the figures were 7,900 and 15,200 tons. In the latter half of the 1920's these two crops contributed on the average 51 per cent. of the total value of Kenya's domestic exports, the only other items of any importance being maize (12$\frac{1}{2}$ per cent.), hides and skins (11 per cent.), and sodium carbonate, still the only significant mineral product (8$\frac{1}{2}$ per cent.).[2] Maize apart, the contribution of non-plantation agriculture to the export

[1] Figures from Kenya Annual Agricultural Censuses, 1922, 1928.
[2] Kenya Agricultural Censuses, 1922, 1929.

trade was inconsiderable, and the export of substantial quantities of maize was achieved only by the profligate practice of continuous cropping. To some extent, of course, concentration on the export figures gives a misleading picture. The wheat-growers and dairy-farmers were helping to feed the urban European and in some measure the Asian population—though at high cost—and the maize-growers, by providing food for plantation and other labourers, were making a large indirect as well as a direct contribution to export production.

One of the most striking contrasts between the economy of the 1920's and that of the pre-war period was the far smaller part now played by independent African production in the export trade. In 1912–13, at a conservative estimate, 70 per cent. by value of the agricultural exports had been 'native produce'. In 1928 the proportion was less than 20 per cent.[1] Even in absolute terms the increase had been small, and since 1925 there had actually been a noticeable decline. Moreover, of the £479,000 contributed from the African reserves, well over half was represented by hides and skins, the automatic by-product of subsistence pastoralism. The export of simsim, once so important to the Kavirondo economy, had dwindled into insignificance. Attempts to establish a cotton industry had been renewed in 1923 but had met with little success; during the 1920's the export value of this crop only once exceeded £10,000. It is true that, here also, exports were not the whole of the story. African farmers were undoubtedly gaining a certain income from the local sale of milk and vegetables; and although their maize was not of export quality some of it was believed to find its way on to the internal market. Since, how-ever, European production was largely in excess of exports, it is hard to believe that African sales were yet considerable. By far the greater part of the output of the reserves, which was very roughly estimated at 1·39 million bags in 1930 (when the European output reached a peak of 1·86 million)[2] must have been consumed on the farm, and can hardly be counted as a result of economic development, except in so far as the substitution of maize for millets, begun in pre-British times, had been greatly accelerated.

The allegation that African economic agriculture, especially

[1] Ibid., 1928.   [2] Ibid., 1930.

in the Nyanza Province, had been deliberately stifled in the interests of European farmers probably has some validity in respect of the early post-war years, when the whole endeavour of Government was directed towards the provision of labour for the settled areas. But, as we have seen, the use of official pressures in this direction was renounced in 1921, and in 1923 the Government formally proclaimed a 'dual policy': henceforward agricultural development was to be fostered in the European and the native areas alike. The reasons for the signal failure of one-half of this policy remain obscure. It should be noted, however, that not only in Kenya but also in Uganda and Tanganyika little or no headway was being made during the middle and later 1920's with African production of marketable crops. It seems that throughout East Africa this was a period in which African wants were more or less static. The native societies, having passed through the first stage of adaptation to a money economy, brought about by the imposition of taxation and the adoption of certain new conventions, such as the wearing of a modicum of cotton clothing, had attained a new equilibrium. European standards of living were altogether beyond their horizon, and after a limited range of needs had been satisfied the marginal utility of money sharply diminished. To probably a large majority of Kenyans, it was still coins, not commodities, that were 'bought'.

This, however, does not explain why the majority of them should apparently have chosen to earn this limited income by wage-labour rather than by the cultivation of their own fields. Certainly the character of European farming had altered out of all recognition since the pre-war period, when rough adventurers demanded that African labour should be put at their disposal, although most of them had very little either of capital or skill to add to the product of African muscles. The Highland farms were now much more capitalized than before, and incomparably more productive than African holdings. Some of them were producing crops of far higher unit value than any in the native repertoire; and even the arable and stock farms, with their steam ploughs and tractors, their dips and fences, and high-grade herds, were capable of exercising a genuine economic attraction. Not only were wages somewhat higher, but housing and feeding had much improved, medical treatment was usually provided, and the general handling of the workers had become very much more humane. Calculations of the relative economic returns are exceedingly difficult to make, but it does none the less appear that the Kavirondo at least could have earned a given income with less effort by staying at home and growing cotton than by engaging themselves for hire. The economic returns, however, are not the only factor to be considered. At the time, it was generally believed that non-economic influences told heavily in favour of peasant farming in the reserves, but this may have been a misconception. There is reason to think that for many of the younger generation a sojourn in Nairobi or on a European farm was actually a welcome relief from the ennui of a tribal life from which most of the vitality had departed.

In the final analysis, however, the basic explanation may well be that the Africans' choice was not even yet an entirely free one. In this period of total docility the wishes of authority, even though not expressed as forcibly as in former times, had a profound influence on African economic decisions, and on the whole the wish of authority was still that the natives should go out to work. Certainly the 'dual policy' was not prosecuted in this period with any great vigour. Alex Holm, who was Director of Agriculture from 1921 to 1930, was a convinced believer in European farming enterprise, the development of which was his primary concern, as it was the primary concern of the Government as a whole.

This bias was most clearly brought out by the issue of the controversy which raged from 1925 onwards over the cultivation of coffee by African peasants. By this time African production, not only of *robusta* coffee but also of the more valuable and delicate *arabica* species, had started both in Uganda and in Tanganyika. But the suggestion that coffee might be introduced into the native reserves of Kenya aroused vehement opposition from the settlers and a mobilization of all the influence that they could command in London. As late as 1932 the assembled coffee planters urged 'the indefinite postponement of a step so utterly unwise'.[1] Even a proposal to experiment with *robusta* in areas far removed from European

---

[1] *Report of the Coffee Planter's Days and Coffee Conference, 1932* (Govt. Printer, Nairobi, 1932). Cf. *Report of the Coffee Conference, 1927* (Govt. Printer, Nairobi, 1928).

plantations was resisted as being the thin end of the wedge. Their views prevailed for the time being. Not only were no positive steps taken to introduce coffee into African agriculture but its cultivation was severely frowned on, which is to say that it was virtually forbidden.[1] The principal ground put forward for this restriction was the fear that ill-tended native gardens would be a breeding ground for the various pests and diseases to which the coffee tree was vulnerable, and would thus be a menace to neighbouring plantations. This fear was not without some foundation, though experience elsewhere was to show that, given careful supervision, African-grown coffee need be no less healthy, and of no lower quality, than any other. Behind the settlers' objections, however, there lay undoubtedly the simple fact that any drastic improvement in the productivity of African agriculture would inevitably raise the price of labour. As one of the more candid of their number put it:

it stands to reason that the more prosperous and contented is the population of a reserve, the less the need or inclination of the young men of the tribe to go out into the field. From the farmers' point of view, the ideal reserve is a recruiting-ground for labour, a place from which the able-bodied go out to work, returning occasionally to rest and to beget the next generation of labourers.[2]

There could be no valid objection to the production of low-value bulk crops like maize, but an infringement of the European monopoly of coffee-growing would have struck at the roots of the settler economy. Nearly half the European landholders were wholly or partly dependent on this crop, which absorbed about a third of the total labour force of Kenya.

So, during the 1920's, European-directed agriculture established and maintained an overwhelming preponderance over other forms of production for the market. The system was constantly expanding and to all appearance was prospering exceedingly. Yet there are grounds for doubting whether it was yet soundly based, or even whether the majority of farmers were making a true profit. The enormous adverse balance of trade—

---

[1] By the Coffee Plantations Registration Ordinance of 1918, every grower was required to take out a licence to the value of 30s. per year, and administrative officers were instructed that such licences should not in any case be issued to African growers.

[2] M. A. Buxton, *Kenya Days* (London, 1927), p. 10.

imports were rarely less than double the value of exports—suggests, even when allowance has been made for the transport and financial services rendered to other territories and for the large import of public capital, that most people were spending beyond their current incomes, and that the whole system depended heavily on a continuing inflow of private funds, which in turn depended on a good yield being before long obtained on existing investments. But this, in spite of the general atmosphere of confidence, was rather problematic. Wheat-growing and dairy farming, besides being very vulnerable to natural disasters, were utterly dependent on a protected market. The maize industry was agronomically unsound and its economic foundations were shaky. The plantation industries were healthy at their core but had a broad fringe of weakness; coffee had been planted in large quantities on unsuitable land and by unsuitable people. Indeed, despite an improvement in the general level of efficiency, much of the European farming was still somewhat amateurish. Of the Baroness Blixen, for example, it could fairly be said that her great talents as a writer were not matched by her capacity for estate management; and the settlers still included large numbers of similar people, to whom the Highlands were the 'happy hunting grounds' and not a place in which marginal revenue needed to be equated with marginal cost. In so far as they provided a market for goods and services, such residents were valuable citizens of Kenya—so long as their incomes lasted. Everything, in fact, turned on a continuance of the good fortune which had blessed the country during the halcyon years of the middle 1920's.

1929–39

But from 1928 onwards fortune deserted Kenya. In the autumn of that year the desert locust came out of the north and ravaged the land, to repeat the process with still greater efficiency in the following season. From 1931 to 1934 there was disastrous drought. And meanwhile the world commodity markets had broken, more resoundingly than they had ever broken before, and for a longer period. Between 1928 and 1934 the local value of coffee was reduced by more than a half, and the value of sisal and of maize by more than two-thirds. Neither the fall in the prices of imported goods, which was generally not of the same magnitude, nor a general wage-cut of about 40 per cent. were sufficient to offset this catastrophic deterioration in the farmer's position, for neither had any bearing on the fact that the real burden of his debt (and nearly all farmers had borrowed to the limit of their capacity) was now much greater than before. The most obvious solution from the producer's point of view, devaluation of the currency, was ruled out by considerations of general policy. Despite strong pressure from the settlers, the Colonial Secretary refused to consider it.[1]

The Government, which also had heavy fixed obligations in the form of debt charges and pensions, was in equally grave straits. It none the less made strenuous efforts to save the European farmers from ruin. In addition to miscellaneous refunds and rebates amounting to £143,000 between 1930 and 1933, loan subsidies of £116,000 were granted on exports of cereals from the 1929–30 crop, and under the Agricultural Advances Ordinance of 1930 a further £113,000 had been lent by 1934 to those of the farmers whose plight was especially desperate. Nevertheless, the situation continued to deteriorate. Few of the settlers actually abandoned the struggle, partly because for the majority farming in Kenya was the breath of life, partly because their assets were unrealizable and their creditors could see no advantage in foreclosing. But between 1930 and 1936 the cultivated area dropped from 644,000 to 502,000 acres.[2] While on some farms costs were being cut in the short run by overworking of the land, others had been put on a care and maintenance basis, their owners seeking to remedy their fortunes by some other method.

To this time of crisis belongs the curious episode of the Kenya gold rush. Gold had long been known to exist in the Kavirondo country, but apart from a little alluvial digging in the 1920's it had never previously been thought worth exploiting. A new and rather more promising discovery had been made in 1931 near Kakamega, but it is doubtful whether much would have been made even of this if it had not been for the rising price of gold (especially after the devaluation of the

---

[1] Cunliffe Lister's pronouncement is reported in full in the *Report of the Economic Development Committee*, 1934 (Nairobi, 1935), p. 169.

[2] Kenya Agricultural Censuses, 1930, 1936.

dollar in 1934) and the desperate situation of a large part of the population. As it was, a crowd of hopeful prospectors flocked into the area and certain of the big mining companies began to take an interest. At its peak in 1935 the industry gave employment to over 600 Europeans and nearly 15,000 Africans. Thereafter, as the alluvial deposits began to be exhausted, the numbers employed declined, but the value of the output continued to rise until 1940, when it reached £640,000. The amount of payable gold, however, was in reality small, and from then on the industry dwindled slowly into insignificance.[1]

While they lasted, the goldfields provided a subsistence for a large part of the European population, as well as fortune for a very few. Meanwhile more solid relief was obtained through the partial recovery of world markets and the reconstruction of European agriculture. One great step forward was the setting up of a Land Bank in 1931 with a capital of £500,000 derived from loan funds, so that normal farm credit was at last placed on a sound footing. Another was a major shift away from maize-growing to more profitable and technically preferable forms of agriculture. The area under maize on European farms declined by more than 50 per cent. between 1929 and 1938. On the other hand, the number of cows increased by about 80 per cent. in the same period and the output of dairy products, supported by an efficient co-operative organization and by still higher protective duties, expanded in even greater proportion.[2] At least equally important was the advent of a new crop, pyrethrum. In 1935 it was discovered that this daisy, whose flowers yielded the most potent insecticide then known, could be made to flourish in the Kenya Highlands, and was indeed more productive there than in most other parts of the world. Thus the farmers of the Highlands had at last found what they had once looked for in flax—a crop which could be grown above 6,000 feet, which needed little capital, and which, nevertheless, yielded a large margin of profit. At first, indeed, the margin was not large, but the price rose dramatically, and by 1937, when it was selling in London at £125 a ton, pyrethrum was making a modest fortune for many of its growers.

[1] H. Fearn, 'The gold-mining era in Kenya Colony', *Journal of Tropical Geography*, xi (1958), 43–58.
[2] Kenya Agricultural Censuses, 1929, 1938.

For the Colony at large, however, it was once again the resilience of the plantation industries that averted ruin. Even at the worst of times coffee and sisal could be made to yield a profit to the more efficient producers, and the output of both crops continued to rise throughout the long years of depression—partly, it is true, because of the maturation of earlier plantings. And to these well-established products there was now added a third. Tea had been grown in Kenya since the early years of the century, but for a long time the large capital sums needed for its production on a commercial scale had not been forthcoming. In 1925, however, this need had been met. Large London interests had entered the industry and big plantations had been established in the south-western Highlands, where alone the rainfall was fully adequate. By the mid-1930's these investments had begun to show results and by 1938 tea was second only to coffee among Kenya's agricultural exports. Further expansion was held up only because Kenya was a party to the international restriction agreement. Even with this reinforcement the proportionate contribution of the plantation industries to the Colony's total exports was not quite as high as formerly, averaging 47 per cent. in the years 1936–8.[1] The main reason was the rise of gold, which now accounted for 10 per cent. of the total.

For the African population as well as for others the depression was a great disaster. The prices of such commodities as hides, ghee, beans, and simsim slumped even more drastically than those of the staples of European agriculture. Wages fell back from 14 sh. to 8 sh. a month, and in spite of this, for the first time in the history of the Colony there was unemployment, in the sense that men actively seeking work were unable to find it. There was, it is true, one very important mitigating factor. Thanks to the so-called Congo Basin treaties,[2] the East African territories were unable to discriminate against cloth and other consumer goods of Japanese manufacture, which now became available at such low prices that, for the poor, the terms of trade

---

[1] Annual Reports of the Department of Agriculture, 1936–8.

[2] The general aim of the conventions known as the Congo Basin Treaties, agreed on in the Berlin Act of 1885 and in the Brussels Act of 1890, was, on the one hand, to lay down certain standards for the treatment of African indigenous populations, and, on the other, to ensure equal conditions for the commerce of all interested nations in a wide area of central Africa.

may actually have improved. On the other hand, although African producers were not burdened by debt, they were faced with the fixed obligation of tax payments, which now became a much heavier burden in real terms. The only solution was to increase production. Whether or not the Africans would have reached this conclusion for themselves, the Government had reached it for them. Some countries at this time were attempting to improve their terms of trade by restricting output, but this would not have been a sensible course for Kenya to adopt, as her exports formed too small a proportion of world supplies of any commodity for changes in their volume to have an appreciable effect on prices. In face of the Colony's evident need for more exports, opposition to the development of native production for the market was melting away; it found only one voice among the members of the Economic Development Committee in 1934.[1] An exception was still made for coffee, but in 1937 the authorities felt able to take the first very tentative steps towards the introduction of this industry in certain native areas.

In less controversial fields, every effort was made to persuade African cultivators to expand production, and with considerable success. The output of seed-cotton in the Nyanza Province shot up from about 1 million lb. in 1930–1 to nearly 24 million in the 1937–8 season; and sales of maize from the reserves steadily filled the gap left by the decline in European production. By the end of the decade they amounted to over 700,000 bags, considerably more than the deliveries from European farms. To the economy of the Colony as a whole this surplus was a very welcome contribution. But it was, of course, much less welcome to those European farmers who were still growing maize, and whose powerful co-operative, the Kenya Farmers' Association, had hitherto had some success in maintaining the price level. They were now being undercut, especially on the more profitable internal market. Here it becomes necessary to explain a curious feature of the Kenya maize industry. European maize production had reached its 1930 dimensions on the basis of a large export trade. Only

[1] *Report of the Economic Development Committee, 1934* (Nairobi, 1935), p. 184. The dissentient voice was that of T. J. O'Shea, elected member for the Uasin Gishu Plateau.

certain qualities of maize—those which kept well and satisfied the special requirements of overseas buyers—could be exported at all. On the internal market, where prices were higher, these qualities were not important. Thus the individual high-quality producer got little or no reward for an effort which, to the industry as a whole, was indispensable. The K.F.A., having established a virtual monopoly of maize marketing, had surmounted this difficulty by paying its members uniform pool prices, scaled according to quality but not according to destination. This arrangement was now endangered by the increasing penetration of the internal market by African producers, who benefited from the fact that a large part of total supplies was monopolistically controlled. The solution was obvious: the European growers must restore their control of the market by buying up African supplies, both in order to sustain prices at a level which would keep them in business and in order to make the African producers share the burden of the less rewarding export trade. Buying agencies of the K.F.A. were therefore set up in the reserves and primary marketing was to a large extent taken out of the hands of the existing Asian dealers. In this process the K.F.A. were assisted by a reform of the marketing system which the Government had introduced in 1934. Henceforward African produce could be sold only in organized markets, and not to the shopkeepers and itinerant merchants who had previously conducted the bulk of the trade. The motives behind this reform, which had been concerted with the governments of Uganda and Tanganyika, were distrust of the petty trader and the desire to reduce the profits of middlemen and raise the prices received by the producer.[1] This object was indeed achieved, though at the expense of the convenience of doorstep purchase, but physical concentration of trade naturally facilitated the growth of monopoly.

During the second world war the intervention of Government in the marketing of maize became much more direct. In 1942, having committed itself to making large contributions to the provisioning of the Imperial forces in the Middle East, it was obliged to establish control over the marketing of maize. There followed, in the early months of 1943, a severe food shortage, due partly to the (very incomplete) fulfilment of the Govern-

---

[1] See *Report of the Economic Development Committee, 1934*, pp. 124-31.

ment's promises of overseas shipments, partly to natural causes, and partly to the dislocation of normal trade by the Maize Control. It had become apparent that unless production could be largely increased Kenya would not only be unable to perform the war-supply function that had been assigned to it but, in an unfavourable season, would not even achieve the self-sufficiency that was essential under war conditions. To induce the necessary expansion on the part of European farmers it was necessary to guarantee much increased prices. Similar increases were not thought to be needed in the case of African growers, whose opportunity costs were much lower. They would, moreover, have caused serious inflation, since the supply of imported consumer goods was regulated, not by effective demand, but by allocations of production capacity and shipping space made in Washington and London. The solution was found in withholding part of the increase from the African producers, the balance being paid into soil-conservation funds controlled by African local authorities. This was the beginning of a system of centralized marketing and managed prices which became a major and permanent feature of the post-war economy, the benefits being shared by the high-cost European producers, the African district councils, for whom the maize cess developed into a major source of general revenue, and to some extent the African growers.

During the 1930's, then, Africans began to play a much larger part in the exchange economy. But as the years passed the problem of stimulating the production of a marketable surplus was overshadowed by another problem of still greater and more permanent import. It began to be apparent that the land itself was in peril. Attention had, indeed, been called to the menace of soil erosion even before 1930, but it was not until after that date that the magnitude of the danger was revealed. By the end of the decade the Department of Agriculture was preoccupied much less with the hope that the land might yield a still larger surplus than with the fear that before long it might fail to provide the peoples of Kenya even with a bare subsistence.

In the first forty years of British rule a profound change had been effected in the economic life of the African peoples, and not least in the nature of their agricultural production. By

virtue of revolutionary changes in the means of transport, of the
creation of a wide area of peace and law, and of the advent of
persons skilled in trade, the market had been greatly extended,
and a value had thus been given to the potential surplus product of African family holdings. But this increase in the value
of products had not been accompanied by any corresponding
change in the methods of production. The techniques of
agriculture were essentially unaltered, apart from the introduction of the steel hoe and in a few places of the ox-drawn
plough, and there had been no fundamental reconstruction of
agrarian organization, so far as the reserves were concerned.
Indigenous practices, varying in detail, conformed to the
general pattern known as 'shifting cultivation'. Land was tilled
until its yield began to diminish. It was then abandoned to the
slow regenerative agencies of nature and new fields were taken
out of the surrounding waste. No attempt was made, by
systematic rotation of crops or the application of manure, to
maintain the soil at a high level of fertility under continuous
cultivation. To do so would not only have been exceedingly
difficult under African conditions but would also have been
entirely pointless. For the system was based on the hitherto
valid premiss that land was not a scarce factor.

What was not scarce naturally had no owner. The community controlled a territory, and within that territory each of
its members had the unquestioned right to cultivate enough
land for the support of his family—a right which followed
logically from his membership, for without cultivating he
could not live. The question of his acquiring more land in order
to produce a saleable surplus did not arise, for there was no
one to buy the surplus. The fields which a family had created
were, of course, its property so long as the fields lasted. But since
there were no permanent steadings, and since land as such had no
marketable value, there was no proprietorship in the soil itself.

The twin assumptions, that land was not scarce and that
cultivation was for subsistence only, remained substantially
valid during the first decades of British rule. In 1900 the density
of population was almost certainly subnormal, at any rate in
the Kikuyu country, and the subsequent increase was checked,
if not annulled, by pestilence and famine in 1918–20. Moreover,
the area of land available to the agricultural tribes had been

largely augmented by the opening up of the former Masai domain, which, as has been shown earlier, was not and could not have been withheld from African peasants. And until after 1930 the volume of production for the market had not been sufficient to make much impact on the land or on the pattern of agrarian activity. After that date a very different situation began to emerge. Population was now definitely on the increase. Since no census was taken during the period covered by this chapter, a precise estimate is not possible, but a careful student of the available data reached the conclusion in 1935[1] that during the past decade or so the rate of growth among the Kikuyu and in part of the Nyanza Province had been of the order of 1·5 per cent. per annum. The density of population in Kikuyu land as a whole was reckoned at 283 to the square mile (or 208 after the implementation of the Carter Report) and at 145 in the three Kavirondo districts. These figures did not in themselves indicate serious congestion, but there were localities in which the density was much higher. Moreover, the demands made on the land by each family were becoming much greater, as production for the market was intensified. In some areas at least, land was becoming scarce, and the necessary adjustments of economic and social relationships were being made to this supremely important change. Holdings were being bought and sold, and a struggle for ownership was developing between the lineage officials traditionally charged with allotment and adjudication, who were endeavouring to set up as landlords, and the individual cultivators, who were seeking emancipation from communal controls. At the same time those peasants who were not members of the locally dominant lineage were coming to be regarded as tenants, and their rights of occupation were becoming increasingly precarious.

Over and above these disturbing changes in the pattern of agrarian society was the serious agronomical deterioration. The premises of shifting cultivation were no longer operative. The land was no longer receiving its proper periods of rest, and, as a result, not only were yields declining but the exhausted soil was being washed away. An irremediable loss of fertility was imminent in many places. In the arid pastoral areas the

[1] Unpublished memorandum by B. Fazan, prepared for the 1935 Economic Development Committee.

situation was perhaps even worse than in the congested agricultural districts. Here, as a result of the veterinary officers' successes in the campaign against epizootic diseases, cattle and goats had multiplied to the point where they began to threaten the permanent destruction of the pastures. Efforts to induce the pastoralists to part with their surplus male stock were of little avail against their continuing conviction that wealth and livestock were synonymous terms. These efforts were not helped by the almost permanent quarantine which was maintained in many of the African pastoral areas for the protection of European stock and which made the organization of stock markets exceedingly difficult. Although the herding tribes were undoubtedly less responsive than most of the agriculturalists to the temptations of western economy and culture, there is a good deal of evidence that their unwillingness to turn beasts into money was by no means absolute.

The worst example of devastation was the country of the Kamba tribe, which was rapidly being converted into a desert by a combination of over-cultivation, over-grazing, and forest destruction. Here compulsory de-stocking was decided on, and special arrangements were made with a meat-processing firm for the disposal of the products. The association of compulsory sale and private monopolistic purchase was, of course, profoundly objectionable. The Kamba, who did *not* possess more cattle than they needed for their subsistence, made an energetic protest, and the project had to be abandoned.[1]

Meanwhile, however, the Department of Agriculture had embarked on the great effort of investigation, experiment, and planning which, in conjunction with the Empire-wide and world-wide assault on the problems of erosion, cleared the way for the strenuous remedial action which was to be undertaken after the second world war. First there were worked out the techniques of protection against erosion—contour-ploughing, strip-cropping, terracing, and so forth. These, however, were clearly seen to be effective only against the outworks of the problem. The ultimate solution lay in the development of a system of husbandry in which the soil would not merely be kept in place but would be maintained at a permanently high level of fertility. Temporary cultivation patches would have to be

[1] See also Chapter VII, p. 368, below.

replaced by permanent, bounded, consolidated farms, in which animal husbandry would be integrated with a planned crop rotation. This transformation was obviously going to be exceedingly difficult to bring about, and it would not prevent the immense social disturbance that was being generated by the growing scarcity of land. For under the new system the unit of cultivation would need to be rather larger, and certainly not smaller, than before. The land might well support a still denser population at a higher standard of living, but it would not be possible for every family to have a piece of its own.

While pressure on the land was building up within the reserves, the safety-valve, emigration to the European-owned areas of the Highlands, was being closed. The 'squatter' system, which had suited both parties in the early stages of development, became less and less appropriate as the land filled up. Precluded by legislation from playing the role of improving landlords, the settlers had to be farmers or nothing; and, as farmers, they increasingly preferred straightforward wage-labour to villein service, which entailed the use, and generally the misuse, of increasingly valuable land by inefficient subsistence cultivators and herdsmen. Up to about 1928 there had been a continuous net inflow of resident labourers and their families, until in that year the number of Africans resident on European farms reached a total of 112,000, of whom 33,000 were adult males. But after 1930 the trend was reversed. By 1938 they numbered 104,000, and of these only 28,000 were adult males, although the total farm labour force had considerably increased.[1] At the same time there was a tendency, assisted by fresh legislation in 1937,[2] to curtail the rights, or privileges, of the labour-tenants, especially in respect of grazing land, which, with the general shift from arable to stock-farming, was becoming increasingly scarce.

Thus at all points the security and freedom of the subsistence peasant were being gradually eroded. The old egalitarian pattern—to each woman her little patch of maize, to each man his little flock of goats—could not much longer be maintained. In the future there would be landless men, dependent on

---

[1] Kenya Agricultural Censuses, 1928, 1938.
[2] Resident Labourers Ordinance, 1937. See C. K. Meek, *Land Law and Custom in the Colonies* (Oxford, 1946), pp. 83–84.

others for the means of life. In our period this impending change, the unavoidable concomitant of economic growth, cast only a faint shadow over the land. But the shadow was there, and it was ominous.

During the inter-war period, and especially in its last decade, economic forces were working towards the gradual assimilation of the two sectors of Kenyan economy and society. The increasingly commercial character of African agriculture and the slow spread of new wants among the masses of the people were beginning to modify the distinction between the modern forms of production and exchange in the White Highlands and the primitive subsistence agriculture of the Reserves. On the other hand, the main weight of policy was now thrust in opposition to this change, and so far as this could be effected by institutional arrangements the lines of cleavage were not less but more sharply drawn and rigidly upheld. Several factors contributed to the shaping of this policy. There was the administrator's concern for the maintenance of traditional mechanisms of social and political control. There was the now virtually unanimous belief of European employers that adequate and reasonably prosperous reserves were in their interest, despite the degree of independence that they conferred on the workers, because they were an insurance against unrest and a protection against the heavy costs and responsibilities of proletarianization; minute wages and rudimentary social services were thought to be unobjectionable, since the workers had their homes and their security outside the European social system. And there was also the humanitarian conviction that the Africans could be protected against the harsh impact of European economic ambition, of 'civilization rampant and greedy',[1] only if a place were set apart for them, if 'a field for the full development of native life' were 'clearly defined and safeguarded'.[2] From this conviction there stemmed the interminable wrangles over whether the natives were or were not receiving a fair return for their taxes.[3] Into this sterile controversy we

---

[1] P. Mitchell, *African Afterthoughts* (London, 1954), p. 124, quoting a diary entry of 1 May 1930.

[2] *Report of the Commission on Closer Union* (Hilton Young Commission), Cmd. 3234 (1929), pp. 40–41.

[3] See *Report by the Financial Commissioner (Lord Moyne) on Certain Questions in Kenya*, Cmd. 4093 (1932); *Report of Joint Committee on Closer Union in East Africa*, H.C. 156 (1931).

need not enter, except to point out that by a 'fair' return was usually meant a return equal to their contribution. In most modern societies, of course, the poor are expected to pay into the public chest much less than they take out. The Africans of Kenya, however, were not regarded as 'the poor' but as a distinct community, to which communal rather than individual justice was to be rendered.

It was in the matter of land rights, however, that the doctrines of communalism found their clearest expression. The idea of excluding immigrants from the lands occupied by the native peoples was as old as Kenya. But it was generally acknowledged in the 1920's that the boundaries of the tribal territories had not always been correctly drawn and were not even yet sufficiently clearly 'defined and safeguarded'. The natives had lost some land which was rightfully theirs, and their friends were not convinced that they might not lose yet more in the future. The Kenya Land Commission was appointed in 1932 to put these matters right. Now, although the Commission paid a good deal of attention to the economic needs of the various African communities, its approach was on the whole historical and legal. After an extremely patient and rigorous inquiry it came to the conclusion that since 1902, when everything began, a certain amount of land which should have been treated as native territory had indeed been wrongfully alienated. The Kikuyu, the chief sufferers, had, it was true indeed, subsequently been allotted larger areas outside their original territory, but these areas were much less desirable than the ones lost, and the Commission's assessment was that the Government still owed the Kikuyu, on balance, $30\frac{1}{2}$ square miles of good land.[1] This debt was to be paid, largely at the expense of the Forest Reserve; and, to meet economic needs as distinct from claims of right, certain additional lands were to be reserved for Africans in areas which had so far neither been gazetted as native reserves nor leased to Europeans—that is, of course, in areas which no one had hitherto found attractive.

Once they had been thus adjusted the ethnic boundaries of Kenya were to remain inviolate. The Africans were to be secured for ever both against dispossession and against the voluntary surrender of their heritage. But conversely they were

[1] Carter Commission *Report*, Cmd. 4556, pp. 129–31.

to be debarred for ever from acquiring rights in the remainder
of the country. When farms had been alienated on the borders
of Kikuyu land in the early years, most of the native occupants
had taken compensation and departed; but some had chosen
to stay, their holdings forming small enclaves in European
estates, and a few such rightholders still remained. Perhaps
the most significant of the commissioners' recommendations
was that these rights should now be extinguished, with due
compensation, in order that *de jure* segregation should be final
and completed. In similar vein they expressed concern at the
number of stock possessed by some resident labourers. It was
vital, they considered, that this arrangement should be essentially a labour contract, and not a tenancy contract, which
would be 'contrary to the purpose for which the European
Highlands have been reserved'.[1] Here we see the final stage in
the semantic evolution of this term. Originally the adjective
was predicative and its antonym was 'Indian'. Now it was used
in a qualifying sense and its principal antonym was 'African'. In
those parts of the Highlands which had not been reserved for
Africans, only Europeans would be permitted to acquire
rights in land. In effect, a European tribal reserve had been
created.

Retrospect and prospect

Throughout the period covered by this chapter Kenya
remained an essentially agricultural country inasmuch as the
cultivation of the soil and the herding of livestock continued to
be the principal occupations of the vast majority of her peoples.
Other forms of primary production, notably the exploitation
of the forests and of the gold and soda deposits, had their place
in the economy, but it was not a very important place. Apart
from the necessary processing of primary products, secondary
industry was very little developed. There were a few small
factories and workshops in Nairobi and Mombasa, engaged
mainly in the final stages of manufacture—clothing and footwear, furniture, aluminium hollow-ware and the like—but
their contribution to the national income was not significant.
The reason for this was not, of course, that Kenya was deliberately reserved as a 'colonial' market. We have seen that

[1] Carter Commission *Report*, pp. 492-3.

the Government was, if anything, excessively kind to infant local industries such as bacon factories and flour mills; and, whereas from 1934 onwards Kenya's exports enjoyed the benefits of imperial preference, she was precluded by the 'Congo Basin' treaties from offering similar consideration to the products of metropolitan industries. The main reason was rather that the potential consumers were so few and so poor that sales could not be expected to justify the heavy fixed costs of factory production. On the other hand, a considerable growth of tertiary industries was a natural and necessary concomitant of agricultural expansion. It is to be noted that, despite the usual connotation of the word 'settler', farmers were at no time a majority even of the non-official white population, being consistently outnumbered by the professional and business classes. (Classification, however, was by no means easy; if there were such a thing as a typical Kenya European, he would be a business man with a 20-acre residential holding ten miles from the centre of Nairobi and perhaps a financial interest in a farm near Nakuru.) The members of the Asian communities were almost exclusively engaged in commerce, in clerical work, and in the building and other service industries. And of those Africans who were employed for hire, much larger numbers were absorbed by transport, construction, and domestic service, taken together, than by agriculture.

The importance of the tertiary sector was enhanced by the fact that many of the services rendered by Kenyans often extended beyond the boundaries of the Colony. Geography and the railway system decreed that they should transport and ship goods for Uganda and part of northern Tanganyika, which was linked to the Mombasa Railway by a line originally built for military purposes in the first world war. Over and above this, Nairobi, as the centre of the only sizeable body of well-to-do consumers in East Africa, was from an early date the natural headquarters for business firms of all kinds, which often operated in the other territories through branch offices or agencies. It thus became in a sense the commercial and financial capital of the whole region. It was certainly by far the largest town in East Africa, with a population which by 1945 was probably approaching 100,000, and Mombasa, about half the size of Nairobi, easily held second place. No other towns in

Kenya, except perhaps Nakuru, the 'capital of the White Highlands', were of any real consequence.

Thus only a very small fraction of the people could yet be described as town-dwellers, and only for a still smaller fraction was urbanization more than partial. Hardly any Africans had entirely severed themselves from their roots in the rural areas, and certainly none were in any true sense detribalized. The urban economy was based in the main, like that of the White Highlands, on the system of migrant or temporary labour. Africans came to work for short periods in the towns, leaving their families to support themselves in the reserves, whither they would return when they had saved a sum sufficient for their present requirements. The system undoubtedly had many advantages at this stage of development. It probably accorded on the whole with the inclinations of the people; and it certainly accorded with the inclinations of the ruling classes, who were enabled to postpone serious consideration of the formidable social and economic problems which would be posed by the emergence of an urban proletariat. This development, in the view of the Administration, would have disrupted the whole existing social and political order—as, indeed, it was to do, throughout Africa, in the 1950's. For employers, the system made it possible to continue paying low wages, which were, in effect, subsidized by subsistence production in the reserves. And employers, taxpayers, and administrators alike were relieved of the enormously expensive task of building towns in which large numbers of people could comfortably live. It was convenient for all parties to believe that Africans did not really live in towns at all, but merely camped briefly in the vicinity. 'The native reserves', declared the Land Commission, endorsing the prevailing official opinion, 'are the proper place for natives whose presence in the towns is no longer required.'[1]

It is now generally acknowledged that these views were short-sighted. The defects of the temporary system are plain—and not least among them is the fact that it postponed consideration of problems which could not be indefinitely evaded, if development were to proceed. Socially, the system produced a large class of men who were neither citizens nor tribesmen, neither workers nor peasants, but moved uneasily between two

[1] Carter Commission *Report*, p. 177.

incompatible and equally unsatisfying worlds. Economically, besides making for the inefficient use of land, which was an increasingly scarce resource, it prevented the accumulation of industrial skills, and so tended to perpetuate the closed circle of low productivity, low wages, low consumption, and a narrow market for industrial goods. Even in our period the system was not so universal as the foregoing remarks may have implied. Some employers could not do without a more or less permanent nucleus of semi-skilled African workers, and it was the largest of these, the Railways and Harbours Administration, that was most prominent in the provision of respectable housing. The Government also provided houses for its own regular employees, and several estates were built during the inter-war period by the municipality of Nairobi, in which provision was made for married as well as for bachelor citizens. By the end of the second world war larger housing and town planning schemes were being taken seriously in hand. Nevertheless, the main pattern of urban life and work still presupposed the predominance of labourers whose efficiency did not warrant and whose needs did not compel anything more than a bachelor wage.

Meanwhile, in 1939, Kenya had been startled by the first signs of concerted action on the part of urban labour. The pioneers of militancy were, as might be expected, the dockers of Mombasa, who now went tumultuously on strike. This outburst was no more than a hint of things to come; union organization was as yet embryonic. Moreover, while some of the workers were becoming more exigent, economic forces were in some ways operating to their disadvantage. In the early stages of development, as we have seen, the overwhelming problem had been the deficiency in the effective supply of labour. Now, however, supply had begun to overtake the effective demand, partly because of the depression but also as a result of longer-run factors—the growth of population and the rise in the demand for goods not available in the subsistence economy, which made it less and less easy for Africans to withhold their labour from the market. Kenya was ceasing to be a 'new' country, lacking chiefly manpower for its development, and was becoming an 'underdeveloped' country of a more usual type, in which labour was the only abundant factor.

Most of the trends visible in the economy of Kenya in 1939

were accelerated by the second world war. The short-run effects of this conflict were, indeed, mainly negative. The demands of war created an acute shortage of manpower, both skilled and unskilled, distracted the attention of policy-makers, and enforced a long postponement of efforts to grapple with the agrarian problem. In the later stages of the conflict, however, more positive influences began to make themselves felt. War conditions provided automatic protection for infant industries, many of which made rapid, though in some cases not entirely healthy, growth in this period. The new political situation which began to emerge with the signature of the Atlantic Charter compelled the authorities to a drastic revision of their ideas about the desirable and necessary rate of economic development. Above all, in 1942 the prices of primary products, both for external and for internal consumption, began to move sharply upward; and this rise, which, contrary to all expectations, was to be sustained for a whole decade, began a revolutionary transformation of the Kenya economy. The influence of the market began to penetrate societies, such as that of the Kipsigis, which had hitherto been almost unaffected, and to intensify the opportunities and the stresses already present among the Kikuyu and the Luo.

The numbers of the people were growing fast, their aspirations faster still. The world market situation was opening up prospects hitherto undreamt of. The Government was imbued with a new sense of urgency, and supplied with funds on a scale out of all comparison with the past. There was to be a new influx of foreign skills and capital. Given a radical reshaping of her social and political institutions, these forces could lead Kenya to prosperity; without it, to disaster.

VI

SETTLERS AND POLITICS IN KENYA

GEORGE BENNETT

The foundation of the colony

IN the first half of the twentieth century Kenya was the scene of an attempt by a small group of European settlers to create a white colony. Coming, as some did, from older areas of British settlement, from countries rapidly becoming self-governing Dominions, they saw in this new land no essential difference from settlement elsewhere; they carried with them the same political aspirations which they expected to achieve also in East Africa. In fact they were at one of the last frontiers of white settlement in British Africa, opened in the first year of the century by the Uganda Railway reaching Lake Victoria, and advertised then by Sir Harry Johnston's Report on Uganda. That and his later writings were the first to draw wide attention to the possibility of 'a white man's country' in the highlands of what was then the Eastern Province of Uganda. To put the railway under one administration, that province, lying between Naivasha and Mount Elgon, was transferred to the East Africa Protectorate, as Kenya was then known, on 1 April 1902.[1] Much of it was empty of inhabitants or but sparsely occupied by nomadic pastoralists. It needed development if the railway was to pay. Johnston had long believed in the development of Africa in racial harmony and so could speak of this land also as a possible 'America of the Hindu'.[2] The troubled story of racial politics in Kenya has belied his hopes.

The Foreign Office, responsible for the Protectorate and particularly concerned to develop the economy and reduce the Treasury grant-in-aid on which the Protectorate depended, pressed settlement, both Indian and European,[3] upon Sir

[1] K. Ingham, 'Uganda's old Eastern Province', *Uganda J.* xxi. 1 (1957), 41–46.
[2] *Report by His Majesty's Special Commissioner on the Protectorate of Uganda*, Cd. 671 (1901), pp. 9 and 7.
[3] Lansdowne to Eliot, 27 Aug. 1901, F.O. 2/443.

Charles Eliot, the new Commissioner, who arrived in East
Africa early in 1901. One member of the British Government
was prepared to go further in extending racial complexities.
Joseph Chamberlain, visiting East Africa late in 1902, suggested
that the Zionists might find there a solution, albeit temporary,
of their troubles.[1] However, in 1905, the Zionist Congress
decided against this, the so-called 'Uganda offer', greatly to the
relief of an increasingly embarrassed Imperial Government. The
idea had come under strong criticism, inside the Government
itself as well as from East Africa, from Eliot, who had argued for
European colonization since May 1901,[2] and from the early
settlers. The incident was typical of much in Kenya's history:
action was initiated without consideration of the political
reactions, and these, when they came, whether in or outside
Kenya, dominated the scene. The need for development
remained.

European settlement was made possible by the railway. Only
a rare family could walk up from Mombasa as the McQueens
did in 1896. They were entering the wilderness to settle, true
frontiersmen, on the very edge of the Kikuyu country, not far
from the site of the present capital.[3] Nairobi's beginnings were
as a shanty town for the railwaymen. There in 1900 T. A. Wood
opened a hotel which quickly became the acknowledged centre
for political meetings. Early in January 1902 twenty-two Europeans met at Wood's to elect a committee to encourage white
settlement. Their letter to Eliot seeking government support
epitomizes the future themes of the settlers in Kenya: land,
labour, and opposition to the Indians. They wanted land to be
granted in freehold, help through the establishment of model
farms and of a forestry department, and the passing of mining
laws; they asked that the natives should be made 'more amenable to European supervision', and described Asiatic immigration as 'detrimental to the European settler in particular and to
the native inhabitant generally'. At the committee's request
Eliot met them. He assured them of H.M. Government's desire
to promote and encourage European settlement and tried to

---

[1] J. Amery, *Life of Joseph Chamberlain*, vol. iv (London, 1951), ch. lxxxvii.
[2] Eliot to Lord Cranborne, personal, 15 May 1901, F.O. 2/447.
[3] J. A. Hunter and D. P. Mannix, *African Bush Adventures* (London, 1954),
pp. 129 sqq.

pacify them on the Indian issue by his belief that the highlands were 'positively distasteful to the Hindu', who might well settle near the lake and on the coast.

The ancient Indian trade connexion with East Africa was marked by the use of Indian coinage and by the extension of British law in the form of the Indian codes. This irked the settlers. Friction developed between European and Indian traders. The settlers' meeting, Eliot reported, 'was very hostile to the Indian element'.[1] They did not need to fear competition from the Punjabi coolies who built the railway, since most returned home. The present Indians of Kenya have come predominantly from Gujarat, the area north of Bombay and round the coast to Cutch. Like the European settlers, they came inland travelling on the railway, though, as with the Europeans, there were a few who penetrated earlier. By 1898 they were trading at Kibwezi and Machakos, and at Nairobi in 1899.

Prominent among them was A. M. Jeevanjee, the head of a firm of contractors, shipowners, and general merchants.[2] He arrived in Nairobi to build, in 1899, the residence of Ainsworth, the government officer,[3] and to engage in much other profitable building and land acquisition. In 1901 he started at Mombasa the *African Standard*. Acquired by a European in 1903, it became the *East African Standard* in 1905, thus passing from the control of the man who became known to the Indians as their 'Grand Old Man', to voice later the ideas and policies of Delamere and Grogan, who at times held a considerable influence in its direction.

These two prominent leaders of the Europeans arrived as white settlement was becoming important. Each had earlier travelled through remote parts of Africa. Captain Grogan's remarkable journey in 1898 and 1899 from the Cape to Cairo, the first time this feat had been achieved,[4] fixed in his mind a view of African primitive savagery which informed his outlook

[1] Dispatches of Eliot to Lansdowne, 21 Jan. 1902, with enclosed, undated letter from the committee, F.O. 2/805; 5 Jan. 1902, F.O. 2/569; and 31 Mar. 1902, F.O. 2/576.

[2] *Daily Chronicle*, 1 Sept. 1910.

[3] Hardinge to Salisbury, 8 Jan. 1900, transmitting Ainsworth to Hardinge, Nairobi, 29 Dec. 1899, F.O. 2/795.

[4] For his own account of this see E. S. Grogan and A. H. Sharp, *From the Cape to Cairo* (London, 1900). He finally retired from the Kenya Legislative Council in 1956.

throughout his long political career in Kenya. He came to East Africa in May 1904 as a partner in a timber business, and rapidly 'acquired'—to use his own phrase—'considerable interests'.[1] The third Lord Delamere had first been attracted by the highlands of East Africa in 1898, when he trekked there on a shooting expedition through the Somalilands and Ethiopia, finishing, according to Sir Harry Johnston's report, with £14,000 worth of ivory.[2] Delamere returned more permanently in January 1903, being followed by his brothers-in-law, Galbraith and Berkeley Cole, sons of the Earl of Enniskillen. European settlement in Kenya has always had a strong aristocratic flavour: one of Nairobi's hotels became known as 'the House of Lords'. But then, and for some years to come, Nairobi's conditions were those of the frontier. Delamere himself appeared as the typical frontiersman, with hair flowing down to his shoulders, wearing disreputable clothes, and capable in irritation of locking the manager of that same hotel in the meat-safe with several dead sheep.[3]

In the frontier, in the meeting between the so-called civilized and uncivilized, there is often violence, as the American frontier has shown; the same has been true of East Africa. Government officials, many with service going back to the days of the Imperial British East Africa Company, reported on this new spirit, explaining that many of the settlers were from South Africa, with the racial prejudices of that country. Frederick Jackson, Eliot's Deputy Commissioner, told the Foreign Office that the Protectorate was becoming a country of 'nigger-' and game-shooters. He described one leading settler as 'a well known filibuster', saying that he and Delamere were 'as thick as thieves'. Moreover, he believed that Eliot had come under Delamere's influence and was kow-towing to the settlers, the majority of whom Jackson regarded as 'a lot of scalliwags'.[4] Hostility soon grew between settlers and officials, who considered themselves as having a long-standing and prior duty to the natives.

Before Delamere finally decided to settle he applied for a government post, giving as his reason his sympathy with the

[1] Letter in *The Times*, 27 Aug. 1904.

[2] R. Oliver, *Sir Harry Johnston and the Scramble for Africa* (London, 1957), pp. 295–6.

[3] E. Huxley, *White Man's Country* (2 vols., London, 1935). vol i, *passim*. This biography gives a fascinating account of Delamere's life and influence on Kenya.

[4] Jackson to Sir Clement Hill, private, 25 May and 4 Aug. 1903, F.O. 2/720.

settlers suffering under official hostility. Eliot offered him one 'specially charged with the affairs which concern the white settlers', and recommended his appointment as a sub-collector, coupled with that of Land Officer as an experiment. He apparently accepted Delamere's views, for he explained to the Foreign Office that Ainsworth, the then Land Officer, had too much to do and was 'quarrelsome with the settlers'. Before the appointment could be concluded Delamere was laid up as the result of a riding accident.[1] Instead of allotting land to settlers, he was soon applying for grazing land,[2] and obtained in November 100,000 acres on lease. Eliot's and Delamere's ideas became increasingly close, so that, to quote Delamere's biographer: 'White settlement in East Africa is largely the creation of these two men.'

Yet Eliot was in a very real sense 'the progenitor'.[3] The Foreign Office records make abundantly clear his part in urging successive concessions to the settlers' wishes, though, until the very end of his time in East Africa, this was not generally known. A man of culture, he came to Africa from a wide diplomatic experience and with considerable gifts as an oriental scholar. He was instructed to develop the country, a policy in which he believed ever more whole-heartedly, more especially because his ideas were those of the period. Africans shocked him by their barbarity and their nudity. He regarded British East Africa as 'the greatest philanthropic achievement of the later nineteenth century', since British rule had ended Arab slave raids and famine. In the style of Chamberlain, he described the Protectorate as 'practically an estate belonging to His Majesty's Government, on which an enormous outlay has been made, and which ought to repay that outlay'—this by European settlement.[4] He looked for development by small men, believing that a capital of £300 to £500 was sufficient. He compared East Africa with New Zealand,[5] and welcomed the provision for sale in freehold—which he had been advocating—in the Crown Lands Ordinance of 1902.

[1] Eliot to Lansdowne, telegram, 16 Apr. 1903, F.O. 2/719, and Huxley, op. cit. i. 91–92.
[2] Eliot to Lansdowne, 7 June 1903, F.O. 2/807.
[3] Huxley, op. cit. i. 131 and 75.
[4] *Report by His Majesty's Commissioner on the East Africa Protectorate*, Cd. 1626 (1903), p. 29.
[5] Eliot to Lansdowne, 28 Jan. 1902, F.O. 2/569.

L

Jackson, Acting Commissioner in Eliot's absence on leave, hedged the offer of sale with such regulations that Eliot reported in January 1903 that not a single application had been made.[1] Settler immigration began in earnest only after Eliot's revision of the regulations. He continued to seek yet greater freedom in making grants without reference home, urging that the settlers were not willing to accept formalities and delays and that 'the enormous land appetites of the colonists, particularly South African' should be considered.[2] In the same month of August 1903 that Eliot penned this he sent off Marsden, his Chief of Customs, to South Africa to publicize settlement prospects, and was also beginning with two South Africans, Robert Chamberlain and A. S. Flemmer, the negotiations which were eventually to lead to his resignation.

Their prospective land was in the Rift Valley, where, late in 1903, the Foreign Office realized there was a danger of a clash between the interests of settlement and of the Masai. They warned Eliot of this, but only after themselves concluding an agreement with the East Africa Syndicate for land there did they forbid him to make further concessions in the area. By then, without informing the Foreign Office, Eliot had already committed himself to a grant—and one, moreover, larger than he had authority to make—to Chamberlain and Flemmer.[3] But the Foreign Office also was at fault in not passing on information. In October Lord Lansdowne had privately to apologize to Eliot, who was protesting because he had heard of the offer to the Zionists only from the press and other public sources.[4] When the friction became public in Eliot's resignation and a Parliamentary Paper, opinion in East Africa could see it as a clash between capitalist influence on the Government in London and Eliot's interest in individuals in East Africa. But there were other issues: Eliot resigned also because the Foreign Office preferred to be guided by two of his subordinates, Jackson and Bagge, on the Masai land question. Eliot's final explosions to Lansdowne made plain where he stood:

Your Lordship has opened this Protectorate to white immigration

[1] Eliot to Lansdowne, 5 Jan. 1903, F.O. 2/806.

[2] Eliot to Cranborne, personal, 10 Aug. 1903, F.O. 2/807.

[3] Lansdowne to Eliot, 8 Mar. 1904, F.O. 2/832, and Eliot to Lansdowne, 7 Apr. 1904, F.O. 2/835.

[4] Lansdowne to Eliot, 5 Oct. 1903. Lansdowne's State Papers, vol. xxix.

and colonization, and I think it well that in confidential correspondence at least, we should face the undoubted issue—viz., that white mates black in a very few moves. . . . There can be no doubt that the Masai and many other tribes must go under. It is a prospect which I view with equanimity and a clear conscience . . . [Masaidom] is a beastly, bloody system founded on raiding and immorality.

In a following dispatch Eliot complained that his 'great practical difficulties' were not understood in London. South Africans had been encouraged to come, but nothing was ready: they were bitterly complaining of the lack of accommodation, transport, and surveyors, and saying that the country was taken up with reserves for Jews, natives, game, and forests—and Eliot thought that their grievances were 'not without foundation'.[1] Yet he himself was to blame for much of the disproportion between invitation and preparation. The simile he used to Lansdowne—'you cannot invite people to dinner and then lock the dining-room door'—was acidly turned against him by Sir Clement Hill at the Foreign Office: 'He has invited his guests to dinner and opened the doors, but forgotten the waiters'[2]—a fitting retort, since many of Eliot's requests for facilities to help the settlers came only after they had begun to arrive.

The quarrel mounted between Eliot and the Foreign Office, so that the officials in Whitehall were relieved to receive his resignation. Unbeknown to them, however, Eliot had already lit the train of a dispute that was to have far wider repercussions. On 14 September 1903 he gave instructions to the Land Officer that no land grants, except of small plots, were to be made to Indians between Machakos Road station and Fort Ternan,[3] to the west of the Rift Valley. No regulations were published, but Eliot gave the settlers an assurance that the area 'from Kiu to Fort Ternan' (i.e. a further extension of sixteen miles) would be reserved for men of their own race.[4] He made no reference to this important policy decision in his dispatches, thus leaving the

[1] Eliot to Lansdowne, 9 and 10 Apr. 1904, *Correspondence relating to the Resignation of Sir Charles Eliot and to the Concession to the East African Syndicate*, Cd. 2099 (1904), nos. 25 and 26.

[2] Eliot to Lansdowne, 5 Apr. 1904, F.O. 2/835, and memorandum by Sir Clement Hill, 9 May 1904, F.O. 2/847.

[3] Acting Commissioner Hobley to Lansdowne, telegram, 19 July 1904, F.O. 2/842. See inset map on p. 208, above.

[4] Lord Delamere, *The Grant of Land to the Zionist Congress and Land Settlement in British East Africa* (London, 1903).

Foreign Office to hear of it first in July of the next year, when a protest reached them from the Indian Association of Mombasa.[1] They immediately cabled to Nairobi for information and asked the Colonial Office if there were precedent elsewhere. The Colonial Office replied with references to the peculiar circumstances of Hong Kong and the Transvaal, but said that such legislation was 'not in accordance with the general policy of His Majesty's Government and can only be defended on special grounds'. They further explained that the Transvaal situation preceded British rule and had given rise to many difficulties, and that conditions there appeared to be 'fundamentally different from those of a tropical protectorate'.[2] Eliot had argued from early 1902 for European and Indian settlement in separate areas[3] but he had no right to adopt a policy of segregation without reference home. He did so without considering the full implications of his action—he was a diplomat, not an official brought up in the Colonial Office tradition of no racial discrimination. The result was that he left a poisoned chalice for the Imperial Government in forming British policy in Kenya. He had, indeed, laid the foundation of white settlement; the Europeans of Kenya were right to remember him.

Eliot may, perhaps, also be considered the godfather of politics in Kenya, since he gave the first official support to the idea of a Legislative Council. This was in a dispatch suggesting one consisting only of officials, but in a final communication to the Planters' and Farmers' Association he said that they must strive for 'some local Government': they could not expect representative government, but they could have a council with unofficial members. He believed that such a council, with some financial power, could have taken the initiative in providing roads and services to intending settlers and thus might have prevented many of the difficulties of the past eight or ten months.[4] This support was a change from the cold way with which he had dis-

---

[1] W. A. Bowen, Secretary, Mombasa, 24 June 1904, explaining that the Association's satisfaction at Eliot's resignation was because of his policy in this matter, F.O. 2/847.

[2] Foreign Office to Colonial Office, 23 July 1904, F.O. 2/848, and Colonial Office to Foreign Office, 15 Aug. 1904, C.O. 519/1.

[3] Eliot to Lansdowne, 5 Jan. 1902, F.O. 2/569.

[4] Eliot to Lansdowne, 10 Apr. 1904, F.O. 2/835, and *African Standard*, 9 July 1904.

missed the first petition for an Advisory Council with unofficial members. This had originated from a group of Europeans and Asians in Mombasa in 1902, but Eliot was not then convinced that his 'so-called arduous duties' would be lightened by such a body.[1] Indeed, until the very end Eliot had a reputation among the generality of the settlers for being unapproachable and 'absolutely despotic'.[2]

But the settlers he called in were British, 'political animals' by national tradition. In 1902 the committee to encourage European settlement had led to the formation of a Colonists' Association, which Eliot had welcomed as a source of valuable advice. Delamere, on his arrival in January 1903, formed the Planters' and Farmers' Association. Concerned initially with the marketing of potatoes in South Africa, it soon turned to a more vital life in politics and superseded the older body.[3] It pressed for the reservation of the Highlands for white settlement, but attained a wider fame in organizing the protest against Jewish settlement. Delamere telegraphed to the Foreign Office on behalf of the association, threatening that they were prepared to resist 'by all means in their power'. On inquiry from Eliot the Foreign Office discovered that the association had only thirty-two members![4] Its day was to come only after the first co-operation between Delamere and a head of the Government had ended with Eliot's departure.

He was succeeded by Sir Donald Stewart, who was recommended by the Colonial Office 'principally on the ground of his successful experience of the white settlers on the Gold Coast'.[5] He assumed office on 1 August 1904 with instructions to attend first to 'the relations between white settlers and natives', more especially between Nairobi and Lake Victoria, where there was a possibility of European colonization on a large scale; on the proper solution of this question 'the future of the Protectorate will largely depend'. Further, he was told that 'the primary duty

[1] Eliot to Lansdowne, 29 Mar. 1902, F.O. 2/570.

[2] *African Standard*, leading article, 25 June 1904, where it opined that Eliot had never set his mark upon East Africa.

[3] Ibid., 22 Jan. and 5 Mar. 1903.

[4] Telegram, Delamere to Lansdowne, 2 Sept. 1903, and Eliot to Lansdowne, 31 Oct. 1903, F.O. 2/785.

[5] This odd statement is in a memorandum by Eyre Crowe, 7 Oct. 1904, in F.O. 2/911.

of Great Britain in East Africa is the welfare of the native races'.[1]
Thus Eliot's talk of 'paramountcy of white interests', a phrase he
used both to settlers and in later writing, received clear denial.
However, the Foreign Office did not carry out its original intention[2] of publishing Stewart's instructions. Public ambiguity
concerning policy remained, thus permitting further concessions
to the settlers, and allowing Eliot's pronouncements to be taken
as a correct interpretation of Imperial policy.[3]

Stewart concentrated his attention on the land problem. He
effected an agreement with the Masai whereby part of the tribe
was to move to Laikipia, thus freeing the Rift Valley for European settlement; but he warned Lansdowne that when the
Masai had grazed down the grass there and made it sweet,
envious eyes would again be cast on their lands.[4] He was right:
Laikipia became a Naboth's vineyard. In November Stewart
appointed a committee to consider the land laws and their
administration. It consisted of two judges, the Crown Advocate,
a nominee of the Planters' and Farmers' Association, and Delamere, who became chairman when the presiding judge was
promoted to Zanzibar.

Before the committee reported, the Protectorate was transferred to the Colonial Office. The settlers had pressed for this,
believing it would lead to a more sympathetic and less miserly
administration; they talked of becoming then a Crown Colony
with a Legislative Council containing elected members. The
Planters' and Farmers' Association meeting in January 1905
called for a council—and also changed their name to the
Colonists' Association.[5] At this time Lansdowne instructed
Stewart to end the differentiation between immigrants, who
were taxed, and natives, who were not.[6]

The Colonial Office takes over

The first Colonial Office reactions were not sympathetic.

[1] Lansdowne to Stewart, 8 July 1904, F.O. 2/833.

[2] Lansdowne to Stewart, telegram, 20 July 1904, F.O. 2/841.

[3] e.g. M. R. Dilley, *British Policy in Kenya Colony* (New York, 1937), pp. 187 and
137, where Sir Edward Grigg, speaking in 1930 in the Legislative Council, is cited
as 'a good witness'. See p. 315 below.

[4] Stewart to Lansdowne, 5 Sept. 1904, F.O. 2/839. For the agreement see
Chapter I above.

[5] *African Standard*, 30 May 1903, 15 Oct. 1904 and 14 Jan. 1905.

[6] Lansdowne to Stewart, 14 Jan. 1905, F.O. 2/913.

Lyttelton, the Secretary of State, doubted if the white population would ever be numerically important and considered East
Africa as 'the natural outlet for Indian emigration'. His officials
disliked the Foreign Office's 'happy-go-lucky style' of making
land grants, and thought Eliot's lease of November 1903 to Delamere was 'an ideal grant for a company monger'.[1] In taking over
the Protectorate they feared trouble with men who would approach
members of parliament and try to 'bounce' them into making
concessions.[2] One settler, Lord Hindlip, was soon worrying the
Colonial Office with complaints, threatening—and later demonstrating—that he had a ready-made forum in the House of Lords.

The first attack on the Colonial Office was launched in both
London and Nairobi. Early in 1905 the Colonists' Association
came increasingly under the influence of new arrivals from
South Africa. They drew up a statement of grievances which
was so extreme that Delamere withdrew his support. The
Association turned to Hindlip, then in England, who explained
to the Colonial Office that 'the chief question' concerned some
form of representation on a council, which Stewart had refused.
Lyttelton found the proposal 'a reasonable one' and it proved to
be the settlers' one gain from their petition.[3] They phrased this
request in traditional terms—'no taxation without representation'—though they could only claim that they paid customs,
rates, stamp taxes, licences, and other fees. They attacked the
Indian codes in another traditional phrase: 'every Englishman
carries the common law of England'.[4] Their remarks about the
natives, however, sprang from South Africa; they professed to
fear an eventual rising as 'an absolute certainty' and so wanted
forts, white police, Imperial troops, and a burgher militia, the
last meaning elected field cornets and commandants with
magisterial powers responsible for law and order.

[1] Minutes on various papers, Aug. 1904, C.O. 519/1.
[2] Minute on Stewart to Lansdowne, 16 Mar. 1905, transmitting documents on
the Lingham and Grogan timber proposals. C.O. 533/1.
[3] Hindlip to Duke of Marlborough, 2 Aug. and Lyttelton to Stewart, 18 Aug.
1905, C.O. 533/10. The *Morning Post* (5 Aug.) published the settlers' 'Demands'.
These were later addressed more formally to the Secretary of State (23 Aug. 1905)
and so appear in *Papers relating to British East Africa*, H.L. 158 (1907), pp. 30-36.
[4] The addition, however, of the words 'into every new country settled by him
over which the King has proved Sovereignty' enabled the Colonial Office to point
out that this was not a colony of settlement but a 'foreign country' under the
Foreign Jurisdiction Act (ibid., p. 39).

Influences from South Africa have played a large part in Kenya's political thinking, but in 1905 officials could report that this petition was the work of unrepresentative agitators—and in all there were only some 600 resident settlers.[1] Nevertheless, their main demand was granted in 1906 by Lord Elgin, Colonial Secretary in the new Liberal Government, and supported by a new Commissioner, Sir James Hayes Sadler, who came from Uganda on Stewart's death in 1905. Although the Protectorate did not become a Colony it was provided with a new constitution: the Commissioner became Governor, with Executive and Legislative Councils, the latter to include nominated unofficial members.[2]

Before these could be appointed, an incident in March 1907 shook Nairobi and drew such wide attention that a Parliamentary Paper was published on it. Captain Grogan, who had been elected President of the Colonists' Association in January, took the leading role in the public flogging of three Kikuyu servants in front of the Nairobi court house. The local press and the evidence given at the subsequent trial made plain that this was a deliberate challenge to the Government, and particularly to the courts: the frontier was seeking to assert itself in a main street of Nairobi. Officials there and in Downing Street urged that the Legislative Council should be withdrawn, but on Sadler's recommendation—and on the consideration that the incident was the work only of a small South African group—preparations for its meeting in August went on. The one modification was that Grogan was not nominated—which had been intended, since he was President of the Colonists' Association.[3]

When the Legislative Council met, the Governor announced a further concession: a Land Board to be appointed with five unofficial members.[4] Settler influence on the all important land policy had begun unofficially in the relations between Eliot

[1] Acting Commissioner Jackson to Lyttelton, 11 Nov. 1905, transmitting his own and Ainsworth's views, C.O. 533/5.

[2] Order in Council and Letters Patent, 22 Oct. 1906. Winston Churchill told the Colonists' Association in Nairobi in 1907: 'Never before in Colonial experience has a Council been granted where the number of settlers is so few' (*East African Standard*, 23 Nov. 1907).

[3] *Correspondence relating to the Flogging of Natives by Certain Europeans at Nairobi*, Cd. 3562 (1907), and Acting Governor Jackson to Elgin, 25 Mar. 1907, and minutes thereon, C.O. 533/28.

[4] *E.A. Standard*, 24 Aug. 1907.

and Delamere, but had received open recognition in Stewart's Land Committee under Delamere. Consideration of their report was delayed by official changes but—and this was typical of Kenya—they also raised issues wider than those in their terms of reference. The committee not only argued for a loosening of the conditions of the Land Ordinance of 1902 on lines suggested by Delamere in a pamphlet in 1903, but they attacked the whole principle of control: speculation was a lesser evil than stagnation. This view the Colonial Office, recalling the history of the Australasian colonies, could not share, and replied by announcing that a Commissioner of Lands would be appointed to report. The committee called for the reservation of the Highlands for white settlement, and in this they were supported by Stewart. Though Judge Cator, the original chairman, favoured a similar reservation elsewhere for Asians, the committee considered it neither possible nor politic 'to restrain the energies and capital of European planters within limited bounds'. They urged the establishment of native reserves, 'few in number but of large extent and far removed from European centres'—something which might have meant wholesale removals, particularly of the Kikuyu. Native villages were to be encouraged on settlers' farms on the basis of cultivation rights in exchange for labour; such natives to be registered, and any unregistered to be removed to reserves. To supervise the operation of this registration policy the committee suggested the appointment of a Commissioner for Native Affairs. They acknowledged that, since so much of Nairobi consisted of government land, they could not have a fully elected municipal council there, but they wanted its unofficial members to be elected—something Stewart queried, since Indians and natives also paid municipal taxes, whilst the Europeans wished to monopolize representation. Finally the committee urged that a Land Board should be established and should include two or more unofficial 'Assessors'.

The new Land Commissioner, Colonel Montgomery, hesitated, then accepted this, as did Elgin.[1] He commented on the concession in the House of Lords in 1907, in replying to a motion from Hindlip, adding that he could not imagine a statement with so little foundation as the settlers' assertion that East

[1] H.L. 158 (1907), *passim*.

Africa was a white man's country, for there were only 2,000 whites in an estimated population of 4 million.[1]

Yet the year before, these few had obtained from Elgin what the Colonial Office had denied to the colonists of 'white Australia' and of Natal: restrictions on land grants to non-Europeans. In May 1906 the settlers, stung by renewed Indian protests against such discrimination, assembled in the largest meeting Nairobi had yet seen, to pledge 'the most determined opposition' to grants to Indians in the Highlands. Sadler, like Stewart, had continued Eliot's policy. Now he was allowed to tell the Colonists' Association that 'a reasonable discretion' would be exercised in dealing with applications by non-Europeans, since the area suitable for Europeans was 'comparatively limited'.[2] This came to be regarded by the settlers as 'the Elgin pledge' and was strengthened in 1908 by a yet more specious reason for breaking with an Imperial policy:

It is not consonant with the views of His Majesty's Government to impose *legal* restriction on any particular section of the community, but as a matter of administrative convenience grants in the upland area should not be made to Indians.[3]

This statement was published at the end of a Parliamentary Paper which clearly demonstrated the continued pressure from settlers, now expressed through the Land Board. At first official control of the Board was secured by the chairman's casting vote, but this soon disappeared. Without reference to London, the Board was given 'a large unofficial majority'. Elgin, noticing this, insisted that it should remain only 'a consultative body'.[4] But, as it was allowed to discuss the draft of an amending Crown Lands Ordinance, it had considerable influence on policy formation.

Labour—with land the twin subject of settler interest—provided the next occasion for a Parliamentary Paper. Eliot's last annual report should have provided warning: settlers and natives wanted agricultural labour at the same times, the natives had little incentive to labour, and considerable feeling

---

[1] *Hansard*, 4th ser., clxxvii, 24, 27 June 1907.
[2] Elgin to Sadler, 17 July 1906, in H.L. 158 (1907), pp. 41–43.
[3] The area concerned was left undefined until this task was given to the Morris Carter Commission in 1933.
[4] Elgin to Sadler, 19 Mar. 1908 in *Correspondence relating to the Tenure of Land in the East Africa Protectorate*, Cd. 4117 (1908), pp. 29–34.

was building up that the Administration should apply pressure to increase the supply.[1] South African solutions seemed natural to the colonists, as the Land Committee report of 1905 showed. In 1906, to the alarm of the Colonial Office, a Masters and Servants Ordinance was promulgated; this, based on the law of the Transvaal, allowed both payment in kind and imprisonment of labourers for breach of contract.[2] In 1907, following a suggestion of the Land Committee, a Secretary for Native Affairs was appointed, his Department being 'specially instituted to deal with the labour supply'.[3] However, the result was not to the colonists' satisfaction. A. C. (later Sir Claud) Hollis, this new Secretary, discovered widespread abuses in labour recruiting. A government circular was sent out prohibiting chiefs from compelling labour, regulations to control recruitment were issued, and officers explained to natives that they need not work unless they wished to. The labour supply diminished and settler protests mounted.

In March 1908 the storm burst. The Colonists' Association claimed that the 'extraordinary labour rules' had at least doubled the cost of labour and called for their immediate withdrawal, saying that the Government's attitude might easily lead to severe breaches of the peace. The Governor held a conference with some 150 plain-spoken settlers who advocated the whip—some acknowledged using it—and Pass Laws to discipline the natives, besides taxation to force out labour. Delamere also urged that the amount of land the natives were allowed to hold 'should be absolutely limited'; they must 'force the native to work', and he hoped that they could rely on the Government. A unanimous resolution was passed calling for new rules to be framed by a Central Board with unofficial representation and for the establishment of a Labour Bureau separate from the Department of Native Affairs, and urging that the Government should fix maximum wages. Sadler expressed his sympathy but would not give any definite answers.

Irritated and dissatisfied, the settlers, led by Delamere and

---

[1] *Report on the E.A.P. for 1903–4*, Cd. 2331 (1905), p. 21.

[2] Sadler to Elgin, 20 Aug. 1906, minutes thereon, and Elgin to Sadler, 21 Nov. 1906, C.O. 533/16.

[3] Minute by Lobb, 17 July 1907, on Sadler to Elgin, 11 June 1907, C.O. 533/29, and Sadler to Elgin, 19 May 1908, *Report of the Committee on Emigration from India to the Crown Colonies and Protectorates*, vol. iii, Cd. 5192–4 (1910), no. 8 (f).

Baillie, both unofficial members of the Legislative Council, marched that afternoon on Government House. They refused the Governor's offer to meet two or three of their leaders inside. Sadler then came out before the excited crowd and tried to speak, but was interrupted by Delamere; fearing further trouble, he withdrew to shouts of 'Resign, resign!' The crowd, after holding a brief meeting, broke up with cheers. The next day Sadler gave his replies to a deputation of Delamere and six others: he refused to withdraw the rules, but agreed to appoint a Board of Inquiry of officials with six unofficial members to consider the terms and conditions of labour supply. In writing home Sadler blamed the whole incident on 'the spirit of political unrest, impatient of any form of government but its own' which had come with European colonization. Not being a historian, he should not have assumed that the Legislative Councillors' action was 'almost without a parallel in the annals of colonial history', but it did give him the opportunity to raise the question of his relations with them. He was in any case weary of Delamere's petulance on the Council and now took the opportunity to suspend both him and Baillie, whom he described as only a puppet.[1] Sadler, a weak governor known to the settlers as 'Flannelfoot',[2] thus imposed the first check on them, though, amiable man that he was, it was not long before he was suggesting Delamere's and Baillie's return to the Council; this the Colonial Office delayed into the new year.[3]

But Sadler took up something even more distasteful to the settlers: the representation of Indians on the Legislative Council. In 1907 Winston Churchill, Under-Secretary of State at the Colonial Office, had queried their omission: 'There can be no reason for excluding this large and meritorious class. Begin early to instil good principles in the East Africa Protectorate!' Sadler had, then, no name to suggest, but he was told not to overlook them.[4] In April 1908 he received a petition from the Indian

[1] Sadler to Elgin, 26 and 27 Mar. 1908, in *Correspondence relating to Affairs in East Africa*, Cd. 4122 (1908), nos. 10 and 11.

[2] Huxley, *White Man's Country*, i. 226.

[3] Sadler to Crewe, 8 Sept. 1908, and Crewe to Sadler, 5 Nov., C.O. 533/47; also Sadler to Crewe, 8 Dec. 1908, and Crewe to Sadler, 28 Jan. 1909, C.O. 533/48.

[4] Minutes on Sadler's telegram, 21 May 1907, and Elgin to Sadler, 26 June 1907, C.O. 533/29.

community and considered that they had 'legitimate claims'; whereupon he was instructed to submit a name. The Colonial Office did not, in fact, receive a nomination until June next year, when A. M. Jeevanjee was suggested by Jackson, then Acting Governor.[1]

By then Sadler had gone to become Governor of the Windward Islands. The Colonial Office had become tired of his weakness and failure to deal with the problems of the Protectorate. Holding a low opinion of the officials there, they considered it necessary to bring in a strong man from outside. Their choice fell on Sir Percy Girouard, who had won golden opinions as Lugard's successor in Northern Nigeria.

Settler advances under Girouard and Belfield

Girouard arrived in September 1909 with instructions to report on the whole East African situation; within two months he produced a masterly survey. He was shocked at the contrast: in Northern Nigeria orderly progress had followed on Lugard's memoranda, but in East Africa there was an 'utter absence of any defined policy'. He found this not only in regard to native administration but generally; the form of land tenure, the 'burning' issue for the colonists, was 'still unsettled', and there was no policy with regard to the Indians. Girouard described them as feared by white and native alike, but he said that they were essential, since their presence as subordinate staff alone made government possible. His references to the Legislative Council made plain how strong the settlers' influence had become: he wanted a strong Colonial Secretary to give a lead on the Council, where he found the officials weak both in numbers and in debate. But he wanted more European unofficial members there also, for their active participation in government was 'essential'. European settlement might have been hasty, but it was now 'an accomplished fact' and demanded 'a broader view of the situation'.[2] Girouard's outlook derived not only from Nigeria but also from experience in South Africa, where, while reconstructing the railways under Milner, he had married into Transvaal society. The Colonial Office should not then have

---

[1] Sadler to Crewe, 10 May 1908, and Crewe to Sadler, 14 July, C.O. 533/43; and Jackson to Crewe, 20 May 1909, C.O. 533/59.

[2] Girouard to Crewe, 13 Nov. 1909, and enclosures, C.O. 533/63.

been surprised at his intention of pressing on with self-government; they were now to be faced with the powerful combination
of settlers and Governor.

Girouard came immediately under Delamere's influence,
believing he would be 'a firm friend'.[1] He cabled recommending
Delamere's re-appointment to the Legislative Council (he had
resigned in May), but questioning that of Jeevanjee, since it
would lead to 'legitimate demands' from the Arabs and Swahilis,
who outnumbered the Indians by two to one—an argument
which should have applied *a fortiori* to Delamere and his
colleagues. Over Jeevanjee the Colonial Office could not give
way: his appointment had been gazetted.[2] But this was only the
first of a series of representations of settlers' views. According to
Girouard they were 'discontented and bitter' because the
economy was 'moribund'. Already in September he urged that
size of holding was of no importance provided the land was
developed[3]—he had accepted the position of the large landowners led by Delamere—and he turned against the small
farmer. In February 1910 he reported on the revision of the
Crown Lands Ordinance, which had been delayed for his consideration: he opposed the writing in of rent revision after thirty-
three years, since before then the settlers would 'very probably'
get self-government—the provision would be an 'unnecessary
aggravation', since it could soon be undone.[4] In the small
society of Nairobi such opinions could not be hid.

In these circumstances it seemed that all the settlers needed
to make their voice effective was unity and a spokesman. Could
Delamere be the man? Already he had lost control of the
Colonists' Association from 1905 to 1907, regaining it only after
the Grogan flogging incident. Often the more extreme settlers, and particularly the South Africans, preferred the more
flamboyant Grogan. Moreover, throughout Kenya's history
there has been a reluctance to accept leadership. Churchill
noted this individualism of the frontier in a visit as Under-
Secretary of State in 1907: 'Every white man in Nairobi is a

---

[1] Huxley, op. cit. i. 240, and Girouard to H. Read, 16 Nov. 1909, C.O. 533/63.
[2] Girouard to Crewe, 23 Sept. 1909, and Crewe to Girouard, 2 Oct., C.O.
533/62.
[3] Girouard to Crewe, telegram, 12 Nov. 1909, C.O. 533/63 and dispatch,
23 Sept. 1909, C.O. 533/62.
[4] Girouard to Crewe, 17 Feb. 1910, C.O. 533/71.

politician; and most of them are leaders of parties.'[1] He received addresses from two associations, the Colonists' and the Pastoralists'. They made many similar points, but the Pastoralists' Association also attacked 'dummying',[2] and the Legislative Council as passing under the influence of one group,[3] by which they meant the large landholders. The Pastoralists' Association had been formed at Nakuru, 'the capital of the Highlands', by Robert Chamberlain, who protested from his arrival in the country against Delamere's large landholding and influence.

Other local associations also sprang up; there was talk of bringing them all together in a 'Confederation'.[4] A 'Central Committee' was set up in 1908, but only in September 1910 was the quarrel between Chamberlain and Delamere sufficiently composed for something more formal: the Convention of Associations, under the chairmanship of Grogan, who then described himself as 'the baddest and the boldest of a bold bad gang'.[5]

The Convention, already dubbed 'the Settlers' Parliament', met first in February 1911. From the beginning it had grandiose ideas: a motion was passed for the Protectorate's representation —and Eliot was nominated for this—at the Imperial Conference. There was talk in Nairobi of responsible government being 'almost within a hand's reach', and the Convention, in meeting, called for the enforcement of the native Pass Laws and discussed 'the Asiatic question'.[6] Delegations went to see the Governor about elective representation, but Girouard told the first group that there was little hope the Colonial Office would accept.[7]

He should have known, for he had recently returned from a visit to London to review the whole situation. He asked to go in May 1910, explaining that the settlers wished him to represent their disabilities in person,[8] and, when he urged the visit in August, permission was granted. The Colonial Office by then welcomed a meeting; they had become tired of a governor who

---

[1] W. S. Churchill, *My African Journey* (London, 1908), p. 21.
[2] i.e. applying for extra land in the name of dependants.
[3] *E.A. Standard*, 16 and 23 Nov. 1907.
[4] Ibid., 13 June and 11 July 1908.
[5] Ibid., 12 Nov. 1910. See also Huxley, op. cit., i. 261–2.
[6] *E.A. Standard*, leading article, 14 Jan. 1911, and 4 Feb. 1911.
[7] Ibid., 5 and 12 Aug. 1911.
[8] Girouard to Crewe, secret, 26 May 1910, C.O. 533/74.

repeatedly put up demands which required financial reference to the Treasury, and who acted without authority.[1]

A clear example of this was provided by the second move of the Masai. Girouard had mentioned this as a possibility, but it began, early in 1910, before he had obtained the Secretary of State's approval.[2] The settlers, under Delamere's leadership, had been urging for some eighteen months that the Masai should leave Laikipia. Though there may have been sound administrative reasons for concentrating the tribe, the fact that Girouard relied for advice about the Masai on Delamere aroused suspicions in London.[3] A Parliamentary Paper was issued, and then, under the pressure of debate and repeated questions, Harcourt, the new Secretary of State, sought to reassure the House of Commons by the statement, in April 1912, that no allocation of land on Laikipia had been made to settlers.[4] He had been misinformed: promises had been made in Nairobi two years before. Harcourt only learned of them in May from Girouard, then on leave in London. A dispute ensued; Girouard resigned and took up a business career. The Colonial Office was left to yield; the Masai moved, the land was granted. The settlers concluded that the man on the spot would always win. But the Masai move had another result: it was the first *cause célèbre* to focus humanitarian attention in England on the East Africa Protectorate. For a while happenings there were more carefully watched.[5]

Thus when the attention of the settlers focused again on labour their words did not pass unnoticed. In 1911 economic developments[6] began to produce a shortage of labour. Govern-

---

[1] Girouard to Crewe, telegram, 16 Aug. 1910, and minutes thereon, C.O. 533/76.

[2] Minutes on Girouard to Crewe, telegram, 21 Apr. 1904 (no. 3 in Cd. 5584, *Correspondence relating to the Masai* (1911)), C.O. 533/73.

[3] According to minutes and a letter bound with Jackson to Crewe, 7 Mar. 1910 (no. 1 in Cd. 5584), C.O. 533/72, the agitation began after Sir Harry Johnston had advocated this second move in the *Nineteenth Century* (Oct. 1908). For details of the move see Chapter I, pp. 36–38 above.

[4] *Hansard*, 5th ser., H. of C. xxxvii. 499, 16 Apr. 1912.

[5] In the crises of the 1920's care was taken to see that the move was not forgotten. Dr. N. Leys published his *Kenya* (1924). His ch. iv is based partly on his participation, which he seeks to conceal, in these events. Leys, a government medical officer, was transferred in 1913 to Nyasaland for the action he took in opposing the move.

[6] See Chapter V above.

ment policy remained as declared by Lord Crewe in 1908: the Government was not to help settlers to find labour; it should impose terms and leave them to make their own arrangements.[1] The problem remained to get the natives to 'come out and work'. In 1912 a Native Labour Commission was appointed to make recommendations. It sat from September to the following April, collecting evidence which provides a remarkable conspectus of views: of settlers, officials, missionaries, Indians, and even Africans. In a colonial tradition, many of them were outspoken.[2] On publication[3] it provoked a series of shocked questions in the Commons. When the matter was raised in debate, Harcourt commented that they should not confuse evidence with the Report, on which he was not then prepared to announce a final decision.[4]

Before the promised Parliamentary Paper could be laid, war intervened. Affairs in East Africa disappeared again from public attention. War has been called the handmaid of constitutional advance. For this the settlers had been clamouring, but other things also became possible after 1914.

In 1915 the Crown Lands Ordinance was at last amended, the Colonial Office giving way to the local pressures. In East Africa officials and governors were quickly converted by settler members of the Land Board and of committees of the Legislative Council. The position of the Colonial Office had been made plain in 1911: it had then rejected the ordinance passed in 1909. Girouard had been told that he had represented the settlers' views 'with much force and ability', but Harcourt was not prepared to yield. He had insisted that Government should share in the increasing value of land by thirty-year revision of rents and by retaining provisions against land accumulation, lest 'the ideal of a large white population in the Highlands' should be seriously prejudiced; his responsibility was for 'the future welfare of the Protectorate'.[5] Publication of this dispatch

[1] Crewe to Sadler, 27 Aug. 1908 in Cd. 5194 (1910), no. 8 (h).

[2] There is a summary of the evidence in W. McGregor Ross, *Kenya from Within* (London, 1927), pp. 92–99. The conclusion of this hostile critic is perhaps worth quoting: 'any such concerted display of negrophobe malevolence as is exhibited in some of the evidence . . . would be impossible in the Kenya Colony of 1927.'

[3] *Report and Evidence of the Native Labour Commission* (Nairobi, 1913).

[4] *Hansard*, 5th ser., H. of C. lxv. 1190–1, 28 July 1914.

[5] Harcourt to Girouard, 3 Feb. 1911, in E.A.P. *Official Gazette*, 1 Mar. 1911, pp. 88–90.

had followed the further halting of the Masai move in February 1911. These events had provoked the settlers to such an extent that Girouard was allowed to announce some small concessions in opening the Nakuru Agricultural Show in March.[1] However, the local authorities could stop neither dummying nor the determination of the settlers to obtain their way over the Land Ordinance.

A new Bill was introduced in December 1913. Though it was referred to a committee with only one unofficial member—the others had resigned from the Legislative Council—this produced a report which met settler wishes; and not unnaturally, since the committee consulted fully with a joint committee of the Landholders' Association and of the Convention of Associations and 'found themselves substantially in agreement . . . on practically every matter of important principle'.[2] The Legislative Council committee recommended, and obtained, 999-year leases—instead of 99 as the Colonial Office wanted—though they did accept thirty-year revision of rents. They approved of the clause in the draft Bill which proposed that the native lands should be called 'Crown Lands', though this did not escape question in London and was to be a source of political trouble in the future. The settlers' main attention centred on ways and means of stopping the transfer of land to Asians: they disliked the proposal that all transfers should be subject to the Governor's veto, obtaining instead that this should apply only to those between persons of different race.[3] Thus the Governor could enforce racial segregation both in the Highlands and in townships. It became a grievance to the Indians that the settlers had obtained a legal consolidation of 'the Elgin pledge' under cover of war conditions. 1915 saw also the passing of a Native Registration Ordinance, following a recommendation of the Native Labour Commission. Designed to control the movement of labour, its enforcement was delayed until after the war, when it became a constant source of complaint among Africans. For the Europeans the two ordinances marked considerable achievements in respect of both land and labour.

[1] E.A. Standard, 11 Mar. 1911.
[2] Leg. Co. Minutes, 18 Jan. 1915, p. 12.
[3] Report of the Special Committee, Aug. 1914, which refers to representations from T. E. Harvey, M.P., against the new status of the native lands, which is referred to in more detail in Appendix I below.

There remained elective representation. After Girouard's departure this was pressed under the new Governor, Sir Henry Belfield, who was regarded initially as unlikely, after twenty-eight years in the Malay States, to be sympathetic to white settlement.[1] Delamere, temporarily out of politics through ill health, marked his return by refusing re-appointment to the Legislative Council in February 1913. He explained to the Pastoralists' Association that they should have elections, since they now paid direct taxation (a poll-tax was started in 1912) and were self-supporting, since the Treasury grant-in-aid had ended. However, Delamere's 'Popular Representation Petition' was not immediately supported.[2] In July, at the Convention of Associations, he caught the political moment, claiming representation not only as a right but as the practical answer to government inefficiencies. He explained that he was asking not for self-government but for a minority elected by the Europeans; 'Natives and Asiatics being subject peoples are represented by the official members on the Council', who also looked after the interests of the British taxpayer. Resolutions were passed calling on the nominated unofficial members to resign.[3] Thus when the Council met again in September the only unofficial present was J. H. Wilson of Mombasa. Settler politics were centred on the Highlands, as the presence of an unofficial from Mombasa throughout the boycott further showed.

The petition for elective representation went home and the Governor gave it his support, but it received a sharp rebuff from Harcourt. He said that it came from 'one section only of the community', which must be considered 'as a whole'; the white population was 'vastly outnumbered'. He asked how the non-Europeans, who provided the greater proportion of the revenue, were to be represented, and raised the question of voters' qualifications, mentioning considerations like education and property. Finally he asked for further information.[4]

The Indians were 'the crux of the situation',[5] for, the Conven-

[1] *E.A. Standard*, leading article, 20 July 1912, commenting on a Nairobi meeting of protest against Belfield's appointment.
[2] Ibid., 22 Mar. and 5 Apr. 1913.
[3] Ibid., 2 Aug. 1913. Some of Delamere's speech—but not the sentence quoted —appears in Huxley, *White Man's Country*, i. 277–9.
[4] Letter of Chief Secretary to Secretary, Convention of Associations, 18 Nov. 1913, in *E.A. Standard*, 29 Nov. 1913.
[5] Phrase of *E.A. Standard*, leading article, 29 Nov. 1913.

tion of Associations replied in January, it was 'obvious' that the natives would not take part in elections 'for many years'; the Convention feared that the Indians would 'vote solid' and so control elections. But this was fencing. The reply continued that the whites were the nucleus on which the government of the future 'must inevitably devolve'. The official majority amply safeguarded the Indians, but, if the Government considered it necessary, they would suggest the appointment of an unofficial European 'directly to represent Eastern interests'.[1] The Indians replied by forming the East African Indian National Congress, which first met in March, when a major complaint was that they had had no representation on the Legislative Council since 1911, when Jeevanjee's appointment had expired.[2] However, battle between the Europeans and the Indians was delayed until after the war.

During the war the Europeans obtained for themselves first a form of election and then the real thing. After the first flush of enthusiasm in 1914 a 'phoney war' atmosphere descended on East Africa in early 1915: settlers drifted back to their farms from the East African Mounted Rifles, and the impression spread that the Administration was unconcerned with the war. From this apathy Grogan, with government support, roused Nairobi in September. He told a crowded meeting that they were a mob without organization, and shamed them by reference to Bonar Law, the new Colonial Secretary, who had said that of the Colonies only British East Africa had not played its part. Grogan blamed 'the bureaucracy' and demanded conscription and the establishment of a small War Council with unofficial members. Supporting speakers included an Indian and a Goan. Bowring, the Chief Secretary, welcomed the meeting and replied by announcing that registration for war work would be introduced, to begin with the Europeans.[3]

The War Council was appointed a week later, under Bowring's chairmanship, with three other officials, two military representatives, and three settlers who included Grogan.[4]

---

[1] *E.A. Standard*, 31 Jan. 1914.

[2] Report of the 1st Session of the E.A.I.N.C., 7–8 Mar. 1914.

[3] *E.A. Standard*, 11 Sept. 1915. Bonar Law's remarks may have been based on *Further Correspondence regarding Gifts from the Oversea Dominions and Colonies*, Cd. 7875 (1915). East Africa was the first part of the Empire to introduce conscription, however.   [4] *E.A. Standard*, 18 Sept. 1915.

Though only advisory, its almost daily meetings soon gave it a power and influence which was virtually executive. It not only discussed the war and conscription problems, but sought to strengthen the European position after the war. From it emerged, during 1916, the idea of a Soldier Settlement Scheme, and Delamere, when he became a member in 1917, tried to make it an instrument of agricultural production.[1]

The most important political gain, the settlers considered, was the concession of elections to the War Council. The first, and appointed, members toured to seek opinions, but were met with resolutions that other members should be added. The Governor agreed. Elections were demanded, but the Government refused to be responsible for any electoral scheme which was left to the Europeans. Belfield, however, agreed to make further appointments after elections from separate electoral divisions,[2] and three were formed. Although the War Council was not formally part of the constitution, the settlers considered that the principle of elective representation 'was won'.[3] In any case the Governor continued to press for it and was proud to announce the success of his efforts in the Legislative Council in October 1916. Bonar Law had approved of its introduction when it should become convenient to work out the details—the qualification of electors, electoral areas, and the best way of representing the 'interests of Indian, Arab, and Native Community' (sic)—but said, it was later disclosed, that this would be impossible until after the war.[4]

However, Nairobi took time by the forelock. In February 1917, unofficials returned to the Legislative Council in order 'to bring into being a form of elective representation'. On the Government's motion a committee was appointed[5] which reported in June. They received representations from the East African Women's League, formed in March as a suffrage

[1] Leg. Co. *Minutes*, 10 Oct. 1916, p. 3, and Huxley, op. cit., ii. 32. See also Chapter V above.

[2] *E.A. Standard*, 30 Oct. 1915; G. A. S. Northcote, Kiambu District Commissioner, speaking at Nairobi meeting, 22 Oct. 1915.

[3] Huxley, op. cit., ii. 22–23, and M. F. Hill, *Permanent Way*, vol. i. *The Story of the Kenya and Uganda Railway* (Nairobi, 1950), p. 353.

[4] Leg. Co. *Minutes*, 10 Oct. 1916, p. 3, and 20 Nov. 1918, p. 35.

[5] Delamere speaking at Nakuru, 26 Jan. 1918, *E.A. Standard*, 2 Feb. 1918, and Leg. Co. *Minutes*, 12 Feb. 1917, p. 5.

organization,[1] and from the Indian Associations of Nairobi and Mombasa. These were all brushed on one side, for the committee were unanimous for giving the vote only to every male British subject of European origin ('whole-blooded descent from European ancestors') on proof of twelve months' continuous residence. Since the coloured races then outnumbered the white, it was 'not desirable that the franchise should be extended to Asiatics or Natives'. They suggested ten European electoral areas delimited to represent interests rather than numbers: one for Nairobi against one for the rural area of the coast, and two for the Uasin Gishu plateau because of its Dutch and other interests. Though Grogan, on war service in German East Africa, protested,[2] it was generally realized that constituencies based on numbers would have meant control by Nairobi and Mombasa, which have always contained about half of the European population. Instead the South African principle of weightage in favour of rural areas was taken to a more extreme conclusion. In the committee the unofficials also raised the possibility of their representation on the Executive Council, but the chairman ruled them out of order;[3] they renewed their pressure by petition later in the year and in a debate in the Legislative Council in February 1918.[4]

The Europeans became irritated because no action was taken. But London had a war to fight; one, moreover, which by the capture of German East Africa raised the question of the future organization of the British possessions in East Africa.[5] There was a lengthy interregnum after Belfield's retirement in 1917 before the military Governor desired by the settlers could take up his office in February 1919. This was General Sir Edward Northey, who had campaigned against the Germans from Nyasaland.[6] In

---

[1] *The Leader of British East Africa*, 17 Mar. 1917, and Ross, *Kenya from Within*, p. 326. Its first president, Mrs. McGregor Ross, told the committee that the women who had shared in the pioneer work and privations of the men were conscious of the problems for legislation (Proceedings and Report of the Committee). The women obtained the franchise in the 1919 Ordinance; the E.A.P. was thus the first part of the Empire where complete adult suffrage was introduced at once—at least for one racial group.

[2] 'The Dodoma letter' in *The Leader of B.E.A.*, 29 Dec. 1917. 'In the final Ordinance of 1919 Nairobi received two seats, the total being raised to eleven.

[3] Unofficial members to the Governor, 28 May 1917.

[4] Leg. Co. *Minutes*, 8 Oct. 1917, p. 3, and 18 Feb. 1918, p. 11.

[5] Ibid., 20 Nov. 1918, p. 38.

[6] Nyasaland was renamed Malawi in July 1964.

opening his first Legislative Council he announced that the time had come, with the Colonial Secretary's approval, for European elections, that the Arabs and Indians would have nominated representatives, and that unofficials would be appointed to the Executive Council.[1]

The Indian controversy

Already Northey had been given a striking demonstration of Nairobi politics. The Convention of Associations, in abeyance during the war, met again in January 1919 and briefed Grogan, their president, for a speech at a banquet of welcome. This turned into 'a violent and insolent tirade'[2] of two hours' duration in which Grogan attacked the Colonial Office and local officials, besides explaining the Convention's wishes on the organization of government, and land and labour policies. He then concentrated on the Asiatic question: the Europeans were 'the guardians of the back door' and owed it to South Africa to keep the Indians out. Finally he promised Northey, according to his attitude, either a fight or 'unswerving devotion'. Northey, feeling his difficult position, replied in restrained terms: he sympathized with the officials and stressed the need for co-operation, concluding with thanks to Grogan, whom he christened his 'godfather'.[3]

Northey had arrived as the Indian question, which was to dominate politics until 1923, was breaking.[4] But there were other issues also, made plain in Grogan's speech and still more in the report in March of the Economic Commission. Appointed

[1] Ibid., 24 Feb. 1919, p. 3.
[2] Phrase of Lord Emmott, in the House of Lords, *Hansard*, 5th ser. 41, 142, 14 July 1920. [3] *E.A. Standard*, 15 Feb. 1919.
[4] This had been touched off by an article, 'A Colony for India' (*Nineteenth Century*, Sept. 1918) urging that German East Africa should be handed to India as compensation for Indians being shut out from the self-governing Dominions. The author, Sir Theodore Morison, then a colonel in the War Office but formerly a member of the Council of India, was reflecting ideas current in the Government of India. A claim that India should be the mandatory for German East Africa was put forward by Lord Sinha, an Indian representative, at the Paris peace negotiations early in 1919 (R. Meinertzhagen, *Army Diary, 1899–1926* (London, 1960), pp. 248–50). Whether the settlers knew all this or not, they took the threat seriously. The ideas in Morison's article were condemned in a Legislative Council debate, 9 Dec. 1918, and in a letter from Bishop Weston of Zanzibar (*E.A. Standard*, 25 Dec. 1918). All this had thus a strong influence on the Convention of Associations' meeting in January and on the Economic Commission's Report, then being drafted.

in 1917 to survey the economic future, it interpreted its
terms in a very wide sense. Not only did the report achieve
considerable notoriety from its immoderate language about the
Indians,[1] but the seven signatories (five settlers and two officials)
discussed the constitution, pressing for further steps to responsible government. They also talked of areas being released from
the native reserves for white settlement[2] and discussed the labour
question. This last became acute in the aftermath of the war and
through the possibility of a further influx of settlers by the
approval of a scheme for soldier settlement. The new Governor
made plain the spirit in which he intended to tackle these issues.
He told a deputation of the Nairobi Indian Association in
March 1919 that 'the principle had been accepted at home that
this country was primarily for European development', and he
confirmed this by letter: 'European interests must be paramount
throughout the Protectorate.'[3]

The dangers of such an attitude were exemplified over both
land and labour. A large area of the Nandi reserve was taken
for the Soldier Settlement Scheme, the Colonial Office being
informed so late that it was not practicable to reverse the
Governor's action.[4] On labour there were the so-called
'Northey circulars'. The first, issued in October over the signature of Ainsworth, the Chief Native Commissioner, provoked a
strong reaction from missionaries. In a reasoned criticism the
bishops of Mombasa and Uganda, with the Reverend Dr.
Arthur, the senior Church of Scotland missionary, showed that,
though compulsion was not mentioned, the wish of the Government for officials, including chiefs and headmen, to help in
producing labour would in effect mean compulsion. This the
missionaries were prepared to admit for work of national im-

---

[1] For this the report was strongly criticized by Milner, Colonial Secretary since
Jan. 1919, in the House of Lords, *Hansard*, 5th ser. 41. 161, 14 July 1920.

[2] At the same time settlers' evidence before the Land Settlement Commission,
1919, laid particular claim to parts of Kikuyu land.

[3] *Correspondence regarding the Position of Indians in East Africa*, Cmd. 1311 (1921),
p. 2, and Ross, op. cit., pp. 327–8. According to Buell (*The Native Problem in Africa*
(2 vols., New York, 1928), i. 333) Northey used a similar expression in the Convention of Associations, words there linked with the labour problem. It is not clear
whether Northey had any authority to make these statements, but such evidence
as I have been able to glean inclines me to think he had not.

[4] *Report of the East Africa Commission* (Ormsby-Gore Commission), Cmd. 2387
(1925), p. 29, see also Ross, op. cit., pp. 81–82.

portance and under conditions, preferring enactment and definite obligation to 'incessant appeals and demands'. Their memorandum and missionary influence in London produced questions and debate in parliament. In writing to Northey, Milner, the Secretary of State, thought a difference between advice and compulsion could be maintained,[1] but this did not satisfy missionary opinion. Pressure was maintained until Churchill, Milner's successor, sent a dispatch stating that officials, beyond giving natives information about where labour was required, were 'to take no part in recruiting labour for private employment'.[2] The Colonial Office had returned to Crewe's position in 1908: this was easy in Downing Street, but difficult for officials caught between their duty and the settlers' pressures.[3]

Missionary influence had been important;[4] Africans were not yet able to exert political pressure. Yet, just when missionaries at Nairobi were suggesting, in 1919 and again in 1921, that they should represent native interests on the Legislative Council,[5] Africans, provoked by European action, were stirring politically. Two bodies were formed: the Kikuyu Association in 1920 and the Young Kikuyu Association in 1921. The first, composed largely of chiefs and headmen, was concerned mainly with the defence of the Kikuyu land, but the second also with grievances of the labourers. Harry Thuku, its secretary, was a government telephone operator, soon dismissed for his activities. He attacked two changes introduced in 1920: the *kipande*, a card bearing finger-prints that adult males were compelled to carry under the new system of native registration, and the doubling of the hut tax and poll-tax, from 5 to 10 rupees. In 1921 this was reduced to 8 rupees, but the African was again hit, for the European farmers, affected by the fall in world prices, enforced a one-third cut in native wages. Thuku began his agitation among the Kikuyu, but, since the grievances were general, seized the opportunity of extending it into the west, visiting Kisumu and

---

[1] *Despatch to the Governor of the E.A.P. relating to Native Labour and Papers connected therewith*, Cmd. 873 (1920).

[2] *Despatch . . . relating to Native Labour, 5 September 1921*, Cmd. 1509 (1921).

[3] e.g. S. V. Cooke in 1925 (Ross, op. cit., pp. 113–14).

[4] R. Oliver, *The Missionary Factor in East Africa* (London, 1952), pp. 248–57.

[5] Representative Council of the Alliance of the Missionary Societies of British East Africa, minutes of meetings, Nairobi, Jan. 1919 and Apr. 1921.

addressing large meetings of Kavirondo. The Chief Native Commissioner maintained that a prayer issued for Thuku introduced an element of religion which might lead to a dangerous situation, the people being told that they were in a state of slavery imposed by the Europeans. The Government arrested Thuku in March 1922, and deported him, as 'dangerous to peace and good order', to Kismayu (then part of Kenya), though not without touching off a riot in Nairobi.[1] African political expression could then be dealt with firmly—or else ignored, as when the Kikuyu Association was denied a hearing in the 1923 negotiations in London.[2] At this time it was considered sufficient to listen to a missionary and to place him on the Legislative Council to represent African interests.

Politics were reserved to the Europeans and the Indians. Had it not been for their rivalry the Europeans might have established their position in Kenya, as in places farther south. In 1919 the Indians, angered by the Economic Commission's report, Northey's cold-shoulder, and the denial of elected representation, were betrayed into utterances almost as wild as those of the Europeans. Their Congress passed a resolution asking for German East Africa to be reserved 'for the purpose of Indian colonization'. On the advice of leaders from India they quickly retreated to a more tenable position, expressing only the hope of sharing equal rights with other subjects of the King.[3]

Behind the battle lines communications stretched to India and South Africa. The Government of India, sensitive to the growing Indian nationalist movement, bombarded Whitehall with dispatches, and South African opinion was heard through the powerful voice of General Smuts. East African politics raised issues of Imperial concern that were discussed at Imperial Conferences.[4]

In 1920, just before the Protectorate became Kenya Colony, Milner sought a solution: he continued the policies of no specific immigration restrictions on Indians, residential segregation, and the bar on land ownership in the Highlands, but he was pre-

---

[1] G. Bennett, 'The development of political organizations in Kenya', *Political Studies*, v. 2 (June 1957), 118–19.

[2] *Hansard*, 5th ser., H. of C. 166. 902, 9 July 1923.

[3] *Report by Sir Benjamin Robertson, dated 4 August 1920*, Cmd. 1312 (1921), p. 3.

[4] W. K. Hancock, *Survey of British Commonwealth Affairs*, vol. i (London, 1937), ch. iv.

pared to establish an area for Indians, and to introduce elected representation for them, though by only two members as against the Europeans' eleven.[1] The Government of India, in a masterly dispatch, shattered this. Relying on Milner's phrase in the House of Lords, 'even-handed justice between the different races', they showed that the official majority in the Legislative Council was no protection: 'the only real safeguard . . . is adequate representation'. They asked for this on a common roll with property and education qualifications, fearing—in phrases recalling the Montagu–Chelmsford Report in India—that separate representation would 'perpetuate and intensify racial antagonism'. They showed that Kenya's land policy was not being implemented with 'even-handed justice'; above all, it was not true that the European area was small in proportion to the amount of alienable land. They could not accept Milner's decisions as a final settlement, and they urged the appointment of a Royal Commission.[2]

In Kenya Milner's solution was accepted by neither party. The battle continued, with a pause only in May 1921, when the Governor called the two parties together in a three-day conference. But this proved abortive. In June the Convention, in a meeting dominated by the Indian question, formulated what came to be known as their 'irreducible minimum'.[3] In the following months resolutions and appeals poured from the two sides, being sent to South Africa and India, and also to Britain, where alone could the final decision be made.

Delamere journeyed to London to see Churchill, and heard him speak at an East African dinner in January 1922. Holding that the democratic principles of Europe were 'by no means suited to the development of Asiatic and African people', Churchill, nevertheless, wished to apply broadly Rhodes's principle of equal rights for all civilized men. Natives and Indians who conformed to well-marked European standards should not be denied the fullest exercise and enjoyment of civic and political rights, but in the definition of these standards the European community had 'a right to be fully consulted'. The Government

[1] Milner to Bowring, 21 May 1920, in *Kenya Official Gazette*, 18 Aug. 1920, pp. 774–6.

[2] Government of India to India Office, 21 Oct. 1920, *Correspondence regarding the Position of Indians in East Africa*, Cmd. 1311 (1921).

[3] Huxley, *White Man's Country*, ii. 122.

would maintain the 'pledge' of the reservation of the Highlands and regulate future Indian immigration. Most notably, Churchill declared:

> We do not contemplate any settlement or system which will prevent British East Africa, or Kenya, as it has now become known, becoming a characteristically and distinctively British colony looking forward in the full fruition of time to complete responsible self-government.[1]

The speech aroused a storm in India, but Delamere returned to Kenya confident of the future.

Moreover, events in Kenya under Northey had gone the settlers' way. There had grown up a system which Delamere later christened 'government by agreement':[2] co-operation in which the Government consulted elected members before introducing Bills, thus giving them the opportunity to suggest modifications. This process worked the more easily since two of these Europeans were from 1919 on the Executive Council, where Northey considered them as 'members of the Government'.[3] Under this régime much of the ill-feeling between settlers and officials disappeared. Northey permitted officials to acquire land and allowed them a free vote in the Legislative Council. There Holm, the new Director of Agriculture from South Africa, said plainly that he would 'always' give his voice for the farming community.[4] The *East African Standard* regarded Northey visiting London as 'Our Ambassador'.[5]

In these circumstances the settlers considered that their chief remaining goal was that of obtaining direct control over the formulation of government policy. The growing economic difficulties of 1922 seemed to provide the necessary opportunity. The Government in considering the appointment of a committee to suggest economies, like the Geddes Committee in England, intended that its members should be civil servants, but critics pointed out that the Geddes Committee was not so composed.[6] The critics won: the Economic and Finance Committee, appointed in March, had but two official members against six

---

[1] *The Times*, 28 Jan. 1922.
[2] Leg. Co. *Debates*, 24 Aug. 1925, p. 770.
[3] In the Legislative Council, 12 Oct. 1921 (*E.A. Standard*, 15 Oct. 1921).
[4] In the Legislative Council, 4 May 1920 (*E.A. Standard*, 8 May 1920).
[5] Title of leading article, *E.A. Standard*, 4 July 1921.
[6] Ibid., leading article, 1 Mar. 1922.

non-officials, of whom one was an Indian. It soon developed on lines similar to the War Council—being again chaired by Sir Charles Bowring. In putting up recommendations its daily meetings created the impression that it was 'effecting a revolution by due course of law in giving the substance if not the name of unofficial control of public affairs'.[1] It killed the income tax, which the settlers had fought since 1920 by such methods as refusal to fill in tax returns.[2] Against Indian protests, this Bowring Committee put forward a policy of high tariff protection for agriculture, one recommendation being a 100 per cent. duty on flour and 50 per cent. on wheat.

Riding thus with the tide, the settlers were the more dismayed when the wave broke in mid-1922. They should have taken warning from Churchill's ending of the official free vote in February and his cut of the proposed duties to 30 per cent. early in June.[3] The Colonial Office was reasserting itself, but the shock came in Northey's abrupt recall by a secret dispatch of 29 June. The *East African Standard* printed this in August with the comment that Northey had been recalled 'in defiance—it is an open secret—of the Economic Committee, of the elected members of the Legislative Council and of the Convention of Associations'; there was 'dismay and indignation' that Bowring had been passed over.[4] On 1 September Coryndon arrived from being Governor of Uganda, telegraphing to a friend: 'Have accepted Governorship of Kenya: no more peace.'[5]

Five days later a second shock reached Nairobi in a telegram summarizing the 'Wood–Winterton report'. This new attempt of the Colonial and India Offices (called after their parliamentary under-secretaries) to settle the Indian controversy affronted 'the irreducible minimum' of the Convention in all but the continued reservation of the Highlands. It rejected immigration restriction, segregation, and Indian representation by nomination. Instead it put proposals for a common roll with property

---

[1] Ibid., leading article, 16 June 1922.

[2] Ibid., 8 May 1920, 24 Dec. 1921, and 1 Apr. 1922. Delamere called the tax 'unconstitutional', saying that for it they should have an unofficial majority. A Taxpayers' Protection League was formed in Dec. 1921 to fight the tax.

[3] Ibid., 18 Feb., and Leg. Co., *Minutes*, 6 June 1922, p. 9.

[4] *E.A. Standard*, 19 Aug. 1922. The dispatch is in Ross, *Kenya from Within*, pp. 358–9.

[5] Huxley, op. cit., ii. 132.

and educational qualifications to produce a 10 per cent. Indian electorate, with four seats reserved for them. The readiness of the Indians to accept was taken by the Government as meaning only that they would raise further demands, whilst the Europeans saw this as the beginning of a move towards their eventual elimination from the Legislative Council.[1] They determined to resist. Plans were drawn up to seize the railway and telegraphic communications and to kidnap the Governor. However, the Imperial Government was not prepared to use coercion. A new Colonial Secretary, the Duke of Devonshire, summoned the Kenya principals to London, a truce being arranged between the local Government and the settlers. In March 1923 Coryndon and two delegations, European and Indian, departed, the latter, as if to indicate both the strength and the weakness of its position, travelling via Bombay.[2]

The London negotiations were conducted against a background of appeals by both delegations to public opinion, Delamere devoting his private means to this end. Yet neither party was pleased with the White Paper which emerged in July. It denied the Indians a common roll, granting them only five communal seats in the Legislative Council, and refused to reconsider the Highlands land policy. The Indians, in determining to continue working for equal status, therefore began a policy of non-co-operation, which reached its extreme in non-payment of taxes in 1924. The Europeans were told that there would be no immigration restriction and that residential segregation in townships must be abandoned; they lost the monopoly of the franchise, and learned that the Imperial Government considered that responsible government was 'out of the question within any period of time which need now be taken into consideration'. The full weight of this rebuff may be measured against the grant of this same status to the Southern Rhodesian settlers in the same year—but they had no Indians to contend with. The Europeans could not rest content with this settlement. For a moment it even appeared as if they might reject the terms, but, through the quick hostile reaction of the Indians, they were able to put a brave face on their defeat.[3] Yet in a way the Europeans had

---

[1] *Indians in Kenya*, Cmd. 1922 (1923), pp. 6–8.

[2] Huxley, op. cit., ii. 136–40.

[3] Ibid., ch. xix, which provides a valuable picture of the negotiations and settlement as seen by Delamere.

won: the Indians were denied political equality and the Europeans gained further recognition of their communal electorate,
a safeguard second in importance only to land reservation.

However, there was a greater significance in the White Paper:
it 'rediscovered the vast majority of Kenya's population, namely
the native Africans',[1] revealing that all the noise had come from
some 10,000 Europeans (including officials) and 23,000 Indians
acting before an estimated $2\frac{1}{2}$ million Africans. The White Paper
not only denied responsible government to the settlers, and any
immediate unofficial majority in the Legislative Council, but it
asserted Whitehall's sole trusteeship on behalf of these Africans.

In the long argument both Europeans and Indians had talked
of native interests, each producing Africans in Nairobi to speak
against the other. In the 1923 negotiations the Europeans went
further. The Convention, knowing the anti-Indian attitude of
the Kenya missionaries, accepted Coryndon's suggestion that a
missionary, Dr. Arthur, should join the delegation to represent
native interests.[2] But there were other missionaries: those in
India and Ceylon were well aware of Asian hatred of racial
discrimination. Reports from both sides of the Indian Ocean
reached J. H. Oldham, secretary in London of the International
Missionary Council, who was at that time concerned about
labour problems in Kenya. He came to see that by stressing the
native question he could resolve the conflict between missionaries, and that this had an application also in the political field.
Supported by Davidson, Archbishop of Canterbury, his idea of
a declaration that native interests should be paramount was put
to the Colonial Office.[3] It provided a welcome way of escape,
but the words of the proclamation—'Primarily Kenya is an
African territory . . . the interests of the African natives must be
paramount'—reversed for the Europeans the paramountcy talk
of Eliot and Northey. It came as a thunderclap, nobody realiz-
ing that it echoed Stewart's instructions in 1904. However, the
qualification was added that 'obviously the interests of the other
communities, European, Indian, and Arab, must severally be
safeguarded'.[4] Thus it remained a question of the relation of
interests; the meaning of paramountcy could be argued about.

---

[1] Hancock, *Survey of Commonwealth Affairs*, i. 224.
[2] *E.A. Standard*, 3 Mar. 1923.
[3] Oliver, *Missionary Factor*, pp. 259–62.   [4] Cmd. 1922 (1923), p. 9.

Delamere, Grigg, Amery, and federation

In the London negotiations Delamere appeared as the settlers' acknowledged leader. It had taken him long to reach this eminence. Indeed, in the first elections of 1920, the *East African Standard* ran Grogan as 'The People's Leader',[1] but he was ignominiously defeated in his constituency; thereafter his main role was the making of sporadic speeches with the verbal fireworks for which he remained famous. In the Legislative Council Delamere tried to organize the unofficial vote by creating 'the Reform Party' in May 1921.[2] The individualist elected Europeans of Kenya always chafed under discipline, but there were other reasons for questioning Delamere's leadership. His early land dealings had not been forgotten—how could they be since he was widely regarded as the leader of the large landowners? In September Captain Coney won a by-election with the cry that the Reform Party was a party of 'the Big Interests', and he mentioned particularly Delamere, Grogan, and the *East African Standard*.[3] After entering the Council, however, Coney joined Delamere's group and became his chief lieutenant. Attacked for this in the election campaign of 1924, he explained that on the Bowring Committee he had realized that 'Delamere was a statesman' and that the Colony was lucky to have him.[4] The crisis of 1922–3 appeared to establish Delamere's position, but he was never beyond question.[5] In 1924 a flood of letters in the *East African Standard* attacked him for his land dealing, particularly because of his relations with Martin, the Commissioner of Lands; the newspaper itself was led to comment that unpleasantness would have been avoided if the action had been more open.[6] Then, in the same year, the publication of Dr. Leys' *Kenya* revived old charges of 'dummying'. Amery, as Secretary of State, ordered investigations: two White Papers were published which provided some defence.[7]

---

[1] Title of leading article, *E.A. Standard*, 26 Feb. 1920.
[2] Ibid., 28 May 1921 letter from Delamere.
[3] Ibid., 3 Sept. 1921.   [4] Ibid., 1 Mar. 1924.
[5] *Pace* Huxley, op. cit., ii. 320.
[6] *E.A. Standard*, leading article, 13 Aug. 1924.
[7] *Correspondence with the Government of Kenya relating to an exchange of Lands with Lord Delamere*, Cmd. 2500 (1925), and *Correspondence . . . relating to Lord Delamere's Acquisition of Land in Kenya*, Cmd. 2629 (1926). For opposing comment see Huxley, op. cit., ii. 174–9, and Ross, op. cit., p. 74.

No longer just the frontiersman—significantly, his flowing locks gave place to a more normal hair style in 1924[1]—Delamere impressed Grigg, the Governor who succeeded on Coryndon's death in 1925, as the great estate owner with the racial ideas of the southern states at the time of the American civil war, who thought of old Virginia as the model.[2] Not surprisingly, his constituents complained of his aloofness, and he found difficulty in controlling public meetings, even in his own Nakuru;[3] and, moreover, he was never a good speaker. The Europeans did not always find it easy to support the policy of 'government by agreement'; like other colonials they feared the possibility of a 'lost leader' joining the irremovable Government. Delamere had urged the appointment of a governor of eminence and obtained an increase in the salary of the new Governor to build up Kenya's prestige.[4] He was—unlike some others—ready for the wider views Grigg was to bring, and with him he attained his last period of influence.

Some received the new-comer with suspicion. They thought his former Liberal membership of parliament for Oldham might indicate a connexion with Manchester cotton interests.[5] These were believed to support native peasant agriculture as producing cheaper raw materials, particularly cotton. Was there not a danger that the 'Dual Policy',[6] proclaimed by Coryndon, of developing European and native agriculture each in its own area, would deprive the settlers of labour?

However, Grigg's thinking was primarily political. In imperial ideas he had long been associated with Amery.[7] As followers of Milner they regarded East Africa in the light of South Africa after the Boer war: for effective growth closer union was necessary. In 1919 Amery had urged this as Milner's Under-Secretary; now, in power, he appointed Grigg to bring it about.[8] Although the Ormsby-Gore Commission had been sent out to

---

[1] Huxley, op. cit., ii. 185. The portrait (ibid., vol. i, frontispiece), hung in the Memorial Hall, Nairobi, in 1924 (*E.A. Standard*, 29 Nov.) shows Delamere shorn.

[2] Lord Altrincham, *Kenya's Opportunity* (London, 1955), p. 205.

[3] e.g. *E.A. Standard*, 23 Jan. 1926 and 19 Jan. 1929.

[4] Leg. Co. *Debates*, 18 Feb. 1925, pp. 17–23, and *East Africa*, 21 Jan. 1926.

[5] *E.A. Standard*, 6 June 1925, and *East Africa*, 6 Aug. 1925.

[6] See Chapter VIII below.

[7] They had been together on the staff of *The Times*, 1903–10 (*History of The Times*, vol. iv (London, 1952), ch. i, 'The new imperialism', especially pp. 16 sqq., also pp. 683–4). [8] L. S. Amery, *My Political Life*, ii (London, 1953), 360–1.

M

examine the East African situation in 1924 and had reported in 1925, Grigg was given instructions, recalling those of Girouard, to report on this again.[1] There was a widespread feeling that greater knowledge and research were needed;[2] it seemed as if Grigg might assemble a new 'kindergarten' to provide this, with Oldham as Director of Research.[3] Like Girouard, Grigg felt immediately the weakness of the officials in the debates of the Legislative Council. He wanted a politician to help in selling his ideas to the politicians of Nairobi. He pressed Amery to remove his chief official, Denham, the Colonial Secretary, and hoped to replace him by Feetham, a South African judge and former member of Milner's 'kindergarten'. The latter came in 1926, but only to report on local government.

If local government was Grigg's first priority, the second was the question of an unofficial majority in the Legislative Council.[4] Grigg found that constitutional custom had developed far more rapidly than he had realized; the official majority had ceased to have any meaning, so that he was 'obliged to proceed, as a general rule, by consent'. Moreover, the majority had 'no moral cohesion', since it contained members with local training whose 'whole instinct' was to vote with the elected members; it could not be relied on in a crisis. Grigg, therefore, asked that the reserve power should be placed in his hands, through 'certification, as in India'.[5] Amery, replying to earlier representations, conceded that the system was 'inherently weak', but, because of the political situation in South Africa, Britain, and India, he was not prepared to make a change which would 'weaken our control over a difficult situation'.[6] However, Grigg, for his part, told the Nairobi Caledonian dinner that the request for progress to self-government had his 'instinctive sympathy'.

[1] Much that follows is based on the private correspondence of Grigg (the Altrincham Papers) and that of Dr. J. H. Oldham. I am much indebted both to the latter and to Mr. John Grigg for the privilege of access to these two most valuable sources.

[2] e.g. House of Lords debate, 20 May 1925, on the Ormsby-Gore Report (Cmd. 2387). In replying, Balfour announced the establishment of the Civil Research Committee (*Hansard*, 5th ser. 61. 412–13).

[3] G. Bennett, 'Paramountcy to partnership: J. H. Oldham and Africa', *Africa*, xxx. 4 (1960), pp. 356–61.

[4] Major E. A. T. Dutton, Grigg's private secretary, to J. H. Oldham, 11 Aug. 1926, Oldham Papers.

[5] Grigg to Amery, 21 Sept. 1926, Altrincham Papers.

[6] Ibid., Amery to Grigg, 22 Sept. 1926.

At the same time he felt constrained to mention the difficulties: even friendly critics questioned the position in Kenya, and he quoted Cromer describing compulsory labour as 'synonymous with slavery'.[1] The comment was pertinent, for Coney had told his constituents in February: 'You will never solve the labour problem until you have control of the country—when you have that you will immediately solve the problem.' He then went on to advocate compulsion.[2] In November the *East African Standard* referred back to these remarks as 'irresponsible' because of their possible effect on British opinion.[3] The paper was developing a series of leading articles urging the institution of an unofficial majority. In 1925 and 1926 the labour situation was acute: there was talk of seeking Indian, and even Chinese, indentured labour, and Delamere, in opposing this, suggested bringing Italians.[4] In this he came close to Grigg's constant view that the solution lay in closer settlement, thus ending the Europeans' dependence on native labour by bringing in Europeans of all classes to build up a white state.[5] Then self-government would follow, whereas for many settlers, agitatedly concerned about labour, it was simply associated as the solution of that problem. Grigg was already willing to have an unofficial majority, but the settler leaders went further: their election manifesto, in December 1926, called for a majority of European elected members,[6] a demand in which they may have been encouraged by Grigg's proclaimed sympathy.

Grigg visited London and submitted his views on East Africa to the Colonial Office in a memorandum in March 1927: this he had first circulated to friends. He thus persuaded Oldham that the position of the 1923 White Paper—trusteeship for the native races as an Imperial responsibility which could neither be delegated nor shared—was untenable because of the influence of the settlers in Kenya and had, in fact, already been given up.

---

[1] *E.A. Standard*, 4 Dec. 1926.

[2] Ibid., 20 Feb. 1926, quoted in Ross, op. cit., p. 117, also by J. H. Thomas, 19 July 1927 (*Hansard*, 5th ser., H. of C. 209. 263) and Olivier, 7 Dec. 1927 (ibid., H. of L. 69. 572).

[3] Ibid., 27 Nov. 1926.

[4] *East Africa*, 23 July 1925, and *E.A. Standard*, 23 May 1925 and 30 Oct. 1926.

[5] The European leaders were so impressed by Grigg's utterances on this subject that they collected them in a memorandum for the Morris Carter Commission. Kenya Land Commission, *Evidence and Memoranda*, Col. 91 (1934), vol. iii, pp. 2882–6.

[6] *E.A. Standard*, 1 Jan. 1927.

Grigg believed that the Europeans would eventually gain control, though his immediate proposals were only for a European unofficial majority composed partly of elected members and partly of others nominated by the Governor to represent native interests. Oldham accepted the need for a new statement of policy that would lead to responsibility being shared with the local Europeans, but he saw also that, after the 1923 White Paper, it would come as 'a great shock to public opinion'.[1]

He was right. Amery's White Paper of July, declaring that the Imperial Government desired to associate local colonists and residents more closely in the trust,[2] appeared as a revolution in policy. Amery defended this in the Commons on the somewhat surprising ground that the early settlers in South Africa had been kept from native policy, and that a hostility had been bred in them towards the Government which thus 'denied them a share in the control of their own affairs'. Amery affirmed that self-government in Kenya would come with 'the growth of a large settled community', and he wanted them to have a 'spirit of trusteeship'.[3] Linked with the declaration of association was an announcement that a commission would visit East Africa to consider federation. Thus Amery's objective was now made public.

If federation was a 'forced card' as Lord Olivier said,[4] it was forced by two influences of which those in Britain who desired to create a great Dominion in East Africa were the prime movers. In Kenya Delamere had opposed the idea in the 1920 elections, believing that Kenya should stand alone until it was self-governing and that its own problems should be digested first.[5] By 1925, however, he was ready for Grigg's federation

---

[1] Oldham to Grigg, 9 Mar., 1 and 10 Apr. 1927, Altrincham Papers, and Oldham to Ormsby-Gore, 6 May 1927, Oldham Papers. Grigg had hoped that the memorandum would be published, but, as Oldham pointed out, it contained much controversial material, particularly regarding Tanganyika, so that this did not prove possible. Grigg later considered that the failure to publish it and some of his evidence before the Joint Select Committee in 1931 mattered little, since his dispatch of 11 Sept. 1930 in Col. 57 was 'a complete résumé of the views which I have expressed since I first formed any in Kenya, and also a complete account of the constitutional steps which seem to me necessary to the welfare of the Colony' (Grigg to J. A. Cable, 22 Mar. 1932, Altrincham Papers).

[2] *Future Policy in regard to Eastern Africa*, Cmd. 2904 (1927).

[3] *Hansard*, 5th ser., H. of C. 209. 291, 19 July 1927.

[4] Ibid., H. of L. 69. 555, 7 Dec. 1927.

[5] Huxley, *White Man's Country*, ii. 83–84, and *E.A. Standard*, 17 Jan. 1920.

plans, and supported the idea of building a Government House at Nairobi to be a worthy centre for the newly established Governors' Conference.[1] He provided an unofficial background to the Governors' first meeting at Nairobi in 1926 by calling a conference, at Tukuyu in southern Tanganyika, of settler leaders from the whole area from Kenya to Nyasaland and Northern Rhodesia.[2] This was succeeded by others, at Livingstone in 1926 and Nairobi in 1927, but the importance of the federation movement for the politics of Kenya was in Delamere's linking of 'safeguards' with it. The first statement of this came at the Nakuru Caledonian dinner in 1925. Delamere announced that Grigg had arrived at 'a psychological moment in the history of Kenya', when it could become 'the centre of opinion and thought in Eastern Africa', with a 'civilizing influence' going southward to meet those radiating north from Rhodesia. But, he added, the door leading to federation was shut, and the only key was an elected majority on the Kenya Legislative Council.[3] This then lay behind Grigg's urging of an unofficial majority.

However, the European pressures were well known. In November 1927, in the House of Commons, Josiah Wedgwood, an old Radical critic of the settlers and friend of the Indians, suggested that the Governor should open the East African Indian National Congress if he opened the Convention of Associations,[4] as had become customary. Perhaps in answer to such criticism, the custom was dropped, but, as if in more immediate response, Grigg did open an Unofficial Conference of the Indian Associations of East Africa later in the same month. This met to consider the appointment of the Hilton Young Commission on federation, but Grigg took the opportunity to point out that Kenya was the one territory in Africa where the Indians had elective representation, adding that the common roll only worked in a homogeneous community.[5]

Grigg's words found no favour in the December meeting of

[1] A plan of the fine mansion designed by Sir Herbert Baker will be found in E. Huxley's *Murder at Government House* (London, 1937), a novel scarcely disguised in its reference to Kenya and its characters.

[2] Huxley, *White Man's Country*, ii. 201 sqq.

[3] Ibid., pp. 198–9, and *E.A. Standard*, 5 Dec. 1925.

[4] *Hansard*, 5th ser., H. of C. 210. 613, 14 Nov. 1927.

[5] *Speeches by H.E. Sir Edward Grigg, 1925–1930* (Nairobi, n.d.), pp. 211, 214.

the Congress, which passed a motion of 'emphatic protest' against his 'generally hostile attitude'.[1] Indian resentment went back to his introduction, in 1926, of separate racial taxation to provide the finance for education by communities, a policy which affronted Asian principles by entrenching communal division in Kenya.[2] Tyeb Ali, the Congress president, in recounting a long series of grievances, referred to 'the iniquitous recommendations' of the Feetham Commission on local government, and spoke of Grigg's 'unholy alliance with Lord Delamere and his henchmen'.[3] Isher Dass, a Punjabi Hindu who had recently arrived to be Jeevanjee's private secretary, was heard for the first time. He had come from India, where the Simon Commission was being denounced as purely European. He now heard Tyeb Ali make the same complaint about the Hilton Young commissioners, and rose to call for a boycott of them also.[4]

Isher Dass became the leading advocate of renewed non-co-operation, the policy of 1923, which had mainly taken the form of refusal to participate in elections, although seats on the Legislative Council had in fact been taken up, between August 1925 and the general election of February 1927, on the basis of the Government nominating those put forward by the Congress, which conducted a form of elections. However, in 1927 a small group broke the Congress ban, put their names on the official electoral roll, and returned A. H. Malik. Despite Congress denunciation and demands for his resignation, he remained on the Council, where he later described non-co-operation as not Muslim,[5] a feeling which was to grow in his community.

Congress hostility prevented any nominations being made in March for the four vacant Legislative Council seats when a special election was offered for them.[6] Grigg continued trying to bring the Indians back into the Council, offering to make nominations on the Congress's advice. In April he said that though he understood their fears that they would compromise their position on the common roll, this would not happen, since

---

[1] *E.A. Standard*, 31 Dec. 1927.
[2] Leg. Co. *Debates*, 5 Nov. 1926, pp. 642–54.
[3] E.A.I.N.C. 7th Session: Presidential Address of Mr. Tyeb Ali.
[4] *Kenya Daily Mail*, Congress Special Number, 6 Jan. 1928.
[5] Leg. Co. *Debates*, 18 July 1929, p. 286.
[6] *E.A. Standard*, 10 Mar. 1928.

the matter would be before the Hilton Young Commission. Further, he affirmed that they would not be committed on the Feetham Report—they could state their objections on the Council. He offered to submit the new Local Government Bill to a Select Committee there, on which Europeans and Indians should be equally represented.[1] However, the Indians would not walk into the parlour: their leaders unanimously expressed appreciation of Grigg's offer but found themselves unable to accept.[2] The Local Government Bill was then referred to a round table conference which met in private. The more moderate Indian leaders conferred, but the non-co-operators persuaded the Indian associations to repudiate their agreement, since by then they preferred to await the publication of the Hilton Young Report.[3]

Rumours had reached them which reversed their original suspicions that the commission was a plot of Amery, Grigg, and Delamere. Originally, too, the Europeans were no less wary, for they feared that the commissioners represented various interests hostile to them. Harper, the chairman of the Convention of Associations, in saying this, added that they could rely implicitly on Oldham's impartiality alone.[4] He was the one member of the commission who had real knowledge of Kenya, from an earlier visit and from the extensive correspondence he had since maintained with missionaries, settlers, and officials. With his transparent desire to seek a solution for their problems in agreement, he played a large part in drafting, with Sir George Schuster, the majority report of the commission.

The various political associations produced memoranda, those of the Indian and African bodies being published; from the Convention all that then appeared was an original draft circulated for discussion. The *East African Standard* denounced this document as widening the racial gulf in the Colony and creating suspicion in both Uganda and Tanganyika. The paper called for an agreement between the communities in Kenya, without which 'the logical outcome' would be that their problems

[1] Grigg, *Speeches*, pp. 251–2.
[2] *E.A. Standard*, 5 May 1928.
[3] Note by H. T. Martin on the position of Indians in Kenya, 12 June 1929, Altrincham Papers: but see also M. Parker, *Development of Municipal Government in Kenya* (Ph.D. thesis, London, 1949), pp. 574–80.
[4] *E.A. Standard*, 22 Oct. 1927.

would be settled for them; further, the Europeans' past policy had 'led to a racial clash' and tended to lead to another—with the Africans.[1] Certainly the Kenya Government later looked back to the coming of the commission as provoking a new development of political activity among the Africans. Their submissions expressed fears of a settler majority on the Council as possibly leading to forced labour and further loss of land; they attacked specifically the Crown Lands Ordinance of 1915, referring to their lack of security of title.[2] This question provoked a first major clash between the commissioners and opinion, both of officials and settlers in Kenya.

Some form of protection for the native lands had long been sought by missionaries and Africans, strong representations being made to the Ormsby-Gore Commission, which discussed the matter at length.[3] Amery gave Grigg verbal instructions to report on the final delimitation of the reserves, with the best means of securing them permanently, and approved the proposals he put up in March 1927. Grigg rejected Lugard's suggestion of dividing the reserves from the rest of the Colony under a separate system of government, preferring to establish a Board of Trustees on which—that they might share in the trust—settlers could be included.[4] His Bill received settler support, but opinion among missionaries was more reserved. While they welcomed the fixing of the reserves by law, they felt considerable doubt about the provisions for leasing of land there. Moreover, the missionaries were particularly anxious about the proposed advisory boards, on which, they suggested, Africans should sit; alternatively, the Local Native Council should have to agree to any alteration to a reserve.[5] In the Legislative Council Canon Leakey, representing native interests, expressed his doubts, but said he would vote for the Bill if the Governor's proposed amendment was accepted: that land taken from a

[1] Leading article, 30 Dec. 1927. The Convention's memorandum was only published when the Hilton Young Report appeared (*E.A. Standard*, 2 Feb. 1929).
[2] Kavirondo Taxpayers' Welfare Association (ibid., 31 Dec. 1927); Kikuyu Association (ibid., 14 Jan. 1928), and Kikuyu Central Association (ibid., 4 Feb. 1928). See also Chapter VII below.
[3] Ormsby-Gore *Report*, Cmd. 2387 (1925), pp. 28–31.
[4] *Papers relating to the Closer Union of Kenya, Uganda and Tanganyika Territory*, Col. 57 (1931), pp. 1–2.
[5] Evidence to Hilton Young Commission, i. 499–509 (mimeograph in Colonial Office library).

reserve would be replaced. The following week Grigg told the Council that although every clause of the Bill had the Secretary of State's 'prior approval', it was to be reviewed at home, on the representation of the Hilton Young Commission. Conway Harvey, European leader while Delamere was ill with heart trouble, dubbed this 'insulting to the people of Kenya and grossly unfair to the natives'; he believed that the commissioners had only acted through 'the intrigues of certain busybodies'.[1] The Bill was still suspended when Amery and the Conservative Government fell in June 1929.

The failure of Closer Union

The publication in January of the Hilton Young Report raised other problems, particularly in respect of the political future of Kenya. Not only did it reiterate the 1923 declaration on 'paramountcy' but it answered the settlers with a new word, one that later was to become an object of policy in Britain's multi-racial territories: 'What the immigrant communities may justly claim is partnership, not control.' There could be an unofficial majority in the Legislative Council only if the interests of the native races were 'adequately represented' and Imperial control was maintained until the natives could take a share in government 'equivalent to that of the immigrant communities' —and this was not in the foreseeable future. Meanwhile Imperial control should be made more effective by the appointment of a High Commissioner for East Africa, who would be responsible for matters of common concern, and particularly for native policy. Thus the settlers' dream of responsible government was brushed aside, and, still more disturbingly, the commissioners re-opened the whole question of the franchise by going back to the Wood–Winterton proposal of a civilization test. They referred to the Donoughmore Commission's attack on communal electorates in Ceylon as accentuating differences and preventing the growth of a healthy political life. In stressing the need for co-operation between the communities of Kenya, all except the chairman went on to urge as an ideal 'a common roll on an equal franchise with no discrimination between the races'.[2]

[1] Leg. Co. *Debates*, 14 June 1928, pp. 321–4, and 20 June, pp. 375–6.
[2] *Report of the Commission on Closer Union of the Dependencies in Eastern and Central Africa* (Hilton Young Report), Cmd. 3234 (1929), pp. 39–41, 239, 144 sqq., 208–11, 244 sqq.

The report shocked the settlers. In a cabled protest to Amery they took their stand on Churchill's declaration of 1922 and affirmed that the communal franchise was an essential part of the settlement of 1923. Faced with the denial of responsible government, they threatened 'more vigorous action . . . to assert their point of view and ambitions'; the theory of waiting 'till the backward races (whom the Report itself describes as twenty centuries behind the Europeans) have reached their standard is an impossible proposition which no virile and governing race could be expected to acquiesce in'. Amery, despite the imminence of a general election, attempted to salvage something of his federation plans: he sent out his Permanent Under-Secretary, Sir Samuel Wilson, to discuss and report on reactions in East Africa. Wilson arrived in April to find an 'atmosphere of suspicion and mistrust' among the Europeans, who even professed a belief that his visit was 'the last move . . . before putting a final stop to white settlement', whilst the Indians, not unnaturally, demanded a common roll before other discussions. Only the commercial community would still consider closer union,[1] which they desired for economic co-ordination, not political reasons. Significantly, Mombasa Europeans, in a public meeting, denounced the terms of the cable to Amery. One leading businessman there asked how, with only 12,000 Europeans of whom some 3,000 were officials, they could expect to run the Government.[2]

Nevertheless, Wilson, after his discussions, considered that 'the great majority of people'[3] in East Africa were agreed as to the desirability of putting the essential economic services under a Central Authority. Since he accepted that the *sine qua non* for this was an unofficial majority on the Kenya Legislative Council, the main part of his work necessarily turned on the Colony. He emphasized to the Indians—a point they had chosen to ignore —that the Hilton Young majority had made the common roll dependent on general agreement locally. Shocked thus on their foundation, many retired into non-co-operation. However, some more moderate Indians at Mombasa led Wilson to conclude

[1] *Report of Sir Samuel Wilson on his Visit to East Africa*, Cmd. 3378 (1929), pp. 31–32, 5, 7–8.
[2] *E.A. Standard*, 23 Mar. 1929.
[3] A curiously significant use of a Kenya European phrase, since Wilson made no reference to African opinion.

that the community might, under certain provisos, accept nomination to the Council. Subsequent events showed that he had played down the influence of the non-co-operators. On the other hand, he gave full weight to the representations of the Europeans, going so far as to include among his three possible schemes one which conceded their demand for a minimum of fifteen elected Europeans, and he accepted their view—not that of the Indians—of the Indian position on the Council.[1] Before he reported, in July, Labour was in power, with Passfield as Colonial Secretary. He at first intended to implement Wilson's Report, and on the basis of such an assurance, Grigg, who was in England, returned to Kenya as Governor.[2] Then, such pressure, organized largely by Oldham working closely with Lord Lugard,[3] was put on the Government that it drew back. The matter remained before a Cabinet committee 'for months'.[4]

The Colonial Office, under its new masters, began to reassert itself on affairs in Kenya in a way that had not been seen since Churchill removed Northey. Demands for such action grew among Labour members of parliament, who had been questioning Amery's policy. They had particularly attacked an ordinance providing for a Defence Force with compulsory service for Europeans, Lord Olivier denouncing it as the burgher force the Europeans had long wanted.[5] Though these protests had not prevented its establishment, Passfield was now able to cut the extra £9,000 which the European elected members inserted in the 1930 budget to pay for it. At the same time he cut £20,000 from the provision for roads and stopped the Europeans' obstruction of educational and medical development. In Kenya a leading European, Lord Francis Scott, told his constituents that Passfield was employing 'a legal right of which no Colonial Secretary had availed himself for many years' in respect of the budget.[6]

The Europeans were already angered by Passfield's amendments to the Native Lands Trust Bill, announced in the

---

[1] Cmd. 3378, pp. 13, 23, 25–28 and unpublished material in the Altrincham Papers.

[2] Grigg to Passfield, 19 Nov. 1930, Altrincham Papers.

[3] M. Perham, *Lugard*, vol. ii. *The Years of Authority* (London, 1960), pp. 686–7, and the Oldham Papers.

[4] Passfield to Grigg, 1 May 1930, Altrincham Papers.

[5] *Hansard*, 5th ser., H. of L. 69. 572, 7 Dec. 1927.

[6] *E.A. Standard*, 7 June 1930.

Commons in November 1929.[1] Of these, the settlers' leaders objected particularly to that for the addition to a reserve of land 'equal in extent, and, as far as possible, equal in value' to any being taken for public purposes. They maintained that this was 'quite impractical as in many cases no such land would be available', that the State should have full power to acquire native land equally with that of others, and that compensation for individuals disturbed was sufficient. They declared that if the proposal were insisted on they would withdraw support from the Bill. Grigg told the Legislative Council in December that his Government had pointed out the difficulty of applying the principle, but that Passfield wanted it laid down, saying that if in the future an impossible case did arise, the Secretary of State would then consider a special ordinance making alternative provision. A stormy discussion ensued before Grigg announced that he would again refer the matter to London, since it was desirable that such a measure should be an agreed one. In April Grigg could only lay Passfield's explanatory reply, and appeal to the Europeans to support the Bill; a week later he was compelled to use the official majority to pass it with the amendments.[2]

Grigg considered that the delay on the Bill had encouraged the growth of African political agitation, especially among the Kikuyu.[3] At this time two issues particularly concerned them: land and female circumcision. This practice, common to many African peoples, was regarded by the Kikuyu as an essential element in their social customs. When, therefore, the Church of Scotland pressed their attack on it in 1929, the Kikuyu Central Association (the Young Kikuyu Association, renamed after the Harry Thuku troubles) picked up a popular issue in springing to its defence. Membership of the Association increased rapidly, and it held large meetings in the Kikuyu reserves, but, more important for the future, a new figure emerged: its General

---

[1] *Hansard*, 5th ser., H. of C. 231. 1034–5, 6 Nov. 1929.

[2] Leg. Co. *Debates*, 20 Dec. 1929, pp. 817–26, 2 Apr. 1930, p. 13, and 10 Apr., pp. 159–81. This question indicates well the difficulty of control from a distance, since Churchill, in a dispatch to the Governor dated 25 Aug. 1921, had laid down that 'in the event of permanent alienation an equivalent area of equal value must be added to the Reserve, if practicable in the same vicinity', and he made similar provision with respect to temporary alienation (Colonial Office to Dr. Arthur, 8 Aug. 1923, in the Arthur Papers, Church of Scotland Office, Edinburgh).

[3] Leg. Co. *Debates*, 16 Oct. 1929, p. 375.

Secretary, Johnstone (later Jomo) Kenyatta, who was also producing Kenya's first independent vernacular newspaper.[1] Its
enigmatic articles and parables,[2] and the anti-Government
songs, caused considerable concern to the Administration.
Grigg strengthened the Native Authority Ordinance to prevent
the collection of money without permits,[3] and the K.C.A.'s
President, Joseph Kangethe, was sentenced to two years' imprisonment and a fine of 150 sh. for taking part in a meeting
prohibited by a headman.[4] Passfield, troubled by these actions,
told Grigg that he could not possibly agree to anything which
could be interpreted as repression, preferring that any seditious
movement should come out into the open and there be dealt
with. He warned Grigg that he could not always cover a divergence of views if action were thus taken without consultation.[5]
Instructions were then issued that licences for monetary collections were to be given as a matter of course to all reputable
bodies, but clearly the Kenya Government did not publicize
this.[6]

The Labour Government tried to grapple with the difficult
problem of maintaining control at a distance by laying down
policy. In June 1930 it coupled with its White Paper of Conclusions of Closer Union another, a Memorandum on Native
Policy in East Africa: 'the Black Papers', as the settlers soon
called them. Funereal they were to the settlers' aims, particularly that of self-government, for here was the Imperial
Government taking up the Hilton Young Report, but without
the unofficial majority. Closer Union was proposed, with a High
Commissioner to supervise the territories by powers of suspension
and initiation of legislation within them; he was also to administer and legislate, with a council, on technical subjects. The
sole change in the Kenya Council was to be an increase of the
representatives of African interests from one to two, but the aim
of a common roll was set forth more definitely, for the High

---

[1] Bennett, *Political Studies* (June 1957), p. 121.
[2] Evidence of G. V. Maxwell to the Joint Select Committee on Closer Union in
East Africa, H.C. 156 (1931), vol. ii, questions 4017–19.
[3] Grigg, *Speeches*, pp. 338–9.
[4] *Hansard*, 5th ser., H. of C. 240. 1255–6, 3 July 1930.
[5] Passfield to Grigg, 1 May 1930, Altrincham Papers.
[6] *Report of the Joint Select Committee on Closer Union in East Africa.* H.C. 156 (1931),
vol. ii. questions 4088–90. Cunliffe-Lister maintained the instructions (*Hansard*,
5th ser., H. of C., 260, 1094, 2 Dec. 1931).

Commissioner was to make an inquiry into action towards this in the immediate future. Responsible government was recognized as the goal 'in Kenya as elsewhere', but defined as by 'a Ministry representing an electorate in which every section of the population finds an effective and adequate voice', something not soon possible, since 'less than one per cent. of the population' was then enfranchised.[1] The Memorandum insisted that in the meantime the trusteeship must rest with His Majesty's Government 'alone'; theirs must be 'the ultimate decision and final control', even if it were later decided that the Kenya official majority should be abandoned. The political development of the Africans should take place through the Local Native Councils until they could share in the government of the territory.[2]

Such bluntness could only provoke a storm in Kenya. Already the affairs of East Africa—which meant really those of Kenya—were so involved in controversy that the suggestion had been made that they should be referred to a Joint Select Committee of the two Houses of Parliament.[3] Passfield accepted this idea in the foreword to the Conclusions, but in that to the Memorandum ordered the immediate application of that paper.

This only added fuel to the flames. Settlers detected an air of self-righteousness and patronage in the wording of the papers; every phrase was scrutinized. Delamere, in an angry cable to the Colonial Secretary, rejected the designation 'immigrant community' as applied to the Europeans, although no objection had been raised to the phrase in the 1927 White Paper.[4] He could not accept the implication of Indian equality in the government of East Africa, for 'East African colonists stand on principle that the white race is the only people which has proved its capacity to govern mixed races'. Against the reassertion of paramountcy he set 'the closer association in trusteeship' of 1927. He also cabled to the South African and Southern Rhodesian governments for support and led a mission to London. They

---

[1] *Statement of the Conclusions of H.M.G. . . . on Closer Union in East Africa*, Cmd. 3574 (1930), pp. 4–8.

[2] *Memorandum on Native Policy in East Africa*, Cmd. 3573 (1930), pp. 4–6.

[3] Lugard in Lords debate on the Hilton Young Report (*Hansard*, 5th ser., H. of L. 73. 461, 3 Mar. 1929), see also letter to the *The Times*, 25 Feb. 1929.

[4] Cf. Passfield replying to Cranworth (*Hansard*, 5th ser., H. of L. 78. 309 and 293, 3 July 1930).

arrived in August before the Joint Select Committee had been
appointed, but were able immediately to see Hertzog and
Havenga, who were there for the Imperial Conference.[1]

In July the settlers' feelings received full expression in a
speech extraordinary for a governor. Grigg, addressing the
Legislative Council, referred to the increasing economic depression, and then said that the Imperial Government's proposals had 'added very considerably to the cloud of anxiety . . .
hanging over the Colony'. He talked of uncertainty for investment and settlement through the fluctuations of Imperial
policy, which he traced back through the 1920's to Eliot's
words and to the general pre-war situation, and he maintained
that there had been a complete change in 1923 through the
proclamation of 'paramountcy'. He welcomed the appointment
of a Joint Select Committee to settle the disputes.[2] Perhaps
Grigg felt free to speak frankly in this, his last address to the
Council before his final departure from Kenya in September.

Within a fortnight, to the settlers' consternation, a new
Governor, Sir Joseph Byrne, was appointed. The *Daily Herald*
was forthright in welcoming him as the 'strong man for a tough
job' needed in Kenya. He came from being Governor of Sierra
Leone, but what was remembered was that he had been a
policeman in the troubles in Ireland. He was a man to take
orders, to enforce policy. Unlike Grigg, he was neither an orator
nor a politician; he only wanted to do a job, he told the press on
arrival at Mombasa in February 1931.[3] Already, in London, he
had said that he had heard that there were reasonable men in
Kenya who disliked politics and publicity, and that he would
seek to work with them; to this the very proper reply was
returned that the elected members were the constitutionally
chosen representatives.[4]

The clash with them came within three days of Byrne's
opening his first Legislative Council in June. There Delamere
was prepared to congratulate him on the economies made in
these first months, but they had been achieved without reference
to the unofficial members. Indeed 'government by agreement'

---

[1] Huxley, *White Man's Country*, ii. 278–81.
[2] Leg. Co. *Debates*, 10 July 1930, pp. 432–446.
[3] *E.A. Standard*, 11 Oct. 1930 and 14 Feb. 1931.
[4] Ibid., leading article, 4 Feb. 1931.

had been abruptly ended. Delamere now moved to refer the financial position to the Select Committee on the Estimates, which had a large unofficial majority; he was voted down by the Government. In broken and incoherent sentences Delamere asked for an adjournment. Byrne at first insisted on continuing with the other business, but shortly relented.[1] The drama of this day and Delamere's death five months later needed only a Kenya story to complete it: that Delamere had died of a broken heart under Byrne's treatment.[2]

Certainly his death seemed to mark the end of a chapter in Kenya's history.[3] But something yet more important had happened elsewhere, in the findings of the Joint Select Committee, hurried to its conclusion by the economic crisis and the general election of 1931 in Britain. Before it officials and representatives of all the communities of Kenya gave evidence, and a new gloss on paramountcy was agreed between the settlers' leaders and Labour members—a thorny problem thus receiving 'decent burial'. At the same time European aspirations heard their doom. When questions elicited the fact that there were only 9,000 Europeans in Kenya qualified to vote, Lord Francis Scott, Delamere's successor as leader, conceded that they were not asking for self-government then, but only as an ultimate goal. As Closer Union was likely to be abandoned because of the depression, they would not ask for any change in the composition of the Kenya Council in the immediate future. The committee was thus able to report in one firm passage: 'an unofficial majority, whatever may be said to the contrary, does morally and in fact become responsible'.[4] Though nobody dared say so at the time, this sentence ended the first theme of Kenya's history: the direct possibility of an independent settler-governed state. Thereafter European leaders might still proclaim the same dazzling goal, but they had to concentrate on secondary objectives—financial control and ministerial office. The main battle had been lost; could power be achieved by sapping and mining?

The committee disposed of one specific controversy of the

---

[1] Leg. Co. *Debates*, 5 June 1931, pp. 53–73.

[2] Expressed by Captain Schwartze in Leg. Co., 12 Aug. 1933, p. 622; see also 'Naughticus' in *Kenya Weekly News*, 18 Aug. 1933.

[3] E. Huxley's conclusion, op. cit., ii. 323.

[4] *Report of J.S.C.C.U.*, H.C. 156 (1931), ii. 717 and 626–30 and i. 41.

1920's by remarking that it was 'impracticable' then to advocate a common roll. From this they turned to the future and African representation, saying that they had been much impressed by the ability of the African witnesses. A difficulty arose with those from Kenya in the need for an interpreter, a fatal bar then for membership of a Legislative Council. Besides, the committee doubted if there were any English-speaking natives who would command the confidence of their own people. In judging this they had been denied by the Government the opportunity of hearing Kenyatta and P. G. Mockerie, who sought to speak for the K.C.A., but the three Kenya African witnesses did include Chief Koinange of the Kikuyu Association and Ezekiel Apindi of the Kavirondo Taxpayers' Welfare Association.

In their examination much reference was made to the Local Native Councils, first formed in 1925.[1] Opinion on the committee was divided as to whether the future of African political development should be in them—with a tier structure through provincial councils to one at the centre, as Cameron was proposing in Tanganyika—or by direct representation on the Legislative Council. The African witnesses were clear in favour of the latter, Apindi asking for equal representation with the Europeans on grounds of African numbers and taxation, and all insisted that this representation should be by Africans. Apindi and Koinange showed no great enthusiasm for the Local Native Councils, which Koinange described as only just being developed; in its report the committee recommended that they should be 'actively fostered'. Seven members of the committee asked for the nomination of three natives to the Kenya Council, but the report went no further than to recommend increased representation of native interests, leaving the Governor to include suitable Africans when he found them available.[2] In fact, the first was not appointed until 1944.

The committee noted other African grievances for 'early and sympathetic consideration by the Kenya Government', starting with Thuku's old one of the *kipande* and the complaints of prohibition of coffee-growing. They found, like the Hilton Young

---

[1] For the establishment of Local Native Councils, see Chapter VII, pp. 350–1, below.

[2] *Report of J.S.C.C.U.*, H.C. 156, i. 42–43 and 73–74, and ii. 400–21.

Commission before them, that the evidence about the incidence of taxation between the various communities was so contradictory that they would not express an opinion on this lively political issue, recommending only an inquiry by an independent authority without delay. Similar treatment was suggested for the main source of native fears—land.[1]

Byrne, Scott, and Cavendish-Bentinck

Action on the report was taken by a new Secretary of State, Cunliffe-Lister. He saw his function as tidying up after the disputes of the 1920's. Closer Union was quietly dropped. Believing that policy statements and the ensuing controversies had been the bane of the past, he sought to make 'action, not talk' the motto of the Colonial Office. In Byrne he had the necessary agent, apt for orders although increasingly unpopular with the settlers, who continued to press their demands. Lord Francis Scott, their new leader, insisted that he would not employ unconstitutional methods and was told, in an open letter, that this completely reversed Delamere's policy.[2] Scott's strongest cards were his London connexions, for there, people in Kenya said openly, he had important ties of both blood and friendship: in 1936 the Permanent Under-Secretary at the Colonial Office was spoken of as his 'old personal friend' and mention was made of his seeing six Cabinet ministers, besides George V.[3] With this new leadership in the Colonial Office and Nairobi, the temper of politics changed—at least at the summit.

For the generality the old quarrels continued, the Indian community providing a good example. Their leaders had come to see the failure of non-co-operation. The more moderate Mombasa group had insisted on staying on the Municipal Board there, and they prevented a new campaign of non-payment of taxes in 1929. 'Abstention has cost us dearly', said the Congress President in opening the Nairobi session in January 1931, but the non-co-operators dominated the proceedings and the meeting broke up in confusion, fearing violence. The scenes recalled those in the parent body, the Indian National Congress, in its meeting at Surat in 1907. In the general election of May,

---

[1] *Report of J.S.C.C.U.*, H.C. 156, i. p. 44.   [2] *E.A. Standard*, 18 Mar. 1933.
[3] Ibid., 5 June and 4 Sept. 1936. Scott's niece, Lady Alice Montagu-Douglas-Scott, married the Duke of Gloucester in 1935.

candidates led by Isher Dass, and pledged not to enter the
Legislative Council, overwhelmed such opposition as appeared.
Four of the five elected were Hindus. This provided an additional reason for Muslim restiveness under the Congress policy.
In 1932 the Muslims withdrew from that body; and, though the
split was repaired, it foreshadowed the final break under the
impact of events in India in 1947.[1]

The weakened position of the Europeans was marked by the
Government's quiet stifling of the Board of Agriculture with its
settler chairman, and the prolonged denial of an Economic and
Finance Committee modelled on that of 1922, to deal with the
depression. This led Scott to comment that the Government
seemed to have taken to heart the Hilton Young Commission's
remarks about the influence of the settlers through committees.[2]
When at last, in February 1932, Byrne did announce the formation of a Standing Economic Committee, it had a parity of
officials and unofficials with only one elected member of the
Legislative Council, Scott. Although he called this a departure
from constitutional practice, he was prepared to be conciliatory,
and Byrne, in response, opened the Convention to mark the
need for co-operation in abnormal times.[3]

Present also on this occasion was Lord Moyne, the Commissioner requested by the Joint Select Committee to review
questions of racial taxation and expenditure. The deepening
gravity of Kenya's economic situation led to his terms of reference being widened to cover the general budgetary position of
the Colony. His report did not please the Europeans. Though
he accepted that there should be no administrative separation,
he did recommend the establishment of a Native Betterment
Fund with a statutory revenue, freed from supervision by the
Select Committee on the Estimates with its majority of European unofficial members. Yet more seriously, he accepted the
constant criticisms that the Africans were heavily burdened
with taxation, whilst the Europeans enjoyed 'the amenities of
civilization in return for a relatively light scale of contribution'.
The increased revenue which he saw as necessary ought, therefore, to come from the non-natives. After considering other

[1] Bennett, *Political Studies* (1957), p. 117.
[2] *E.A. Standard*, 12 Dec. 1931.
[3] Ibid., 6 Feb. and 5 and 12 Mar. 1932.

methods he concluded in favour of an income tax, and thereby re-opened an old issue.[1]

The attempt at conciliation between Scott and Byrne was thus drowned in a new flood of polemics. The Europeans contended that the introduction of an income tax should not precede the report of the Expenditure Advisory Committee appointed in May. This view, rejected by the Government,[2] found further expression in a manifesto and meetings, which culminated in a conference of Europeans from all parts of East Africa at Nairobi in September to protest at London's insistence on the tax. Cunliffe-Lister reacted strongly to their resolutions, saying, in a published dispatch, that after the threats of non-co-operation and obstruction, no Secretary of State could agree to consider their representations. He therefore demanded and obtained an immediate disclaimer from their delegation in London; then ten days of discussion took place in the Colonial Office.[3] However, the delegation, which included Grogan, the most extreme opponent of income tax, succeeded in leaving on Cunliffe-Lister a most unfortunate impression, which Scott had later to seek to eradicate. The fact remains that the support of the majority of the settlers was obtained against the tax, although the economic conditions were then such that only a few big men would have paid it. The dispute led to the Europeans concentrating on a demand for financial control.

Before this could happen a new crisis occurred over land. Gold was discovered at Kakamega, in a native reserve, and settlers, hit by the continuing economic difficulties, flocked there from their farms. For effective working it was considered necessary to remove the area on lease from the reserve, but in such a way as to entail an amendment to the Native Lands Trust Ordinance of 1930. Wade, the Chief Native Commissioner, was frank in introducing the Bill in December: they had got to hurt the natives' feelings and violate 'some of their cherished and possibly even sacred traditions', yet, despite the principal ordinance, there had been no reference to the Local Native Council, since this would be 'merely a farce'.[4] The Bill provoked

[1] *Report by the Financial Commissioner (Lord Moyne) on Certain Questions in Kenya*, Cmd. 4093 (1932), pp. 48, 38, 27, 58–60.

[2] Leg. Co. *Debates*, 28 July 1932, pp. 236–62.

[3] *E.A. Standard*, 1 Oct. and 26 Nov. 1932.

[4] Leg. Co. *Debates*, 20 Dec. 1932, pp. 511–12.

an explosion of opinion in the British press and debates in both Houses of Parliament. The original ordinance had been regarded as a final settlement, a pledge; Lang, the Archbishop of Canterbury, found it very difficult to understand how, after the declarations of 1930, the amendments had been rushed through which removed the two main provisions of the ordinance—consultation with the Local Native Council and the need to add an equal area for land taken. Allegations were made of breach of faith and action in an air of secrecy. Before all this Cunliffe-Lister stood firm, relying on practical necessities, but the incident shook confidence and was long remembered. In Kenya it increased African mistrust of the Land Commission appointed to make the survey requested by the Joint Select Committee, for, it was announced, the commissioners had agreed to the amendments.[1] Already this Morris Carter Commission had been criticized, since its members included two settlers, one of whom was a retired official. The Commission gave very full opportunity to the politicians, from Kenyatta in London to Europeans, Indians, and Africans in Kenya, and a vast mass of wide-ranging evidence was recorded. Although the commissioners digested this into a report by July 1933, publication was delayed until the following May.[2]

Until then financial questions remained the main topic of concern. The Moyne Report prejudiced opinion in England against the settlers over taxation. At least the Nairobi Chamber of Commerce saw that if they were to maintain an opposition to income tax on principle they would have to put forward alternatives, and the Government did agree to appoint a committee to consider these.[3] Meanwhile, a noisy agitation continued on two lines: the signing of a petition against income tax, and the renewal of the demand for financial control, Delamere's other 'safeguard' before federation. Two methods were considered: one, an adaptation of that most singular constitutional device then operating in Jamaica, by which any nine of the fourteen elected members had power to hold up a money Bill; the other, the establishment of a statutory Standing Finance

[1] *Hansard*, 5th ser., H. of L. 86, 560–3, 8 Feb. 1933; and H. of C. 274. 203–48, 372–6, 8–9 Feb. 1933.

[2] *Report of the Kenya Land Commission* (Morris Carter Report), Cmd. 4556 (1934) and Col. 91 (3 vols. of Evidence) (1934).

[3] *E.A. Standard*, 18 Mar. 1933.

Committee with a majority of European unofficial members. Though protests were made that they did not thereby wish to control the natives or native finance, Captain Guest, a member of parliament who called himself a Kenya settler, knew what this meant. He said in the Commons that he had told the Convention of Associations that asking for more effective financial control 'was tantamount to asking for self-government'—a comment that was subsequently accepted by the Europeans in the Legislative Council. In March 1933 Scott, who had spoken of visiting Britain for health reasons, agreed to fly there with the anti-income tax petition. He then started on lengthy discussions with the Colonial Office.[1]

Their first outcome was that Cunliffe-Lister, in a dispatch to Byrne in early June, announced that 'where the choice lies between alternative means of taxing particular sections of the community that method is to be preferred which is the more acceptable to those upon whom the tax is to be levied'; he was prepared to adopt as 'an experiment' Nairobi's alternative proposals: a graduated poll-tax and various indirect taxes. The settlers hailed this as 'the greatest constitutional victory in the history of the Colony' and Cunliffe-Lister was attacked in the Commons for surrendering to them:[2] a criticism that had some meaning, since the imposition of income tax had been taken as Imperial policy. Yet the victory was hollow: the principle announced was constitutionally unexceptionable[3]—although in immediate application it ignored the Indians' expressed approval of the income tax; but more significantly, three years later the Europeans had to accept this detested tax.

Scott's negotiations also led to agreement that a Standing Finance Committee should be established. Even here the victory was incomplete. Byrne delayed the committee's appointment until July 1934 by insisting that the groups on the Legislative Council should agree, or the idea would be dropped; and the committee was established by a procedural amendment—it was not statutory. It was to consist of three officials, three unofficial Europeans, one Indian, and one European, a nominated repre-

---

[1] G. Bennett, 'Early procedural developments in the Kenya Legislative Council —II', *Parliamentary Affairs*. x. 4 (Autumn, 1957), 471–2.

[2] Dilley, *British Policy in Kenya*, pp. 122–5.

[3] Cf. Ormsby-Gore to Byrne, 22 Oct. 1936, in *E.A. Standard*, 4 Dec. 1936.

sentative of African interests. The Europeans, who had not obtained their desired majority, could only hope that the representative of African interests would be sympathetic to them and that they would thus achieve parity, while a later enlargement of the committee might shift the balance towards them.[1]

Cunliffe-Lister had already shown, on a visit to Kenya in February 1934, that he could speak forcefully to the Europeans; he gave the impression that he had come to preach, not to learn. He told both groups, Europeans and Indians, that the constitutional question was closed, but the home truths on finance that he delivered to the Europeans were rendered no more palatable by being spiced with forceful ripostes to their remarks.[2] In May he acted with authority, publishing with the Morris Carter Commission Report the Government's decisions.[3] The settlers were left to protest that he had allowed no discussion in Kenya.

To obtain this they had to request a special session of the Legislative Council in October. In the lengthy debate a new leader emerged, Major (later Sir Ferdinand) Cavendish-Bentinck. As the Europeans' Secretary and Whip he managed to organize them effectively for the first time. They were particularly incensed at being denied the Leroghi plateau, which they claimed as repeatedly promised, and called for the establishment of a Board, similar to that for the Native Lands, to protect their Highlands. J. B. Pandya, the Indian leader, twitted 'the most advanced' and 'powerful race' with feeling this weakness. Nevertheless, the fact remains that the Europeans were now being forced on the defensive over land, as they had already been on constitutional questions. Indeed, the remarks of Archdeacon Burns, representing native interests, aroused their full ire. Yet Burns did not voice all the African grievances, though he had been put in touch with representatives of the Kikuyu associations by a committee of the Kenya Missionary Council, and Isher Dass was left to read into the record their joint memorandum.[4] In this major debate African views received only an indirect hearing, but the Europeans had to struggle on for five years before obtaining their 'protective' Board.

[1] Bennett, *Parliamentary Affairs* (1957), p. 472.
[2] *E.A. Standard*, 21 and 28 Apr. and 5 May 1934.
[3] *Kenya Land Commission Report: summary of conclusions reached by His Majesty's Government*, Cmd. 4580 (1934).
[4] Leg. Co. *Debates*, 16-25 Oct. 1934, pp. 492, 518-653, 663-708.

European fury mounted against the 'tyrannical dictator',[1] Cunliffe-Lister, and his agent Byrne, especially because of increased taxation in the new budget and the discovery that the Standing Finance Committee gave the Europeans no immediate greater control. The perennial complaints against Scott's moderation found a new and more potent spokesman in Cavendish-Bentinck. His impulsive walk-out from the Legislative Council in August 1935[2] was taken as a challenge by Scott. The quarrel was patched up, but Scott had to agree to become chairman of a Vigilance Committee set up by the Convention in September.[3] At the time many saw that this was a mistake: its title recalled that of the body which planned the rising in 1922, and now there were Africans, increasingly politically conscious, who might learn from any example of anarchy. Though the Vigilance Committee soon appeared 'moribund'[4] it was, in fact, maintained to the end of Byrne's governorship.[5]

Within a few days of the formation of the committee Byrne sent home a dispatch concerning the Kenya Defence Force. This became known in March 1936, with the publication of the Secretary of State's reply approving the disbandment of the force; it was to be replaced by a proper territorial organization, the Kenya Regiment. Although Scott thought that Byrne might have advocated suppression because of fears that the Vigilance Committee might use the K.D.F. to overawe the Government,[6] he was deeply hurt at the Governor's completely ignoring him over the force, in which he took a keen personal interest. With Cavendish-Bentinck, he resigned from the Executive Council, and in so doing expressed his long sense of grievance at the change from Grigg's days: this was only a 'last glaring instance', an affront to the whole European community,[7] who had been shut out from effective discussion of policy. There remained the appeal to Caesar.

This resort became increasingly attractive as Scott nursed his

[1] Phrase of Lord Erroll, *E.A. Standard*, 8 Dec. 1934.
[2] Leg. Co. *Debates*, 1 Aug., 1935, p. 544.
[3] *E.A. Standard*, 20 Sept. 1935.
[4] *East Africa*, leading article, 16 July 1936.
[5] Minutes of the (European) Elected Members' Organization, meetings of 4 Aug. 1936 and 1 Mar. 1937.
[6] Ibid., 7 Apr. 1936.
[7] J. H. Thomas to Byrne, 5 Feb. and Scott to Byrne, 8 Mar. (*E.A. Standard*, 6 and 13 Mar. 1936).

grievances. In early March he told a Nairobi meeting that he was leaving to discuss with the Secretary of State the whole economic and political situation, which had been rendered more acute by the Italian invasion of Ethiopia and the talk of returning Tanganyika to the Germans. He advocated a change in the constitution: the Executive Council to be reduced to an equality of official and unofficial members, three or four of each, with departments joined 'under a sort of Minister' who 'in due course' might be an unofficial member.[1] The appointment of unofficial ministers had first been proposed to the Hilton Young commissioners; they had seen the difficulties, but their chairman had been prepared to recommend the innovation, and the specific case of an unofficial Minister of Agriculture had already been fully discussed some years earlier.[2] Scott's essential aim, in reviving this idea and submitting it to the Secretary of State, was to shift the ground from the Legislative Council, where no change was possible, to the Executive, the policy-forming body. In London Scott's path was eased, for shortly after his arrival a new Secretary of State, the third within a year in the Baldwin Government, was appointed: Ormsby-Gore, an old acquaintance, whose attitude Scott found to be 'extremely cordial and sympathetic'.[3] Yet he returned to Kenya in July without any decisions having been made; little more could be done than to spread the impression of the effectiveness of his eminent contacts and to announce that it was hoped that Cavendish-Bentinck would carry the matter further in London.[4]

In early September Sir Alan Pim's report was published. The European leaders had requested this further outside examination of Kenya's financial position in the belief that, despite the committees on economy which they had forced on the Government, no sufficient action had been taken. Already, in Pim's appointment, their chagrin had been roused by the addition of taxation to his terms of reference; now they were faced with a fresh advocacy of income tax. In concluding with this recommendation Pim gave warning against a repetition of the events of 1921 and 1933, for there were natives, 'diligent students of

[1] Ibid., 8 May 1936.
[2] Cmd. 3234 (1929), pp. 199–201, and *Report of the Agricultural Commission* (Hall Commission), (1929), pp. 2–4.
[3] Interview in *East Africa*, 25 June 1936.
[4] *E.A. Standard*, 4 Sept. 1936.

the newspapers', who 'might apply to their own case lessons learned from such controversies'.[1] However, Grogan maintained his intransigence on the issue, commenting that they had asked for bread and got a 'Mill's bomb'.[2] Rumour quickly went round that Byrne, defeated on the issue in 1933, was determined to rush through the tax as the last thing he did.[3] Yet the explosion did not take place. Scott believed that the settlers were tiring of the constant political ferment and might not continue to support him over this issue. Moreover, private advices from London told him of the Imperial Government's determination to insist this time on the tax:[4] negotiation was essential. This took place in the secrecy of the Standing Finance Committee. A 'compromise' was worked out: the Europeans accepted a reduction of native taxation, as urged by Pim, and the imposition of a 'light Income Tax' on the Rhodesian model, in return for Ormsby-Gore's promise that the new Governor would inquire into the reconstitution of the Executive Council.[5] Scott was about to attain his desired objective: influence at the source of authority and action.

The appointment of the new Governor, Air Chief Marshal Sir Robert Brooke-Popham, had been made in November. Cavendish-Bentinck, still in London, had the opportunity to see him and inform him of the Kenya situation as the Europeans saw it. Brooke-Popham arrived in Nairobi in April 1937. Finding him sympathetic, Cavendish-Bentinck promptly agreed to rejoin the Executive Council.[6] In August its new composition was announced: Scott's suggestion of parity between official and unofficial members was accepted, but the form was a multi-racial one exactly paralleling that of the Standing Finance Committee. European hopes of the Indian member being removed were thus dashed, and there was no mention of ministerial office. What possibilities then lay in Brooke-Popham's announcements that he would use the Executive Council to

---

[1] Report ... on the Financial Position and System of Taxation of Kenya, Col. 116 (1936), p. 235.

[2] E.A. Standard, 9 Oct. 1936.

[3] Ibid., 2 Oct. 1936: Letter from G. Williams of the Convention of Associations.

[4] Minutes of the (European) E.M.O., 28 Oct. and 14 Dec. 1936, and 4 Jan. 1937.

[5] Report of the S.F.C. on the Draft Estimates for 1937, pt. ii (1936), p. 1.

[6] Kenya Official Gazette, 27 Apr. 1937, Govt. Notice 339, dated 21 Apr. 1937.

develop policy in a constructive sense?[1] In fact, he shortly provided a most striking demonstration, the complete reverse of Byrne's, of the flexibility of a constitution of the British type, which so much depends on the manner in which it is operated. As a result, Scott, in a general election speech early in 1938, could report on a great change in relations with the Government, and Cavendish-Bentinck went on to claim that the settlers took a considerable part in the government of the country, having a bigger 'say' than ever before.[2]

It remained to consolidate their position. Cavendish-Bentinck took the lead in promoting further European settlement and in pressing, through repeated debates in the Legislative Council, for action on the Morris Carter recommendation of an Order in Council to define the Highlands.[3] This was a matter of considerable embarrassment to an Imperial Government conscious of Indian nationalist feeling, since it appeared to mean the translation of an administrative discrimination into a legal enforcement of a colour bar. Yet Ormsby-Gore had said in the Commons, in July 1936, that no legal disabilities on grounds of race, colour, or creed would be included,[4] and this did not please the settler leaders. Indeed, after an official memorandum on the forthcoming Order in Council had reiterated this point, Scott told his constituents that the absence of the word 'European' in the definition of the Highlands was a 'defeat' for them. He took comfort from the promised supervisory Highlands Board, with its majority of settlers, since it would be 'very rare' for the Governor to overrule such a body.[5]

After the promulgation of the Order the deep Indian feelings at this entrenchment of the old administrative practice were expressed in measured terms in the Legislative Council by A. B. Patel, the Mombasa lawyer who was later to assume the leadership of the community. He roused Nicol, the European member for Mombasa, to repeat the Indian question whether it was fair that foreigners, and even ex-enemies, should have privileges denied to British subjects. Only Isher Dass voiced African opinion, reading into the record, in the face of European

---

[1] Leg. Co. *Debates*, 12 Aug. 1937, pp. 387–8, and 29 Oct., p. 13.
[2] *E.A. Standard*, 28 Jan. and 11 Mar. 1938.
[3] e.g. Leg. Co. *Debates*, 11–13 Aug. 1937 and 28–29 Apr. 1938.
[4] Hancock. *Survey of Commonwealth Affairs*, i. 234–5.
[5] *E.A. Standard*, 2 Sept. 1938.

protests, the petition of the K.C.A. and the K.T.W.A. to the Secretary of State against the Order.[1]

Such indirect representation by an Indian provided the only means for the African political associations to be heard. At this time they were weak through factionalism and tribal division, but the Government did not make their path any easier. It dismissed them as unrepresentative, since the mass of the population was 'not concerned with politics',[2] and considered it sufficient, when Archdeacon Burns left the Legislative Council in 1938, for African interests to be represented there by two retired officials. The appointment of the second, the former Chief Native Commissioner, gave rise to widespread criticism, the *East African Standard* even advocating his replacement by the outspoken missionary, Archdeacon Owen of Kavirondo, whom it criticized for fighting for the right things in the wrong places, namely outside Kenya,[3] as in writing to the *Manchester Guardian*. Certainly the Kenya Government did, in 1939, consider appointing Owen, and even an African, but in the end no change was made.[4]

A war-time 'Coalition Government'

The outbreak of the second world war produced a suspension of politics. Because of the war the Indians decided to halt their agitation against the Highlands Order in Council,[5] and on the eve of war with Italy in East Africa in 1940 the Government suppressed a number of African political organizations, including the K.C.A., and interned their leaders.[6] In the meanwhile, European political expression died away as the European leaders exerted considerable influence in the war-time Government. The Legislative Council fell into abeyance, action being taken by the Executive Council through such instruments as Defence Regulations, which could in any case be made without reference to the Secretary of State.[7]

[1] Leg. Co. *Debates*, 21 Apr. 1939, pp. 256–310.
[2] Bennett, *Political Studies* (1957), pp. 123–5.
[3] Leading articles, 8 Apr. 1938 and 27 Jan. 1939. The former C.N.C.'s appointment was also questioned in the Commons (*Hansard*, 5th ser. 335., 693–4, 3 May 1938) and by *East Africa and Rhodesia*, 12 May 1938.
[4] Unpublished material, Nairobi Secretariat.
[5] E.A.I.N.C.: Speech by A. B. Patel at Nairobi Conference, 26 Dec. 1942.
[6] Bennett, *Political Studies*, p. 126.
[7] *Hansard*, 5th ser., H. of C. 371. 836, 7 May 1941.

The Kenya practice of committees and boards—often criticized in the past for being so effective a source of European
influence—displayed a vigorous development. Some thirty-one
new and often powerful ones were formed in the first two years
of the war.[1] Thus the whole economic life of the country came
under executive control; in this those settlers who acted as
Controllers of various primary products played a leading part.
Most prominent was Cavendish-Bentinck, who also represented
Kenya in missions to London, Delhi, and Cairo. Unofficials had
become 'semi-official Members'[2] of the Government, but yet
remained in the curious and anomalous position of sometimes
attacking and sometimes defending the Government in the
Legislative Council.[3] Nevertheless, Lord Francis Scott considered the experience sufficient, by August 1943, to show that
unofficial ministers would be possible after the war.[4]

If the Europeans had during the war 'increased their influence in government to a very considerable degree',[5] yet that
government remained one under supervision from London.
There Kenya's labour legislation, repeatedly questioned in
parliament, aroused further comment: Labour members, led by
Creech Jones, the future Colonial Secretary, paid particular
attention to a Defence Regulation of 1942 whereby compulsory
labour on European farms was allowed as an 'Essential Undertaking' for the war effort.[6] Repeated questions ensured that the
system was controlled, and even suspended for a period in 1943.[7]
At that time also a Trade Union Bill was passed to make Kenya
legislation conform to that of Britain, something which, said E. H.
Wright, the then European leader, was accepted only through
force majeure.[8]

Already the highly independent and critical settlers had
shown that they were not prepared to remain silent, despite the
growth of their leaders' influence. The reassembly of the Legislative Council was obtained, and in April 1941 Mrs. Olga

[1] List dated 16 Sept. 1941, in Nairobi Secretariat.
[2] *E.A. Standard*, leading article, 15 Mar. 1940.
[3] e.g. Cavendish-Bentinck attacking the raising of the petrol tax, 19 Aug. 1942,
pp. 213–14, but defending over Maize Control, 21 Aug., pp. 348–66.
[4] Speech at Nakuru, *E.A. Standard*, 6 Aug. 1943.
[5] *Hansard*, 5th ser., H. of C. 395. 1908, comment of Creech Jones, 17 Dec. 1943.
[6] Ibid. 378. 2199–227, 26 Mar. 1942.
[7] Ibid. 390, 2074, 7 July 1943.
[8] Letter in *Kenya Weekly News*, 28 July 1944.

Watkins won a by-election which the *East African Standard* interpreted as a revolt against 'complacency and apathy in high
places', the European leaders being 'a group of "yes-men" to
Government'.[1] Nearly a year later Mrs. Watkins was instru-
mental in the formation of the Total Defence Union, to stimulate the Colony's war effort. The Government responded by
setting up a Civil Defence and Supply Council, though not the
suggested War Council.[2] Although this reminiscent title did
not reappear, Cavendish-Bentinck's appointment to the new
council may be taken as again portending the ministerial
development to which Scott was looking. Yet European agitation still mounted. In 1943 there was a demand for a general
election; and new local political associations were formed which
joined in February 1944 to become the Electors' Union to
replace the defunct Convention of Associations.[3]

Much of this agitation was anti-Indian in intention. War
conditions gave the opportunity to deal with the old enemy:
immigration could at long last be controlled through Defence
Regulations. Although the wording did not imply racial discrimination, Indians, in both Nairobi and Delhi, where the
matter was taken up, knew very well that the Admission of
Male Persons Regulations, 1944, were aimed at the Asian community.[4]

The Europeans were again using a war in the attempt to
consolidate their position. This was so also over the Highlands,
on which two Bills were introduced in April 1944, one even
legislating to control inter-racial transfers of shares in companies with land in the area. Yet was it possible to construct
effective dikes against the future? A strangely significant portent
was the intervention on the Land Control Bill by the new and
vigorous representative of African interests, Archdeacon (later
Archbishop) Beecher. He was bold enough to demand African
representation on the Select Committee appointed to discuss the
Bill in order to reciprocate European interest in the African
lands. Cavendish-Bentinck, who had throughout taken the lead
in building the defences of the Highlands, replied forcibly. The

[1] Leading article, *E.A. Standard*, 10 Apr. 1941.
[2] *E.A. Standard*, 13 and 27 Mar. 1942.
[3] Bennett, *Political Studies*, (1957), p. 115.
[4] Leg. Co. *Debates*, 18–19 Apr. 1944, pp. 142–67 and 170–80, and Indian Council
of State, *Debates*, 6 Apr. 1944, pp. 654–68.

language used foreshadowed the future clash over this, the central keep of the Europeans.[1]

There were some who saw that the European position in Kenya could not be maintained fully and indefinitely. In August, Commander F. J. Couldrey, editor of the *Kenya Weekly News*, was the first leading European to say openly, in a B.B.C. broadcast directed to East Africa, that they could not achieve self-government by Europeans alone; it could only be 'on the basis of all races co-operating'.[2] These words raised a storm amongst Europeans in Kenya, and may have cost Couldrey the position of Deputy Leader of the European group on the Legislative Council.[3]

Couldrey saw that it was necessary to bring Africans on to the political stage: he and some others, notably S. V. Cooke, the independent-minded member for the Coast, were urging their appointment to the Legislative Council.[4] When the new Council was formed in October it included the first such nominee. This was E. W. Mathu, the son of a Kikuyu medicine-man and a product of Balliol College, Oxford. His career thus typified—a point sharpened by his polished speeches—the rapidity of change in this part of Africa. This had come about in politics pre-eminently through the example and stimulus given by the settlers. It was, therefore, fitting that Kenya should have the first African member of a Legislative Council in East Africa.

Couldrey had said that he supported such appointments, since the interests of Europeans and Africans were 'absolutely interwoven',[5] but this was an old European argument in making points against the Indians. Now this 'eternal triangle' of Kenya politics took on a new form. Mathu's appointment and the support he had from the political organization he helped to create in 1944 (the Kenya African Union, briefly known as the Kenya African Study Union), marked the emergence of the African on to the full stage of Kenya's politics. He would there be courted by Asians and Europeans alike. Whose was the power of the future? The appointment of Cavendish-Bentinck, in the Government re-organization of August 1945, as a

---

[1] Leg. Co. *Debates*, 12–14 Apr. 1944, pp. 6–48, 51–85, and 88–108.
[2] *East Africa and Rhodesia*, 17 Aug. 1944.
[3] Ibid., obituary of Couldrey, 2 May 1946.
[4] e.g. *E.A. Standard*, 15 Sept. 1944, article by S. V. Cooke.
[5] *East Africa and Rhodesia*, 6 July 1944.

quasi-minister, under the title of Member for Agriculture, caused Africans and Asians to join together in common opposition to what appeared like another European advance.[1] But some looked forward: Couldrey, even as he advocated Africans being on the Legislative Council, realized that it was likely that in the future the Europeans would be 'the strongest opponents of self-government'.[2]

By the end of the war it was clear to the perceptive that the European attempt to build a 'white man's country' in Kenya must fail. Ministerial office was no substitute for self-government. Yet optimists could still talk of the other races accepting European leadership in a transfer of power from Westminster. The idea itself was typical of the aristocratic mentality of the Kenya settler community. The Kenya Europeans had failed, until it was too late, to act upon the warnings of Harcourt and Grigg of the need to build up their numbers. Perhaps, in any case, the attempt would have been doomed to failure: the Kenya Highlands could hardly have supported a large white population, and the original idea of developing a new South Africa was from the beginning an unrealizable dream. In 1945 the settlers formed only a minute European island in tropical Africa, an island that was shortly to be overwhelmed in the tide of African nationalism rising in the revolution of the end of colonial rule.

[1] Leg. Co. *Debates*, 18–25 July 1945.
[2] *Kenya Weekly News*, 22 Sept. 1944.

VII

KENYA: ADMINISTRATION AND CHANGES IN AFRICAN LIFE
1912–45

JOHN MIDDLETON

The indigenous peoples and early administration

THE period 1912–45 was one of far-reaching and radical changes in the pattern of life of the African inhabitants of Kenya. In 1912 it was a country of many small tribes, each living in the centre of its own small world, hardly aware of the world outside its own cultural and linguistic or dialectal boundaries. By 1945 it had become a country wherein at least the articulate of its African members were aware of their common identity and interests, even if not of their community of interests as Kenyans with other ethnic groups, Europeans, Asians, and Arabs. Whereas in 1912 Kenya consisted of many small social systems each largely independent of the others, by the end of the period it had become a single economic and political system. The scale of social relations of the traditional units of Kenya society increased in the economic, political, and religious fields. And as it increased so did the values held by its members change. Whatever the cultural differences between tribes and between African, European, Asian, and Arab at the beginning of the period, by the end of it Kenya had become a single society, even though deeply divided within itself.

Change had always occurred in Kenya before the coming of the Europeans. Whether the pre-European age was golden or one of unredeemed barbarity is irrelevant—and neither is true. There had always been change, but it had been slow. By 1912, when the administration of the African areas was made more systematic, rapid change had hardly begun. It was to mark the coming decades.

In this period a tribal organization was transformed into one

N

based upon a community wider than the tribe. Traditional tribal consciousness was slight, and in Kenya the tribe, except for the small state of Wanga in Kavirondo, was never a single political unit acting as a single polity. In parts of Uganda and Tanganyika the tribe was such a polity, and this difference between these territories and Kenya was to have a marked significance in their later reactions to economic and political developments. In Kenya the effective political unit was smaller, a segment of a tribe. Although the traditional societies varied among themselves in detail, in all of them the basic social group consisted of kin. A man lived among his kin, his first loyalty was to his kin, he helped them and they helped him. Outside Wanga and the coast there were no indigenous kings, no systems of tribute which maintained aristocracies, no great differences in standards of living or differences of caste, class, or rank. Wealth lay in influence, in prestige, measured by the number of kin and friends a man had. Men of high genealogical seniority held authority over their juniors, and some men acquired high position by being divinely favoured to prophesy. But their influence was only temporary. In many tribes, especially the pastoralists and those living near them, seniority in age and experience was all-important and gave authority. But this did not give rise to hereditary classes and authority.

At the beginning of the period there were five main clusters of tribes in Kenya, each of which was sufficiently uniform in its composition to be taken as the basis for a distinct provincial administration.

These clusters each consisted of several tribes, distinct, but usually related culturally or linguistically or both. In Nyanza there were two main groups—the Nilotic-speaking Luo and the several small Bantu-speaking Luhya or 'Bantu Kavirondo', with the Bantu Gusii in the south of the area. All these tribes had a similar economy, based upon grain-growing and cattle rearing, and a similar political organization: small communities were each formed round the core of an agnatic lineage of three or four generations. There was one exception, the Wanga in North Kavirondo, among whom there had developed a chiefship which played an important part in the political history of this area. In the centre of Kenya was the Kikuyu–Kamba cluster of agricultural Bantu-speaking tribes—Kikuyu, Kamba, and the Meru and Embu groups in the north. In all of these, villages based upon small lineages were the foundation of social organization, but age-sets were found (probably copied from the neighbouring Masai), and there are records of several important Kikuyu and Kamba war-leaders who wielded considerable although transitory influence. Between these two tribal groupings was a belt of Nilo-Hamitic-speaking tribes, most of them scorning agriculture and preferring the keeping of cattle on the steppes of the Rift Valley region. These included the Masai, the Nandi, Kipsigis, and Pokot, and the smaller peoples of the Eldama Ravine area, the Marakwet and Keyo. They were mainly transhumant, needing a large area of grazing through which they moved slowly season after season: they were controlled by the authority of prophets and had age-set systems which provided highly efficient military organizations. Near the coast were the smaller Bantu-speaking tribes of Teita and Taveta, and, on the Swahili coast proper, the Giryama, Digo, and Duruma, and to the north the Pokomo of the inhospitable Tana river. Finally, there were the various transhumant and almost nomadic pastoralists of the Northern Frontier Province, the Nilo-Hamitic Turkana and Samburu, and the Hamitic Boran (Galla) and Somali, who had no ambitions but to be left alone to capture and graze cattle and camels.[1]

Despite the differences in the cultures and organizations of the various tribes and tribal clusters, which were always apparent to administrative officers, it is clear that from the viewpoint of general long-term government policy these differences were minimized except where they were so great as to make the application of a common policy impossible.

Despite divergent views as to the ends to be pursued in administration, in the early years of Kenya Colony, at any rate, the general view of the Government was that traditional tribal culture was not in itself desirable, that indeed on balance it was often highly undesirable, and that its preservation would make the efficient development of Kenya society difficult. The

[1] It is unnecessary to give a long list of books dealing with the indigenous economic and political systems of Kenya. The best summaries are J. E. Goldthorpe, *Outlines of East African Society* (Kampala, 1958) and L. P. Mair, *Primitive Government* (London, 1962).

'native' was noble and admirable in his own state, provided he lived far enough away from the European areas to be of little or no value as a potential labourer or a potential buyer of local or imported produce, or of little or no danger as a potential rival as producer of goods of value in the export market. Yet labour was required, and to make him into a labourer taxation was introduced, with the intention also of 'educating' him in 'citizenship'. With the introduction of taxation he had to earn money either by selling his labour or by growing cash crops. Owing to the need of European farmers for labour and for freedom from competition, the former came to be the accepted way in which Africans could acquire cash.

In spite of frequent contradictions and changes of policy, the prevailing aim of the Government seems to have been to fashion a country in which white settlers played a main economic and political role, with Indians in a subordinate economic capacity and with Africans playing subordinate roles in their own tribal areas. It was inevitable that the greater economic and political capital and skills of the Europeans should for a long period give them a great advantage. And likewise the resources—especially in the form of labour and education—of some of the African tribal clusters (notably the larger ones of Kavirondo and Kikuyu) were to give them a leading position in tribal economic and political life. As they took over this leading position, however, they were to find that tribal organization was inadequate to changing needs, and they began to form new organizations modelled largely upon those possessed by Europeans.

The main factors in differentiating governmental political and economic policy between one area and another were the possibility of alienation of land to non-Africans and the supply of labour to non-African enterprises. No one ever wanted either the land or the labour of the peoples of the Northern Frontier region (although their cattle played a part in the Kenya meat industry), and on the whole they were left alone to develop slowly at their own pace. Indeed, their administration was a mainly military one, kept apart from that of the rest of the country. The other groups were affected by land policies in different ways, all being subject to some degree of alienation and restriction of the land available for growing populations.

Those tribal clusters which could supply labour were mainly the Kikuyu, the Luhya, the Luo, the Taita, the Giryama, and later the Nandi and the Kipsigis. These tribes, which responded to calls for labour migration and for the growing of cash crops, mainly as a consequence of land shortage, taxation, good communications, and the influence of missions, became closely integrated into the total Kenya economy, an economy largely controlled by interests concerned with the development of European farming as the best basis for the future of Kenya. These were the tribes most seriously affected by the depression of the 1930's, by the discovery of gold, and by regulations as to the types of export crops permitted or not permitted to be grown by African farmers.[1] They were the tribes which made 'progress', but which also suffered so perennially from the 'indiscipline' which featured so largely in reports of the Native administration. It was they who provided the spectacular and threatening development of political and religious associations which came to occupy so much of the time and thought of the Government.

Population, land, and labour

The African population of Kenya has increased markedly during this century. Population figures before the 1948 census are unreliable, generally being estimates based on the numbers of adult male taxpayers. Figures quoted by Goldthorpe[2] show an increase from perhaps $2\frac{1}{2}$-3 million about 1912 to $5\frac{1}{4}$ million in 1948. A steep increase in the population during the 1930's and 1940's seems to have taken place as part of a regular cycle of population increase and decrease under conditions typical of underdeveloped, non-industrial, rural subsistence societies subject to periodic famines, epidemics, and wars. The end of the last century and the beginning of this were marked by several famines and epidemics, and there was considerable mortality during and immediately after the first world war. The most reliable estimate for the rate of natural increase of the African population of all East Africa between 1931 and 1948 is between 1 per cent. and 1·75 per cent. In 1948 the census showed a very

[1] See Chapter V above.
[2] See appendix vii to the *Report of the East African Royal Commission, 1953-1955* (Dow Commission), Cmd. 9475 (1955), pp. 464-7.

high ratio of children—over 40 per cent. of the rural population; the adult population had to support this heavy proportion of dependants. Since from some areas a great part of the male population were always absent as labour migrants, the proportion of dependants in these was even higher.

Most of Kenya is not a fertile country. The annual reports of the Kenya Government from 1912 until 1945 mention the frequent occurrence of drought and famine, and occasional plagues of locusts, in all but the highland areas of Kikuyu, Nyanza, and the White Highlands. In most other parts of Kenya the chances of 30 inches of rain per annum are not more than thirty in a hundred years.[1] Thus the poorer areas were unable to produce a surplus of crops for export and tended to become little more than areas of economic stagnation, and there were periodic movements of people from famine and drought regions to more favourable areas. Agricultural tribes experienced both overcrowding and some restriction upon growing cash crops, especially coffee,[2] and these led to much anti-European resentment. Lest stock disease spread to the European areas, efforts were made to control native stock movement, so that the marketing of much African stock was difficult and often impossible.

The principal economic factors which affected tribal life included land shortage and deterioration, the introduction of money and the possibility—and necessity—of earning money by wage labour, and variations in the prices received by native growers of marketable crops. Some of these have been discussed in previous chapters, but something should be said here about land shortage, which was of far-reaching importance among the Kikuyu and the tribes of Nyanza. Changes in land use and tenure, with an increase throughout the period in the importance of cash farming, provided the basic framework for other changes in African life in Kenya. Among the African population fear over land was at the bottom of most of the insecurity and sense of injustice which played so great a part in the African response to European impact. Their traditional

[1] See maps 2 and 3 at the end of the Dow Commission *Report*.
[2] Coffee-growing was restricted between 1934 and 1937; at other times local administrative restrictions were imposed, mainly in Kikuyu. See also Chapter V pp. 245–6, above.

economies, whether agricultural or pastoral, had as their foundation the enjoyment of joint rights over land, rights held by the main social units of indigenous African society, small villages, clan-groups, and so on. Changes in land policy and land conditions had immediate and deeply felt reactions on all aspects of African life.

The Kikuyu of the Central Province provided most problems for the administration. For the Kikuyu land seems traditionally to have had a deeper significance than for most other East African peoples. Their land system is usually known as the 'githaka' system. A githaka is a plot of land owned jointly by the members of a small localized lineage, the mbari, the basic unit of Kikuyu society. The Kikuyu moved through their formerly wooded country from north to south, arriving in what is now Kiambu only towards the end of the last century. As they moved southwards they cleared the forest, cultivating for a few years until the soil fertility was depleted, then moving south to more forest. Local groups, of different clan affiliations, became remarkably interspersed, each with its own githaka which gave its members a sense of unity. They were not merely a group of kin but a corporate land-owning unit. Without a githaka their sense of unity was lost and they became merely an aggregate of landless and resentful people. It seems to have been mainly the younger Kikuyu without ithaka, and those who feared the loss of theirs, who took such a prominent part in later political developments in Kikuyu.[1]

During this period the land situation in southern Kikuyu came to be a source of immense dissatisfaction. There was increasing pressure on land. There was also some alienation of land suitable for coffee-growing. At the time the Europeans entered the country the Kikuyu had suffered a series of epidemics and it was thought that much of it was empty, although it is certain that in fact rights in it were held by Kikuyu lineages. There was also a small amount of forcible acquisition.[2]

The question of the alienation of Kikuyu land, which came to have such an important role in Kikuyu political aims, is

[1] There is a good deal of published information on the Kikuyu land system, of variable quality. It is summarized in J. Middleton, *The Kikuyu and Kamba of Kenya* (London, 1953).

[2] See Kenya Land Commission (Carter Commission), *Evidence*, Col. no. 91 (1934), vol. i.

dealt with in the Report of the Kenya Land Commission (the Carter Commission) of 1932. Out of a total of almost 1,800 square miles the actual amount of alienated land was only 109·5 square miles. The alienated land was, however, fertile, and became valuable as coffee-growing land, and its value was also enhanced by its proximity to Nairobi.[1] To say, as became general Kikuyu opinion, that the alienation of land led to overcrowding, erosion, and the virtual destruction of the Kikuyu way of life was manifestly a convenient political myth. A more valid point was that the drawing of a boundary round the land occupied by the Kikuyu at the turn of the century, and calling it a reserve, meant that there was no room to expand into the many almost unused areas to the west and south. The Government replied that this land had traditionally been empty, forest, or Masai land, and the argument raged unsettled until the Mau Mau troubles after the second world war. However, suggestions that to add extra areas at the edge of the reserves would compensate for the loss of *githaka* land showed a lack of understanding of the meaning of land for the Kikuyu. In his evidence to the Kenya Land Commission, the Commissioner of Lands stated:

In the early days of European immigration at any rate the theory appears to have been followed that, provided adequate arrangements were made for any natives who happened to be on the land, and compensation was paid for disturbance and any loss of crops, Government was fully entitled to regard the land concerned as available for alienation.[2]

The Chief Native Commissioner commented on this that

the whole fallacy of such a theory appears to be contained in the word 'adequate'. There can be no adequate arrangement for a man evicted from the only spot on earth where he has the right to live.[3]

The density of population in Kikuyu rose considerably during the period. The resident population in the reserves rose from 452,000 at a density of 254 per square mile in 1902, to 489,000 at a density of 283 per square mile in 1931.[4] By 1948 they had a total resident population of 745,000; Kiambu

---

[1] See *Report of the Kenya Land Commission*, Cmd. 4556 (1934), ch. vi, with map.
[2] Carter Commission, *Evidence*, i. 28.   [3] Ibid., p. 43.
[4] Carter Commission *Report*, p. 26, para. 67. The figure of 283 for 1931 refers to the reserves proper and does not take into account the Mwea grazing area.

District contained 258,000 people at a density of 420 per square mile, Fort Hall District 304,000 at a density of 411, and Nyeri 183,000 at a density of 272.[1] The high density in southern and central Kikuyu was largely a consequence of the growth of Nairobi, with its opportunities for wage labour and for selling cash crops, charcoal and similar products. At the end of the period the Kikuyu formed about 45 per cent. of the city's African population, and many Kikuyu of Kiambu became commuters, working in Nairobi and returning to their family plots at night.

In Kiambu, in particular, land acquired high value both as a means of growing cash crops for sale in the city and also for residential purposes. A consequence was the introduction of outright sale of plots of land in place of the traditional systems of tenancy, and the holding of land in freehold, a development unique in the African parts of Kenya. With sale and the commercialization of land went the breakdown of the *githaka* system and the changing of the nature of the rights held both by members of lineages and by their tenants. The head of a lineage tended to become a landowner, and the commonest form of tenant in the old system, *muhoi*, came to mean a tenant who rented land for cash. A member of the lineage ceased to exercise merely temporary rights of user by virtue of his membership of the group, and took his share of the group's land as his own freehold plot.[2]

Developments in western Kenya, in the Kavirondo or Nyanza area, were rather different. Here live the two largest tribal groupings after the Kikuyu, the Luhya (or Bantu Kavirondo), who were 654,000 in 1948, and the Nilotic Luo, numbering 697,000 in 1948. In 1948 the three districts of the area were North Nyanza, with 634,000 people at a density of 236 per square mile, almost all being Luhya; Central Nyanza, with 463,000 at a density of 185, mostly Luo; and South Nyanza, with 545,000 at a density of 145, consisting of Gusii, some Luo, Kuria, and other smaller tribes. There was in Nyanza proper comparatively little alienation of land,[3] and as most of the

[1] *East African Population Census, 1948* (Nairobi, 1948). These figures exclude Kikuyu living in other districts of Kenya.

[2] See Middleton, op. cit., pp. 52-56.

[3] Land was alienated in the north and east of the area, but much was grazing land and not the rich agricultural land that was to be such a source of controversy.

province has favourable soil and climate it was to become the richest producer of native maize and cotton in the country. Despite the discovery of gold at Kakamega in 1931 and the absence of many labour migrants from all parts of Kavirondo, the area remained one in which there was far more continuity of traditional life than in Kikuyu; while the wealth and density of population of the area led at the same time to a 'progress' that was to be marked by the development of missions, education, and political groupings to a high degree.

The other mainly agricultural areas of Kenya are scattered. The changes in the economic life of the many small tribes at the coast may be summed up by saying that with the startling growth of Mombasa, whose population trebled between 1921 and 1946, went an increasing stagnation of rural life in the surrounding areas. Except for the narrow coastal strip (occupied by Arabs and Swahili tribes and ethnically mixed), the Teita hills, and the banks of the Tana river, most of this region is inhospitable semi-desert, the *nyika*. The coast itself had been under Arab suzerainty for many centuries, although the effective power of the small Arab city-states had waned many years before the beginnings of European contact.

Apart from the areas occupied by Arabs, a good deal of land in the coastal belt was early alienated to Europeans; sisal and other crops were grown, but most of the alienated land was never used and remained occupied by Africans from neighbouring tribal reserves. The Teita of the Teita hills, with the highest rate of increase of all Kenya tribes,[1] had lost some 1,300 acres in the middle of their country[2] and much of the surrounding plains which had been used for grazing and some farming but not for residence. The hills became overcrowded, and many Teita migrated to Mombasa as wage labourers, composing about 10 per cent. of the labour force there. The Digo and Duruma had a good deal of land taken for European estates and for various small settlements of Arabs and Swahili, but little of this land was ever used and much of it was occupied by Digo squatters. The Giryama, after having been moved and having revolted in 1914, were left to their own uneventful life, and the Pokomo of the Tana river continued their poverty-

---

[1] Carter Commission, *Report*, p. 319, para. 1237.
[2] Later restored on the recommendation of the Carter Commission.

stricken existence virtually undisturbed up to the second world war,[1] after which it was found that the Tana might provide enough water for extensive irrigation and settlement schemes.

The remaining important agricultural groups are the Kamba and the various small tribes, closely related to the Kikuyu, which are generally classed together as the Embu and Meru. The Kamba occupy two districts, Machakos, a fairly fertile agricultural area, with a population in 1948 of 357,000, and Kitui, an arid region mainly suitable for herding only, with 211,000 people in 1948. There was little alienation, although in Machakos District some fertile farms were taken which were to become valuable through their proximity to the markets of Nairobi. On the whole Kamba remained an impoverished area, struggling against almost persistent drought and aridity until after the second world war, when dam-building and other works were to change the situation. The Embu (202,000 in 1948) and Meru (313,000) dwell on the eastern slopes of Mount Kenya. They suffered little alienation of land, but the remoteness of their countries and their rugged terrain were to make cash crop production of little importance (although some coffee was being grown by the mid-1930's), and there was some overcrowding with consequent labour migration, mostly to Nairobi, Mombasa, and parts of Kamba country.

The pastoral peoples of Kenya were affected differently by changing economic conditions. They suffered especially from alienation of land, water supplies, and saltlicks. By their traditional systems of grazing, much of the land used by them was at any given time empty of men and herds; consequently much of it was taken for European ranches by a government which assumed that it was unused.

The deprivation of the Masai of much of their grazing has already been described.[2] The Uasin Gishu Masai had suffered more than did the other Masai groups, mainly from civil war and from epidemics, and had ceased to exist as a tribe by 1883, but all Masai were left in comparatively poorly watered areas, with inadequate grazing for their needs as they traditionally saw them.[3] Whatever the merits or demerits of their case, there can be little doubt that the Masai regarded themselves as badly

[1] Carter Commission *Report*, ch. xv.   [2] See Chapter I above.
[3] Carter Commission *Report*, p. 247, paras. 915 sqq.

treated, and they turned away from European contact and reverted to a narrow tribalism. Their reserves became overcrowded and overgrazed, and attempts by European veterinary and administrative officers to better their lot met with steady opposition and distrust.

The smaller pastoral tribes of the Nandi and Kipsigis found themselves in territory which, being healthy and fertile, was early coveted by European farmers. Although alienation of land was not particularly extensive, it had serious repercussions, as the areas formerly occupied by these tribes were in any case small. The Nandi reserve in 1932 was 757 square miles, of which 61 square miles were alienated; of the remainder, 156 square miles were forest reserve. It was admitted that much of the alienated land had actually been occupied by Nandi, as compensation had been paid for huts standing on the farms when taken over.[1] The Kipsigis lost rather more land. The Kenya Land Commission Report stated that it was 'undisputed' by European farmers that 130,000 acres of alienated land had originally been used by Kipsigis, and also stated that of the 200 square miles of alienated land at Sotik and south Nyando 'a good proportion' had formerly been occupied by Kipsigis tribesmen. Land had been alienated partly to establish a buffer zone between the Kipsigis and the tribes of Kavirondo, to the west, and also in an effort to 'depastoralize' the Kipsigis.[2] Throughout the period the Nandi and Kipsigis came to depend as much on farming as on herding for sustenance, and, indeed, after the second world war the Kipsigis were to become perhaps the most 'progressive' of all African farmers in Kenya.

To the north the smaller tribes of Tuken (Kamasia), Keyo, Marakwet, Pokot, Njemps and the other peoples of the Baringo region were left largely in peace,[3] apparently because no one else wanted their difficult and arid mountainous lands. In the far north, in the lava deserts and semi-deserts of the northern frontier, there was little direct European impact.

The various developments to do with land which had the greatest impact on the African peoples of Kenya were, therefore, the fixing of tribal or 'reserve' boundaries, and the alienation

---

[1] Carter Commission *Report*, p. 271, paras. 1031 sqq.
[2] Ibid., p. 302, paras. 1149 sqq., 1165.
[3] Although the Kony were removed to North Kavirondo in 1921.

of land to European and other farmers. The former prevented the traditional migration-drift of agricultural tribes across the country. This would not have mattered if the population had not increased and if the growing of cash crops had not become not only desirable but essential. As things were, the need for expansion from the more crowded areas became inevitable. This was recognized by the Kenya Land Commission of 1932, and was taken into account in its recommendations for changes in reserve boundaries. Unfortunately, few of these recommendations were ever to be put into effect.

A simplified but not inaccurate picture is that of three main blocks of fertile farming land: Nyanza, producing maize and other cash crops in abundance, with little land alienated and, despite the high population density, largely self-supporting; the Kikuyu highlands and the neighbouring areas, with a high density of population and needing land for expansion, and with a somewhat exaggerated but none the less real grudge with regard to land alienation; and the coast, with much alienation, a high population density, and a good deal of economic stagnation. Between Nyanza and Kikuyu were the pastoralists, much of their lands alienated and much of the remainder ill-used by overgrazing, and the people little interested in turning their livestock or labour into cash.

The most obvious response to this situation, in particular for the agricultural peoples, was emigration from the reserves. General government policy was to inhibit the settlement of members of one tribe in the reserves of others, as this led to difficulties in local administration. It could not be prevented altogether, but the main emigration was into the towns and into European and forest land.

The African population of Nairobi grew from 12,000 in 1921 to 27,000 in 1931, 40,000 in 1938, and over 70,000 in 1947. Mombasa grew from 18,000 in 1921 to 57,000 in 1946.[1] Reliable figures for the tribal composition of the towns before the 1948 census are rarely available, but this gives an indication of the position at the end of the period. In Nairobi municipality, 45 per cent. of the African population were Kikuyu (of whom almost half were from Kiambu), 16 per cent. were Luo, 9 per

---

[1] Figures quoted from various sources by M. Parker, *Municipal Government in Kenya* (Ph.D. thesis, University of London, 1950), pp. 2-3.

cent. Luhya, 5 per cent. Kamba, and 5 per cent. Embu. In Mombasa island 18 per cent. of the African population were 'Nyika' (Giryama and Digo), 14 per cent. were Kamba from Kitui, 10 per cent. Teita, 10 per cent. Luo, and 4 per cent. Luhya. In Nakuru, 44 per cent. were Kikuyu, 14 per cent. Luhya, and 10 per cent. Luo.[1]

Besides moving into the towns, Africans also settled in white farming areas as squatters. They were of two types: those who stayed on the land on which they had always lived, but which had been alienated; and the majority, land-hungry Africans who settled on European lands in return for their labour. Squatters were classed officially as 'resident native labourers', but differed from ordinarily employed labourers in certain important ways. Under the Resident Native Labourers Ordinance of 1925, squatters entered into a contract with a landowner. This ensured them a plot of land for cultivation and building, and prescribed the number of livestock which could be grazed on the farm. (It thus implied the right to pasture livestock, and this was perhaps the most important aspect of the contract for the squatters themselves.) A squatter was obliged to work for 180 days in the year at a specified wage. Originally this system ensured at least a regular supply of labour for farmers. In time, however, it became clear that there was room for considerable abuse. Squatters—and their livestock—increased in numbers, and besides squatting on occupied farms lived on alienated but unworked lands, which thus became in effect extensions to the reserve areas in which people could live without working for Europeans at all. In 1933 the Kenya Land Commission estimated that there were about 110,000 Kikuyu living outside the Kikuyu reserves, and of these the majority were squatters on European farms.[2] Although most squatters in the colony were Kikuyu, there were also over 13,000 Nandi[3] and at least 4,000 Kipsigis

[1] Figures from *Kenya: Geographical and Tribal Studies, 1948* (East African Statistical Dept., Nairobi, 1950).

[2] Carter Commission *Report*, p. 144, paras. 498–9. The report adds that there were also some 41,000 Kikuyu labourers outside the Kikuyu reserves who were not counted as squatters; and there were also considerable numbers of Kikuyu living in the Masai Reserve and at the coast.

[3] G. W. B. Huntingford, *Nandi Work and Culture* (H.M.S.O., London, 1950) p. 73. These lived outside the Nandi Reserve, mostly in the districts of Nandi, Uasin-Gishu and Trans-Nzoia. The squatters amounted to about one-quarter of the entire tribe.

squatters; much of the alienated but unopened land at the coast was occupied by Teita, Giryama, and Digo squatters, who had no contracts with anyone. In 1931 there were also 52,000 Africans from Kavirondo away from their reserves, but detailed figures of their whereabouts are not obtainable.[1] There were also many Africans living illegally in forest reserves.[2]

By the early 1930's there were many complaints of the abuse by squatters of their rights—they had too many cattle for the available grazing,[3] many of them used land but did no work in return, and their homes were the scenes of drunkenness and the refuges of thieves and raiders of cattle from European farms. Some employers turned a blind eye to over-grazing, and some provided dispensaries and small schools, but the squatters as a rule lived wretchedly. Reports of the Labour Department stressed that the wording of the ordinance 'shows the low standard of living expected for these people'.[4] In order to remedy some of the abuses a new ordinance was enacted in 1937. This laid out the obligations of both landowners and squatters in detail.[5] In 1945 there were some 200,000 squatters.

The position of townsmen and squatters was alike in two important respects. Neither had permanent ties in the place in which they worked. If they retired through old age, or became sick, or lost employment, as during the depression of the early 1930's, they had to return to their reserves, which thus took the place of insurance and pension schemes. In both cases, especially in the towns, there was an unequal ratio between the sexes, an imbalance that was reflected in the reserves from which they came. In 1948, for example, certain areas had a far higher proportion of men than women: Nairobi District, with 72,000 adult men to 16,000 women; Mombasa, with 29,000 to 14,000, and the white farming areas of Thika, Nanyuki, Kericho, Trans-Nzoia, Uasin-Gishu, and Nakuru,

[1] Carter Commission *Report*, p. 271, paras. 1031, sqq.; pp. 287-8, para. 1092; p. 303, para. 1156; p. 320, para. 1247, sqq.; p. 328, para. 1288.

[2] Including the Dorobo, who had traditionally lived in the forests, but whose occupancy was regarded as 'illegal' by the Government.

[3] In 1932 it was reckoned that in Trans-Nzoia alone there were about a quarter million African-owned cattle and the same number of goats and sheep. Carter Commission *Report*, p. 508, paras. 2038-9.

[4] Native Affairs Department Report, 1930.

[5] Details are summarized in C. K. Meek, *Land Law and Custom in the Colonies* (London, 1946), pp. 83-84.

in all of which the proportion of adults was some two-thirds men to one-third women. And in the major labour-exporting reserves of Kiambu, Fort Hall, Nyeri, Embu, Meru, Machakos, Kitui, the three Nyanza districts, and Giryama there were more women than men; some, such as Central Nyanza and Nyeri, had only 98 men to 146 women and 38 men to 58 women respectively. In the other reserves, which supplied little labour, the figures were more or less equal.

The growth of local government

By assuming control of the African areas the Government became responsible for general law and order, the collection of tax, the efficient administration of justice, and the control of population movements. In the early years only the first two of these aims seemed important, or at least immediately feasible; after about 1910 the other two became of equal importance. Besides the need for control of 'indiscipline' and the administration of justice came the need for development and guided change from a primitive and seemingly barbarous way of life to a more civilized one. The Government had to be represented to the people and its orders transmitted downwards, and the wishes of the governed had to be presented to the Government. In the earlier part of this century the former need was paramount, but the latter became of increasing importance throughout the years, and by the 1930's was an important aim of the central Administration.[1]

Lord Hailey has written that the system of native administration in Kenya has been distinguished from those of most other East and Central African territories in that it has generally been based on the use of appointed authorities rather than on that of traditional native chiefs.[2] This was due mainly to the form of the indigenous political systems of Kenya. In southern Uganda the British found existing native governments with kings, councils, and appointed chiefs; it was comparatively simple to take over these systems for the purposes of colonial

---

[1] There are full accounts of the growth of local government and judicial organization in Lord Hailey, *Native Administration in the British African Territories*, vol. i (London, 1950), and in A. Phillips, *Report on Native Tribunals* (Nairobi, 1945).

[2] Hailey, op. cit., pp. 87, 91.

administration. But in most parts of Kenya there was nothing remotely approaching this situation. In almost every tribe local government was in the hands either of the heads of small clans and lineages (as in Luo and Luhya) or of local councils composed of elders in an age-set system (as in Kikuyu, Kamba, and the pastoral Nilo-Hamitic groups). These systems of government had serious disadvantages from the viewpoint of a central government. The heads of clans and lineages and the members of councils exercised jurisdiction over very small groups, and the sanctions behind their authority were usually religious. Elders were chosen by genealogical position, or by age, and in both cases once acquired the positions were held for life. And elders could not exercise authority over persons not traditionally members of the particular kinship or local groups concerned. Any efforts to widen their authority would meet with opposition and would, in any case, be largely ineffective since traditional sanctions would not operate. There were some exceptions. One was in the small state of Wanga, in North Nyanza, where there existed a kingship with some authority and influence over neighbouring tribes; a second was the institution of war-leaders among the Kikuyu, Luhya, and Kamba, important men whose influence was, however, temporary and non-hereditary; a third was the position in some of the small towns of the coast of the *liwali*, a functionary who was the representative of the Sultan of Zanzibar, the nominal owner of the coastal strip.

The first legislation concerned with local native administration, the Native Courts Regulations of 1897, had empowered administrative officers to supervise the administration of justice by the 'chiefs and elders' of certain tribes. The Village Headmen Ordinance of 1902 had provided for the appointment of official headmen in charge of villages or groups of villages. Some of them were those holding traditional chiefly authority, but certainly in many cases such traditional authorities were not recognized for the simple reason that they did not exist. The men chosen were usually those who had come into some kind of contact with Europeans, often as traders, guides, even messengers and donkey men. They were given the duty of imposing some kind of peace and of collecting tax, but very little more. There are in the library of the Secretariat at

Nairobi some memoranda written by various district commissioners about 1912, pointing out that these so-called chiefs, especially in Kikuyu,[1] were often little but partly detribalized riff-raff who had made themselves useful to early officers but who enjoyed no confidence among their own people. They had in many cases usurped the authority of traditional elders and other tribal functionaries, had taken to themselves unofficial perquisites and were in general a hindrance to efficient administration. In some areas the situation was almost ludicrous: among the Galla, for example, as late as 1925 two of the four headmen were not even Galla but former Galla slaves, one from Nyasaland and the other from Kamba.[2]

From the middle of the 1920's, however, this situation was effectively changed. The main feature of local government in Kenya came to be the Local Native Councils, which led to more efficient representation of the people and to their playing a more responsible part in local administration. Amendments to the Native Authority Ordinance, in 1924 and 1933, provided for the setting up of local councils, of which the district commissioners were to be presidents. These councils provided for considerable representation, both formal and informal, of local interests, the majority of members being elected by popular choice. They were to provide a stimulus both to interest in local government matters and also to the creation of a sense of unity throughout the district, which often contained more than one tribe and was usually a larger unit than that recognized under any indigenous organization. Councils were established during 1924 and 1925 in many districts. Their deliberations, although effective, were usually limited to consideration of local opinion, without legislative power except for the passing of resolutions which had the effect of by-laws. They were not concerned with wider matters of a more 'political' nature, nor with modification and changes in traditional law and custom.[3]

The topics considered at council meetings included matters

---

[1] Hailey, op. cit., p. 123, mentions the example of 'one Kinanjui', appointed at an early stage as 'Paramount of the Kikuyu', which was 'merely the recognition accorded by the officer who subsequently became the first District Commissioner of Fort Hall to a man who had proved useful to him in Southern Kikuyu'. See Chapter I, p. 45, n. 1, above.

[2] Native Affairs Department Report, 1925, p. 11.

[3] See Hailey, op. cit., p. 130.

to do with agriculture and land betterment, education, communications, registration of marriage and deaths, and other matters of purely local administrative concern. The councils were early given some financial autonomy, and were not meant to be merely rubber-stamp committees for the decisions of administrative officers. They were empowered to collect rates and land fees and to levy taxes for education and other communal purposes. In 1926 the total income of all Local Native Councils in Kenya was almost £37,000 and by 1938 it had risen to over £112,000. In 1926 their total expenditure was just over £17,000, and this rose to £103,000 in 1938. Of this last sum £18,000 was spent on education and almost £20,000 on agriculture, forestry, and water-supplies. Almost half the total income and expenditure was accounted for by the councils of Nyanza Province.[1] It was reported in the same year that the demand for education was insatiable, and that the main difficulty of the Administration was to curb the enthusiasm of native councils in voting large sums of money for education and educational buildings.[2] Although the progress made by some of the smaller and more remote councils was naturally limited, the success in local administration of those in the more central areas was certainly notable.

The administration of justice early presented serious problems; there were no indigenous judicial authorities other than informal councils of elders. Tribunals, under the direct authority of chiefs and headmen, had been recognized by the Courts Ordinance of 1907. The Native Tribunal Rules of 1911 recognized the constitution of councils of elders in accordance with traditional custom. In many cases, however, the authority of the indigenous judicial bodies had been so severely weakened that they were unable to function as efficiently as was hoped. The traditional sanctions had usually been destroyed by the prohibition of the use of force by any but agents of the central government. The Native Authority Ordinance of 1912 enlarged the formerly relatively minor powers of headmen and laid down that they were to be appointed over specific areas, later to be

[1] Native Affairs Department Report, 1938, pp. 39-41.
[2] For example, the Native Affairs Department Report, 1946-7, stated (p. 49): 'Most of the Local Native Councils of the large agricultural tribes and some of those of the semi-pastoral tribes would be prepared to vote almost all their ordinary revenue and all their surplus balances for the furtherance of education.'

known as locations, and whose boundaries were in most cases drawn on a tribal or ethnical basis. It took several years for the boundaries to be decided upon, and it was not until 1926 that a definitive demarcation of reserves and locations was completed.

The annual reports of district commissioners, provincial commissioners, and the Native Affairs Department from 1912 until 1939 all contain references to the situation of conflict between the chiefs, the traditional elders, and their councils, on the one hand, and on the other the younger and more educated men who demanded a greater share in local administration and who seemed to be so liable to the 'indiscipline' that made the everyday work of the Administration so difficult. Chiefs could collect tax, but in most cases they were not efficient administrators of justice; traditional elders could administer justice, but only in matters covered by native custom (and so by the use of traditional sanctions and traditional rules of evidence, neither of which were always compatible with Western notions of justice) and only over the members of their own small local groupings. The more educated younger men were, whether the Government or elders liked it or not, the men of the future, who had therefore to be taken into account and who, moreover, increased both their numbers and their power as the years went by. These conflicts became acute at different times in different areas, first among the Kikuyu, next among the Nyanza tribes, and later among the more remote and poorer tribes of Kenya; but the conflicts found expression in all areas in the course of the period.

The expression took the form of complaints of the general inefficiency of the administrative and judicial system in the native areas. Charges of corruption and inefficiency were common; what seemed to the Administration to be unnecessary litigation increased to such a degree in some areas, especially Nyanza and Kikuyu, as to threaten to choke the system altogether. The difficulties were due partly to the facts that traditional elders could not deal, by traditional custom, with such criminal offences as tax default; that an increasing number of cases dealing with land and marriage were between parties not members of the traditional tiny local groups beyond whose boundaries the authority of traditional councils could not run;

that young men could more and more easily escape from areas of traditional jurisdiction by moving to towns or European farms; and that an appellate system was set up by which appeals from native tribunals went to European courts, which did not always administer justice by native custom, but by considerations of European law.

In 1930 the Native Tribunals Ordinance tried to better the position by giving tribunals jurisdiction over all Africans within their area, irrespective of tribe, by debarring advocates from native tribunals (thus removing a factor leading to irresponsible use of the appeal system), by setting up a dual jurisdiction by which appeals from native tribunals went to native commissioners rather than to the Supreme Court, and by establishing native courts of appeal without restricting them to consideration of cases involving native custom only. The Native Tribunals (Amendment) Ordinance of 1942 laid down that cases involving land within the reserves must first be taken to the local native tribunal and not to European courts. After 1930 many changes were made in the organization of native tribunals, such as the payment of members, which had the general effect of departing from traditional custom. These changes reflected the growing importance of the new elements in native society and the decrease in importance of traditional authority and sanctions. Part of this process was the setting up of special courts to deal with cases between Africans living in towns and on European farms, for whom the judicial system had until then made no provision. In 1944 there were 139 native tribunals in Kenya.[1]

White settlement and the demands for labour

The more or less traditional pattern of life that existed in Kenya until 1912 was changed considerably by the first world war. In all 163,000 Africans from Kenya were employed at various times as carriers in the armed forces. Some 47,000 Africans from East Africa died on war service; and the Kikuyu alone lost 120,000 in deaths from war casualties, famine, and influenza.[2] Although there was no fighting on Kenya soil, the

[1] Forty-two in Central Province, 29 in Nyanza Province, 25 in Coast Province, 22 in Rift Valley Province, 11 in Masai District, and 10 in the Northern Frontier District. See Phillips, *Native Tribunals*, p. 6.

[2] Figures quoted from F. B. Welbourn, *East African Rebels* (London, 1961), pp. 121, 125.

disturbances among the African population were considerable. This was the first time that large numbers of men had been moved away from their homes, away from the authority of their chiefs, and had mingled with Europeans and members of tribes other than their own.

The period up to the early 1920's was one of consolidation of European farmers, who were in competition with African farmers. Before the war the African share in export production was some 70 per cent. of the total; after it the proportions were more than reversed.[1] To achieve higher production Europeans demanded more and more labour, regardless of whether or not this disrupted African farming, and the war caused both an additional demand and also a scarcity. By 1920 the labour position had become one which threatened the livelihood of the African population in the central areas, and the early 1920's were marked by a reaction. In brief, until 1920 the demands of the European sector had been paramount, and Africans seem to have been too shocked by the strength of European impact to protest; they were still in the first stage of colonial contact. After 1920 they began to realize that the effects of this impact were within the control of the Europeans, rather than being merely a change of the kind which they had known traditionally, due to famines, tribal wars, and epidemics; and, with a clearly defined enemy, they began to organize themselves to assert what they regarded as their rights.

Before discussing the political movements of the 1920's it is necessary to say something of the labour conditions at the time, in particular as seen by the Africans. The evidence of the 1912–13 Labour Commission Report gives a picture of the situation.[2] European farmers needed labour and wanted to increase African taxation to ensure a larger and more regular labour supply, although several government witnesses stated that in fact an increase in poll-tax would have little effect upon it as African manpower was limited. Africans needed money for taxes and consumer goods, but needed also the time to work on

---

[1] See Chapter V above.

[2] *Report of the Labour Commission, 1912–1913* (Nairobi, 1913). The evidence to the commission contains much detail, and was given not only by government officers and European and Indian employers but also by a few African labourers. Extracts from the evidence may be found in W. McGregor Ross, *Kenya from Within* (London, 1927), ch. vi.

their own land. Administrative officers found themselves under pressure to persuade labour to come forward, but on the whole objected to having to do so. Chiefs found themselves in a similar position, but in the words of a witness to the commission, 'chiefs did not object to natives leaving the reserves to work for Europeans, for they were not sufficiently powerful to do so'. Some chiefs were bribed by labour recruiters to ensure a regular supply, and there cannot be the least doubt that the position was one that needed immediate amelioration: there were many cases of brutality, of cheating unsophisticated labourers, of providing what was virtually forced labour, including women and children. In general all Africans, including chiefs, classed all Europeans as having the complete support of an all-powerful government, and the activities of labour recruiters were regarded as official. The evidence showed that chiefs were weak as against the farmers, but all-powerful as regards their subjects, and that for Africans European employment, although almost the only way of acquiring money, was unpopular and under-paid.

The recommendations of the settler-dominated Economic Commission of 1917,[1] the Resident Natives Ordinance of 1918, and the instructions in the 'Northey circular' on labour issued in October 1919,[2] led to a situation of great African discontent. The Resident Natives Ordinance of 1918 defined the status of African squatters on European farms. Although this had the effect of extending the acreage of land available for Africans (especially as much European land was held by absentee owners), it led to a widespread feeling of insecurity and to breakdown in tribal and domestic authority. The instructions of the labour circular were that it was the 'wish' of the Government that 'tribesmen' should 'come out into the labour field', and administrative officers were to encourage them to do so. Chiefs and elders should assist 'as part of their duty', and lists were to be prepared of those who were 'helpful' or 'not helpful'; employers and recruiters 'will be invited and encouraged to enter freely any Native Reserve' to recruit; and in areas near the farms women and children should also be

---

[1] *Final Report of the Economic Commission* (Nairobi, 1919). Later repudiated by the British Government.
[2] See Chapter VI, pp. 292-3, above.

recruited. By implication the encouragement of African farming within the reserves was not part of government policy.

The demand for labour became ever more acute, and native poll-tax was increased from 12 sh. to 16 sh. a head. In 1921, by a change in the financial year, tax was collected twice in twelve months. Visible returns for taxes, in the form of services for the African population, were not at that time very apparent.[1] In 1920 previous registration ordinances, which had been introduced largely with South African pass laws in mind but which had not been put into effect, were repealed and a new ordinance was passed. It laid down that every African male over the apparent age of 16 years should be registered and should carry with him a registration certificate (the *kipande*). By the end of 1920 195,000 Africans were registered, a number which rose steadily to reach over half a million by the end of 1924; in March 1923 the system was extended in the Nakuru District to boys of 12.[2] The main purposes of these measures were to stabilize the labour supply, to ensure payment of taxes, and to make possible the apprehension of 'deserters' from European farms as well as that of ordinary criminals.

In 1921 an attempt was made by the Convention of Associations, the body representing European farming and political interests, to reduce African wages by a third. Although this was not unanimously supported, either by individual farmers or by government departments, and was in the event not put into effect, it received wide publicity and provided an immediate cause of African unrest.

The growth of political consciousness: the Kikuyu

For several reasons the Kikuyu were the first group among which political associations developed, and they were to remain in the vanguard of political organization throughout the entire period. There is also much more material available upon Kikuyu political developments than on those among other

---

[1] See, for example, an official witness to the East African Commission of 1925 who stated: 'If we left the [Kitui Kamba] district tomorrow the only permanent evidence of our occupation would be the buildings we have erected for the use of our tax-collecting staff', *Report of the East Africa Commission* (Ormsby-Gore Commission), Cmd. 2387 (1925), p. 187.

[2] By proclamation of the Governor: *Official Gazette*, 21 Mar. 1923; quoted in Ross, op. cit., p. 193.

Kenya peoples, and emphasis is therefore given to them in this account.[1]

Their first expression was the formation of a Kikuyu Association in Nairobi in 1920. This was an essentially moderate body, but in the following year another organization, the Young Kikuyu Association, was formed under the leadership of Harry Thuku[2] and took up a more radical position. A government report stated of it:

> The formation of a Kikuyu Association with a membership composed largely of office boys and domestic servants in Nairobi is a sign of the times. The old machinery of representation through Native Chiefs and Councils is not suitable to progressive modern conditions,

and added that 'native agitators' were active.[3]

The Association had as its expressed aims the change of labour conditions, the withdrawal of the *kipande*, a decrease in poll-tax, and the return of alienated land to the Kikuyu. Its formation was also a response to the rapidly changing social conditions among the Kikuyu, conditions which were blamed largely upon the chiefs appointed by the Government, many of whom were highly unpopular for the part they played in the recruitment of labour. The movement spread throughout Kiambu and into Fort Hall; Harry Thuku also visited Kisumu in Nyanza. Meetings were held in Nairobi; in March 1922 Thuku was arrested, and a crowd in Nairobi was fired upon by the police, about twenty-five people being killed or dying later of wounds. Leaders were arrested, and Thuku was exiled to Kismayu. The threatened wage reductions were then dropped as they were leading to an ever more serious shortage of labour. In the same year there was also formed an East African Association, a more militant body which claimed to speak for all the Africans of East Africa.

[1] Information is from several sources, including the annual reports of the Native Affairs Department, the report *Historical Survey of the Origins and Growth of Mau Mau* (Corfield Report), Cmnd. 1030 (1960), and the works of Welbourn and McGregor Ross already mentioned. The fullest is perhaps the work of Corfield, but the criticism of it by Welbourn (op. cit., p. 252) is fully justified, and it should be treated with caution. There is a brief account in G. Bennett, 'The development of political organizations in Kenya', *Political Studies*, v. 2 (June 1957), 113-30.

[2] Then a telephone operator at the Treasury in Nairobi. He was discharged for political activity and afterwards devoted his career to politics. Some personal details of him are given by Ross, op. cit., p. 227.

[3] Native Affairs Department Report, 1921.

The associations marked the first political appearance of younger men who felt themselves as a new occupational grouping ('office boys and domestic servants') rather than as junior kinsmen as such, and the East African Association marks the emergence of a trans-tribal consciousness, although it was not as yet to be successfully effective. Whereas the support for Thuku was generally considered to be limited to a few urbanized Kikuyu, the Rev. J. W. Arthur of the Church of Scotland Mission at Kikuyu, an acute observer, wrote:

The development of the native peoples in Kenya in one short year is simply past thinking. They are almost now able to safeguard themselves against oppression and exploitation. What is much more to be feared is native risings led by young educated Christians and resulting in bloodshed and serious setbacks to their whole life . . . (Thuku) has now got hold of . . . the majority of the young Kikuyu Christianity . . . but not the older Christians. . . . These latter however are called by the others Judases. The movement is anti-European and anti-Missionary.[1]

A new association, the Kikuyu Central Association, came into prominence in 1925. It was under the leadership of Joseph Kangethe and Jesse Kariuki, both of whom were later to become known as extremist Kikuyu politicians. The first political action of the Kikuyu Central Association was to petition the Governor for the removal of restrictions on coffee-growing by Africans,[2] for the publication of the laws of the country in Kikuyu, for the appointment of a Kikuyu paramount chief, and for the release of Harry Thuku. It thus showed itself to be concerned mainly with Kikuyu economic and political advancement, and a wider sense of African consciousness was not yet apparent. The Native Affairs Department Report for that year showed the attitude of the Government towards it. The movement was described as 'an indeterminate collection of malcontents, with no constitution, no representative authority and no constructive programme of reform', which had 'achieved a notoriety and a prominence out of all proportion to its merits or its influence'. The report stated that the Kikuyu had shown

---

[1] J. W. Arthur to J. H. Oldham, 14 Mar. 1922, quoted in Welbourn, op. cit., pp. 127-8. The young Christians were C.M.S. (Church Missionary Society) in Fort Hall, C.S.M. in Nyeri (Welbourn, personal communication).

[2] See Chapter V, p. 246 above.

a great fear for the security of their land, 'which has intruded itself into all their Councils, has formed the subject of numerous petitions and memoranda and has tended to overshadow genuine attempts towards political development and social progress'. It is noteworthy that this year marked the change of ruling generation-set among the Kikuyu. Traditionally the senior generation-set held authority, both political and ritual, for some twenty years, which was handed over to the succeeding generation-set at a series of ceremonies held throughout the Kikuyu country, called the *itwika*. The ceremonies were elaborate and marked by much disturbance of everyday life. After them the new generation-set 'ruled' the country for a further twenty years until it handed over power in its turn. This traditional system of government was clearly incompatible with the new one by government-supported chiefs and headmen, who were chosen for ability rather than by seniority in the age-set system, and who could hardly be expected to retire in this way *en bloc* every twenty years. The expected hostility between the generations, expressed very vividly in the *itwika* rites, was transformed to some extent into that between the elders who held government authority and who wished to maintain tribal tradition, and the younger men who wanted education and the benefits of modern progress. The paradox, of course, was in the fact that at this juncture it was the elders, who wished to remain with government authority, who were going against tribal tradition, and the younger men who wished to retain it. However, it was remarked by the District Commissioner, Fort Hall, that in the establishment of the newly formed Local Native Councils many of the elder men supported the election of some of the younger and more educated men, 'indicating that the senior generation is beginning to rely upon the younger', as indeed they would have done by traditional custom.

The Kikuyu associations continued to grow. The Native Affairs Department Report for 1926 states:

Though native political aspirations have not manifested themselves by any serious outburst, it is nevertheless necessary to realise that they exist, and that agents are continually at work, in some cases with quite honest intentions, though often misdirected. One association at least in the Kikuyu Province seems bent on a campaign to subvert tribal discipline, and is active in spreading propaganda which ascribes sinister motives to all actions of Government and to any schemes which are initiated for promoting native welfare. The leaders of this movement are all young people who appear to live on their own wits and other people's ignorant credulity. They are adherents of a notorious deportee[1] and have representatives in Nairobi, as well as in the native reserves, whose efforts are devoted to undermining the loyalty of the native population, and, with this end in view, to winning over the official headmen. Money is collected from the ignorant and foolish who are led to believe that great benefits will accrue to them therefrom, but it appears to be spent chiefly on the personal requirements and luxurious tastes of the collectors. Minor demonstrations have occurred, such as the uprooting of seeds planted in the gardens of mission outschools; this was doubtless the outcome of a carefully circulated, but, of course, quite unfounded, rumour to the effect that the planting of trees and crops was an attempt to establish a title to the land and thus take it from the natives.[2]

This statement refers to all the significant factors that made this movement so important in Kenya's history.

Dissatisfaction among the Kikuyu increased, or it would perhaps be more accurate to say that articulate organization of dissatisfied persons continued to develop. The Native Affairs Department Report for 1927 says:

There has . . . been evident among a section of the Kikuyu tribes a continuous undercurrent of semi-articulate agitation which has commonly found expression in vague plaintive generalities, voiced sometimes at secret assemblies of unofficial associations and sometimes by the dissatisfied at regular meetings of official councils.

and:

To the younger men the conservation of constituted authority seems to be a fatuous relic of discredited barbarism, by the elder the progressive doctrines of unregulated maturity are regarded as the mischievous propaganda of an unhallowed anarchy.[3]

By this time the various strands that made up this discontent were becoming very clear: young men were the leaders in anti-European agitation, and also in that against the chiefs and headmen. These, as always in a colonial situation of this kind

[1] Presumably Harry Thuku.
[2] Native Affairs Department Report, 1926, pp. 12–13.
[3] Native Affairs Department Report, 1927.

(at least in Africa), had to compromise themselves by alliance to the Europeans if their authority was to be effective at all. The Europeans had prohibited the exercise of traditional power, sanctions, and punishments, and had substituted a power which they, and only they, controlled. A chief who attempted to exercise traditional authority in any but domestic situations stood in danger of becoming regarded as out of touch with and unsympathetic to modern developments, if not positively disloyal, by the European officers.

By the end of 1928 the political associations were losing some of their momentum owing largely to the fairly efficient operation of Local Native Councils, which had in most areas accepted the representation of the younger and more rebellious element and were able to express at least some grievances and discontent. In October 1926 the progressive demarcation of native reserves had been started, and as a result immediate fear of further alienation of native lands had died down. The Native Affairs Department report for 1928 mentioned expressly that by then the Kikuyu were turning to the question of individual security of tenure within the reserves, a problem which was to remain important and insoluble until after the Mau Mau movement. The report states that there were then four associations working in Kikuyu, the Kikuyu Association, the Kikuyu Central Association, the Progressive Kikuyu Party, and the Catholic Association; the first two were to some extent working in opposition, the third was confined to Nyeri, and of the fourth the report says its 'activities were not very apparent'. It adds that 'the views of all native associations are well represented on the Local Native Councils, which are rapidly assuming their proper functions as the legitimate media of expression of native public opinion'. As the events of 1929 were to show, this assessment was somewhat optimistic. In spite of mention of the militant nature of the Kikuyu Central Association in earlier reports, the report for this year stated that

It is energetic, virile and enterprising and among its activities publishes a monthly newspaper in Kikuyu, *Muiguithania*, the contents of which have been for the most part quite unexceptional and deserving of much commendation.[1]

[1] Native Affairs Department Report, 1929.

The editor of *Muiguithania* at the time was Jomo Kenyatta, who had become General Secretary of the Association in 1928.

The conflicts inherent in the situation of change among the Kikuyu, between Kikuyu fears of further alienation of land and destruction of tribal custom, the ambitions of Kikuyu tribal and political associations, and the Christian missions with their general control of education, were crystallized in the female circumcision controversy of 1929. This led to a break between the Kikuyu and the missions and Government in the field of education which was to have far-reaching political consequences.

The Kikuyu practised initiation of both boys and girls at puberty; boys were circumcised and girls underwent the operation of clitoridectomy, often known as 'female circumcision'. Both the operation and the whole series of rites of which it was but one part, although perhaps the central one, were known as *irua*. The actual physical operation varied from one area to another, but the essential part was the excision of the clitoris, usually with small cuts on the *labia majora*; the operation was performed by a woman specialist. The initiation was regarded by the Kikuyu both as a sign of acceptance by society as an adult, and as a necessary preparation for participation in sexual intercourse, before marriage, of a limited kind known as *nguiko*, in which the partners achieved sexual satisfaction without physical penetration being permitted. It was necessary for a bride to show physical virginity, and pre-marital pregnancy was a disgrace for both partners and their families.

In most cases the operation, although severe, had no ill effects, but in some there was considerable formation of scar-tissue and difficulty in child-bearing later. It seems that the authorities became concerned partly because, with growing trust in European doctors, more cases of complications were finding their way to the hospitals; because, with an increase in the use of untrained operators, especially in and near urban centres, complications were in fact more common and certainly the operation was more severe; and because when young men and women discovered that the Government prohibited the traditional penalties for pre-marital pregnancy, more girls were becoming pregnant who had barely reached puberty and there was a corresponding rise in the mortality rate in early childbirth. Also, the amounts of livestock payable at marriage in bridewealth had been increasing for several years, so that young men had to wait longer before marrying and were not content with the traditional form of limited intercourse. The missions themselves had aggravated this difficulty by insisting on a complete single payment of all bridewealth cattle before registering the marriage. Traditionally a token payment had been made, the remainder being transferred over a long period during the marriage.[1]

In the late 1920's missionaries and doctors were growing concerned at the practice of clitoridectomy, and determined efforts to prohibit it were made by the Church of Scotland and the Africa Inland Mission. Although these led to a sudden outburst of sentiment, they were the culmination of a long conflict over the retention of the operation. Teaching by missions against the practice had begun in 1906 at the Church of Scotland Mission at Kikuyu and at the Africa Inland Mission at Kijabe. After the first world war many Kikuyu themselves began to put forward demands for its prohibition.[2] The Government recognized the harmful effects of the operation—it was discussed at the Conference of East African Governors in 1926[3]—but in general was neutral in the controversy, regarding education as the best means of ensuring its gradual disappearance. According to most authorities the practice was in fact beginning to die out. But attacks by missions were taken as attacks not on the severity of the operation itself but on the whole initiation ceremony and so on the whole body of traditional Kikuyu custom. Since initiation made a child into an adult, it was rightly held by Kikuyu to be at the very heart of their traditional life.

Conflicts between missions and the mass of the Kikuyu population became open during the late 1920's, missions being accused of wishing to destroy Kikuyu culture and to acquire Kikuyu land. The Kikuyu Central Association entered the arena as the champion of traditional Kikuyu custom, and was joined by a society called the *Miti-ya-Kenya* (the trees of Kenya),

[1] See L. S. B. Leakey, 'The Kikuyu problem of the initiation of girls', *Journal of the Royal Anthropological Institute*, lxi (1931), 277–85, and Welbourn, *East African Rebels*, ch. vii.

[2] Ibid., pp. 136 sqq.

[3] Native Affairs Department Report, 1926, p. 10.

whose members vowed to practise polygyny and to re-establish female circumcision.[1]

By the beginning of 1929 all Local Native Councils among the Kikuyu except for Nyeri had passed resolutions restricting the operation to the simple removal of the clitoris, and not including that of parts of the *labia majora* as well. It was certainly accepted that these resolutions were little more than formal; but, urged by interested parties in the missions, the Local Native Council in Kiambu began prosecutions for disobedience to the resolutions, and in April 1929 two women were each fined 30 sh. for performing a more severe operation. It was soon apparent, however, that the chiefs and councils did not have the support of the mass of the people.

Certain stations of the Church of Scotland Mission thereupon required their elders to sign a paper renouncing the practice on pain of expulsion from the Church. Their lead was followed by the Africa Inland Mission and the Gospel Missionary Society. The consequence was immediate, and the provincial commissioner estimated that nine-tenths of the congregations deserted the churches. In November the Church of Scotland Mission dismissed all its out-teachers who would not sign and lost four-fifths of its school-children; the other two missions lost even more. The agitation spread to Embu. In March 1930 a woman missionary was murdered at Kijabe. After that the tension died down.

The circumcision controversy, although it marked rather than caused the conflict between European and Kikuyu, played a considerable part in the emergence of the Kikuyu as a single people conscious of its past and present unity. It also marked the emergence of effective political associations in the primarily religious field, and of a definitely expressed anti-European sentiment, a sentiment that was reflected in action. Welbourn writes of it:

It enabled a general unrest and desire for independence to be focussed at a point—in the churches and church schools—where rules could be disobeyed and independence asserted with the least danger of interference by an all-powerful Government. At the same time, it became a protest against what was seen as a specifically

[1] Welbourn, op. cit., pp. 130-1. Welbourn does not give the exact date of the formation of this society, but implies that it was in the mid-1920's.

western, rather than a Christian, element in the missionary culture. The greater part of the rebels wished to remain Christian, in more than name, provided they could be free of missionary control and free to practise their tribal customs. . . . Female circumcision was no more than a symbol of a greater issue. But it was the *casus belli*.[1]

The most important and immediate outcome of the conflict was the appearance of the independent schools movement. Although the Government controlled and supervised almost all African education, the actual teaching had been in the hands of Christian missions. It would not be unjust to say that for the majority of Africans who received any form of mission teaching it was the education rather than the Christian teaching which they wanted. Education was seen as the main road to the acquisition of European power. Most Africans of Kenya accepted Christianity as a necessary part of European values as such rather than as a system of belief and ethics which could be accepted by peoples of all races. To be like a European, to be a civilized man, had meant living in a brick house, being monogamous, and at least nominally Christian. The Kikuyu adherents of the independent schools movement, most of whom were, as Welbourn has pointed out so vividly,[2] sincere Christians although against mission influence and control, were the first people in Kenya to realize that education and mission evangelization were not, in fact, necessarily linked.

By 1912 there had been in all some forty main mission schools in various parts of Kenya, mainly on the coast, in Kavirondo, and in Kikuyu. By 1930 there were some ninety main schools with over 2,000 out-schools attached to them. There were in all some 85,000 children attending some kind of mission school, of whom 60,000 were in Kavirondo. (The Kikuyu schools had lost large numbers of pupils in 1929.)[3]

---

[1] Ibid., p. 142.   [2] Ibid., ch. viii.

[3] The missions working in Kenya which had schools were the Church Missionary Society (mainly in Kikuyu, Teita, and the coast); the Holy Ghost Fathers (Kikuyu and Teita); the Mill Hill Fathers (Kavirondo); the Church of Scotland (Kikuyu); the Consolata Fathers (Kikuyu); the Friends' African Mission (North Kavirondo); the Africa Inland Mission (Kamba, Kikuyu, and the Baringo area); the Seventh Day Adventists (South Kavirondo); the Salvation Army (Kavirondo, Kikuyu, and Kamba); the Nilotic Independent Mission (Luo); the United Methodist Mission (Meru and Digo); the Gospel Mission (Kikuyu); the Pentecostal Assemblies and the Lumbwa Industrial Mission (Kipsigis); the Church of God (Kavirondo); and the Neukirchen Mission (Tana river).

O

There had already been some dissatisfaction with mission-controlled education. The obvious problem was that despite the insatiable demand for education the opportunities for educated Africans were very few, except at the lowest level of semi-literate labour. This not unnaturally led to resentment and a realization of the operation of what seemed to be (and often was) a colour bar in occupations in which Africans might come into competition with Asians and Europeans. After the clitori-dectomy controversy, two educational bodies appeared among the Kikuyu, the Kikuyu Independent Schools Association (to be referred to later as K.I.S.A.), and the Kikuyu Karinga Educational Association (K.K.E.A.). The K.I.S.A. wished to organize schools not controlled by missionaries, but attempted for a long time to work with the government education author-ities to provide adequate alternative facilities. Its object was 'to further the interests of the Kikuyu and its members and to safeguard the homogeneity of such interests relating to their spiritual, economic, social and educational upliftment'. Its membership was open to 'all natives of Kenya and negroes generally' who were expected to be 'faithful and loyal to His Majesty the King' and to 'follow principles of the "African Independent Pentecostal Church" '. And its original objectives included the establishing of dispensaries, the instruction of mothers in hygiene and morality, and the holding of quarterly teachers' conferences.[1] It is noticeable that economic, political, social, religious, and educational aims were all involved: the Association's founders realized that these were indivisible.

The K.K.E.A.[2] was based far more on Kikuyu tribal values, and from its inception strongly resisted any form of government supervision. Whereas the K.I.S.A. was offered and accepted financial assistance from both Government and Local Native Councils, the K.K.E.A. became increasingly involved with the Kikuyu Central Association, and, indeed, many of its leaders were also those of that association.

The depression began to be felt in Kenya during 1930 and continued for some years. Wages fell, and the amount of employment available, both on farms and in the towns, lessened

---

[1] Welbourn, op. cit., pp. 145–6.
[2] *Karinga* means 'unadulterated', a reference to the desire for traditional Kikuyu education purified of European influence.

substantially. Food could still be grown: it was money that was short. All tribes found it very difficult to pay their taxes (these were not in general lowered), and tribes such as the Kikuyu which depended upon a high income from wage labour suffered very considerably. The Kikuyu Central Association was less active during 1930, but the Native Affairs Department Report for that year stated:

It is impossible to prophesy in what form the at present comatose agitation will break out, but sporadic attempts are almost bound to occur unless the more intelligent and progressive elements in the Association can keep the unintelligent and extremely mercenary elements in check.

It added:

It is certainly helpful to find that a large number of the Association members are progressive and far from unintelligent, and it is certainly conspicuous that where they are in large numbers, there you find better houses, better *shambas* (farm plots), and cleaner children.[1]

The Kikuyu scene became rather more complicated at this time. Harry Thuku was released in 1930, and before release had undertaken to oppose the Government by constitutional means only. In 1932 he became President of the Kikuyu Central Association, defeating the more extremist Jesse Kariuki and Joseph Kangethe. However, the latter tried to continue in office, and after much wrangling Thuku left in 1935 to found the Kikuyu Provincial Association, which offered co-operation with the Government. Although there were later attempts by Thuku at a *rapprochement*, both associations continued in competition until the second world war, the Kikuyu Central Association finally gaining the greater membership.

In 1931 the Kikuyu Association, the original group founded in 1920, was renamed the Kikuyu Loyal Patriots, a name chosen to stress its loyalty and to distinguish itself from the Kikuyu Central Association. It was led by chiefs Koinange and Waruhiu and concerned itself mainly with the land question in Kiambu. The Progressive Kikuyu Party had been formed in 1929, based upon South Nyeri, and supported the Church of Scotland in the circumcision controversy. These three associations were still largely local, the Kikuyu Central Association having most of

[1] Native Affairs Department Report, 1930.

its support in Fort Hall, and the Kikuyu Loyal Patriots and the Progressive Kikuyu Party in Kiambu and Nyeri respectively. There was still little tribal-wide Kikuyu sentiment.[1]

The Kikuyu Central Association was to become the most powerful group in the years after 1935. It revived its newspaper *Muiguithania* and maintained close touch with its representative in England, Jomo Kenyatta. It soon had branches outside Nairobi, in Thika, Fort Hall, Limuru and other parts of Kiambu, Nyeri, and in the European farming area of Laikipia. By May 1938 its membership was still under 300, but rose to almost 2,000 by March 1939. During this period it opposed many government projects which it thought disfavoured the Kikuyu or might lead to greater European encroachment on the land. It also, significantly, spread beyond the borders of Kikuyu and the Kikuyu squatter areas. In 1938 it became involved with agitation against destocking of cattle among the Kamba, and the Ukamba Members Association was formed, although with the same Nairobi offices as the K.C.A. itself. It assisted with agitation against land measures in the Teita hills, which led to the founding of the Teita Hills Association, and was also concerned in the Mombasa dock strike of 1939. Although it failed to win support among the Nyanza tribes, it had by the beginning of the war widespread support in many parts of Kenya, and in Mombasa at least was actively concerned with matters of industrial employment. In May 1940 it was declared an illegal society, and its leaders were arrested as being seditious. At that time it claimed a paid-up membership of 7,000. The Kikuyu Provincial Association supported the war and was not proscribed. The leaders of the K.C.A. were released in 1943 and 1944, and it was reported that it was in fact kept in being between 1940 and 1944 under the name of the Kikuyu Farmers' and Traders' Association, perhaps an indication of the interests of at least its livelier members.[2]

During the late 1930's the independent schools movement continued to grow, and its relationship with both political and Kikuyu religious movements was close. Both the K.I.S.A. and K.K.E.A., besides providing education and being closely associated with religious aims, had a formal and new type of

---

[1] Bennett, *Political Studies* (1957), pp. 122–5.
[2] Ibid. See also Corfield *Report*, pp. 46 sqq.

organization, which, in the classical manner of new associations of this type, provided means of advancement to positions of authority and responsibility for persons who obtained no satisfying social status outside. Welbourn writes:

Both Karinga and K.I.S.A. distinguished between committees for church and school and gave a definite place to women. Church committees consisted of the local elders, possibly with a specially appointed 'preacher' for each congregation. Schools had parallel committees of men and women (in Nyeri the number was the apostolic twelve). But the women's committees were concerned chiefly with the raising of funds and had to consult the men over important decisions. At least in K.I.S.A. the chairman of the men's committee was expected to be a member of the church and to lead daily prayers in the school. Members of committees were representative of the villages near each school, and, in Karinga, there were only *ad hoc* committees for special purposes at a higher level. K.I.S.A., which was a much larger organization, had formal committees in each district and at provincial level.[1]

The immediate policy of the associations was to run their own schools without mission supervision, and in consequence it was hardly to be expected that their standards should be other than very low. One reason was the desire for the use of English as a medium of instruction in the higher forms. Swahili, the lingua franca of East Africa, was unwanted, as being associated with settler domination, whereas English would emphasize the ties between Africans of different tribal vernaculars and the independence of Africans from local white domination. Replacement of trained teachers, especially, became almost impossible, as the missions continued to control the teacher training schools. For a time, after 1936, the Department of Education tried to assist the independent schools, a special Inspector of Education being appointed for them, but later Local Native Councils and District Education Boards were asked not to subsidize the more inefficient schools, a somewhat drastic measure which merely, as might have been foreseen, spurred the movement on to greater independence. Many mission schools, especially those in the Rift Valley and other white areas, which catered for the children of squatters, were also extremely inefficient, and by 1939 many of these were in fact controlled largely by the

[1] Welbourn, op. cit., p. 153.

independent associations.[1] By this time the number of independent schools associations had grown. The K.I.S.A. was strong in Fort Hall, Kiambu, Nyeri, and Embu, and was linked with the African Independent Pentecostal Church; the K.K.E.A. operated mainly in Kiambu, linked with the African Orthodox Church; in Nyeri there was a breakaway group of the K.I.S.A. linked with the African Orthodox Church; in Fort Hall there was also a Kikuyu Parents' Secondary Schools Association, and an African Christian Church and Schools;[2] while in Meru a single association called itself at various times the Kikuyu Independent Schools Association, the African Private Schools Association, and the South Mwimbi African Community Schools Association.[3] In 1940 the leader of the K.K.E.A. claimed twelve schools in Kiambu and eleven in the Rift Valley and Kericho; in 1952 there were reported to be over 150 K.I.S.A. schools.[4]

In 1939 the Kenya Teacher Training College was founded at Githunguri in Kiambu. The aim of the college was to provide teachers for the Kikuyu independent schools.[5] It began with 225 pupils and by 1947 had over 500.[6] It later fell largely under the control of the K.C.A. and Jomo Kenyatta, who returned to Kenya in 1946. It was closed, and the K.K.E.A. and the K.I.S.A. were proscribed during the Mau Mau emergency in 1952, and most of the independent schools associations' leaders were arrested. One hundred and eighty-four independent schools were closed, 149 K.I.S.A., 21 K.K.E.A., and 14 under other independent management. Only those in Nyeri under Johana Kunyiha[7] were allowed to remain open, as he handed them over to the District Education Board.[8]

In 1935 the K.I.S.A. had become more closely linked with

---

[1] Corfield *Report*, p. 175.

[2] This was in a rather different category. It split from the Africa Inland Mission over the control of church property, not over doctrinal questions; it was notably 'loyal' during the Mau Mau emergency (Welbourn, personal communication).

[3] Welbourn, op. cit., pp. 150 sqq.

[4] Corfield *Report*, pp. 175, 190; Welbourn, op. cit., p. 155.

[5] Welbourn, in a personal communication, states that later it came under K.K.E.A. control. For a description of the college, see P. M. Koinange, *The People of Kenya Speak for Themselves* (Detroit, 1955), ch. iv.

[6] Corfield *Report*, p. 183.

[7] The president of the K.I.S.A. in 1934. See Welbourn, op. cit., p. 146 for biographical details of Kunyiha.

[8] Welbourn, personal communication.

the Kikuyu Central Association, and in the last years of the movement the connexion between political, educational, and religious organizations became very close.

The independent schools movement was intimately connected with religious reform and the formation of churches which, although Christian, would be free from European control. The earliest would seem to have been formed about 1922, when Daudi Maina wa Kiragu founded a small independent church in Fort Hall, whose adherents were drawn from the unbaptized.[1] After the circumcision controversy, mission control was withdrawn from the adherents of the independent schools. In 1933 the independent groups in Fort Hall attempted to co-operate with the missions, mainly in order to acquire priests to baptize their members. This attempt proved unsuccessful,[2] and, largely on the advice of Jesse Kariuki of the K.C.A., a negro archbishop, Daniel William Alexander, the Primate of the African Orthodox Church in South Africa, was invited to Kenya.[3] It was claimed that the African Orthodox Church was 'a Church (of the Africans, governed by the Africans, and for the Africans) to make daily supplication to Almighty God led by priests who have the welfare of Africans at heart'.[4] The

---

[1] Welbourn, *East African Rebels*, p. 144.

[2] Ibid., p. 147, quotes Daudi Maina: 'In these troubled days we reckoned that religion was necessary to a good and progressive educational system. We found it necessary to have churches where we could pray every day to our Creator and Father. We thought of places where our people could train as ministers so that they could teach others about God and his Son Jesus Christ. The need for clergy of our own was obvious in these troubled days, since none of the other clergy came to our help. They left us to struggle and continued to laugh at us, while they knew very well that we needed their help and that God had charged them to look after us. We read from the scriptures that you were asked to feed his lambs; but, instead of doing this, when the sun grew hot you ran away to shelter and left our Lord's sheep in the sun.'

[3] The African Orthodox Church sprang from the Universal Negro Improvement Association of Marcus Garvey, in the United States. Archbishop Alexander visited Uganda in 1931, where he worked with Reuben Spartas. The African Orthodox Church obtained its orders, by devious and illegitimate routes, from the Jacobite (Monophysite) Patriarch of Antioch. It is not recognized by either the Monophysite or Orthodox Churches. A good deal of information is given by Welbourn, op. cit., from whose account it is evident that the patronizing treatment of Archbishop Alexander by Corfield is both uninformed and unjustified. Corfield apparently overlooked the sincerity of at least the majority of the people concerned in this and allied churches at the time.

[4] From *Report and Constitution of the Kikuyu Independent Schools Association*, quoted in Welbourn, op. cit., p. 148.

archbishop was paid a salary of £750 a year, and was to stay for eighteen months in order to devise a new Christian dogma for the particular use of independent schools, and to organize the new Kikuyu African Orthodox Church. During his stay he spread the tenets of his Church and baptized large numbers of adherents, mainly in Fort Hall, Nyeri, and the Rift Valley. He returned to South Africa in 1937 having ordained four Kikuyu ministers (one of whom was the Daudi Maina who had started his own church in the early 1920's). A schism then appeared, two of the ministers forming—as K.I.S.A. had always intended —the African Independent Pentecostal Church, free of all external control; the other two remained faithful to the arch-bishop, forming the African Orthodox Church, which (at least in Kiambu) was closely associated with K.K.E.A.[1] The episode was significant as marking the linking of Kikuyu political, educational, and religious organizations with international African nationalist aspirations, and indirectly with Negro move-ments in the United States. The horizon of Kenya African nationalism was widening.

Little is known about most of the Christian sects among the Kikuyu and other tribes. They were in most cases ephemeral, consisting of a leader and a handful of followers, some of whom would soon break away to form a new sect under a new leader. They were mostly splinter sects from the Protestant mission churches. They frequently advocated polygyny, practised speak-ing with tongues, and behaviour which symbolized their African and anti-European sentiments. They provided an important means of expression for anti-European feeling, giving mem-bers opportunity for self-expression and the exercise of power, which were to a large extent denied them both in traditional political life and in the life of the Christian missions. They were, in their own eyes at least, truly Christian, although they often tried to include some elements of traditional custom.

The best known were the *Watu wa Mungu*, 'the people of God'. They came into existence during the 1920's, their leaders being known as *arathi* (seers). These believed their actions to be dictated by the Holy Ghost, who gave them the power to see both into the past and into the future. The seers gave up their property, wore no European clothing, and carried bows and arrows as

[1] Welbourn, personal communication.

signs of their fight against the forces of evil; later these arms became rather symbols of the fight against Europeans and missions. They wore beards, prayed facing Mount Kenya, and claimed supernatural powers, including that of striking dead all those whom they touched. They became associated with the Kikuyu Central Association, and brought themselves into local disrepute by their immoral behaviour and disregard of tribal authority.[1] It is at least probable that the first appearance of this sect was associated with the circumcision controversy. But it came more to public notice in 1934 after an affray with the police in which several people were killed. The carrying of arms was then forbidden, and by 1942 its members no longer refused to wear European clothing, although they were still opposed to mission influence and supported by the Kikuyu Central Association. By 1947, according to the only published material on it at this time, it had divided into two sects.[2] The *Dini ya Jesu Kristo* ('religion of Jesus Christ') was the extremist wing; its members wore skins and were known as 'skin-men', and whereas the original sect fought against 'the enemies of God', the new sect fought 'the enemies of the Kikuyu people'. There were bloody encounters with the police in 1947. The other wing, according to Rawcliffe, was the Mau Mau movement, but there is no evidence published to show whether in fact this is correct.[3]

The growth of political consciousness: Nyanza

In Nyanza the emergence of a political consciousness was expressed largely in terms of struggles between the many small tribal and clan groups in the region for political independence one from another, and in the formation of mainly tribal political associations and of small religious separatist sects. There were also conflicts between the main linguistic groupings, the Bantu

[1] Welbourn, op. cit., p. 140, quoting from a personal memorandum by Dr. J. W. Arthur dated 1931. There is also an account in D. H. Rawcliffe, *The Struggle for Kenya* (London, 1954), pp. 30 sqq. Rawcliffe suggests that the title of Kenyatta's book *Facing Mount Kenya* referred to the *Watu wa Mungu*, and it would seem that Kenyatta's famous photograph of himself wearing skins and fingering a spear is in the guise of a seer.

[2] Rawcliffe, op. cit., p. 32.

[3] Rawcliffe suggests that the name was onomatopœic, referring to the sound like the roaring of lions made by the members of the *Watu wa Mungu* when praying facing Mount Kenya.

Kavirondo or Luhya,[1] the Luo, and the Nandi-Kipsigis. These various rivalries were growing in importance throughout the 1920's and 1930's.

The Bantu areas of Kavirondo were distinguished by a very high density of population, a high degree of tribal intermingling, and the occurrence of the small centralized state of Wanga, the only one of its kind in Kenya. In 1912 the population density of North Nyanza was estimated to be 122 to the square mile; in 1948 the census showed densities ranging from 145 to 236, although densities in individual locations were in some cases as high as 1,000 a square mile. In the early days of administration these tribes were divided into locations by the Government. Most of these were intended to be tribally homogeneous, but with the high density of population and land shortage, movements of small groups looking for land led to considerable interpenetration, which resulted in much confusion and resentment. This phenomenon was not unique to Nyanza, but it was certainly more extreme there than in other parts of Kenya.

These small tribes were ruled by chiefs, but their power was confined to their own tribe only, and they were usually appointed as much for personal qualities as for any particular genealogical status; their authority was very limited and unformalized. The early British administrators found only one exception to this state of affairs, in the small state of Wanga, where there ruled a king, the famous and long-lived Mumia, with marked political and ritual powers.[2]

In 1909, when the administrative organization of the region was first put on a proper basis, it was generally accepted by the Government that Mumia was to be regarded as *de facto* paramount chief; this was not, however, accepted by either the Luo or the non-Wanga Bantu groups, who resented any attempts to put them under Wanga authority. Mumia's influence was due largely to the fact that he had increased his power very considerably in the early days of contact by support-

[1] The latter is a comparatively recent term coined by the people themselves to cover all the Bantu-speaking groups of the area; the former is used only by Europeans. Each Bantu tribal group has also, of course, its own tribal name.

[2] Most of the following material is taken from a series of reports prepared in 1930 by the Provincial Commissioner, Nyanza, which are in the library of the Secretariat, Nairobi. They are unpublished.

ing Swahili and Arab slavers and traders, who had supplied him in return with arms. In 1909 it was regarded as 'inevitable' that a relative or nominee of Mumia should be placed over the various locations of North Nyanza. None the less, it was also reported in the same year that despite Mumia's personal influence and that of his expected successor, his brother Mulama, non-Wanga chiefs and headmen showed 'a decided tendency to ignore him'. Mumia was proclaimed Paramount Chief of all North Kavirondo in 1909, in the face of Luo hostility; but the Administration decided to give him their complete support, which continued for several years. The Native Affairs Department Report for 1929 states:

In the early days the Administration found a family of conquerors —the Wanga—in this District, very much superior to the indigenous people who were completely sunk in barbarism. As it was impossible to appoint chiefs from these indigenous peoples who could exercise any authority whatsoever, the practice was adopted of putting Wanga natives in charge of the different locations.[1]

However, by 1914 the district commissioner wrote that although when Mumia was originally appointed his friendliness to Europeans was most useful, in recent years his influence had greatly waned and he was content merely to sit in his village and draw his pay. He had lost much prestige and authority, was growing old and sick, and the respect accorded to him was due more to past traditions than to his present authority. He seemed also always to be antagonistic to the Luo. By 1916 the situation was worse and the Administration was thinking of refusing to recognize a paramount chief after Mumia's death.

During this period Mumia and his kin had increased their power by becoming allied not only to the Administration but also to other European, Arab, and Swahili interests. They had been involved in labour recruiting for the building of the railway through North Nyanza and for European farmers.[2] But by about 1919 the Wanga dynasty had begun to lose popular support. Their labour-recruiting activities were apparently unpopular, and so also was their use of Swahilis; these had originally been employed in connexion with certain royal rites at the Wanga court as soldiers and medicine-men, and later as traders,

[1] Native Affairs Department Report, 1929.
[2] See *Evidence* to the Native Labour Commission, 1912-1913 (Nairobi, 1913).

recruiters, and Muslim missionaries. This alliance may have increased the range of Mumia's power, but it also undermined the traditional religious influence of Wanga and separated the ruler from his pagan and Christian subjects.[1] As in Kikuyu, the lead in later actions to diminish the political power of such early chiefs came from mission-trained Africans, and especially from the over-populated tribal area of Bunyore. In 1920 the district headquarters were moved from Mumia's to Kakamega, which still further diminished the chief's influence and prestige. By this time some of the Luo locations had been transferred to Central Kavirondo, and so outside Mumia's authority. The district commissioner in his annual report for 1925 stated that the establishment of the Local Native Council had further detracted from Mumia's authority, and he retired in 1926. He was succeeded by hiss on and, after the latter's conviction on a criminal charge, by a nephew, Osundwa. Neither was much respected by Administration or people.

Later years were marked by the attempts of the Wanga to maintain and to increase their authority over neighbouring groups, and by the attempts of these other tribes to set up their own headmen and councils. The Native Affairs Department annual reports from 1927 onwards contain references to fights and affrays along the borders of locations, to the need for administrative officers to support the Wanga, on the one hand, but, on the other, to permit the legitimate aspirations to independence of the other tribes. Within the Luhya locations small pockets of Luo repeatedly attempted to detach themselves, and many small associations were founded, most of them, however, ephemeral. Small clans and tribes tried to amalgamate their scattered sections, and to have headmen of their own, even where the authority of these headmen would have had to be exercised over small clusters of people dispersed across several locations. Not unnaturally the Administration could not agree to all these demands. None the less, the enchantment of the Administration with the Wanga dynasty was fading. The Report of the Native Affairs Department for 1932 remarks:

It will be observed that Wanga location is concerned in all these

[1] This has been suggested by Mrs. E. M. Chilver in an unpublished essay on 'Native administration and political change in North Nyanza District'.

political movements. It is difficult to resist the conclusion that the Wanga were more generously treated in the fixation of boundaries in the old days than they should have been. The astuteness of Chief Mumia, in allying himself with the newcomers in the early days of European occupation of Kavirondo, must have given him an over-whelming advantage, of which Mulama and the other Wanga chieftains were not slow to take advantage.[1]

In 1934 the Administration considered that it was time for the removal of Wanga sovereignty over some of the locations in which Mumia's brothers had been made chiefs. This met with general popular support and was considered desirable also on purely administrative grounds.

An event of great importance was the discovery of gold at Kakamega in 1931.[2] Despite promises made earlier that this was part of the native reserve land of Kavirondo, the Crown owned the mineral rights and European prospectors and miners were admitted to the area. Although great care was taken to avoid racial incidents and to provide for payment of com-pensation to Africans who were disturbed by mining, there was not unnaturally considerable feeling that the Africans had been deceived. In fact all parties behaved with care and tact, and the situation never led to any very acute trouble. By 1934 there were some 400 Europeans engaged in prospecting and mining. At the peak of the boom, in 1934–5, there were about 7,000 Africans employed at and near Kakamega.

During 1937 the administration in Nyanza Province was reorganized with the election of headmen. Headmen now held authority over territorial areas, irrespective of clan member-ship. They replaced the former government-recognized clan and lineage elders; the latter continued to exercise authority in clan matters, as official but unpaid arbitrators and assessors. Luhya–Luo hostility continued unabated, as did inter-clan hostility, now that the common Wanga enemy had been re-moved. This hostility led to continual outbreaks of violence, especially in competition to build separate tribal and clan churches. Also, much to the relief of the Administration, it was expressed somewhat less bloodily in football matches. The end of the period before the second world war was one of growing

---

[1] Native Affairs Department Report, 1932, p. 8.
[2] See Chapter V, pp. 248–9, and Chapter VI, pp. 320–1, above.

prosperity, based largely on the growing of maize and cotton. This was accompanied by continual litigation in the reformed courts and tribunals, but this was partly no more than a symptom of overcrowding (land cases were a large proportion) and partly a sign that the system was working effectively. It was again reorganized in 1941–2.

Apart from local tribal rivalries, which centred upon the efforts to limit Wanga supremacy and upon Luo–Luhya conflict, political associations of the Kikuyu type also appeared in Nyanza. These were, however, much less anti-mission and anti-government in sentiment than were the Kikuyu associations, and were tribal benefit associations rather than purely political ones aiming at acquiring power in the centre of the political stage.

The first important association was the Kavirondo Taxpayers' Welfare Society, founded in 1923 by Archdeacon Owen, with government encouragement, from the Young Kavirondo Association which had recently come into existence.[1] This was an effort to canalize political development along constructive lines. The 1926 Native Affairs Department Report stated of it:

The Kavirondo Taxpayers' Welfare Association, of which the Founder and President is Archdeacon Owen, is a native society with a laudable list of avowed objects, namely: (i) better food; (ii) better clothing; (iii) better houses; (iv) better education; and (v) better hygiene. It is undoubtedly capable of much good if carefully directed on such lines, but its activities appear to be chiefly political and of a nature likely to damage the reputation of the Association, for natives use the meetings for airing grievances, often imaginary, instead of going to their Administrative Officers. This is especially unfortunate in an Association which is directly connected with a missionary society.[2]

There was also founded in Nyanza at this time a Native Catholic Union in opposition to the primarily Church of England Taxpayers' Welfare Society; it became moribund, however, after a few years. By 1925 tribal rivalries had split Archdeacon Owen's Association into Bantu and Luo branches. It became increasingly a Luo organization, and in 1934 a mainly Luhya Association was formed, with the title of the North Kavirondo

---

[1] Bennett, *Political Studies* (1957), p. 120.
[2] Native Affairs Department Report, 1926, p. 13.

Central Association, apparently on the model of the Kikuyu Central Association. Its principal aim was the creation of a Luhya paramount chief.[1] Recruits came from mission-educated young men, and it was joined by Chief Mulama, Mumia's brother, who was named by the association as Paramount Chief Presumptive of north Kavirondo. As a consequence he was dismissed from his post by the Administration and the ambitions of the Wanga dynasty came to an end.

Nyanza was the seat of many independent sects and churches. Welbourn states that the problem of independent churches in Nyanza sets a more complex problem than do these churches elsewhere in Kenya,[2] but there is little information as to their development. Probably the earliest was the *Dini ya Roho* ('religion of the Spirit'). Rawcliffe states, without giving evidence, that it began among the Luo in 1916.[3] It soon faded in importance, but seems to have been resuscitated in 1927 as one of several similar movements deriving from the influence of Canadian Pentecostal missionaries; it was centred on the Friends' Mission at Kaimosi.[4] It gathered more strength in 1935 under a leader Lowe, who had visions after the death of its original founder. Cult activities included drumming, speaking with tongues, and possession; tobacco and alcohol were forbidden, and members were allowed two wives each; they refused to wear European clothes. One branch refused medicine and kept the Saturday Sabbath.[5] The cult's leader was unfortunately killed while foraging for female converts among neighbouring Bantu villages.

Another early movement, although differing from the *Dini ya Roho* in not being Christian, was the Luo cult known as Mumboism. It was a retreat from western ideas, whereas the *Dini ya Roho* was rather an attempt to make a positive adjustment to western influence. The Mumbo cult began in 1921, with worship of a god Mumbo who demanded sacrifice and forbade the wearing of European clothes; members wore skins and neither cut their hair nor washed. It subsided among the Luo

---

[1] Native Affairs Department Report, 1935, pp. 7–8.
[2] Welbourn, *East African Rebels*, pp. 98, 232–3.
[3] Rawcliffe, *Struggle for Kenya*, p. 27.
[4] Welbourn, personal communication.
[5] Rawcliffe, op. cit., p. 27; Welbourn, op. cit., p. 47, and personal communication.

but in 1933 appeared among the Gusii of South Kavirondo; it was a direct consequence of the drought, locust plague, and general economic depression of the time. It died down after its leaders were deported to the coast.[1]

There were in Nyanza many adherents of the Revival movement within the Anglican Church, a movement which began in Rwanda in 1929 and spread into Uganda and Kenya.[2] A number of independent congregations in Nyanza were organized, by Archbishop Alexander's successors in Kikuyu, into the African Orthodox Church. During the Mau Mau emergency they became associated with what was by then the African Greek Orthodox Church in Uganda.[3] Welbourn suggests that the great number of independent churches in Nyanza was due largely to the confused missionary situation in the area, with many small missions, many with a 'highly congregational policy', often operating in competition. Another reason may have been the high density and the intermingling of population,[4] so that each little church may have represented a tribal segment in opposition to neighbouring segments of different tribal affiliation.

The growth of political consciousness: the Nilo-Hamites

Among the southern Nilo-Hamitic peoples of Kenya, the Masai, Nandi, and Kipsigis, the reaction to colonial rule was somewhat different from that of the agricultural Bantu tribes. The main problems of the Nilo-Hamites arose from the restriction of their traditional movement of men and herds in search of water and grazing over wide areas of the Rift Valley, much of which was taken for white settlement, and from the prohibition of their traditional raiding and warfare in search of more livestock.

Among the Masai the chief issues were those of the now unemployed warriors and of the *laibons* or prophets. The warriors, the *moran*, who would traditionally have raided and fought on behalf of the various Masai tribal groups, had no

---

[1] 'Nyangweso', 'The cult of Mumbo in central and south Kavirondo', in *Journal of the East Africa and Uganda Natural History Society*, xxxviii–xxxix (1930), 13–17.

[2] Welbourn, op. cit., p. 9.

[3] Ibid., pp. 83, 97–98, and personal communication. In 1958 there were 119 congregations thus connected in North Nyanza and two in South Nyanza, most of which were polygamous.

[4] Ibid., pp. 165–6, 168.

obvious function after the advent of administration and the cessation of warfare. Annual administration reports throughout the period complain of the 'indiscipline' of the *moran*, who seemed to be growing degenerate with nothing to do. Periodically there were affrays between the warriors of different tribal sections, and there was almost continual raiding of cattle along the borders, from the Kamba, Arusha, Gusii, Kuria, and on many occasions from European farms. It was not until after 1945 that the Administration succeeded in harnessing the energies of the warriors to some kind of tribal benefit.

Traditionally the Masai *laibons* were of three categories: diviners, rain-makers, and the senior *laibons*, one to each of the tribal groups into which the Masai were divided. These last sanctioned war and made protective war medicine, authorized the circumcision and age-set ceremonies, performed rites for the fertility of people and land, and made rain. Some of them also prophesied future events. These senior *laibons* were all members of the Il-Kidoni sub-clan of the Il-Aiser clan, and so all related. Until 1918 the chief *laibon* in Kenya, at Ngong, was accepted by the Administration as a paramount chief; but in 1918 it was recognized that in fact his authority was much more limited, and a system of Local Native Councils and locations was introduced.

About 1860 the Nandi, in imitation of Masai practice, had accepted the ritual authority of the *laibon* of the Uasin Gishu Masai, who came to live in Nandi country and was known there as *orkoiyot*. His descendant, Koitalel (also known as Samwei), was shot by the British in the Nandi rebellion of 1905, and was succeeded by other *orkoiyots* of the same clan, the Talai, and peace prevailed.[1] In 1920 100 square miles of reserve land were excised (a violation of a promise of 1907 made that the reserves would remain Nandi land for ever), and in the same year there was an outbreak of rinderpest. In 1911 the *orkoiyot* had died, to be replaced by the Administration by Arap Kipeles, the son of Koitalel's father's brother. However, the real successor was Parserion Arap Samwei, the son of Koitalel, who was violently anti-British. He plotted a rebellion in 1923 to coincide with the assembling of all Nandi warriors for the ceremony of 'handing over' by one ruling age-set to its

[1] See Chapter I above.

successors, and threatened death by witchcraft to any man who failed to attend. The Government, however, got wind of the rising, and Parserion was deported to Meru until 1930, when he again attempted to spread sedition but without success.

The Kipsigis copied the example of the Nandi, and imported one of the Nandi *orkoiyots*, Kipchomber, as their own *orkoiyot* some time before 1895. His clan soon became influential and wealthy from cattle-raiding. The *orkoiyots* arranged continual raids by Kipsigis warriors of cattle from neighbouring Luo and Bantu tribes and also from European farms. A series of reports by the Administration[1] show that the *orkoiyots*, who, as among the Nandi, were greatly feared for their powers of witchcraft as well as revered for their powers of leadership, organized an effective system for the planning of raids and the disposal of stolen cattle, of which they took a share. In 1934 it was decided to remove the entire *orkoiyot* clan from the Kipsigis reserve, and they were deported to Gwassi, in South Kavirondo, the removal being effected by 1938. Subsequently they provided great difficulties for the Administration, which felt itself responsible for their welfare, as they were not absorbed by the surrounding tribes. The main trouble was marriage, despite efforts to provide likely brides for the younger men. In 1944 an *orkoiyot* school was established at Kericho, in Kipsigis country, the scholars being allowed to marry locally with other Kipsigis.

The responses of the Nandi and Kipsigis *orkoiyots* were those of uninstitutionalized tribal leaders, the sanctions for whose powers were entirely religious ones. They attempted to continue to guide their people in traditional ways (in this case, cattle-raiding) and to stand up for them in the face of a superior colonial power. The fact that they were ritual leaders only was a main impediment to their being absorbed as chiefs into the administrative machine: attempts to turn them into chiefs with more than clan authority, as was done among the Masai, were accepted as failures, and efforts to establish efficient organs of administration among the Nilo-Hamitic pastoralists were very largely unsuccessful. Until after 1945 none of these groups, except for the Kipsigis and Nandi, took kindly to agriculture, and the virtual destruction of their traditional economies soon lost them the political pre-eminence that was theirs at the end

[1] Unpublished; now in the Secretariat library, Nairobi.

of the nineteenth century. Thereafter, however, both became prosperous as agriculturalists, the Kipsigis in particular developing progressive agricultural techniques which were to place them in the vanguard of the 'progressive' peoples of Kenya.

The Nilo-Hamitic tribes seem not to have been affected by separatist cults, except for the remote Suk. In 1935 an epileptic adherent of the Friends' Mission, Elijah Masindi, who had played football for Kenya, left the mission after having been refused permission to take a second wife; he married the wife and set up a new faith known as *Dini ya Masambwa* ('religion of the spirits of the dead'). He prophesied that the tribal dead would reappear and that the perfect traditional way of life would be revived. This group came into prominence after 1945, with the killing of several policemen, after the leader had been certified insane but released from asylum.[1]

The growth of national consciousness: the minor tribes

Outside these main clusters, the Kikuyu, the Nyanza peoples, and the Nilo-Hamitic pastoralists, change was not as clearly marked during this period, although the general trend among some of the other tribes was similar. Among the Meru and Embu, for example, small tribes to the north of Kikuyu and closely related to them, the traditional organs of local government, the councils of elders and young men, had been reorganized by the Embu as early as 1923, mainly in efforts to control heavy drinking among young men, a sign of dissolution of tribal authority. Despite the lack of information available, today it is clear that these northern tribes were not living in peace and contentment, but that there was continual unrest and confusion just under the surface. They were not, indeed, directly affected by the presence of white settlers living on what they claimed to be their lands. The racial bitterness was absent, but other factors of change were present. Although Christian independent churches and schools spread among both Meru and Embu during the 1930's,[2] on the whole the response to modern change was the appearance of secret societies, to which adherents were bound by secret oaths, a sign of internal ferment concerned with matters such as the conflict of authority between young and old rather than with xenophobic sentiment. Such

[1] Rawcliffe, op. cit., p. 28.   [2] Welbourn, op. cit., pp. 156–7

societies included the Athi society, which probably went back
to pre-British times, but which came to be a group that terrorized the population into providing them with meat and other
objects. Adherents joined by oath-taking, and after the group's
suppression the tribe was cleansed by special medicine-men,
a foreshadowing of the oathing rites which were later to become
so marked among the Kikuyu tribes.[1] The 1923 Native Affairs
Department Report refers to a poisoning league called *Mndio*,
which tried to combat witchcraft, usually a sign of increased
social tension, and to curb the growing power of unpopular
chiefs and headmen.[2] A society called *Kagitha* is also mentioned,
the members of which contented themselves with dancing and
sexual orgies.[3]

On the coast, except for the Teita and Giryama—tribes much
affected by labour migration to the growing port of Mombasa
and the European plantations on the coast to the north of
Mombasa—the general story was one of stagnation—economic
and social. The Giryama had been the first large tribe in Kenya
to be deeply affected by European impact. Missionaries worked
among and near them from the mid-nineteenth century, and
for centuries before that, of course, they had been in close
contact with Arabs, who even in the twentieth century regarded
themselves as the natural overlords of these humble savages.
In 1914 came the Giryama rising, led by prophetesses ('witch-
doctors' in the official reports of the time). This amounted to
a refusal to pay tax and to send out young men as labourers for
government projects and to nearby European plantations, set
in what the Giryama claimed to be their own traditional home-
lands. The prophetesses attempted to invoke the spirits of tribal
ancestors at the Giryama *kaya*, or fortified citadel, where these
spirits lived. The revolt was soon put down, and the Giryama
reverted to a state of resignation and despondency which was
to last until the second world war.[4] The Duruma, south of
Mombasa, boycotted government-appointed headmen in 1922
and 1923, and forced the Government to appoint the members
of the *ngambi*, the traditional Duruma organ of government,
in their place. The Teita, although supplying many men as

[1] Rawcliffe, op. cit., p. 30.
[2] Native Affairs Department Report, 1923.   [3] Rawcliffe, op. cit., p. 30.
[4] See annual reports of the Native Affairs Department during this period.

labourers to Mombasa, remained, in the words of the Native Affairs Department Report for 1927, 'placid and contented ... their particular vice is drink'. The wretched Pokomo of the Tana river were, according to the 1925 report, 'pleasant featured, timid, shy, simple-minded, ignorant, unambitious, unenter-prising, lethargic, disease-racked', which presumably implied that they were not, at any rate, organizing themselves into politically active associations; and of the Taveta the 1927 Report stated merely that 'their traditional customs are un-speakable' and that they had a rooted antipathy to work. It was not until after the second world war that the coastal tribes began organized political activity, when they established the *Miji Kenda* Union (the Nine Towns Union), referring to the traditional nine tribes of the Nyika, the coastal desert region.

The emergent society

By the close of the period, that is by the end of the second world war, certain changes were discernible in the form of Kenya society, marked by the decreasing importance of tradi-tional social groupings—especially those based upon kinship—and the emergence of 'individualization' on the one hand, and of new occupational, religious, and political associations on the other.

The concept of 'individualization' implies here the appearance of the individual as the unit of production and of residence. A single man, often helped by his wife and children, came to be the producer of cash crops, or the labourer or squatter in urban and rural areas alike. Women also moved to the towns to work, as individuals.[1] The traditional lineage and neighbourhood work-groups, although still functioning in many areas,[2] were losing importance. Ties and obligations of kinship and neigh-bourhood were irksome to the men who could earn money and aspired to a new way and standard of living. Individual

---

[1] One consequence was the large number of associations which appeared at this time whose main aims were to return women to their tribal areas, and especially to prevent prostitution.

[2] Efforts were often made to use these groups within a modern framework of cash-crop farming, See, for example, N. Humphrey, *The Liguru and the Land* (Nairobi, 1947); J. Hughes Rice, 'Soil conservation organization in Fort Hall District as adapted from the indigenous "Ngwatio" system', *E.A. Agricultural Journal*, xii (1947), 200.

ownership of property, especially in money, and in some places of land, was developing, with consequent changes in the respective roles of senior and junior men in the traditional system. Distinctions of wealth and power appeared within tribal units where traditionally there had been few or none. People emerged with more wealth than anyone could formerly have possessed, and, significantly, these were generally drawn from those who were not traditionally the holders of wealth or power. There was a marked increase in social mobility, both in spatial terms, with widespread labour migration to the towns and European farming areas, and also in class terms, with the growth of incipient classes and class distinctions.

The second world war was an event of major importance for the peoples of Kenya. Out of a total of 280,000 men recruited into the East African Forces (including men from Nyasaland, Northern Rhodesia, and British Somaliland, as well as from the East African territories proper), some 75,000 came from Kenya, a figure representing a little under 20 per cent. of its total adult male African population. During the war a considerable amount of money in family allowances was paid into the reserves, and in most areas the demand for agricultural and livestock products by the army ensured a steady market for those tribes able to produce for it. Against this were the absence of men, the direction of other men on to European farms as essential labour, and the dearth of administrative and technical government officers to organize agricultural output and social development.

But the main consequence was certainly the immense widening of the experience of most of the men recruited. Many served in the Middle East and the Far East, as well as nearer home in other parts of Kenya, Madagascar, and Ethiopia. They came into contact with men of other tribes, and with Europeans, Indians, and Arabs of all classes. They saw that the traditional superiority of European and Asian was by no means accepted outside East Africa. And in their army training they were given both formal and informal education—it was, for example, the policy of the army to make as many *askari* as possible literate and also able to speak basic English. Many soldiers received technical training of various kinds, and after the end of the Japanese war the army opened schools of general and technical training, at a simple level, for soldiers before their disbandment. Although the prognostications of many officials in 1945—that the experiences of the troops would lead to immediate disturbances after their return to the reserves— were not fulfilled in the event, none the less these experiences were to have a lasting effect. In the more remote areas soldiers seem to have settled down again into tribal life without much stress. But in the more 'progressive' areas there were many changes. For the first time Africans entered into retail trade in large numbers in direct and open competition with Indian traders; they also entered the market as buyers of local produce, in which they had a considerable advantage over the Indians, and in both Nyanza and Kikuyu they captured a large share of this trade. Their position as retailers was recognized by the Government, who fixed quotas for the distribution of retail goods so that Africans could not be squeezed out by the refusal of Indian wholesalers to deal with them.[1]

The economy of the African areas in the years during and immediately after the war was a prosperous one for those which could produce cash crops or meat. In 1948, for example, well over £1,000,000 came into the Central Province reserves in exchange for exports of wattle bark, vegetables, eggs, and other produce, and exports from Nyanza Province, mainly cereals and animal products, were worth over £500,000. The coast and the main cattle-rearing areas of northern Kenya also had a large export trade.[2]

Besides the primarily political[3] African associations that developed during the period before the second world war, there were many others, in most cases short-lived, and with a bewildering history of schism, amalgamation, and frequent changes of name.[4] The continual founding and splitting of small

[1] See Report of the Native Affairs Department, 1946–7, pp. 69–70.

[2] See ibid., 1948, p. 48.

[3] It is, of course, not possible to say that the associations which have been mentioned were purely political. The Kikuyu Central Association, for example, had in 1931 as one of its objectives 'the negotiation and settlement of differences that may arise between members of the Association and employers . . . by means of collective bargaining or agreement or by other legal action'. *East African Standard*, 9 May 1931; quoted by Mary Parker, *Municipal Government*.

[4] Amalgamations and divisions tended to reflect divisions in local society. For example, the Report of the Native Affairs Department, 1946–7, stated that the Kikuyu General Union 'had to contend with a host of fragmentary bodies representing age-grades, locations and sub-locations. Many of these were short-lived and came to grief through peculation of funds' (p. 81).

groups of this kind owed much to European and Indian example;[1] associations, both political and occupational, were organized by both European and Indian groups early in the period. An Indian Association was founded in Mombasa in 1900. In the early years of the century various European planters' and settlers' associations were formed, mostly based on a particular area. Eight associations and two chambers of commerce amalgamated to form in 1910 the Convention of Associations, a group that was to have very considerable political and other influence in Kenya in the succeeding years.[2] In 1918 was founded the Asian Railway Union, and in 1934 the Indian Trade Union of Kenya, which in 1936 widened both its ethnical and territorial range to become the Labour Trade Union of East Africa. The Chief Native Commissioner in his annual report for 1926 made the somewhat jaundiced remark:

From observation I am satisfied that native indiscipline, whether individual or corporate, is born of non-native indiscipline. Natives see non-Natives commit offences against law, custom or good manners, sometimes with comparative impunity, and naturally think that they can do the same. Native agitators take their cue from non-Native agitators, and native political bodies adopt their tone and seek to emulate what they gather to be their attitude towards those whose views or interests do not coincide with theirs and towards constituted authority.[3]

And ten years later, Leakey wrote:

Another result of the perusal of the reports of political meetings held by settlers, is that the Africans get the impression that so long as a group of people call themselves an 'Association', they are entitled to attack Government as much as they like! Consequently not a few active political associations have been formed.[4]

African associations were of many types: occupational, tribal benefit, residential benefit, tribal recreational, residential re-

---

[1] Besides the example of European and Indian associations, there was also at several periods direct personal influence by individual European and Indian helpers on African associations. The former included many missionaries, such as Archdeacon Owen in Nyanza; most of the latter seem to have been more overtly political in their interests and are therefore often referred to in reports as 'agitators'. The names of many, of both races, are given by McGregor Ross, Welbourn, Bennett, &c.   [2] Ross, *Kenya from Within*, ch. x, and Chapter VI above.

[3] Native Affairs Department Report, 1926, pp. 8–10.

[4] L. S. B. Leakey, *Kenya* (London, 1936), p. 110; quoted in Welbourn, op. cit., p. 123.

creational, tribal political, nationalist political, trade union, class, tribal religious, and national religious. None of these various categories were exclusive: a tribal dancing club would always have political overtones, sometimes in tribal terms, sometimes as being restricted to members who performed in European evening dress, an important symbol of wealth and class-consciousness. A welfare or commercial association was bound in time to become anti-European or anti-Indian or to lose its membership, finding that its activities were directed against Indian traders, European farmers or missionaries, or government chiefs, who were seen as the agents of the central government. And tribal or residential groupings (often the two criteria were co-terminous) tended to develop into trans-tribal groups. Occupational associations, moreover, often followed tribal or residential lines. In Mombasa, for instance, there were after the second world war associations of traders, barbers, charcoal sellers, chicken and egg dealers, all of which tended to be Kikuyu: the barbers came mostly from Fort Hall, the charcoal burners and sellers from Nyeri. There were also Meru snuff sellers, Luhya basketwork sellers, Kamba and Luo handicraft hawkers, Luo domestic servants, while Kamba tended to predominate in technical work for the railway and post office. In Nairobi there were similar tribal-occupational associations, including Kikuyu eating-house keepers and landlords—the landlords of Pumwani location banded themselves together as the Pumwani Housing Committee. In Mombasa, faced with Indian expansion into formerly African quarters, they formed the Mombasa Landless Houseowners' Association.[1] It has been pointed out that these occupational associations were moved not so much by the spirit of the medieval guild as by that of the American trade protection society.[2] Many of them were extremely wealthy: in 1945 the Nairobi Eating House Keepers Association bought property in the Nairobi Bazaar for £15,000, and the payment of even larger sums for Nairobi properties is mentioned.[3]

The ending of the war in 1945 saw a remarkable growth in the number of African associations: an army report in that year

[1] Parker, op. cit., p. 38.
[2] Nairobi *M.A.A.O. Report, 1941*, quoted in Parker, op. cit., p. 38.
[3] Parker, op. cit., p. 22.

lists 200 of them, many very ephemeral, reported by East
African soldiers. Of these thirty-eight were Kenya tribal welfare
and educational associations and twenty-two were commercial
and co-operative associations; in both cases the majority were
in Kikuyu and Luhya. Comparatively few were avowedly
political, but it is significant that these included most of the
associations of long standing—the remainder of these long-
established ones being mainly religious movements which were
essentially political in significance. There the Kenya
African Study Union, which ran its own newspaper, *Sauti ya
Mwafrika*—'The Voice of the African'—and which aimed at a
pan-tribal movement for Kenya; the Kikuyu Central Association, with Jomo Kenyatta as its representative in England;
the Kikuyu Provincial Association, led by Harry Thuku; and
three associations from the coast—the Coast African Association, the *Miji Kenda* Union (the 'Nine Towns' of the nine
tribes of the coast), and the Teita Hills Association. These were
all important, well founded, financed, and administered, all
except Harry Thuku's group anti-Government, and all connected with both religious and trade union activities.

A later list of associations, compiled in 1947,[1] shows changes
in emphasis. Of the further 130 African associations known in
Kenya alone over fifty were restricted to Kikuyu, and in many
of the others in Nairobi Kikuyu certainly predominated. On the
other hand, only twelve had education as their explicit aim,
and only nine were overtly religious—fifty being tribal welfare
associations with various aims[2] and fifty commercial and trading associations.[3] These last reflected the appearance of a new
mercantile class in African Kenya.

An African middle class was clearly emerging. The term
'middle class' implies a position in a total class system which
covers all sections of Kenya society, despite the distinctions
so often held between members of different racial groups.
The new African middle class took its main criteria from the

---

[1] In the Secretariat library, Nairobi, unpublished.
[2] Some were ex-soldiers' associations, others groups of tribesmen who were
labour migrants in one of the towns; several were formed to improve the status of
women—all, however, apparently composed of men with the exception of the
Tumu Tumu Fashion Girls, whose aim was to reduce the inflationary amount of
bridewealth payable, which was condemning them to perennial spinsterhood.
[3] Over half in Nairobi, and at least twenty of them Kikuyu.

European ways of living; clothing, house, use of English, a fairly high educational standard, Christian monogamy, and importance attached more to trans-tribal class ties than to purely tribal and kinship bonds. In short, this class consisted of members of different tribes who regarded themselves as having thrown off the shackles of tribal loyalties and ignorance; they saw themselves as the vanguard of a new African way of life.

Like all classes and groups, and especially new ones, they had a mythology and a common aim; otherwise they would have formed not a class but merely a collection of ambitious individuals. Yet these were—perhaps by their very nature—in contradiction. And it is from this contradiction that there sprang so much of the internecine hostility and strife between modern African political and industrial leaders. The mythology relates to the past, the aims to the future. The past was one of tribal exploits and grandeur, one of a peaceful and perfect tribal life, in which ties of fraternal kinship between tribesmen and of wise guidance and authority between young and old were idyllic and without strain or stress. The future was to be one of a perfect life for all the peoples of Kenya—certainly all the African peoples—in which tribalism, and at least by implication traditional kinship and authority, would have no place. The aim was to succeed to European wealth, power, and education, things which in their very nature could mean only the destruction of tribal life.

The mythology of a perfect African past is expressed in several books published by Africans of the period. The best-known and perhaps the most telling, as it was written by a man who had had every opportunity to acquire an objective knowledge of Kenya's traditional life, was Jomo Kenyatta's *Facing Mount Kenya*, published in 1938. This, an anthropological account of the Kikuyu, contained much material which is historically inaccurate; it provided a pseudo-scientific mythology for the Kikuyu. What was significant was that in seeing the need for such a mythology, which would at least imply that all that was unlovely in contemporary African life was due to the Europeans, it was necessary to describe a past in tribal terms. To describe a general idyllic past for Kenya would have been impossible: a Kikuyu, for example, could hardly idyllize the past of his traditional enemies the Masai.

The future aim was, at least until the end of the second world war, only vaguely defined. First much had to be done in an immediate present: to open the White Highlands to African use, to break the hold of the Asians on wholesale and retail trade, to rid the educational system of mission control, and even to secure enough money and food to bring up a family in the material ways both elders and missionaries laid down as being desirable. The overall European enemy was there, to provide a common sense of grievance and justification for political activity, independent schools, and the rest. The wider aims of a pan-African state were little discussed in this period. And it must be emphasized that any such political discussions, even after 1945, let alone during the 1930's, were confined to a numerically minute fringe of educated men drawn mainly from the larger agricultural tribes. The more distant aims were difficult to define as well as to realize, because of the insidious appeal to tribal loyalties. If the White Highlands were to be opened up, how would they be distributed? They had never been in Kikuyu territory, so why should Kikuyu enter them? Any organization with members from many tribes had to have leaders, but from which tribes should they be drawn? In 1945 there were many lines of dissension apparent: pastoralists against agriculturalists, Bantu Kavirondo against Luo of Kavirondo, all other tribes against the Kikuyu. This last antagonism became very apparent when the Mau Mau movement failed so signally to spread beyond the borders of Kikuyu.

In short, the tribalist had become the nationalist—had had to become so if he were ever to be more than a petty local politician. As nationalist he was bound to appeal for popular support to a racialism in which the enemy was obvious but whose overthrow could lead to a resurgence of tribal antagonism. Fifteen years after the end of the period covered by this chapter this same dilemma was still only too apparent and perhaps still as difficult of solution.

Map 6. Uganda: Administration and Communications, 1939–40.

VIII

THE UGANDA ECONOMY
1903–1945

CYRIL EHRLICH

THROUGHOUT the modern history of Uganda the principal determinant of economic growth has been the condition of world markets for certain primary commodities. It was a temporary shortage of cotton in the early years of the century which gave the first impulse to what was to become the country's principal export. It was the collapse in prices of 1920 which crippled plantation agriculture and emphasized the already emerging dominance of peasant production in the economy. It was the enormous rise in cotton and coffee prices after 1943 which made possible the great social progress which the country enjoyed in the immediate post-war years. It has become fashionable to decry the dependence of 'underdeveloped' countries upon a few staple exports and the vagaries of world markets. But a preoccupation with the need for an ill-defined 'stabilization' should not blind us to the fact that most of the development which has taken place has been due to the existence of such markets and the ability of primitive economies to enter them. Professor Frankel has powerfully argued this thesis: that the discovery or propagation of viable export crops is perhaps 'the most important single factor in the economic development of backward areas'.[1] The economic history of Uganda offers striking evidence for this view.

Within the limits set by this dependence upon world markets three separate groups have shaped the evolving pattern of Uganda's economy: the Administration, Indian immigrants, and, often more acted upon than acting, the indigenous peoples. Others have, on occasion, made their presence felt. The missions were, of course, an omnipresent influence, notably in the field

---

[1] S. H. Frankel, 'United Nations primer for development: reply', *Quarterly Journal of Economics*, lxvii (1953), 280–5.

of education, though neither the Catholic nor the Protestant ethic did much to engender a spirit of capitalism among their converts. Another important group, at least up to 1921, were the European planters, who, astonishing as this seems to contemporary Ugandans, once constituted a substantial and inevitably articulate and influential class. But essentially the economic history of Uganda is one of the three separate groups symbolized by Entebbe, 'an exquisite oasis of order in the rank untidiness of Africa',[1] the duka town, and the shamba, less tidy, but no less fruitful of economic growth.

For all three groups, though they have not always seen it in these terms, the essential problem has been the creation of a viable economy; above all, the production of exports that could be sold to the rest of the world. By 1903 the railway had linked a land-locked Uganda with the world economy, but the link was slender and fragile. Exports were negligible and their main item, ivory, was a wasting asset. Yet both Government and people desired the products of the developed world. The Government saw its immediate task as the production of a local revenue which would emancipate it from subservience to a parsimonious British Treasury. Less urgently, but fairly consistently throughout our period, official policy was motivated by the desire to prove that Uganda was an economic asset and not merely a strategic and evangelical acquisition. This was to be achieved by making Uganda a useful market for British products, an aim which was hampered by an open-door policy, based on the Congo Basin treaties,[2] that gave Ugandans the full benefit of cheap foreign manufactured goods, and by an occasional reluctance on the part of British manufacturers to compete in a difficult field. More dubious was the belief that Uganda might supply cheap tropical goods to the mother country, an idea which found its strongest advocacy in the years immediately following the first world war, when goods were scarce and universal elixirs abundant. But such aberrations were short lived, and it is noteworthy that Uganda's principal export has gone mainly to India rather than to Lancashire, the home of the Empire cotton movement. This absence of metropolitan

---

[1] G. H. Jones, *Uganda in Transformation, 1876-1926* (C.M.S., London, 1926), p. 52.
[2] See Chapter V, p. 250, n. 2, above.

greed for exports or import markets leaves slight opportunity for the historian who would interpret Uganda's story in Marxist terms of imperialist exploitation; nevertheless, at least one writer has not been deterred by these facts.[1]

For traders and peasants the immediate motives were simpler. To the Indian immigrant trader Uganda offered the opportunity of making good in a country where his skills and aptitudes were scarce and valuable. For the African peasant economic development promised a new and better life—for though it is not the economist's task to pontificate upon ultimate values, it must be emphasized that economic development involves the widening of men's access to alternatives. Moreover, it is certain that in Uganda there was never any question of foisting 'meretricious trade goods' upon a reluctant naïve populace. The peoples of Uganda, despite that high preference for leisure which is common among pre-industrial men, eagerly demanded the products of the developed world. In 1893 Lugard was convinced that 'all the wants of an infant civilization are present—tools, utensils, glass, stationery, anything and everything'.[2] By 1900 Johnston, the Special Commissioner, reported that they were 'greedy for cloth and for almost every manufactured article up to a phonograph and a brougham'.[3] They lacked only the means with which to make these demands effective.

Uganda in 1903

In 1903, ten years after the assumption of the British protectorate, the economy of Uganda was essentially one of peasant subsistence production, with markets and cash playing only a peripheral role, and barely that outside Buganda. Internal sources of government revenue were quite inadequate for the provision of even basic administrative services; a grant-in-aid from the British Treasury paid for some 84 per cent. of government expenditure. Exports were limited in quantity and value. Ivory, valued at £26,000, was by far the largest item, but even this was a rapidly diminishing asset.

[1] R. Mukherjee, *The Problem of Uganda: a study in acculturation* (Berlin, Akademie-Verlag, 1956).

[2] F. D. Lugard, *The Rise of our East African Empire* (2 vols., Edinburgh, 1893), i. 401.

[3] H. Johnston, 'Preliminary Report on the Protectorate of Uganda'. Enclosed in Johnston to Salisbury, 27 Apr. 1900, F.O. 2/298.

The native population of the country, after the loss of the old Eastern Province to the East Africa Protectorate, was perhaps some $3\frac{1}{2}$ million.[1] The immigrant population consisted of some 200 Europeans and about 500 Asians; the former consisting predominantly of missionaries and administrative and military officers, the latter of traders. This population occupied an area of some 94,000 square miles (of which about 14,000 square miles is open water), an average of between 40 and 45 persons a square mile. But the density varied considerably, from perhaps 6 per square mile in Karamoja to over 100 in parts of Buganda and the Eastern Province.

There were considerable regional differences in habitat and economy, and these differences persisted throughout our period or were perhaps even widened. Where communications are poor, economic history is perforce regional history, and in a real sense there was no 'Uganda economy', for no unifying market existed. Such differences were not solely a matter of physical environment and location; differences in social structure were perhaps of equal importance. Probably the most useful classification for our purpose is that which distinguishes the area inhabited by the 'interlacustrine Bantu'[2] from the rest of the Protectorate. The former area, consisting of the whole of Uganda to the west and south of the Victoria Nile with an extension eastwards in Busoga, contained peoples whose societies were comparatively advanced before the coming of British administration. Outstanding among these interlacustrine societies, of course, were the Ganda. These were a permanently settled banana-growing people whose system of agriculture was essentially individualistic, in contrast to those of most other traditional East African societies, and maintained the people at a tolerable level of subsistence. Ganda traditional society was strongly ranked, with considerable inequalities of power and even of wealth. Chiefs enjoyed a style of life appropriate to their station, and peasants were accustomed to accept such power and wealth as the normal perquisites of the 'upper classes', though some social mobility was possible, mainly through

[1] See R. R. Kuczynski, *Demographic Survey of the British Colonial Empire*, vol. ii (London, 1949), 235–9, for a detailed analysis of the various estimates of population at this period.

[2] Cf. A. I. Richards in *East African Chiefs* (London, 1960), ch. i.

patronage at the Kabaka's court. Admittedly such differences in the social scale can be exaggerated. Except in a purely quantitative sense a chief's material standard of life differed little from the peasant's; his hut was merely a big hut and his food equally monotonous. Yet all this stands in marked contrast to the virtually 'chiefless' society of the Gisu of Mount Elgon, for example, and was a factor of considerable importance in the later development of the Protectorate.

Instruments of change, 1903–13

It was Uganda's good fortune that, at the very time that the Administration was becoming concerned with the development of a viable export crop, world market conditions were uniquely favourable for such experiments. Markets for raw materials were buoyant and prices were commencing their first considerable upsurge for a generation.[1] Most important, raw cotton prices were rising steadily. Many mills in the United States, England, and on the Continent were running short time because of the scarcity of raw material. In Europe this led to a revival of the cotton scare, with its attendant interest in the promotion of raw material supplies alternative to the American source, which had been forgotten since the American Civil War. In 1901 a committee of the Oldham Chamber of Commerce began to lobby the Colonial Office and colonial officials on the subject, and published a report which maintained that 'suitable cotton for the Lancashire trade could be grown in various parts of the British Empire'.[2] This report was circulated among other Lancashire chambers of commerce and a powerful pressure group began to take shape. In June 1902 the British Cotton Growing Association was formally inaugurated. The cornering of the American cotton market by Sully in the following year, raising the price from $5\frac{3}{4}d$. in 1903 to $9d$. in January 1904, added a further stimulus to the Empire cotton movement. By 1904 the question was of sufficient importance to be included in the King's Speech: 'The insufficiency of the supply of raw material upon which the great cotton industry of this country depends

[1] In 1906 Sauerbeck's Index of Raw Material Prices reached 83, its highest level since 1880.

[2] J. A. Hutton, *The Work of the British Cotton Growing Association* (Manchester, 1914).

has inspired me with deep concern. I trust that the efforts which are being made in various parts of my Empire to increase the area under cultivation may be attended with a large measure of success.'[1]

Uganda's first bid for economic development was therefore well timed. But if we are to explain the country's response to this buoyant market we must look for the initiators of economic change. We shall find them among government officers, anxious to initiate cash crops so that taxes might be paid; among traders and planters seeking a profit; and among some of the indigenous people themselves, groping hesitantly towards a new form of economic life.

The Government's problem was simple to define but inordinately difficult to resolve. Its most pressing need was a continuous and increasing flow of revenue with which to finance its multifarious tasks, for at that time Imperial financial policy was one of self-sufficiency, in contrast to later ideas of development and welfare. In every year since the beginning of British rule the Uganda Government's revenue had been totally inadequate to meet even a modest level of expenditure. The gulf was bridged by annual grants-in-aid from the British Treasury, but it seemed self-evident to the early commissioners and governors that one of their first duties was to end this state of affairs. 'I cannot tell you how earnestly I look forward to a fair return from native taxation during the current year,' wrote Johnston to Bishop Tucker in 1900, 'more than anything else this will encourage the British Treasury to keep its heart and to go on for some time supplying funds for the development of Uganda.'[2] Not that that organ was ever greatly overworked on Uganda's behalf. The total of British grants-in-aid, for the whole period from 1893 until their cessation in 1915, amounted to a mere £2½ million. This could have put little strain on an economy whose national income was about £2,000 million in 1911, and whose public expenditure, even in 1900, was some £35 million.

Direct taxation was established in 1900 with the imposition of a hut tax of 3 rupees (4s.). But in the absence of cash people were at first allowed to pay in labour or produce. Moreover, the

---

[1] *Hansard*, 4th ser., H. of C. 129. 4, 2 Feb. 1904.
[2] Johnston to Tucker, 13 May 1900, Entebbe Secretariat Archives (hereinafter 'E.S.A.') A7/6/Misc.

demonetization of cowrie shells in 1901 greatly inhibited the peasant's ability to pay in cash. The resulting influx of goods was embarrassing in its diversity and inutility. Only about two-thirds of the first year's nominal collection of £82,000 was actually received in cash or in ivory which was easily sold. The remainder was paid either collectively in elephants (one young live elephant paid for 1,000 huts), hippopotami (100 huts), and zebras (20 huts), or individually in pigs or one month's labour. The Government's attempts to convert these into cash met with some success at Entebbe, but in outlying districts gluts at collection points resulted in prices which were absurdly low. In succeeding years the system was more carefully organized. Payment in livestock or perishable foodstuffs was discouraged except where a market was assured. Minimum acceptable prices for tax produce were announced, and merchants were required to bid at auctions as the goods came in. Representative minimum prices in Buganda in 1904, for example, were 1 rupee for 40 lb. of ground-nuts or simsim, 20 lb. of chillies, 25 lb. of unhusked coffee, or 10 lb. of cotton. It was hoped in this way to encourage the cultivation of a wide range of produce.[1]

The payment of hut tax in labour presented many problems. It was difficult to supervise except in the immediate vicinity of an administrative station. Chiefs were sometimes unscrupulous in their interpretation of the law. They would send 'old, decrepit and footsore Wanyoro' into Entebbe, or would pay the tax in cash on behalf of their tenants and then exact work from them on their personal estates for anything up to five instead of the legal one month.[2]

By 1904 hut tax in the vicinity of Kampala was generally paid in specie. The local administrator even complained that it was difficult to procure sufficient labour for government porterage. Considerable increases in revenue were secured by 'constant stimulation of rivalry between the *saza* chiefs as regards their returns'. Thus in the Kakumiro District of Buganda hut tax proceeds increased from 3,871 rupees in 1903 to 12,951 rupees in the following year. But it was very different in outlying districts where, as one administrator complained, 'markets are few and traders practically absent'. A severe famine in Busoga in

[1] *Uganda Gazette*, 15 Oct. 1903.
[2] Jackson to Lansdowne, 13 July 1901, F.O. No. 145, p. 218.

1908, and the appalling sleeping sickness epidemic which resulted in the death of tens of thousands of taxpayers, were also great setbacks to the collection of revenue.

It was self-evident that the solution of Uganda's economic problem, both in the narrow administrative sense of providing revenue, and the broader economic sense of developing a backward society, lay in the establishment of an exchange economy. For this to succeed markets were essential: lack of markets is one of the principal features of a primitive economy. In many areas the mere establishment of law and order provided some inducement to truck and barter, and the improvement of communications was another obviously vital task facing the Administration. But in the absence of any tradition of indigenous enterprise, or of large-scale concessions to immigrant settlers, the Government's role, while scarcely embracing that 'practical experiment in State socialism' advocated by Winston Churchill,[1] extended far beyond the mere establishment of 'peace, justice and roads', to the active promotion of economic development. And all this was to be done on the proverbial shoestring.

While the encouragement of local markets was an important part of this process, the most vital need was for a viable export crop, and much of the Administration's slender resources was expended on propaganda to this end. Thus the collectors in Ankole and Toro were urged to 'impress on the chiefs the importance of inducing their people to work up all the products their country is capable of producing as it is the only means by which they may hope to progress'.[2] In similar vein, a charming letter from Hayes Sadler to the 'Kabaka' of Toro urged: 'My Friend . . . advise your chiefs and people to grow produce for sale. I wish to see Toro advance like Uganda [i.e. Buganda] and the other parts of the Protectorate, and I think this is also your wish.'[3]

The fact that cotton proved to be, overwhelmingly, the successful answer to these prayers must not be allowed to obscure the fact that many crops were tried. M. J. Dawe, of the Scientific and Forestry Department, forerunner of the Agricultural Department, would tour the country advising Africans on the cultivation of a wide range of experimental

---

[1] W. S. Churchill, *My African Journey* (London, 1908), p. 123.
[2] 28 Aug. 1905, E.S.A. A14/2.   [3] 1 Nov. 1905, E.S.A. A14/3.

crops—cotton, coffee, rubber, chillies, wheat, simsim, ground-nuts, sugar. It was even thought that tea, cacao, and vanilla might prosper on the Sesse islands. Great hopes were set on sansevieria, and enthusiastic claims were made on its behalf, but nothing came of it. Results with other crops were similarly disappointing.

There was thus nothing premeditated or inevitable about the emergence of cotton as the dominating crop. To the Administration the problem was simply to find something—anything—which would provide a healthy base for development and replace slaves and ivory, those well-matched bed-mates of the primitive economy.

Cotton had long been known in Uganda; it was noted between 1862 and 1893 by Speke, by Baker, by Emin, and by Lugard. But before 1903 its commercial value was negligible. The question as to who deserves the credit for introducing cotton as an economic crop has been a matter of some controversy. Probably Kristen Borup, a Danish lay missionary of the Church Missionary Society and later first manager of the Uganda Company, was the first to import seed.[1] But it would certainly be difficult to exaggerate the importance of the Government's role in establishing Uganda's cotton industry. In April 1904 it imported 1½ tons of three different types of cotton seed from the Khedivial Agricultural Society of Egypt and distributed it among selected chiefs 'for trial cultivation by peasants in all likely and accessible parts of the Protectorate'.[2] Such was the interest among chiefs that a further 3 tons of seed were distributed that September, mainly in Buganda, Bunyoro, and Busoga. Different types of seed were issued in an attempt to discover which strains were most suited to the local conditions. This mixture of seeds was to contribute to a major crisis a few years later. Meanwhile the Uganda Company had distributed a further 2½ tons of five different types of seed among twenty-seven chiefs in eight districts of Buganda. At the first harvest it was evident that the American seed which had been distributed by the Uganda Company was by far the most successful, so the Government procured another ton of this and gave it out in

---

[1] Cf. C. Ehrlich, *The Uganda Company Ltd.: the first fifty years* (Kampala, 1953), ch. iii.

[2] 5 July 1908, E.S.A. 759/09.

Buganda, Busoga, Bunyoro, and Ankole. It should be noted that these initial distributions of seed extended throughout the administered area of Uganda.

Instructions to cultivators were rudimentary and optimistic. A pamphlet was issued to advise them 'on the preparation of commercial products', with notes on ramie, rubber, ground-nuts, chillies, simsim, and cotton, offering further evidence that cotton was at first regarded merely as one among many possible crops. Three tiny experimental stations were established to investigate suitable varieties of seed and soil, but growers were meanwhile advised that 'the best strains and most prolific varieties' could be secured by selecting seed from heavily bearing plants. The encouragement of hand-ginning also appeared to be a reasonable policy, for there were no power-ginneries outside Kampala, where the Uganda Company had erected one in 1904. Ginning separates cotton by weight into approximately two parts seed and one part lint; with poor and costly transport it was therefore obviously desirable to gin as near to the fields as possible. Sixty-two hand-gins were there-fore sold at £1 each, and another forty-three were given away to chiefs. Men who were completely ignorant of the simplest form of machine were then expected to use these gins with the aid of an instructional pamphlet and occasional demonstrations at administrative centres.

It is hardly surprising that these 'do it yourself' attempts to encourage the rapid spread of cultivation, while unavoidable in the absence of adequate staff and resources, led to serious quality problems within a few seasons. Yet their success in starting the industry is an important demonstration of how much can be achieved by the often underrated effects of en-thusiasm and a healthy market. By 1907-8 nearly 4,000 bales of cotton were produced, worth more than £51,000, and equivalent to about 35 per cent. of the total value of Uganda's exports.

In 1907, however, alarming reports began to come in from the British Cotton Growing Association on the state of cotton arriving from Uganda. Much of it was badly stained, and several different varieties would commonly be mixed in the same bale. This state of affairs, was, of course, anathema to spinners, who require clean cotton of consistent strain. Moreover, it was thought to be a dangerous situation for a country whose product was new to the world and had yet to establish a firm reputation in a highly selective market. The B.C.G.A., which existed for this very purpose, directed a stream of propaganda on this subject towards the Colonial Office and the Uganda Administration, and made a personal approach to the Governor, Hesketh Bell, when he visited England in 1907. Some of this was, perhaps, exaggerated by professional enthusiasm leading to an undue emphasis upon 'quality production' of a new cash crop. But at this early stage it seemed evident that drastic steps would have to be taken if Uganda cotton was ever to gain a firm hold in world markets.

The cotton legislation of 1908 completely reversed official policy in a vigorous attempt to establish the industry on a sound basis. Only one type of seed was to be grown, which was distributed by the Government. All cotton plants were to be destroyed after the harvest had been gathered. To stop bad ginning and prevent the use of inferior seed, all hand-gins were withdrawn and destroyed. As Hesketh Bell admitted, such drastic legislation was only feasible in a country enjoying the 'somewhat unusual conditions applying in Uganda'. Such was the authority of the chiefs that their 'bare orders' were sufficient to ensure the effective execution of these drastic demands. Bell also declared that the regents[1] and chiefs 'readily appreciated the necessity for maintaining a high standard in the quality of cotton exported'.[2] In practice, however, government inspectors toured the country to ensure that the rules were obeyed.

It was a dangerous gamble to attempt such ruthless reforms in a society whose people were only just beginning to accept a new crop. As the manager of the Uganda Company reported to his directors: 'In seeking to improve the cotton there is no small danger that they may improve it altogether away.'[3] Yet the effects of this draconian policy on the size of the crop were amazingly slight. The quantity of cotton exported fell slightly in 1908-9, but by the following season it had substantially increased and the quality had undoubtedly improved.

[1] The Kabaka of Buganda, Daudi Chwa, was at this time a minor. See Chapter II above.
[2] H. Bell, *Report on the Introduction and Establishment of the Cotton Industry in the Uganda Protectorate*, Cd. 4910 (1909).
[3] 27 Oct. 1908, Uganda Company Archives.

Meanwhile the Government had attained its primary objective: a viable export had been developed and revenue was becoming buoyant. Between 1903 and 1910 revenue increased fourfold, and the value of exports eightfold. Even self-sufficiency in public finance, merely a pious hope in 1905, had by 1910 become an attainable, if questionable, objective. Table I illustrates how effective and how rapid was the establishment of the new economy.

TABLE I

(£'000)

	Grant-in-aid	Revenue	Expenditure	Total exports	Cotton exports*
1900-1	204	82	252	25†	—
1901-2	172	74	229	49†	—
1902-3	135	41	204	30	—
1903-4	130	51	187	43	—
1904-5	140	60	173	60	0·2
1905-6	103	78	191	90	1
1906-7	112	97	192	116	11
1907-8	85	114	196	147	52
1908-9	95	103	256	127	44
1909-10	103	165	240	126	60
1910-11	96	191	252	307	169
1911-12	65	203	284	368	237
1912-13	45	239	292	437	266
1913-14	35	257	290	512	331
1914-15	10	283	289	523	369

* Including cotton seed.
† Mainly ivory, probably includes some in transit from Congo Free State.

Sources: Uganda Blue Books; Uganda Annual Reports; Kenya and Uganda Annual Trade Reports.

When we turn to the traders' role in these early years we find it difficult to exaggerate the importance of their contribution to the economic development of Uganda. As willing purchasers of native products they created and continuously widened those markets upon which development was fundamentally dependent. As sellers of trade goods they both satisfied existing needs and created new incentives for further production. Their transactions injected a stream of cash into the economy. In fact, the widening of the exchange economy, which is synonymous with economic development, would have been impossible without them. These are truisms, yet they demand emphasis in an area where 'development' is often regarded as attainable only by grandiose projects, and where ancient fallacies about the 'unproductivity of trade' persist. Moreover they are given peculiar force in the history of Uganda by the fact that the overwhelming majority of traders were immigrants from India. Our estimate of their contribution to the development of Uganda will greatly depend on our understanding of the general function of the trader in undeveloped societies.[1]

It is difficult to document their story, for, in the tradition of most small traders, they have left few accessible records, and their activities usually escaped official notice except when they offended against government policy. Fortunately, a long tradition of administrative attempts to regulate commerce has at least had the beneficial result of providing some documentary material for the historian.

Contrary to popular myth, the Indian traders of Uganda are not the descendants of the coolies who were imported to build the railway. Most of them were Gujerati-speaking Muslims or Hindus from Bombay Presidency and Kathiawar who came first to Zanzibar or Mombasa, specifically to trade, and later moved up country when they had acquired some financial backing. The first Uganda census, in 1911, revealed that there were 1,852 male and 364 female 'Asiatics' in the country, almost all of them employed in trade. Few of them arrived with much capital, but many brought a spirit of enterprise and commercial acumen which were rare and desirable qualities in Uganda. 'Within the term of my special commission' (1899–1901), wrote Johnston, 'Indian traders advanced their posts from Kampala to Toro and the vicinity of the Congo Free State, to five places in Bunyoro, and all the posts at which European or native soldiers were established in the Nile Province, besides opening bazaars at all the stations in the Eastern half of the Protectorate.'[2]

Not all of them were enterprising, of course, and some began, even at this early stage, to betray that apathy to change which has become the curse of East Africa's 'bazaar economy'. The

[1] Cf. P. Bauer, *West African Trade* (Cambridge, 1954), ch. ii, 'The multiplicity of traders and the productivity of trade.'

[2] H. H. Johnston, *The Uganda Protectorate* (2 vols., London, 1902), p. 294.

C.M.S. missionary, C. W. Hattersley, in 1908 shrewdly observed: 'it is very hard to see how they expect to thrive, as almost every store is the exact counterpart of its neighbour. However, whether they trade or not seems to be a matter of complete indifference to the storekeeper, judging by the placid way in which he sits among his goods, and the nonchalant air he adopts when asked his prices.'[1] Yet in a country whose peoples, with the possible exception of some Ganda, were totally ignorant of business and trade, this immigrant mercantile class played a unique role in the early stages of Uganda's development.

Typical in origin but quite outstanding in achievement among these immigrants was Allidina Visram, perhaps the most important individual in the early economic development of East Africa. Born in Kera in the province of Kutch in 1863, he migrated to Zanzibar as a young boy. By the 1890's he was a leading figure in the Zanzibar merchant community, that extraordinary group whose influence and commercial services extended into the far interior, to the amazement and gratification of many an early traveller and missionary. 'So, in an African wilderness, 500 miles from Zanzibar, this stranger Arab handed me a fine Muscat donkey with saddle and trappings in exchange for a dirty piece of paper with an order written in English for 110 dollars.'[2]

By the turn of the century Allidina's trading empire, based on Zanzibar, boasted over thirty up-country branches, extending throughout German and British East Africa and Uganda, even to the remote outposts of Wadelai, Nimule, and Gondokoro. These sold the usual range of piece-goods and provisions, but their functions went far beyond those we usually associate with a village store. In addition to buying all kinds of produce, the trader acted as banker, supplying credit to local government officers and even, on occasion, to peasants, though the latter activity was often suspect in official circles. A detailed chronology of Allidina's commercial activities, if it could be compiled, would trace an effective map of the moving traders' frontier in East Africa. Even the few letters on official files add up to an impressive picture.

---

[1] C. W. Hattersley, *The Baganda at Home* (London, 1908), p. 85.
[2] R. P. Ashe, *Two Kings of Uganda* (London, 1889), p. 249.

The long list of Allidina Visram's branches is a striking indication of the advancing frontier of trade, never far behind the
establishment of administration and sometimes even ahead of
its realization of law and order.[1] In Lango District in 1909, for
example, where 'each village appears to live in constant dread
of being raided by the neighbouring villages', one of his agents
arrived, selling 'little or nothing except to the police and staff'.[2]
It was in such remote areas, moreover, that the educational role
of commerce was most important. 'It would appear', reported
the district commissioner, 'that they only cultivate sufficient for
their own requirements and that they have no idea of the value
of such little produce as they have to dispose of . . . for a few
handfuls of sem sem they expect to be supplied with any article
they choose to select from Allidina's stock.'[3] Thus the administrative station and the trader formed an oasis of potential
economic development in a desert of backwardness.

For the first two decades of this century it was by no means
certain that the Uganda economy would be firmly based on
African peasant agriculture. Admittedly the transfer of the old
Eastern Province to the East Africa Protectorate in 1901 removed much of the land that was likely to attract white settlers,
and Nairobi by 1908 had a white population of over 1,000
against Uganda's total of some 450, which included government
officials and missionaries. But even if climatic conditions were
not conducive to permanent white settlement, there appeared
to be no self-evident reason why development should not be
attempted primarily through the agency of large-scale plantations under alien ownership and management. This had been
the generally accepted method of developing tropical dependencies, particularly when rapid results were required. There
was ample historical precedent for the large-scale alienation of
land and very little for reliance on the indigenous peoples to
produce 'grass roots' development. In German East Africa
during the same period, although tentative experiments with
peasant crops were being made, extensive alien plantations were
common and were implicitly regarded as synonymous with
'development'.[4]

---

[1] Cf. Chapter II, p. 57, above.
[2] Lango District Monthly Reports, 5 May 1909, E.S.A.
[3] Ibid., 19 June 1909, E.S.A.   [4] Cf. Chapter IX below.

Certainly the Uganda Administration had no clear-cut policy of support for peasant in preference to planter farming. Nor was there a clear directive from the British Government along these lines. On the contrary, Hayes Sadler's instructions on his appointment as Commissioner in 1901 were that 'every encouragement is to be offered to capitalists and settlers'. But despite numerous inquiries from prospective immigrants there was no rapid inflow of planters until the second decade. There were several reasons for this: the greater attractions of British East Africa, to which many applicants were referred; the attitudes of successive governors, whose personal influence on policy was inevitably very great; the surprisingly rapid success of cotton as a peasant crop; and, perhaps most important, the absence of a clearly defined land-alienation law, offering favourable terms to planters.

The attitudes of Uganda's first commissioners and governors were essentially pragmatic. In the same way as they were willing to try any crop, they were prepared to encourage any method of production. But although it is true that 'what interested them most was revenue', it is not true that they 'troubled themselves very little with imperial planning or social theorising'.[1] On the contrary, their anxiety for rapid development was tempered by a notable solicitude for the welfare of their subjects. Thus Johnston argued cautiously, as he had in Nyasaland, that land alienation was permissible to those who would use it productively, and, unlike his successors, he was willing to extend this privilege to Indian 'agricultural colonists who would make the desert blossom as the rose'.[2] But 'he had stricter views than most of his generation about the prevention of speculation and about the alienation of permanent freehold title'.[3]

Sadler's views were more orthodox. In his extensive General Report of 1904 he admitted that Uganda would never be a 'white man's country in the sense that South Africa and parts of East Africa will prove to be' but he clearly envisaged a planter economy in which 'the work would be done by paid native

---

[1] W. K. Hancock, *Survey of British Commonwealth Affairs*, vol. ii, pt. 2, *Problems of Economic Policy* (London, 1940), p. 180.

[2] Johnston to Salisbury, 26 Oct. 1900, F.O.C.P., no. 18.

[3] R. Oliver, *Sir Harry Johnston and the Scramble for Africa* (London, 1957), p. 220.

labour under the superintendence of the settler and his assistants'. Hesketh Bell was a pragmatist *par excellence*. While acknowledging the role that alien planters could play, he was 'convinced that every effort should be made to avoid the intrusion of alien interests in land'. On the other hand, he was well aware of the prevailing ignorance and apathy which bedevilled a peasant economy, and of the risks which faced any individual attempting to break through this crust of custom. Therefore, he argued in his diary,

it should be the duty of the Government to make agricultural experiments in the first place. Failures are as valuable as successes. A Government can afford to 'buy experience' in testing an enterprise: a small capitalist cannot. The loss of a single pioneer's resources has a deplorable effect on other ventures and may be remembered for a long time. On the other hand, any success proved commercially by the Government is at the disposal of the whole community.[1]

The fact that all this had to be done on a shoestring, although 'exasperating', was no deterrent. £50 was devoted to an experimental cotton scheme at Jinja to 'demonstrate that cultivation can profitably be carried on in Busoga', and, in the lengthy correspondence on such schemes Bell's reiterated advice was 'persevere and keep careful accounts'. In all this activity he was able to draw upon his earlier experience in the West Indies, much of which was directly relevant to the promotion of peasant production.

Not all the members of the Administration were agreed about the emphasis to be placed upon peasant production. For some of them it was difficult to conceive of development except in terms of European enterprise and capital. But throughout the pre-war period successive governors—Johnston, Sadler, Bell, and Jackson, who was even more 'pro-African' than his predecessors—were powerful advocates of peasant enterprise.

The brilliant success of cotton has already been described, but its principal effect, from the planters' point of view, was to intensify their labour difficulties. As early as 1908 the Uganda Chamber of Commerce was beginning to complain of labour scarcity and to lay some of the blame for this upon 'the encouragement of Government and missionaries of local agriculture,

[1] H. Bell, *Glimpses of a Governor's Life* (London, 1946), p. 140.

whereby the peasant is able to produce all he wants in the way of money from his own garden, as is seen by the great increase in the cotton growing industry'.

This criticism was to develop into a major controversy over the Government's policy towards plantation and peasant enterprise, culminating in the Development Commission of 1920. The detailed history of land policy is discussed elsewhere.[1] In striking contrast to conditions in British East Africa, considerable restrictions were imposed upon land alienation. Freehold grants were allowed under the Crown Lands Ordinance of 1903, but any allocation exceeding 1,000 acres required the special permission of the Secretary of State, and it was general policy severely to restrict freehold allocations. In 1907 even the leasehold of more than 10,000 acres was forbidden. But apart from these restraints and the various views held by local officials on the desirability of plantation agriculture, the curious fact was that although the authorities were theoretically in possession of 8,000 square miles of land in Buganda, the legal and administrative difficulties were such that there was very little that they could offer to planters. The alternative was for planters to acquire land by sale or lease from native owners. At first this process was not encouraged by the Government, but as the demand increased and as the difficulties of alienating Crown land became increasingly apparent, the official attitude began to change. It was argued that, in the interests of 'development', African landowners should be allowed, or even encouraged, to sell land which would otherwise lie idle. Nevertheless, the Governor ruled that landowners should not normally be allowed to sell more than half their total holdings.

The effects of these restrictions are difficult to assess. Certainly the planters thought that they were being given insufficient encouragement. But the state of the market for tropical products was probably at least as responsible as land policy for the slow increase in plantation agriculture before the war. Cotton was not sufficiently remunerative to attract planters. Two products, coffee and rubber, were of primary interest, though cocoa was also planted. Coffee prices had recovered from the depths of 1902-3, but the recovery was slow. The *Statist* index number for coffee (1867-77 = 100) during this

[1] See Chapter IX below.

period rose from 69 in 1903 to 85 in 1914. Rubber, however, was extremely attractive; the London price of standard quality reaching the incredible height of 12s. 9d. a lb. in 1910. Thereafter prices fell steadily, but even the range of 2s. to 3s. in the years immediately preceding the war was sufficient to attract capital to rubber planting in Uganda. Total costs of Uganda rubber c.i.f. London were reckoned at about 1s. a lb.

By far the most ambitious venture during this period was the Mabira Forest (Uganda) Rubber Company Limited, which was launched in London in 1906 with an authorized capital of £120,000 and anticipated annual profits of £80,000. It received a lease for twenty-one years of 100 square miles, over which it planned to collect wild rubber. But this proved hopelessly uneconomic, and the company had to resort to the more arduous promotion of plantation agriculture, with little success. The East African Trading Company was given similar rights to collect wild rubber in the Budongo Forest over an area of about 60 square miles. In awarding these concessions the authorities were constantly on guard against the undue dominance of one firm. Thus Elgin's reaction to the Mabira Company's application for land in Budongo was to refuse, on the grounds that 'the interests of the Protectorate will best be secured by the introduction of a certain amount of commercial competition'.[1] Other rubber ventures were on a much smaller scale, notably the plantation at Namukekera, about 40 miles from Kampala, which was undertaken by the Uganda Company in 1908. One hundred and fifty-three acres were cleared and 19,400 trees planted, to the amusement of local African cultivators, who were convinced that crops could not be grown on this land. This was not the last occasion on which local traditional lore was to prove superior to alien knowledge and technique, and it was finally only by ignoring orders from London and planting on the hill slopes that the local managers were able to grow rubber with any degree of success.

By 1911 there were about twenty alien estates in Uganda with some 2,000 acres under permanent crops, of which rubber was by far the most important. In 1910 a Planters' Association was formed which boasted forty members by 1913. The launching of the *Uganda Herald* in 1912 is some reflection of the growing

[1] Elgin to Acting Commissioner, 8 May 1907, Africa no. 869 (1907).

importance of European planters, and for some years it faithfully reflected their views, providing the historian with a useful but prejudiced source for the period.

The gestation period between planting and harvest is, for coffee, about three years, and for rubber seven,[1] so the contribution of plantation crops to the Uganda economy was still small by the outbreak of the first world war. There were by then approximately 130 plantations, mostly in Buganda, with a total acreage of some 50,000, of which about 20,000 acres were under cultivation, 15,000 in Buganda. In 1914 exports of coffee were valued at £23,000, and of rubber at less than £3,000. But in the same year, total exports were worth more than £500,000, of which 65 per cent. was contributed by cotton, and another 10 per cent. by chillies, hides, and skins, all of which were produced by native enterprise.

The alacrity with which Uganda Africans responded to economic stimuli during this first decade of development deserves comment and demands explanation. Contemporaries were obsessed by this theme, and the Ganda in particular were singled out for extravagant praise. There was 'no more progressive type of negro to be found throughout the length and breadth of Africa'; they were the 'Japanese' of the continent; they were lauded, and sometimes condemned, for their 'innate love of trade'. 'Wherever prospects of trade open up, the Baganda will go', wrote a missionary in 1906.

One explanation of this eagerness for cash (a rare and significant quality among backward peoples) was advanced by Sir Charles Eliot; Uganda 'presents a feature totally lacking in East Africa,[2] namely a large native population which is assimilating European ideas and is anxious to purchase European goods. At present the purchasing power is wanting, but if any plentiful and paying article of export can be found . . . a great increase in imports and revenue will certainly result.'[3] Among the 'European ideas' which were most effectively transforming Africans into economic men was the teaching of Christian missionaries.

If the African Christian was to abandon his place on the old

---

[1] That is, in Uganda. In most rubber-growing areas, at much lower altitudes, it is four years.

[2] i.e. the East Africa Protectorate.

[3] C. Eliot, *The East Africa Protectorate* (London, 1905), p. 202.

ladders of economic prosperity and social prestige by practising monogamy, he must be compensated by learning a trade or new methods of agriculture which would open the way to new ambitions. If his children were to sleep at home and live a Christian family life, he must have a house with two rooms instead of one. If he was to read his Bible, his house must have windows to admit the light, and therefore its shape must be square and not conical; nor could he afford to build it every five years to meet the needs of shifting cultivation. If his children were to be educated, he must learn to do without their services on the farm and yet earn enough to pay their school fees. Again, to pay the government tax and his Church tithe he must have ready money; and if he was not to leave his family to work on a railway or a plantation, he must produce not only for himself but for the market.[1]

The changing pattern of African consumption during this first decade of development is indicated in Table II below. Not all of the imported goods were consumed by Africans, of course, but the comparative insignificance of the immigrant population means that the table gives a reasonably accurate picture of African consumption.

TABLE II

Selected imports ($£'000$)*

	Total retained imports	Unbleached calico (Amerikani)	Other† textiles	Bicycles and accessories	Books and stationery
1904	115	21	24	—	—
1905	143	24	29	—	2
1906	196	36	34	—	2
1907	255	45	63	—	2
1908	311	32	66	4	4
1909	337	46	66	4	5
1910	360	57	60	3	5
1911	504	60	82	7	7
1912	576	76	110	14	7
1913	710	85	135	19	9
1914	940	108	185	27	14

* All figures rounded to nearest £1,000.
† Cotton, wool, and silk manufactures.

It is noteworthy that imports of superior textiles, in contrast to mere 'Amerikani', rose quite rapidly. The importance of

[1] R. Oliver, *The Missionary Factor in East Africa* (London, 1952), p. 214.

bicycles both as an index of prosperity and as an aid to its furtherance will be obvious to anyone who has visited Africa; their astonishing range of uses is too well known to need detailed description. The figures for books and stationery are also interesting. Once they had learned the art, the Ganda became great readers and writers. Sir Apolo Kagwa, for example, left a collected correspondence whose dimensions and self-consciousness rival those of many nineteenth-century British statesmen. It is impossible to distinguish the quantities of other imported goods which were being purchased by Africans, but they were certainly growing perceptibly even outside Buganda. In Bunyoro, where in 1910 people, especially those living in the neighbourhood of trading centres, were reported as 'discarding their bark cloths in favour of the more up to date imported garments', a few were buying tea, sugar, and biscuits, and some were discarding their native pottery for enamelled basins, kettles, and mugs. Three Africans had houses roofed with corrugated iron that year—a major advance in health and security. A few of the 'better class chiefs' bought bicycles at about £20 each. The superiority of these imported articles over indigenous products was unquestionable and could be regretted only by the most sentimental of observers.

But the mere desire for higher standards of living is inadequate as an explanation of the speed with which peasants, accustomed only to the subsistence production of food, became producers of cotton. No thorough change from subsistence to cash farming took place; in fact Uganda has still not yet experienced a thoroughgoing agrarian revolution. But even the integration of a cash crop into a predominantly subsistence agriculture demanded a human effort greater perhaps than the merely passive provision of labour for alien enterprises or the docile acceptance of government edict. A change so rapid and so fundamental would have been inconceivable without some measure of enterprise on the part of the people and their leaders. We must not exaggerate this. In a strictly economic sense the African's role at this stage was limited—he ventured no capital, took no risks, and was required to do little but respond, for his own benefit, to an alien stimulus. His seed was issued free with abundant advice on how to cultivate it. A ready market was provided, with no effort on his part except the carrying of goods to the place of sale. Even the hand-gins originally issued by the Government were provided free or below cost. Moreover, when it was seen that hand-gins were unsuitable, the Government repurchased them at their original price before destroying them. All this is in striking contrast to the early history of the Gold Coast cocoa industry[1] and the Nigerian palm-oil industry,[2] the success of which owed much to African initiative and enterprise.

Nevertheless, if the demands made upon the people of Uganda were limited, their psychological achievement in breaking through the accumulated crust of peasant custom and inertia was considerable. In all this the role of the chiefs was of unique importance. Thus in Masaka in 1909, the district commissioner reported bitterly that the chiefs had to 'literally stand over these people to ensure any cultivation at all'. A few Ganda chiefs were particularly enterprising and commercially minded, though once again we must avoid an uncritical acceptance of contemporary panegyrics. Thus Johnston's assurance to a bank which proposed opening a Kampala branch, that it 'would meet with a great deal of business amongst the wealthier Baganda chiefs, *all* of whom can read and write and have very clear ideas already about banking and a great desire to place their funds in security' was mere special pleading. Fifty years later an authoritative work declared that 'the East African (in contrast to the West African) has not yet advanced to that stage of economic development at which he uses banking facilities'.[3]

In practice the principal economic role of the chiefs was to see that administrative orders were obeyed, but there can be little doubt that their eagerness to promote an economic crop was enhanced by the knowledge that they would enjoy a disproportionate share of its proceeds. The precise allocation of income between chiefs and people cannot be measured, but such was the chief's authority, backed both by tradition and by the new Protectorate Government, that it can safely be assumed that his reward was more than adequate. Not only in Buganda, but throughout the cotton-growing areas, the crop was established by essentially collective means in central fields under the chief's

Cf. W. M. Macmillan in C. W. Meek, W. M. Macmillan, and E. R. J. Hussey, *Europe and West Africa* (London, 1940).

[2] Cf. K. O. Dike, *Trade and Politics in the Niger Delta, 1830–1885* (Oxford, 1956).

[3] W. T. Newlyn and D. C. Rowan, *Money and Banking in British Colonial Africa* (Oxford, 1954), p. 85.

control. Gradually, as the attractions of the market became apparent, an increasing number of peasants began to grow cotton on their own account, in addition to working for their chief. But this process was slow, particularly outside Buganda, where the money economy and the stimulus of the market were weaker. Thus in Bukedi in 1910 growers taking their crop to market 'had to be held back whilst their cotton was weighed in order that they might receive payment for it; all they wanted to do was to bring it to the white man and they were satisfied'.[1]

But the white men, or at least most government officials, were by no means satisfied, for they recognized the need to promote a genuine interest in the new crops among the mass of the peasantry. Yet this desire often conflicted with their natural wish to back the authority of the chiefs. The administrative officers in Toro complained in 1912 that many chiefs were so rapacious that the peasants believed that new products such as beeswax and cotton were the chiefs' perquisites. Therefore, they argued, 'the first step is to teach the peasant that new crops are introduced for his own gains and not as an additional burden imposed upon him by the Government and his chief'. An even more fundamental dilemma, which was never fully resolved, was also beginning to face the Administration in its pursuance of development through the indigenous peoples. Inherent in government policy was the conflict between the need to encourage native enterprise and the natural desire for a quiet life and tidy administration. Enterprising men are not always scrupulous and are rarely docile, but the degree of approval and of restraint which society affords them is a strategic factor in the economic development of that society. Because of their social and educational background, and because of the intrinsic difficulties of their job, most British officials were rarely disposed to favour enterprising Africans who, almost by definition, were likely to be misfits both in their own traditional societies and in the new paternal régime. Considering the difficulties facing them, therefore, it is surprising that any Africans took much initiative in shaping the new economy. Yet a few did, notably in Buganda, and in the pre-war period Ganda middlemen were to be found in the cotton industry wherever the crop was grown and marketed. Most of them were financed by Indian and

[1] *Uganda Notes* (journal of the Church Missionary Society), July 1910.

European ginners and traders each buying season, and some of them began in this way to acquire the rudiments of commercial practice. The reason for their disappearance almost before they began to emerge as an effective class is a highly controversial question, the answer to which depends upon the relative weight the historian gives to official discouragement and Indian immigration. That it was a tragedy in the social history of the country, the outcome of which is perhaps the most serious economic problem facing modern Uganda, is beyond all question.

A fundamental barrier to economic progress in Uganda was the inadequacy of its transport system. The completion of the railway in 1902 had, admittedly, opened up communications with the outside world, and had enormously reduced transport costs. A striking example of the fantastic costs of transport to the coast before the coming of the railway is given in the following analysis by the firm of Smith Mackenzie & Co. The cost of a 'load' (about 65 lb.) of pink beads, delivered to Kampala in 1898, was accounted for in the following way:

	Rupees	Annas
First cost, ready marked in tins	35	0
Duty, at 5 per cent.	1	12
Shipping, &c., to Mombasa and landing . .	1	4
Transport, Mombasa to Kampala . . .	140	0
Interest on 178 rupees at 15 per cent. per annum[1] .	26	10
Profit at 15 per cent.	26	10
	231	4

In addition to the obvious risks of damage or loss to goods in caravan or in open canoes, there were additional human factors such as the discovery that a nail in a tin of kerosene could lighten a porter's load. The railway and the launching of 4 steamers, 13 dhows, and 2 steel boats on Lake Victoria had changed all this by the beginning of our period. Freight costs from England to Kampala fell to about a tenth of their former level. Deliveries of imported goods were quicker, more certain, and more regular, thus greatly reducing the amount of capital which had to be tied up in the form of stocks. As we have seen,

[1] Note the high price of credit even to a firm of Smith Mackenzie's standing.

the railway also made possible the growth of exports. In all these vital respects its impact upon the Uganda economy cannot be gainsaid. But it did not bring about a 'transport revolution' in the sense that that phrase is understood elsewhere.[1] Both in its construction and in its running it had virtually no effect for many years on local markets for labour, capital, or enterprise. It was truly an alien enterprise, and apart from the provision of the all important link with the coast, its impact upon Uganda's economy and society can easily be overrated. To contemporaries the most significant fact about the Uganda Railway was that not a mile of its lines was laid within Uganda's borders. Exports had first to be transported to a lake port and then across to Kisumu.

The problems of land transport continued to be practically insurmountable. In Uganda, as in most other parts of Africa, disease made the use of animal transport almost impossible. Until the establishment of rail communication and the later coming of the motor-lorry, this problem was never really solved, although various expedients were tried. Despite serious attempts to organize ox transport, and experiments with elephants (Hesketh Bell imported an Indian elephant and mahout in a fruitless attempt to train African animals) and even domesticated zebras trained by an optimistic German in Kenya, the 'only available beast of burden was man, the weakest and most costly of all'.

Where adequate roads existed, *hamali* carts were used. These were long narrow four-wheeled carts carrying about 1600 lb. and pushed by ten men. But native techniques of road-making and bridge-building, while highly developed by local African standards, were wholly inadequate for wheeled transport. Thus in 1905 it took two months to transport goods by cart from Entebbe to Butiaba on Lake Albert, a distance of some 150 miles. Practically every bridge, consisting of a few bamboo poles covered with earth, collapsed *en route*, and each wagon had to undergo extensive repairs after every trip. Attempts by the Government to improve conditions were severely limited by inadequate resources. Road improvements were undertaken but often had to be abandoned a few miles out of Kampala. Even main routes were incomplete. For example in 1912 the metalled

---

[1] Cf. L. H. Jenks, 'Railroads as an economic force in American development', *Journal of Economic History*, iv (1944), 1–20.

road from Kampala to Toro ceased 55 miles from Fort Portal, and included a hazardous gap of 14 miles. Along this and similar routes the bulk of goods was carried on men's heads.

It is difficult to exaggerate the deleterious effects of this 'porter system' upon the peasant economy of Uganda. It has been estimated that a railway train of average capacity and engine-power will do the work of from 15,000 to 20,000 porters for one-fifth to one-tenth of the cost.[1] The failure of the hand-ginning scheme and the lack of up-country ginneries meant that vast loads of unginned cotton had to be transported long distances. Moreover, the demand for this labour came precisely at the time when it was most needed for preparing the land for food crops. It is hardly surprising, therefore, that there were constant complaints about the inadequate supply of porters.

To some extent this burden was relieved in the Eastern Province by the opening in 1912 of the 61-mile 'Busoga' railway, which connected Jinja and Namasagali on the Victoria Nile. But so rapid was the expansion of the crop in this area that in 1913 it required about half a million porters' loads for its marketing.[2] In Bukedi in 1912 the lack of transport facilities and resulting scarcity of buyers meant that cotton was bought at 'ridiculously low prices', leaving the peasant no incentive to grow cotton the following season.[3]

It was becoming increasingly evident that future development would be dependent more upon an adequate system of communications than upon any other single factor. It will be recalled that the original distributions of cotton seed were widely dispersed throughout the country. The Government's leading cotton expert suggested in 1909 that there were 'large tracts of land' in the Nile Province and Toro which might be suitable for this crop, but that 'in view of transport difficulties it is not feasible to even consider them for the present'.[4] Nor were they considered for many years to come, and thus was

---

[1] S. H. Frankel, *Capital Investment in Africa* (London, 1938), p. 32. A resolution of the Uganda Chamber of Commerce, typical of its period, reads: 'Unless porters can be obtained the cotton industry will be ruined . . . carts are unable to approach interior districts, therefore porters are the only means of transport' (Uganda Chamber of Commerce *Minutes*, 12 Mar. 1910).

[2] Uganda Agricultural Department Report, 1913–14.

[3] Ibid., 1913.

[4] M. Dawe, 'Notes on the history of the cotton industry in Uganda', 5 July 1909, E.S.A., Agricultural Dept., 759/09.

perpetuated one of the most serious problems that Uganda has had to face—the enormous regional disparities of income and wealth within its borders.

The boom, 1913–29

The first world war was disastrous for a Uganda economy which was just beginning to find its feet. Most European plantations were left without adequate supervision and government departments were hopelessly understaffed, often with grievous results. Thus the loss of some 200,000 head of cattle through rinderpest would almost certainly have been averted by the presence of a few veterinary officers. In the whole of the Eastern Province in 1918 there was only one agricultural officer who for part of the year had to combine his duties with those of an administrative officer. About 63,000 Africans were recruited for the Carrier Corps, and many of those who eventually returned brought with them smallpox, meningitis, and plague. Shipping from Mombasa to Europe was extremely limited and hopelessly dislocated during the final year of war. The importation of capital for new enterprises virtually ceased. The Lake Victoria trade, which had been expanding rapidly, was greatly disorganized by the commandeering of all but two steamers for lake patrol work. This in turn led to acute congestion along the railway, and goods had to be stored for indefinite periods in godowns along the line.[1]

When the war ended many European planters and government officers returned home for leave, 'whilst the discharged natives for the most part were content to enjoy a few months' idleness on the fruit of their savings during active service'.[2] Considering the chaotic nature of demobilization in Europe at that time it is hardly surprising that there was little planning for post-war rehabilitation in Uganda. To make matters worse 1918 was a year of drought, with famine in some areas and serious shortages of food in all. The deaths of more than 4,000 people from starvation in the Eastern Province, despite emergency imports of food, were a grim reminder of how slender were the resources of a primitive economy.

[1] V. C. R. Ford, *The Trade of Lake Victoria*, East African Studies no. 3 (Kampala, 1955), pp. 24–25.
[2] Uganda Annual Reports, 1918–19.

It is remarkable, in view of all this, that the total value of exports, which had exceeded half a million pounds for the first time in 1913, never fell below that figure, and raced ahead to £1·2 million in 1918. To some extent this was the easily won fruit of rising world prices, but even the physical quantities were impressive, as can be seen in Table III below.

TABLE III

Selected exports, 1913–19

	Total exports	Ginned cotton		Coffee		Hides	
	(£'000)	('000 cwt.)	(£'000)	('000 cwt.)	(£'000)	('000 cwt.)	(£'000)
1913–14	512	85	272	12	23	14	53
1914–15	523	107	320	20	41	16	55
1915–16	504	91	239	43	87	18	64
1916–17	638	78	349	49	104	19	53
1917–18	785	99	537	20	39	23	77
1918–19	1,247	98	966	54	105	15	64

The immediate post-war years were a period when the level of economic discussion reached a low ebb throughout most of the world. This was the age of the Treaty 'without nobility, without morality, without intellect'—and Lord Keynes's indictment of Versailles might serve equally for the policies of the Empire Resources Development Committee, whose 'farrago of cant and greed' reflected all that was worst in contemporary ideas of imperial development.[1]

In Uganda these ideas were mirrored by the report of a Development Commission in 1920. Its terms of reference were sensible enough: 'to consider generally the steps which should be taken to forward the commercial and industrial development of the Protectorate having regard to the interests of the different communities resident therein' and to pay special attention to the question of transport facilities. Yet at a time when the peasant sector was producing at least 80 per cent. of Uganda's total exports, the commission was not merely unrepresentative of those who were making such progress possible, but was antagonistic to their very existence.

[1] Cf. Hancock, *Survey of Commonwealth Affairs*, vol. ii, pt. i, pp. 106–10.

Essentially a planters' charter, the product of a small, unrepresentative, and frustrated group of men, the Development Commission Report[1] reads like a caricature of the prejudices of white men in tropical Africa. A few quotations will suffice to convey its tone and approach. On the incidence of venereal disease among the native population: 'in certain districts . . . about 90 per cent. are infected', and this, long before any adequate medical statistics were available. On native education: 'We are opposed to any extensive education for the general native population . . . half educated natives are a menace.' But its wildest paragraphs were devoted, despite the presence of three government officials on the commission, to a vituperative attack on the Director of Agriculture for 'failing to identify himself with the planters' interest as he should have done'. The Government was also attacked for having 'tacitly accepted the position'.

There was truth in these allegations, if not in the implicit assumption that the interests of the planters and of the Protectorate were identical. S. Simpson, Director of Agriculture from 1911 to 1929, made no secret of his antipathy towards the planters and of his wholehearted enthusiasm for native agriculture. While his department did not wholly neglect the plantation sector, its main attentions had since its inception been devoted to the promotion of the cotton industry. But Simpson was not alone in his refusal to be browbeaten by an articulate planter group and by the contemporary fashion of equating 'development' with alien enterprise. Despite the presence of a governor, Sir Robert Coryndon, who, in contrast to his predecessors, openly supported the planters, several men among the Provincial Administration shared Simpson's views. Most notable among them was Frederick Spire, who had come to Uganda in 1894 as Colville's batman[2] and had risen to become Provincial Commissioner of the Eastern Province. The opposition of men like Simpson and Spire to bland assumptions of planter superiority both reflected and contributed to the growing body of support for development through indigenous institutions which was to find its fullest expression in the work of Sir Hugh Clifford and Lord Lugard in West Africa. In Uganda

---

[1] *Report of the Development Commission* (Entebbe, 1920).
[2] Oliver, *Sir Harry Johnston*, p. 310.

these ideas were remarkable for their early appearance and their effectiveness in the face of considerable local opposition.

The essential argument of the Development Report was that future economic progress would be wholly dependent upon the expansion of plantation agriculture, for native agriculture was limited by idleness, apathy, and ignorance. It therefore attacked the Government's 'unnecessary interference' in land transactions. In Buganda, where Africans were 'in possession of practically the whole of the cultivable area . . . hardly any development was taking place'. To a great extent this was the result of the banana, 'a crop which requires little industry or care on the part of the producer, and the tendency to idleness which is inherent in the native is encouraged thereby'. This could be overcome, the report argued, by simplifying the alienation of land, and by a tax on undeveloped land, for 'it is not proper that areas up to 50 square miles should be in the hands of private individuals who spend not one penny in improving it'.

But scarcity of labour affected the planters even more than their alleged shortage of land; and there was little point in demanding more land if insufficient labour was forthcoming to work upon the small areas they had already secured. Here lay a fundamental conflict between plantation and peasant agriculture. The people of Uganda were, on the whole, able to satisfy their subsistence needs through the traditional economy. Their demand for cash was increasing, as we have seen, but was tempered by their natural reluctance to work as unskilled 'porters' (a word of humiliating connotation in Uganda) on plantations. The cultivation of cotton in their own gardens offered a far more satisfactory way of supplying their cash needs. It was therefore inevitable that official encouragement of the cotton industry should meet with opposition. Nor were the planters the sole opponents; it was, for example, a young official in Kampala, who, appalled by the idleness of the Ganda, protested to the Chief Secretary, 'The root cause of the present difficulties is the unwillingness of the peasant to work steadily owing to his growing prosperity derived from cotton.'[1] Such complaints continued to be voiced for many years. Even the Ormsby-Gore

---

[1] 1919 E.S.A. Secretariat Minute Paper (hereinafter 'S.M.P.') 5711.

Commission, which was by no means unsympathetic towards native agriculture, admitted that: 'It would be idle to pretend that this shortage is not in part due to the rapid extension of native agriculture and that the rich rewards that the native can reap by the production of economic crops for export does not affect the labour supply.'[1]

There were two possible ways in which the Government might be persuaded to improve labour supplies—either by discouraging the extension of cotton-growing or by exercising direct coercion. The first was unlikely to succeed if only because cotton was by now the basis of Uganda's economy and of the Government's finances. In 1920, for example, the export tax on cotton contributed 7 per cent. of total revenue, and native poll-tax, most of which was paid out of income received from cotton, contributed 50 per cent.; another 21 per cent. came from customs duties, most of which was again dependent upon cotton earnings. A pattern had emerged which was to be the dominant feature of the Uganda economy for the rest of our period: a whole series of annual variables, such as the level of personal and public incomes, and the level of imports, particularly those of consumer goods bought chiefly by Africans, such as bicycles, depended each year upon the value of the cotton crop. In contrast to this the planters could offer little to Uganda save optimistic promises and doubts of the future expansibility of peasant agriculture. It is not surprising therefore that the Government emphasized 'the necessity for extending the existing areas of cotton cultivation as well as for introducing and encouraging the production of the crop in suitable localities throughout the Protectorate'.[2] What is surprising is the fact that the Government did not pursue this policy with much enthusiasm; the reason for this can be understood if we digress for a moment to consider the problem of labour migration, which had by now become acute.

The distinctive features of labour migration into and within Uganda have been its concentration upon Buganda and the fact that immigrants have come to work not only for alien planters and the Government, but also for Ganda farmers. A thorough

---

[1] *Report of the East Africa Commission, 1924–5* (Ormsby-Gore Commission), Cmd. 2387 (1925), p. 40. For this commission, see Chapter VI, pp. 301–2, above.
[2] 16 Mar. 1919, E.S.A./S.M.P. 3457.

analysis of these movements is beyond the scope of this chapter,[1] but a few of their more obvious causes and effects are perhaps relevant to our narrative. Migration can be explained in terms of 'push' and 'pull' and of the relative ease with which journeys can be undertaken. In this case population pressures, occasional famines, such as those in Ruanda Urundi[2] and Tanganyika in 1928, the desire to escape compulsory labour, and above all, the need for cash, all prompted people to move from the less developed areas of Uganda, Tanganyika, and Ruanda Urundi into Buganda. The attractions of Buganda's comparatively prosperous cash economy were much enhanced by the opportunities of acquiring land and growing cash crops.[3] Under British administration the mere establishment of law and order enabled men to move with reasonable confidence, and it was probably this rather than any physical improvements in transport that eased the flow of labour. Throughout our period the majority of immigrants travelled on foot under conditions of considerable hardship.[4] Unfortunately, meaningful statistics of the migration are unavailable until the late 1930's, by which time the annual inflow was measured in tens of thousands. But it was substantial even during the early years of the century, and by 1924 there were some 15,000 to 20,000 immigrants employed in Buganda, *excluding* those working on Buganda farms.[5]

Among the deleterious effects of these flows was a general tendency to depress wages in Buganda, not only because of the constant availability of abundant 'cheap, poor labour',[6] but also because a high labour turnover left employers with little incentive to improve conditions and establish a stable working force. Similarly, health authorities had to fight constantly against the swamping effect of a continuous inflow of peoples with appalling standards of nutrition and hygiene. Equally serious

[1] See in A. I. Richards (ed.), *Economic Development and Tribal Change* (Cambridge, 1954); P. G. Powesland, *Economic Policy and Labour: a study in Uganda's economic history*, East African Studies no. 10 (Kampala, 1957).

[2] Now Rwanda and Burundi.

[3] By 1937 there were over 28,000 non-Ganda settled in homesteads in Buganda (Richards, op. cit., p. 50).

[4] One woman told Dr. Richards, 'No, I had no trouble at all on the journey. My baby died in the camp last night.' (Ibid., p. 60.)

[5] For a detailed analysis of the statistics 1935-51, see P. G. Powesland's note in ibid., pp. 254-6.

[6] Powesland, *Economic Policy and Labour*, p. 55.

was the effect on the societies from which the migrants came. To suggest this is not to argue that migration *in itself* has harmed these areas, for against the deprivations arising from a loss of young people must be balanced the income opportunities which lead them to migrate, and we know little of this balance.[1] What is apparent, however, is the effect that this migration had upon the Uganda Government's attitude towards regional economic development. In 1925, for example, when an agricultural officer in the West Nile District succeeded in stimulating cotton production and thereby hindered the recruitment of labourers for Buganda, the Director of Agriculture was informed that it was official policy 'to refrain from actively stimulating the production of cotton or other economic crops in outlying districts on which it is dependent for a supply of labour for the carrying out of essential services in the central or producing districts'.[2] It was added that the intention 'was not, and never had been, to prevent cotton planting in any district by natives wishing to do so', but in a paternal society this abdication of responsibility for the direct promotion of cash crops was effectively an acquiescence in the continuance of subsistence economies outside Buganda and the Eastern Province. It could be argued that different climatic conditions, remoteness from markets, and inadequate transport facilities were at least equally responsible for regional disparities in development, but the significance of official policy is well illustrated by Powesland's speculation: 'if the country that is now the Uganda Protectorate had been opened up from the direction of Khartoum instead of from the Coast, would there have been a stage when the development of Buganda had to be postponed until after the solution of labour difficulties in the Northern Province?'[3]

The planters' second approach to the labour problem was to persuade the Government to 'exert direct pressure', as the Development Commission phrased it; this to be done, of course, in the interests of 'the country' and of the 'natives themselves'. It was even possible to quote a Luganda proverb in support of the coercion: 'You thank, when the day dawns, the man who dragged you out of your bed at night.' But despite their sancti-

[1] Cf. W. Watson, *Tribal Cohesion in a Money Economy* (Manchester, 1958), an important Northern Rhodesian study of migration without social disruption.
[2] Quoted in Powesland, op. cit., p. 40. [3] Ibid., p. 41.

morious language the planters were here on firmer ground. The Government had itself employed compulsory labour since 1908 for road-making, porter transport, and other public services. While this *kasanvu* system was theoretically intended to serve only official needs, it aided private employers both directly and indirectly. It was not unknown for officially conscripted labourers to be turned over to planters, and in any case exemption from the levy of those already in employment acted as a powerful aid to recruitment by private employers. Moreover, the mere existence of compulsion tended to depress wages below the level which would have existed in a free market.[1] Planters had been tolerably satisfied with this system, but their complacency was being disturbed by the Government's increasing difficulty in getting chiefs to co-operate by sending in the men required. As alternative sources of income became available, notably through cotton-growing, men were gaining a new independence of traditional tribal authority. The Development Commission expressed the planters' growing dissatisfaction with this state of affairs in language curiously remote from present-day discussion of Uganda affairs. 'More than one of the prominent tribes of the Protectorate is becoming rotten to the core, and unless industry and thrift can be substituted for idleness and immorality, they will soon be but shadows of their former selves.'[2] Any hopes of increased compulsion, however, were swept aside in the following year by a Colonial Office dispatch arising from the dispute over the Kenya 'Northey circulars',[3] which ruled that it would no longer be tolerated save for specific public works. Thus *kasanvu* ended throughout the Protectorate in 1922.

The Development Report marked the apogee of European planters' influence in Uganda. Within four years of its publication many planters had failed and either left the country or moved into the cotton industry. Never again were they able to dominate public discussion. Their failure was partly fortuitous and partly due to fundamental economic weaknesses. It was their misfortune that just as they were beginning to reap the harvest of their investment they were grievously hurt by the

[1] Ibid., ch. ii.
[2] *Development Commission Report 1920*, para. 105.
[3] See Chapter VI, pp. 292–3, above.

combined impact of a slump in prices and of acute currency instability. The effects of the slump were obvious and disastrous. The best Uganda coffee, which had fetched £160 a ton in 1920, fell to £80 in 1921. Rubber fell from an average of 1s. 10d. a pound to 10d. A prolonged crisis in East African currency arrangements was equally damaging and requires more detailed explanation.[1]

The Indian silver rupee had been established as a standard East African monetary unit in 1906 at an exchange rate of 1s. 4d. to the rupee. In 1918 rupee notes were accepted as equivalent to silver rupees. Meanwhile, however, the value of silver had risen and the Indian rupee began to appreciate in terms of the pound, reaching an exchange value of 2s. 9d. in February 1920. This difference in exchange and intrinsic value naturally caused great confusion in East Africa, and it was decided to create a Currency Board similar to the one already established in West Africa. But in order to operate East Africa's currency on a sterling exchange system it was necessary to isolate it from the fluctuating rupee and fix its value in sterling. This was done in July 1920; a new coin, the florin, was introduced, based on the current Indian rupee exchange value of 1 florin = 2 shillings = 1 rupee. But no sooner had this been done than the rupee began to *depreciate* in terms of sterling. To make confusion worse, rupees were not immediately withdrawn from circulation in East Africa because the new florins were not yet available. Indian coins and notes therefore circulated at an artificially high exchange value, and many were inevitably smuggled in through Zanzibar. On 8 February 1921 Indian rupee notes were demonetized in East Africa without previous warning. Smuggling of coins into East Africa continued, at least until June, when they, too, ceased to be legal tender. Even then a certain amount of smuggling went on because Africans, who were by now completely bewildered, continued to accept 'worthless' coins, and the Government was therefore forced to extend the period of redemption. Nor was this an end to the fiasco, for there was considerable pressure from planters in Kenya to devalue the florin in order to make their export prices more attractive. These efforts failed, but the florin was replaced by a shilling currency in January 1922.

[1] Cf. Chapter V, pp. 234-5, above.

The effects of this long period of monetary instability were serious throughout the Uganda economy, but the planters were particularly affected. During the period of rupee appreciation their principal markets, which were in the United Kingdom, were most unremunerative for reasons quite separate from the co-existent depression in prices. Unlike the cotton exporters, who could send their produce to Bombay, planters were forced to accept payment in sterling whose value to them fell by half, while having to meet their local current costs in rupees. Imports of capital from the United Kingdom were, of course, discouraged. The overvaluation of the rupee in 1921 perpetuated this situation, planters receiving only 10 rupees or florins for every pound. The effect was to increase their wage costs and debt charges by half. Meanwhile bankers at first refused to accept drafts on London, and then only agreed at a rate of 1s. 3¾d. to the florin. At this stage there was a clear-cut division between the various interests in the country. This was demonstrated at a public meeting in Kampala which was attended by the major groups, including the civil servants, and missionaries representing native interests. The planters, missionaries, and the Indian Association were unanimously against the existing rate; officials, ginners, and the Chamber of Commerce were unanimously in favour of its continuance. Despite considerable pressure from the planters and the Uganda Government, the Colonial Office stood by its original decision, and the currency situation remained confused for several years.

These price and currency misfortunes, in addition to their oft-lamented labour and land difficulties, might be regarded as sufficient explanation of the planters' failure; certainly this was their own interpretation of the matter in a long series of meetings and letters to the press. Yet to accept this view would be to neglect the more fundamental weaknesses of plantation agriculture in Uganda. The fact was that they faced overwhelming odds, which had been temporarily obscured by high post-war prices for their crops and the artificially depressed wages of their labour. In the first place their costs, particularly those of European managers unable to 'live off the country', were far too high and inflexible to withstand even a short depression. Secondly, and probably more significantly, they had not succeeded in producing any crop of sufficient value to sustain these costs. Cocoa was a failure, perhaps because of inadequate capital and skill. Rubber was seriously affected by the slump of 1921, made a good recovery in the mid-1920's, but ultimately, mainly because of inadequate rainfall, proved to be a peripheral crop, profitable only when world conditions were abnormally favourable. Its chequered history is illustrated by the table below, and by the fate of the Mabira Forest Company, which, it will be remembered, was launched with such high promise in 1906. The company's annual profits never remotely approached the £80,000 which had been anticipated when it was formed. During the early 1920's it suffered severe losses and added its voice to the protests against the Government's encouragement of cotton-growing. In 1925 it announced the largest profit in its history—£18,600, which was followed by smaller profits during the next few years. In 1926 it surrendered its original vast concession for a modest leasehold of 4,000 acres. Dry weather was responsible for a loss of nearly £3,000 in 1929, which was followed, of course, by further losses during the ensuing slump. The company's reports throughout the 1930's are a sad tale of annual losses relieved occasionally by tiny profits—£45 in 1932, £57 in 1937. The war years were more favourable, particularly after the Japanese overran Malaya, but in 1947 the company was relieved to sell out for a few thousand pounds.

TABLE IV

Rubber in Uganda, 1910–33

	Acreage	*Crop*	*Value*
	('000 acres)	(centals)	(£'000)
1910	3	5	0·1
1913	5	194	2·9
1916	8	720	5·8
1919	20	3,885	25·9
1922	15	1,248	3·7
1925	16	8,058	68·7
1928	13	11,312	54·9
1931	13	1,334	2·3
1933	11	356	0·3

Sources: Uganda Blue Books; Annual Reports of Uganda Department of Agriculture.

The final overwhelming disadvantage facing planters in Uganda was that they had to market their produce by inadequate and costly road and water transport, thence along 700 miles of single-track railway, and finally over several thousand miles of ocean. When all these facts are considered, the brief rise of the planters can be seen as a remarkable aberration in Uganda's history. After 1922 those who remained made a desperate attempt to persuade the Government to reduce wages, but this ran directly counter to the new official policy of 'bringing the Government into credit as an employer'.[1] Henceforth those who survived had to make their way in a cold, competitive market, unaided by the coercive power of the State. A few succeeded despite all odds, but none made a fortune, and very few were rewarded even by modest prosperity.

There was, however, a notable exception to this general failure of plantation enterprise. The history of sugar in Uganda is of particular interest as an example of a completely successful plantation crop. Jaggery, or unrefined sugar, had been crudely produced on a small scale for many years. Most of it was consumed locally, but a small export trade grew up after 1910, when 257 cwt., worth £200, were exported. Modern sugar production, however, commenced in 1924, when Nanji Kalidas Mehta, an Indian entrepreneur already prominent in cotton-ginning, acquired some 5,000 acres of derelict plantation land in the Kyagwe district of Buganda and built a sugar factory at Lugazi, near Jinja. The enterprise faced those difficulties which were by now becoming familiar. Transport was inadequate—there was, for example, no railway between Jinja and Kampala. The recruitment and training of labour was costly, for the local people, with a satisfactory cash crop, preferred to farm their own holdings, and immigrants from Ruanda and the West Nile therefore had to be recruited and trained. As most of them were 'target workers' who returned home after securing their limited cash needs, labour turnover was very high, and labour costs commensurately increased, particularly in the factory, where skills were more difficult to acquire and were consequently of greater value to the employer. Machinery was expensive to maintain because of the lack of skilled mechanics and outside

[1] Powesland, *Economic Policy and Labour*, p. 35.

repair shops. The factory was forced, in fact, to be a completely self-contained unit with its own repair shops and large stocks of spare parts. Even basic agricultural knowledge of the methods of cultivation suitable to local conditions of climate and soil was virtually non-existent. Nevertheless, the enterprise was success-ful, and by 1926 Lugazi was producing about 4,000 tons of sugar a season, rising to 5,000 tons by 1928. An important by-product was industrial alcohol, of which Lugazi produced 150,000 gallons each year. In 1929 Muljibhai Madhvani opened a second sugar factory at Kakira, in Busoga, on a planta-tion of some 4,000 acres. Under the protection afforded by customs tariffs and transport costs, the sugar industry made rapid progress until, by the early 1930's, production outstripped local consumption.

The success of sugar is explicable partly in terms of its climatic suitability and of the outstanding entrepreneurial skills and energies of Mehta and Madhvani, but the industry also enjoyed three advantages not shared by coffee and rubber plantations. In the first place sugar is particularly suitable for plantation development; it requires extensive factory equipment for pro-cessing near the place of origin, and the cane must be ground immediately it is cut. This by no means excludes the possibility of peasant production—in the Caribbean, for example, factories buy cane from small farmers—but it does lead to considerable economies of scale. Sugar's second advantage lay in the exis-tence of a local market which, if small, was capable of expansion as African incomes rose, and was comparatively stable in con-trast to the notorious fluctuations of world markets during the 1920's and 1930's. If Lugazi and Kakira had been forced to depend upon exporting their product they would undoubtedly have been defeated by the costs of transport to the coast and by fickle world markets. Unlike other plantation crops, however, sugar was eagerly demanded by Africans, who are notoriously sweet-toothed. A large potential market therefore existed, though its immediate impact was tempered by high prices and lack of purchasing power. Local prices were extremely high for a sugar-producing area, averaging $2\frac{1}{2}d.$ a lb. for an inferior product, which was the cost of the finest refined sugar in Eng-land. In 1929 East African consumption per head averaged only 3 lb. a year, in contrast to the United Kingdom's 101 lb., India's

27 lb., and Egypt's 26 lb.[1] Clearly there was plenty of scope for expansion. A final and significant advantage was that these businesses were managed by Indians who were willing to accept lower wages and living standards than their European counterparts. The resulting economy gave Lugazi and Kakira, like many subsequent Indian enterprises, a very great competitive advantage.

While plantation crops experienced the varying fortunes described above, peasant-grown cotton strengthened its hold upon the economy. Its progress was affected by the war and the slump of 1921, but in both of these crises it proved remarkably resilient. In 1914 shipping difficulties, a temporary fall in the world cotton market, and the closure of some local firms, resulted in negligible demand for the crop. As growers were unable to store their cotton they neglected or burned it. Buying started in a desultory fashion early in 1915, but the rains came a few weeks later, making transport difficult, staining cotton, and encouraging growers to ignore it and concentrate on planting their food crops. In most areas prices were half of those ruling in the previous season. But in the following year eager buying and high prices encouraged growers to plant heavily again. The Agricultural Department happily reported that this refusal of the growers to be discouraged by temporary fluctuations offered conclusive proof that the crop was now well established.[2] A similar pattern of events occurred five years later. In 1920 cotton prices reached their highest level since the American Civil War, a peak that was not touched again until 1946. In Uganda growers received up to 54 cents a pound. Stimulated by such rewards, they produced a bumper crop in the following season, only to find that prices had dropped to a tenth of their former level. But again recovery was rapid and output continued to expand steadily, except for a poor crop in 1927 which was the result of drought.

The most remarkable expansion was in the Eastern Province, where the cotton acreage, after a threefold increase between 1912 and 1917, again trebled in the following five years. Statistics of acreage for this period are admittedly unreliable, but the

[1] Empire Marketing Board, *Report of the Imperial Sugar Cane Conference, London, 1931* (1932), p. 17.
[2] Agricultural Department Annual Report, 1916, p. 7.

general pattern is confirmed by other evidence, such as the increase in poll-tax revenue from the Eastern Province at that time. Meanwhile cotton production in Buganda was increasing at a much slower rate, partly because alternative income opportunities were available to the people, but probably mainly because the efforts of the Agricultural Department were concentrated upon the Eastern Province. The precise nature of these efforts merits detailed explanation, for it was at this stage that the Government began to erect a structure of control over the industry which was to become increasingly complex, restrictive, and inflexible.

For about a decade after the introduction of cotton, the Government's main purpose had been to establish seed supplies and to persuade the peasant, with varying degrees of pressure, to grow the crop in the manner prescribed. By 1913 it had established control over seed supplies, and cotton had emerged as the country's leading staple. It was therefore logical to concentrate upon the extension of its acreage. The most effective way of doing this was to improve transport, and loans from Imperial funds, totalling some £300,000, were used mainly for the construction of the Busoga Railway and of roads in the Eastern Province. But the very effectiveness of these measures in extending the area of production led to new difficulties. After the failure of the hand-ginning scheme, processing of the crop was dependent upon a few power-driven factories, most of which were situated in Kampala. The Government wished to encourage new ginneries, but it was particularly anxious that they should be erected 'up-country', for two reasons. In the first place, as the area under cultivation became more extensive, cotton had to be transported over longer distances before ginning. In a country where the 'dry' marketing season is often interrupted by rain, this costly transport also resulted in staining and general deterioration in the quality of the crop. Secondly, the medical authorities were becoming increasingly alarmed at the risk of plague in the towns, which was increased by the presence of cotton stores harbouring rats. The ginners, on the other hand, were naturally reluctant to forsake the economic advantages and social amenities of the towns so long as they were able to secure adequate supplies of their raw material. The improvement of transport made it easier for them to secure such supplies either by sending their representatives up-country, or by purchasing from independent middlemen.[1] But to any firm that was contemplating the erection of an up-country ginnery, the presence of such middlemen was a serious disincentive, as they represented a continuous threat of competition for local supplies of cotton. Thus the middlemen became the centre of a long controversy, hated and decried, yet constantly employed, by ginners.

The principal inducement that could be afforded to ginners was to grant them a measure of protection from competitors. With this purpose in mind the Government, in addition to its general policy of trying to improve the quality of the crop, began to exert control over primary marketing. Its first attempts were made in the new cotton areas of Lango and Teso in 1910, growers being required to bring their crop to central buying points where marketing could be supervised. The prohibition of itinerant buying placed a considerable burden of transport upon the growers, but it was thought that they would gain by protection from cheating by unscrupulous buyers. In 1913 this system was extended throughout the whole of the Eastern Province.[2] Fifty-seven markets were 'gazetted' and the only other legal purchasing centres were the three ginneries in the province. In order to encourage the building of ginneries it was also made clear that any new ginnery would be similarly gazetted.

But the new system was not in itself sufficient to persuade ginners to move up-country, for buying licences were still freely available, and the middlemen could thus continue to compete. The Government therefore made various attempts to restrict their activities. First it tried the drastic policy of limiting buying licences to the representatives of 'any well-known firm'. But this could not be sustained in the face of vigorous opposition, notably that of the British Cotton Growing Association, which successfully lobbied the Colonial Office, arguing that restricted licensing favoured ginners at the expense of merchants, and that competition, not 'harassing restrictions', was the growers' best safeguard.[3] Licences therefore became freely available again, competition continued, and the marketing system was subjected

---

[1] Throughout this chapter 'middlemen' refers to intermediaries between growers and ginners. This is the normal Uganda usage.

[2] *Uganda Gazette*, Cotton Rules, 1913.

[3] British Cotton Growing Association Annual Report, May 1914.

to a mounting storm of abuse. Ginners demanded protection from 'volatile' middlemen without a 'real stake in the country', who would cream off easy profits in good years, cheating gullible peasants, and would abandon Uganda in bad years.

There was much confusion and special pleading in such arguments. A certain amount of cheating was indeed inevitable so long as growers remained unsophisticated and inexperienced in the ways of the market. Nevertheless, they obviously gained from the presence of several buyers competing for their crop, and the few who were articulate held this view. But in a paternalist society the welfare of the great majority clearly depended primarily upon the attitude of the Administration. Most local officials favoured competition, but some were led by devious routes to support the ginners' case for protection. Thus in Teso District they argued that it would not merely attract ginners to remote areas, but would enable them, in contrast to the middlemen, to pay 'full prices'. This is a fallacy which commonly arises when agricultural marketing is discussed; it ignores the cost of bulking minute quantities of a crop into manageable units, a function which has to be performed even if intermediaries are avoided. In practice ginners, whenever they were able to exercise a monopoly in buying, consistently paid *lower* prices, partly in order to cover bulking costs, but chiefly through the exercise of their bargaining strength.

The Government was therefore faced by a conflict of loyalties. On the one hand, it wished to encourage ginners, which, it thought, demanded the granting of monopoly privileges. On the other hand, it wanted to protect growers, which was most easily done by the maintenance of competition among buyers of the crop. This dilemma was often obscured by complexities of argument and legislation, and was greatly affected by contemporary views on 'rationalization' of industry, but it bedevilled policy throughout our period. Nor was the problem merely one of an individual ginnery's bargaining power, for from the outset ginners attempted to form associations which would share out the market and guarantee monopoly rights to the members. These associations were invariably short-lived at this early stage, but their effectiveness in lowering prices was well understood by Africans, and the 'syndicates' became a regular subject of complaint and petition to the Government.

For a few years no further steps were taken to resolve this controversy, if only because shortages of staff made effective control impossible. Even the existing level of supervision was difficult to maintain. Yet the experience of the war years strengthened the move towards control. To some extent this was merely an example, on a small scale, of what was happening in other countries: governments grew accustomed to increased power and to dealing with 'the industry', by which they meant a few large firms. There was obviously a considerable temptation for a poor understaffed government to administer economic controls through a few leading European firms, particularly those with London offices who had ready access to the metropolitan government. But apart from these general trends there were two incidents which strengthened the Government's resolve to exert firmer control over the cotton industry, and particularly to limit the activities of middlemen. First, the collapse of marketing in 1914 appeared to provide evidence of inherent instability in marketing arrangements; and although the entry of middlemen in 1915 was most welcome, the view gained ground that ultimate salvation lay in their discouragement and in the establishment of ginners as sole buyers. Second, and perhaps more significant, were the events of 1918, when the Government made a disastrous attempt to control prices. The original motive for this step was the fear that acute shipping difficulties would prevent any cotton being bought despite rapidly rising prices in the world market. While lengthy discussions took place in London, shipping facilities proved to be much easier than anyone had anticipated. Despite this, and against the advice of the Agricultural Department, the Government fixed prices to the growers at a level far below those justified by market conditions.[1] The obvious result was that middlemen were able to make easy profits by buying at the fixed price, and selling to ginners at the rising market price. There was frantic competition for the crop; many buyers offered non-monetary inducements such as salt and cigarettes above the legal price to growers, and some were prosecuted for such offences. Traders who normally did not deal in cotton joined the rush and even seventy Africans took out buying-licences.

[1] *Uganda Gazette*, 31 Jan. 1918.

In the remoter areas the growers were apparently satisfied with their modest share in this boom, being content to receive sufficient cash to pay their taxes and buy a few simple requirements. But in the 'more civilised parts the action of the Government was not understood'.[1] As the middlemen continued to profit by this extraordinary situation the complaints of growers, government officials, and ginners rose to a deafening crescendo. But such was the demand for cotton that ginners continued to buy from the hated middlemen. A typical cable from the London office of one prominent firm, in answer to requests for a ruling on what price to pay, read 'exercise your judgement, but the Company must get cotton'.[2] The Government next attempted to control middlemen's profits by fixing prices for the sale of cotton to the ginners. In so far as this edict was obeyed its effect was merely to pass the benefit on to ginners and exporters, for there was no control over the price they received for lint. To some extent this step, by removing the obvious demonstrable abuse, served to quieten African criticism, which had by now become sufficiently incensed for an appeal to be made to the Government by the Kabaka and his ministers.[3] But it is probable that the ordinance was extensively ignored. In any case, although the Government raised the price half-way through the season, it is evident that growers gained a smaller proportion of that season's proceeds than they would have done in the absence of controls. Finally, in November all attempts at price fixing were abandoned.[4]

In a long dispatch to the Colonial Secretary, the new Governor, Sir Robert Corydon, attempted to assess the lessons to be learned from this crisis. He was prepared to admit the necessity of the middlemen's functions, particularly in a country where 'the European cannot trade in such a small way, and the native has not yet learned to do so on any extensive scale'. But while there was 'nothing improper in such trade in itself' he argued that it could not be allowed to assume such proportions again as it had done in 1918, when

hundreds of little known and usually immoral speculators without

---

[1] Agricultural Department Report, 1918.
[2] Uganda Company, Board of Directors' *Minutes*, 20 Feb. 1918.
[3] 31 May 1918, E.S.A., Agricultural Dept., Minute Paper 486(ii).
[4] *Uganda Gazette*, 30 Nov. 1918.

any stake or interest in the industry or in the country, turned the cotton markets into pandemonium; evaded or overrode nearly all control; made without risk or work enormous profits largely at the expense of the peasant grower who had put his labour into his crop and of the ginner who had invested thousands of pounds in machinery; and finally brought into their trading a most pernicious element of chicanery.[1]

Although the crisis had arisen through unforeseen circumstances which were unlikely to occur again, it was essential, he argued, that legislation should be introduced which would definitely prevent its recurrence. For the following decade a great part of the energies and limited resources of the Government were expended in elaborate attempts to formulate such legislation.

It should be noted that a fairly clear racial division was envisaged between African growers, Indian middlemen, and European ginners. But none of these categories was clear-cut or impermeable; a number of Africans were beginning to attain a measure of success as middlemen. Those who could raise a little capital enjoyed the advantage over Indian competitors that during the greater part of the year, when no cotton was marketed, they could return to their smallholdings. Any attack by the Government upon middlemen was therefore also an attack on practically the only activity in which Africans could gain some experience of business. Moreover, the pre-eminence of Europeans in the ginning and exporting of cotton was being challenged by Indian firms.

After 1916 rising cotton prices and the expansion of the Indian and Japanese textile industries stimulated interest in Uganda cotton on the Bombay market, and this resulted in a considerable flow of Indian capital and enterprise into Uganda and of cotton exports to India. Neither of these factors of production were new-comers to Uganda, but they now assumed a wholly new significance. Before the war Allidina Visram had been the only Indian entrepreneur of real consequence, but even his activities were essentially those of a general trader with an 'amateur' interest in cotton, and his links with India as a source of capital were probably slight. Moreover, his death in

[1] 31 May 1918, E.S.A., Agricultural Dept., M.P. 486(ii).

1916 was soon followed by the collapse of the trading empire that he had created.

The new wave of Indian influence was heralded by the arrival in 1916 of Narandas Rajaram & Co. Ltd. This was a well-known cotton firm, launched in 1860, and the first Indian company to be represented on the Bombay Chamber of Commerce. Its director, Sir Purshotamdas Thakurdas, was an outstanding figure in Indian commerce and public life.[1] Backed by considerable authority, experience, and capital, the firm made an immediate impact upon the Uganda cotton industry. It began by purchasing cotton for export to its Bombay mills, but soon acquired and built ginneries. Other firms followed suit until by 1925 there were 145 ginneries in Uganda of which approximately 100 were Indian-owned. Many of these firms naturally retained or opened up links with the flourishing Bombay market, where mills were eager to acquire long stapled cotton, and a link was forged which has, with rare breaks, continued until the present day. The ginning boom, the influx of Indian firms, and the rise of the Bombay market, are shown in Table V below. Sterling exchange difficulties probably account for the sudden rise in exports to India during 1921 and 1922, but independently of these temporary advantages Bombay, both as an ultimate market and as an entrepôt for the Japanese trade, regularly absorbed at least half of Uganda's

TABLE V

	Cotton exports	Cotton exports to U.K.	Cotton exports to India	Ginning factories	Indian-owned factories
	('000 bales)	(% total)	(% total)		
1913–14	28	75	1	20	1
1915–16	26	74	12	19	Not known
1917–18	28	67	33	33	Not known
1919–20	36	66	29	58	17
1921	81	37	62	74	Not known
1922	48	29	70	83	Not known
1923	88	42	56	101	59
1925	196	57	40	155	100

Sources: Kenya and Uganda Annual Trade Reports; Annual Reports of Uganda Department of Agriculture.

[1] Cf. F. Moraes, *Sir Purshotamdas Thakurdas* (Bombay, 1956).

cotton by the 1920's. For most of the 1930's it was by far the biggest market, sometimes taking as much as 90 per cent. of Uganda's total cotton exports.

One of the Government's first acts after the war was to introduce new cotton rules[1] which were intended to effect a drastic reform. In the Eastern Province and Buganda posts were established where continuous buying was allowed throughout the season. Ginners were protected in various ways. 'Irresponsible buyers' were discouraged, for example, by reducing the number of posts from 75 to 35. Probably the most effective measure, however, was the 'Five-mile Rule' which guaranteed the removal of a buying post from within 5 miles of any ginnery. The rule did not at first appear on the statute book, but its existence is revealed by the protests it evoked from the Chamber of Commerce.[2] Not only buying-posts but even new ginneries were excluded by the rule, and thus the Government's policy of encouraging the building of ginneries was increasingly modified by its desire to protect those already in existence. In 1920, at the peak of the boom in cotton prices, numerous applications for ginning sites were refused on the ground that the area in question was 'sufficiently served with ginneries erected or approved'.[3] Opposition to the rule came not only from middlemen and those wishing to erect ginneries but also from growers, who were by now well aware of the advantages of competition for their crop, and were 'unanimous on this subject'.[4]

Torn between conflicting desires to appease growers, established ginners, and potential ginners, the Government vacillated in applying the rule. In 1920 its application was restricted to those ginneries already enjoying its protection. Later that year, after many complaints including protests from the Lukiko, it was abandoned in Buganda, but in 1924 it was reinstated 'as a guiding principle to be applied as far as circumstances permit'.[5] By now the ginning boom was forcing the Government into a complete reversal of its previous policy—from a fear of dearth it had swung to a fear of glut, and 'overcapitalization' became, paradoxically, a dreaded word in a society starved of capital.

[1] *Uganda Gazette*, 30 Nov. 1918.   [2] *Uganda Herald*, 3 Jan. 1919.

[3] 1923 Cotton Committee, *Evidence*, Annexure iv, 24 Sept. 1919.

[4] Ibid., annexure xv, 20 July 1923.

[5] *Uganda Gazette*, no. 155, 1924.

These ideas were, of course, keenly supported by established ginners, who after 1924 were able to influence policy not only through the indirect methods employed in the past, but through their direct representation on the newly created Cotton Control Board, which was empowered to consider applications for new ginning sites. But although vested interests were clearly at work, much as canal companies had opposed the building of railways in nineteenth-century England, it is true that there was real cause for disquiet.

The essential problem was that of ginning 'throughput'. Cotton-ginning is an industry in which machines and buildings lie idle for part of the year and fixed costs account for a large proportion of total costs. It follows that average costs fall considerably as more cotton is processed, and every ginner therefore attempts to maximize his purchases of cotton. But during the 1920's this could only be done by vigorously competing for the crop, because cotton production was not increasing as rapidly as the building of ginneries. Moreover prices failed to retain their 1920 level. The minimum throughput that would sustain a ginnery was probably about 500 bales, although ginners argued that 1,000 bales were necessary to ensure a 'modest' profit. But many ginneries were failing to secure even the minimum quantity; one ginner complained in 1923 that he was able to purchase the equivalent of only 300 bales, 200 of which were purchased at great distance and cost. An added difficulty was that there were few alternative outlets for capital and enterprise during the long period between cotton seasons. Some ginners were also in wholesale or retail trade, but generally losses incurred one season could not be made up during the year. It is hardly an exaggeration to say that most ginners were forced to make a year's profits in three months. The ultimate sanction was bankruptcy, but the Government was unwilling to see this happen on any scale for fear that it would 'bring the credit of the country into disrepute' and discourage future investment.

But if this was the plight of a few peripheral firms, for the majority ginning was reasonably profitable throughout the twenties. Certainly the complaints of ginners need not be taken at their face value. They were an articulate group with several outlets for publicity—the chambers of commerce, the Cotton Association, and the local press—and a formidable array of representatives who could exert pressure at home. Moreover, the very anxiety of the Government over their position stimulated a constant flow of advocacy, reaching flood-tides in 1923 when an official committee collected voluminous evidence without publishing a report, and in 1929 when a Commission of Enquiry was appointed. Support for the growers' case was, by contrast, pitiably inadequate. Ginners' profit margins were probably lower than those which the pioneers had enjoyed during the immediate post-war years, but it is difficult to believe that many were actually experiencing losses. The enthusiasm with which firms continued to enter the industry reflected an optimism which may have been irrational but which must have been based on some knowledge of its profitability. In 1925 the Director of Agriculture reported the erection of twenty-two new ginneries, 'in spite of every effort being made to induce prospective ginners to refrain from building', and complained in similar terms the following year. The few factories that changed hands during this period fetched good prices—over £5,000 in Buganda, over £10,000 in the Eastern Province. The ginners' disgruntlement was probably due more to the disappointment of optimistic anticipations than to the experience of real losses.

We have already noted that many attempts had been made to form buying associations, without much success. A more determined and successful effort was made in Buganda in 1927, leading to the formation of the Buganda Seed Cotton Buying Association, whose aim, when stripped of the high-flown language common to such organizations, was the elimination of competition for the crop. The government reaction to this was to do nothing, provided 'reasonable' prices were paid by the Association. It even welcomed the Association on being assured that 'by superior organization' and the elimination of the costs which resulted from 'unrestricted and rather wild competition' the grower would receive a *higher* price.[1] The growers' response was inevitably very different. The Lukiko refused an invitation to send a representative to the meetings of the new Association; and the Kabaka's nominee on the Cotton Control Board attempted, unsuccessfully, to persuade the Government to intervene and 'protect' the growers. Such was the extent of

[1] Governor's speech to Legislative Council, 5 Feb. 1929.

African opposition that the Provincial Commissioner of Buganda was moved to publish an elaborate apologia for the Association,[1] the logic of which was assailed by the fact that prices were higher wherever competition existed. In the Eastern Province, where competition still existed in some areas, there was wide disparity between prices in 'free' and 'association' markets; in four areas where monopoly buying was enforced, prices were at most two-thirds of those ruling where buying was competitive. An estimate made by the Agricultural Department suggested that in Buganda, as a result of the Association's activities that season, growers received some £136,000 less for their crop than they would have received 'under normal competition'.[2]

A serious limitation of the Buganda Association's effectiveness was the fact that in the Eastern Province ginners had so far been unable to form a province-wide syndicate. Ganda growers were therefore able to get higher prices in 1928 by taking their cotton across the Nile into Busoga, where competition still existed. During the following season the Buganda Association therefore attempted to consolidate its monopoly by persuading the Government to forbid the removal of cotton in this way. The Cotton Control Board's rejection of this request, which was only carried by means of the Director of Agriculture's casting vote, was a crucial and controversial decision, for it marked the fine but vital distinction between passive acquiescence in monopoly and its active support by the Government.

Meanwhile a flood of propaganda for the Association poured forth, couched in euphemisms like 'co-operation', 'stabilization', and 'rationalization', which were catchwords of the day in England, where influential pressure groups echoed these sentiments. The British Cotton Growing Association, no longer an impartial outsider and champion of competition, but involved through its Uganda ginneries, asserted that improved transport facilities in the Eastern Province offered 'a splendid opportunity' for reducing the number of ginneries, but would necessitate a 'combination of ginners'.[3] The chairman of the Empire Cotton Growing Corporation claimed that ginning 'ought to be a monopoly, or at least ought to be rigorously controlled'. This

[1] Official Communication to the *Uganda Herald*, 16 Mar. 1928.
[2] 10 Aug. 1928, E.S.A., Agricultural Department, 1294/491.
[3] B.C.G.A. Annual Report, 1928.

might reduce growers' proceeds but would not discourage cultivation, for Africans had few other sources of income. Moreover, they had been 'slightly and not unnaturally demoralised by an easy success'.[1] The Hilton Young Commission[2] also voiced its support for monopoly buying in vague terms, as assisting to 'strengthen the position'.

Two groups in Uganda stood firmly against these views. Indian middlemen formed a 'Free Traders Union' and resolved to take 'all constitutional steps' against associations, demanding that the Government declare them illegal, increase buying posts and middlemen's representation on the Cotton Control Board, and appoint a Royal Commission to investigate the industry. But, as a leading firm of ginners remarked, 'the names of the leaders of this movement did not indicate ability to influence the Government or public opinion in Uganda'. More significant was the unanimous opposition of Africans to the 'syndicate'. The Provincial Commissioner of Buganda confessed that when on tour he was constantly 'bombarded with questions on the subject', and there were many letters from Africans to the press. Nor could these sentiments be dismissed as the work of political agitators or the foolish repetition of middleman propaganda, for the Lukiko and the Kabaka also expressed their opposition with considerable force. In the Eastern Province the 'Young Busoga Association' was formed with the main object of persuading growers not to sell to members of the Association.[3] Even in the more backward areas African opposition, though less articulate, was sufficiently active to worry the administration. In the West Nile District, for example, where a buying association was active, the district commissioner reported that 'a lot of cotton has been held back because of the ridiculous prices offered. It is going to be extremely difficult to get the West Nile natives to grow any cotton next year.' His fears were warranted, for in the following season the cotton acreage fell from 8,000 to 100 acres.

It was against this background of 'hostility and distrust of associations'[4] that a Commission of Enquiry was appointed in 1929. But far from being an expert Royal Commission with

[1] Empire Cotton Growing Corporation, Lord Derby's speech at meeting of Council, 1928.
[2] See Chapter VI, pp. 307-8, above.
[3] Uganda Provincial Commissioners Annual Report, Eastern Province, 1929.
[4] Uganda Gazette, 16 Sept. 1929, Governor's speech to Legislative Council.

open terms of reference, it was a local body with the avowed object of fixing 'fair' prices to growers under monopolistic conditions.

The commission produced a report[1] which was a remarkable exercise in tortuous *non-sequitur*. It freely admitted that 'excessive competition' benefited the growers, but alleged that this was true only 'for the time being' because 'it is obvious that an industry cannot go on indefinitely paying more for its raw product than is economic'. Those ginners who had not been driven out of business by competition would then combine and buy cotton at prices low enough to compensate themselves for past losses. Growers would therefore suffer unless new firms were to enter ginning, but this they would do only at the expense of existing firms which had 'built up the industry'. Meanwhile internecine competition would have lowered 'the credit of the country in the financial world'.

Therefore, the report concluded, both in the interests of the 'industry' (meaning the ginners) 'and those of the country generally', the revival of competition would be most undesirable. But—and here was the crux of the matter—it was by no means certain that buying associations could survive 'unless definite encouragement be given to them'. Therefore, provided the owners of four-fifths of the gins either east or west of the Nile agreed to form an association for ten years, the Government should *compel* recalcitrant ginners either to join the relevant association or surrender their ginning rights. If an association were formed in only one area, then the Government should safeguard it by preventing the movement of raw cotton from its area into a free area. Such action was justified by a government's right to 'curtail individual rights for the benefit of the community generally'. But if associations were to be protected, so also must growers; this was to be effected by minimum price legislation, with the Government prepared to enter as buyer of last resort. A final suggestion, which was to become a matter of some controversy, was that growers should be able if they wished to get their cotton processed without selling it to a ginnery. To prevent 'overcapitalization' the Government should prohibit any increase in the capacity of existing gin-

[1] *Report of the Commission of Enquiry into the Cotton Industry of Uganda* (Entebbe, 1929).

neries, in addition to continuing to refuse licences for new ginneries, as it had been doing since 1928. Finally, 'redundant
ginneries' should be eliminated and their owners compensated
out of a fund subscribed by ginners, the Government, and the
growers.

A thorough analysis of the paralogisms contained in this
extraordinary report would require undue elaboration, but a
few comments must be made. First, the commission's arguments
appeared to rest on two assumptions: that buying associations
would automatically reduce costs, and that the benefits of this
would be passed on to the growers. Neither of these assumptions
was valid either theoretically or historically. Secondly, the fact
that the growers were unanimously and sensibly, in the light
of their experience, opposed to associations, was at no stage
seriously considered. The minimum price legislation which the
commission recommended could be attempted only by reference to estimates of processing costs, an exercise to which they
devoted a great deal of calculation. But such estimates could
bear little relation to an efficient, or even an 'average' firm, for
this would involve a large number of firms falling 'below the
line' and result in those bankruptcies which it was a paramount
aim of policy to avoid. Moreover, the 'Table of Costs' calculated
by the commission[1] was based upon the hoary fallacy that
capital assets can be valued at their original money cost. Its
attitude towards the writing down of capital was based upon an
amalgam of sentimentality—the belief that established capitalists have 'a stake in the country' which entitles them to unlimited protection from new-comers—and capitulation to a
highly articulate vested interest. Finally, the belief that growers,
by contributing towards compensation of 'redundant' ginners,
should pay for something which they unanimously opposed, was
an extraordinary interpretation of the role of Government.

Far from expressing their delight, the ginners were not satisfied with the report.[2] The 'very greatest exception' was taken
to the commission's mild criticism of the prices paid to growers
in recent seasons, and proposals for the elimination of ginneries
were strenuously opposed. It was argued that the Government

[1] Ibid., Appendix 3.
[2] Joint memorandum by the Uganda Cotton Association and the Buganda Seed
Cotton Buying Association, Kampala, 13 Aug. 1929.

had shown insufficient zeal in 'persuading' growers to produce more cotton. Production, they considered, was not primarily a function of price and climatic conditions, but of administrative control. 'Overcapitalization' indicated a lack of raw material rather than an excess of ginneries. The commission's recommendation that growers should be able to get their cotton ginned without selling to a ginnery was opposed because it would 'lead to a new class of middlemen'. Most significant was their opposition to compulsory association membership, a reflection of the incipient instability of the associations.

African opposition to the report was unanimous and well argued. At a meeting of the Buganda Lukiko it was subjected to close and damaging scrutiny. Associations lowered prices, therefore the Government must not encourage them. Ginneries and stores should not be reduced in number, because this would seriously inconvenience farmers. Africans should be helped to enter the ginning industry, and should be educated to understand the cotton market by the publication of price statistics. These were the unanimous views of the Lukiko, and the Governor was requested to forward them to the Colonial Secretary. Finally, the Kabaka wrote to the Governor in identical terms. Similar views were voiced by 'the Association of Uganda Farmers' in a 'letter to the people' and in petitions to the Colonial Secretary, the Governor, and the Kabaka.

The Government's attitude was explained at a meeting of ginners' organizations and chambers of commerce in October. 'The essential condition of any legislation to encourage the formation of 100% associations' was that they should agree to gin cotton on behalf of growers at an agreed 'fair price'. Given this, the Government was prepared to meet most of the ginners' demands. But early in 1930, before any action could be taken on the commission's recommendations, the associations broke up and ginners again began to compete for the crop. The reason for this collapse was a poor harvest due to bad weather. Rather less cotton had been planted than in the previous season, probably because of growers' general disgruntlement and fear of the associations, though reasonable weather would have resulted in a crop only slightly smaller than that of 1928-9. But the customary dry spell failed to materialize in October, and continuing rains encouraged the spread of blackarm disease, while the lack of sun gave cotton no chance to mature. The final crop was less than half that of the previous season. Ginners ignored their association commitments and competed wildly for a share of this greatly reduced quantity. In the Eastern Province, which was most seriously affected, the average number of bales per ginnery fell from 1,100 to 300. Even in Buganda, where it had been thought that a '100% Association' was assured of at least ten years' life, competitive buying forced prices up from 12·50 sh. to 20 sh., and the Buying Association disintegrated.

Thus, twenty-five years after its inception, the cotton industry and the Government's cotton policy had reached a watershed. Up to the early 1920's attempts by ginners to form buying associations had emerged as a natural reaction to the uncertainties of an increasingly competitive market situation. During this period the Government was at first unwilling to do much more than hold the ring, but this liberal attitude was increasingly influenced by the desire to control quality, to encourage ginners, and to protect growers against cheating. Then in the mid-1920's, with the increasingly fierce competition for a slowly expanding crop, the idea of 'rationalization' began to emerge as an elixir which it was thought would benefit growers and ginners alike. Encouraged by the apparent respectability of this cult, whose advocates included articulate interests in England, and obsessed by a growing fear of bankruptcies and social distress, the Government was naturally disposed to welcome a solution of apparent neatness and simplicity. There remained only one obstacle to its wholehearted support of ginners' associations: the unanimous opposition of the growers to monopoly and their desire for competition. The 1929 Commission Report, which purported to be an expert and unprejudiced analysis of the situation, removed this lingering doubt. The growers were to have monopoly buying forced upon them and to be protected from exploitation by a system of minimum price legislation. Finally, at the brink of this imposition, the collapse of the associations left the Government with a clear choice. Either it could accept the growers' wishes, allowing, or even enforcing the continuance of competitive buying, or it could attempt to re-establish the associations and impose regulated monopoly buying.

The decade after 1920 witnessed the triumph of African farming as the leading sector of Uganda's economy, but it also saw a remarkable change in economic relationships within that sector. During the early years of cotton-growing the chiefs had played a dominant role and enjoyed a liberal share of the new wealth. The Government had regarded them not merely as indispensable agents for the imposition of British rule, but as potential leaders in the process of social and economic change which stemmed from that rule. But whatever their success in the former role, the chiefs proved to be sadly deficient in qualities of economic leadership. With few exceptions they were content to enjoy the easeful life of country gentlemen, financed by ill-defined but lucrative rents, taxes, and tributes. The Government was probably affected less by these deficiencies than by a growing awareness that many of the chiefs offended against British standards of effective and tolerable local government, and perhaps by the knowledge that they were becoming less indispensable as administration became firmly established. But other influences helped to define a changing official attitude towards chiefs and peasants.

There was the simple argument that peasants would work harder and produce more if they were allowed to retain a greater proportion of the proceeds of their labours. Economic incentives might therefore become more important as less use was made of the old coercive methods of encouraging production. In October 1924, just before the arrival of the Ormsby-Gore Commission, a circular was issued to all provincial commissioners, deploring 'the excessive zeal shown by chiefs in fining and imprisoning natives for failing to show sufficient activity in planting'. But in 1925 native court returns showed that people were still being tried and punished for failing to plant cotton, and the instructions were repeated, although 'legitimate influence in propaganda' was encouraged. But, as the commission remarked,[1] the days of coercion were passing and could not be revived. It will be remembered that the ginners attributed the slow growth of cotton production to this relaxation of pressure upon the growers. This was denied by the Government, who argued that the reduced crops of 1926 and 1927 were 'due almost entirely to climatic conditions, a factor

[1] Ormsby-Gore *Report*, Cmd. 2387, p. 34.

which even the most autocratic and omniscient Government could not hope to control'.[1] There was truth in both views. While little could be done to cushion the economy from the influence of climate, a factor which has remained a leading determinant of Uganda's annual income to this day, mere propaganda was an inadequate alternative to direct pressure upon growers. A lively promotion of market incentives might have proved more effective, but neither the ginners nor the Government were willing to face the full implications of such a policy. However, the idealization of the peasant flourished in the new social and moral climate of the 1920's. If the rapacious demands of white masters, as characterized by the 1920 Development Commission, could be rejected, were the assumptions of black masters to remain unassailed? Moreover, the cult of the peasant and the denigration of the landowner were a prominent feature of Europe's intellectual climate during this period.

Thus the ultimate aim of policy, as stated by Jarvis, the Acting Governor, in 1922, became 'the division of the land among a large number of peasant producers. On this basis the economic prosperity and social development of the tribe can be most surely developed.' The new policy was even more clearly expressed in a public statement in 1926: 'whether the ownership of large freehold estates should vest in one individual or another is, looking to the interests of the country as a whole, of less importance than the safeguarding of the interests of the native tenants.'[2] Thus in Buganda the transfer of land to peasant ownership was to be encouraged and tenants were to be protected against exploitation. Outside Buganda chiefs would not be granted freehold titles and would be converted from feudal overlords into salaried officials.

The impact of this significant change in policy upon one important society has been described by an anthropologist with an intimate knowledge of Busoga.[3] The political system of Busoga had been 'Ganda-ized' by Semei Kakunguru, a Ganda chief who was appointed as paramount chief in 1906.[4] In each county chiefs were granted *bwesengeze* (personal estates) on

[1] Governor's speech to Legislative Council, 16 Sept. 1929.
[2] Quoted in H. B. Thomas and A. E. Spencer, *A History of Uganda Land and Surveys* (Entebbe, 1938), p. 72.
[3] L. A. Fallers, *Bantu Bureaucracy* (Cambridge, 1956), ch. vi.
[4] For Kakunguru's career, see Chapter II, pp. 88–91, above.

which they could demand personal tributes in produce and labour from their tenants. The introduction of cotton stimulated the commutation of these tributes into money payments, which were regularized in 1922. Each peasant was required to pay 10 sh. or one month's unpaid labour a year, which could, of course, be employed in the cultivation of cotton on the chief's private lands. Additional income was received in the form of rebates from poll-tax revenue. In 1924 it was estimated that the biggest county chief was receiving an annual income of more than £3,500 from these various sources. It is hardly surprising that 'chiefs who served during the period of the *bwesengeze* system speak of it with nostalgia'.[1] In 1926 the system was abolished; tribute was reduced to 4 sh. or 12 days' labour, poll-tax rebates were forbidden, and the chiefs were paid fixed salaries and pensions. In 1936 all tributes were abolished and the chiefs became salaried officials.[2]

Meanwhile in Buganda, peasant proprietors with holdings of 10–100 acres were beginning to emerge of their own volition. Inheritance without primogeniture was breaking up the great estates that had been created by the Uganda Agreement, and men were purchasing land in order to escape the 'chiefs' pernicious outside influences' and to establish their rank in society. This process was slow, but the Administration's desire to hasten it was given further stimulus by the agrarian discontent revealed during the *bataka* controversy of 1922. A detailed examination of this movement is beyond the scope of the present chapter,[3] but whatever the merits of the movement itself, it certainly encouraged the Protectorate Government to take effective action. The *Busulu* and *Envujo* Law[4] 'probably the first instance of a rent restriction act in tropical Africa',[5] regulated the peasant's obligations and secured his rights of occupancy. *Busulu* was fixed at 10 sh. a year or one month's unpaid labour. *Envujo* was fixed at 4 sh. in most counties. 'Thus having given unprecedented

[1] Fallers, *Bantu Bureaucracy*, p. 149.

[2] For the political aspect of these changes, see Chapter IX, pp. 494-6, below.

[3] See Chapter IX below.

[4] Uganda Protectorate Ordinance 1927, Appendix C. Native Laws, p. 278. '*Busulu* is a commutation in money of the labour obligations by a tenant to the landlord. *Envujo* is a commutation in money of the customary present of a part of the produce or a calabash of beer.' See A. B. Mukwaya, *Land Tenure in Buganda*, East African Studies no. 1 (Kampala, 1953), p. 20.

[5] Thomas and Spencer, op. cit., p. 72.

privileges of freehold to the chiefs and notables in 1900, the Government subsequently limited the powers of these landlords in a way which would be thought unusual in other countries with individual land tenure.'[1] But it would be misleading to emphasize the immediate benefits that peasants derived from the fixing of these obligations. While prices and incomes remained low their real burden was considerable. It was only in the years following the second world war that rising prices and increasing land values really benefited tenants at the expense of landlords.

A peasant economy's resilience to world depression, 1929–39

Uganda's reaction to the great depression was, at first glance, surprising. 'The economy shuddered briefly, then went forward rather faster than before.'[2] Some statistics of this change are shown in Table VI below.

TABLE VI

Prices and production, 1929–38

	Cotton		Coffee		
	Average price to growers	*Production*	*Average price f.o.b. Mombasa*	*Exports*	*Total domestic exports*
	(sh./100 lb.)	('000 bales)	(sh./100 lb.)	('000 cwt.)	(£m.)
1929	17	203	86	41	4·3
1930	15	130	63	49	2·1
1931	11	190	46	70	1·9
1932	11	203	51	87	2·2
1933	9	291	42	100	3·5
1934	10	278	38	154	3·8
1935	12	249	37	126	3·6
1936	10	322	33	229	4·5
1937	13	331	32	258	5·7
1938	8	424	23	280	4·6

These figures illustrate the comparative resilience of a peasant economy to the onslaught of depression. Uganda's experience of the 1930's was happier than that of countries dependent upon plantations for their income.[3] Her own small plantation sector

[1] Richards, *Economic Development and Tribal Change*, p. 128.
[2] C. C. Wrigley, *Crops and Wealth in Uganda*, East African Studies no. 12 (Kampala, 1959), p. 60.
[3] Cf. A. Pim, *Colonial Agricultural Production* (London, 1946), p. 44.

was sharply affected by falling prices, apart from sugar, which enjoyed a local market, and tea, which became a useful subsidiary crop after the mid-1930's. The area under non-native coffee fell from approximately 20,000 acres in 1929 to 13,000 acres in 1938.

Peasant production was comparatively buoyant, but it would be wrong to deduce from this that peasants were 'perverse' in their reactions to price changes, i.e. that they produced more *because* prices were falling. In the first place the available statistics are inadequate and misleading. Thus the increased production of 1931 was a result of improved weather after the disastrous previous season. Acreage figures would give a better indication of the growers' response to price, but they are quite unreliable for this period. Secondly, any attempt to correlate prices and production during this period founders upon the simple fact that 'other things' were by no means equal. Improved communications and the effects of the Government's agricultural policy were at least as important as market forces in influencing output.

The retirement of Simpson as Director of Agriculture, and the appointment in 1929 of Dr. J. D. Tothill as his successor, marked the end of an era in agricultural policy. To some extent this reflected the differences in background and temperament of two outstanding men holding a key position in the economy. Working with meagre resources and few precedents, Simpson had created a department with a tradition of support for the peasants, in opposition not merely to planter interests but sometimes even to government policy. Thus in 1918 his published departmental report had been openly critical of the Government's attempts to fix cotton prices. His consistent regard for the growers is demonstrated by the care with which his department collected evidence of the effect of ginners' associations upon the prices they were receiving. It was presumably this evidence that led him to use his casting vote on the Cotton Board to prevent the Government from closing the Busoga free market to Buganda cotton. The importance of this decision in the ginners' struggle for monopoly is demonstrated by the vicious attack which was launched upon Simpson, his second ordeal by slander in a decade. An anonymous correspondent to the *Uganda Herald*, evidently a member of the Cotton Board, described him as 'a

domineering old man who held the balance in his own hands
and ruthlessly used his power in an antagonistic attitude against
the Buganda ginners'.[1] There can be little doubt that Simpson
was a great colonial administrator whose single-mindedness
in the advocacy and promotion of peasant agriculture was an
important contribution to the progress of Uganda Africans.[2]
Tothill was, by contrast, an agricultural scientist whose expert
technical knowledge was accompanied by an ignorance of business intrigue which often led him to an uncritical acceptance of
'the industry's' views on commercial matters. Moreover, the
very fact that he was a new-comer limited his ability to take a
strong, independent line in the tradition of his predecessor, who
had served under four governors.

But the change of personalities was merely one aspect of a
fundamental change in the nature of agricultural policy during
these years. The 1930's saw the rise of 'scientific agriculture' in
Uganda. In 1914 the department's total staff had consisted of
the Director, six district agricultural officers, a ploughing in-
structor, an entomologist, and a botanist. By 1931, despite the
depression, there were no less than forty-two members of the
department of whom virtually all were professionally qualified
and many were specialist technicians. After 1930 the department's annual report became an elaborate document, consisting
of two parts: the first a review of administration and 'the
agricultural position of the Protectorate'; the second, a report
on the scientific work and results of experiments conducted
during the year. Another influence towards scientism was the
work of the Empire Cotton Growing Corporation. Whereas the
British Cotton Growing Association had, since 1904, subjected
Entebbe to a fairly constant stream of advice, criticism, exhortation, and warning of incipient danger, the younger E.C.G.C.,
without replacing its predecessor, added a new-found and far
more technical enthusiasm.

The new technology made numerous significant contributions towards the ultimate improvement of agriculture in
Uganda, where much of the basic environmental knowledge
essential to progressive agriculture was lacking, and where

[1] *Uganda Herald*, 2 Nov. 1928.
[2] Cf. in contrast the work of Kenya's Agricultural Department during this
period, Chapter V, pp. 245-7, above.

techniques and equipment were often crude, inadequate, or even harmful. In crop studies, disease control, anti-erosion measures and agricultural education, the work of the department and of outside technical bodies added considerably to the country's store of knowledge.[1] But a traditional agrarian society responds slowly to the stimulus of new ideas and techniques, and what happens to the network of economic relationships is usually more significant for development than the accumulation and improvement of technology. Moreover, it could be argued that the advance of technology itself brought concomitant disadvantages. Two demand our special attention: the economic implications of quality control, and the relegation of market forces to an inferior status in the economy. Neither was wholly new in economic policy, but they acquired an added significance during the 1930's.

The Agricultural Department's attitude towards the development of motor transport offered an interesting demonstration of the conflicts that can arise between the demands of quality control and those of economic development. The use of lorries began to increase substantially during the mid-1920's. No statistics of vehicle registration are available before 1930, but it is known that by 1927 many cotton-growers were using lorries to transport their crop to ginneries. By 1930 nearly 1,500 motor-lorries were licensed in Uganda, and it was 'the exception rather than the rule for the grower to market his crop by direct head-load'.[2] Imports of motor-spirit doubled between 1924 and 1926 and had again doubled by 1930. Nor was this of importance only to the cotton industry. Wherever transport was required, the lorry supplemented the bicycle in a country with neither a substantial network of railways nor effective animal transport. As cotton-marketing lasted for only three months, vehicles were available for the rest of the year to perform a multitude of tasks. They provided immediate pleasures of travel; they acted as feeders to the railway, which in 1931 at last reached Kampala; and they generally served to lower costs and to extend the area of the cash economy. Uganda by now enjoyed a good road system, in contrast to Kenya's and Tanganyika's inadequacies; by 1920 the Provincial Commissioner of the Northern Province

---

[1] Cf. J. D. Tothill (ed.), *Agriculture in Uganda* (Oxford, 1940).
[2] Agricultural Department Report, 1930.

was boasting that the 1,400 miles of roads in his province were 'swept throughout every Monday'. But until the coming of the motor-vehicle there was little transport to disturb the dust. By 1932 not only were there 1,800 miles of good main roads in the country, but they were being used, and road transport promised to 'open up the country' in a way that the railway never achieved.

It is necessary to appreciate the full meaning of this hackneyed but pregnant phrase. Individual centres of trade had existed since the beginning of our period; by 1935 there were 108 'gazetted' townships and twenty-seven trading centres. But each was a comparatively isolated market with a limited radius of impact upon its surrounding area. A few miles outside even the main towns, prices of imported goods were higher, wages lower, and the influence of new ideas and new techniques slight. Improved transport alone could not push this economy, hovering between subsistence and cash, into sustained growth, but it could facilitate the linking of these isolated pockets of development into the complex network of interconnected markets which distinguishes a healthy growing economy. Finally, transport was itself an industry providing employment and incomes where they were sorely needed.

Yet despite these obvious advantages the growth of motor-transport encountered a growing body of criticism which demanded its restriction. Lorries were said to facilitate the cheating of cotton-growers, who could be conveyed to a remote ginnery with their cotton and then forced to accept a low price or face a long walk home. They were also alleged, in some unspecified way, to 'demoralize the native'. An effective answer to these complaints was given by a district agricultural officer:

The average native has passed the stage of 'spoon feeding' and in the majority of cases is well able to look after his own interests. The use of motor transport is after all only a sign of the times, and it is difficult to understand how it will 'demoralise the native' . . . it would appear rather to be a progressive movement, which should tend to popularise the cultivation of cotton, inasmuch as it does away with one of the most distasteful duties in connection with the raising of the crop.[1]

[1] 31 Jan. 1927, Jinja Agricultural Department Archives.

Nevertheless, an effective attack upon the unrestricted development of lorry transport was launched by the Agricultural Department. Its 1931 Report admitted that lorries had 'undoubtedly facilitated the sale of cotton by producers', but was distressed by their 'agricultural effects'. These were seen entirely in terms of quality control, by which standard lorry transport had two serious disadvantages. First it tended to increase the distribution of such pests as pink bollworm and blackarm, which were carried in seed cotton, and therefore made it increasingly difficult to issue 'clean' seed. Secondly, it encouraged the mixing of different growths and of good and bad qualities of the same growth. To these complaints the department added the curious argument that improved transport *raised* costs: 'when cotton prices were high its (transport) cost was of secondary importance. With pre-war prices now ruling, however, the original value of the system has largely disappeared, because although producers can sell their cotton readily, the cost of lorry transport causes a substantially lower price to be paid'.[1] An ideal system of marketing, argued the department, would ensure the 'economical' use of lorries, and avoid quality deterioration, by dividing the country into zones within which cotton would be sold and processed and out of which no seed-cotton could be moved. The Cotton Zone Ordinance of 1933[2] imposed this policy and thus resolved the dilemma which had faced the Government since 1929, for it led inevitably to the rebirth of ginning associations.

Thus it was the agriculturalists' demand for quality control that led to, or provided justification for, not merely restrictions on the use of lorry transport, but the final implementation of monopoly buying. Moreover, zoning ensured the future survival of the syndicates by removing the threat of competition between zones, and was therefore a complete reversal of Simpson's decision in 1928. The fact that the Government was aware of these implications is revealed by the ordinance's provision for the fixing of minimum prices, and by the curiously worded statement of a later Cotton Commission: 'The pools were constituted by a series of individual agreements between ginnery owners; it cannot be said that direct official encouragement was

---

[1] Agricultural Department Report, 1931, p. 10.
[2] *Laws of Uganda*, no. 16 of 1933.

given by Government to the formation of the pools, although no obstacles were presented, while assistance and advice were rendered by the Department of Agriculture during their organisation.'[1]

Direct limitation of the use of lorries arose therefore from a misconceived desire to prevent 'uneconomic' transport, and from a policy of quality control which could probably have been implemented without resort to draconian legislation. It was also strengthened by the wish to protect the railway from competition. Indirect limitations were also placed upon the benefits arising from improved transport. These were the restrictions placed upon the activities of traders, a policy originally based upon the desire to protect Africans and to maintain law and order, which now hardened into an inflexible code of great complexity. In 1904 the Trading Ordinance was a simple document. By 1938 it consisted of ten pages of detailed regulations governing every conceivable activity that a trader might contemplate, and couched in language which would be incomprehensible or at least forbidding to men in societies far more advanced than Uganda. Thus, it was unlawful for non-natives to trade outside established trading centres or within 'scheduled' areas. It was also unlawful for natives to trade in such places on behalf of non-natives, an obvious barrier to emergent African businessmen without capital. Trading licences could be refused on numerous grounds, including failure to make 'satisfactory provision for the keeping of proper books of account'. Explicable in terms of the protection of native interests, these restrictions severely impeded the spread of the money economy.

They were strengthened by an increasing tendency to create an artificial division between 'agricultural' and 'commercial' problems, and to regard 'production' as a purely technical matter which could be divorced from market considerations. This is well illustrated by the new division of responsibilities between the B.C.G.A. and the E.C.G.C.: 'the Association made themselves responsible primarily for the commercial side, particularly ginning, baling, and marketing, while the Corporation concentrated upon production with its relevant agricultural and scientific problems and requirements.'[2] A similar attitude

---

[1] *Report of the Uganda Cotton Commission 1938* (Entebbe, 1939), para. 33.
[2] 'Empire Cotton Growing Association 1921–1950', *Empire Cotton Growing Review*, xxviii. 1 (1951).

R

was embraced by the Uganda Agriculture Department and 'agricultural and scientific problems and requirements' were usually given priority while markets were regarded as peripheral, rather than at the heart of the productive process. Thus the 1936 Cotton Committee asserted that 'in general, while deprecating further increase of markets to any extent, we realise that there are places where new markets may be required from time to time *on account of* increase of crop'.[1]

The fallacy is obvious but fundamental. To regard increased production as leading to, rather than resulting from, the extension of the market, is to reverse the entire logic of development in a free economy. Such a policy might succeed in a fully planned totalitarian society, but in Uganda neither the political philosophy nor the elaborate machinery of control were in existence. Allied to this 'non-market' approach to development was the desire to impose high technical standards which were often inappropriate to local abilities or even to market demand. It was commonly assumed, for example, that in the absence of controls, competitive buying would lead to the undesirable purchase of 'inferior' qualities. Restrictions were therefore devised and buyers would be prosecuted for 'buying below grade'.[2] This was a repetition of ideas which had some justification in 1908, but by now the situation had changed. Uganda's cotton was established in world markets, and presumably primary buyers could be expected to have some conception of the market's needs and some respect for the losses they would incur through buying inappropriate qualities. Nor were these restrictive attitudes confined to cotton, although the Government's preoccupation with that crop and its prominence in this chapter accurately reflect its importance in the economy. In no year during the 1930's did cotton exports account for less than 77 per cent. of the value of total exports, and in most years it was well above 80 per cent. Brief mention must be made, however, of developments in the production of coffee, sugar, and tea, for the idea of diversifying the economy was an important element in economic policy.

In 1923, as part of the drive for peasant production, it had been decided to encourage Africans to grow coffee. The esti-

---

[1] *Report of the Cotton Committee* (Entebbe, 1936), para. 43.
[2] Agricultural Department Report, 1933.

mated acreage increased in the following decade from about 1,500 acres to some 27,000 acres, but it was not until after the second world war that coffee became a serious rival to cotton as a major source of income. In certain areas, however, where cotton had not penetrated, coffee assumed considerable local importance. Thus in the tiny area of Bwamba, in the Western Province, it introduced the people to cash. Between 1936 and 1945 the Amba's annual income from their coffee rose from approximately £2,000 to over £9,000.[1] The fact that coffee was a more remunerative crop than cotton gradually became apparent, and by 1937 there were in the whole of Uganda about 48,000 acres under the crop. Most of this was *robusta* coffee, a type indigenous to Uganda—the Sesse islands contain trees known to be over 100 years old. But in Bugisu, on the slopes of Mount Elgon, where conditions are suitable for the cultivation of finer coffee, a highly organized scheme was developed for the production of *arabica*. When the first seedlings were introduced in 1912, the Gisu had enjoyed few opportunities of earning cash at home. A few grew cotton on the lower slopes, but many migrated to Kenya or Buganda as plantation workers. Gradually the Government established nurseries, introduced simple processing machinery, and attempted to encourage the high standards of quality which are necessary for *arabica*. Production rose from 11 tons in 1915 to 260 tons in 1930, worth £8,700 to the cultivators. The subsequent history of the scheme is one of repeated attempts by the authorities to organize a comprehensive co-operative, a full appraisal of which would require consideration of the period after 1945, which lies outside the scope of this chapter.[2] But whatever the failure of the scheme in engendering a true spirit of co-operation among the Gisu, it was successful in directing a flow of income into the area. An official history of the scheme[3] gives little indication of the size of growers' proceeds, and published statistics are sporadic and haphazard; but by the mid-thirties growers were probably receiving more than £14,000 a year. Production increased to over 4,000 tons of *arabica* coffee by 1940.

[1] Cf. E. H. Winter, *Bwamba Economy*, East African Studies no. 5 (Kampala, 1955).
[2] Cf. *Report of the Commission of Inquiry into the Affairs of the Bugisu Co-operative Union Ltd.* (Entebbe, 1958).
[3] 'The history of the Bugishu Coffee Scheme' (undated), in Mbale District Office.

The rise of sugar as a successful plantation crop has already been described, but while this was happening the world sugar situation steadily deteriorated. In May 1920 sugar had sold in world markets at 10*d*. a lb.; by December it was 2*d*., and in the following year 1*d*. After a slight recovery in 1923 it fell again, and by mid-1930 was ½*d*. Meanwhile Uganda production had grown to about 10,000 tons, greatly in excess of Uganda sales, and Kenya production was also increasing. Spurred by this chaotic price history and by fears of local over-production, East African producers hastened to form an association, which was joined in 1931 by all five of the Kenya producers, but by only one of the two Uganda firms. The association was unable to enforce restriction of production so long as one Uganda firm was 'recalcitrant' and, largely because several of the Kenya firms were high-cost producers, its sugar was being driven out of the Uganda market into the perilous export market. This, and rumours that production was about to begin in Tanganyika, drove the association to approach the Governments of Kenya, Tanganyika, and Uganda with a plan for 'rationalization' of the industry, which came before the Governors' Conference in 1933. The governors faced a dilemma. On the one hand, they favoured low consumer prices as being intrinsically desirable and likely to promote the growth of a healthy local market for sugar. On the other hand, they were inevitably affected not merely by the pleas of local producers and current beliefs in the efficacy of 'rationalization', but also by the international discussions on sugar restriction which were taking place at that time. A Commission of Enquiry into the sugar industry was appointed, but did not publish its report. In 1937 an international restriction scheme imposed an export quota of 27,000 tons a year on East Africa, of which Uganda's share was 12,000 tons, equivalent to less than half her total production in that year and less than one-third of her 1938 output. The Uganda Sugar (Control) Ordinance[1] gave effect to this scheme, empowering the Government to fix the level of sugar exports and stocks.

Similar restrictions were imposed upon tea, a crop which, like sugar, offered considerable opportunities of plantation development based initially upon local markets. Only 2,000

[1] *Laws of Uganda*, no. 1 of 1938.

acres were allotted to Uganda for the first restriction period, ending in 1938, and a further 1,450 acres were allotted for the next five-year period. Within these limitations tea production advanced and both local (i.e. East African) and export sales increased as illustrated in Table VII below.

TABLE VII

Tea production and exports (lb. million), 1937–45

	Total production	Exported	Consumed locally
1937	0·4	0·1	0·3
1939	0·7	0·3	0·4
1941	1·4	0·9	0·5
1943	1·7	1·1	0·6
1945	2·8	2·0	0·8

But restrictive policies were confined neither to cotton nor to those crops affected by international restriction schemes. The Native Produce Marketing Ordinance (No. 20 of 1932) imposed severe limitations on the marketing of virtually every other cash crop grown in Uganda, including ghee, hides and skins, ground-nuts, chillies, coffee, and tobacco. The measure was unanimously opposed by traders and met such opposition as was possible in Legislative Council, but, as the Governor explained, it was 'the intention of the Government, in administering the Ordinance, to guard against the over-capitalisation and the consequent reckless competition in buying which constitute today such unsatisfactory features of the cotton industry'.[1]

It is difficult to reach a just appraisal of the overall effects of these restrictive policies. Criticism could imply untenable surmises as to 'what might have been' which neglect the economic and intellectual climate in which the Uganda Government's policy evolved. Clearly it was unfortunate that, at a time when the interests of the infant Uganda economy lay in an expansionist and liberal approach, circumstances in the mature British economy encouraged men to think in terms of restriction and 'rationalization'. Superficially, 'development' was considerable during this period; the cotton crop of 1938 reached an all-time record of 418,000 bales. But how much of this took place in spite of, rather than because of, official policy is

[1] Speech to Legislative Council, 5 Dec. 1932.

impossible to ascertain. Undoubtedly much was due to the stimulus of bicycle and motor transport, despite the limitations set upon their use. But whatever conclusions are reached on the effectiveness of policy from a merely statistical viewpoint, its effects upon the people's capacity for further development were almost certainly deleterious. The undeniable fact is that the majority of Uganda Africans were unable to identify themselves with the country's economic development.

There is much evidence for this statement. It can be seen in the constant opposition of growers to the controlled marketing system. In 1934, for example, all the *saza* chiefs in Busoga signed a letter to the provincial commissioner, expressing their alarm at the re-establishment of syndicates, and their dislike of zoning, which 'gives an opportunity to the cotton buyers to reduce the prices of cotton, knowing that people cannot remove their cotton and sell it in other neighbouring districts, which pay a fair price'.[1] During that season ginners complained that members of the Young Busoga Association, including chiefs, were picketing ginneries and persuading growers to withhold their cotton. Similarly in Budama, a Native Cultivators' Association petitioned a group of visiting British M.P.s against the zoning legislation, 'not only on the cotton but . . . on the business in general. . . . The business should be running freely; that is to say that every seller may make a bargain according to his wish but not the buyer to have a fixed price.'[2] In Buganda the district commissioner at Masaka considered that 'the majority of growers are entirely ignorant of ginning and buying pools systems, and consequently are extremely suspicious'. His colleague in Mengo asserted that 'the existing system of cotton purchase is tolerated by the grower only because it is the only way in which he can dispose of his crop. Without exception all growers distrust and dislike the pools . . . and regard them as being formed solely to depress the price, and as the pools arose from government policy so is Government also implicated.'[3] A 1938 letter from the Buganda Native Government quoted the Kabaka's letter of 1929 and repeated the familiar attack upon monopoly.

---

[1] 16 Jan. 1934, Agricultural Dept., Jinja, File 2/24.
[2] 3 Dec. 1935, loc. cit.
[3] Agricultural Dept., Entebbe, File 23, undated, but presumably 1938.

Even more significant than the continuation of African opposition to controlled marketing throughout the thirties was an increasing number of complaints that Africans lacked opportunities of entering the processing industry. In 1926 the first African to apply for a ginning licence was refused, not on racial grounds, of course, but because of the general policy of restriction. In 1930 an ambitious attempt to enter the industry was made by a group of Africans who formed a company with the intention of buying cotton and ultimately acquiring ginneries, but the scheme collapsed after a bout of litigation and fraud. This fiasco led inevitably to a dampening of enthusiasm; for several seasons African entrepreneurs were distrusted by growers, ginners, and the Government. The official reaction to this incident was that Africans were inexperienced and incapable of entrepreneurship, 'eager to run before they could walk'. But there were few opportunities for them to learn to walk, not merely because of the presence of Indian competition, though this was the common excuse of both Africans and officials, but also because 'petty trade' was frowned upon and excluded. By 1935 there were only forty-four independent middlemen in the cotton industry, handling less than 3 per cent. of the crop,[1] and it was commonly held that 'no useful purpose would be served by their re-entry'.[2] Similar attitudes prevailed against hawking and petty trade.

An alternative way into commerce was through the formation of co-operative societies, fifteen of which were operating by 1938, but these too were not popular with the Government. There were good reasons for this, for, apart from their insouciant recklessness, the innocence of their members offered tempting opportunities to unscrupulous leaders. The 1938 Cotton Commission listed their major faults as follows:

1. Scattered membership.
2. Dealing in cotton by buying in markets from non-members.
3. Admitting to membership in an agricultural society persons who are not agriculturalists.
4. Complete lack of knowledge of the elementary principles of business.

It concluded that they served 'little useful purpose; indeed they

---

[1] 1938 Cotton Commission *Report*, p. 53.　　　　[2] Ibid., p. 77.

may to some extent militate against orderly marketing since working on their present lines they are functioning as irregular middlemen'.[1] It was not until 1946 that a Department of Co-operation was set up with the object of helping African co-operatives to become effective organizations.

The 1938 Commission, after arguing that 'on purely economic grounds' there was nothing to be said for the encouragement of co-operatives, agreed that 'the desire of Africans to have a share and quite possibly a controlling share in the industry is legitimate and deserving of every encouragement', but that 'they should aim at becoming owners of ginneries as part of the present organisation'. But few, if any, Africans possessed the necessary qualities to do this. After considering how these deficiencies might be overcome, it recommended an apprenticeship scheme under which Africans might be trained for 'ultimate entry into the business in a controlling capacity'. By opposing petty trading co-operatives and advocating apprenticeship in their stead, the commission accurately represented official thinking on this problem and inadvertently exposed its deficiencies. Technical apprenticeship and formal commercial education can teach technical skills and book-keeping, but they cannot inculcate those commercial abilities which are essential pre-requisites for success in business. These can be learnt only by tactical experience in the market.[2] Such experience was available to few Africans in Uganda.

Thus by 1939 Uganda had become essentially a static society. Cash crops had been appended to the traditional peasant economy, and the people received a trickle of cash income in addition to the products of their subsistence agriculture. But there were few signs or even possibilities of a thoroughgoing economic revolution. The instruments of change which had launched Uganda into the world economy were now modified almost beyond recognition, and no new forces had arisen to take their place. The world market for primary commodities remained an important source of income but was insufficiently buoyant to offer the opportunity of lifting the economy on to a higher plane of activity. The Government which had begun as

[1] 1938 Cotton Commission *Report*, p. 78.
[2] Cf. W. A. Lewis, *Theory of Economic Growth* (London, 1955), ch. iv.

an active initiator of economic development had been transformed into an administration that valued stability above economic progress. The first generation of active chiefs had been succeeded by a group of civil servant chiefs with little scope or inclination for drive and initiative, and an indolent country gentry. The Indian merchant pioneers had been replaced by an entrenched monopoly of ginners and myriad small traders operating within a rigidly controlled framework of commerce. There remained the peasants enjoying a life of easeful poverty, for 'to work eight hours a day instead of four in order to be able to buy two shirts a year instead of one was a course of action which, comprehensibly, the average man was not tempted to adopt'.[2]

The war years, 1939–45

The second world war did much to disturb this state of unruffled calm. There was, in the first place, some draining away of manpower. At the peak of recruitment in 1944 nearly 55,000 men were serving in the army, and many more spent short periods in military labour organizations. Secondly, food production was given a new emphasis in agricultural policy, not merely in order to meet local needs, but also for military supplies to the Middle East. Maize production increased from 49,000 tons in 1938 to a yearly average of over 100,000 tons after 1942. The stimulus of this demand, however, was seriously offset by adverse weather conditions; 1939 was one of the driest years on record, and the short rains failed in both 1942 and 1943. To meet the ensuing threat of famine large areas were planted with famine reserve crops, principally cassava and sweet potatoes. Thirdly there was a large increase in the demand for a wide range of commodities vital to the war effort. Cotton was, of course, one of these, but the fixing of extremely low prices as an anti-inflationary precaution and in order to encourage food production was a serious disincentive to producers. In some areas, notably Buganda, their response to low cotton prices took the form of greatly increased production of coffee, which although similarly controlled yielded much higher incomes than cotton. This move was greatly accelerated in later years but was already evident by 1945.

[1] Wrigley, *Crops and Wealth*, p. 59.

Coffee, tobacco, hides and skins, oil-seeds, timber, tea, and sugar all benefited from war demand. After the fall of Malaya even rubber was profitable. This war-time pattern of exports is illustrated in Table VIII below.

TABLE VIII

Principal exports from Uganda, 1940–5 (£'000)

	Total exports	Cotton	Coffee	Tobacco	Hides and skins	Tea	Rubber
1940	5,155	3,760	483	71	92	24	35
1941	5,709	4,262	615	131	124	54	44
1942	4,841	2,861	703	275	155	96	57
1943	5,659	3,238	1,162	474	152	73	72
1944	7,531	5,043	1,045	607	110	88	57
1945	9,938	7,026	1,162	681	141	120	49

But these were essentially temporary and superficial changes in the economic landscape. More significant were two developments whose full impact was not felt until after 1945—the new concept of colonial development and welfare, and an enormous increase in Uganda government funds arising from high export prices and export marketing policies. Between 1939 and 1945 ordinary revenue doubled after having stagnated throughout the previous decade. Even more important was the fact that far larger sums than those accruing through normal revenues were accumulated in the newly created cotton and coffee funds as a result of the great difference between the export value of these crops and the sums paid to their producers. These funds were theoretically intended to be used for future stabilization of cotton and coffee prices,[1] but in practice they provided the Government with finance for general purposes on a wholly unprecedented scale. Meanwhile a new consciousness of the need for development was beginning to affect colonial policy; the West Indian Royal Commission of 1938 and the 1940 Colonial Development and Welfare Act provided early evidence of this new thinking. We must not exaggerate the nature or the pace of this change. Direct government intervention in economic and social development was, as we have shown, no new thing in

[1] Official statement in *Uganda Herald*, 3 Feb. 1943.

Uganda. Nor were the full effects of this new trend evident by 1945. In a period of rapidly rising prices government revenue only doubled between 1939 and 1945, while it was to increase fivefold during the next decade. The Cotton Fund, standing at approximately £1½ million in 1945, was over £21 million by 1954 and a further £15 million had accrued to the Coffee Fund, despite the removal of over £21 million from both funds for various 'development' schemes. Against these astronomical figures and the grandiloquence which they engendered among some post-war administrators, changes before 1945 appear modest and unspectacular. Yet it is perhaps not merely the wisdom of hindsight which discerns the genesis of an economic revolution before 1945.

Certainly, viewed against the experience of the 1930's the war years can be seen as a period of fundamental change in official resources and attitudes. The feebleness and incoherence of government economic policy had been clearly demonstrated in the 1936 report of the Development Committee. Whereas the 1920 Commission, which we have castigated for its planter bias, at least had the merit of presenting suggestions for the development of the country's resources, its 1936 successors were primarily concerned with the provision of a few new government offices. Their sole contribution to economic planning was an extremely modest proposal for the improvement of rural water supplies. The exaggerated caution of the report's £1,142,000 programme, equivalent to less than one year's revenue, reflected two attitudes that were typical of pre-war colonial policy. One was a sheer lack of enthusiasm for development. An engineer visiting Uganda in 1936 contrasted the prevailing apathy with activity in the Belgian Congo, where 'the Belgians hurry on with exploitation' while 'native welfare can be left to traders and missionaries'. He did not point the moral that without development there can be little welfare, but it is certainly true that before the war development ranked low in the Uganda Administration's set of priorities. The second attitude referred to above was an all-pervading sense that revenues were stagnant and would probably remain so. The chairman of the 1936 Committee represented this view when he refused to postulate any rise in revenue during the five years ahead and would therefore admit no scheme committing the Government to an increase in recurrent expenditure. This, and the implicit assumption that no funds would be forthcoming from the Imperial exchequer, were explicable rationalizations of contemporary economic conditions, but they exerted a crippling effect upon any attempt to think in terms of economic progress.

The Uganda economy had in fact reached an impasse by 1939. It had successfully emerged from a primary stage of subsistence into a secondary stage of subsistence plus a useful market sector linked to the outside world. But it was seemingly quite unable to break through into the third stage, the 'take-off into sustained growth'. The 1940's offered both an opportunity and a psychology that were conducive to this 'take-off'. The new mood was personified by Sir John Hall, who became Governor in 1944. For the first time since Sir Hesketh Bell's period of office Uganda was to be led by a man whose primary aim was to lift the economy on to a new plane of activity. In a foreword to the 1946 Development Plan for Uganda,[1] in words unburdened by circumlocution or false tact, he outlined the barriers that would have to be overcome if development were to take place without resort to 'regimentation and dragooning'. Chief among these were 'a predominantly peasant agriculture and an inefficient labour force'. But given better feeding, medical services, and conditions of employment, and the stimulus of consumer goods, he argued that it was 'surely not unduly sanguine to look for a marked improvement in the matter of idleness, indifference, and irresponsibility which are such disturbing features of the present day African labourer and cultivator'.

An appraisal of Sir John Hall's policies would take us beyond the period covered by this chapter,[2] but it is clear that a new phase in the economic history of Uganda was beginning in 1944. The war years were therefore prosperous ones for Uganda, but only in the sense of increasing export proceeds and government revenues. For the mass of the people they were a period of great hardship. Peasants were paid a fixed price for their cotton which was allowed to rise very little above the average for the 1930's and was consistently below those paid between 1924 and 1929.

[1] E. B. Worthington, *A Development Plan for Uganda* (Entebbe, 1946), foreword by H.E. the Governor of Uganda.

[2] Cf. Sir John Hall, 'Some aspects of economic development in Uganda', *African Affairs*, li (1952), 124-32; D. Walker and C. Ehrlich, 'Stabilisation and development policy in Uganda: an appraisal', *Kyklos*, xii (1959), 341-53.

Their share in the total proceeds of the crop fell catastrophically, as can be seen in Table IX below.

TABLE IX

Cotton-growers' prices and proceeds, 1940–5

	Cotton lint and seed exports proceeds	Total payments to growers	Total payments as percentage of 1930–8 payments	Payments to growers as percentage of export proceeds
	(£m.)	(£m.)		
1930–8	3·0	1·8	100	60
1940–1	4·2	2·1	112	50
1941–2	2·9	1·3	72	45
1942–3	3·2	0·9	50	28
1943–4	5·1	1·6	89	31
1944–5	7·1	2·7	150	38

The burden of taxation upon these low incomes was extremely heavy. One effect of war-time marketing arrangements[1] was that the whole of the cotton export tax was paid by the growers, for both ginners and exporters now worked on generous fixed margins and therefore made no contribution to this important source of revenue.[2] In addition all male Africans paid an annual poll-tax varying from 8 sh. to 21 sh. according to district, and import duties of 22 per cent. *ad valorem* affected many goods commonly purchased by them.

In terms of real, as distinct from money, income, the peasants' plight was even more serious than is suggested by these figures. Prices of most of the goods purchased by them increased at least twofold during the war. In the case of cheap textiles, the cutting off of Japanese supplies led to a fivefold increase. There can be little doubt that economic distress and particularly low producer prices were significant factors in the riots which occurred in 1945. The official report on these disturbances practically admitted this, but added that 'in all the circumstances the prices

[1] War-time marketing of colonial products is thoroughly examined in C. Leubuscher, *Bulk Buying from the Colonies* (London, 1956). For Uganda see especially pp. 60–64. See also C. Ehrlich, *The Marketing of Cotton in Uganda, 1903–1939* (Ph.D. Thesis, London, 1958), ch. viii.

[2] In 1945 the revenue from cotton tax amounted to £540,000 and was equivalent to 20 per cent. of the total payments to cotton-growers that year.

paid are proper and reasonable. They are far higher than what the growers used to receive before the war.'[1] No evidence was produced for the first of these statements; the second was demonstrably untrue.

But it would be misleading to close on this note of discord and distress. In Uganda, as elsewhere, 1945 was a year of jubilation and hope, and, so far as the condition of the people was concerned, the war years were in no way representative of our period. At the end of an economic survey of this kind it is fitting to ask: what were the effects of the changes we have described upon the life of the common man? The representative common man was, throughout our period, a peasant, and there can be little doubt that his lot had improved. If British administration had done nothing else, it would deserve credit for having first reduced, and then removed, the age-long dread of famine. Not that this was a gradual process of constant improvement; serious famines occurred as late as 1919, and there were lean years during the second world war. But improved agricultural production, and particularly improved communications, had by the end of our period eliminated the scourge of dearth.

Changes in agricultural techniques had been simple but far reaching. Improved seeds, imported hoes, a few ploughs, most notably in Teso, and a slow process of agricultural education, were beginning to have some effect. More striking perhaps was the participation of *men* in agricultural production with the spread of cash crops. During the nineteenth century agriculture had been essentially a feminine occupation while the men concentrated upon fighting and politics. During the twentieth century agriculture began to absorb some of the energies previously devoted to warfare, although there was probably little abatement of political discourse.

But it was as a consumer that the peasant was clearly better off than his predecessor. He was more consistently, if not more nutritiously fed, better clothed and better housed. He enjoyed the small but significant luxuries of oil-lighting, sugar, tea, perhaps a bicycle. Above all he might, if fortunate and enterprising, have access to some education. To say this is not to

---

[1] *Report of the Commission of Inquiry into the Disturbances which occurred in Uganda during January 1945* (Entebbe, 1945), para. 31. In contrast cf. E. M. K. Mulira, *Troubled Uganda* (London, Fabian Colonial Bureau, 1950), p. 50.

impose European judgements of cultural values but merely to accept African valuations, for no western commodity is more universally desired in modern Africa than education. After fifty years of British administration Uganda had not yet experienced a thoroughgoing economic revolution, but it had made contact with the cash economy, and at least some of its people were on the threshold of the modern world.

IX

ADMINISTRATION AND POLITICS
IN UGANDA
1919–1945

B Y the end of the first world war the first task which the
British had set for themselves in Uganda was achieved; a
financially self-sustaining framework of administration was
established throughout the whole Protectorate. Each district in
Uganda had its district commissioner and its hierarchy of native
authorities. Regular taxes were collected. A system of supervised
native courts was functioning. The Protectorate Government no
longer relied on an annual Imperial grant to supplement its recurrent revenue. Moreover, general revenues, though still most
modest, were increasing, and there was some scope for expenditures beyond the initial essentials of administration, police,
communications, and epidemic control.

If 1919 opened a new phase of colonial rule in Uganda, the
second world war closed it. The disturbances in Buganda in
1945 served to announce that Uganda, in common with so many
other colonial areas, was moving into a period of more active
and more hostile political activity. Before 1945 there had been
signs that the climate of political opinion was changing slowly
in this direction. Still, throughout the years between 1919 and
1945 British rule rested to a quite remarkable extent upon the
unforced acquiescence of the populace.[1] During these years
there was no African political activity against colonial rule *per
se*. The Administration had in the native governments and
authorities a hierarchy of subordinates who were loyal to the
Protectorate Government and who had real authority and
influence within their own community. These, then, were the

---

[1] There were in 1920, for example, only 59 administrative officers and only
19 police officers for the whole of the Protectorate. Fourteen of the 59 administrative
officers had been appointed within the previous year. Uganda Blue Book for the
year ending 31 Mar. 1920.

years of constructive, unhindered administration. Limited by its still meagre revenues and by its inevitable ignorance of the institutions and values of those it ruled, the British Administration was yet able to rule and develop Uganda as it wished without the constant harassing by political nationalists and self-confident tribal leaders that was to become so important a feature of colonial rule in most parts of Africa after 1945.

The issue of plantation or peasant agriculture

The Protectorate Government, however, in 1919 was still of two minds on how best to develop Uganda. Sir Keith Hancock has illuminated the constitutional controversies in Kenya from 1919 to 1923 by reference to two competing British views of empire, the one concerned primarily with Britain's international position and the interests of her economy and her colonial settlements, the other viewing colonial policy primarily as an exercise of trust on behalf of the colonial peoples.[1] These same views of British responsibility are discernible in the controversy over economic policy in Uganda.

The two schools of thought on economic policy are easily summarized. William Morris Carter, Justice and then Chief Justice in Uganda and also chairman of a crucial committee on land policy,[2] was the chief spokesman for the majority view that the Government ought to facilitate as much as it could the development of European-owned plantations. In contrast Frederick Spire, Provincial Commissioner of the Eastern Province from 1909 until 1918, and S. Simpson, Director of

[1] W. K. Hancock, *Survey of British Commonwealth Affairs*, vol. ii, pt. 2 (London, 1942), ch. i.

[2] In 1911 a committee was appointed to consider land policy in Ankole, Bunyoro, Busoga, and Toro. It produced seven reports, its last being in 1921. These four districts were the very districts in which plantation development was expected if land could be alienated for that purpose. The committee was thus in effect considering whether or not the Government ought to encourage large scale non-African participation in the economy, for were it to recommend a land settlement in these four districts which would preclude or severely limit the alienation of land, this would be to recommend against the development of plantations. *Report of the Committee Appointed to Consider the Question of Native Settlement in Ankole, Bunyoro, Busoga and Toro* (Entebbe, 1914), and the subsequent Report of this committee in typescript in Entebbe Secretariat Archives (hereafter 'E.S.A.'), Secretariat Minute Paper (hereafter 'S.M.P.') 2198; H. B. Thomas and A. E. Spencer, *A History of Uganda Land and Surveys and of the Uganda Land and Survey Department* (Entebbe, 1938); C. C. Wrigley, *Crops and Wealth in Uganda*, East African Studies no. 12 (Kampala, 1959).

Agriculture from 1911 until 1929, felt that African peasant cultivation of cash crops ought to be the basis of the economic development of Uganda.

This point of dispute was not merely a question of emphasis or a matter of degree. The controversy was in fact fundamental and of far-reaching significance. The two policies—plantation development or African cash farming—were competitive rather than supplementary. Each implied, indeed required, land and labour policies that were incompatible with the other, and each had vastly different social and political consequences. Plantation development would have required large-scale alienation of land to non-Africans.[1] This, it can safely be predicted, would have had two accompanying consequences. Because of the difficulties of securing an adequate labour supply the planters would demand government pressure upon Africans to enter wage employment and would oppose the promotion of cash crop cultivation by Africans.[2] Second, as the European community grew in numbers and in importance, it would have demanded special and important political concessions. In contrast to these developments which would probably follow any major alienation of land to Europeans, reliance upon peasant farming would preserve the security of African land rights, and be far less destructive of the indigenous social institutions. Its political results, though perhaps not anticipated, were important. Because the non-African communities would be smaller and less influential, they would be less likely to win any major share of political representation or to enjoy great political influence.

The dispute over economic policy was therefore at heart a

[1] The Third Report of the Land Settlement Committee, which was submitted to the Colonial Secretary in 1915, would have resulted in 84 per cent. of Ankole, 89 per cent. of Bunyoro, 73 per cent. of Busoga, and 85 per cent. of Toro being available for alienation. The remaining areas were for African use. They were calculated on the basis of 4 acres for every five Africans. No provision was made for population increases, for cash crop cultivation, or for shifting agriculture. *Report of the Land Settlement Committee.*

[2] Already in Uganda the tiny planter community was hostile to the efforts of the Department of Agriculture to encourage peasant farming of coffee. See, for example, the criticisms of Simpson in the *Report of the Development Commission* (Entebbe, 1920). This commission included leading planters and traders and as well three senior government officials. The pressure from this community was sufficient to cause the Government to hold back the introduction of cash crops in several labour supplying districts. See P. Y. Powesland, *Economic Policy and Labour: a study in Uganda's economic history,* East African Studies no. 10 (Kampala, 1957), also Wrigley, op. cit., p. 35.

dispute both over the capacity of the Africans of Uganda and over British responsibility towards them. Morris Carter, Sir Frederick Jackson, Governor from 1912 to 1917, and Sir Robert Coryndon, his successor, assumed that the African's main productive role would have to be as a wage labourer.[1] They accepted, indeed welcomed, the prospect of a major increase in non-African participation in the economy of Uganda, and Coryndon anticipated the demand for political representation from the immigrant communities, whose role he sought to increase, by introducing a Legislative Council in 1921 in which these communities alone formed the unofficial side.

Spire and Simpson, in contrast, had taken over the confidence of earlier missionaries in the capacity of the African and particularly the Bantu peoples of Uganda.[2] 'Every development', minuted Spire in 1915, 'must be carried out by natives.'[3] And Spire and Simpson could and did point to the substantial economic achievement already in the cultivation of cotton by Africans. Their opposition to plantation development was reinforced by a hostility to the disruptive social impact which extensive alienation of land to Europeans would have entailed.[4] But they were not arguing primarily that traditional institutions ought to be shielded and preserved. They were concerned to establish that peasant cultivation was the better and more effective way of developing Uganda.[5] Their concern was much more for the welfare of Africans, their advancement and the development of their country than for the preservation intact of their indigenous institutions.[6]

---

[1] Neither the Third Report nor the Seventh Report of the Land Settlement Committee (the Third being accepted by Jackson in 1915 and the Seventh by Coryndon in 1921) made any provision in the four districts for the reservation of land which would be developed economically by Africans. Allen, the Land Officer and a member of the committee until 1917, suggested in an appendage to the 1915 Report that in the foreseeable future all Africans in these districts would be absorbed into plantations as wage labourers. *Report of the Land Settlement Committee.*

[2] See, for example, A. R. Tucker, *Eighteen years in Uganda and East Africa* (2 vols., London, 1908), and C. W. Hattersley, *The Baganda at Home* (London, 1908).

[3] Wrigley, op. cit., p. 31.

[4] Wrigley stresses the importance of this (op. cit., p. 32).

[5] Throughout the voluminous files on land policy in the E.S.A. I found no indication of a significant concern on the part of either Spire or Simpson to value *per se* the preservation of indigenous institutions. (R.C.P.)

[6] For an interpretation that lays greater stress on the conservative aspect of their hostility to plantations see Wrigley, op. cit., especially p. 32.

Spire and Simpson initially were a minority of two within the senior ranks of Government in their opposition to the proposals of the Morris Carter Committee. In 1915 these proposals went forward to the Colonial Secretary with the Governor's approval.[1] The Uganda Government, however, had lost touch with the trend of opinion within the Colonial Office. There, on the basis of West African experience, peasant cultivation rather than plantation development was favoured for tropical countries unsuited to permanent European settlement. Bonar Law, who was then briefly Secretary of State, accepted this view and rejected the 1915 proposals with a blunt 'I am not satisfied that the arrangements contemplated are in the best interests either of the peasants or of the development of the territory'.[2]

It is, however, easier for a Colonial Secretary to veto a policy than to secure the introduction of an alternative policy which lacks the support of the local colonial administration. Jackson referred the whole matter back to the same committee whose proposals had just been rejected. For several years this committee, still under Morris Carter's chairmanship, left the issue open, meeting only occasionally, requesting extensive further information of district commissioners, and producing several inconsequential further reports. Not until Morris Carter saw an opportunity to win approval for the policy rejected in 1916 did the committee prepare again a detailed set of proposals. In 1921 the Seventh Report was presented.

Expectations concerning the proposals for plantation development in Uganda were high during 1919 and 1920. Moreover, there was in Britain a brief upsurge of support in high places for blatant economic imperialism.[3] Sir Robert Coryndon, Lord Milner, who was Secretary of State from 1919 to 1921, and his successor Winston Churchill, were all imperially minded and

---

[1] Jackson to Bonar Law, 17 July 1915, E.S.A./S.M.P. 2198.

[2] Bonar Law to Jackson, 13 Jan. 1916, E.S.A./S.M.P. 2198. The Uganda proposal involved as well a strong recommendation that freehold grants of land be made to the chiefs of the four districts with which the committee was concerned. It was a particularly ill-timed recommendation and was a further cause of the Bonar Law veto. The Colonial Office had strongly opposed the continued granting of freehold titles to Kenya settlers (see Chapter V above, and Appendix I on Land Policy in Kenya below) and was, therefore, unlikely to accept their introduction for African notables in a neighbouring protectorate.

[3] See Hancock's discussion of this, *Survey of Commonwealth Affairs*, vol. ii, pt. i (Oxford, 1940), pp. 106 sqq.

receptive to the view that major non-African participation was essential in Uganda and that in this participation preference ought to be shown to Europeans rather than Asians. In the few years from 1919 to 1921 the general direction of policy in Uganda received a sharper, less ambivalent definition. A Legislative Council was introduced in which representation was weighted in favour of the European and against the Asian. Urban segregation received official support.[1] The Government did its best to assist planters to secure labour and held back the introduction of cash crops from labour-supplying districts.[2] In 1920 the 1916 veto from London upon any further sale of African freehold land to non-Africans was lifted. In the same year the seventh and final report of the Land Settlement Committee, recommending much the same proposals as it had in 1915 and to the same pro-plantation effect,[3] was submitted with Coryndon's approval to Churchill as Colonial Secretary. His approval was given in April 1921. Morris Carter after nine years of controversy appeared to have carried the day.

Yet within a year a quite remarkable reversal occurred in both the labour and the land policies of the Uganda Government. In July 1922 Coryndon asked the Colonial Secretary for what was in effect a reversal of the Morris Carter proposals which he had approved the year before. Happily it fell to a new Secretary of State, the Duke of Devonshire, to reply, and in February 1923 he accepted this new direction of land policy in Uganda.[4] In the same year compulsory labour, which had been given a clear sanction in the Native Authority Ordinance in 1919, was abolished save under very limited and carefully controlled conditions.[5] From 1923 onwards the Uganda Administration was thus firmly committed to a land policy which accepted the security of the African population as its first responsibility and an economic policy which recognized African peasant agriculture as the basis of Uganda's economic development.

---

[1] See p. 512, below.   [2] Powesland, op. cit., pp. 26 sqq

[3] One senior official minuted the truth bluntly in these terms: 'The whole tenor of the Committee Report shows the object aimed at therein is the securing of the largest possible area of land in each district for alienation' (11 Jan. 1922, E.S.A./S.M.P. 2198).

[4] Thomas and Spencer, *Uganda Land and Surveys*, pp. 157–8.

[5] Ordinance no. 14 of 1923.

African opposition to both the land and the labour policies of the Government was of some influence in winning this reversal. The Lukiko, for example, passed a law in 1921 to invalidate the Government's decision of the previous year that *mailo* estates[1] could be sold to non-Africans. The chiefs opposed, and proved largely incapable of collecting, the paid forced labour for public purposes (*kasanvu* labour) which the 1919 Ordinance permitted.

The major explanation of the shift in policy in 1923, however, lies in the sudden collapse of the earlier high expectations about the future of European plantations in Uganda. By 1920 requests for new land allocations had dwindled to very few, and in 1921 the slump in coffee prices hit the existing plantations so hard that it was not till 1936 that plantation acreage reached again the 1920 level. Simpson and Spire had been right all along. Uganda was not a planter's country.[2]

Not only had events proved that their judgement was sound, but during the years from 1919 to 1923 the trusteeship values that had informed and reinforced their stand became widely accepted within the Provincial Administration. The initial phase of colonial rule was over; the British position was secure and unchallenged. The next concern which was to give shape and character to British policy was a concern for the welfare of the ordinary African. It influenced native administration policy, in which the Government began to look beyond the chiefs to the peasants whom they ruled. It helps to account for the opposition of the Provincial Administration by 1921 to the land policy proposals of the Morris Carter Committee.[3] It contributed to the increasing concern for medical services for Africans[4] and for better labour conditions.[5]

Without doubt the fact that African peasant agriculture was proving economically superior to foreign-owned plantations greatly increased the influence and strength of these values. But this economic fact reinforced the values rather than created

[1] For the origin of *mailo* land, see Chapter II above.

[2] See Chapter VIII above for an analysis of the economic collapse of the plantations. Also Wrigley, *Crops and Wealth*, pp. 36 sqq.

[3] Thomas and Spencer, op. cit., p. 57. In 1922 the provincial commissioners took the unusual step of asking that their memorandum opposing the Seventh Report of the Land Settlement Committee be forwarded to the Colonial Secretary. E.S.A./S.M.P. 2198.

[4] See p. 485, below.   [5] Powesland, op. cit., p. 46.

them. The trusteeship concern for the security, the development, and the welfare of Africans was no mere rationalization of an economic necessity. It was a strongly held conviction that was itself an important determinant of policy in Uganda.

Moreover, it met with a sympathetic response at the Colonial Office. With the appointment of the Duke of Devonshire as Secretary of State late in 1922, colonial policy again attached the greatest importance in land policy to the security and adequacy of African holdings. The Duke of Devonshire, when he agreed to reverse the policy that had been recommended to his predecessor by the Morris Carter Committee, was in effect returning to the position held by the Colonial Office in 1915. In his dispatch[1] he asked that the Protectorate Government prepare a Land Ordinance along the lines of the 1923 Tanganyika Land Ordinance, whose preamble affirmed that the Government was the trustee of the land primarily in the interests of the indigenous population. London as well as Entebbe had thus come to regard Britain's responsibility as a trustee for the African population as her first obligation in Uganda. Both regarded Uganda primarily as an African territory dependent for its development upon African peasant farming. These views were never again seriously challenged.

Despite this important, fundamental clarification of policy, the Protectorate Government had no grand design, no master plan of the Uganda it wished to create. However, the decisions made and the policies introduced do reveal several values and assumptions that underlay British rule and explain its character and general shape. There was first of all the increased concern for the welfare of ordinary Africans to which reference has already been made. There was an unquestioned confidence in the advantage to Africans of British rule, and in the judgement of the colonial Administration on what in fact constituted African interests.[2] There was a preoccupation with economic

[1] Duke of Devonshire to Coryndon, 1 Feb. 1923, E.S.A./S.M.P. 2198.
[2] This is illustrated in the interesting difference in the manner in which land and labour policy shifted. The change in land policy was the result of a request from the Uganda Government to which the Colonial Secretary acceded. The abandonment of paid forced labour was the result of instructions from the Secretary of State reluctantly accepted in Entebbe. The Provincial Administration had too much confidence in its judgement on how Africans ought to use their labour and on the need to train Africans to disciplined work to welcome the abandonment of forced

development partly because it was a prerequisite of every other
advance and partly for the immediate benefits it would bring to
Africans. This concern for African welfare was, of course, always
social and economic, rarely political. Any concern to prepare
Uganda for self-rule was completely absent. Africans and British
alike assumed throughout the whole period that British rule
would last a very long time. As late as 1939 Sir Philip Mitchell,
then Governor, wrote that 'we have an almost unlimited time
in which to make our dispositions'.[1]

After 1923 the Protectorate Government was able without
divided purpose to devote its expanding though still very limited
revenues to the development of the economic potential of
Uganda's peasant agriculture and to an increase in the welfare
services which it provided for her people. In the financial year
1917–18 the total revenues of the Protectorate Government had
been £326,366. In 1923 they were nearly £1 million and in
1935 over £1 million. A major beneficiary of these improved
revenues was the Public Works Department.[2] The Uganda
economy, peasant-based and just moving from subsistence
farming, had to bear the cost of a central government whose
standards and expectations were derived from those of much
wealthier states. The housing, the offices, and the public buildings which the Protectorate Government felt necessary
absorbed a much higher share of public revenues than in
wealthier countries, leaving less for other more productive
works expenditures.[3] Nevertheless, communications did receive
increased attention, especially after the grant of a substantial
Imperial development loan in 1921. The railway was extended
from Kenya into Uganda, reaching Jinja in 1923 and Kampala

labour. Indeed, until the instruction from the Secretary of State, government
departments had relied entirely on *kasanvu* labour for their labour force. Thomas
and Spencer, Wrigley, and Powesland, all cited previously; and E.S.A./S.M.P.s
5711 and 2195.

[1] P. Mitchell, *Uganda Protectorate: native administration* (Entebbe, 1939), p. 23.

[2] Protectorate Government Revenue and Public Works Expenditures:

	1919	1925	1929	1932	1938
Total revenues (£)	495,595	1,479,289	1,652,918	1,402,528	1,863,863
Public works* (£)	45,287	252,872	404,910	59,378	556,828

  * Including only those expenditures from current revenue. *Source*: Uganda Blue
Books for these various years.

[3] In the years 1927–9, for example, £394,213 was spent on public buildings and
£103,713 on roads. From the Uganda Annual Reports 1927, 1928, and 1929.

in 1931. The total mileage of all-weather roads maintained by
the Public Works Department increased from 600 miles in 1919
to over 2,000 miles in 1938.[1]

The activities of the Medical, Agricultural, and Veterinary
Departments were also expanded as fast as resources permitted.[2]
Over the nineteen-year period from 1921 to 1939 the number
of veterinary officers in Uganda increased from 3 to 13; of
agricultural officers from 13 to 29; of medical officers from 24 to
43; of nursing sisters from 4 to 25.[3] In 1919 the Medical Department still had as its major responsibility the health of the
European officials and the control of epidemics.[4] The Department of Agriculture still limited its activities to Buganda and
the Eastern Province, and the Veterinary Department was so
understaffed that it was unable to control the disastrous rinderpest and pleuro-pneumonia epidemics in the years 1919–21.
Over the next two decades ordinary medical services were
extended throughout the whole Protectorate.[5] The Veterinary
Department mastered the control of epidemics and moved to
the promotion of better livestock care. The Agricultural Department succeeded in increasing greatly the acreage of coffee and
cotton under cultivation by Africans.[6] After 1926 it extended its

[1] Annual Reports of the Public Works Department, 1919, 1938.

[2] Education expenditures were also increased, but there were ideological factors
which hindered their full increase. See pp. 520–7, below.

[3] These figures are drawn from the Annual Reports of the departments concerned for the years 1921 and 1939.

[4] In the whole of the Western and Northern Provinces in 1920 there were
2 medical officers, 1 assistant surgeon, 4 compounders, and 47 subordinate staff.
There were hospital beds for 37 Africans. Uganda Blue Book for the year ending
31 Mar. 1920.

[5] The expansion of government medical services to Africans is indicated by
these figures:

	1919	1928	1938
African hospitals	10	23	21
Beds therein	231	1,251	1,300
Dispensaries	—	59	108
New African cases	62,405*	573,234	1,048,689

* Including non-African cases.

Sources: Annual Reports of the Medical and Sanitary Department and Uganda
Blue Books for the years 1919, 1928, and 1938.

[6] Total acreage devoted to cotton cultivation in Buganda and the Eastern
Province rose from 173,000 to 999,400 in 1945. In 1925 there were 1,349 acres of
coffee cultivation and in 1945 137,400 acres. Annual Reports of the Department
of Agriculture for 1920, 1925, 1945. (The Lango District figures have been deducted
from the 1920 estimate for the Eastern Province.)

activities into the Western and Northern Provinces and sought
other crops that might be more appropriate for cultivation
there.[1] In 1919 expenditure on administration, police, prisons,
and the military absorbed 28·9 per cent. of government revenue,
and the Public Works, Agriculture, Education, Veterinary, and
Medical departments accounted for 24·2 per cent. In 1938 these
percentages had become 16·6 per cent. and 50·7 per cent.
respectively.[2] The whole character and emphasis of government
spending had changed.

[1] There were few government activities which could more directly and immediately aid the African peasant than these attempts to help him to break from the
rigid limitations of subsistence farming. Where they succeeded, hope was aroused
and a vitality generated amongst peoples who were often in despondent apathy.
A provincial commissioner who observed this transformation in the Western
Province in the mid-1930's described it in these terms: 'I am confident that further
prosperity can only be achieved by way of material prosperity. I have visited parts
of this Province during the last five years where the atmosphere of depression was
comparable to that prevalent in the "distressed areas". Most of the men are stated
to be away from home "looking for work" and there was everywhere an air of
listlessness and lack of interest. But where some economic crop can be grown
a new spirit appears. The population returns. New tools, and clothes, are to be
seen. Better houses are begun, new roads are proposed, questions asked about
alternative crops, plans made for the education of children or for spending money
yet to be earned. The circulation of a little money changes the whole outlook.'
(Annual Report of the Provincial Commissioners, Eastern and Western Provinces,
1936.)

[2] The following table of revenue and expenditures in four selected years between
1919 and 1938 demonstrates the change that occurred in the character of colonial
rule in Uganda during this period:

		1919	1928	1932	1938
	Total Revenue (in £):	351,834	1,519,237	1,402,528	1,863,563
I	Secretariat and Governor	4,036	22,960	22,379	26,433
II	Provincial Administration	29,400	99,686	88,236	116,793
III	Police and prisons	28,969	91,738	91,562	110,439
IV	Military	39,187	66,051	54,795	55,501
V	Sub-total I–IV	101,592	280,435	256,972	309,166
VI	Public works	40,757	315,118	160,564	556,828
VII	Medical	30,365	144,795	147,801	185,035
VIII	Agriculture	}11,953	36,121	45,079	65,771
IX	Veterinary		25,651	30,296	32,008
X	Education	2,100	49,556	68,463	105,128
XI	Sub-total VI–X	85,175	571,241	452,203	944,770
V	as a percentage of total revenue	48·9%	18·5%	18·3%	16·6%
XI	as a percentage of total revenue	24·2%	37·6%	32·2%	50·7%

Source: Uganda Blue Books, 1919, 1928, 1932, and 1938.

Administration and traditional institutions

The Provincial Administration had always depended heavily upon the native authorities. But in the first decades of British rule the main activities which the Administration called upon the chiefs to perform were those, such as maintaining order, building roads, and recruiting labour, which were most likely to be within their competence. With the expansion of medical, veterinary, and agricultural services the native authorities were drawn into less familiar activities. The central government departments and the local administrations were not self-contained, each with their separate responsibilities and their own field staff. The government departments could not hope to recruit and train the personnel needed to carry their policies down to the village level. They had to use the chiefs who already were responsible for local rule throughout the Protectorate. Moreover, many of the new services required the co-operation of the general public if they were to succeed. Often this co-operation was not easily obtained. Sanitation improvement, for example, and venereal disease control, strip-cropping, famine storage, rat-catching, and bull castrations could be introduced only with the active assistance of the chiefs. Their leadership and exhortation was needed to overcome initial fears and misunderstandings. Moreover, when the short cut of legal coercion was judged necessary to secure local co-operation in the first stages of a new policy, the chiefs were called upon to assert their authority directly. The increase in the range and complexity of government activities did not lessen the importance of the chiefs; rather it underlines the Government's administrative dependence upon the native authorities. But it was also to affect their development and to set in train a variety of reforms.

There were three distinguishable types of native administration systems in Uganda. In Buganda there was a native government in treaty relationship with the protecting British. Because of the terms of the Uganda Agreement and because it had co-operated effectively with the Protectorate Government, the Buganda Government had been allowed to enjoy a wide degree of internal administrative autonomy during the first two decades after 1900. This Government, though somewhat modified in structure from its traditional form, was still its clear and accepted derivative. It was headed by a traditional king, the Kabaka, and included both a ministerial central government and a three-tier hierarchy of appointed chiefs organized regionally into *sazas*, *gombololas*, and *mirukas* (counties, sub-counties, and villages).

The native governments of Bunyoro, Toro, and Ankole were also traditional native kingdoms, two of them at the beginning of the period under review having their own agreements with the British. However, neither the terms of these agreements nor actual administrative practice gave these native governments an internal autonomy comparable with that enjoyed by the Buganda Government. In its actual operation their administration in fact compared more with that of the other districts of Uganda than with Buganda, with which they had much in common constitutionally.[1]

Outside the four tribal kingdoms of Uganda the native administrations were British-organized copies of the Buganda three-tier hierarchy of chiefs. In most of these districts, and especially in the non-Bantu areas, this system of rule was completely foreign. Local rule after 1900 was basically a direct rule by British officers through appointed chiefs, sometimes local men, sometimes trusted Ganda, who were the direct subordinates of the district commissioner, and who derived their authority from their appointment alone. Neither they as individuals nor the system itself had any traditional foundations. Because there were so few administrative officers these chiefs did exercise a good deal of unsupervised power, but it was not by right under an agreement nor collectively as a native government. There were no legal and very few practical or policy restrictions on the control which the Administration could assert over a chief on any matter to which its attention was drawn.

Three ordinances in 1919 gave legal definition to the responsibilities and powers of the chiefs outside Buganda. The first and most important of these, the Native Authority Ordinance, defined their executive responsibilities. It made few innovations. It was, to quote from a minute paper of the time, 'really a code of administrative regulations cast into the form of an Ordinance for the purpose of enforcing them with legal sanctions'.[2] The ordinance established the mandatory responsibility of the chiefs

---

[1] For their early administration, and the Toro and Ankole agreements, see Chapter II above.

[2] Unpublished material, E.S.A.

to maintain law and order, and it gave them the authority
necessary to that end. Secondly, it sanctioned 'any order which
such Chief may issue by virtue of any native law or custom in
force for the time being in his area'.[1] As many chiefs in fact had
no traditional status, it might be thought that this power was of
little significance. However, by a happy and convenient fiction
they had acquired wide and undefined powers, which were
assumed to be customary. In many districts these included the
assumption that customary law required obedience to the chief,
and on this simple and clear premiss, rather than on the basis
of the complex articles of the Native Authority Ordinance, the
authority of the chief was enforced in the native courts.

The ordinance also lists a series of specific purposes for which
the chief could issue orders. This list reflects the matters on
which the Government was then expecting the assistance of the
chiefs. It included the provision of porters and food for *safaris*,
the control of the manufacture and consumption of intoxicating
drink, and the prevention of the pollution of streams, the spread
of disease, the evasion of taxes, and the wasteful destruction of
trees. Provision was also made for the chiefs to require their
able-bodied natives to work unpaid on local public works for up
to thirty days a year, or at a time of threatening famine, and to
work as paid labour for up to sixty days a year for various
government purposes. The ordinance provided that a provincial
or district commissioner could require a chief to issue any
orders that he felt necessary. To emphasize further the directly
subordinate nature of the chief's position, the ordinance concluded with provision for the punishment by fine or imprisonment of neglectful or disobedient chiefs.

The second ordinance was the Courts Ordinance,[2] part of
which defined the jurisdiction of the native courts and the
supervisory and revisionary powers of administrative officers. It
was a further exercise of a concern to regularize the native courts
and improve the quality of the justice they dispensed, which the
Provincial Administration had long regarded as an important
part of its responsibilities.

The third ordinance,[3] the Native Laws Ordinance, also
applied outside Buganda. It gave legal recognition to the

[1] Ordinance no. 17 of 1919, section A, para. 7.
[2] Ordinance no. 24 of 1919.   [3] Ordinance no. 31 of 1919.

district councils which, because of their administrative usefulness, had already been organized by district officers in several districts. The actual powers which this ordinance gave to the councils were very limited. Under the ordinance they could propose changes in the customary law and recommend the punishments for offences against it, which, once the Governor had approved them, would become law. It was a step, but a very preliminary, cautious step, towards the establishment of district native governments. The district commissioners were still the controlling and unifying factor in the native administrations and were their chief executives.

But in British colonial territories it is often not legal form but official policy that shapes the relations that develop between the colonial governments and the native authorities under them. At no time was this truer than in the British territories in Africa from 1919 to 1945. In territory after territory the doctrine of Indirect Rule won the strong allegiance of governors and senior administrators, and the major preoccupation of their native policy became a search for traditional authorities who could be made the agents of local rule.

Native administration in Uganda, at least in the kingdoms, with their traditional rulers and their formal agreements, might well be regarded as excellent examples of indirect rule. Yet much in fact distinguished their administration from the normal indirect rule pattern. The traditional rulers were not the operative heads of their administrations, and on most matters district officers communicated directly with their subordinate and non-hereditary ministers and chiefs. The rulers for their part welcomed their detachment from day to day administration, for it shielded them from the criticism of being too submissive to the ruling British. This was particularly true in Buganda, where administrative relations had never been adjusted adequately to accommodate an adult Kabaka. Although the Protectorate Government had in the early years of Daudi Chwa's adulthood favoured a strong Kabaka, it had been unwilling to relax the close working relations between district officers and the chiefs. The Kabaka remained partly on the outside of an administration theoretically his own. He tended to be brought into particular issues only when his prestige might be exploited to overcome local hostility. By the 1930's he had reacted to this with an increasing hostility to his ministers and with an open lack of co-operation with the Protectorate Government.[1]

Buganda thus differed from the indirect rule model in two different and partly contradictory ways. Constitutionally, because of the Uganda Agreement, it had a more independent status than a native authority under Indirect Rule. Administratively, by contrast, the Ḳabaka was far less active and British control far more direct and continuous than Indirect Rule, at least in theory, would require. The districts outside Buganda and the other kingdoms bear much less relation to Indirect Rule. The principle which the Government followed was in fact

the creation in each district of a District Native Administration of which the district commissioner was the controller and chief executive operating through a hierarchy of chiefs and subordinate chiefs in charge of territorial units. . . . The basis of their authority lay . . . in the place they occupied as part of an official or semi-official organization, the District Native Administration.[2]

The difference between native administration in Uganda and in such British territories as Nigeria and Tanganyika was more than one of legal status and administrative practice. It reflected an important difference in emphasis. Uganda had not had, at least until 1935, a governor who took a major interest in native administration. The Provincial Administration never came to regard rule through traditional authorities as a central objective of policy. Indeed, the pattern was the reverse. The Provincial Administration had inherited a native government in Buganda with more autonomy than this Administration felt was justified, and until 1936 it was concerned to limit this autonomy rather than to increase it.

The existence of the kingdoms, their rulers, and their agreements had led many to interpret the native policy of Uganda in terms of Indirect Rule.[3] Yet by 1920 the agreements and the

---

[1] D. A. Low and R. C. Pratt, *Buganda and British Overrule* (London, 1960), pp. 246 sqq.

[2] Lord Hailey, *Native Administration in the British African Territories* (London, 1950), p. 28.

[3] Bishop Willis, for example, told the Hilton Young Commission 'Uganda's special contribution to native policy was to build up native states', *Report of the Commission on Closer Union of the Dependencies in East Africa* (Hilton Young Commission), Evidence taken in Uganda, i (1929), 4.

native governments were accepted elements of the political terrain rather than assets to be cherished for their traditional worth. Outside Buganda there is little evidence that might suggest that Government on occasion wished to promote the growth of native states. Of this evidence the most important items were the willingness of the Government to meet half-way the Busoga request for a paramount chief in 1919, the offer of an agreement to Busoga a few years earlier, and the agreement with Bunyoro in 1933. Even in these few cases every effort was made to limit the native state implications of the decisions. They were, much more, marginal acknowledgements to tribal sentiments within the framework of a policy whose main direction was towards greater control and increased bureaucratization.

The Protectorate Government was in fact more concerned with economy, efficiency, and welfare than with the maintenance of traditional institutions. Because the chiefs were important for the administration of the new services the Protectorate Government sought to control and supervise these chiefs more closely. The Government no longer doubted for a moment that it was secure. It was concerned with more than public order, tax-collection, and road-building. It was concerned to administer Uganda more closely, more efficiently, and with increasing benefits to the ordinary African, and it did not doubt the wisdom of its policies. It therefore wanted its native authorities above all to be effective subordinate agents of the central government. It was unlikely that the Government would postpone a policy it felt was desirable because it might require some interference with, or control upon, the native authorities.

The Government was drawn to supervise and reform the native authorities for reasons of social policy. As officials became less preoccupied with the native authorities and with their loyalty and more able to look beyond them to the people themselves, they became more sensitive to the possibility of abuses of power by the chiefs and to the impact of their rule upon ordinary Africans.

Certainly at the beginning of our period there was much to concern them. The burden of government weighed heavily upon the ordinary citizen, to the advantage of the chiefs. There was until 1923 the obligation already mentioned to perform up to two months' labour a year on public projects (*kasanvu* labour). Labour and produce tributes were due to the chiefs, or, in Buganda (where they were known as *busulu* and *envujo*), to the owner of the *mailo* land on which the peasant lived. In Buganda the *busulu* required either twenty-eight days' labour a year for the chief or a cash payment of 7·50 sh. later increased to 10 sh. The *envujo* was expected to be approximately one-tenth of the peasant's produce from his land. Elsewhere in Uganda equivalent tributes were paid to the chiefs, though the alternative of a cash commutation had not yet been widely introduced. A third obligation was *luwalo* labour, a month's unpaid labour on local public works. This labour, called out, organized, and directed by the chiefs, maintained the local roads and footpaths, and built many of the native administration buildings. It was in many areas a continuation of a customary obligation which had been a feature of the more highly organized political systems in southern and western Uganda. Though *luwalo* labour was disliked, especially by Africans of some social standing or education, it was not bitterly resented, perhaps because the chiefs enforced it mainly upon the less articulate, more submissive peasants. There was in fact a provision, first in Buganda then elsewhere, that the permanently employed could commute this obligation by a 10 sh. payment. In Buganda in 1930, and within a few years in almost all districts, this right to commute was extended to any who wished to pay the cash alternative.

The main direct tax which Africans paid was the poll-tax, a *per capita* tax which in 1921 was 15 sh. in the more prosperous areas and from 6 to 10 sh. elsewhere. The tax was collected by the native authorities and paid into the protectorate revenues. From these revenues the chiefs in turn received a rebate of 10–30 per cent. of the taxes they had collected. Initially, therefore, the tax had served not only to raise revenue but to encourage a co-operative and loyal attitude amongst the chiefs. It also provided a strong indirect pressure on Africans to engage in some economic activity. In the cotton-growing areas this aspect was no longer significant. The normal economic incentives had begun to operate, and the amount of cotton grown far exceeded that needed for tax payments. In less fortunate areas the income with which to pay the tax could often be earned only by working on the non-African plantations, for government departments, or for Buganda farmers. Many were thus forced each year to leave home and tribal area and migrate long distances in search of work. In many districts it proved impossible for most Africans to earn an income equal to their fixed tax obligations, and personal hardship was widespread and intense.[1] Only after 1933, as prices rose, as new crops were introduced, and as communications improved, did African incomes in other parts of Uganda become substantially larger than the total taxes which they had to pay.[2]

What were heavy impositions upon the peasants were the chiefs' main source of income, and hence an important reason for their loyalty. In the case of the senior chiefs in each district, this income was by no means negligible, especially as the distribution of the rebates and tributes amongst the chiefs of various ranks was weighted very much to their advantage. In Busoga, to quote an extreme example, the chief of the largest county received more than £5,000 from these sources.[3] In addition he received (as did many other chiefs) further substantial income by using *busulu* labour to grow cash crops. In Buganda another and sometimes most important source of income were the large rent-bearing official estates of the *saza* chiefs.

In the immediate post-war period the Government, though not happy about this system of remuneration, hesitated to abolish the tax rebate and the personal tribute of peasant to chief, lest it weaken the chief's authority and lessen his loyalty. But considerations of this sort soon gave place to a desire for reform. In 1923 in Toro the first experiment was made to convert the personal tribute into a local tax and to pay both it and tax rebate into the Toro Native Government Fund from which fixed salaries were then paid to the chiefs. The system was introduced in Busoga in 1927, and during the next ten years

[1] The hardships which the poll-tax caused in Bunyoro were described by the Acting Governor to the Legislative Council on 15 Dec. 1926 (Summary of the *Proceedings* of the Legislative Council, 6th Session, p. 82).

[2] A sure indication of this improvement in the middle and late 1930's was the great increase in the number of Africans with sufficient income to be able to commute their *luwalo* labour obligations.

[3] This is calculated from details which had been carefully collated by the district commissioner of Busoga in 1927. 20 Sept. 1927. L.10, Provincial Commissioner's Archives, Jinja (now transferred to Mbale). The next most highly paid chief received approximately £2,250 from these sources.

throughout the whole Protectorate. In every case the rebate and the new tax were paid into the native administration funds. This not only permitted the payment of fixed salaries to the chiefs but also provided some revenue for local projects.[1]

The replacement of personal tributes by a direct tax and fixed salaries was strongly opposed by the chiefs of Toro and Busoga when it was first introduced. The change not only reduced the high incomes of some of the senior chiefs but contributed to a radical and unwelcome transformation of their position. The personal tribute had been a witness of an acknowledged authority. It had confirmed the position of the chiefs as local rulers rather than paid employees. Its replacement by a local tax weakened this authority. Their new fixed salaries were proof of their subordinate, dependent relationship with the Protectorate Government. They complained, and petitioned, about these changes, but they had finally no alternative save resignation. One group of chiefs did in fact choose this latter alternative. In Busoga, at the lowest rank of the traditional hierarchy, there were *mitala* and *kisoko* chiefs, local leaders over small communities, whose position and authority rested not on any delegation of power from a superior but on a traditionally based acceptance from below. When the salary scheme was introduced in Busoga in 1927 the district commissioner had proposed that 1,700 of these chiefs should form the first level of the hierarchy of official, salaried chiefs. The *mitala* and *kisoko* chiefs *en masse* rejected this. They refused to have any official status and they willingly rejected the proposed salaries in order not to compromise their local authority. They still enjoyed a real local prestige in their own right. They recognized that it rested on the intimacy and immediacy of their relations with those under them and they valued it above any of the perquisites of office.

Their choice brings into focus the position of the vast majority of chiefs who accepted the imposed salary scheme. Their status, their authority, and now their income were largely derived from their official position. If they lost that, little would distinguish them from ordinary subjects. In consequence they chose to

[1] There was an interesting reason for this decision. The Provincial Administration, which would in fact directly run these native administration funds, was anxious to keep this local revenue under its own direct control rather than have it disbursed by the Treasury.

remain in office, accepting, however reluctantly, the changes in their position which the Protectorate Government had introduced.

The decision to force through this important change in the status of the chiefs is a measure of the Government's greater determination to protect and promote the interests of the ordinary African. The Government, in its pursuit of this objective, was willing not only to face the dissatisfaction of the chiefs but also to weaken their authority within their districts. Reasons of efficiency as well as considerations of welfare without doubt influenced this decision to change the basis of the chiefs' remuneration. But on a further issue, closely connected with it, the Government's new concern to revise the relations between the chiefs and the people was more clearly the dominant consideration.

In 1919 it was still not clear what powers over land the Government was willing to concede to the chiefs of Toro, Bunyoro, Ankole, and Busoga.[1] In each of these districts the ruling hierarchy had long hoped to receive the same rights and privileges over land as the Ganda chiefs had been granted under the 1900 Agreement. They had good reason to expect this, for it seems clear that early administrators had promised that such *mailo* land grants would be made. Moreover, in each of these four districts district commissioners had acquiesced in the introduction by the chiefs of various expedients to secure for themselves tribute-paying subjects similar to the rent-paying tenants on the *mailo* estates in Buganda.

These expedients are worth recording. In Toro, the 1900 Agreement assigned 376 square miles to the Mukama, the chiefs, and the leading personages of the tribe, for official and private freehold estates. Despite the clear injunction of the agreement that these estates were to be waste or uncultivated land, they were in fact declared in the richest and most heavily populated areas of Toro. In addition, without any authority under the agreement, the Mukama distributed most of the remaining occupied land as further official estates or as fief holdings to retired chiefs, members of the ruling clans, retainers, and court favourites. By thus adding to itself these important powers over

[1] This question was an integral part of the land settlement for these districts which is discussed above, pp. 81 sqq.

land, the ruling oligarchy in Toro securely entrenched its dominant position.[1]

In Bunyoro the Protectorate Government had initially insisted that all tributes should be paid only to official chiefs and that neither retired chiefs nor traditional authorities should receive any. Gradually the Mukama of Bunyoro tried to restore the position of the older hierarchy. He assumed the right to grant estates. The new *kibanja* owners rather than the official chiefs received the tributes and services of the people living on these lands. By 1931 6,000 of the 22,000 tax-payers lived on such private *kibanjas*.[2]

In Busoga the development towards a *mailo* system had not been pushed quite so far. All adult male Africans still owed tribute to their official chiefs. However, each *saza* (county) had been divided between areas to be administered as the personal estate (*bwesengeze*) of the office-holding chief and areas to be ruled through officially appointed subordinate chiefs. There was no governmental control over the appointments made by the *saza* chief to subordinate posts or over the share of the tax rebates and tributes which he gave to their holders. The chiefs hoped and half-expected that the Protectorate Government would grant these *bwesengeze* areas to them as freehold estates.

In its First Report and in its subsequent reports, the Morris Carter Committee[3] urged that large private and official estates should be given to chiefs and tribal leaders in Busoga, Toro, Bunyoro, and Ankole. Indeed, the first report recommended that the whole of the land to be reserved for Africans should be distributed in this way. Such estates, it argued, had been promised to the chiefs and were necessary to secure their loyalty more firmly. They would make the land policy in these districts consistent with that in Buganda, and as privately held freehold is more easily sold than communal lands, the introduction of private estates for the chiefs would facilitate land alienation. The committee's proposals to grant these estates and its refusal to recommend substantial and definite native reserves thus formed a coherent whole, united by a concern to assist planta-

[1] The Toro situation is discussed in *Enquiry into the Grievances of the Mukama and the People of Toro* (Entebbe, 1926).

[2] See *Enquiry into Land Tenure and the Kibanja system in Bunyoro, 1931, Report of the Committee* (Entebbe, 1932).

[3] See pp. 478 sqq. above.

tion development as much as possible. The provincial commissioners, who, it will be remembered, rallied to effect a final
sudden reversal of the Morris Carter proposals in 1922, were
equally hostile to both these main recommendations of the
committee. Their main concern was to protect the native inhabitants and promote their welfare. They wanted to give
Africans secure tenure on land adequate to their needs. They
opposed large estates for the chiefs in order to protect Africans
from any further increase in the power of the chiefs over them.
The reversal of the Morris Carter proposals, which the provincial commissioners won in 1922, included a victory on both
these issues. The land policy announcement of 1924 promised
that adequate African reserves would be demarcated, and
added as well the categorical statement 'the *mailo* system which
is in force in the Kingdom of Buganda will not be introduced
except in so far as the Government is bound by the Toro and
Ankole Agreements'.[1] It thus brought to an end a controversy
over land policy which had divided opinion in Entebbe for
twelve years.

The announcement, however, did not bring peace to the
districts. In all four of the affected districts the chiefs were
bitterly disappointed at this rejection of an ambition they had
long nourished. In Toro, moreover, a further group, the ex-
chiefs and the Babito,[2] were also aggrieved, for they lost the
tributes they had long enjoyed and were suddenly without any
acknowledgement of their higher status. The Mukama himself
joined their protests until in 1925 he was called to Entebbe for a
stern warning that opposition to the new system must cease.

In Bunyoro hostility was such that in 1933 the Protectorate
Government offered Bunyoro a formal agreement on the model
of the Toro and Ankole agreements to assuage its grievances.
Although its actual terms did not include freehold grants and
were little more than a formal statement of the very full controls
actually exercised by the Protectorate Government, the offer
was accepted and did help to restore the self-esteem of the
Nyoro.

Opposition to the 1924 announcement was equally strong
amongst the Soga chiefs. They continued for years to petition

---

[1] Statement on Land Policy, 29 Jan. 1924. Unpublished material, E.S.A.
[2] The Babito were members of the ruling clan.

for freehold grants in the hope that a policy that they had seen
fluctuate so frequently could be induced to take one final turn
in their favour. In 1930 the Protectorate Government, in an
effort to placate them, offered the Busoga chiefs 85 square miles
of freehold land and a Busoga Agreement.[1] Despite the attraction of the latter, which would greatly enhance tribal prestige,
the chiefs held out for a much larger freehold grant until, in
1935, the offer was withdrawn, and the chiefs had reluctantly
and slowly to accept that they would not receive freehold grants.

In Buganda freehold land rights had, of course, been granted
under the 1900 Agreement. These rights could hardly be taken
away, but they could perhaps be limited. The Protectorate
Government's efforts to do this led to the most serious political
and administrative crisis in the inter-war years. In 1918 the
bataka[2] renewed their previous agitation against the land settlement, hoping to win from Daudi Chwa concessions which they
had not secured from Apolo Kagwa and the Lukiko. Many of
them organized the Bataka Association and presented their
complaints formally to the Kabaka. He acknowledged that the
1907 land settlement had ignored important traditional rights.
He suggested that the Lukiko should agree to allocate *mailo*
estates to any *bataka* who could prove that they had lost their
rightful *bataka* land. These new land grants could then be exchanged voluntarily for their *bataka* estates if their present
owners were willing. This proposal, though coming from the
Kabaka, and involving no coercion, was rejected by a 3 to 1
vote in the Lukiko.[3]

The issue then began to acquire a wider political importance.
The *bataka* were local leaders intimately connected with the
traditional pattern of life. They were outside the ruling hierarchy. Thus they were ideally placed to become the spokesmen
for the more general discontent against the land system which

---

[1] This was approved by the Colonial Secretary in a dispatch of 27 Feb. 1930.
The offer is discussed in K. Ingham, *The Making of Modern Uganda* (London,
1958), p. 196.
[2] The *bataka* were the clan heads, many of whom had lost their traditional
ownership of their clans' burial grounds under the Buganda land settlement. See
Chapter II, pp. 78–81, above.
[3] See Thomas and Spencer, *Uganda Land and Surveys*, pp. 69–72, and Low and
Pratt, *Buganda*, pp. 233–6, for discussions of the whole land controversy in Buganda
from 1918 to 1926.

had begun to develop when the *busulu* and *envujo* exactions were increased.

After the Lukiko rejected the Kabaka's compromise, the Bataka Association in 1922 appealed to the Protectorate Government to intervene. Although a government committee fifteen years previously had recommended that the *bataka* claims could justly and properly be ignored,[1] the Protectorate Government in 1924 appointed the Provincial Commissioner, J. R. Sturrock, and the new Chief Justice, Sir Charles Griffiths, to investigate the whole question afresh. They showed much greater sympathy towards the *bataka* claims than had the earlier government committee. They agreed that the land settlement had wrongly ignored and violated customary *bataka* rights and they recommended that a land arbitration court be empowered to investigate individual claims and to restore the *bataka* estates to their earlier owners. They had not consulted the Land Office at all in preparing their report and seem to have had little idea of how difficult it would be to carry out their proposals.

In 1926 the whole matter was referred to the Colonial Secretary, L. S. Amery, for a final decision. In October of that year his reply was read to a most anxious Lukiko.[2] He rebuked the regents in very strong terms for the way in which they had used their powers at the time of the land allocation. However, he announced that practical considerations made it impossible to reopen the whole issue. Certainly there were many such considerations. The number of cases that would have had to be investigated was enormous. The passage of time would frequently have made it extremely difficult for any court to be sure of the justice of its particular decisions. If compensation were to be paid the sum involved would be prohibitive, while outright expropriation after so many years would have been extremely unjust. The restoration of *bataka* lands to the clan heads would have created a hybrid land-tenure system in Buganda, partly modern and partly traditional, which, because the *bataka* estates would not have been freely transferable, might have hindered agricultural development.

[1] This committee, under the chairmanship of Justice W. Morris Carter, reported in March 1907. The report is summarized by Thomas and Spencer, op. cit., p. 53.

[2] His reply was outlined to the Legislative Council by the Acting Governor in Dec. 1926 (Summary of the *Proceedings* of the Legislative Council, 6th Session, p. 79).

There was a further factor. A whole new aspect of land policy had intruded upon the consideration of the *bataka* claims.[1] In the first years after the land settlement of 1907 the peasants' obligation to their landlords had continued to be the traditional *busulu* and *envujo*. With the rapid extension of cotton cultivation in the early 1920's, the landlords began to levy an *envujo* on the cotton crops of their tenants as well as on their beer and food produce. In 1920 a Lukiko law was passed authorizing a 10 per cent. levy by landlords on any crop. It was, however, vetoed by the Governor. Levies on cash crops persisted, and in 1926 a government committee claimed that as much as one-third of the cotton crop was frequently commandeered by the landlord. To many officers, the *busulu* and *envujo* issue was a further and final proof that the chiefs and landowners were a special interest group concerned above all with promoting their own welfare. Reinforcing the willingness to intervene on this issue was the further feeling that a high *envujo* on cotton would discourage peasants from increasing its cultivation. Feeling ran so strongly that in 1926 a government committee suggested that the Lukiko law on this matter was repugnant to justice and morality and that the Lukiko should be advised and if necessary compelled to abolish the *envujo* altogether.

The Provincial Commissioner in Buganda held to a steadier course. He recognized that the British Administration rested on an alliance with the landed classes which would be sorely tried by any effort to convince or coerce the Lukiko into abolishing the *envujo*. He succeeded in negotiating a compromise with the Native Government which pleased neither his superiors nor the Buganda Government but which both accepted. The compromise was embodied in the *Busulu* and *Envujo* Law, which the Lukiko passed in 1927. This law fixed the size of the *busulu*; it limited the *envujo* that could be charged for any holding of 3 acres or less, and it gave security of tenure to the tenants as long as they met these limited obligations. Each of these provisions was a major restriction on the economic power of the landowners, and the Lukiko accepted the law only under great pressure from the Protectorate Government.

Financial considerations reinforced this administrative concern. The increasing commutation of *luwalo* labour and the

[1] Low and Pratt, op. cit., pp. 236 sqq.

introduction of local salary schemes for the native authorities greatly increased the annual revenues of the native administration funds. In 1931, for example, their estimated revenue was £328,792. This, and the importance of the items on which these revenues were spent, led the Protectorate Government to control them most carefully.

In the districts without a formal agreement with the Protectorate, there were no legal and very few political obstacles to the extension of central control over the chiefs and over the native administration funds. Chiefs were appointed, dismissed, and promoted by the Governor on the advice of their district commissioners. Though the senior chiefs were often consulted when there were vacancies to be filled amongst the lower chiefs, the final recommendations on which the Governor acted were from the Provincial Administration. Similarly, though the district commissioners consulted local district finance committees, they themselves administered the native administration funds and decided what expenditures to make from them. This was as true in Toro, Bunyoro, and Ankole as it was in the other districts outside Buganda. Despite their agreements, the authority of the Protectorate Government was so unquestioned in these three kingdoms that district officers could control and supervise their governments and chiefs with equal effectiveness.

In Buganda the situation was more complicated. The attempt to secure a similar control over the chiefs and over the native government revenue broke an existing pattern of relations within which Buganda had enjoyed a wide autonomy in its internal affairs. A major controversy was perhaps inevitable and it occurred in due course. The main point in dispute was the right of government officers to deal directly with the chiefs in Buganda. This was happening more and more as the chiefs became involved after the war in a wider range of functions. Understandably, the *katikiro* and the Kabaka felt that this diminished the importance of their own positions and threatened the status of Buganda as a native state. Moreover the agreement itself clearly stated that 'on all questions but the assessment and collection of taxes the chief of the county will report direct to the King's native ministers from whom he will receive his instructions'.[1] Despite this, the Protectorate Government insisted that

---

[1] Article 9, Uganda Agreement, 1900.

its officers must supervise and instruct the chiefs directly. To surrender this right and to rely upon the Buganda Government to convey all instructions to the chiefs and to supervise them would have greatly lowered administrative efficiency in Buganda. The Governor even speculated that if the agreement appeared an obstacle to this control, then by a happy fiction the district officers could be regarded as the agents of the Kabaka in their relations with the chiefs.

In 1925 the issue came to a head. A sharp and bitter clash of wills occurred between the provincial commissioner, J. R. Postlethwaite, and the *katikiro*, Sir Apolo Kagwa, over a relatively minor issue, the issuing of beer licences in the Kibuga.[1] The dispute, as it developed, widened in scope until it centred on the right of direct communications between government officers and Ganda chiefs. While the Governor decided against Postlethwaite on the immediate initiating issue of the crisis, he refused to concede that all advice and instructions to the chiefs of Buganda had to be communicated through the Native Government. The antagonism between Postlethwaite and Kagwa was too intense for any *modus vivendi* and after first appealing to the Colonial Secretary, Kagwa, an ill and ageing man, agreed to resign.

In part this controversy marked the readjustment of relations between Buganda and the Protectorate Government which was necessary if the new government services were to be administered successfully. In part it was a clash of personalities, Kagwa used to authority and unwilling to concede, Postlethwaite assuming a superiority as of right. But its implications were perhaps wider. It brought into open conflict two vastly different views of the relationship between the British and the Ganda. Kagwa led a government which he felt was the ally of the British. He remembered their debt to the Ganda in the early years of the Protectorate and particularly to himself as leader of the loyal faction. He could not believe that the Governor would now give preference to a younger man with less service and experience. Postlethwaite for his part felt unquestioningly that, as a British officer, he was owed the obedience of any native official. Though his superiors might regret Postlethwaite's lack

[1] The Kibuga, a heavily populated African area on the outskirts of Kampala, is the seat of the capital of Buganda.

of tact, once the controversy with Kagwa had become public knowledge, it was Postlethwaite and not Kagwa whom they supported. Sir Apolo Kagwa's error was to suppose that the recognition of the Kabaka, the importance given to the agreement, and the preservation of the status of the Native Government were in the last analysis other than techniques through which a British administration ruled a colonial people.[1]

Kagwa's resignation in 1926 marked a turning-point in Protectorate–Buganda relations. It witnessed the determination of the Protectorate Government to secure the controls over the Buganda Government which it felt necessary. The Buganda ministers who came to office after Kagwa's resignation drew from it the obvious political moral. For the rest of this period the Provincial Administration received from them all the co-operation which it could wish. Through the indirect method of consultation and advice the Provincial Administration exercised in the 1930's a measure of control over the Buganda Government not much different from that exercised in the rest of Uganda.

African political activity in Uganda, though never directed against the British presence, was, nevertheless, important and varied. Perhaps its most significant forms were the protests which the native governments and the native authorities made to the Protectorate Government against the increased control and supervision which it began to exercise over them. But these protests were political activity of a special kind. They were levied at the Protectorate Government by men who despite their local authority were nevertheless still dependent upon the Protectorate Government. Moreover, the issues about which they protested often centred on their own privileges and prerogatives. They were not issues on which the chiefs could hope to rally widespread popular support. For example, in the *busulu* and *envujo* controversy, in which the Government faced the united opposition of the Kabaka, the ministers, and the Lukiko, the Government was defending the economic interests of the African peasants. It is hard to imagine that the peasants regarded the Lukiko and the Buganda Government as asserting other than their own special interests. In any case, throughout the controversy the mass of the Ganda remained passive observers.

[1] Low and Pratt, *Buganda*, pp. 212 sqq.

There were, however, a few occasions when chiefs or a native government did receive the open support of their people in an effort to change a government decision. The most frequent of such efforts occurred wherever tribal or local loyalties had been ignored or inadequately accommodated in the new native administrations that the British organized. In Bugisu, Bukedi, Toro, Acholi, and the West Nile there was popular hostility to the use of Ganda 'Agents',[1] and in many districts there was agitation to have *saza* boundaries redrawn to acknowledge older political units whose identity had been unrecognized. The Protectorate Government was normally willing to make what accommodation it could to such local sentiments. The Ganda Agents were withdrawn as fast as satisfactory local replacements could be found, and there were frequent boundary revisions.

But there was one important grievance of this type which the Protectorate Government was unable to settle. The Nyoro continued to complain of the inclusion within Buganda of several important Bunyoro *sazas*. The hostility of the Protectorate Government to Bunyoro, which had been apparent in the 1890's,[2] had long subsided, and under the governorship of Sir William Gowers it switched to a benevolent concern to promote the welfare of this depressed people. Yet on this issue of the counties which had been lost to Buganda, the Protectorate Government would not act, for Buganda's possession of them was the result of an earlier British policy and was entrenched within the 1900 Agreement. The Government knew how great would be the Ganda opposition to any attempt to amend these articles of their agreement and it never thought the issue worth the trouble.

In these still early years of British protection, African interest in and understanding of British policies tended to be limited to policies affecting land and the native administrations.

Issues other than these were still very few, and the African political activity that resulted was of limited effectiveness. It was in each case a tribal activity. It never led to organized inter-tribal co-operation. There was no unifying national political consciousness. No general sense of racial grievance had yet issued from the various sources of insecurity and unrest. Africans

[1] For the extension of administration through these Ganda 'Agents', see Chapter II, pp. 89–91, 105–6, above.   [2] Chapter II, pp. 68–71, above.

remained content to seek objectives which were possible within the framework of British protection. There was no articulate hostility to British rule itself. Africans did not question the continued presence of the British any more than did the British. This is not to say that there was very little political activity in Uganda. There was in fact a great deal, but it took place within the framework of British rule, and concerned itself not with government policies but with authority and political office within the African communities.

This political activity was accelerated by a most important shift that was occurring in the foci of power in Uganda. In many districts the first chiefs and native officials under British rule had commanded authority in their own right. They were either traditional clan heads, chiefs appointed by a traditional ruler, Ganda chiefs or generals with retinues of their own, or powerful local figures who had allied themselves at an early stage with the British. Their co-operation thus increased the power of the Protectorate and added to its authority. There were very few chiefs of whom this could still be said in the 1930's. The whole cultural transformation that was taking place lessened many of the traditional values and attitudes that might have kept their subjects passive and submissive. Independent sources of income, education, Christianity, freedom to travel, all increased the independent-mindedness of Africans and made it likely that the chiefs would not long be able to command unquestioned obedience. Many government policies indirectly contributed to this decline in their authority. The use of the chiefs to promote unpopular policies, the growth in the bureaucratic aspects of their work, the open control of the district officers, all underlined their dependence upon the Protectorate Government and lessened their local authority. By the third decade of this century the ability of most chiefs to command obedience was derived from their appointment. They no longer brought an independent authority to supplement that of the protecting power. Rather, their own authority was derived from the final power and authority of the British. Most chiefs were thus in a much more exposed position politically than their predecessors. They were often appointed chiefs whom the British urged to be leaders, rather than leaders who had been made chiefs.

The method of their appointment and promotion further

contributed to the insecurity of their office. It was the responsibility of district commissioners to recommend who should be appointed as a chief and who promoted. District officers had no easy, clear guide to a chief's integrity and loyalty. They were bound to rely on the advice of their senior chiefs, especially in the case of *gombolola* (sub-county) and *miruka* (parish) appointments. Moreover, even when a district commissioner chose to assert his own opinion, it was bound in part to be a product of the views and opinions that had casually or deliberately been conveyed to him. Thus there was ample scope for intrigue and for nepotism. In each district factions formed and re-formed about local leading figures in a constant struggle for power within the native governments and native authorities.

A further factor contributing to the pattern of tribal politics was the heritage of loyalties and institutions from the earlier pre-British institutions. Their influence was complex and is difficult to trace in detail, for it varied with the character of the indigenous political institutions and with the degree to which they were ignored by or accommodated within the new system of native administration. However, certain generalizations are possible.

In many parts of Uganda there were traditional clan and village heads whose authority continued to be an important feature of tribal life. These minor tribal authorities were admittedly under pressure. The impact of British rule had loosened the older loyalties on which their position depended, and the appointed official chiefs had begun to take to themselves some of their traditional rights and functions. Yet these very chiefs could not ignore them. Often only these minor traditional leaders could exercise effective authority at the village level, and where this was true the senior chiefs had no choice but to rely upon them as the local agents of the native authority. But it was an incongruous situation. These minor chiefs were unlikely to comprehend or to be sympathetic to many of the policies they were requested to enforce. Often they regarded the superior chiefs as usurpers. Clearly the occasions were numerous for friction and misunderstanding between these minor traditional leaders and their British-appointed superiors. Here then was one important traditional source of political tension and social strain.

A second source was the presence of the descendants of a conquering tribe or the members of a ruling princely clan, who in Bunyoro, Toro, Ankole, and to a lesser extent Busoga, still formed a social *élite*. The Government had always hesitated to entrench the power of these *élites*. In Toro and Bunyoro, where many of their number had acquired important *de facto* powers over land, the Protectorate Government finally rejected the demand that these be converted into full freehold rights. The Government also refused to agree that these princely sections of the population had any special claim to official chieftainships, and in the inter-war years more and more commoners were in fact made chiefs. Though these *élites* continued to enjoy a higher social prestige, by 1939 they had lost any monopoly of political office which they may once have enjoyed.

In Busoga and in West Nile, government policy was somewhat different. The indigenous social and political institutions of the Soga and the Alur were vastly different, but in each case the tribe had been grouped into fairly small-scale political units that were not large enough to become districts under British rule but were often equivalent in size to counties. Where this was true, the county boundaries of the native administration were normally drawn to coincide with these earlier divisions, and for most of the inter-war period the Governor appointed the traditional chiefs of these areas to be their official county chiefs. Gradually the considerations of efficient administration broke down this practice until in Busoga, where it had been followed most consistently, it was openly abandoned in 1938 and the traditional and the official positions were kept distinct.

A certain acknowledgement of traditional leadership occurred also in Lango and Acholi, where traditional clan heads were often appointed to be county chiefs, though in these districts, in contrast to the situation in Busoga and West Nile, their new responsibilities extended far beyond the boundaries of their older authority. Neither these Lango and Acholi appointments nor the respect for tradition in the Busoga and Alur appointments can be interpreted as evidence of a serious concern to protect and promote the interests of traditional authorities. All that was involved was the employment within an official hierarchy of some who had in addition an older claim to authority in the area. Where this was done, the new hierarchy inherited some of the older loyalties. When it was abandoned, those enjoying these loyalties tended naturally to become a focus of discontent and hostility to the new ruling oligarchy. The political life of most districts was marked by a rivalry between the official hierarchy and these various groups who had had traditional authority in the tribe but who were now without official status. The *bataka* in Buganda, the minor *mitala* and *kisoko* chiefs in Busoga, and, after 1938, many of the chiefs of the old Busoga chiefdoms, the clan heads in Acholi, Teso, and Bugisu: these were often the leaders and instigators of local hostility towards the appointed chiefs who were exercising authority under the British Protectorate.

Rivalry between adherents of the main Christian missions was the third main source of political factions within many Uganda tribes. The struggle between the Protestant and Catholic factions had been most important in Buganda in the 1890's[1] and these religious antagonisms had not died out. Catholics and Protestants continued to organize themselves separately to promote their interests within Buganda. Ganda Agents, catechists, and teachers carried this rivalry into other parts of Uganda. The missions themselves sometimes encouraged it, for there were many advantages in any area where the chief was a loyal convert. These religious loyalties were the one strong allegiance of a non-traditional nature then present in African society, and, understandably, they often became the basis of the major political factions within the ruling oligarchies.

The close connexion between religion and politics can also be discerned in the separatist Christian movement, the *abamalaki*, which suddenly became a serious challenge to the established Christian sects in Buganda in the early 1920's. The hostility of the *abamalaki* to any form of medical attention and their practice of mass baptism without prior instruction can no doubt be explained in theological terms. But the success of the *abamalaki* appeal was a product of non-religious factors.[2] Many Ganda desired to have a Christian name but did not wish to undergo the religious instruction which was required by the established missions before baptism. The unconditional baptism offered by

[1] See ch. xi in vol. i of this *History*.
[2] F. B. Welbourn, 'Abamalaki in Buganda, 1914–1919', *Uganda J.* xxi. 2 (1952), 150–61.

the *abamalaki* met this demand. Their hostility to medical treatment also coincided with local hostility to rinderpest inoculations of cattle and an anti-venereal disease campaign. Many Ganda must have been attracted to the *abamalaki* by the religious justification they gave for refusing all medical or veterinary services.

But one need not rely only on surmise to establish a link between the *abamalaki* and the political and social issues that disturbed Buganda society. The sect attracted to itself many of the Ganda who were hostile to the ruling hierarchy for political reasons. There were clear connexions between the leadership of the *bataka* movement and the *abamalaki*.[1] Kakunguru, Kagwa's greatest Ganda rival of an earlier decade, became a strong and influential supporter of the *abamalaki*. This is not to suggest that the religious protest was a product of the political or the reverse. But so closely allied were the chiefs and the missions that anyone who was in opposition to the one would be likely to oppose the other as well.

These various factions, religious, personal, and traditional, were not, of course, mutually exclusive. In the case of the *abamalaki* and the *bataka*, for example, they were in fact supplementary. This was the normal pattern rather than the exception. Many personal factions represented religious groups, and many traditional groups were headed by a single man or a group who had wished for personal reasons to arouse the cohesion of the group involved. Nor were the various types of faction everywhere of equal influence. Traditional factions were especially important in multi-tribal districts or in districts where an important section of the tribal society was aggrieved at the new administrative system. Religious factions were most important in Buganda, Bukedi, Bugisu, Kigezi, and Lango. But whatever their basis, factional disputes for office and influence in the native governments and native authorities were a major aspect of the political life of every district.

The immigrant communities

No mention has yet been made in this discussion of the European and Asian minorities. It is, of course, true that from 1922 on the Government was committed by economic realities and

---

[1] See Welbourn, loc. cit.

by its own conviction to developing the Uganda economy on the basis of African peasant agriculture. Yet the minorities did not disappear, and no discussion of political activity in these years is complete if it ignores their part, for though small, both these minorities were articulate and had a clear idea of what they required of the Government.

The European community was extremely small. In 1931 there were 2,001 Europeans of whom only 385 were privately employed.[1] Moreover, since 1922 they had had no doubt that they would remain a very small minority. Their numbers, their relative unimportance as primary producers of wealth, and the fact that so very few of them in any case regarded Uganda as their permanent home, meant that they never developed strong political ambitions as a racial minority. Their political behaviour differed from that of European minorities who are intent on turning a colonial territory into a white man's country. The Europeans in Uganda ignored the two main preoccupations of a self-conscious and politically ambitious racial minority— increased immigration and increased political representation. When they acted politically it was to promote their several economic interests rather than to increase their collective influence as a racial minority.

This interest in economic rather than racial considerations showed itself in their reaction to the proposals for a closer union of East Africa which were widely canvassed in the 1920's. Although such a union was expected to increase the political influence of the Europeans settled in East Africa, the Europeans in Uganda opposed it. Any sense of a common racial cause uniting Europeans throughout East Africa was overridden by the fact that the dominant group in such a union would be the larger Kenya community, whose economic interests differed sharply from those of the European trading community in Uganda.

This lack of ambition as a racial minority also explains why Europeans in Uganda were so much freer of open political hostility towards the Asian minority than were the Europeans in Kenya. Examples of this comparative lack of prejudice were many. The Uganda Development Commission of 1920, which included both European and Indian members, agreed that

[1] H. B. Thomas and R. Scott, *Uganda* (Oxford, 1935), p. 360.

there was no need for urban commercial segregation or for government-enforced residential segregation. The all-European counterpart in Kenya recommended both. The Uganda Chamber of Commerce, unlike the Kenya Chamber, had both Indian and European members. The 1930 Local Government Committee, which included leading European and Indian unofficials, recommended *inter alia* that there should be a Kampala Municipal Council elected by a common roll of all property owners. Nowhere else in East Africa were Europeans ready to accept at any level of government a common roll on which at some future date they might be outnumbered by either Asians or Africans.

In 1931 there were 14,860 Asians in Uganda.[1] Many of these planned to settle permanently, although a majority of them were still recent immigrants.[2] As a community of traders and small businessmen living in a foreign territory amongst alien peoples, the Asians were at first content to be without any political power. However, in 1920 they were stirred to political action by the impact upon them of the politics of neighbouring Kenya. The initiating incident was a dispatch of 21 May 1919 in which the Colonial Secretary, Lord Milner, attempted to settle the questions of land, of urban segregation, and of political representation in Kenya, all in a manner most favourable to the Kenya European community.

The detailed story of the controversy that followed this dispatch is largely but not entirely a Kenya story. The initial dispatch was understood to apply *mutatis mutandis* to Uganda and was first announced in Entebbe as well as Nairobi. The Government of India's vigorous response to it[3] included a strong recommendation that the Uganda Government reassure its Indian population that it would not impose new disabilities upon them. Such reassurances were not forthcoming. Instead the one recommendation of Milner's dispatch which could easily be transposed to Uganda, that suggesting urban racial segregation, became official policy. But it was not this that aroused the Asian community so much as the representation

[1] Thomas and Scott, op. cit., p. 361.

[2] Hailey estimated in 1938 that 60 per cent. of the Asians were permanently settled (Lord Hailey, *An African Survey* (London, 1938), p. 342).

[3] This dispatch is published in *Correspondence regarding the Position of Indians in East Africa (Kenya and Uganda)*, Cmd. 1311 (1921).

which Coryndon planned to give Asians in the Legislative Council which was being established.

It will be remembered that Coryndon expected that the non-African commercial and planter interests would become much more important in Uganda and he was anxious to provide for their early political representation. But it was the European rather than the Asian minority whom he was particularly anxious to encourage and to placate. This was an attitude which Milner shared. In his policy towards the Kenya legislature he had done his best to secure the dominant position of the Europeans from any encroachment by the Asian community. Milner was unlikely therefore to wish to grant the Asian minority in Uganda a representation equal to that which the Europeans were to receive. After consultation between the two in London the composition of the Legislative Council was announced. There were to be 8 members—5 officials, 2 European unofficials, and 1 Asian.

The Asian community, which knew itself to be much larger than the European community and more important economically, reacted with understandable hostility. They saw this 2 : 1 ratio as a suggestion of inferiority and as a denial of their equal right to contribute to the public life of Uganda. For five years the Asian community boycotted the Council in protest, and in 1926, when the first Asian did accept an appointment, it was on the clear understanding that this would in no way prejudice their case for increased representation.

Despite this omen Asian fears (on this ground) proved unfounded. In fact the economic depression of 1921 and the shift in the underlying social values of government both ruled out the possibility that the Kenya pattern would be extended to Uganda and that legislation and policy would be prejudiced against the Asian but to the advantage of the European. The question of European-Asian relations never became a serious issue, though until 1934 it lingered on because of the greater European representation in the Legislative Council. In its place the relations between Asian and African became the more important problem.

Once the Government saw its role in trusteeship terms it became a difficult problem of public policy to decide how much immigrant participation in the economy of the territory was compatible with the protection of African interests. In Uganda the Asians were the crucial minority in this regard. It was they who, as clerks, semi-skilled workers, and petty traders appeared to many officials to block African progress. In an effort to preserve an open field for African advance, the Government restricted Asian activity in several important ways. In 1933 Asian traders were required to confine their trading activities to special trading centres and were excluded from trading in the Kibuga.[1] A slight increase in the leasing of *mailo* land to Asians in the early 1930's generated intense official fears that Ganda landowners might sell large areas of their freehold to Asians. So strongly did the Buganda Provincial Commissioner feel about this that he permitted himself to conjure up a picture of Uganda overrun by indiscriminately multiplying Indians, and tried to get the Kabaka and the Lukiko to forbid any further leases of occupied land to non-Africans. Several efforts were made to encourage the greater employment of Africans in government departments by making conditions of employment less attractive for Asians. In 1923 the starting salaries of Asian recruits were significantly reduced, and in the following year the native Civil Service was formed, which provided for many classes of posts until then almost entirely held by Asians. The effort was renewed in 1929, when the government departments were instructed that all new clerical staff should if possible be African and that all new Asian appointments should be temporary, with provision for dismissal on a single week's notice.

The aim and first consideration of these various restrictive measures was to protect the interests of Uganda's Africans. But in introducing them there were fewer inhibitions than there would have been had the minority affected been European, for the Asians were weak politically and shared neither common racial and national loyalties, nor a common social life with the British administrators. Perhaps the bluntness with which some of these measures were pursued was encouraged by a lack of sympathy in Government towards the Asian minority. This is suggested by the following reply, given by the Attorney-General to a query on the civil service regulations: 'The natives of the country should be encouraged to take a larger share in the public services, a principle which he had no doubt Indians would endorse even though it would involve a gradual replacement of Indians by

---

[1] See p. 503, n. 1, above.

Africans, since this was precisely the principle which they claimed should be applied in their own country.'[1]

The implication of this statement, and indeed of government policy, was that the Asians in Uganda were to be regarded not as natives of Uganda but as impermanent immigrants with another homeland. By the 1930's this was untrue of the majority of Asians in Uganda. The Government was very slow to recognize this fact and the problems it might entail. Little was done to facilitate the tranquil integration of the Asian minority into Uganda life. Government education, land, internal trade, and medical policies accentuated their separateness. Official equivocation over the position of the Asian community was neatly revealed by an Orwellian indiscretion by the Chief Secretary in 1928, who, when asked if he regarded the Asians as permanent residents in Uganda, replied that 'the Government recognizes many Asiatics as permanently settled in the country but considers that natives are still more permanent'.[2]

This odd mixture of trusteeship values and prejudice was also apparent in the government attitude towards Asian representation on the Legislative Council. From 1924 until 1934 the Government always insisted publicly that the three unofficials might be of any race and that they were meant to represent the interests of the whole community. Yet in fact, though appointments and substitutions were frequent during these years, Asian always followed Asian and European, European. Never was the 2:1 ratio disturbed. This policy was never questioned by the Colonial Office until Lord Passfield raised the whole issue when he was Colonial Secretary. Sir William Gowers, who was then Governor of Uganda, met his queries with a denial that the existing representation was racial. He must have realized that this denial would not sound convincing, for he went on in his dispatch to give what was in effect a defence of a European majority on the unofficial side. 'I think that there is much truth in saying . . . that the people of Uganda in accepting the British Protectorate accepted the protection of the British race.'[3]

Passfield was soon out of the Colonial Office and it was left to

[1] Summary of the *Proceedings* of the Legislative Council, Tenth Session, 1930–1, p. 6.
[2] Minutes of the Legislative Council, 1928, *Uganda Gazette*, 1928, p. 546.
[3] Gowers to Passfield, 4 Nov. 1931, unpublished material, E.S.A.

Gowers's successor, Sir Bernard Bourdillon, to raise the issue again. On his initiative the right of the Asian community to a representation equal to that of the tiny European community was at last conceded. It was a small victory, but it did remove the last remaining legacy from the Coryndon–Milner attempt to make the European community into a major participant in Uganda life.

The determination of the Asians to win this open recognition of their equality with Europeans in Uganda was intensified by efforts in Kenya to place social and political restrictions upon the Indians there. This Asian concern was more than a natural concern to check the spread of undesired policies. There were strong influences at work to see that the Asian community within East Africa should speak with a single political voice. Many leading Indians in Uganda had economic interests in Kenya, and were as concerned with developments there as in Uganda. So, too, were those Indians who were representing Indian firms with East African investments.

A further influence came from the Government of India. Not only did it hold an effective watching brief on behalf of East African Indians, but on several important occasions it sent representatives to East Africa to assist in the presentation of the Indian viewpoint. Naturally the Government of India was closely concerned with the Kenya situation, and its influence within East Africa increased the sense of common cause amongst the Indian communities there. On several important issues these communities did present a common political front. They were careful not to advocate contradictory policies in their submissions to the Ormsby-Gore and Hilton Young Commissions in 1924 and 1928 and to Sir Samuel Wilson, the visiting Commissioner in 1929.[1] It is also probably not pure coincidence that in 1926 the Indian communities in Kenya and Uganda both decided to accept the representation on the Legislative Council which they had in each case rejected over the preceding five years. Finally, the Uganda Indian leaders, though in fact much more concerned to secure the recognition of their equality as a community with the Europeans, were always careful to repeat their support for a common roll, which was a main political objective of the Indians in Kenya.

[1] For these commissions, &c., see Chapter VI above.

It is, however, extremely easy to exaggerate the degree to which the Indians in Uganda acted politically as a united community. When they did so act it was in reaction to pressures which seemed unfairly aimed against them. Such pressures, except during the short 1919–21 period, were never strong in Uganda. In consequence whenever issues arose which touched the very real religious, sectarian, and caste subdivisions to which the Indians belonged, the unsubstantial nature of the unity of the Indian community revealed itself. In 1915 a government proposal to establish a common burial ground for the use of all sections of the Indian community aroused sharp assertions of these sectarian divisions. So also did the attempt by the Government in 1925 to decide which Hindu and Muslim sects should be given plots of land in townships at reduced rentals. Again, after 1927, when the Government began to support Indian education, the various subdivisions consistently resisted the Government's efforts to have common schools for all Indian students. These divisions, although fundamental, were little affected by most government policies, and in consequence only occasionally determined Indian political behaviour. Over the wider range of political issues Indians did not act as members of sectarian factions, nor, save when under pressure, did they act as a racial minority. Their political activities, like those of the European minority, were shaped much more by economic than by racial considerations.

There was a strong campaign by Asian traders against the official policy over the marketing of African grown crops.[1] Both communities objected to railway policies which they felt were prejudiced in Kenya's favour.[2] There were strong protests for this same reason in 1928 against proposed changes in the customs and excise tariffs. When it happened that the representation of Asian and European opinion reinforced the views which the Government of Uganda was itself putting forward to the Colonial Secretary, then for that reason they were of some importance.[3]

[1] See Chapter VIII above.

[2] M. F. Hill, *Permanent Way*, vol. i. *The Story of the Kenya and Uganda Railway* (Nairobi, 1950), chs. xiv–xvi.

[3] For example, in 1929 it was of some assistance to the Governor of Uganda, when he was opposing strong Kenya pressure for higher protective tariffs on agricultural produce, to be able to refer to the unanimous opposition of the unofficial side of the Legislative Council to the proposed rates.

But when the minority communities attempted to block a policy which the Uganda Government supported they were much less successful. Neither minority had the political power which was needed to influence government policy in major fashion. The Government could with little political embarrassment ignore their occasional protests against its 'West Coast' preoccupation with African affairs.

Social and political development and Buganda nationalism

With the increased services, improved communications, secure framework of law and order, and expanding educational facilities, and with the evangelizing of the missions, Uganda was experiencing the very developments which in other African territories led to the growth of supra-tribal nationalism and to the decline in the authority of the traditional chiefs. Yet in Uganda there was much in the nature of their impact to weaken their socially disintegrating effects and to lessen the likelihood of any supra-tribal integration about new institutions, symbols, and values.

In the first place their impact was much more intense in the south and south-east than elsewhere in Uganda. The evangelizing and the educational work of the missions, and the medical services of the Government, though spreading out from Buganda into the rest of Uganda, remained more heavily concentrated in the Eastern Province and Buganda.[1] The economic development of the territory was equally unbalanced. Cotton, the main peasant cash crop, was first grown in Buganda, and while it was most successfully extended into the Eastern Province, there were large areas of the Western and Northern Provinces where neither cotton nor any other economic crop could be extensively cultivated.[2] The gap between large sections of the Bantu south and the Nilo-Hamitic north, and more specifically between Buganda and the rest, was accentuated rather than narrowed.

[1] The missions, for example, claimed 364,215 followers in Buganda in 1930 and only 186,902 in the Western and Northern Provinces. Uganda Blue Book, 1930, pp. 105–17; Annual Report of the Department of Education, 1930, p. 47.

[2] In 1930 cotton acreage in Buganda was put at 194,129 acres, in Teso 118,813 acres, and in Busoga 132,890 acres. In contrast, in the whole of what is now the Northern and Western Provinces there were less than 110,000 acres under cotton and nearly two-thirds of this was in Lango (Uganda Blue Book, 1930, pp. 326–30). These figures cannot be more than guesses, but they do reveal the heavy concentration of cotton cultivation in a few districts.

Moreover, the impact of these forces even in Buganda tended not to overwhelm but to be absorbed by the traditional institutions. Cotton brought substantial incomes to many without seriously disrupting their traditional pattern of life or their accepted system of land tenure. Education did not lead to the growth of an uprooted minority in open hostility to the whole native administrative system. The early close connexion between the missions and the chiefs continued. A substantial proportion of school-children were sons of the chiefs. Many of the educated Ganda thus had close and intimate connexions with the ruling hierarchy. In addition this hierarchy was 'open to the talents' rather than confined to any one lineage group, clan, or set of families. Thus ambitious, educated men, rather than reacting in full hostility to the whole government system, tended instead to aspire to it.

Nor did Christianity directly undermine the tribal political institutions. The Kabaka, the ministers, and the chiefs were almost all practising Christians. They had themselves enforced the Witchcraft Ordinance, enacted as early as 1912,[1] interpreting it widely to drive into illegality many pagan practices. The introduction of Christianity did not lead to the creation of a believing minority alienated from the whole tribal society. Rather, Christianity became in a real sense the new religion of the tribe, with the missionary societies and the ruling chiefs and ministers each strong supporters of the other.

The one major issue that threatened seriously to divide the Government and Africans in Uganda had the effect of increasing the tribal and separatist loyalties of the Ganda, rather than of stimulating a supra-tribal nationalism. For a whole decade, until the Joint Select Committee of 1931 finally reported against a closer union of the East African territories, this issue disturbed the political life of East Africa. It touched a most sensitive fear on the part of the Africans, the fear of losing their land and the control of their local affairs to European settlers. Uganda Africans wanted to be completely free of any constitutional relations with Kenya. The point was bluntly expressed by the Kabaka in a supplementary memorandum to the Joint Select Committee in 1931:

It has always been my fear that as a result of the establishment

---

[1] Ordinance no. 6 of 1912.

of a Federal Council any changes of the Uganda Protectorate will necessarily affect adversely the present status and position of the Buganda Kingdom since it is certain that such a Federal Council will of necessity be composed of a large number of unofficial members of the various immigrant races possessing vast interests in their deliberation in such Council. It is needless to point out that the interests of foreign and immigrant races in a Country must inevitably be in conflict with the interests of the Natives of the Country.[1]

Federation was not wanted: it was deeply feared. The African's response to pressure was to hold the more firmly to their older tribal loyalties. Moreover, in the case of the Ganda, the separate status guaranteed in the Uganda Agreement gave them constitutional grounds on which to fight the proposed federation, and they clung to the agreement. Serwano Kulubya, *omuwanika* (treasurer) of the Buganda Government, illustrated this in his evidence to the same committee: 'the Buganda Agreement is the very life blood of us as a nation . . . our one desire is to be left alone to carry on in the same way as we have been going since the Solemn Promise which marked the signing of the Agreement'.[2]

This Buganda separatism, and the tribalism of other tribes, was never challenged by the Protectorate Government. The Government agreed that the tribe was the natural and proper unit of African political life. The British as well as the Africans were content to regard the Protectorate Government as a British affair. Sure of their policies and sure that they would rule in Uganda for a very long time, the British were not concerned about the entirely alien character of the Uganda administration nor the lack of political integration amongst the tribes of Uganda. The African development which Government was anxious to encourage was always social, economic, and administrative. It was never political and national. The Government saw its objective in Uganda in terms of ruling Uganda well and developing its resources. Training for self-government belongs to a later era.

Proof of these attitudes and evidence of their influence can be seen in the Government's policy towards African education and

[1] Joint Select Committee on Closer Union in East Africa, Vol. iii. *Minutes of Evidence*, H.C. 156 (1931), p. 99.
[2] Ibid. ii. 551.

towards the central legislature, two issues that become the preoccupation of both nationalists and governments once self-
government is expected and the advance towards it is planned.
Until after the first world war, African education in Uganda
was entirely the responsibility of the mission societies. Happily
it was a responsibility to which they attached great importance,
and in Uganda as elsewhere the village mission schools were an
important and integral part of the Christian expansion.[1] In 1920
there were, moreover, a variety of other mission schools[2] with an
enrolment of over 13,000.[3]

After the first world war there was a cautious recognition
by the Government of a responsibility to develop educational
services. It had already begun, most tentatively, to spend some
public moneys on education. At first such expenditures were
nominal block grants to the missionary societies. In 1918 they
totalled £2,100. Then, in 1922, in response to strong pressure
from local employers, the Government opened a school at
Makerere outside Kampala to train young Africans in carpentry
and mechanics. But the Government soon felt that it could not
leave primary and secondary education entirely to voluntary
societies without either adequate assistance or supervision. In
1924 Eric Hussey, an able educational administrator from the
Sudan Government, became Uganda's first Director of Education. Under his leadership the education policy of the Government was quickly defined. The Government decided against
assisting the thousands of village mission schools. They were too
numerous, and too badly staffed, to be incorporated into a co-
ordinated school system, and it would not have been possible to
train or supervise all their teachers. Instead some fifty of these
schools were selected to become the first stage of a government-supported education system. These schools remained under
mission ownership, but were subject to syllabus controls and
government inspection. District and provincial boards were

[1] In 1920 the missions reported a total enrolment of 102,360 students in these
schools. In 1939 this figure was up to 269,227. Enrolment and other statistics on
mission schools appear in great detail in each edition of the Uganda Blue Book
from 1919 to 1945, when its publication ceased.

[2] These included 70 central schools, 11 normal schools, 13 technical schools,
and 6 high schools. Uganda Blue Book, 1920.

[3] Almost all of these were in the early years of primary education. Jesse Jones
estimated that there were 500 in Standard III and IV and an additional 100 beyond
that level (T. J. Jones, *Education in East Africa* (New York, 1925), p. 152).

established, under the chairmanship of administrative officers, to supervise these schools and to allocate amongst them the limited funds, mainly grants from the native governments and native authorities, which the boards had at their disposal.

Some policy such as this was doubtless essential if an organized, properly supervised school system was to be established. Something, however, was lost in the process. The village mission schools, though bearing witness to new values and a new way of life, were an integral part of the village communities. They were something which the people felt to be their own. By leaving them outside its education system the Government neglected an institution which, because of its acceptance within the African community, might have been a vital agent of social change. Africans for their part were suspicious of the Government's policy.[1] The purpose behind the supervision of the few selected schools was not understood, while the decision to leave large numbers of village schools without any official standing or support was resented. Many felt that the work of men who were trusted and admired as village teachers and catechists was being contemptuously dismissed as useless. In education, as in local government, a contradiction was thus revealed between the controls needed to secure efficiency and competency and the autonomy necessary to assure continued genuine popular acceptability.

Hussey had initially hoped that the mission central and high schools might be taken over by the Department of Education and run as government schools. In this, however, he was out of harmony with Colonial Office policy, which was willing to leave the ownership and immediate management of African schools to the missions. Behind this British policy was more than a practical desire to retain the advantages of missionary participation. There was also an official fear that education would undermine the traditional social order and that this would have unfortunate moral, social, and political consequences. Missionary participation in education was supported in the hope that the missions would succeed in introducing new beliefs and new social values as substitutes for those being undermined and thus provide an alternative basis for a stable, tranquil social order. This coldly

---

[1] Annual Report of the Department of Education for 1925, p. 4, and J. V. Taylor, *The Growth of the Church in Buganda* (London, 1958), pp. 64–65, 156–60.

utilitarian view of religion may well merit J. H. Oldham's sarcastic 'It cannot in the long run be to the advantage of Christianity to be treated as an economical substitute for a police
force'.[1] Nevertheless, it did for the moment strengthen the
missions' position against those who would remove the schools
from their charge. Hussey quickly abandoned his initial intention and for the next sixteen years the Government limited its
role in primary and secondary education to the provision of
grants to the missionary societies, the training of teachers, and
the exercise of a general overall supervision.

In addition to these activities the Department of Education
itself started several technical schools which provided training
in such crafts as carpentry, tailoring, building, and mechanics.
It also began to make relatively large expenditures on Makerere
College, the government school which was later to evolve into
Makerere University College. In its early years, however, the
emphasis of the college was vocational rather than academic. It
had been started in 1921 to meet the needs of local private
employers. Within a few years several government departments
requested courses to train African assistants for their growing
rural services. In 1922 a medical course was added to the initial
curriculum of carpentry and mechanics, and within a few years
there were also veterinary, surveying, and agricultural courses.
Teacher-training also became an important part of the programme at Makerere.

Throughout the decade from 1925 to 1935 educational development in Uganda was beset by many difficulties over and
above the inevitable problems of inadequate finance and too few
teachers. Most of these difficulties derived from an ambivalence
within the Government itself on the question of African education. There were several serious disagreements between the
missions and the Education Department in these years. The
department was anxious to limit the number of mission secondary schools doing regular academic training and to develop the
remaining post-primary schools into semi-vocational central
schools which would prepare students for a purely local and
largely practical examination. The department hoped that these,
rather than the secondary schools which prepared students for

[1] J. H. Oldham, 'The educational work of missionary societies', *Africa*, vii. 1
(1934), 56.

the more academic Makerere entrance examinations, would receive the majority of the students who proceeded beyond the elementary vernacular schools. This policy was strongly pushed, and by 1935 there were 2,866 students in these central schools and fewer than 2,000 in the middle and junior secondary schools.[1]

Despite this official pressure the missionary societies were never too happy with these central schools. From the establishment by the C.M.S. of King's College, Budo, in deliberate imitation of an English public school, the mission societies had attempted to bring to Africans what they felt to be the best in British educational practice. Many missionaries saw in the argument that African education should be essentially practical and manual a suggestion that Africans should receive a second-best education, and for this reason opposed it. The missionary societies did not wish merely to provide trained Africans for employment by government or private employers. They were concerned to train a new Christian *élite* whose leadership and example would benefit the whole African community. For this high objective, technical and vocational education hardly sufficed. At the more mundane level the missionary societies doubted whether the 'practical' education which the Government desired would in fact meet the career needs of their students. A substantial number of these would in time become chiefs, native government or native authority officials, or would go on to the professional courses at Makerere. For these students a regular secondary school education was felt to be more appropriate and more valuable than any less academic training.

The missions were strongly supported by Africans in this preference for academic rather than technical, manual, or agricultural education. Africans turned to education to secure a command of English, an ability to read and write, a knowledge of the outside world, and thus to be the competitive equals of the European. Articulate African opinion pressed for changes that would increase rather than lessen the western character of African education. Government suggestions that school curricula should be revised to increase their 'African' or their practical content invariably met with strong African opposition. By 1935 this combined opposition of Africans and missions succeeded in

[1] Annual Report of the Department of Education, 1935, pp. 18–20.

winning from the Department of Education a most reluctant admission that the central school experiment had not succeeded.

Africans and missionary societies united against the Government on another important policy. In 1927 the governments of Uganda, Tanganyika, and Kenya decided to promote Swahili as a common 'African' language throughout the whole of East Africa. There was more in this policy than a concern to maintain an African content in education, for it would have been a great administrative convenience for these governments if a single vernacular were understood throughout the area. Critics of this policy also suspected that the introduction of Swahili was connected with the movement for a closer union of the three territories.

There was very great missionary and African hostility in Uganda to this attempt to introduce Swahili into the schools. Students walked out in protest when Swahili was introduced at the Kampala Technical School. The Buganda Lukiko and the Anglican Synod protested, and the Uganda Advisory Council on Education opposed the innovation in 1931 with a 17 to 1 vote. The four bishops in Uganda joined in a common petition to the Colonial Secretary, and African leaders carried the issue to the Joint Select Committee on Closer Union in 1931.

This widespread opposition contained two rather different types of protest. The government policy greatly offended the Ganda, who wished that their language should become the main vernacular in Uganda and who wished to learn English as their second language. Their resistance was so intense that within a few years the teaching of Swahili in Buganda and in neighbouring Busoga was abandoned. However, it continued to be official policy to promote Swahili as a lingua franca throughout the whole of East Africa save amongst these two tribes. In the rest of Uganda African opposition was less and owed more to the part played by the missions; nevertheless, in the end it was successful, and this attempt by Government to promote an 'African' element in education, which neither Africans nor their teachers desired, was abandoned.

The general conclusion is inevitable that the Government was much more hesitant and cautious in the expansion of its educational services than it was with its medical, agricultural, or

T

veterinary services. This is not because of the prior occupation
of the field by the missionary societies. Later they were to prove
no barrier to a rapid expansion of the government educational
services. The explanation is really ideological. The Government
in fact doubted the value of too much education. The Department of Education wished to limit the number of schools which
provided formal academic training, so that no more students
would graduate with a western-type education than were required by government departments, the native administration,
and private employers. The department's estimate of such needs
was extremely cautious, and in 1933, at a time when there were
sixty-nine successful graduates from the junior secondary
schools, the Director of Education judged that there was
no need for any further expansion of secondary education in
Uganda.[1] At Makerere the development of the various technical
and professional courses was determined by the needs of the
relevant government departments. The clerical course which
began in 1929 was in direct response to the government decision
of that year to try to replace its Asian civil servants by Africans.
The first academic class introduced in 1926 was a preparatory
class for students who would later enter the professional courses.
Finally, when full secondary-school training began at Makerere
in 1933, all the students who took it were required to promise
that after graduation they would enter one of the professional
courses and thus eventually become protectorate government
civil servants.

Several things are clear from this. The society whose needs
the Education Department felt it had to meet was a society for
whom the British already provided the ruling class and the
senior bureaucracy. Education beyond that which was needed
to provide subordinate staff was suspect. There was little
enthusiasm for the civilizing value of a humanist education, no
appreciation of the worth of an highly educated African *élite*,
and no suggestion that a vast educational programme was
required to effect a great social transformation. Rather the
reverse. Formal western education was suspected by many
administrators because of the adverse impact it would have
upon the vitality of tribal values and loyalties, and because of
a practical fear that Africans with such schooling were likely to

[1] Annual Report of the Department of Education, 1932, p. 11.

become the spokesmen of a disruptive political extremism. 'The central difficulty', said a British White Paper of 1925, 'lies in finding ways to improve what is sound in the indigenous tradition . . . in imparting any kind of education which has not a disintegrating and unsettling effect upon the people of the country.'[1] These sentiments were more bluntly repeated by the Director of Education in Uganda who expressed hostility towards 'a policy of ruthless westernization accomplished through the medium of education'.[2] Clearly the Government did not see its job as training the African legislators and civil servants of a future independent Uganda.

The same general lack of concern about political development at the national level is seen in government policy towards the central legislature. The Legislative Council was started when Coryndon was Governor and Milner was Colonial Secretary. It was part of their general policy of preparing the way for a greater non-African role in Uganda. The Council was to assure the minority communities and particularly the Europeans that they would have a regular and constitutional right to be consulted on all government legislation. The Council was not regarded as the beginnings of a supra-tribal African institution. Neither at its beginning nor until 1945 was a single African made a member. The Council was a concession to the minority communities. It had nothing to do with 'native policy'.

These minorities did not grow into the important communities for which Coryndon and Milner had hoped. In consequence the Council failed to become a vigorous and obviously important body on which Africans might wish representation. The few unofficial members did not represent politically aggressive communities anxious finally to assume full local control. Neither the European nor, after 1934, the Asian minority pressed for any increase in their representation. Their representatives on the Legislative Council acted as the representatives of special interest groups. They never seriously attempted to make the Council a genuine forum for the discussion and debate of the whole range of government policy. Nor was the Government anxious to encourage this. A large majority of protectorate laws were in fact passed by a special procedure which permitted all

---

[1] *Education Policy in British Tropical Africa*, Cmd. 2374 (1925), pp. 4, 8.
[2] Annual Report of the Department of Education, 1926, p. 6.

three readings of a Bill to take place on the same day. In this way sessions of the Council lasted very few days, with many measures being passed without any debate at all.[1] The few matters that were given full and lively discussion, such as the reorganization of the cotton industry or the custom and excise arrangements with Kenya, were those which directly affected the immigrant communities. None of the major policies affecting Africans was the subject of even an occasional close debate. Almost all ordinances that were primarily concerned with African affairs passed without discussion, their three stages being handled in a single day. It is small wonder that the Council did not become an accepted local institution, nor even an assembly in which Africans wished to participate.

This situation troubled neither the Government nor the African. What little African reaction there was to the establishment of the Council in 1921 came from the Ganda. The Kabaka and ministers wrote to the Governor, not to argue for African representation, but to seek assurances that the new legislature would not affect the 1900 Agreement. Then, as always, the Ganda preferred to see themselves as a tribal nation in a protected but quasi-diplomatic relation with the British rather than as part of a larger African territory. Ten years later Serwano Kulubya explained the Ganda attitude in these terms:

If we get a representative on the Legislative Council it is quite possible, say, with one or two representatives that he will be outvoted then by the majority and when he has been outvoted in that way it will be very difficult for us to open the questions because we have our representative there. So if you leave it as it is we have every chance of complaining on anything that might be passed by the Legislative Council and we can always approach the Secretary of State if nothing is altered.[2]

The Protectorate Government was willing at this time to allow this native-state view to stand unchallenged. When the

[1] The following table reveals how limited were the debates in the Legislative Council during the inter-war years:

	1928	1932	1935
Number of days in session	3	9	6
Number of bills passed through all stages on the same day	14	27	17
Total number of bills passed	14	32	20

[2] Joint Select Committee, 1931, *Evidence*, ii. 517.

Governor, Sir Robert Coryndon, opened the first Legislative Council he went out of his way to promise that 'the constitution of this Council will not in any way affect or supersede the rights, the responsibilities or the status of the Native Government'.[1] Ten years later official policy still did not regard the Legislative Council as a possible African national legislature.

The more educated and progressive natives will be well advised to devote their energies, for some time to come, to improving the calibre and the organization of their own native administrations and their own native courts, and that this line of action will be more to the advantage of their own people than if they take part in proceedings designed rather for a European than an African setting.[2]

The net result was a serious contrast between the very heavy concentration of services and functions in the hands of the central government and the lack of any African loyalty towards or participation in the affairs of this Government. That this unbalance was never regarded as a serious challenge by the Government and that stable and effective government could continue despite it, are both explained by two assumptions which almost no one doubted throughout the inter-war years. The first of these was that British overrule would last for a very long time and would throughout continue to enjoy a high and unquestioned prestige. This overrule was provided by the central government. Its high prestige sustained it, and it was able to rule tranquilly and with a remarkable absence of force. The second assumption was that the native governments and native authorities would continue to command widespread local authority and to co-operate willingly with the supervising British administrators. Their authority and co-operation assured reasonable local administration and the absence of any serious trouble due to tensions within the African community. On the basis of these assumptions, which seemed entirely reasonable and justified, the problem of who would rule an independent Uganda and through what institutions, seemed academic and far distant.

The first of these assumptions, that British rule would continue indefinitely, was unchallenged throughout the whole of

---

[1] *Summary of the Proceedings* of the Legislative Council, First Session, 1921, p. 11.
[2] An official statement quoted before the Joint Select Committee 1931, *Evidence*, ii. 871.

the period under review. But Sir Philip Mitchell, who became Governor in 1935, was one of the first officials in Uganda to question the second assumption that the native authorities and native governments would continue to have secure authority over their communities. Earlier in his career Mitchell had been an important subordinate of Sir Donald Cameron in Tanganyika. He shared Cameron's conviction that traditional authorities ought to be the basis of local administration, but like Cameron he recognized that this was not itself an ultimate objective of policy, and that if the people 'are not prepared to accept the orders of the so-called authority unless we compel them to do so then of course the administration we set up is not indirect and the native authority set up on such a basis is a sham and a snare'.[1] Mitchell brought to Uganda a sensitivity to the political position of the native authorities and a concern about the quality of leadership in the African community. As a result he gave to native administration policy and to education policy a lead that was long overdue.

The political situation within Buganda required his immediate attention. Eighteen months previously the Lukiko, at the instance of the provincial commissioner, had passed a resolution opposing the leasing to non-Africans of *mailo* land on which there were African tenants.[2] The Kabaka, himself a major landowner, objected to this limitation upon property rights. Without consulting the Governor or any British official he published a pamphlet defending a wider interpretation of the rights of *mailo* landowners and distributed it to all Lukiko members.

The pamphlet introduced a constitutional point of some importance, for it was an open challenge to a declared government policy. After stern private discussions with Sir Bernard Bourdillon, Mitchell's predecessor, the Kabaka agreed to withdraw the pamphlet, and the Government did not pursue further the constitutional question of the Kabaka's right to oppose government policy in this open fashion. In May 1934 the Lukiko repeated its earlier resolution. For ten months the Kabaka failed to forward it to the Governor, and when he was

---

[1] D. Cameron, *The Principles of Native Administration and their Application* (Lagos, 1934), p. 6.

[2] For the constitutional controversy of 1934–5 see Low and Pratt, *Buganda*, pp. 239–41.

specifically requested to do so he sent it on without his counter-signature. Strong pressure was again brought to bear on him by the Governor[1] and he finally agreed to sign the resolution.

It was at this point that Mitchell arrived as Governor. He was most anxious to establish the unquestioned final authority of the Protectorate Government. He regretted that the Uganda Agreement had come to assume the status of a binding constitutional document, for he saw that its terms did not, in any straightforward reading, give the Protecting Power complete and overriding authority. For example, in the controversy over the right of the Kabaka to withhold his assent to Lukiko resolutions, the section of the agreement that was specifically relevant seemed to support Daudi Chwa's view rather than Bourdillon's.[2] Bourdillon had, nevertheless, obliged the Kabaka to retreat by firmly asserting the undefined final authority of the Protectorate Government.

Mitchell recognized that the growth of tribal self-confidence and racial antagonism would make similar exploitations of the general position and prestige of the British more difficult.[3] He wished, therefore, to establish openly and categorically the complete final authority of the Protectorate Government. To this end he was determined to avoid a repetition of the recent crisis with Kabaka Daudi Chwa over Lukiko resolutions. A supplementary agreement was projected that would have required the Kabaka to follow the advice of the Governor on the rejection as well as the implementation of Lukiko resolutions. It was dropped only after Mitchell had won Colonial Office approval for the view that such an obligation could be assumed to exist under Article 6 of the agreement.

Mitchell was not only concerned to assert the final authority of the Protectorate Government. Within the framework of that authority he was anxious to grant more autonomy to the Buganda Government. He recognized that the official districts

---

[1] 'A holiday in the Seychelles' is believed to have been mentioned as the likely response of the Government if he continued to be obstinate.

[2] Article 11 required only that the Kabaka must seek and follow the advice of Her Majesty's Representative before giving effect to a Lukiko resolution. To require the Kabaka to approve a Lukiko resolution the Governor had to rely on the general obligation in Article 6 to co-operate loyally in the administration of Buganda.

[3] Low and Pratt, *Buganda*, pp. 260–2.

in Buganda, each under a district commissioner who took direct executive action through the chiefs in the district, was inconsistent with Buganda's status as a protected native state. Despite the opposition of the provincial commissioners in Buganda, Mitchell hoped that the Provincial Administration could in time become the adviser of the Buganda Government, allowing it to do much of the supervision, inspection, and administration that was then done by district officers. As a first step towards a functional reorganization of the Provincial Administration which would make it better suited for advisory functions, Mitchell appointed a judicial adviser to take over the court work formerly done by the regular district officers. To mark the new emphasis which he wished to secure he changed the title of the senior British officer in Buganda from Provincial Commissioner to that of Resident. This introduction of a term in common use in India and Northern Nigeria is revealing. Mitchell's efforts to secure a clearer definition of the responsibilities of the Protectorate and Buganda governments, a definition which would recognize the final authority of the former and a wider autonomy for the latter, amounted in many ways to an attempt to bring administrative relations in Buganda into line with the classic Indirect Rule pattern in Northern Nigeria.

Outside Buganda, Mitchell judged that the Provincial Administration had come by a process of self-deception to regard the official chiefs as if they were in fact traditional native authorities, accepted by their people and with strong customary claims upon their loyalty. In most districts, these chiefs had been brought into district councils which were assumed to be able to speak for the districts and were given the right to propose amendments to customary law. Yet in fact these chiefs were an appointed and an almost entirely non-traditional oligarchy, responsible to the district commissioner and deriving their authority from him. Mitchell saw and was distressed by the parallel between this situation and that in Eastern Nigeria before the 1929 riots.[1]

---

[1] In 1929 a series of women's riots occurred in Eastern Nigeria which demonstrated how insecure was the position of the non-traditional 'warrant' chiefs whom Britain had placed in positions of local authority. See Reports of the Commissions of Enquiry . . . into the Disturbances at Opobo, Abak, and Utu-Etim-Ekpo (Sessional Paper no. 12 of 1930) and in the Calabar and Owerri Provinces (Sessional Paper no. 28 of 1930).

In Uganda, too, there were signs that the more advanced sections of the community were becoming restive under the chiefs' rule, and that its efficacy was diminishing. By the late 1930's complaints appear regularly in the district reports of the declining authority of the chiefs. 'The early stages of the system known as indirect rule', wrote the Provincial Commissioner of the Western Province in 1937, 'are often more promising than the second.'[1]

Under Mitchell's direct initiative several important reforms were introduced into the organization of these native authorities. In Busoga and West Nile, where there had been a confusion of traditional and official chieftainships, the official positions were separated from the local traditional chiefdoms so as to leave no doubt of their subordinate and appointed nature. In the more advanced districts of the Eastern Province the councils, which had been composed entirely of chiefs, were enlarged. Traditional leaders and, where it seemed necessary to assure their representative character, indirectly elected members and representatives of the main religious communities, were introduced into the councils. In one or two districts the first steps were taken to create a district local government with the appointment of an African district treasurer.

These changes were introduced in only a few districts and they were not given any statutory basis. Yet these several reforms were informed by a clear conception of the final objective of local administrative policy. Under Mitchell's leadership the aim of native policy was to build a local government system in which the chiefs and the new district officials would be the local civil servants of a popular and representative district council which would include as strong a traditional element as local sentiments justified.

Mitchell's impact on educational policy was just as dramatic as his impact on native policy. Unlike his Education Department, Mitchell regarded the development of higher education as one of the Government's most important responsibilities. He was not unduly worried by fears of how educated Africans would be subsequently employed or of what their political influence would be. Though always respecting tribal institutions as long as they were vital, he also saw the need to produce an

[1] Annual Report of the Provincial Commissioners, Eastern, Northern, and Western Provinces, for 1937, p. 50.

African *élite* which would be the European's equal in education, culture, and sophistication. A quotation from Renan appears in his diary as an expression of his own attitude.

The countries which . . . have created a considerable popular instruction without any serious higher instruction, will long have to expiate this fault by their intellectual mediocrity, their vulgarity of manners, their superficial spirit, their lack of general intelligence.[1]

In 1936, in order to promote a general change of policy, he secured the appointment by the Colonial Secretary of an outside expert commission to consider the future development of higher education in East Africa. This commission, under Earl De La Warr's chairmanship, recommended a rapid expansion of higher education facilities, including the development of Makerere to the full status of a university college as soon as possible.[2] With Sir Philip's enthusiastic support these recommendations became the basis of government policy.

This development of Makerere necessarily implied a similar expansion in secondary education. Government grants for this purpose increased substantially, and every effort was made to raise standards and to enlarge enrolment. The semi-vocational central schools were converted into regular secondary schools. Enrolment in secondary schools rose from 226 in 1935 to 1,335 in 1939. The number of full primary schools increased from 23 to 78 over the same period.[3] Government recurrent and special expenditures for education from ordinary revenue rose from nearly £79,000 in 1936 to over £386,000 in 1939.[4]

The war, of course, slowed down the pace of expansion. It was not until 1945 that expenditure on education consistently reached a high level. However, the decisive policy changes had already been made. The development which has occurred since the war has been along the general lines of policy which were formulated and incorporated into legislation between 1936 and 1942.

The war years

The years 1939–45 must be treated in a brief and summary fashion. However, the main pattern of their political and

---

[1] Quoted in P. Mitchell, *African Afterthoughts* (London, 1954), p. 181.
[2] *Report of the Commission on Higher Education in East Africa*, Col. 142 (1937).
[3] Annual Reports of the Department of Education, 1935 and 1939.
[4] This includes a special grant of £250,000 to Makerere.

administrative events does stand out clearly and can be outlined with some confidence.

Inevitably the war greatly reduced the regular administrative work which district officers were able to carry out. Recruiting of new officers ceased. Many of the younger serving officers begged to be transferred to one of the fighting services, while those who remained undertook a wide range of urgent war-time functions in addition to their regular duties. In many districts touring had for long periods to be almost completely suspended. Everywhere the gap between administrative officers and their peoples increased, and with it misunderstanding and lack of sympathy. In this situation the chiefs proved their continued administrative worth to the Protectorate Government. They were active in encouraging enlistments into the armed services; they administered the attempts to stabilize the price of local foodstuffs; they raised the compulsory labour which after May 1940 the Government was empowered to enlist; they enforced the quite sweeping government instructions designed to increase the cultivation of maize and other food crops. These and other war-time responsibilities were undertaken with tolerable efficiency by the chiefs without any breakdown of their normal administrative activities and under much less direct supervision from district officers than had been normal.

There was little open hostility to Uganda's participation in the war. The link with Britain was still accepted as both desirable and lasting. No political leader thought to exploit Britain's position to secure political concessions. Chiefs and rulers were quick to affirm their loyalty, and many thousands enlisted for service in the Pioneer Corps, the East African Medical and Labour Service, and the King's African Rifles.[1]

Yet there developed in the war years a hostility towards the European which became sufficiently general to have a serious effect upon government policy. Its origins long pre-date the war. E. M. K. Mulira dates the first signs of strained relations between the British and Africans in Uganda to about 1925.[2] Dauncey Tongue, a senior administrative officer, wrote in 1935

[1] Total accepted enlistments in Uganda were 76,957. *Annual Reports of the Provincial Commissioners of the Eastern, Northern, and Western Provinces of Uganda, 1939–45.*

[2] E. M. K. Mulira, *Troubled Uganda* (Fabian Colonial Bureau, London, 1950), p. 16.

that 'the native is under no delusion as to our shortcomings and no longer regards us as superior moral beings. . . . He is no longer prepared to take us on trust.'[1] Even before the war this suspicion of the British occasionally had its effect on government policies. It was, for example, a factor in the rejection by the Lukiko of the Protectorate's offers of a trained European to supervise its public works department and of another to review the financial structure of the Buganda Government.

The declining contact between ordinary Africans and district officers and the increased exercise of unpopular authority by the chiefs deepened the general suspicion and hostility of Africans towards the Government. The return of large numbers of servicemen from the Abyssinian campaign, and the increasing number of secondary-school graduates and of Africans who were ambitious to establish themselves as traders, created a new and politically restless element in African society. Finally, for many Africans, the war involved serious hardships. Neither the price of their main economic crops nor wages kept up with the rising cost of living. Xenophobia and a general political restlessness were thus strongly reinforced by an economic discontent that was both widespread and often severe.

By the early 1940's both Government and the missions were affected by this deterioration in social and political relations and attitudes. The number of Christian communicants began in these years to decline. The C.M.S. became involved in several public disputes in which African suspicions of European motives were a major influence. In 1940 the decision of the Native Anglican Church to turn over the mineral rights of its lands to the Protectorate Government met with a most hostile reception and was widely regarded as a European intrigue upon African land instigated by the bishop. In the next year the *namasole*, the widow of the Kabaka, Sir Daudi Chwa, wished to remarry. Although this offended a traditional rule that no *namasole* should remarry, it was, of course, perfectly legitimate in Church law, and the bishop agreed to the service. The Ganda reaction was extremely hostile, and even amongst the Christian chiefs very few accepted the legitimacy of the marriage. A further important example of the antagonism towards the British and towards

[1] E. Dauncey Tongue, 'The contact of races in Uganda', *British Journal of Psychology*, xxv. 5 (1934-5), 363.

those who co-operated with them was the very strong Ganda opposition to the proposal that the Protectorate Government or the Kabaka himself should be given compulsory powers of land acquisition. Although government spokesmen urged that such powers were needed to secure adequate land for Makerere College and the Empire Cotton Research Station, a very large number of Ganda feared that the proposal was an elaborate ruse of the British to rob them of their land.

To this political situation Sir Charles Dundas, Governor from 1940 to 1944, made his own important contribution. Like Sir Philip Mitchell he had served under Cameron in Tanganyika, and despite the preoccupations of war-time government he also made the reform of the native administration system one of his main interests. Much that he sought to do was consistent with the reforms initiated by Mitchell. About Protectorate policy towards Buganda he readily expressed his views to the Lukiko in the bluntest terms:

> In the past . . . the chiefs were under two masters and the people particularly in the more distant parts of Buganda looked to the District Commissioners as much as to your Government for adjust-ment of their affairs. . . . Such was perhaps necessary but the stage has now been reached at which it should no longer be necessary for us to go beyond the scope set by the Agreement in the way of super-vision of your administration and I do not wish to perpetuate a system which I believe was not contemplated when the Agreement was concluded.[1]

Though he was less subtle and less cautious than Sir Philip Mitchell, Dundas was nevertheless expressing here the same general approach to the internal administration of Buganda as his predecessor.

There were, however, major differences between these two governors. Dundas was without Mitchell's concern to establish the close and unquestioned final authority of the Protectorate Government. Much more than Mitchell he believed that the reform of the native authorities must come from the authorities themselves, that protectorate officers must limit their role to the offering of advice and criticism. He was thus more willing than

[1] Speech to the Lukiko, Oct. 1944, quoted in the *Report of the Sub-committee of the Lukiiko set up to examine the recommendations made by the Hancock Committee* (Entebbe, 1955), p. 47.

any of his predecessors to leave the native governments and authorities to their own devices. In Buganda in particular, where the agreement strengthened the case for greater autonomy, he gave this view its fullest application. In the judgement of a Commissioner who investigated the 1945 riots, Dundas believed 'apparently . . . that British supervision was being given in a way which prevented the Buganda government from developing self-reliance and proper progress . . .'.[1]

The controversy over the *namasole*'s remarriage provided an important occasion for him to allow the Ganda greater internal autonomy. The Lukiko requested the dismissal of Martin Luther Nsibirwa because of his willingness to accept the remarriage. Although Nsibirwa had had an able and loyal record since his appointment as *katikiro* in 1928, Dundas did not support him but instead agreed to his dismissal. He then appointed as his successor Wamala, the candidate nominated by the Lukiko.

It was a particularly inappropriate issue on which to allow greater autonomy. Nsibirwa's decision to support the *namasole*'s right to remarry was hardly one that the Governor could criticize. Moreover, the agitation against Nsibirwa was strongly coloured by the personal ambitions of other factions within the Buganda hierarchy. Agreeing to abandon the *katikiro* was not yielding to a healthy assertion of local autonomy; it was surrendering to local intrigue. Nsibirwa's resignation was a turning-point in Buganda politics. The Governor's willingness to surrender to Lukiko pressure on such an issue as this gave great incentive to further intrigue and factious agitation. The confidence and security of loyal chiefs was greatly weakened, and many of them began quietly to ensure that they did not become fully alienated from those who were successfully manipulating political sentiments within and outside the Lukiko.

Dundas, however, was undismayed, and in 1944 he proceeded with a major reorganization of the whole relationship of the Protectorate Government with Buganda. In October of that year he announced that all official dealings with the Buganda Government would be conducted through the Resident and a staff of two assistant residents. These assistants would be stationed in Kampala alone, and, though they would tour

[1] *Report of the Commission of Inquiry into the Disturbances which occurred in Uganda during January, 1945* (Entebbe, 1945), p. 5.

Buganda, they would not directly supervise the chiefs. They would report to the Resident, who would then give what advice he thought necessary to the Kabaka and his ministers. They alone would be responsible for the control and detailed supervision of the chiefs in Buganda.[1] Dundas was thus conceding in one major and rapid reform what had been denied to Sir Apolo Kagwa twenty years previously.

Dundas accepted that the government to which he was thus granting more autonomy was unrepresentative. He had few illusions about the Lukiko and he realized that as then constituted it represented an already very powerful landowning hierarchy. However, he would neither give positive directions to the Kabaka nor exert strong pressure upon him to secure greater unofficial representation. Largely relying on the future leadership of the still young Mutesa II, he hoped that the native government would itself initiate the desired democratic reforms.[2]

If this was Dundas's expectation, if, as Sir Norman Whitley suggested, 'it was apparently hoped that a sense of pride would speed the Baganda to move on their own initiative towards more progressive liberal ways of Government',[3] then the hope was ill-founded. Some of the ministers and many of the chiefs were unpopular. Any democratization of the Lukiko would only add to their difficulties. As the war progressed, the growing political unrest was mobilized by their rivals further to threaten the position of these ministers and chiefs. More and more the energy and abilities of the Ganda chiefs were directed inward into intrigue and political manipulation.

In January 1945, three months after these Dundas reforms, serious riots occurred in many centres in Buganda and these in turn stimulated less serious disturbances in a few centres outside Buganda.[4] The increased economic pressure of rising prices, the intrigues and insecurity within the hierarchy, the growth of a general hostility and suspicion towards the British, and the appearance of an active political group of younger Africans outside the hierarchy were all important underlying factors. But the dismissal of the *omuwanika* Serwano Kulubya was their

[1] Low and Pratt, *Buganda*, pp. 278 sqq.
[2] C. C. F. Dundas, *African Crossroads* (London, 1955), p. 212.
[3] *Report . . . into the Disturbances . . . in Uganda during 1945*, p. 5.
[4] Ibid., *passim*.

most clearly articulated objective and the unrest subsided when he announced his resignation.

The riots were evidence of a political malaise far more serious than had yet faced the Administration in Uganda. The Government acted firmly to restore order and to punish the leaders of the riots, but they did not seek out its more fundamental causes. The Provincial Administration had never favoured Dundas's reforms of Protectorate–Buganda relations and the riots seemed to substantiate its judgement. Quietly on its advice the new Governor, Sir John Hall, attempted to re-establish a relationship with Buganda similar to that which had existed before the Mitchell and Dundas reforms. Assistant residents were again posted to district headquarters in Buganda, and from there they renewed their previous supervision of the chiefs. Prominent Ganda, including Prince Suna, uncle of the Kabaka, and S. Wamala, the *katikiro* whom Dundas had appointed, were arrested and deported from Buganda. M. L. Nsibirwa was brought back as *katikiro*, Kawalya-Kagwa, son of the late Sir Apolo Kagwa, was appointed *omuwanika*, and many chiefs whose loyalty to the Protectorate had proved unreliable were dismissed. As if to mark the change, the Resident, with the strong support of the new ministers, again urged the Lukiko to give the Kabaka power to acquire land compulsorily for public purposes. Finally, and most reluctantly, the Lukiko agreed. Sad evidence of the intensity of the fears of some Ganda over this issue came immediately. On the day following the Lukiko vote, Nsibirwa was murdered. Again the Protectorate responded firmly. Kagwa became *katikiro*, the ranks of the chiefs were further pruned, and nineteen more Ganda were deported without trial. After these demonstrations of its readiness to assert its authority and its determination to secure a native government and a body of chiefs who would co-operate fully with it, the Provincial Administration swiftly re-established the close relationship of control, supervision, and advice which had existed in the 1930's.

In the districts outside Buganda, Dundas had not impressed his views upon the native administrative system to the same extent. There was in consequence not the same dramatic reversal of policy in 1945 as occurred in Buganda. But the pattern that the Government intended to follow was everywhere the same. Throughout Uganda the Protectorate Government entered the post-war years still relying upon and ruling through a hierarchy of appointed chiefs. In 1945 as in 1939 the Protectorate Government continued to rest its policy on the twin assumptions that chiefs could be found who would be administratively efficient and politically acceptable to the people they ruled, and that British rule would and could continue for a long time on that basis without any major recourse to force or the show of force. It would not be long before political realities were to demonstrate how inadequate these assumptions had become. The period of tranquil and accepted British rule, of stable and manageable relations between the Protectorate Government, the native government and authorities, and the people was, in fact, soon to draw to a close.

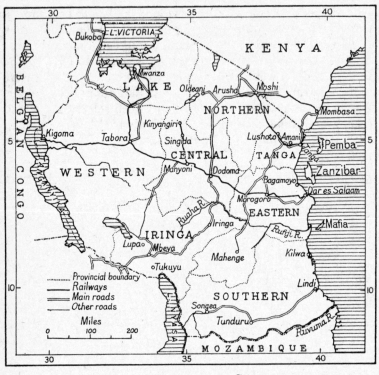

MAP 7. TANGANYIKA: ADMINISTRATION AND COMMUNICATIONS, 1939–40

X

TANGANYIKA
THE MANDATE AND CAMERON
1919–1931

KENNETH INGHAM

The mandate

THE decision to administer German East Africa as a mandated territory under the supervision of the League of Nations was reached by a complicated series of stages.[1] General Smuts, who played an important part in the discussions leading up to the creation of the League of Nations, appears at one time to have intended that the German colonies in Africa should be annexed by the powers which had conquered them. German East Africa, he thought, would then form a valuable link between Rhodesia and the British protectorates north of Lake Victoria. Even President Wilson, whose role in extending the system of mandates to Africa was vital, drafted his original Fourteen Points under the assumption that Germany's African colonies would be annexed by individual powers.

The policy of no annexation first emerged in relation to the former German, Austrian, and Turkish possessions in Europe and the Near East. The object was to avoid creating frontiers along which the victorious powers might come into conflict with each other and with their former enemies. In some of these regions it was possible to create self-governing states which would act as buffers against the conflicting interests of the powers. Where, on the other hand, territories were not ready for immediate independence, a system of trusteeship by one of the great powers, under the supervision of the League of Nations, appeared to offer a reasonable means of avoiding international friction.

[1] H. D. Hall, *Mandates, Dependencies and Trusteeship* (London, 1948). This book contains a detailed study of the background to the mandates and forms the basis of the early pages of this chapter.

The extension of this system of mandates to the African continent was a later development, but it was not a surprising one. European diplomacy had been occupied for nearly forty years in trying to prevent the colonial rivalries of the great powers in Africa from resulting in a European war. At the same time, the desire to introduce into Africa the benefits of western civilization had not been limited to any one power, so that since the Berlin and Brussels Conferences[1] it might be said that there had been some attempt at an international approach to the problems of tropical Africa.

It was, then, a bold variation upon an existing trend when the British Labour Party proposed, in August 1917, that the whole of tropical Africa between the Sahara and the Zambesi should be transferred to the League of Nations and administered by an impartial commission as a single, independent, African state. The adoption of this striking plan was more than the colonial powers as a whole were prepared to accept, although in May the British Foreign Secretary, Mr. Balfour, had already expressed to the American Ambassador the hope that the captured German colonies would be internationalized. Nevertheless, a favourable climate of opinion was gradually developing, and eighteen months later a Foreign Office memorandum was drafted which urged the establishment of a system of mandates for the backward territories including those in tropical Africa. This memorandum was adopted as the basis for British drafts of a covenant for the League of Nations. Shortly afterwards, in December 1918, President Wilson announced that in his opinion, too, the German colonies 'should be declared the common property of the League of Nations', and the first American draft of the Covenant to be circulated to the Allied powers contained a mandates clause which included the German colonies in Africa. Thus, by the time that the final text of the League Covenant came to be drafted by the great powers, there was evidence in several quarters of a willingness to introduce a system of mandates for Africa.

It was Article 22 of the Covenant[2] which embodied these

---

[1] See ch. x in vol. i of this *History*.

[2] Article 22 was in fact closely based on a resolution moved by Smuts at the Peace Conference. See W. K. Hancock, *Smuts*. vol. i. *The Sanguine Years, 1870–1919* (Cambridge, 1962), p. 507.

proposals and which defined as a sacred trust the well-being and development of the inhabitants of the mandated territories. It went on to distinguish between those countries which might be provisionally recognized as independent, subject to the administrative assistance of a mandatory power, and those in which the mandatory authority must be responsible for the administration. A third category was listed comprising those territories which could be best administered as integral parts of the mandatory power or its dependencies. It was in the second, or B class, that German East Africa was placed, and the powers accepted without argument that the mandates should be allotted to individual nations and not to groups of powers.

The task of drafting and allocating the mandates fell to the Allied Supreme Council of the five great powers—Britain, France, Italy, Japan, and the United States. The fact that it was the victorious powers, and not the League of Nations, which were responsible for instituting the system of mandates was to be one of the chief arguments put forward by British settlers in East Africa against undue interference by the League in the 1930's. But this was clearly a misinterpretation of the powers' intention. Although the League did not come into existence until January 1920, while the B and C mandates had already been allocated in May 1919, the great powers unanimously accepted that the mandatory system could not take effect until the League was in being and that the supervision of the mandates would be the League's responsibility. In the event the formalities involved resulted in still further delay. The texts of the mandates were drafted in July and August 1919, but they were not presented to the League Council until December 1920. In February 1921 a further delay was created when the United States asked for the postponement of their confirmation until the American public's views had been ascertained. Negotiations continued until July 1922, and only then were the B mandates finally confirmed by the League Council so that they could come into force. It should be added that in October of the previous year the British Prime Minister, Mr. Lloyd George, had suggested to President Wilson that America should undertake the trusteeship of German East Africa, but the United States had rejected the proposal. East Africa then fell to Britain.

In spite of their talk of international supervision, the victorious nations, all of whom possessed considerable overseas dependencies, had no intention of imposing severe restrictions upon the countries administering the mandates. The Permanent Mandates Commission, which was set up on 4 October 1921 to be directly responsible for supervising the working of the mandates, made this position clear. The members, who were supposed to be acting in a personal capacity, confidently defined their duties as being to determine the extent to which the principles contained in the Covenant and the mandates were being truly applied, while at the same time doing all in their power to assist the mandatory governments in carrying out their tasks. These two functions were not considered to be incompatible, since it was expected that the administering powers would fulfil their responsibilities conscientiously.

The whole machinery through which the system of mandates worked was so designed that excessive interference by the League of Nations was impossible, although moral pressure could be, and indeed was, brought to bear upon any power capable of responding to such an approach. The mandatory powers were required to submit to the Permanent Mandates Commission an annual report drawn up according to a standard pattern. The commission examined the reports some time after the events described in them had taken place. It did so in the presence of an accredited representative of the mandatory power and it transmitted its observations to the Council of the League to which it acted solely as adviser. The League Council then passed on the observations to the mandatory power, usually in the form of requests for further information. This arrangement was made still more innocuous by the fact that since the commission sat in Geneva it had to rely heavily upon the goodwill of the mandatory power for the information upon which it based its opinions. On the initiative of Great Britain, however, the League introduced a system whereby it could receive petitions from the inhabitants of mandated territories, although this formed no part of the Covenant or of the texts of the mandates. Little advantage was taken of this scheme, however, either because it was scarcely known to exist, or because it proved unnecessary, or perhaps because the petitions had to be submitted through the mandatory administration. In effect the functions of the Permanent Mandates Commission were to act as the conscience of the mandatory powers rather than as a stern and powerful master and to help the administering authorities by constructive suggestions.

Tanganyika after the war

While the great powers continued their discussions, the administration of Germany's former East African dependency, soon to be renamed Tanganyika, remained in the hands of the victorious Belgians and British. On 31 January 1919 Sir Horace Byatt, who since 1916 had been Civil Administrator of the northern sector of German East Africa, was appointed Administrator of the whole territory occupied by British troops. The area of British responsibility was further extended on 22 March 1921 after it had been decided that the Belgian mandate should be restricted to the populous territory of Ruanda-Urundi.

Byatt was a cautious man, and ill health further undermined his determination. Faced with the task of creating a new administration and a new economy upon the ruins of German enterprise, he was convinced that there should be no sudden innovations to disturb the African population. These latter, having so recently suffered the appalling ravages of war, were still undergoing successive blows from famine and influenza epidemics. There were, however, many difficulties to be overcome, of which the shortage of experienced administrative officers was not the least. Tribes had been scattered by the war or had abandoned their former homes to seek refuge from the military forces. The system of communications which the Germans had constructed with infinite labour had been destroyed by them with equal thoroughness to hamper the advance of the British invaders. Until the whole of the Central Railway was under British control the lucrative transit trade to the Belgian Congo could not be fully developed. Meanwhile, the finances of the territory needed bolstering from every available source. Although there was a surplus balance of £230,483 on 31 March 1920, this did not take into account the cost of the three battalions of Kings African Rifles forming the garrison of Tanganyika, for whose maintenance at a cost of about £240,000 a year the Civil Administration had become liable on 1 February 1919. Furthermore, exclusive of the cost of the garrison, expenditure for 1919–20 exceeded revenue by £120,929, so that for the year 1920–21 it was necessary to obtain a grant-in-aid of £330,000 from the Imperial Treasury.[1]

Since Tanganyika relied heavily for its income upon customs dues and hut and poll-taxes, little improvement could be expected until the productivity of the country had been restored. But the loss of Ruanda-Urundi, while restricting the area to be administered, at the same time cut off one of Tanganyika's wealthiest and most heavily populated regions. In addition, the former German estates from which the country had derived much of its income before the war were now derelict: their previous owners were refused permission to restore them to production and were driven from the country. An attempt was made to relieve this situation by making the sisal estates available on annual leases, and a number of Greeks seized the opportunity thus offered to lay the foundations of a profitable participation in the country's agricultural development. Even then there were difficulties, for until 1920 the lack of shipping space greatly hampered the recovery of the sisal industry, and this situation was scarcely rectified when there was a sharp drop in the value of sisal in the world market. During 1919 a number of shipping lines established agencies in Dar es Salaam and Tanga, but the services they provided were irregular and depended heavily upon the inducement offered by way of inward and outward freights. In the uncertain condition of the sisal industry a steady flow of exports could not be relied upon, and until European farming and other activities could be renewed imports consisted largely of cheap textiles from India and Japan. Cotton cultivation, too, which was mainly the work of African peasants, could not hope to supply the need for exports until the population had once more settled down to a peaceful routine, although every effort was made by the Administration to revive cotton-growing and 100 tons of seed were imported from Uganda for distribution in the territory.

The reconstruction of public services imposed a further strain upon the country's finances. The first public works programme was drawn up by the new Administration in 1918 when the war was still in progress, and a more extensive pro-

---

[1] *Report on Tanganyika Territory from the Armistice to the end of 1920*, Cmd. 1428 (1921), pp. 42–44.

gramme was undertaken in 1919. Needless to say, this was mainly concerned with repairing the damages of the war period, since virtually no maintenance work had been done for five years. Roads, bridges, urban and rural sanitation, sea-walls, lighthouses, and other public buildings all required attention, while the water-supply and drainage system of Dar es Salaam, the new civil headquarters, were in need of immediate improvement. Hospital buildings were generally found to be satisfactory, but in the medical field shortage of staff was the limiting factor. The educational system, too, which under the Germans had achieved such praiseworthy results, could not be restored overnight. Authority was given in December 1919 to reopen some of the former German schools, and a Director of Education was appointed in September of the following year with the task of framing a comprehensive scheme of education for the African population. But there was a shortage of staff to make the programme effective. Many former teachers were hard to trace, while others had obtained alternative employment which they did not wish to leave.

In addition to these problems there were sporadic outbursts of crime after the armistice which taxed the resources of police and administrators to the full. Many of the worst offenders, it is true, were Africans from other territories who had been brought to Tanganyika by the war, but their activities placed yet another burden upon the limited resources of trained manpower in the territory.

By insisting that no action should be taken which might prejudice the terms of the mandate before they were officially known, Byatt himself did little to improve the situation. It may be, too, that he adopted this conservative doctrine as a means of justifying his own policy of caution, for it is clear that as far as the great powers were concerned the Administrator was behaving with excessive prudence. In the economic sphere Tanganyika's position as a mandated territory was to present the British with certain initial benefits. For example, to assist economic reconstruction it was agreed that the territory should be taken over free of all public debt. The administering authority was also able to acquire the Central Railway for the nominal sum of £33,995, and even in the derelict condition in which it had been left by the Germans its true value was many times greater. Subject, too, to the general ruling that native laws and customs should be taken into account and the rights and interests of the African population safeguarded, considerable latitude was given in the formulation of a land policy.[1] And, bearing in mind the achievements of the German settlers and the need to maintain and build upon the foundations they had laid, Britain was not required to hand back to Africans the land which the settlers had acquired. The mandatory's responsibilities in regard to the control of labour conditions were similarly modest and did not contemplate the introduction of any measures which the British authorities might not have been expected to enforce on their own initiative.

Potentially more serious, perhaps, was the clause in the mandate calling for equal opportunities for the trade and commerce of all other members of the League.[2] Under this ruling Tanganyika could not negotiate for reciprocal concessions with other trading nations so as to guarantee a good market for her exports. Nor could she discriminate against imports from any foreign country which might indulge in unfair business methods. The first of these restrictions had no more than a theoretical significance between the two wars, and Tanganyika herself did not suffer economically from the existence of an open market for the imports of all members of the League. But the arrangement gave rise to considerable criticism from British merchants when it was seen in the 1930's that Japan in particular was taking advantage of the situation to increase her imports while purchasing virtually nothing from Tanganyika in return.

The establishment of British administration

Within the framework of international supervision, British administration in Tanganyika Territory was formally established by the Tanganyika Order in Council of 22 July 1920.[3] By the terms of the order the title of the chief representative of His Majesty's Government was changed from that of Administrator to Governor and Commander-in-Chief. Subject to the

---

[1] The British Mandate for East Africa, Article 6. See Appendix II below.
[2] Ibid., Article 7.
[3] Tanganyika Territory, *Ordinances, Proclamations, &c.*, vol. i (London, 1921), 92 sqq.

Colonial Secretary's general power of disallowance, the Governor was then empowered to make ordinances for the good government of the country, provided he respected existing native laws and customs. He was to be assisted in his work by an Executive Council consisting of the Chief Secretary, Attorney-General, Treasurer, and Principal Medical Officer. In addition there was to be a High Court possessing full criminal and civil jurisdiction over all persons in the Territory. This court was to be superior to all other courts in the country with the exception of a Special Tribunal appointed primarily to deal with civil cases which had arisen before the implementation of the order in council and which, so far as circumstances would permit, exercised jurisdiction in conformity with the law and procedure in force at the time when the action arose. In all other cases the Indian Civil Procedure, Criminal Procedure, and Penal Codes formed the basis of jurisdiction, supplemented where necessary and appropriate by English common and statute law. It was also ruled that where Africans were parties to any case, whether civil or criminal, courts should be guided by native law if it was applicable and if it did not conflict with justice, morality, or any order in council or ordinance. Such cases were to be decided according to substantial justice without undue regard to technicalities of procedure and without undue delay.

In spite of the considerable powers vested in him by the order in council, patience and prudence still remained the dominant themes of Byatt's policy. The twenty-two administrative districts into which the Germans had divided the territory were retained. So, too, where possible, were the services of the experienced *akidas* whom the Germans had formerly employed in some areas, although their status and privileges were to be gradually reduced.[1] But this conservative approach had a number of disadvantages. The retention of the *akidas* militated against the revival of the customary tribal authorities upon which Byatt hoped to found the stable development of future administration. At the same time, European administrative officers were left a remarkably free hand in the formulation of their own local policies and in changing those of their predecessors. The emergence of any constructive plan for the

---

[1] *Report on Tanganyika . . . to 1920*, Cmd. 1428 (1921), p. 37. For the German use of *akidas*, see Chapter III above.

uniform administration of the large number of districts into
which the territory was divided was consequently threatened
with indefinite delay.

The same lack of stimulus from the centre was noticeable
in the terms of the Native Authority Ordinances of 1921[1] and
1923.[2] These enactments sought to revive indigenous authorities
by requiring any chief, headman, or council of elders recognized
by the Governor to maintain order and prevent crime and by
empowering them to issue orders covering a wide field of
offences and regulating a number of public services. But the
same powers were simultaneously given to the *akidas*, while the
initiative in developing the powers into a useful instrument of
local government was left largely to the discretion of local
administrative officers. Gradually, however, it became clear
that the need for a co-ordinated administrative policy was
growing rapidly more pressing. In 1924, when Byatt had left
the country, a conference of senior officers was convened to
review the situation. Their basic recommendation was that
Tanganyika should adopt the system of administration then
enjoying considerable popularity under the title of 'Indirect
Rule'. To ensure the uniform application of this scheme it was
also proposed that the twenty-two districts should be grouped
into provinces under senior officials and that the office of
Secretary for Native Affairs should be created.[3]

Land policy and land use

Byatt's *laissez-faire* attitude towards native administration
disturbed only a few of the more senior among his administrative officers. His apparent inaction over economic matters and
more particularly over land issues produced a lively flow of
criticism from the handful of unofficial Europeans in the territory. One of their chief complaints was levelled against the
delay in disposing of the land formerly owned or leased by
German settlers. In 1919 a number of firms were anxious to
buy the extensive sisal plantations abandoned by the Germans
and to take advantage of the favourable prices then being
offered for the crop. The delay in meeting these demands was

---

[1] Tanganyika Territory, *Ordinances*, vol. ii. *1921* (London, 1923), pp. 92 sqq.
[2] Ibid. vol. iv, *1923* (Dar es Salaam, 1924), pp. 204 sqq.
[3] C. C. F. Dundas, *African Crossroads* (London, 1955), pp. 132–3.

due to no fault on the part of Byatt himself, but to the fact that there could be no distribution of enemy property until the proclamation of the Tanganyika Order in Council. The Governor was, however, firmly opposed to agricultural experiments by Europeans who possessed inadequate capital and experience, so that in spite of the pressure exerted by the *Dar es Salaam Times* he resisted the proposal to introduce a soldier settlement scheme similar to the one in Kenya.[1]

Neither the justice of Byatt's case nor the failure of the Kenya scheme as a result of the economic depression of the early 1920's won for the Governor the sympathy of his critics. These latter, moreover, considered themselves to be still further justified in their opposition by the gap of over two years which intervened between the publication of the order in council and the promulgation of a Land Ordinance on 26 January 1923. In the meantime, they argued, the availability of land on yearly leases made it impossible to do more than grow annual crops. Pursuing their criticisms further, they seized upon every morsel of evidence which might be said to support their growing conviction that the Governor cared nothing for the interests of the European unofficial. The *Dar es Salaam Times*, for example, ever vocal in its condemnation of Byatt's policy, published a leader on 1 April 1922 criticizing the Administration's last-minute decision to reserve for African use a parcel of former German land which had been advertised as being for sale.

This display of concern for the native population is merely ostentatious [the leader ran] for the condition of the average native today is infinitely worse than it has ever been. What a native wants is labour, with its attendant results of money in his pockets, food in his stomach, clothes on his back and the other comforts that the possession of money brings. These he has not had for the past few years, and cannot get them because there is so little European production going on that he cannot find labour.[2]

The ill-founded nature of this attack was clearly demonstrated by the annual report of the Tanganyika Administration for the year 1922, which pointed out that only 30,000 acres out of more than a million and a quarter which had been alienated by the Germans were restored to Africans. Furthermore,

[1] *Dar es Salaam Times*, 10 Dec. 1919 and 10 July 1920.
[2] Ibid., 1 Apr. 1922.

although the Administration possessed the right of pre-emption when ex-enemy property was sold, the Tanganyika authorities themselves acquired only 92 out of a total of 1,000 plots auctioned by the Custodian of Enemy Property.[1]

Once again European unofficial opinion was incensed when the *East African Standard* reported in June 1922 that while on leave in England Sir Horace Byatt had informed the East African section of the London Chamber of Commerce that the future of Tanganyika lay in developing African cultivation. It is true that there was no absolute objection among Tanganyika's Europeans to the principle of encouraging Africans to grow the sort of economic crops which were particularly suited to peasant small-holdings, such as ground-nuts and cotton, but they were convinced that such measures could never produce the wealth which, as the Germans had demonstrated, could be obtained from plantation-grown sisal and coffee. Even to accept the principle that Africans should grow economic crops was not without its dangers, they argued, since the tribes most likely to produce the best results from peasant cultivation were the ones most suited to provide the labour force essential to successful plantation development.

Again the critics did Byatt less than justice. It was a desire to avoid unprofitable experiments rather than any fundamental opposition to European settlement which underlay his policy. For, urgent though the need to re-establish Tanganyika's economy may have been, it was even more important that so fundamental an issue as the control and disposal of the land should be based on sound principles and the best available information. Experience in the Gold Coast had shown that the recommendations contained in the mandate were wholly justified. The period which elapsed before the publication of the Tanganyika Land Ordinance in 1923 was therefore spent in a careful investigation of German records. And when the ordinance did appear it was seen to follow in a number of respects the pattern already adopted in Northern Nigeria, which in its turn had been largely influenced by the difficulties experienced in other dependencies.

The drafting of the Land Ordinance left something to be desired, in that many of its terms appeared to be mutually

[1] *Annual Report for the Year 1922* (1923), p. 26.

contradictory. All land, whether occupied or not, was declared to be public land; yet this did not invalidate existing titles and interests which had been lawfully obtained, and it was specifically stated that existing customary rights should be protected. The public land was then placed under the control of the Governor to be used for the common benefit of the indigenous population of the territory, having regard to native laws and customs. Africans as well as others might obtain rights of occupancy and the terms of the ordinance appeared to require them to do so. In practice, however, this rule was not insisted upon, and while it was not clear from the ordinance whether an African obtaining a right of occupancy ceased automatically to hold his land according to native custom, in fact his customary tenure was not affected. It was also laid down that no title was valid without the Governor's approval, but in practice this was intended to apply only to land acquired by non-Africans. More specific was the statement that no new grants would be made in freehold and that land could only be leased for a maximum period of ninety-nine years. Moreover, so far as non-Africans were concerned, a right of occupancy to more than 5,000 acres could only be obtained henceforward with the approval of the Colonial Secretary.[1]

Although the terminology of the ordinance was confused, it worked satisfactorily, for the Government was clear as to its intentions even if it found difficulty in setting them down in legal form. But a law which was so patently designed to protect African interests in fulfilment of the mandate could not hope to do more than fortify Byatt's European critics in their conviction that they were justified in describing him as a 'negrophilist'.

Still further criticism was aroused by the Governor's attitude towards the cultivation of *arabica* coffee by the Chagga on the slopes of Mount Kilimanjaro, an experiment which was initiated by an administrative officer, Charles (later Sir Charles) Dundas. Dundas had been selected as a member of the British political staff during the East African campaign because of the intimate knowledge of German which he had acquired during seventeen years spent in Hamburg as the son of a British consular official. In 1916 he had noted with surprise a reference in a German

[1] C. K. Meek, *Land Law and Custom in the Colonies* (London, 1946), pp. 101–3.

report to coffee-growing by the Chagga. In Kenya at that time Africans were debarred from growing coffee. Posted to the Kilimanjaro region after the war, Dundas was impressed by the need to introduce an economic crop among the Chagga in addition to the purely subsistence cultivation which was then being pursued. Coffee appeared to be an ideal choice, partly because of the suitability of the soil and climate and partly because it could be grown in the shade of the banana trees which provided the staple diet of the tribe and would not, therefore, adversely affect the production of food. Dundas then sought out the former growers, only to find that they had almost entirely abandoned their coffee bushes because they could find no market for their crop. With his encouragement they renewed their activities, and Dundas next applied himself to the task of extending the experiment so as to produce a crop of saleable size. He met with willing support from the Chagga themselves, and in 1924 the latter formed a union of coffee-growers with the title of the Kilimanjaro Native Planters' Association.[1]

The success of this scheme aroused the opposition of European coffee planters, who professed to see a danger that coffee disease might be spread as a result of the laziness and carelessness of the African growers; they were, too, more than a little anxious about the future of their labour supply. European settlers in Kenya gave vocal aid to their neighbours over the border and the issue was raised in the House of Commons. Even Byatt himself had stated as late as November 1923 that in his view coffee, with the exception of the *robusta* variety, was essentially a European-grown crop;[2] but he supported Dundas loyally when he saw the success which the latter had achieved.

Exasperated by the Governor's policy, some of the European planters began briefly to flirt with the idea of transferring the Kilimanjaro region to Kenya, but Byatt's departure from Tanganyika in April 1924 enabled them to retreat from a position which the more sober spirits among them had already begun to question.

Labour problems

In the event planters' fears of coffee disease on Kilimanjaro

---

[1] Dundas, op. cit., pp. 123–5.　　[2] *Dar es Salaam Times*, 17 Nov. 1923.

were never justified, but their more fundamental concern over the supply of labour was not without foundation. This was an issue which did not affect the Chagga alone. In the years immediately following the war, labourers had been recruited for government work in Kenya from parts of Tanganyika where there were insufficient opportunities of obtaining local employment. The Dar es Salaam Chamber of Commerce and other bodies criticized the Administration for allowing this arrangement to continue. In September 1920 the Acting Secretary to the Administration replied that the policy could only be a passing phenomenon, which must soon disappear when full economic activity was resumed in Tanganyika. In the meantime some control would be exercised by limiting the period of employment to six months in the first instance and by reserving the right to refuse any extension. This did not satisfy the Chamber of Commerce, which asked for the scheme to be withdrawn, not without some suggestion that the current lack of opportunities for employment in Tanganyika was due to the inertia of the Administration.[1] Nevertheless, labourers still continued to cross the border and a number were recruited from the Mwanza region to work on the extension of the railway in Kenya.[2]

With the revival of Tanganyika's economic life this situation could not continue, and in 1924 the Administration pointed out in its report to the Permanent Mandates Commission that the impression that Tanganyika had an ample reservoir of labour to be tapped at will could no longer be considered valid. It was not so much the demands of external employers as the Government's own development programme, coupled with the growing demands of the Tanganyika planters, which by 1924 had created a serious labour problem. Most of the plantation employment was of a seasonal character, which meant that there was an uneven demand at different times of the year. Although this created problems for the employers who were competing for the labour supply, it suited the labourers themselves, since it enabled them to maintain a foothold in the villages in which their lives were still rooted. The visits to the plantations simply

[1] Ibid., 11 Sept. 1920.
[2] Department of Overseas Trade, *Report on the Trade and Commerce of East Africa revised to September, 1922* (London, 1923), p. 25.

U

took on the character of an annual adventure which served the added purpose of providing money to meet the demands of taxation and to purchase goods which were now once more becoming available.

In some areas, like Tabora, the attractions offered by the opportunity to grow economic crops tended to discourage potential labourers from leaving home. In other regions, however, there seems to have been no lack of volunteers to go in search of temporary employment, a situation which was encouraged by the introduction of a hut and poll-tax on 1 April 1923.

In spite of criticisms the Administration was constantly alert to ensure satisfactory conditions of labour. It was not just that in June 1922 the requirements of the mandate were fulfilled by the abolition of slavery.[1] Although no compensation was given, this result was achieved with little opposition, perhaps because the people affected were not the most vocal element in the community. But on 1 January 1922 the Administration had already announced fixed rates of pay for its own unskilled employees, rates which were based upon the results of inquiries carried out by a commission appointed for the purpose. This was followed shortly afterwards by the appointment of a permanent Labour Board to deal with questions of rates of pay for government labourers throughout the territory, since it was seen that there might be a frequent need to revise the rates fixed earlier in the year.[2] In 1923 a Masters and Servants Ordinance was promulgated which, although vague in many of its requirements, was a useful advance towards the regulation of relations between employers and labourers. In the following year a still more important step was taken with the appointment as Special Labour Commissioner of Major C. St. J. Orde Brown, whose task it was to investigate and report upon labour problems generally. This concern for the welfare of the labouring community was one of the most marked features of Tanganyika's administration throughout the 1920's. The increasing demand for labourers undoubtedly provided a stimulus to the policy, but there is much to suggest that the Administration was

[1] Tanganyika Territory, *Ordinances*, vol. iii. *1922* (Dar es Salaam, no date), p. 99.
[2] *Annual Report for the Year 1924*, Col. no. 11 (1925), p. 22.

still more impressed by the need to fulfil its mandatory responsibilities.

Revenue and expenditure

The growing demand for labour and the expanding government development programme were indications of an economic
revival which could not be solely accounted for by grants from
the Imperial Treasury amounting between 1920 and 1922 to
£408,109, nor yet by loans from the same source during the
next four years totalling £3,085,891. These sums undoubtedly
gave an impetus to development, but at the same time Tanganyika's revenue from its own sources rose from rather more
than half a million pounds in 1919–20 to over a million pounds
in 1923–4, and by 1926 the revenue was sufficient to cover the
country's expenditure. The creation of a customs department
on 1 June 1922[1] and the introduction on 1 January 1923 of
a regular system of tariffs,[2] together with the hut and poll-
taxes, were mainly responsible for this promising situation. The
hut tax was payable on every hut, while the poll-tax was paid
by all males of sixteen and over who were not liable to the hut
tax.[3] Both taxes were generally fixed at 10 sh., but might be
varied at the discretion of the Governor, or even commuted by
a tribe into a lump sum payable annually in money, labour, or
kind. In 1924 the taxes ranged from 2 sh. in the Kigoma
District to 9 sh. in the prosperous Bukoba region. In 1924, too,
nearly all domestic exports were, for the first time, significantly
greater than they had been in 1913, the last complete year of
German administration. Sisal had made a good recovery, but
rubber, except in the inflated conditions of the second world
war, never again regained its importance because of the vast
increase in production by Malaya. The coffee crop grown by
Africans in the Bukoba region amounted to 3,535 tons in 1924,
giving to the growers an income of £100,000. Four-fifths of the
crop was *robusta*, but in the Kilimanjaro area, where Africans
grew only *arabica* coffee, there were already 700,000 bushes of
which 140,000 were in bearing.

Regulations published in 1921 to control mining rights produced a ready response from prospectors. Meanwhile, the mica

---

[1] *Ordinances*, vol. iii. *1922*, pp. 17 sqq.　　　　[2] Ibid., pp. 197 sqq.
[3] Ibid., p. 99.

mines in the Uluguru mountains, which had been the chief mineral-producing area in German times, were operated by the Civil Administration until March 1920, when they were closed, after which gold became the new attraction to prospectors. In the Mwanza and Musoma districts to the south and east of Lake Victoria, reefs were discovered in 1922, and in the same year there were finds of alluvial gold along the Lupa river near Lake Rukwa in the far south-west. The Lupa river field attracted a varied collection of people because alluvial mining required little in the way of capital or equipment, and the output of gold showed promise of good profits in the future. Between 1923 and 1924 the amount produced in the Lupa goldfield rose from 1,639 oz. to 6,805 oz.[1]

During this period the improvement of communications went along with economic development in general. Byatt had particularly recognized that if the potentialities of Tanganyika's wealthiest zone, the Lake Victoria region, were to be tapped, there was need for a rail link with the Central Railway to Tabora. It was left to his successor to put the plan into effect, but it was due to Byatt's efforts that in August 1924 the Colonial Secretary sanctioned the extension of the line northwards from Tabora.

Commentary on Byatt

These developments in no way inhibited the steady flow of criticism which was levelled against an Administration described as spineless and all too prone to attribute all its difficulties to the terms of the mandate. Yet, although Byatt lacked the ability to capture public imagination, it was perhaps his failure to consult public opinion, more than a genuine failure to revive Tanganyika's economy, that made him the constant butt of hostile critics. Legislation was promulgated without any previous attempt to sound unofficial reactions as to its possible effects. Particularly where such legislation affected trade and commerce, European and Asian traders alike were resentful. It was, therefore, with overt relief that the *Dar es Salaam Times*, reflecting the views of both European planters and commercial men, announced the departure of Byatt on 9 April 1924. It

[1] J. P. Moffett (ed.), *Handbook of Tanganyika*, revised edn. (Dar es Salaam, 1958), p. 96.

is, too, some measure of the extent to which Byatt had been subjected to adverse comment from European unofficials that the Earl of Buxton saw fit to mention the criticisms when introducing Byatt as the speaker at a luncheon meeting of the African Society on 9 July 1924.[1]

Yet few of these criticisms found their way to Britain. With the exception of an ordinance to impose a tax on profits, which gave rise to a number of exchanges in the House of Commons,[2] the questions asked about Tanganyika were unimportant in character and few in number. Sir Robert Hamilton drew attention to the temporary movement in favour of the transfer of part of northern Tanganyika to Kenya and was assured by the Colonial Secretary that the British Government had no intention of supporting any such proposal.[3] Colonel J. C. Wedgewood, a fairly regular inquirer about the affairs of Tanganyika, went so far as to applaud the terms of the Land Ordinance of 1923,[4] while Sir Sidney Henn posed a question with important implications for the future when he asked if there was any limit to the duration of the mandate. He was told that there was not.[5] For the rest, inquiries ranged over relatively trivial topics and displayed no profound knowledge of Tanganyika on the part of the members of parliament.

Thus Byatt's achievement in establishing Tanganyika upon a firm footing after the troubled war period was underestimated in the territory itself because he adopted no spectacular methods and because he failed to carry European unofficial opinion with him. Of African opinion nothing is recorded. In England he had neither critics nor defenders, for few would have claimed to understand the true nature of Tanganyika's problem.

That the criticisms of Byatt in Tanganyika reflected the urgent enthusiasms of a pioneer community, rather than the constructive programme of a business-like organization, was made clear by the hearty and hasty welcome accorded to his successor, John Scott, who became Acting Governor on Byatt's departure. For Scott was a recent arrival in Tanganyika who knew relatively little of the country and who, as Acting Gover-

---

[1] *Journal of the African Society*, xxiv (1924–5), 51.
[2] *Hansard*, 5th ser., H.C. 163. 10–12, 718, 992, 1183, Apr. 1923.
[3] Ibid. 175. 931–2, 30 June 1924.   [4] Ibid. 167. 539, 25 July 1923.
[5] Ibid. 173. 1395, 14 May 1924.

nor, could not be expected to initiate any striking changes in policy. Consequently the fickle nature of his welcome was soon demonstrated, and even during the brief months in which he held office there was noticeable a growing undercurrent of dissatisfaction with him.

Details of total revenue and expenditure, 1917–26

	1917–18	1918–19	1919–20	1920–1	1921–2	1922–3
	£	£	£	£	£	£
Expenditure	167,698	383,097	790,026	1,389,354	1,807,890	1,811,872
Revenue						
Total	337,325	461,842	669,097	1,262,844*	1,070,301†	1,228,586
Customs	116,976	118,949	140,709	188,200	209,867	267,940
Licences and taxes	196,369	290,373	308,887	442,268	418,872	475,077

	1923–4	1924–5	1925–6
	£	£	£
Expenditure	1,901,158	1,747,578	2,235,624
Revenue			
Total	1,315,188	1,558,982	1,975,400
Customs	337,157	426,725	501,065
House, hut, and poll-tax	426,333	561,625	674,973

* Includes grant-in-aid by Imperial Treasury of £316,000.
† Includes grant-in-aid of £92,109.

Main imports, 1920–5

	1920	1921	1922	1923	1924	1925
Imports	£	£	£	£	£	£
Total	1,734,731	1,426,125	1,386,212	1,799,038	2,062,646	2,863,917
Cotton piece-goods	811,552	587,908	590,466	722,325	811,679	954,689
Foodstuffs	208,157	129,157	141,312	132,179	175,467	282,380
Iron and steel manufactures	14,553	34,218	24,769	192,278	108,318	294,271
Machinery	13,628	37,930	17,811	82,445	94,514	115,967

Throughout this period a very large proportion of imports were from the United Kingdom.

Main exports, 1920–4

	1920	1921	1922	1923	1924
Exports	£	£	£	£	£
Total	2,210,125	1,426,125	1,441,584	1,733,229	2,695,284
Sisal	571,887	238,171	289,388	367,228	644,835
Cotton	164,565	118,620	140,750	177,710	373,753
Coffee	138,867	138,397	203,784	204,987	352,529
Ground-nuts	78,522	141,475	190,553	264,129	359,918
Gold	—	—	—	5,937	30,349

The United Kingdom was the most important market for Tanganyika's produce.

The East Africa Commission

It was during Scott's interregnum that the arrival in Tanganyika of the East Africa Commission under the chairmanship
of W. Ormsby-Gore brought to its first climax the issue of
closer union between the East and Central African territories.[1]
During his governorship Byatt had not regarded the question
of closer union as being a matter of prime importance, and in
1924 unofficial opinion on the subject was only just beginning
to crystallize. Nevertheless, the question of a closer relationship
between the East African territories had exercised the minds
of the non-African population in Tanganyika ever since the
end of the war. It was Ormsby-Gore himself who, in November
1921, had drawn the attention of the Colonial Secretary to a
resolution passed at a mass meeting of European unofficials
in Dar es Salaam on 1 September protesting against the principle of assimilating the financial, fiscal, and economic system
of the territory to that of Kenya. When Ormsby-Gore went
further and asked for an assurance that all fiscal and administrative connexion between two such disparate territories
should be severed, the Colonial Secretary pointed out that no
administrative connexion in fact existed, and, although there
were obvious advantages in retaining the same currency and
the same rates of customs duties in the neighbouring territories,
even this arrangement was subjected to revision on the recommendation of the territories concerned.[2] Subsequently,
however, the advantages of creating a larger economic unit in
East Africa were widely canvassed in Britain in the early
1920's and continued to cause concern among the non-African
communities in Tanganyika. The report of Colonel F. D.
Hammond, Special Commissioner for Railways in East Africa,
which was published towards the end of 1921, provoked
a particularly lively reaction.[3] One of his proposals was that
the Voi-Kahe railway should be re-aligned so as to make
Kilindini the port for the Kilimanjaro region, and, not surprisingly, this was deemed to amount to the virtual transfer

[1] The whole subject of closer union, as it affected all the East African territories,
will be discussed in the third volume of this *History*.

[2] *Hansard*, 5th Ser., H.C. 147. 1965, 3 Nov. 1921.

[3] F. D. Hammond, *Report on the Railway Systems of Kenya, Uganda and Tanganyika*.
pt. i (London, 1921), appendix i, pp. 163-71.

to Kenya of the wealth of one of Tanganyika's most valuable
regions.[1]

Disappointment with Byatt's policy was largely responsible
for the first change in the attitude of some of the Europeans
in Tanganyika. In December 1923 an editorial in the *Dar es
Salaam Times* commented favourably upon the growing discussion about the possibility of a federation of East African
territories, and urged the people of Tanganyika to get rid of
their 'parish pump' outlook on political matters.[2] It stressed the
unanimity of interests in the three territories and the similarity
of their problems, and pointed out that the inter-territorial
boundaries were simply imaginary lines which created unnatural divisions in what might well be a single administrative
unit. The President of the Dar es Salaam Chamber of Commerce was also in favour of increasing reciprocity between the
East African territories, but at the annual general meeting of
the chamber, held early in 1924, he gave warning that not only
he but several of his associates were nervous of Kenya's coming
to dominate the whole East African region. The *Dar es Salaam
Times*, still sanguine, dismissed the chamber's fears and even
argued that the extension of the railway from Tabora to Mwanza
might prove more acceptable to Kenya after federation, when
there would no longer be a feeling of competition. It went on to
draw attention to the recent request of the Europeans in Arusha
and Moshi for the transfer of their two districts to Kenya
Colony.

This, however, was the high-water mark of European support
for federation with Kenya during the earlier 1920's. The absence
of direct communications between Kilimanjaro and Dar es
Salaam had undoubtedly influenced opinion among the
planters of Arusha and Moshi, who had been already incensed
by the Government's attitude towards the cultivation of coffee
by the Chagga. But on Byatt's departure more reasonable
councils triumphed. When the annual general meeting of the
Kilimanjaro Planters' Association was held in August 1924,
the fevered temper which had led some members to respond
to the blandishments of Lord Delamere a few months earlier
had been replaced by a more sober, even suspicious, attitude
towards Delamere's proposals for the annexation of Kilimanjaro

---

[1] *Dar es Salaam Times*, 14 Jan. 1922.   [2] Ibid., 15 Dec. 1923.

to Kenya. Delamere, it was pointed out, was opposed to the construction of the Tabora–Mwanza railway, and it was alleged that he wished to annex to Kenya the whole of northern Tanganyika from the coast at Sadaani to the Belgian frontier, thereby depriving Tanganyika of the whole of its labour supply at a time when labour was vital for the extension of sisal and cotton production. The fear of Delamere's influence now became the most powerful factor affecting European unofficial opinion in Tanganyika, and the assurance given by the Colonial Secretary, J. H. Thomas, early in July, that the Government had no intention of changing Tanganyika's boundaries, did not wholly restore confidence, for Delamere was known to be a man of determination and resource. By this time, too, even the *Dar es Salaam Times* had changed its tune. In June 1924 it attacked the campaign in Kenya for the transfer of the Kilimanjaro area, pointedly arguing that Kenya's claim that such an arrangement was no more than a fair recompense for the arbitrary cession of Jubaland to Italy would have carried more weight if Kenya had previously uttered any objection to the loss of Jubaland.[1]

The hostility towards closer union which had thus sprung up among European unofficials meant that the Ormsby-Gore Commission encountered a fair degree of unanimity in Tanganyika opinion. For the Indian community was too disturbed by the conflict between European settlers and Indians in Kenya to welcome any arrangement which held out the possibility of subjecting the affairs of Tanganyika to control by her neighbour. Race relations in Tanganyika were reasonably friendly, not least because Europeans and Indians alike were unanimous in criticizing the Administration. More fundamental was the fact that so far there had developed no rivalry between the two races over the occupation of land. Thus, while some Europeans criticized the closing of Indian-owned shops in Dar es Salaam in 1922 as a protest against the arrest of Gandhi, they did so primarily because they regarded the action as an unwarranted introduction of racial disputes into a country where none existed.[2] Eighteen months later, when the Indians again closed their shops as a gesture against the terms of a recent Trades Licensing Ordinance, about which the Governor had failed to

[1] Ibid., 14 June 1924. [2] Ibid., 18 and 25 Mar. 1922.

consult unofficial opinion, they had the whole-hearted support of the European commercial community.[1]

There appears to be little evidence of African opinion either for or against closer union. It is unlikely that the issue penetrated to the villages, where Byatt's policy of non-interference had left large sections of the native population free to pursue their local problems without concerning themselves with issues of a wider importance. The Ormsby-Gore Commission did, however, report that it had encountered African opposition to the idea of transferring the Kilimanjaro region to Kenya in the area concerned.[2] The Administration, meanwhile, deprived of its natural head by the departure of the Governor, was in no position to give a strong lead to the commission. The commission's recommendation that there should be conferences of governors at reasonable intervals seemed, therefore, at the time, to satisfy most groups in Tanganyika.

Other proposals and comments made by the commission were also in line with unofficial opinion so far as it was known. Their insistence upon the need to extend the system of road and rail communications and, in particular, to build a line from Tabora to Mwanza, won wholehearted approval. This scheme, together with a further proposal that a line should be constructed from the Central Railway at Ngerengere, some 70 miles west of Dar es Salaam, in a south-westerly direction along the rich alluvial Kilombero Valley to Manda, on the north-eastern shore of Lake Nyasa, was intended both to open up the economic resources of the territory and to facilitate administration. The commission also stressed the importance of developing African administration, and the recommendation that there should be a Secretary for Native Affairs was one which, as has been seen, had already been accepted by the senior administrators of the country. Educational problems, too, elicited comments from the commission as a result of which a new educational programme was formulated.

The creation of a Legislative Council

The report of the Ormsby-Gore Commission provided an en-

---

[1] *Dar es Salaam Times*, 17 Nov. 1923.

[2] *Report of the East Africa Commission, 1924* (Ormsby-Gore Commission) Cmd. 2387 (1925), p. 123.

couraging starting-point for the activities of the new Governor, Sir Donald Cameron, who took up office in April 1925. Cameron, formerly Chief Secretary to the Government of Nigeria, was appointed Governor and Commander-in-Chief of Tanganyika by the short-lived Labour Government of 1924. A West Indian of Irish parentage, he was largely self-educated; tall and thin, with a severe set of countenance, his appearance suggested a character more likely to arouse criticism than to win friends. Though bold in the conception of ideas and energetic in putting them into effect, he was a shy man, repelled rather than excited by the prospect of physical violence. He was, too, over-anxious to justify himself. Nevertheless, if the European unofficial community were looking for action, Cameron was the man to give it to them. Before leaving England he had taken the opportunity to discuss some of Tanganyika's problems with Ormsby-Gore, and in the course of his conversations had learnt that the commission was considering recommending the creation of an Advisory Council in Tanganyika. The relevance of this proposal was immediately confirmed upon Cameron's arrival in Dar es Salaam, where he recognized the urgent need for introducing some constitutional means of consulting public opinion if he was to satisfy the complaints of the unofficial Europeans. This suited Cameron completely, for he was anxious not only to maintain the support of the unofficial communities but also to associate them so closely with his policy that they would feel a sense of responsibility for the Government's decisions. To achieve this end he considered that nothing short of a Legislative Council with a high proportion of unofficial members would suffice. Nevertheless, there was a certain disingenuousness in his suggestion that the unofficial members of a legislature, in which there was a permanent official majority, could be held responsible for the decisions of the Council.

After their experience of Byatt's methods it came as a surprise to the Dar es Salaam Chamber of Commerce when Cameron announced at a dinner held on 16 January 1926 that Tanganyika would have a legislative assembly within a few months.[1] By this time the Ormsby-Gore Commission had already reported in favour of a Legislative rather than an Advisory

[1] *Tanganyika Times*, 18 Jan. 1926.

Council, on the ground that they had found a general demand for such a body among the unofficial European communities of Dar es Salaam and other parts of the territory. Yet, when faced with the immediate prospect of achieving what it had so long demanded, the Chamber of Commerce reacted in a guarded fashion, arguing that its members had not previously believed the country to be ready for such an advance.[1] As the prospect of political action opened before them, however, European officials began to look more favourably upon the proposal. Indeed, when nothing further appeared to have happened by June, there was some concern as to whether the Council was in fact to come into being.

Characteristically, Cameron had definite views regarding the composition of the Council. It would be a mistake, he thought, to overload it with officials, who, quite obviously, could not all attend the meetings of the Council. He suggested, therefore, that the number of official members should be 14, while the unofficial members should number not more than 10, leaving an official majority of 4. It was better, he believed, to avoid having a mere handful of 3 or 4 unofficial members if a larger number of suitable men could be found, since a small council could not hope to fulfil all that he expected of it.

The selection of the unofficial members was not an easy problem. Mr. L. S. Amery, the Colonial Secretary, believed with Cameron that they should be individuals nominated without regard to representation of particular races or interests and that they should be chosen for their capacity to assist the Governor in carrying out his responsibilities. In practice, however, Cameron was forced to admit that he would have to be influenced to some extent by the occupation of the individuals he chose, both in order to obtain men of experience and also to win the confidence of the unofficial community. To gain these two objectives he believed it would be advisable in the first place to nominate five Europeans, two of whom would be planters and two commercial men (one interested in shipping if possible, and one a banker). In addition he thought it would be politic to include two Indians on the unofficial side of the Council. He considered that it would be impossible to obtain an Arab with an adequate command of English to fulfil the

[1] *Tanganyika Times*, 20 Jan. 1926.

duties of a council member, nor for the time being could any African be nominated. The type of young African who might be sufficiently qualified in English would not, in Cameron's opinion, be likely to command support in the tribal areas. Until a new generation emerged it was his view that African interests would be adequately protected by the Governor himself, by the Chief Secretary and by the Secretary for Native Affairs.[1] In the meantime he foresaw a number of stages by which Africans might advance towards full participation in the country's political life. Within a few years it might be possible to form regional councils in which the chiefs could discuss subjects of common interest, and later there might emerge a Central Native Council to deal with issues affecting Africans all over the territory. This latter council might then become a General Native Council, sending delegates to sit with other delegates from a non-native council in order to perform the functions of a Legislative Council. In this way the gap between the African population and the more advanced non-African communities might be bridged in an amicable fashion.[2]

The Tanganyika Legislative Council held its first sitting under Cameron's presidency on 7 December 1926, with thirteen official and seven unofficial members. Because of its wider composition it was immediately more active and influential than the Legislative Council in Uganda.[3] This was as Cameron wished. His readiness to consult unofficial opinion did not, however, extend to unofficials of nationalities other than British. When a number of German settlers who had been allowed to return to the country asked for representation in the Council early in 1929, Cameron's reaction was adamant. He had no intention of nominating 'aliens' to a Legislative Council in a territory administered under a British mandate. His view was that a British mandate could not be shared and that both administration and legislature must be British.

In order to win British unofficial support still more completely, Cameron further decided not to lay down any one

---

[1] Tanganyika Legislative Council *Debates*, First Session, 1926–7 (Dar es Salaam, 1927), pp. 5–7, address by Sir Donald Cameron.

[2] Sir Donald Cameron, *My Tanganyika Service and some Nigeria* (London, 1939), p. 115.

[3] See Chapter IX, pp. 527–9, above.

place in which the Legislative Council should meet. This was a decision which was to serve a valuable purpose in December 1929 when, after a dispute with the European planters in the Kilimanjaro area, Cameron was able to demonstrate his confidence in them by arranging for the budget session of the Council to be held in Arusha. It is unlikely that the planters fully appreciated the administrative problems which this change involved. Any divergence, however small, from general orders had to be reported to the Colonial Secretary. Communications between Dar es Salaam and Arusha involved a journey by sea to Tanga as well as a railway journey from Tanga to Arusha. Accommodation for the members of the Council had to be improvised. But Cameron spared no pains to make the occasion a success, even to the extent of transporting by special trains the band of the 6th Battalion King's African Rifles and a guard of honour from the same unit. In the event, the unofficial British community was sufficiently appreciative of the importance of the Legislative Council for the European Association of Dar es Salaam to propose, in February 1930, that the unofficial representatives should have an established connexion with public bodies whose advice should be sought by the Governor when making his appointments.[1] Already, in 1929, Cameron had added two further Europeans and one additional Indian to the unofficial side of the Council, and it was characteristic of his enthusiasm for the Council's work that although he himself presided at its meetings he never hesitated to take an active part in the debates.

Local government

In spite of the success of the newly created Legislative Council, it was Cameron's native administration policy which won him the widest renown and at the same time brought down upon him the fiercest criticism. His creative spirit was troubled by the apparent lack of direction of the country's administration which persisted at the time of his first arrival in Tanganyika. His attention was drawn to this state of affairs within a month of his taking office. Formerly, before the introduction of European rule, it had been the practice for the African population

---

[1] *Tanganyika Standard*, 19 Feb. 1930.

to pay tribute to their chiefs in the form of produce and labour. In a subsistence economy this did not result in vast profits for the chiefs, but it did enable them to maintain a comfortable standard of life in return for the services they rendered as judges, leaders, counsellors, and rain-makers. In addition, the tribute paid in produce might be used as a reserve in times of famine. When it became possible under European administration to sell the produce, some of the chiefs became more demanding and all of them were anxious to ensure that their tribute was paid regularly. Before Cameron's arrival there had been an attempt to regularize the new situation by a decision to commute the tribute into the payment of a monetary tax which was to be added to the hut and poll-taxes. The chiefs affected would then be compensated by the central treasury. The new scheme had taken effect on 1 April 1925, only a few days before Cameron's arrival, and before the completion of an investigation into which tribes still paid tribute and service, and into the nature of those payments. In an attempt to improve upon this unsatisfactory arrangement until a more organized system of local government could be introduced throughout the country, Cameron decided that the sums roughly assessed as equivalent to the tribute should be paid into a sort of civil list for each tribe, from which the chiefs would be paid stipends.[1] For a man of his temperament, however, this could be no more than a short-term expedient. Writing some years later, Cameron said that it was this problem which induced him to decide upon the introduction of a system of Indirect Rule into Tanganyika. It is more than likely that this would in any case have been his decision. His experience in Northern Nigeria, together with his conviction that this experience was in full accord with the spirit of the mandate, led him to conclude that the only sure way to achieve sound administrative progress was to build upon existing institutions.

The creation of eleven provinces was the first step towards gaining more control over administrative policy, and the appointment of a Secretary for Native Affairs ensured that there would be one man directly responsible for the execution of Cameron's plan. First to hold that office was Charles

[1] Cameron, op. cit., p. 32.

Dundas, whose interest in native affairs had already been demonstrated by his work among the Chagga, and he was succeeded by Philip (later Sir Philip) Mitchell, who admitted to having an abounding zeal for ensuring that Cameron's policy should work.[1] The problem, as Cameron saw it, was to secure the future of the African population not only as producers but also as full members of the State. He did not believe this could be done by subjecting them to alien systems of law and foreign forms of organization. His policy, therefore, was to carry on administration through traditional native authorities and in accordance with customary law, the latter being adapted as proved necessary and acceptable to meet modern requirements. If he could build upon a system which the tribes had inherited, he hoped to avoid a breakdown in discipline and authority. At the same time he anticipated that the Government's economic and social policy would be more effectively promoted through the agency of traditional chiefs and councils whom the people already recognized and respected. By these means, too, he was hopeful of avoiding a clash of interests in the political field between the African population and the more advanced immigrant communities.

Under Cameron's enthusiastic direction the search for indigenous authorities was launched with tremendous energy and at times was carried to extreme lengths. District officers who were rarely qualified social anthropologists were called upon to investigate until they were satisfied that they had found the true authorities in each area. It was to their advantage that the destruction of the indigenous authorities by the German system of administration was probably not as complete as has been frequently claimed. Although the German Government had exercised its rule through *akidas*, many of whom were aliens in the regions where they held sway, life within the tribes and clans had, to a large extent, continued to depend upon the leadership and counsel of the traditional leaders. The removal of German administration during the war had also provided an opportunity for the revival of tribal authorities. In many areas, therefore, it was not difficult to discover who exercised control. It was not always equally easy to assess the nature of that control and its sanctions. In the coastal regions, however, the position

---

[1] Mitchell, *African Afterthoughts* (London, 1954), pp. 127–35.

was very different. There for generations the Arabs had
exercised their sway and had introduced Islamic law and their
own form of organization. The removal of the Arab *akidas* from
the coastal zone meant leaving a serious vacuum. So anxious
was Cameron to introduce his own system, however, that it was
only with difficulty that he was persuaded to retain even the
liwalis in the main towns.

The triple basis upon which Cameron's system was founded
consisted in making provision for the native authorities which
he recognized to exercise certain executive functions, in authorizing them to administer justice, and in providing them with
their own treasuries. The first of these foundations was laid
by the promulgation of the Native Authority Ordinance of
1926. This amounted to a complete revision of the 1923
Ordinance. Under the new ordinance the main functions of the
native authorities recognized by the Governor consisted in
maintaining order and collecting the hut and poll-taxes. Additional duties were added as the authorities became more competent. The responsibility for collecting taxes carried with it
a double advantage. In the first place it was much cheaper to
collect taxes in this way than to employ the officers of the
central Government to do the work. Secondly, it helped to
emphasize the power of the native authority over the people
for whom it was responsible. Out of the revenue collected a proportion was remitted from the Treasury to the native authorities,
and this sum was augmented by the native courts' fines and
fees. The amount thus made available was then spent on paying
the wages of native authority employees or on works and services of benefit to the local community.

The European unofficial community was not opposed to
Cameron's policy, although the speed and energy with which
he implemented the Native Authority Ordinance aroused a
certain amount of criticism.[1] The judicial aspect of Cameron's
plan aroused considerably more opposition, however. At the
outset the limited judicial powers granted to the native authorities were conferred under the Native Courts Ordinance of 1920.
By the provisions of that ordinance appeals from native courts
lay to a subordinate or supervisory court and thence to the
High Court. In practice effective control of the native courts

[1] Leg. Co. *Debates*, Third Session, 1928–9, pt. 2 (Dar es Salaam), p. 33.

stopped at the level of the supervisory courts. Although this position was unsatisfactory, Cameron considered that it would be disastrous if the High Court, with all its powers, were called upon to intervene too directly in the affairs of his infant native authorities. It was, too, the Governor's opinion that in the eyes of the peasantry the executive and judicial duties of the chiefs could not be separated. Thus he came to the conclusion that native courts should be treated as part of the Administration rather than as subject to the High Court.

Inevitably this conclusion was disputed by the legal branch of his Administration, although when he came to write his autobiography Cameron defended himself by stating that he had never intended that administrative officers should dispense justice with anything but the strictest regard for the evidence on record.[1] Whatever his design, a new Native Courts Ordinance was passed in 1929 which removed the native courts from the control of the High Court and placed them under the supervision of administrative officers, in spite of the criticisms of the Chief Justice. Under the terms of the ordinance a provincial commissioner might establish native courts having both civil and criminal jurisdiction over Africans within limits which he would define. The courts were to be constituted in accordance with local native law and custom, and certain more serious crimes were excluded from their jurisdiction. The punishments they were empowered to award were relatively small, and appeals lay first to native courts of appeal and thence in succession to a district officer, a provincial commissioner, and finally to the Governor himself. The courts of the *liwalis* at the coast, which dealt for the most part with questions of Muhammadan marriage and inheritance, retained their former relationship with the High Court.[2]

The strength of European and Asian unofficial opposition was reflected in the manner in which the new ordinance became law only by virtue of the official votes in the Legislative Council, with the unofficials in unanimous opposition.[3] Nor could it be argued that Cameron was confused in his objectives, since in introducing the second reading of the Bill the Attorney-

---

[1] Cameron, op. cit., p. 203.
[2] *Annual Report for the year 1929*, Col. no. 46 (1930), pp. 16–17.
[3] Leg. Co. *Debates*, Third Session, 1928–9, pt. 2.

General openly declared that the main innovation consisted in making the native courts an integral part of the native administration, instead of treating them as part of the legal system.[1] In the event the native courts handled with considerable efficiency a large volume of cases, many of them involving marriage claims, with which European officers could never have hoped to deal satisfactorily.

In the early days of Cameron's native administration policy it was clear that many of the native authorities were too small to be effective in any but the most restricted fields. But Cameron wisely sought to avoid any artificial enlargement of traditional units until the benefits of such amalgamation were recognized by the local population. The chiefs of Sukumaland and of Unyamwezi were among the first to appreciate the financial advantages, in the shape of more extensive public works, which might be derived from the formation of larger units. In 1927 and in 1928 respectively the Sukuma Federation and the Nyamwezi Federation were gazetted as superior authorities. That the chiefs concerned had not fully understood the implications of their action soon became evident, however. Although the Nyamwezi chiefs began by agreeing to accept the decisions of a majority in their council, the Sukuma chiefs were most unwilling to surrender their individual authority over their own peoples. Less than two years more had elapsed when the Nyamwezi chiefs followed their example. Early in 1930, therefore, it became necessary to deprive both councils of their executive authority, although the chiefs continued to meet as a court of appeal and to enjoy the benefits of a joint treasury. The Mwanza region provided a further example of the difficulty which even the more progressive tribes found in understanding the various implications of Cameron's system. It was the Governor's hope that where federal councils were established the chairman would in time come to be recognized as paramount chief, and thus act as a visible symbol of the union. In Mwanza Province this hope appeared to have been fulfilled when the office of paramount chief was recognized. On closer investigation, however, it had to be recognized that the people, although not unwilling to adopt the title, had no intention that the paramount chief should become anything more than the

[1] Ibid., p. 26.

president of the council. This was proof, not so much of the essentially democratic character of Bantu institutions, as claimed by the Administration in its report to the Permanent Mandates Commission in 1929,[1] as of the anxiety of the lesser chiefs to protect their own local authority from the overall control of one of their number.

One of the most striking examples of co-operation was achieved in 1929 between two sections of the Ngoni tribe in Songea. This was the result of no hurried decision, but was the product of four years of discussion among the chiefs and people concerned. The immediate social outcome of the new arrangement was the construction with local government finance of a boarding school combined with an agricultural instruction centre at the headquarters of the new association. On the administrative side an official was appointed, jointly by the two chiefs, whose main responsibility was to supervise the executive work of the Administration. This office had traditional importance among the Ngoni, and its revival illustrates the manner in which Cameron tried to encourage local variations within the overall pattern of his administrative scheme, provided they were in accordance with tribal custom.

Many of the practical problems arising from Cameron's native administration policy did not become visible until he had left the country. This did not protect him from considerable criticism in the latter part of his period of office. Just as at an early stage he had been condemned for the speed at which he had introduced reforms, so now it was said that his wholehearted methods tended to place undue emphasis upon the rapid development of the African population at the expense of the more profitable development of Tanganyika's resources through the agency of non-Africans. Not surprisingly, the bulk of this criticism came from the unofficial European community. The African population, meanwhile, did not immediately notice any great change in their lives. Nor were there among them men of sufficient education or experience of other administrative systems to criticize Cameron's policy, as it was later to be criticized, on the ground that it was alleged to encourage tribalism and thereby to retard the development of Tanganyika as a nation.

[1] *Annual Report for the Year 1929*, Col. no. 46 (1930), p. 17.

European settlement

The Europeans' suspicions of Cameron were far from being justified. Although he was not always confident in the presence of unofficials, the Governor was fully conscious of the contribution they could make to the development of the country. This attitude was clearly reflected in his approach to the question of European settlement in Tanganyika. Soon after assuming office he met in Dar es Salaam a number of Europeans wishing to take up leases of land in the neighbourhood of Iringa, in the Southern Highlands, where Lord Delamere had already bought a farm from the Custodian of Enemy Property and had promoted a company to encourage British settlement in Tanganyika. Cameron informed them that their applications would be forwarded to the district officer to see whether land was available. In the meantime he offered to discuss with the district officer the terms on which land could be offered.

While the Governor was on tour a new factor arose which made it a matter of urgency to take a decision on settlement by non-Africans. In June 1925 the Ex-Enemies Restriction Ordinance of 1922 lapsed. This ordinance had forbidden the entry of ex-enemies into the territory without the Governor's licence. It seemed unreasonable to Cameron that if such persons were permitted to return to Tanganyika they should not be allowed to hold land, and a new ordinance was accordingly enacted in November 1925 which made this legal. A number of Germans soon made their way to Tanganyika and, finding the land formerly owned by their fellow countrymen no longer available, applied for leases in the Iringa area. Most of these immigrants were anxious only to grow coffee, although the district was far more suited to mixed farming, and their persistence led many of them to disaster during the depression of the early 1930's.

To Cameron, who was deeply conscious of Britain's responsibility in Tanganyika, the encouragement of British settlement to counter the activities of the Germans appeared as a matter of the greatest importance. He was startled, therefore, to learn from the Colonial Office that he should discourage the earlier applications for land near Iringa, at least until adequate railway communications had been constructed. Cameron was as conscious as Byatt had been of the frustrations and disappointments to be encountered by farmers with inadequate capital. But he was convinced that where experience and capital were available and where settlers were prepared to agree to a revision of their rents at stated intervals so that the Government might benefit from any unearned increment which might accrue—for example, from the construction of better communications—no restriction should be placed upon British settlers. Two considerations weighed with him over this matter. First, he was not unaware of the stimulating influence which the example of competent European farmers might have upon the neighbouring African population. Second, he was reasonably sure that there was land available for settlement without encroaching upon the present or future requirements of the African population. A similar view was expressed at a conference of settlers from Tanganyika, Kenya, Nyasaland, and Northern Rhodesia which was convened by Lord Delamere at Tukuyu in southern Tanganyika in October 1925, and their opinion was endorsed by the Governors of the East African territories at their first conference early in 1926. Cameron, therefore, was not alone in supporting settlement, and before proceeding to the Governors' Conference he announced to the Dar es Salaam Chamber of Commerce that he would be willing to admit European settlers, a policy which he reaffirmed in his opening address to the Legislative Council in December 1926.

Although the opinion was widely held that there was no shortage of land in Tanganyika, there had been no scientific assessment of the position. Indeed, in 1923 a number of districts had been closed to further settlement because of the heavy pressure upon the land. In these circumstances Cameron welcomed the recommendation made by the Hilton Young Commission on Closer Union in 1929[1] that there should be a survey in East and Central Africa to show which areas were available and which were best suited for a systematic policy of European settlement. A survey team consisting of three senior officers—an administrator, an agriculturalist, and a surveyor— was sent first to the Southern Highlands Province, where 637 square miles of land in the Iringa area were deemed to be available for alienation. Moving then to the Eastern Province,

[1] For the circumstances leading up to the appointment of this commission, see Chapter VI, pp. 304 sqq., above, and pp. 588 sqq., below.

the surveyors recommended that 7,705 out of a total of 12,776 square miles in the Morogoro and Kilosa districts could be made available for settlement.[1] The survey continued until 1932 and provided a scientific basis upon which the Government could formulate its policy. Meanwhile, in 1930, a number of other areas in various parts of the country were closed to non-Africans for agricultural purposes unless they could prove that they had sufficient capital to start work on a sound basis and particularly to provide adequate water-supplies.[2]

In order to take advantage of the land development survey, Cameron appointed in December 1929 a committee consisting of European and Indian unofficial members of the Legislative Council, together with Lord Delamere, to investigate the various aspects of European settlement in Tanganyika. Not surprisingly, in view of its composition, the committee submitted a report early in May 1930 recommending that a settlement scheme for non-Africans was essential to the development of the territory. It was further proposed that a Land Settlement Board should be set up, with an agent in London, and the need for an agricultural development fund to provide assistance for present and future immigrant settlers was also stressed. This latter idea was not an original one, since the Colonial Development Fund Committee in England had suggested in 1929 that the Tanganyika Government should establish a fund of this sort, and discussions were taking place in Kenya which were to result in the creation of a Land and Agricultural Bank in that colony.

In spite of Cameron's efforts and of the favourable attitude of the European unofficial community in Tanganyika, the question of European settlement made little further progress. The world economic depression which began to be felt in Tanganyika late in 1930, together with subsequent fears that the territory might be transferred to Germany, acted as severe deterrents to settlement. Moreover, more favourable opportunities appeared to be offered in Kenya, where the depression was looked upon as providing an added justification for taking

[1] Tanganyika Territory, *Land Development Survey*, Fifth Report, *1931, Eastern Province* (Dar es Salaam, 1932).
[2] C. Leubuscher, *Tanganyika Territory: a study of economic policy under mandate* (London, 1944), p. 32.

steps to assist the settler community, and where, as a result, a Land Bank was established in July 1931.

Cameron's views on the part to be played by Europeans in Tanganyika did not prevent him from coming into conflict with one group of settlers at an early stage in his governorship, and it was only towards the end of his career in Tanganyika that more friendly relations were established. The European coffee planters in the Moshi area took the opportunity of Cameron's arrival in East Africa to press for the prohibition of coffee cultivation by Africans in the Kilimanjaro region. Once again they argued, as they had argued with Byatt, that inefficient methods of cultivation were liable to result in coffee disease which might spread to the European crops. Cameron was reluctant to restrict the activities of the Chagga, but he agreed to introduce measures to deal with the possibility of coffee disease appearing in the African-grown crop. The Chagga had become increasingly enthusiastic over coffee cultivation and in 1925 they asked Cameron for permission to export their own coffee through the Kilimanjaro Native Planters' Association, since the Indian merchants through whom they had previously marketed their crop had combined to force down the prices to an unreasonably low level. Cameron readily agreed to this proposal, for he saw in the Association a potentially sound instrument through which to disseminate information to control the spread of coffee disease. Moreover, through the working of the Association, measures of control did in fact prove entirely satisfactory. But the Moshi planters continued to urge the Government to adopt Kenya's policy of preventing Africans from growing *arabica* coffee.

These differences of opinion between the European planters and the Government reached a climax towards the end of 1928, when the planters and the Chagga growers simultaneously came to the conclusion that the Government was working against them. This misconception arose out of an incident which had no bearing whatsoever upon the question of who should or who should not grow coffee. On 15 October 1928 news was received in the Secretariat in Dar es Salaam that a difference of opinion had arisen between Captain F. C. Hallier, the district officer in Moshi, and the Acting Provincial Commissioner over the conduct of the affairs of the township authority in Moshi. It was decided on 29 October that Hallier should be transferred away from the district. Here the issue would have ended if Hallier had not in the meantime caused unrest among the Chagga by suggesting that individual African land-holdings should be limited in size and that the Kilimanjaro Native Planters' Association should be discontinued. The first proposal had actually originated as a result of the fears expressed by Chagga chiefs that the practice of selling land was threatening to result in the accumulation of large acreages in the hands of a few individuals and in consequent restrictions upon the area available for use by the rising generation. While the issue was under discussion Hallier's own opinions as to how it should be dealt with gave rise to the rumour that the Government intended to reduce existing land-holdings. This groundless fear particularly affected the coffee-growers, who were still further disturbed by Hallier's proposal that their Association and its funds should be entirely absorbed into the structure of the native administration. This was Hallier's own view and it did not have the support of the Government, although the Governor himself was willing to see an attempt made to bring the coffee-growing industry into a clearer relationship with the native administration, which had come into being since the Native Planters' Association was founded.

Faced with two apparently serious threats to the industry which they had built up with so much labour and enthusiasm, the Association's members drafted a petition to the Government which they believed responsible for the change of policy. A number of meetings were held and there was a certain amount of excitement bordering upon disorder. When news of these events reached the Governor in November, he wrote at once in the clearest terms, giving an assurance that the Association would continue in existence and that its duties would in no circumstances be transferred to the native administration. He added that he was sending the Secretary for Native Affairs, Dundas, to Moshi to sort out the trouble. Dundas was a man in whom the Chagga placed unlimited trust, and in the four days after his arrival all dissension came to an end.

In the meantime the European planters in the Moshi area had watched events with deep concern. On 15 November 1928 two of them sent a telegram to the Governor alleging that the

Kilimanjaro Native Planters' Association was agitating against all Europeans, against the Government, and against the Chagga Native Authority. Four days later a meeting of European planters was held in Moshi at which similar allegations were made, which later appeared in the press. The transfer of Hallier, although for entirely unrelated reasons, coupled with the arrival of Dundas, the known friend of the Chagga, appeared to the planters to provide clear evidence of the Government's intention to put African interests before the well-being of the planters themselves and of the country as a whole. On 6 December 1928 a further meeting took place at which the planters demanded a commission of inquiry. Cameron did not consider that such measures were necessary and added that, in his view, to institute inquiries would only stir up feeling between Europeans and Africans when there was every reason to think that the matter could be closed.[1] With some hesitation he agreed to meet a deputation of seven planters to discuss their grievances, and after an airing of opinions the dispute ended. During the course of 1929, however, the Governor did his utmost to assure the planters that the Government was not indifferent to their welfare. The opening of the railway extension from Moshi to Arusha provided an opportunity for a suitable ceremony, and in December, as has already been seen, the Legislative Council held its budget session in Arusha.

Whatever the criticisms levelled against Cameron, his period of governorship was one of increasing prosperity for European planters and African farmers alike until, in the closing months of 1930, the economic depression struck its paralysing blow. Sisal exports, which had reached 20,834 tons in 1913, had risen to 45,728 tons in 1929. In similar fashion the output of coffee increased from 1,059 tons in 1913 to over 10,000 tons in 1928, falling to 8,857 tons in the following year only because of the lack of rain. Of the latter total the African coffee-growers in the Bukoba district produced no less than 6,666 tons. The output of gold also increased steadily, particularly from the Lupa goldfield, where alluvial mining continued to account for a high proportion of the total produced.

---

[1] *Annual Report for the Year 1928*, Col. no. 39 (1929), pp. 87–91; and *Tanganyika Times*, 5 Jan. 1929.

Labour policy

These years of prosperity placed a heavy strain upon the supply of labour and drew the Government's attention to the need to scrutinize the conditions under which labourers were employed. By 1925 it had been noted that employees were quick to discriminate between those plantations offering good working conditions and those which did not. One of the main problems, however, arose from the fact that the labour supply was usually many miles away from the areas where employment was available. Conditions of travel were bad and many labourers succumbed to ill health on the way to obtain work. Cameron was opposed to the adoption of any means which would force labourers to leave their homes in order to work on European-owned estates. He rejected, too, the suggestion, which was heard even in the Tanganyika legislature as it had been in Kenya, that the Government should take responsibility for all labour recruitment.[1] He did, however, issue a circular to administrative officers in 1926 calling upon them to urge the people of their areas to work in their own fields, and, if this were not possible, to offer their services first to the Government where work was available, and where it was not, to private employers. In an age when the paternal relationship between administrative officers and African peasants was still unbroken, such advice might, it is true, have been misconstrued as an order at times, but that was not Cameron's intention.

Throughout the 1920's and 1930's forced labour continued to be necessary for public purposes such as the construction of roads and railways. In these circumstances labourers were generally paid, and it should be added that their number steadily decreased. The main field in which compulsory unpaid labour did in fact continue was in the fulfilment of certain communal projects undertaken by native authorities. This particular branch of work was simply a prolongation of the tradition of communal labour to be found in most tribes and was not resented by the participants. Nevertheless, it came in for criticism from the Permanent Mandates Commission.[2] In a similar

[1] Leg. Co. *Debates*, Second Session, 1928, pt. i, pp. 57-60, 63-65, 69-70, 113-15, 121.

[2] Permanent Mandates Commission, *Minutes* of the 5th Session, July 1929, pp. 123-4.

category, too, might be included the unpaid work done for the
Government in lieu of direct taxation, but in permitting this
arrangement to continue the British authorities, unlike their
German predecessors, laid it down that labourers could not
be assigned to private individuals who were willing to pay the
outstanding tax.

Faced with no light task in ensuring an adequate labour
force, the Tanganyika Government in the later 1920's took the
lead among the British tropical African dependencies in formulating a sound labour policy. Acting on the report of the
Special Labour Commissioner, Major G. St. J. Orde-Browne,[1]
Cameron set up a Labour Department in 1926 which consisted
of a labour commissioner and four assistants, together with a
subordinate staff. Orde-Browne himself was appointed to the
senior post and the other vacancies were filled by officers of
the provincial administration. The headquarters of the department were established in Morogoro, and labour officers were
stationed at Muheza in the plantation area of Tanga Province
and at Kilosa, an important junction along the routes taken by
the majority of the labourers. At the latter centre the first
labour camp was opened to accommodate labourers travelling
to and from the plantations.

The functions of the new department were numerous. It was
required to collect information and to compile statistics concerning labour requirements and the supply of labourers; it
examined labour conditions and advised employers on all
aspects of the supply and care of labourers; it was to supervise
and consider the effects of existing and proposed labour legislation; and it was required to make recommendations on the
care of labourers both during their employment and while
travelling to and from their work. It was not concerned with
the recruitment of labour for private employers. A new Masters
and Servants Ordinance was passed in the same year which
made compulsory the payment of wages in cash and the reporting of serious injury to an employee. Perhaps most important
of all, it gave legal recognition to the existing practice by which
a contract with locally engaged labour could be made for the
performance of a certain number of days' work within a reason-

[1] *Report by Major G. St. J. Orde-Browne, O.B.E., upon Labour in the Tanganyika
Territory, with a covering Despatch from the Governor*, Col. no. 19 (1926).

able time. By fixing the maximum number of working days under this arrangement at thirty, and the maximum period allowed for the completion of the contract at sixty, the new ordinance went far to ensure that labour was not wasted simply because employers took on too many labourers so as to secure an adequate number when they were needed. The advantage of the system lay in the fact that locally employed labourers could perform useful tasks on plantations while still having enough time to cultivate their own plots.

During 1927 and 1928 the labour supply improved. This was partly due to the improved medical care provided in the labour camps and partly to the wider use of motorized transport to carry labourers to and from their places of employment. In 1929 72,055 labourers were given accommodation in labour camps while travelling to and from their work, and of these 11,358 were treated for minor ailments in the dispensaries provided. By the beginning of 1930 a total of seven camps had been opened. The various native authorities were also beginning to take an interest in opportunities for employment for members of their tribes. The initial fear that men who left their homes in search of work would never return was steadily overcome, and the more progressive native authorities encouraged their menfolk to seek paid employment as they grew to appreciate the benefits to be derived from the circulation of greater wealth within the tribe.[1]

Education

The comparative prosperity of the later 1920's encouraged Cameron to initiate a number of projects not so immediately concerned with increasing the wealth of the territory. Education in particular attracted his attention from the earliest months of his governorship. According to Ormsby-Gore's East Africa Commission of 1924–5 the education of the African peoples had not exercised the minds of administrative officers as extensively as they believed to be necessary in a country which, for climatic reasons if for no other, must be mainly an African territory. The commission had noted that there were seventy-two government elementary schools for Africans in rural areas, as well as

[1] Permanent Mandates Commission, *Minutes* of the 5th Session, July 1929, p. 124.

central schools in Dar es Salaam and Tanga, special schools for
chiefs' sons in Tabora and Bukoba, and a government school
in Mwanza in the charge of a White Father. Compared with
the fairly active interest shown in education by the German
Administration, this was not an impressive achievement,
although it should be added that a further 100,000 children
were on the books of various mission schools. These latter
institutions, however, concentrated upon teaching literacy and
the rudiments of religion. In the light of its review the commission recommended that there should be closer co-operation
between the Government and the missionaries as well as a
marked increase in the numbers and salaries of both European
and African teachers. These conclusions were not wholly
surprising, in that a distinguished advisory committee on
Native Education in the British Tropical African Dependencies,
of which also Ormsby-Gore happened to be chairman, had
almost simultaneously published identical recommendations.
The Education Committee, which reported in March 1925,[1]
a month earlier than the East Africa Commission, also suggested
that the Government should be prepared to give grants-in-aid
to efficient schools run by voluntary societies.

Tanganyika's reaction to these suggestions was commendably
swift. In October 1925 an education conference was summoned
in Dar es Salaam by the Director of Education and was attended
by representatives of government departments, missionary
societies, and the planting, commercial, and Indian interests,
and also by two Africans. As a result of their deliberations a
Central Advisory Committee was set up under the chairmanship of the Director of Education, consisting of representatives
of the various groups attending the conference. The committee
was to meet periodically in Dar es Salaam and would be
assisted by provincial and district committees on which native
authorities as well as the missionary societies and government
departments would be represented. Its object was to encourage
co-operation in formulating educational policy for the whole
territory. In addition, the Government agreed to make grants-
in-aid to voluntary schools which fulfilled certain standards of
efficiency.[2]

[1] *Education Policy in British Tropical Africa*, Cmd. 2374 (1925).
[2] *Annual Report for the Year 1925*, Col. no. 18 (1926), p. 65.

The African Education Ordinance authorizing the scheme of grants-in-aid came into effect on 1 January 1928, and government expenditure on education, exclusive of buildings, rose from £15,754 in the financial year 1924–5, a sum equivalent to 1·18 per cent. of the total revenue of the territory, to more than £80,000, or 3·35 per cent. of the territory's revenue, in 1928–9. The latter sum, although still small when compared with the amount spent on medical services or when cited as a percentage of the whole expenditure of the territory, nevertheless indicated a genuine concern for African education, a concern which was further reflected in the cautious but determined attempts to establish a government boarding school for girls.

The Agricultural and Medical Departments were also considered by the East Africa Commission to be as understaffed as the Education Department, and their report drew attention to the fact that the acceptance of a mandate should imply a readiness on the part of the mandatory authority to incur considerable expenditure on behalf of the country and people placed under its jurisdiction. This was a point of view which the Imperial Government was slow to accept, accustomed as it was to regard 'paying their way' to be among the most praiseworthy achievements of its dependencies. Cameron, however, was inhibited by no such principle, so that he incurred still further expenditure in encouraging the expansion of both these departments.

Closer Union

In spite of the relatively happy financial circumstances enjoyed by Tanganyika in the later 1920's, Cameron's policies were not put into effect without considerable effort on his part. Moreover, the whole of his governorship was carried on against the background—to him disquieting—of the campaign for closer union. When, in pursuance of the Ormsby-Gore Commission's recommendations, he attended a meeting of the Governors of East Africa late in 1925 to draft the agenda for the first Governors' Conference, he was unaware that his neighbour, Sir Edward Grigg, had been sent to Kenya by the determined Amery with instructions to secure agreement to closer union by conference and discussion.[1] In any event he considered that the meeting was premature, since none of the three governors had held office for a year. Consequently he was both shocked and angry when he discovered that, immediately after their preliminary meetings, Grigg and Sir William Gowers, Governor of Uganda, had sent a joint cablegram to the Colonial Secretary urging strongly that the Government of Tanganyika should be ordered to cease work upon the Tabora–Mwanza railway line. It was fortunate for Cameron's relations with Grigg that in May 1926 the Colonial Office accepted a recommendation from the Joint East African Board in London that the Tabora railway should be extended northward, not only to develop the potentialities of the Lake Victoria region, but also as the first stage in the development of international communications. Nevertheless, the action of the Governors of Kenya and Uganda was little calculated to win Cameron's support for closer union.

Cameron's insistence upon the construction of this railway was not based upon any desire to damage Kenya. He considered that the trade of the Tanganyika side of the lake should pass through Dar es Salaam rather than Kilindini; but he believed that the lake region could provide ample business for both railway systems and that Kenya's fears of excessive competition were unjustified. His opposition to closer union, which grew steadily, was based rather upon his fears of its effect upon his own programme in Tanganyika and more particularly upon his native administration policy.

While Cameron now developed into one of the leading opponents of closer union, the European unofficial opposition to association with Tanganyika's neighbours was declining. The change of outlook was mainly due to a growing conviction that the interests of Europeans in Kenya and Tanganyika were closely linked, an attitude which Lord Delamere had done much to encourage. Paradoxically, Delamere was as wary of closer union as Cameron himself, for he was suspicious of any arrangement which might threaten the hoped-for position of predominance of the European settlers in Kenya. But these two dominating personalities could not enter into an alliance, for

---

[1] Lord Altrincham, *Kenya's Opportunity* (London, 1955), p. 71. See also Chapter VI above.

Delamere feared Cameron's influence upon his schemes for
European leadership in East Africa, while Cameron was equally
afraid of the effects of Delamere's views upon his own work in
Tanganyika.

When Cameron was summoned to England in May 1927 and
was presented with proposals for closer union drafted by Amery
for the scrutiny of the East African Governors, he was immediately up in arms.[1] Believing himself to be in a minority of one
among those concerned in the projected discussions, he was
nevertheless determined at all costs to defend his freedom of
action in Tanganyika. The methods he employed won the dis-
approval of Sir Edward Grigg, for he did not hesitate to lobby
members of all parties in parliament and even threatened to
resign if the Colonial Secretary persisted in his plans for closer
union.[2] Grigg tried to convince Amery of the need to summon
a Cabinet committee so that he and Gowers might have an
opportunity to put their point of view to those responsible for
initiating policy. But no committee was summoned and the
Cabinet in any case appeared to be divided over Amery's proposals.

This division was reflected in the White Paper on Future
Policy in East Africa[3] which was presented to parliament in
July 1927. Amery's conviction that closer union was absolutely
necessary in East Africa appeared indeed as the starting-point
of the White Paper's argument; but this assertion was later
modified when the White Paper went on to state that a commission would be necessary before the Government could reach
any final decision on its policy. How far Cameron's attitude
and activities had influenced this conclusion it is difficult to say;
but Amery's departure on a Commonwealth tour after appointing only the commission's chairman set the seal on the failure
of his plans. For the divergent interests of the members who
were ultimately appointed and the uncertain character of their
terms of reference resulted in their becoming entangled in so
many purely local controversies that the production of a unanimous report became virtually impossible.[4]

[1] Cameron, op. cit., pp. 224–5.   [2] Altrincham, op. cit., p. 213.
[3] *Future Policy in regard to Eastern Africa*, Cmd. 2904 (1927).
[4] *Report of the Commission on Closer Union of the Dependencies in Eastern and Central Africa: 1928–9* (Hilton Young Commission), Cmd. 3234 (1929).

X

So far as support for Amery's closer union policy was concerned, the Hilton Young Commission received their most
friendly welcome from the Europeans of northern Tanganyika.
The same, too, might be said of Sir Samuel Wilson, who was
sent in April 1929 to salvage what he could of the ideal of
closer union from the debris of public opinion left by his
predecessors. The European Association, in a memorandum
presented to Wilson, deprecated the suggestion contained in
the Hilton Young Report that the British community in Kenya
and therefore in East Africa was unfit to rule East Africa. It
went on to support a unanimous resolution of the Tanganyika
Congress of Associations in favour of the principle of the closer
union of Kenya, Uganda, and Tanganyika.[1] The Dar es Salaam
Chamber of Commerce also gave its approval to closer union,
provided that some control could be exercised over the actions
of a Governor-General through the medium of executive and
legislative councils.[2] The Indian community was not so well
disposed towards the plan. The Management Committee of the
Indian Association drafted a resolution in April 1929 opposing
closer union on the ground that it was liable to affect the autonomy of Tanganyika and was bound to prejudice the status of
the Indians.[3]

Cameron himself gave lukewarm agreement to the Hilton
Young proposals for closer association, but remained uncon-
vinced of the merits of the whole scheme. When Wilson arrived
in Tanganyika, therefore, the Governor was glad to take up
the issue once again. Invoking Article 22 of the League
of Nations Covenant, he urged the appointment of a highly
authoritative committee or commission which would sit in
England and hear the views of those who opposed the Hilton
Young recommendations.[4] In this instance an appeal to Britain's mandatory obligations served as a useful instrument in
Cameron's hands, but his whole career suggests that he would,
in any case, have carried on his struggle against closer union
to the end of his governorship. Consequently the new Labour
Government's decision to appoint a Joint Committee of both
houses of parliament entirely suited Cameron's purpose.

---

[1] *Tanganyika Times*, 27 Apr. 1929.
[2] Ibid., 15 May 1929.   [3] Ibid., 27 Apr. 1929.
[4] *Report of Sir Samuel Wilson on his Visit to East Africa*, Cmd. 3378 (1929), p. 36.

The support of Tanganyika's European unofficials for closer
union was now at its height, and they at once announced that
they were ready and anxious to send representatives to give
evidence before the Joint Committee. From their opposing
viewpoint Tanganyika's Indians were equally anxious to make
their opinions known. In these circumstances the Tanganyika
Government considered it only equitable that Africans should
be enabled to present the Joint Committee with an African
point of view. The three men chosen for this latter purpose were
selected by the Secretary for Native Affairs. They were the
chief clerk from the District Office in Tanga, a chief from
Shinyanga, and the secretary of the chiefs' council in Bukoba.
Although one was a Protestant, one a Catholic, and one a
Muslim, they were unanimous in their view that Tanganyika
should remain under the control of the Colonial Secretary and
the British parliament for as long as they could foresee. Engaged
as they were in a multiplicity of tasks contributing to the development of Tanganyika, they preferred to be left to their work
and not to be disturbed by questions of association with their
neighbours. It might be argued that these men, who were
nominees and friends of the Secretary for Native Affairs, were
unlikely to oppose the Governor's views. Yet they were probably
as representative as any other three Africans of what might be
described as African opinion in Tanganyika. In any event, the
introduction of a common customs tariff for Kenya, Uganda,
and Tanganyika in 1923, together with an arrangement which
permitted goods manufactured in any of the three territories
to enter the other territories duty free, had already laid the
unobtrusive foundations of a more effective association than
was envisaged by most of the critics of closer union.

Another body which maintained a watchful interest in the
closer union proposals was the Permanent Mandates Commission. The first reaction of its members to the Hilton Young
Report was that, while the recommendations it contained
appeared wholly legal, it was doubtful whether their implementation would benefit Tanganyika either economically or from
the point of view of her native policy. Particular attention was
drawn, too, to the statement that one of the duties of a Governor-
General of East Africa would be to secure Imperial interests,
since that did not seem compatible with the terms of the

mandate.[1] When the commission had had more time to consider the issue, however, serious doubts began to arise. Some members readily agreed that the type of association which the British Government appeared to be considering for the East African territories was within the terms of the mandate. Yet they wondered if the mandate itself was not at fault, in that it tended to weaken the concept of Tanganyika's right to a separate existence and failed to stress the fact that the authority which Britain exercised was only a delegated authority. There was thus a danger that the mandatory power might overlook its duty of preparing the people of Tanganyika for political autonomy and ultimate independence. Other members, in a more critical vein, argued that the proposals for closer union offended against the more fundamental principles laid down in Article 22 of the Covenant of the League of Nations.[2]

Initially, all these comments arose from a genuine desire to protect the interests of Tanganyika. With the revival of Germany's concern for her former overseas dependencies, however, a new spirit entered into the committee's deliberations. In November 1930 the members took note of a communication from the president of the Women's League of the German Colonial Society which was accompanied by a resolution, signed by seventy-four German women's associations, protesting against the closer union movement.[3] The full impact of this new factor was not felt immediately, however, since it was then agreed to postpone further discussion until the recommendations of the Joint Select Committee were available to members.[4]

The Joint Committee's conclusion that the time was not ripe for closer union was hastened by the imminent fall of the Labour Government, while the world-wide economic crisis pushed the issue into the background so far as interest in Britain itself was concerned. One member of the Permanent Mandates Commission nevertheless took the opportunity to urge the commission as a whole to state categorically that the time for political and constitutional union never would be ripe so long as the mandate was in force.[5] But for the time being

[1] Permanent Mandates Commission, *Minutes* of the 15th Session, July 1929, pp. 103–6.   [2] Ibid., pp. 168–70, 202–4.
[3] Ibid., *Minutes* of the 19th Session, Nov., 1930, p. 26.
[4] Ibid., pp. 143–50.
[5] Ibid., *Minutes* of the 22nd Session, Nov. 1932, p. 120.

Cameron had won his campaign, as he had won so many others during his six years of office, and he could leave Tanganyika secure in the knowledge that, in the near future at all events, his work would not be undermined by Kenya's ideologies. Yet in many ways this was only half a triumph, for already the slump was beginning to threaten greater damage to the territory than all the disputes which had absorbed the energies of Tanganyika's population in the 1920's. If Byatt's governorship had been a period of caution and consolidation, Cameron's term of office had been one of both conflict and construction. There were soon to be those who argued that the development of the social services under Cameron had been carried to a level which Tanganyika could not maintain in less prosperous times. There were others who saw in the difficulties encountered in developing Cameron's native administration policy evidence of a fundamental weakness in the principle underlying it. Yet there is much to suggest that Tanganyika's survival during the slump of the early 1930's was due not only to the enthusiasm and careful direction of Cameron's successor, and to the goodwill of both official and unofficial communities in Tanganyika, but also to the impetus given to Tanganyika's development and to the life infused into the territory by Cameron's unquenchable energy.

XI

TANGANYIKA:
SLUMP AND SHORT-TERM GOVERNORS
1932-45

KENNETH INGHAM

EVEN before Sir Donald Cameron left Tanganyika, the economic advance of the Territory was beginning to encounter difficulties. In 1930, for the first time in ten years, a check was seen in the country's economic progress. During the first three months of the year heavy floods interfered with railway transport and damaged crops in the more low-lying areas. The roads remained unfit for motor traffic for some months after the rains had ended, and the cotton crop was seriously depleted by a plague of rats. Through the enthusiasm of the cultivators these local calamities were overcome, but towards the end of the year the fall in world prices struck a more deadly blow. Sisal, the country's most valuable export, showed an increase of 4,234 tons but fetched a price of only £1,172,315, £313,278 less than in 1929. By the end of the year it was selling at £21 a ton, compared with £32 in 1929, and it was shortly to fall as low as £12. The quantity of coffee exported also increased by 30 per cent., but its value was 33 per cent. lower than in 1929. This latter fall in prices mainly affected the *robusta* crop grown in the Bukoba Province, and the growers held over a considerable quantity of their coffee in the vain hope of an improvement. The ground-nut export crop also reached a record level and would have been still greater if the growers had not preferred to retain some of their produce for their own consumption rather than to sell it at the low price offered.

As a result of the fall in prices the purchasing power of the African population was swiftly and seriously affected. Imports were reduced and there was a consequent shortfall in revenue from customs.[1] By 31 March 1931, the country's surplus

[1] *Annual Report for the Year 1930*, Col. no. 60 (1931), pp. 34–37.

balance, which had stood at £933,192 a year earlier, had been reduced to £580,169. By 31 March 1932 it had fallen still further, to £281,609. Meanwhile, the Territory's revenue fell from £1,992,675 in 1929–30 to £1,749,478 in 1930–1 and £1,552,368 in 1931–2. This latter situation was due in part to the fall in customs duties already mentioned and in part to the decrease in revenue from the hut and poll-taxes, which in many areas could be collected only with the greatest difficulty. The income from the working of the Central Railway also began to show signs of drying up. A not inconsiderable proportion of the railway's freight had consisted of goods travelling to and from the Belgian Congo. This traffic had already been threatened by the construction of new railways which would provide an outlet for Congo produce via the west coast, and with the Congo trade now affected by the depression the situation became still more serious.

Simultaneously there was a sharp reduction in the demand for labour, while lower wages were paid to those who remained in employment. Yet in spite of these factors, and in spite, too, of the very low prices offered for economic crops, there is little to suggest that the African population suffered any serious hardship as a result of the slump. Their subsistence crops were little affected and they had not yet become dependent to any marked extent upon imported goods. The reversion to hides, skins, and bark-cloth as clothing, which took place in a number of areas, was an indication of the absence of even the small sums of money needed to purchase the astonishingly cheap Japanese goods which were flooding the market. But it did not indicate genuine hardship for the people concerned.

Far more serious was the effect of the slump upon the general development of the country when it had just begun to gain momentum. African peasants, who at first had responded with some reluctance to the Government's encouragement of economic crops, now found their produce unsaleable and became disillusioned. Rudimentary native authorities which had reached the critical stage of accepting increased responsibility for the conduct of local affairs found their revenue seriously reduced.

Capital projects also suffered, and this in some cases had repercussions upon the country's overall economic development. The extension of trade routes by road, rail, and sea, which had contributed so largely to the rapid increase in Tanganyika's trade in the 1920's, had been financed for the most part from loans guaranteed by the British Government. The fundamental importance, indeed the absolute necessity, of this expenditure was not in doubt, but one result was that Tanganyika's public debt had reached a figure which clearly precluded further borrowing until the revenue improved. Consequently, a number of railway projects had to be postponed, including developments south of the Central Line and a connecting link between the Central and Tanga lines. Meanwhile, the consolidation and extension of the road services were dependent upon any funds which might become available from time to time.[1] But the years of comparative plenty with which Cameron's term of office had concluded had resulted in a casual attitude towards expenditure, so that it was some time before the country was willing to accept restrictions. As a first step towards tightening up the country's economy, therefore, a Retrenchment Commission was appointed on 3 March 1931 under the chairmanship of the Treasurer and consisting of both officials and unofficials.

The maintenance of production and the improvement of marketing arrangements

Sir Stewart Symes, formerly Resident and Commander-in-Chief in Aden, became Governor of Tanganyika on 23 May 1931, and took office when the country's economic prospects were at their darkest. He was faced with a difficult task, and in dealing with it he had at his disposal few resources save his own energy and the support of his administrative officers. Early hopes that other exportable crops would offset the fall in the price of sisal were unfulfilled, for neither cotton nor ground-nuts was a success in 1931.

Symes's policy fell into two parts. In the first place he introduced a programme of retrenchment, coupled with measures to increase revenue from taxation, and then he set on foot a long-term scheme to increase Tanganyika's prosperity by means of a productivity drive. In the formulation and execution of this latter undertaking Symes was greatly assisted by the Director of Agriculture, E. Harrison. It was Harrison who, with a bold

[1] Permanent Mandates Commission, *Minutes* of the 22nd Session, Nov. 1932, p. 133.

disregard for current price trends, inaugurated a 'grow more crops' campaign. The chiefs were clearly informed that the Government could not control world prices, but that whatever the future might hold there was everything to be gained from continuing to work the land and to increase the output of crops. Food crops were Harrison's priority, but at the same time he paid special attention to the introduction of improved types of cash crops and better methods of cultivation. The sisal-growers, meanwhile, set a sound example, for in spite of having to reduce their labour forces they were able to maintain and increase their output by the use of more efficient methods.

In the event the response of the African peasants to the Government's policy was remarkably good, and the Government was able to turn its attention to evolving more efficient marketing of the crops. Here the Director of Agriculture was anxious not only to increase the country's revenue but also to maintain the quality of the crops and to ensure a fair return to the growers. To achieve this he proposed to introduce closer government control of the whole marketing system. Even in the cotton trade, which was already to some extent controlled, there was something to be gained from keeping a closer watch upon the issue of buying licences. The benefits of private enterprise by middlemen buyers in good seasons, when every available buyer was needed to handle the large crop, could so easily be offset by the poor prices then offered to the growers. Coffee presented similar problems, with the added difficulty that it was a crop which ripened daily and which was produced in small parcels. Thus the employment of African collectors to gather up the produce and take it to the processing works, though cumbersome and uneconomic, was unavoidable until an adequate number of organized buying posts and licensed curing works had been provided or co-operative marketing societies had been established to undertake bulk sales. The need to secure better returns for growers of ground-nuts, simsim, rice, and leaf tobacco was equally important, though usually most of these crops were bartered for other goods instead of being sold for cash.

In all these cases custom was hard to disturb, and to the innate conservatism of the peasants the vested interests of the dealers added their quota of difficulties. The dealers were in fact beginning to face considerable hostility from their customers, although during the depression at least the criticisms levelled at them were not always justified. For, under the stress of economic difficulties, racial feeling had one of its rare periods of activity. In more sober moments the importance of the contribution made by Indians to the development of trade in Tanganyika was readily recognized by both Europeans and Africans. Financiers in Bombay and wholesale dealers in the coastal towns of East Africa played their valuable role in this development. Even more important, however, were the small but widespread services rendered by a few thousand Indians, domiciled in Tanganyika, who procured credit for the African population and who carried trade to the remotest parts of the country. These services were usually carried on in relatively uncongenial surroundings and were not sufficiently profitable to attract European firms or their agents. Meanwhile the African population had not reached the stage when they could provide the services for themselves.

Without doubt some of the Indian shopkeepers and pedlars had cheated their customers or had resorted to extortionate practices. Owing to the slump, too, the number of these sharp practices may have increased, for there was a loud outcry from both Africans and European officials. As a result the Government was pressed from many quarters to introduce discriminatory legislation against the Indian community. Symes, however, was convinced that less drastic measures were called for, both because such proposals were unfair and also because of the impossibility of replacing the Indians' contribution to the country. He discussed the problem with the Indian leaders and obtained their co-operation in trying to bring the malpractices of the traders to an end. The negotiations were carried on privately and were so successful that before many months had elapsed there were reports from all parts of the country of an improvement in the traders' behaviour.[1]

Fiscal reform

While these developments were taking place more immediate steps were being taken to increase revenue. New methods of collecting the hut and poll-taxes were considered, including payment by instalments or by deducting the tax from the

[1] S. Symes, *Tour of Duty* (London, 1946), pp. 172–4.

wages of employees. In 1932 a levy ranging from 5 per cent.
to 10 per cent. was imposed upon official salaries, but only
brought in rather less than £40,000 a year instead of the anticipated minimum of £46,000.[1] In 1932, also, a Bill was published
in which it was proposed to substitute a graduated poll-tax for
the existing non-native education tax, and civil servants would
be liable to pay this tax in addition to the 5 per cent. levy. The
education tax had been instituted only as recently as 1930, with
the primary object of affording security to the Government for
the repayment of loans made to non-African communities for
building schools. Any balances were to be used to supplement
annual votes for European and Indian education. In practice
the levy was simply a poll-tax, for every adult European and
Asian male was required to pay it whether he was likely to get
any educational benefit or not. But not unnaturally every little
isolated community throughout the territory had begun to
expect additional educational services in return for their payments and had become aggrieved when these were not forthcoming. There was, therefore, a sound practical reason for an
immediate revision of the particular tax, whatever the merits or
demerits of the graduated poll-tax might be. In any case, in the
straitened circumstances of the times, it was scarcely possible
to employ the argument that non-Africans contributed heavily
through indirect taxation to the revenues of the country as a
justification for exempting the wealthiest section of the population from a direct form of taxation which the Africans had been
paying for ten years. Indeed, consideration was given to the
introduction of an income tax, but this was rejected as being an
impracticable arrangement. Instead it was proposed that there
should be a graduated poll-tax ranging at first from 20 sh. on
an income of £50 a year to £30 on incomes of £2,000 or more.
This was subsequently revised so that the minimum payment
was £2 and the maximum £500 on incomes of over £10,000.
Provision for non-African education would then be made from
the general revenue. It was hoped to collect £40,000 a year from
this new tax, but in 1933 it raised only £31,534.

The criticism that the poll-tax was in effect an income tax
under a different title was voiced in the press[2] and in the debate

[1] Tanganyika Legislative Council *Debates*, Sixth Session, 1923, pt. i, p. 18.
[2] *East African Standard*, 30 Jan. 1932.

on the second reading of the Bill in the Legislative Council.[1] The *East African Standard* even went so far as to denounce Sir Stewart Symes as 'a slave of an oppressive bureaucracy' and 'a mere tool or puppet of Downing Street'.[2] The Dar es Salaam Chamber of Commerce, meanwhile, petitioned the Legislative Council to withdraw the Bill, arguing that similar legislation in Kenya had had to be repealed after experience had shown it to be impracticable. In the Legislative Council itself more responsible criticisms were forthcoming. The two principal ones were, first, that the tax was clearly an income tax, and, second, that although it was small now it might increase in the years to come and so act as a deterrent to capital investment in the territory. But the Governor persisted in his determination to solve the country's problems in the way which he considered to be most effective, and even took it upon himself to reply to the debate in place of the Treasurer, who had introduced the Bill.

Another important step was taken in March 1932, when permission was received to float a £750,000 loan on the London market to provide funds to tide over the period until the country's economy could be stabilized. Only a few weeks earlier, Symes had also obtained the agreement of the Lords Commissioners of the Treasury to a proposal that Sir Sydney Armitage-Smith should carry out an investigation into the basis of public revenue and expenditure in the Territory. In his report, published later in the year, Armitage-Smith was extremely critical of Tanganyika's economic policy under Cameron's governorship.[3] Somewhat surprisingly, in view of the figures, he maintained that there had been undue expenditure on social services in proportion to the limited nature of the country's financial resources. He also considered that the practice of budgeting to the hilt on the basis of revenues obtained in a period of prosperity had involved the country in a high recurrent expenditure which could not be sustained even in a period when trade was normal, still less at a time of recession. This criticism was in marked contrast to the Colonial Office's comments on Uganda's conservative budgeting immediately before the depression, and it should be added in

---

[1] Leg. Co. *Debates*, Sixth Session, 1932, pp. 68 sqq.
[2] *E.A. Standard*, 20 Feb. 1932.
[3] *Report . . . on a Financial Mission to Tanganyika*, Cmd. 4182 (1932).

Cameron's defence that his policy had received the encouragement of the Permanent Mandates Commission.

In the circumstances of the early 1930's the Tanganyika Government had already considered it necessary to reduce expenditure on education, on the Medical Department, and on the Department of Lands and Mines. At the same time the Labour Department, which in spite of its limited resources had achieved so much in recent years, was completely abolished in 1931, the responsibility for labour issues then reverting to the Provincial Administration. But the fact that a country wishing to be self-supporting must gear its social services to its income could have been little consolation to those who had hoped to see Tanganyika's progress in the 1920's carried still further in the 1930's. With so much to be done, every reverse must have appeared to threaten a return to the starting-point. Even more disturbing from a long-term point of view was the possibility that the depression might produce a permanent change in the country's economic situation.

A further target for Armitage-Smith's criticism was Tanganyika's participation in what amounted almost to a customs union with Kenya and Uganda. He argued that the maintenance of a high tariff on certain imports, while protecting some of the products and infant industries of Kenya, benefited Tanganyika not at all, but simply increased the price of imported goods. Similarly the absence of customs barriers between the three mainland territories, admirable though it might seem in principle, worked to the detriment of Tanganyika, since she exported little to her neighbours but imported very much more. The Tanganyika Government did not accept Armitage-Smith's opinion on this issue, but the Permanent Mandates Commission, some of whose members had already advised against a customs alliance which might seriously undermine Tanganyika's financial independence,[1] was unwilling to dismiss Armitage-Smith's strictures light-heartedly. Sir Stewart Symes, however, argued strongly that the increase in prices due to the common tariff did not make the cost of imported goods in any way excessive for Tanganyika.

Meanwhile the 'grow more food' campaign was meeting with

[1] Permanent Mandates Commission, *Minutes* of the 15th Session, July 1929, pp. 117–18; *Minutes* of the 22nd Session, Nov. 1932, pp. 136–7, 139–41.

success and widening the basis of the country's production. At the end of 1932 valuable results were already to be seen, and by the middle of 1933 Tanganyika was once again living within its means. This recovery was due in part to the general improvement in the world economic situation, but equally to the response of all communities in Tanganyika to the Government's varied plans for reconstruction. Sir Harold MacMichael, formerly Civil Secretary to the Sudan Government, who arrived in Tanganyika on 19 February 1934 in succession to Sir Stewart Symes, was thus encouraged to contemplate additional measures which would both strengthen the country's economic position still further and assist in the overall development of the Territory. He therefore proposed the repeal of the African hut and poll-taxes and the substitution of a new Native Tax Ordinance involving the introduction of a system of graduated personal taxation based on the wealth of the individual taxpayer.

This was a surprising piece of legislation, since a conference of advisers on native affairs in the three East African territories held in Mwanza as recently as August 1933 had recommended that hut or poll-taxes, graduated by districts, should be retained because of the ease of collection,[1] and in May 1934 the Governors' Conference had endorsed the proposal. So far as Tanganyika was concerned, however, the new tax appeared to have certain advantages. The task of assessment would be carried out by the native authorities, who would thus gain experience in work of a responsible nature. Moreover, the ordinance was permissive, and it was proposed to apply the new system in the first place only to the Bukoba, Arusha, and Moshi districts, where many Africans were obtaining considerable incomes from coffee and where native authorities were sufficiently advanced to carry out the assessment. The native authorities would also benefit directly, since hitherto they had derived 80 per cent. of their revenue from hut and poll-taxes, and an increase in the money collected from the new tax would mean an increase in the funds available to local governments themselves.

Local government

One of the encouraging aspects of the depression period was the continued effectiveness of the majority of the native

[1] *Report of the Conference of Advisers on Native Affairs* (Nairobi, 1933).

authorities. This was doubly surprising in that all of them were disappointed by the fall in their revenues, while some of them were beginning to prove unsuited to the novel demands placed upon them by Cameron's administrative policy. In Masasi District the clan heads who had been recognized as native authorities were shown to have been an unsatisfactory choice. Their traditional authority was exercised over individuals rather than over districts. With the increasing tendency for people to move from one area to another there arose the anomalous situation in which native authorities, in their position as clan heads, were claiming control over persons living outside the areas of authority recognized by the Government, while other individuals, newly arrived within the sphere of a native authority, were looking to the jurisdiction of their own clan leaders in some distant region. Again, if a more important clan leader came to settle in a region where a lesser leader had already been recognized by the Government as the responsible native authority, some of the clan members in that area transferred their allegiance to the new arrival. It was seen that these problems might be overcome if clan leaders voluntarily co-operated in carrying out their administrative duties. In 1938 it was recommended that this practice should be formalized throughout the district.

The development of a native authority among the Masai presented a different problem. Under the terms of the Native Authority Ordinance the *laibon* of the Tanganyika Masai had been recognized as a superior authority with the title of Chief of Masai. At the time this seemed a reasonable step to take, since he was the only person within the tribe who could be said to exercise any general influence. His traditional influence, however, was that of a respected adviser and religious leader whose views were regularly sought but who was not accustomed to exercise either executive or judicial powers. In spite of his new title, therefore, the *laibon* made no attempt to adapt himself to the role expected of him. Instead he delegated the powers granted him as a superior authority to a body of elders who from time to time reported to him the decisions they had taken and received his approval. As the power behind the executive authority the *laibon* remained of the greatest importance, but neither he nor the rest of the Masai aspired to change the situation.

In Tanga Province difficulties arose for the most part from the inability of the people to comprehend the implications of the Government's administrative system. From the start it had proved impossible to find indigenous authorities to exercise the powers which Cameron had hoped to impose upon them. It became necessary, therefore, to select anyone to act as native authority who appeared capable of undertaking the responsibilities of office. Under this arrangement the population was unable to distinguish between the new authorities and the old *akidas* whom Cameron had abolished. In vain did the administrative officers strive to explain the difference between an *akida* who had been simply an agent of the Central Government and an appointee of the same Government who was intended to provide the germ around which local government would develop. It would be untrue to suggest that the discontent voiced by a number of troublemakers stemmed solely from these difficulties. The critics were found to be personally opposed to the office holders in their district and may well have been opposed to authority in general. Nevertheless, the fact that they were able to secure a following was due to some extent at least to the unsettled nature of the administrative system.

In Dar es Salaam, where the more standard version of indirect administration was unsuitable owing to the mixture of tribes living in the neighbourhood of the town, the experiment was tried of bringing together a number of village headmen with a view to creating a council which would fulfil the duties of a native authority.[1] The weak character of the headmen, however, prevented them from shouldering the unquestionably heavy burden of responsibility which the Government hoped to be able to impose upon them.[2]

The situation in southern Uluguru similarly demonstrated the problems which might arise when there were no obvious candidates for the position of native authority. In this region, for want of a likelier candidate, a clan leader who possessed some reputation as a rain-maker had been appointed native authority in 1926. He abused his powers, but because of his magical skill the people were reluctant to complain. Ultimately

---

[1] Permanent Mandates Commission, *Minutes* of the 22nd Session, Nov. 1932, p. 143.

[2] Ibid. 23rd Session, June 1933, pp. 55–56.

he was deposed by the provincial commissioner, but the difficulty of finding a replacement was increased by the widespread
fear of displeasing the former office holder. The Government,
therefore, took the bold decision to amalgamate the affected
area with a neighbouring district which was already under the
control of an able chief. This solution was readily accepted, so
that in this case satisfaction was obtained by departing from the
principle of supporting traditional authorities.

Although these examples serve to illustrate the problems
encountered in the application of the system of native authorities envisaged by Cameron, they were in no sense representative
of the country as a whole. Cameron's successors were faced with
a number of difficulties inherent in the development of a system
rapidly introduced with, perhaps, too great an emphasis upon
basic uniformity. But they had much to be grateful for in the
way in which the local authorities functioned in the 1930's. This
degree of efficiency may not, however, in every case have reflected credit upon Cameron's policy. It is not unreasonable to
assume that in a number of areas the native authorities, instead
of developing a life of their own, displayed a not unnatural
tendency to become the agents of an efficient district commissioner. This was the other aspect of the problem set by
Cameron's fundamental intransigence on the subject of indirect
administration.

The revival of German interest in Tanganyika

If the economic depression was the most serious problem with
which Tanganyika was faced in the early 1930's, during the
later part of the decade it was yet another problem originating
outside the territory which created the most profound disturbance. This was the re-emergence of Germany under Hitler's
leadership. This new factor, whose effects upon Tanganyika had
already been foreshadowed by the interest shown by Germans
in the deliberations on closer union, became prominent during
the discussions of the Permanent Mandates Commission in 1933.

The event which provided Germany with her opportunity to
criticize British policy in Tanganyika was the establishment of a
postal union between Tanganyika and her two northern neighbours in 1932. The Indians of Tanganyika addressed a petition
to the Permanent Mandates Commission in which they argued

that the union was not in the interests of the territory. Shortly afterwards, the President of the Koloniale Reichsarbeitsgemeinschaft of Berlin, Dr. Schnee, former Governor of German East Africa, also addressed a brief petition to the commission which professed to represent the view of all colonial associations in Germany. In it he wrote that the postal union was incompatible with the letter and spirit of Article 22 of the Covenant of the League of Nations. The issue was referred to by M. Rappard and expanded by Dr. J. Ruppel during the course of the twenty-third session of the Permanent Mandates Commission in June 1933. In reply Sir Stewart Symes argued that Britain had no intention of infringing the Covenant. He gave warning, however, that too rigid an interpretation of the mandate would lead to the erection round Tanganyika of an ideological Chinese wall which would hinder the country's development. But Dr. Ruppel persisted in his criticisms, cleverly pressing towards his objective with the suggestion that the exclusion of men who were not British subjects from membership of the Legislative Council simply because they could not take the oath of allegiance to King George V was not in the best interests of Tanganyika. The Belgian and Dutch members, however, agreed that Britain's actions were well within the terms of the mandate, and although Dr. Ruppel refused to associate himself with their view, the commission finally decided to suspend judgement until there had been some experience of the working of the arrangement. In the meantime it was suggested that the Council of the League should ask for further information about the postal union.[1]

This demonstration of German interest in East Africa, coupled with Germany's unchecked annexations elsewhere, made the British in East Africa anxious to obtain a convincing reassurance from their Government that Tanganyika would not be handed back to Germany. In Tanganyika itself the German population was becoming increasingly aggressive under the influence of events in Germany. Offshoots of the Nazi organization were gaining a foothold in the country, and the number of German settlers was increasing to such an extent that, notably in the Moshi area, they had gained a dominant voice. This situation was reflected in an incident which occurred in October

---

[1] Permanent Mandates Commission, *Minutes* of the 23rd Session, June 1930, pp. 45–54, 64–74, 77–80, 171–80; and *E.A. Standard*, 28 Jan. 1933.

1933 when Sir John Sandeman Allen, chairman of the Joint East African Board, was debarred by German members of the local chamber of commerce from discussing closer union and other allied questions, including the mandate, at a public meeting in Moshi. During the course of his visit to East Africa Sir John had frequently laid stress upon the need for accepting the economic unity of the three territories, and this point of view conflicted fundamentally with German aspirations.

In spite of their concern about the future of the Territory, there was not as yet any opposition among British settlers in East Africa to the idea of Germans obtaining land in Tanganyika. So strong was their desire that Europeans should play a greater part in determining East Africa's future that any industrious settler was sure of a welcome. What was both feared and resented was the Germans' tendency to retain close political links with their homeland. It was, therefore, because it was thought by many British residents to provide the best defence against the possibility of the Territory's being transferred to Germany that the idea of closer union lingered on in Tanganyika long after it had been shelved by the British Government.

Verbal assurances of Britain's determination to hold on to Tanganyika were not lacking, however. Speaking in June 1934 at an East African dinner in London, the Colonial Secretary, Sir Philip Cunliffe-Lister, urged the communities of East Africa not to worry about the political aspects of closer union but to work for the true foundation of that union, which lay in day to day co-operation between the three territories. He added that no British Government would ever surrender the trust reposed in them in holding the mandate for Tanganyika.[1] Early in 1935, nevertheless, a memorandum was sent to the Colonial Secretary affirming that the time had arrived when the identity of economic and social interests of all communities of Kenya and Tanganyika demanded a union of the two territories. This should be accompanied by a greater measure of control in administrative and financial affairs by the unofficial permanent residents if the welfare and security of both territories was to be assured in the future. The memorandum originated at a conference held in Arusha on 15 and 16 March and attended by Europeans from both Kenya and Tanganyika. No

[1] *Tanganyika Standard*, 22 June 1934.

representatives of Uganda were present. It was subsequently
endorsed by a number of European associations in Tanganyika
as well as in Kenya and by the unofficial European members
of the Tanganyika Legislative Council.[1] In reply, however, the
Colonial Secretary, Malcolm Macdonald, simply reaffirmed
the views of the Joint Select Committee of 1931.

As Germany's aggressions in Europe continued and German
colonial feeling grew stronger in Tanganyika, the atmosphere
of uncertainty among the British residents increased and soon
communicated itself to Britain. Questions were repeatedly asked
in parliament about the Government's intentions regarding the
transfer of territories to Germany. On 18 December 1935 the
Prime Minister, Stanley Baldwin, stated that no British territory
and no territory under British protection or mandate would be
transferred from British sovereignty without the fullest regard
being paid to the interests of the peoples of the territories concerned. On 27 April 1936 he added that no action would be
taken in regard to any transfer without full discussion in parliament. Troubled still by the Prime Minister's refusal to answer
a supplementary question concerning the Government's future
policy on mandates, a deputation from the Conservative Imperial Affairs Committee attempted on 19 May to obtain from
Baldwin a still more categorical assurance. The deputation was
headed by Earl Winterton and included such prominent figures
in the formulation of British colonial policy as L. S. Amery,
Sir Edward Grigg, Duncan Sandys, and Colonel Ponsonby.
To strengthen their case they took with them a telegram which
had just arrived from Major F. W. Cavendish-Bentinck writing
on behalf of the Europeans in Kenya, and which stressed the
anxiety they felt over the uncertainty as to Tanganyika's future.
The deputation, however, was unsuccessful. On succeeding
Baldwin as Prime Minister, Neville Chamberlain reiterated
the latter's statements in answer to further questions in parliament on 10 November 1938, and added in reply to yet another
question four days later that the Government was certainly not
contemplating the transfer of any of the mandated territories.
Furthermore, lest there should still remain any lingering doubts
arising from a suggestion that the Prime Minister's answers had
not been in the definite form reported in *Hansard*, the Colonial

[1] *Uganda Herald*, 30 Oct. 1935.

Secretary authorized the governors of Kenya and Tanganyika to issue statements confirming that no transfer was contemplated on any terms.

These various replies by members of the British Government were subjected to a minute and apprehensive scrutiny by an association founded in 1938 with the title of the Tanganyika League. This society numbered among its members some of the leading citizens of all three East African territories, and its basic object was to prevent the transfer of Tanganyika to Germany. Its headquarters, however, were in Nairobi, and its chairman and organizer-in-chief was a prominent Kenya resident, Major F. W. Cavendish-Bentinck. The league organized meetings in the main centres in Kenya and Tanganyika, it issued circulars to members to keep them informed of the progress of the campaign, and its chairman gave a weekly broadcast. Cavendish-Bentinck also moved a motion in the Kenya Legislative Council on 10 November 1938 calling upon His Majesty's Government to give an early and unequivocal assurance regarding Tanganyika's future.[1] In the course of his speech introducing the motion he referred to the uncertainty felt in England as well as in East Africa, and mentioned that Lloyds were quoting a rate of 36·15 per cent. for a contingency insurance against possible loss arising from the return of Tanganyika to Germany. He stressed, as the Tanganyika League had consistently done, with limited historical accuracy, that the mandate had been granted to Britain by the victorious Allied powers and not by the League of Nations, that Germany had surrendered her sovereignty to those powers in 1919, and that by the mandate Tanganyika had become as much a part of the British empire as any colony or dependency. Money and effort, he argued, had been invested in Tanganyika on this understanding.

This simplified version of the complicated discussions leading up to the introduction of the mandates system won widespread acceptance among the British unofficials of both Kenya and Tanganyika, and under the pressure of German policy the theme of closer union steadily gained a hold upon them. On 20 July 1939 a convention met in Iringa. It was attended by representatives of business and professional interests, among

---

[1] Kenya Legislative Council *Debates*, 2nd ser., vol. vi (10 Nov. 1938), cols. 222–30.

whom were three legislative councillors from Tanganyika's coastal region. It was these latter who urged that the main subject of discussion should be the means of achieving the complete unification of the East African territories. A month later the executive of the Dar es Salaam Chamber of Commerce once again placed on record its conviction that the amalgamation of the three East African territories under a completely unified system of administration was essential for the prosperity and well-being of East Africa. The chamber as a whole was less confident of the wisdom of this proposal, and was only prepared to support the recommendation of its executive if adequate safeguards for the rights and privileges of the native and Indian population were retained.[1] Indian opinion played an important part in bringing about this modification of the original proposal, and only a few weeks earlier the Dar es Salaam Indian Association had reacted to the discussions held in Iringa by reiterating its view that the unification of the East African territories was not in the interests of the vast majority of the inhabitants of Tanganyika and would amount to a violation of the principles of the mandate.[2] With the outbreak of war against Germany in September, however, the whole issue of closer union became much more a matter of practical expediency than of emotional concern. The fear that Tanganyika would be handed back to Germany then disappeared in the struggle to prevent a German conquest of the whole of the British Commonwealth.

Economic recovery

Beneath this cloud of political uncertainty Tanganyika's recovery continued in an unspectacular but fairly solid fashion. By the end of 1935 the price of sisal had risen once again to £29 a ton, and in the same year the value of sisal exported from the country exceeded £1 million. There was a revival, too, in cotton-growing, and in 1939 the crop of 65,145 bales, valued at £557,358, was the highest on record. In the same year the coffee crop amounted to 16,599 tons, worth £466,026, in spite of the low prices offered as a result of over-production in Brazil.

The efficient marketing of African-grown crops, which had received the attention of the Government during the slump, continued to be used as a means of encouraging the more ex-

---

[1] *Tanganyika Weekly Standard*, 18 Aug. 1939.   [2] Ibid., 11 Aug. 1939.

tensive production of economic crops. The Native Authority Produce Markets, which had come into being in the more heavily populated Lake and Central Provinces during the depression, were now growing in importance as centres both of economic activity and of social life. But it was found impossible to create similar markets in the more sparsely inhabited areas because the distances which the producers would have had to travel were so great that alternative methods of marketing were inevitable.

In an attempt to diversify the country's economy two new estate crops had been introduced. The area of land which might be used for growing tea was limited by the International Tea Restriction Scheme, but in 1934 2,900 acres were allotted to Tanganyika and were soon fully planted, so that in 1938 a further allocation of 2,050 acres was made. These plantations were located in the Southern Highlands Province and the Usambara mountains region, the most suitable areas for tea-growing. The other new crop, sugar, was introduced in the lowland area of Moshi District in the Northern Province, and by 1938 the output amounted to 5,000 tons. Most of this was exported, because the Tanganyika market had already been captured by sugar-growers in Kenya and Uganda. By comparison only about 60 per cent. of Tanganyika's tea crop was exported. This, however, was due to international regulations, which laid down that the proportion of tea exported must be measured against the amount consumed in the territory.

Another important export during the later 1930's was gold, which was now being produced in ever larger quantities. In 1938 the output exceeded 100,000 ounces for the first time, and the following year its value was almost £1 million, second only to sisal among Tanganyika's exports.

One feature there was of Tanganyika's economy which aroused unfavourable comment, namely the pronounced increase in the percentage of goods imported from Japan, which was not counterbalanced by any similar increase in Japanese purchases from Tanganyika. In 1929 Japanese goods imported into Tanganyika amounted to no more than 6 per cent. of the country's total imports. By 1937 they accounted for 23·8 per cent. Meanwhile, Japanese purchases from Tanganyika, which had comprised no more than 3·3 per cent. of the Territory's total exports in 1929, sunk to a mere 0·2 per cent. in 1937. As far as Tanganyika was concerned this was not a serious matter. Indeed, the availability of cheap Japanese goods, even though of inferior quality, might be regarded as having been beneficial to the African population. The chief critics of this situation, therefore, were British exporters, who found themselves faced with difficulties in trying to sell more expensive British-made goods. It is, perhaps, an indication of Britain's estimate of the relative unimportance of the small East African market that British industries in general were reluctant to go to the trouble of producing cheaper goods in order to compete with their trade rivals in this area.[1]

New labour problems

The increase in plantation agriculture and in gold-mining in Tanganyika during the later 1930's placed a heavy demand upon the country's labour supply, and once again the question of working conditions became a matter of concern for the Government. The abolition of the Labour Department in 1931 had attracted the attention of the Permanent Mandates Commission, but the Tanganyika Government had given an assurance that the labourers would not suffer as a result of this action.[2] Now, however, some thousands of Africans were becoming involved in alluvial gold-mining in southern Tanganyika, often as employees of men with limited capital who were unable to offer any guarantee of adequate wages and reasonable working conditions. Many of these labourers came from Nyasaland, and the Government of that territory sent the Reverend W. P. Young to the Lupa goldfield to investigate conditions there. Young was far from satisfied by what he saw, and it was his report which first drew attention to the need for reform. The Permanent Mandates Commission took up the issue, urging the Tanganyika Government to intervene.[3] Special labour officers were posted in the goldfields, and in 1937 a committee was appointed to advise on the supply and welfare of

[1] Department of Overseas Trade, *Report on Economic and Commercial Conditions in British East Africa, 1936–37* (London, 1937), p. 3.

[2] Permanent Mandates Commission, *Minutes* of the 21st Session, Oct. 1931, p. 37; and of the 23rd Session, June 1933, pp. 62–63.

[3] Ibid., *Minutes* of the 25th Session, June 1934, p. 115; and of the 27th Session, June 1935, p. 145.

the labourers. As a result of the committee's recommendations a standing Labour Advisory Board was set up in 1938 under the chairmanship of the recently appointed Chief Inspector of Labour. In this instance, therefore, the existence of the mandate and the supervisory role of the Permanent Mandates Commission played a particularly important role in Tanganyika's affairs. It should be added, however, that it was the open-door policy upon which the mandate insisted which was partly responsible for the problems which the Tanganyika Government had to face in regard to the working conditions of the labourers. The mixture of nationalities to be found among the miners in the Lupa goldfield made it difficult to enforce uniform standards of employment, just as, for the same reason, it had not proved easy to obtain the co-operation of the sisal planters in establishing joint health services for the labourers on a number of plantations.[1]

Land use

The questionable influence of the open-door policy towards immigrants in Tanganyika was to be seen again in the wide variety of nationalities among the landholders in the Territory. In 1938 no less than sixteen nationalities were represented. Germans occupied 32·8 per cent. of the holdings as compared with 26 per cent. held by families of British origin. In actual area, however, the British occupied a greater amount of land, although the acreage held by Germans increased from 389,609 acres in 1930 to 476,351 acres in 1938. The more recently arrived Germans had for the most part obtained leases in the Southern Highlands, although there was evidence that they were also buying from Indians in other regions. Apart, however, from the particular significance of German political influence in Tanganyika, it was also open to question whether the open-door policy, under which land was allotted by auction to the highest bidder, was the ideal method of choosing European immigrants.[2] There were, too, some indications that among the German landholders some of the holdings were of a less than economic size. During the depression there had been a tendency to reduce

[1] C. Leubuscher, *Tanganyika Territory: a study of economic policy under mandate* (London, 1944), p. 69.

[2] For the development of land policy following the end of the first world war, see Chapter X, pp. 552–5, above, and Leubuscher, op. cit., pp. 30 sqq.

the size of holdings among all non-African settlers in Tanganyika. This had been part of a natural process whereby the earlier random allocations of land had been subjected to a more careful scrutiny so as to avoid wasting capital and energy. In certain instances, however, the reduction in size of the German holdings had gone beyond this normal economic adjustment and thus threatened to produce the sort of white settler with precarious prospects whom Byatt and Cameron had wisely striven to discourage.[1]

The Government, meanwhile, was anxious to promote a higher standard of land use by Africans. The fulfilment of these hopes was threatened by the customary system of land tenure among the African tribes. Individual tenure in the sense in which it was known in Britain was foreign to African ideas. The Government was consequently reluctant to press this system too strictly upon the people, lest in so doing they should undermine the tribal organization upon which the country's administrative system had been deliberately based. It was possible, however, to take advantage of cases where overcrowding produced a greater willingness to move to new areas. In regions where the overcrowding coincided with a relatively advanced level of agricultural techniques, the people concerned provided particularly suitable material for agricultural experiments. The first new settlements were started at Ukiriguru in 1933 and in Uzinza in 1935, both in the Lake Province, and in Kingolwira in the Eastern Province. The sites chosen were in the neighbourhood of experimental cotton farms, and the Empire Cotton Growing Corporation provided financial assistance for their development. Individual tenure formed the basis of the experiments and the object was to introduce mixed farming. In such a setting new agricultural methods, including systems of crop rotation to replace the traditional pattern of shifting cultivation, could be taught in order to ensure more profitable use of the land. The numbers involved in these experiments were small, however, and although the schemes met with an enthusiastic reception at first, they were not a permanent success.

The social services

A field of development in which the native authorities made

[1] Leubuscher, op. cit., pp. 33–38.

a useful contribution was in the provision of better medical facilities. The depression had imposed unfortunate restrictions upon the activities of the Medical Department at the very moment when the value of European medical treatment was beginning to be more widely appreciated. In these circumstances the establishment of a system of native authority dispensaries equipped with drugs and medical staff was of the greatest significance. Even during the depression this work had continued to expand, so that by 1934 nearly half a million patients were receiving treatment in the course of a year in 310 dispensaries scattered about the country. Four years later the number of patients had increased to over three-quarters of a million.[1] The importance of these activities was rendered proportionately greater by the fact that the energies of the Medical Department itself had to some extent to be concentrated on the control of the sleeping sickness epidemics which ravaged the Kahama District in the early 1930's and threatened the Liwale District in 1936.

The native authorities were less prominent in promoting education, although they were responsible for running a few schools financed by the Government. Throughout the 1930's education remained the responsibility of the missions and of the Central Government. A review of Tanganyika's educational system in 1934 showed the serious effects which the depression had had upon development. Moreover, it was seen that the policy which the Government had adopted after 1926 of providing slightly more advanced education in a number of central schools had proved unsatisfactory. The standard attained by African pupils in those schools was still not high enough to qualify them to compete for the more remunerative types of employment, so that the money would probably have been better spent in providing more generous opportunities for elementary education. At the same time the seven industrial schools opened by the Government, together with the fifteen assisted mission schools, were found to have been supplying more boys with industrial training than were needed by the country's undeveloped economic system. As a result of this review there was a marked reaction against central and in-

[1] J. P. Moffett (ed.) *Handbook of Tanganyika*, revised edn. (Dar es Salaam. 1958). pp. 111 and 116.

dustrial schools, a reaction which later in the 1930's was proved
to have gone too far when a number of government departments
found it necessary to provide their own schools in order to
ensure an adequate supply of recruits for clerical and artisans'
appointments. Furthermore, with an eye to providing still more
advanced opportunities of training for Tanganyika's Africans,
the Governor agreed in 1938 to contribute £100,000 to the
development of Makerere College in Uganda, which provided
training for some of the lower qualifications in the professional
field.

Better times did at last appear to lie ahead. In 1936 Tanganyika's ordinary revenue exceeded £2 million for the first time
and in 1937 it increased still further. There was a slight reduction in the following year owing to the fall in the prices paid for
Tanganyika's produce and in particular for sisal, and for the
first time since 1933 expenditure was slightly in excess of
revenue. In itself this was not a serious set-back, and in December 1937 a Central Development Committee had been established in order to plan a large-scale development programme
with a view to demonstrating the country's confidence in its
own future. But the committee's deliberations were interrupted
by the outbreak of war in September 1939.

The second world war

In the second world war Tanganyika was not a battlefield as
it had been twenty-five years earlier. Nevertheless, the serious-
ness of the world situation impressed upon the people the need
to investigate every means whereby Tanganyika could contribute to the Imperial war effort. Tanganyika's revenue, exclusive
of income from the railway and from loans, amounted in the
whole of the inter-war period to no more than £33 million, so
that there was little possibility of a large sum of money being
available as a direct contribution to the campaign. Indeed, the
extent of the developments which had taken place in Tanganyika between the wars was remarkable on the basis of such
a restricted income. Yet before the end of 1940 willing contributions amounting to £200,000 had been made to the British
Government from Tanganyika's reserve funds, which were
exhausted in the process.[1] During 1941, also, the Tanganyika

---

[1] Leg. Co. *Debates*, Fifteenth Session, 1940–1, pt. i, p. 4.

Government relieved the United Kingdom Government of the responsibility for maintaining the enemy aliens interned in the Territory. Even the news, received in February 1940, that a greatly increased colonial development fund had been created, aroused, along with feelings of gratitude, a certain amount of concern among the British inhabitants lest a gesture of that sort, coming at a time of extreme gravity, might lead to some weakening of the all-out effort which the country was prepared to make.[1]

Tanganyika's financial position in the latter part of 1939 was indeed not so strong that the Government could look forward unconcernedly to the demands which a Commonwealth war economy would involve. It was clearly necessary to make a diligent search for new sources of revenue. Two years earlier, in 1937, the Permanent Mandates Commission had suggested that the possibility of introducing an income tax might be considered, but once again the proposal had been rejected in Tanganyika, although it was accepted in Kenya. Faced with the demands of war, however, the attitude of the critics changed. In 1940 a tax was introduced on all incomes over £350 per annum, and in 1941 the lower limit of taxable incomes was reduced to £200 a year.

By these and other means the country's revenue was undoubtedly increased, but the fact that it doubled between 1939 and 1945 was due mainly to the rapid rise in prices of primary products. This was not accompanied by any expansion in the country's social services except in the improvement of communications. For it was obvious that a road and rail system which had been barely adequate in peace-time conditions was still less suited to the exigencies of war, when the rapid movement of troops and supplies became a matter of vital importance. The strain imposed upon Tanganyika's transport system soon demonstrated where the weaknesses lay, and improvements had to be made without too closely counting the cost. By contrast, educational developments had to be curtailed, while the country's medical services were increasingly concentrated upon military objectives. Tanganyika's main contribution to the war thus lay in supplying manpower and raw materials and, perhaps above all, in striving for self-sufficiency so as to avoid

[1] *Tanganyika Standard*, 7 June 1940.

making demands upon the goods and transport system of other
member states of the Commonwealth.

The large number of enemy aliens in Tanganyika at the outbreak of war created surprisingly few difficulties for the
Government. In 1939 there were 3,205 Germans in the territory, including 1,858 males, as compared with 4,054 British
residents of whom 2,440 were males. But the months between
Munich and the declaration of war had enabled Tanganyika
to make preparations, and the internment of enemy aliens went
forward without incident. Nevertheless, the ease with which
this programme was put into effect was probably due less to the
efficiency of the Government's preparations than to the fact
that the local German leaders, confident of an early victory for
the Fatherland, had instructed the German settlers not to resist
capture. Herr Ernst Troost, the Führer of the Tanganyika Nazi
bund, was on his way to Moshi by car when he was halted by a
picket outside the township and taken into custody expressing
surprise that war had already been declared. Some of his
lieutenants, including Dr. Mergner and Herr Kageler, leader
of the Tanganyika Hitler Youth, were also arrested.[1]

The question of how best to administer the German estates
then became a matter of immediate importance, since their
produce was vital to the country's economy. When war had first
threatened, the German planters had approached the Government with the proposal that in the event of the German population being interned one man should be left in charge of each
estate to maintain productivity. This suggestion was not
accepted, and shortly after the outbreak of war a Custodian of
Enemy Property was appointed. Under his direction the more
scattered German holdings were placed under the control of
neighbouring British farmers, who acted as managing agents.
In areas where the Germans had been settled in considerable
numbers, and particularly in the Mbulu District of the
Northern Province, members of the Custodian's staff were
appointed as group managers, while in the Southern Highlands
Province the Brooke Bond Tea Company was appointed
managing agent of the former German tea estates. In this
manner continuity was maintained.

Italy's tentative invasion of northern Kenya appeared for a

---

[1] *Tanganyika Standard*, 8 Sept. 1939.

few brief months to threaten the security of East Africa, but a firm rejoinder by a relatively small force of troops soon put an end to Italian dreams of African conquest. Tanganyika soldiers of the King's African Rifles took part in the campaign in Somaliland and Ethiopia which simultaneously destroyed the Italian empire in East Africa and brought to an end the fighting in the East African theatre. The entry of Japan into the war soon required the East African forces to turn their front to face eastward, while the uncertainty regarding the attitude of the Vichy French in Madagascar involved a further campaign in that island in 1942, in which Tanganyika troops again played their part.[1] In June 1943 they also formed part of the 11th (East African) Division which sailed for Ceylon in preparation for the campaign in Burma. This was the first occasion on which the King's African Rifles had been engaged in active operations outside the African continent and the islands around its shores.

Tanganyika's attempt to remain self-supporting as far as possible did not easily meet with success. A number of unfavourable seasons, coupled with the absence of so many able-bodied men on military duties, made it necessary to import maize, one of the country's main food crops, in 1941, 1942, 1944, and 1945. In an attempt to provide even a partial solution to this predicament, wheat was grown in the Northern Province from 1942 to 1945. Apart from any other issues which might have been involved, the resulting reduction in the demand on shipping for imported wheat was a most significant contribution to the war effort.

The disappearance of alternative sources of raw materials also had its effect upon the character of Tanganyika's agricultural programme. Rubber, which had ceased to be of importance among the products of the territory even before the first world war, became a vital crop when Malaya fell into Japanese hands. Every possible source of latex was exploited, so that, like wheat, rubber made its contribution both to Tanganyika's economy and to the prosecution of the war from 1942 to 1945. The Japanese successes in the middle period of the war also affected the sisal industry. Restrictions upon shipping in the opening years of the struggle had made it impossible to export all the sisal which Tanganyika could produce. But when the

[1] See H. Moyse-Bartlett, *The King's African Rifles* (Aldershot, 1956), ch. 23.

Japanese victories in the Pacific deprived the western powers of other sources of sisal, Tanganyika's crop immediately became of vital importance. Cotton, too, was in heavy demand, but since it was more easily affected by unfavourable weather than the more hardy sisal and because as a peasant-grown crop it suffered more acutely from the manpower shortage, Tanganyika's output actually decreased during the war. Rice, also, almost ceased to be exported, except to Zanzibar, but since it was valuable as a food crop in Tanganyika, the loss in revenue was made up in other ways. Coffee, although basically an export crop, remained at the same level of output throughout the war, mainly because it did not have a high priority in the world market. Yet the rise in prices more than compensated the growers for the changes which had occurred in the country's economic pattern. The value of coffee to the producers doubled during the war period, while sisal fetched £5½ million in 1945 compared with £1½ million in 1940 without any increase in output.

The demand for food crops created its own repercussions. Before the war, when the majority of the people of Tanganyika produced their own food, and when the cost of transporting food from one part of the territory to another would have been so high as to render the whole process uneconomic, there had been no reason to produce more foodstuffs than were actually needed for local consumption in any particular area. Now, however, when food was short in some regions and prices were stabilized so as to ensure an adequate food supply throughout the Territory, improved communications encouraged growers in some of the more remote areas to produce more food than they themselves required. Gold, too, acquired a new importance until the introduction of lease–lend reduced the demand for it as a medium of exchange. In 1940 and again in 1941 the value of Tanganyika's gold production exceeded £1 million. After that date the interest in gold-mining declined, and by the end of the war the annual output was valued at considerably less than half a million pounds. In the meantime the discovery of diamonds by Dr. Williamson near Shinyanga resulted in a striking increase in the value of Tanganyika's output, from £12,600 in 1940 to £638,383 in 1945.

Throughout the war the morale of the African population

remained high in spite of the preoccupation of the administrative officers with a wide variety of tasks; in spite, too, of problems over food supplies and the inevitable reduction in social services. Immediately before the war, German miners in the Lupa goldfield had circulated rumours to the effect that on the outbreak of hostilities the British would seize property owned by Africans. This aroused some fear among the labourers, and when war was declared about half of the labour force, which numbered some 20,000, hurried back to their homes to protect their possessions. Apart from this isolated occurrence there were no other signs of unrest.

None the less, the war did threaten to affect adversely the development of Tanganyika's system of native administration. The encouragement given by the Government to the native authorities to accept increasing responsibility had meant that in many cases the members of the local authorities had acquired a considerable status among the people under their control. This was particularly noticeable where the native authorities had been individual chiefs, since they had had frequent and direct contact with European administrative officers, with the result that their importance in the eyes of their own people had been greatly enhanced, while they themselves had broadened their outlook upon a variety of subjects. Their relative wealth had also ensured greater opportunities for their dependants, more particularly in the field of education and in obtaining remunerative employment.

Any excesses which might have resulted from this system would in former days have been controlled by the traditional influence wielded over the chiefs by recognized advisers. In this way in the past the division between chiefs and people had not become too pronounced. Under war-time conditions the control exercised over the chief by the elders of a tribe became less effective. Administrative officers demanding efficiency tended to look for results from the native authorities and could spare little time to consider the constitutional or social implications of the demands they made upon the chiefs. This change should not be over-emphasized, however. Its importance lay in the fact that an existing trend was being encouraged by special conditions. But plans were already being made to curb undesirable developments of this sort. Even before the end of hostilities the

Y

central Government was beginning to think of a post-war period when, having gained experience overseas and in the course of military service, large numbers of young men would be demanding to play a greater part in the administration of local affairs. This would automatically lead to a wider dissemination of responsibility, and it was decided that it would be necessary to introduce a number of reforms in the field of local government to widen the basis of authority. Somewhat surprisingly, however, the Government's prognostication was not fulfilled, and it was almost ten years before younger Africans began to take an interest in controlling the affairs of their own country.

In 1944 the progress of the war had begun to demonstrate the need for post-war planning in a variety of other fields. The feeling almost akin to a sense of blasphemy which had been kindled by suggestions for social development in 1940 was now replaced by the recognition that considerable reconstruction would be needed with the return of peace. The task of planning for this new era was approached with a certain degree of awe as well as of determination. Little could be guessed about Tanganyika's financial position at the end of the war. It was seen that with very little increase in production the value of the country's exports and consequently of its revenue had multiplied several times over during the war years. But it was impossible to assess how peace would affect this situation. Nevertheless, valuable exploratory work was carried out by the Central Development Committee, whose work had previously been interrupted by the outbreak of war. While it was thought that the rehabilitation in civilian life of the men serving in the armed forces would present the first problem of any magnitude, it was recognized that a programme for the overall economic development of the territory was even more fundamental. The concern for the attitude of the ex-soldiers indeed proved to have been unnecessarily exaggerated, but the wisdom of planning for economic reconstruction was soon to be recognized. At the end of 1944 a memorandum was published entitled *An Outline of Post-war Development Proposals*. This embodied a programme which would provide the framework within which future developments could be set on foot while leaving the detailed plans to be formulated when the war came to an end.

One field in which the pattern of post-war development was very largely determined by war-time events was that of co-operation between the three East African territories. The need for a co-ordinated plan of defence and for joint action in providing manpower and foodstuffs had become self-evident even before the end of 1939. Closer co-operation was then no longer a question of communal interests or commercial crystal-gazing but of dire necessity. At a meeting of the Governors' Conference in Nairobi on 1 August 1940, it was decided to set up an East African Economic Council so that the three territories could be handled as a unit in so far as economic and commercial matters were concerned. The chairman of the council was to be Sir Philip Mitchell, deputy chairman of the Governors' Conference, a post created only a short time before in recognition of the need for continuity in the direction of the joint action of the three territories. Sir Philip Mitchell, a former Governor of Uganda, was firmly wedded to the view that the closest possible co-operation between the East African territories was necessary in war-time conditions, and was even prepared to counter any opposition from the Governor of Tanganyika, Sir Mark Young,[1] with the reply that *inter arma silent leges*.[2] Although this co-operation was soon said by Uganda to be working far too much in the interests of Kenya, there is little doubt that it was necessary. The new situation was recognized by the Colonial Office after the war in a White Paper on Inter-Territorial Organization in East Africa, in which it was stated that the loose arrangement of conferences of governors was no longer adequate to deal with the increasingly complicated nature of the association between the three territories.[3]

What distinguished Tanganyika from Uganda or, indeed, from Kenya in the war years was that there was no urgent pressure for political or administrative reform from the African population. The movement for reform came in fact from the Government alone, which, in the dawn of the trusteeship era,

---

[1] Sir Mark Aitchison Young, K.C.M.G., formerly Governor of Barbados, became Governor of Tanganyika on 8 July 1938 in succession to Sir Harold MacMichael, who left the country on 25 Jan. 1938. Young held office until 1941 and was succeeded in the following year by Sir Wilfred Edward Francis Jackson, G.C.M.G., who continued as Governor until 1945.

[2] P. E. Mitchell, *African Afterthoughts* (London, 1954), p. 188.

[3] *Inter-Territorial Organisation in East Africa*, Col. no. 191 (1945).

was thinking of its responsibilities towards the African population rather than reacting to African pressure. Tanganyika, therefore, emerged from the war not as Uganda did, with her feet already marching towards the excitement of a new era, but rather with shoulders braced to meet the task of reconstruction as they had been after the first world war and after the depression of the early 1930's.

XII

TANGANYIKA:
CHANGES IN AFRICAN LIFE
1918–45

MARGARET L. BATES

At the end of the first world war Tanganyika was in a disrupted and chaotic state. Much of the Territory had been fought over; labour for porterage or food for the armies had been commandeered from most tribes; others had dispersed to avoid the fighting. British and German forces had executed or deported some of the leading chiefs. In 1918 the great influenza epidemic reached Tanganyika, and the following year the Territory suffered its worst recorded famine. In the African phrase, 'when elephants fight, it is the grass which is trampled'.

The effects of German occupation had been felt unevenly throughout the Territory. In the west, effective European control was hardly ten years old. African tribes had reached different stages in their contact with western civilization, but they had all felt its tremendous fascination and force. Isolated villages were coming more into touch with the habits and thoughts of others. The process of detribalization, that ambiguous term which is nevertheless indispensable, had begun.

The physical and economic environment

In 1918 the trade and communications of the Territory were still heavily dependent on head porterage despite the existence of two German-built railways. In the 1920's these were extended and a skeletal road system worked out; Africans themselves undertook the building of local roads and paths. The requisitioning of labour for porterage, permitted under mandate provisions only for government purposes, was used mostly for district touring, and progressively declined, so that by 1938 it was seldom possible to find Africans able or willing to make more than local foot *safaris*.[1] The road system remained rudimentary, but it made the country-side more accessible than ever before. Migrant labour routes followed the new dirt roads, railway passenger returns indicated a much enlarged patronage, and buses and lorries, as yet far too expensive for the ordinary African to own, became familiar in the settlements and on the main roads.

Improved communications made it possible to cope more successfully with the outstanding problem of the Territory: food supply. Famine was a recurring spectre, especially in the drought-ridden Central Province and in areas where tsetse encroachment made necessary concentration of settlement. After 1925, when chiefs' tribute in kind was commuted, famine relief had first call on the finances of the newly established native treasuries, while communal labour on roads, on water-supplies, and on tsetse-clearance measures was encouraged by the Administration. Government powers to prohibit export of local foodstuffs and to enforce cultivation of famine-resistant crops were still used in most areas in 1945. A growing knowledge indicated how small a proportion of the land really had adequate rainfall, while in Southern and Western Provinces the map showed only a vast expanse of tsetse bush, with a few small villages striving to keep their land clear. In 1936 it was estimated that 62 per cent. of the land was uninhabited. In turn, increasing population pressure on the good land brought problems. In Uchagga there were probably 600 people to the square mile by 1945. The population of the Territory increased from perhaps 4 million inhabitants in 1921 to more than 7 million in 1948.[2]

Better communications and administrative encouragement to peasant agriculture produced export crops of coffee, cotton, tobacco, rice, hides and skins, and beeswax, which increased slowly but fairly steadily. Coffee was worth £342,990 in 1936,

---

[1] Cf. reports to the International Labour Organization after the application of the International Convention on Forced Labour in 1931; M. Fortie, *Black and Beautiful* (London, 1938).

[2] C. Gillman, 'A population map of Tanganyika Territory', in *Annual Report . . . on Tanganyika for 1935*, Col. no. 113 (1936); Lord Hailey, *Native Administration in the British African Territories*, i (London, 1950), 279. See also maps on rainfall reliability and tsetse infestation in *Report of the East Africa Royal Commission, 1953–1955*, Cmd. 9475 (1955).

£896,301 in 1945. After 1933 the formation of co-operative societies helped with the two major production problems of finance and standards of quality, and by 1947 fifty-five African marketing societies were in existence. This development, however, was highly localized, and occurred in those areas most favoured by nature. A subsistence economy producing barely enough in the good years, and not enough in the bad, would be a much more characteristic picture of Tanganyika in the inter-war period. Eighty-two per cent. of the land cultivated was devoted to crops consumed locally. In Usukuma and Ugogo, cattle continued to be the indication of wealth, and overgrazing and soil erosion problems were serious. In 1944 parts of Shinyanga District, opened to settlement only eight years previously, were already grazed out.[1] Attempts to impose soil conservation and cultivation measures, or to introduce stock dipping or cattle culling, were almost universally unpopular and constituted one of the few sources of friction between Africans and the British Administration.

In many areas the new monetary economy was not firmly established until the 1940's. Currency changes from rupees to shillings in the 1920's, and the depression of the 1930's, seriously deterred its spread. Hut and poll-tax could still be paid in labour in 1945. And while there is no contemporary statistical material which allows us to be very accurate, a later survey would suggest that in 1945 more than 50 per cent. of the national income was still generated by the subsistence, rather than the monetary, economy.[2]

Standards of living

By 1945 some 340,000 Africans were in regular employment; a large percentage of these were migrant labourers on the sisal estates of Tanga, the mixed farms of the Northern Province, and the Lupa goldfields in the south.[3] On the whole the number

---

[1] *Report of the Commissioner for Co-operative Development* (Dar es Salaam, mimeo, 1947); *Annual Report on Tanganyika, 1947*, p. 87; Annual Reports of the Provincial Commissioners, 1944, p. 33.

[2] A. T. Peacock and D. G. M. Dosser, *The National Income of Tanganyika, 1952–54*, Colonial Research Publication no. 26 (London, 1958).

[3] *Annual Report on Tanganyika, 1947*, appendix x. A small number of Africans from the southern districts also went to work in Northern Rhodesia and the Union of South Africa.

of African men absent from their homes never reached in
Tanganyika the high level it did in Nyasaland or the Rhodesias,
although the figure of 46 per cent. was actually recorded in
Njombe in 1944.[1] The Chagga no longer went out to work,
having discovered in the 1920's the profits of coffee cultivation,
and this came to be true also of the Haya. Employers depended
on the Sukuma, Nyamwezi, Ha, and the southern tribes,
especially Ngoni, Nyakyusa, and the Mawia of Portuguese East
Africa; government policy encouraged migration only from
those areas where production of export crops was not feasible.
Tanganyika in 1926 was the first British African dependency
to establish a Labour Department, only to abolish it for
budgetary reasons during the depression. Reports from the Lupa
and some of the sisal estates showed extremely low standards
of housing, nutrition, and sanitation. It was a commentary on
rural conditions that these areas continued to attract labour
and, in the depression, were offered more than they could use.[2]

African standards of living improved very gradually. Stone
or cement court-houses and schools were built at native administration headquarters, while inland Africans imitated coastal
Arabs or Swahili and constructed rectangular houses of
latticed poles covered with mud, with windows and sometimes
more than one room, to replace the rondavel; village pride
might be seen in the spread of intricate patterns of roof thatch-
ing, and the first attempts at village sanitation. The flat-roofed,
low *tembe*, however, continued to be characteristic of Ugogo,
and the skin-covered hut of Masailand. More than 1,300,000
Africans attended government hospitals in 1944 as they became
increasingly popular especially for maternity cases, yet witch-
doctors probably had a comparable practice. The first trained
African doctor entered government service in 1940, but the
major diseases of malaria, yaws, leprosy, and blindness were
hardly touched; the incidence of venereal disease probably

---

[1] This figure occurred during the re-imposition of forced labour during the
second world war. Conscription in the area was stopped. Report of the Labour
Department, 1944, p. 13.

[2] Sessional Paper 2 of 1926; G. St. J. Orde-Browne, *Labour in Tanganyika
Territory*, Col. no. 19 (1926); *Report of the Committee Appointed to Consider and Advise
on Questions Relating to the Supply and Welfare of Native Labour in the Tanganyika
Territory* (Dar es Salaam, 1938); G. St. J. Orde-Browne, *Labour Conditions in East
Africa*, Col. no. 193 (1946).

increased with social mobility; and malnutrition affected three-quarters of the population. In Ufipa in 1940 one out of three men was rejected as medically unfit for military or labour service, in Uha nine out of ten.[1]

African diet was still built upon the local staples of millet, maize, rice, bananas, or sorghum. Salt had always been traded for; the Iramba still made a semi-annual salt safari. Consumption of meat and milk increased in wealthy areas, but sugar and tea remained a luxury for most rural Africans. A study several years after the second world war noted that apart from textiles the 'average' family in Tanganyika consumed very few goods not of African manufacture; to the foods above might be added matches, lamp and body oil, soap, possibly metal pans and dishes. An important purchase was usually an imported hoe (some 443,000 reached the Territory in 1945), but many were still content with the products of the Fipa smith or even the wooden digging stick. Shorts and white shirts became increasingly the desired uniform for men, and the coastal *kanga* replaced simple calico for women. Yet the second world war lowered rural standards of dress, and in Unyakyusa, Ufipa, and Uha, bark-cloth or skins remained normal articles of wear.[2] Canvas shoes were popular on the coast, but inland the sandal made from an old automobile tyre was more often found. European products were put to ingenious second-hand usage, from the 4-gallon kerosene tin which became an oven, to the tops from soda-water bottles which were used as ear-stretchers.

By 1945 the most notable point about African consumption habits was their variety, due now as much to differences of income as to tribal affiliation. As Africans moved out of the subsistence economy to become teachers, or native administration employees, or to sell export crops, a pattern of increasing consumption might be discerned: a better house, wooden furniture, a bicycle, some European food or beer, more cattle, another wife. African petty traders were numerous, though the rate of failure was high. Until 1937, indeed, Africans had to obtain the permission of the district officer to buy on credit

---

[1] Report of the Medical Department, 1944; Annual Reports of the Provincial Commissioners, 1940, p. 74.
[2] F. C. Wright, *African Consumers in Nyasaland and Tanganyika*, Colonial Research Publication no. 17 (London, 1955); M. Wilson, *Good Company* (Oxford, 1951).

terms. Low cash income precluded much capital expenditure. In the Southern Highlands Province in 1943 average annual income per taxpayer was estimated at 51 sh.[1] On the sources of income a survey in Kahama district in 1938 yielded some interesting and probably typical results. Of 16,663 taxpayers in the district that year, 4,618 had earned money to pay tax by sale of ground-nuts, rice, tobacco, root crops, or millet for beer; 3,349 through collection of honey and beeswax; 1,257 through government or native administration employment; 2,411 by the sale of livestock; 4,405 through other work including labour in local mines or on coastal plantations; 506 were artisans, mainly blacksmiths, and 117 had borrowed money.[2]

Many inter-African transactions were now, however, conducted in cash rather than in barter or any form of trade goods. Changing habits and prices could often be seen most vividly through changes in bridewealth, which everywhere increased and came to be expressed almost exclusively in cash and in cattle, while the bride-service of the matrilocal tribes virtually disappeared.

Tribal law and institutions

One of the major results of the introduction of the British administration was a renewed interest in the maintenance of tribal society and government. Since tribes were no longer independent, however, this was modified tribal authority, and changes in structure soon occurred. In most areas the powers of the chief tended to increase, while traditional checks on his power declined; the Bena 'constitutional opposition' was for years unknown to the district administration, and the tribal councillors of Sukumaland, trying to use traditional powers to depose an unpopular chief, found themselves accused of subversion. In Makonde and Usukuma the traditional matrilineal succession became patrilineal when inheritance of the chiefdom was involved. The *laibon* of the Masai and the clan elders of the Gogo, Makua, and Zaramo acquired greater power than in the past, but were often unable to carry out their new responsibilities. Law and order were well maintained; there was

[1] Annual Reports of the Provincial Commissioners, 1943, p. 70.
[2] Ibid., 1938, p. 93.

apparently little difficulty in making the transition from a German to a British régime.[1]

African courts acquired a recognized place in the hierarchy of government, although they now administered far more than native law and custom. Witchcraft cases, removed from their jurisdiction, were often settled locally and unofficially, while an increasing proportion of cases came to deal with offences against territorial legislation—soil conservation measures, hut and poll-tax prosecutions, violations of the native liquor ordinance. There is more evidence of change in court procedure, such as handling of witnesses and keeping records, than of change in African law itself, for the law was unwritten and the courts unbound by precedent. The native courts and the High Court system were after 1929 entirely separate,[2] and there was little attempt to bring British and African law into harmony; it was possible for an African to be prosecuted in one court for carrying out an action required of him by another. The courts, in fact, acted as courts of equity; the major problem for them, as for their predecessors, seems to have been enforcement of judgements. Generally they were regarded as satisfactory and as ensuring justice, while in Bukoba and Tukuyu litigation became a popular hobby, and a substantial proportion of family income might well go to appeal a case from court to court.[3]

The concept of tribe itself seemed in fact to be undergoing redefinition. The census of 1921 listed 72 tribes, that of 1948 120. In the south the Ndendeuli and Matengo, previously dominated by the warrior Ngoni, reasserted their separate identities, while elsewhere the Chagga began to absorb the Kahe, and the Nyakyusa several small tribes living on their boundaries. In the Rufiji Valley and along the coast tribal origins were difficult to establish and seemed frequently to be

---

[1] A. T. and G. M. Culwick, 'What the Wabena think of Indirect Rule', *Journal of the African Society*, xxxvi. 143 (1937), 176–93; H. Cory, *The Indigenous Political System of the Sukuma and Proposals for Political Reform*, East African Studies, no. 2 (Nairobi, 1954); H. Fosbrooke, *A Sociological Survey of the Masai of Tanganyika Territory* (Dar es Salaam, typescript, 1938); Annual Reports of the Provincial Commissioners; District Books for Lindi, Tunduru, Newala, Kisarawe, and Dodoma.

[2] See Chapter X, pp. 573–4 above.

[3] M. Wilson, op. cit.; R. E. S. Tanner, 'The sorcerer in Northern Sukumaland, Tanganyika', *Southwestern Journal of Anthropology*, xii. (1956) 437–43; Annual Reports of the Provincial Commissioners; J. P. Moffett, 'Native courts in Tanganyika', *Journal of African Administration*, iv. 1 (1952), 17–25.

of less importance than economic affinities or other new relationships. In Tanga District it was possible to speak of a process of
re-tribalization, as emigrant labourers from Unyamwezi or Uha
settled among the coastal people and adopted their way of life.[1]
In many rural areas families in search of better land and water
moved into neighbouring districts. Such penetration was
accepted without friction where sufficient land existed, and
native administrations had little trouble in enforcing their
authority over 'stranger' Africans.

Up-country, small villages and trading centres began to
appear around the *bomas* and on the new travel routes. A mixed
population emerged as African teachers were shifted from
school to school or literate clerks were imported to run the
native treasury of a backward tribe. It was not unusual, in
townships like Iringa or Kilosa, to find Africans from all over
Tanganyika and from Kenya and Nyasaland as well. Africans
found it possible to step outside their tribal society, and new
customs and laws were developed. The levels of wages, sanitation, and education were higher than in the surrounding
country-side, and resident Europeans and Asians were the
models for new ideas and standards. Of the real problems of
urban life, however, Tanganyika was still largely unconscious.
Dar es Salaam, with a population of 67,000 in 1945, had not
yet achieved municipal government, but unlike many other
African cities it imposed no stringent pass laws, and it
permitted indigenous African housing in many areas. Tabora,
the largest town in Arab and German days, declined when the
railways replaced the caravan route, and other towns grew
slowly.[2] In 1945 the first African welfare centres were organized.
Town administration, however, had little or no connexion
with the native administration, and Tanganyika remained overwhelmingly rural both in population and in outlook.

[1] P. H. Gulliver, 'A history of the Songea Ngoni', *Tanganyika Notes and Records*,
xli (1955), 16–30; M. Wilson, *The Peoples of the Nyasa-Tanganyika Corridor* (Cape
Town, 1958); E. C. Baker, *Report on Economic and Social Conditions in the Tanga
Province* (Dar es Salaam, 1934); M. J. B. Molohan, *Detribalization* (Dar es Salaam,
1957).

[2] The 1945 figure for Dar es Salaam is an estimate. Annual Reports of the
Provincial Commissioners, 1945, p. 31. Figures for the larger towns were as follows
in 1948: Dar es Salaam, 69,227; Tanga, 20,619; Mwanza, 11,296; Tabora,
12,768; Dodoma, 9,414; Lindi, 8,577; Morogoro, 8,173; Moshi, 8,048.

Manners and mores

Changes in religion are particularly hard to document, but it is probable that Islam was increasing its following more rapidly than Christianity. This occurred generally without formal proselytization, although an Ahmadiyya mission existed in Tabora. The acceptance of Islam was regarded as a sign of progress, status, and prestige; its outward manifestations were adoption of a Muslim name and the wearing of the *kanzu*. A tendency to refer to oneself as 'Swahili' rather than using a tribal name might also be characteristic of the Muslim convert, although he probably did not cut himself away from communal tribal values as markedly as did the Christian. There are instances of the conversion of entire tribes to Islam; that of the Asu (Pare) was reported in 1932. Tribal law, especially on questions of personal status, was changed to bring it into accord with the *sharia*, although the extent to which Muslim law has been applied to inheritance of land is in doubt. Muslim law was regarded as the variant and customary law as the norm, but the use of Muslims as judges, and the Government's classification of Muslim as a type of native law, allowed much individual variation. By territorial law Swahili were held to be Muslim unless proved otherwise; for other groups the opposite still prevailed. The change from pagan to Muslim was a gradual one, and beliefs and ways of living did not alter quickly or radically; the *liwali* of Dar es Salaam stated that he did not expect strict compliance with all the rules of the *sharia* from converts or even first-generation Muslims. There is little evidence that Islam discouraged witchcraft practices, or that many tribal ceremonies disappeared, even where Ramadhan and Id-el-Fitr, for instance, were observed by a whole community. Most of our information on the influence and spread of Islam, however, is fragmentary, and further investigation is needed.[1]

Membership in the Christian churches increased greatly, but the effects of Christianity were often localized; areas such as Songea or Bukoba or Moshi reported a high percentage of converts, but adjoining districts would be virtually untouched. Wide variation in belief among the missions in Tanganyika

[1] J. N. D. Anderson, *Islamic Law in Africa*, Colonial Research Publication no. 16 (1954); L. Harries, *Islam in East Africa* (London, 1954); D. J. Richter, *Tanganyika and its Future* (London, 1934); Molohan, *Detribalization*.

may perhaps account for the fact that no important indigenous African churches were established. Minor cults were reported occasionally; none of them reached the importance of Watch Tower in Rhodesia or the *Dini ya Yesu Kristo* in Kenya. There were, however, interesting modifications within the missionary churches themselves. The Moravians in Tukuyu worked out a special marriage service for African Christians, and the Universities Mission in Masasi accepted, in modified form, tribal circumcision rites. Africans began to contribute increasingly to church financing, and on Kilimanjaro a movement for African control of the church appeared, but the number of African ministers remained very small.

Pre-eminent missionary influence came in matters other than doctrine. Around mission stations, villages appeared to be neater and houses more carefully built. In Usambara, Ubena, and Unyamwezi, continued development of Christian villages changed patterns of tribal administration and clan structure. Lutheran missionaries introduced a new education for marriage among Zaramo women, and Roman Catholics formed African novitiates to combat declining moral standards among Haya women. Mission hospitals and schools played a major role.[1]

Many of these were bush schools, minor evangelistic centres, but they provided the only education available for most African children, and ensured that much of the new generation was exposed to Christian doctrine, while the number of educated Muslims remained disproportionately small. In 1925 the Tanganyika Government began a programme of building its own schools and aiding mission ones which reached a certain standard of performance, but financial difficulties kept the programme to a minimum. In 1945 only 7·5 per cent. of Tanganyika's children attended school. Few of them got beyond standard IV, which promised bare literacy, and no school in the Territory could yet prepare students for the Makerere entrance examinations. On the other hand, the local school had become a fixture in many villages, and the attainment of literacy a widespread ambition. Among the Chagga, schools

[1] R. Oliver, *The Missionary Factor in East Africa* (London, 1952); Richter, op. cit.; G. A. Chambers, *Tanganyika's New Day* (London, 1931); B. Sundkler, 'Marriage problems in the Church in Tanganyika', *International Review of Missions*, xxxiv. 135 (1945), 253–66; G. M. Culwick, 'New ways for old in the treatment of adolescent African girls', *Africa*, xii. 4 (1939), 425–32.

could not be built quickly enough, though their next-door neighbours, the Masai, still refused to send their sons. What should be taught always created a controversy, and the schools were accused of being too European. Tabora school particularly tried to educate the sons of chiefs, while Malangali planned its organization and curriculum on African lines. Traditional tribal schools generally disappeared, although there is at least one instance, in Ubena, of an attempt at resuscitation. It is worth remarking that by 1945 writing paper and pencils were part of the stock in trade of every small trader, and that the Education Department's monthly paper, *Mambo Leo*, had a circulation of 25,000.[1]

Despite a particular lag in women's education (no Tanganyika African woman graduated from a university until 1956) the position of the African woman was changing. Where modern techniques and perennial crops were introduced her agricultural role became less important; her legal position improved in the courts; European influence tended to change ideas about her marital status and her personal importance. Schools and mission work provided some choice besides *shamba* cultivation, although it is probable that the alternative of prostitution also became more common.

One earlier social reform had by 1945 been almost forgotten. Except on the island of Mafia, the abolition of the status of slavery in 1922 had been accepted without repercussion. On Mafia coco-nut plantation owners could no longer obtain labour, and economic life stagnated.

Emerging patterns

Many of the changes chronicled above were not startlingly new. The process of change had begun much earlier, as a reading of Chapter IV indicates, and it had simply been continued and intensified during the inter-war period. By 1945 it was possible to discern some emergent patterns.

The first of these might be called detribalization and its variants. Many persons lived away from their own tribal areas, and census figures showed this to be an increasing movement. Some of these Africans had entirely lost contact with their

---

[1] W. B. Mumford, 'Malangali school', *Africa*, iii. 3 (1930), 265–90; Report of the Department of Education, 1936, 1937; *A Ten-year Development and Welfare Plan for Tanganyika Territory* (Dar es Salaam, 1946).

families and homes; some had become pseudo-Europeans. Larger numbers retained their tribal identity while abandoning individual customs which they regarded as outmoded. In the towns, tribal associations appeared, to act as combined bene-volent societies and liaison groups with the home districts. Tribal nationalism or particularism appeared in Uchagga and Usambara, urging tribal reform and more democratic institu-tions, but fiercely protective of the tribe itself.[1]

The possibilities of re-tribalization have been referred to, and in the 1940's a trans-tribal organization also emerged. The African Association, formed in 1930 mainly to safeguard the interests of African civil servants, moved into the political sphere in Bukoba as early as 1937, more positively in Pare in 1942 and 1944. Although it was yet premature to speak of a feeling of nationality, the association brought together many of the more forward-looking elements in African life, and they began to think beyond tribal boundaries. Members not infrequently had been together at Tabora school or Makerere College, and they shared a common language. Swahili, encouraged by Govern-ment as a territorial language for administrative and educa-tional purposes, provided a basis for inter-tribal communication. By 1945 it is probable that almost every male African in Tanganyika understood at least some Swahili, Masailand being, as so often, the exception to the rule.

If the average African did not yet think of himself as a Tanganyikan, he did think of himself as an African in contrast to the Europeans, Asians, and Arabs who also inhabited the country. This feeling of Africanism manifested itself in one major sphere—concern for the land. As population increased and settled cultivation became the rule, sensitivity about control of land increased markedly. The Chagga nearly rioted in 1933 over a suggestion that certain European species of trees be planted, believing that this might give Europeans rights in the land involved; in the 1940's alienation was felt to be a major grievance in Sukumaland, although no agricultural land in that area had ever passed to a non-African.[2]

By 1945, also, it was no longer necessary to discuss African

---

[1] Annual Reports of the Provincial Commissioners, 1942, 1944.
[2] Annual Reports of the Provincial Commissioners, 1933, p. 52; D. W. Malcolm, *Sukumaland: an African people and their country* (London, 1953).

developments and attitudes only as they appeared to the European observer. Government reports and anthropologists' accounts provide invaluable testimony, but we can draw as well on that of Africans themselves. A changing Tanganyika is thus very well seen in Martin Kayamba's story of his life from his childhood in Usambara to his appointment to an important position in the Central Secretariat, in his discussion of contemporary African problems, and in the account by Yosua Hermas of his missionary life among the Haya.[1] The first independent African newspaper, *Kwetu*, began publication in the late 1930's, and in November 1945 the first African members were appointed to the Legislative Council. Chief Kidaha Makwaia of Usiha and Chief Abdiel Shangali of Machame represented the old tradition and at the same time, as educated men, the new. That Kidaha was a Sukuma and Shangali a Chagga was significant: the Sukuma were the largest tribe in Tanganyika, the Chagga probably the most advanced.

The discussion of this chapter has indicated how very complex the pattern of social change could be, and this unevenness of scale is a continuing and fundamental problem in Tanganyika today. We cannot classify the Tanganyika tribes according to some single criterion of social advance, nor divide them into clusters as is possible in Kenya. It is possible to reach one geographic conclusion: the tribes which by 1945 were the most sophisticated in terms of their knowledge of the western world were those on the edges of the Territory—the coastal tribes, the Chagga, Sambaa, Haya, Nyakyusa, perhaps the Sukuma. Generally, these were the groups which lived in well-watered territory, and which through the development of export crops had acquired an income above African average. A certain correlation might also be made with the success of tribal administration, the local attitude to schooling and the spread of Christianity, but this correlation would by no means be complete, and the word 'sophistication' cannot be taken to mean necessarily either moral or material progress or western education. The numerous tribes in the centre of the territory moved much more slowly into the modern world.

[1] M. Perham (ed.), *Ten Africans* (London, 1936); M. Kayamba, *African Problems* (London, 1948); Yosua Hermas, *Von meiner Heimat in Ostafrika* (Bethel bei Bielefeld, 1953).

Even here, however, there had been a tremendous expansion of scale. The remote family groups of Upangwa or Usafwa or Ufipa, collecting honey or beeswax for export, buying quinine from the district post office, or listening to radio broadcasts from Dar es Salaam or Nairobi, had contact with a world beyond the tribe, beyond even Africa, as none of their fore-fathers had. In a society in which some members still recalled pre-European days and ways, a westernized and entirely twentieth-century generation was beginning to appear. In the second world war some 87,000 Tanganyika Africans were con-scripted for war service, and as they returned after 1945 an acceleration of pace was to be expected.

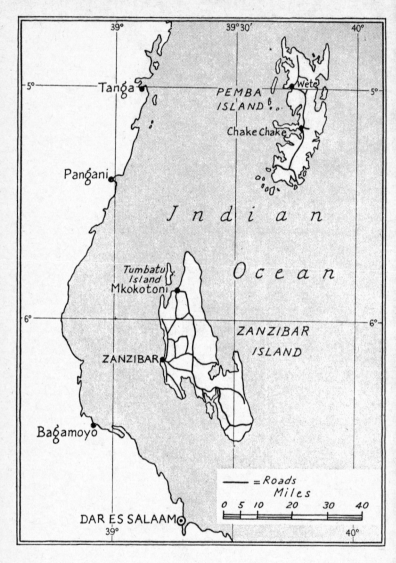

ZANZIBAR, 1939

XIII

ZANZIBAR
1890–1950

J. E. FLINT

The destruction of Arab political control

WHEN Britain officially assumed her protectorate over
the Sultan of Zanzibar's dominions in November 1890,[1]
British politicians and officials had no clear idea of any
positive policies to be pursued in Zanzibar.[2] They were aware
that the anti-slavery movement in Britain would force upon
them some considerable interference in the internal affairs of
Zanzibar, but it seems clear that at first the Foreign Office,
which was responsible for the affairs of the Protectorate up to
1913, intended to work through the Sultanate and its Arab
administrative institutions. The Sultan himself, and the Arab
aristocracy of the court, had been led to believe that this would
be so. Euan-Smith, the British Agent and Consul-General,
explaining the meaning of the proposed Protectorate in June
1890, had stressed its negative character and the need to prevent
German control. The Sultan would transfer all matters concerning foreign relations to the protectorate officials; in return
the Sultan and his successors would be made secure on their
thrones and allowed to nominate their successors, subject to
British approval. Put this way the Protectorate was a constitutional gain for the Sultanate, not only securing it against
foreign interference, but also regularizing the traditional 'election' of the Sultan, with its dangers of factional strife and
anarchy. Euan-Smith made no mention of any British control
over internal administration.[3] In the British House of Commons

---

[1] See *London Gazette*, 4 Nov. 1890, for full text.

[2] Throughout this chapter 'Zanzibar' refers to the Sultan's island possessions,
excluding the mainland territories.

[3] Euan-Smith to Salisbury, most secret, 19 June 1890, F.O. 84/2062, L. W.
Hollingsworth, *Zanzibar under the Foreign Office, 1890–1913* (London, 1953), p. 43.

in July 1890 the Under-Secretary for Foreign Affairs denied any intention of interfering with the Sultan's authority, but spoke of 'exercising a friendly influence' and allowing the ruler to use his 'independence'.[1]

In the few months whilst Euan-Smith remained as Agent and Consul-General, this spirit of guidance rather than control held sway. Sayyid Ali was persuaded to sign the Anti-Slavery Decree of 1 August 1890, prohibiting all sales or exchanges of slaves, closing down the slave markets, declaring the slaves of a childless master free on his death, forbidding the wives of Indians to hold slaves, threatening punishment of masters for ill-treatment, and permitting slaves to purchase their freedom. But the Sultan successfully resisted Euan-Smith's proposal for a total abolition of slavery within fifteen years, and in face of Arab opposition the Sultan tempered the decree with a proclamation eight days later upholding the master's right to inflict just punishments, and making clear that masters were not bound to accept money offered by slaves for purchasing freedom.[2]

The arrival of Gerald Portal to succeed Euan-Smith in August 1891 produced a radical change in the relationship between the British Agent and the Sultan. Portal was a trained administrator from Cairo, and brought with him a belief in the need for British control over internal affairs. He reacted violently against what he saw of the Arab administration. For him it was 'an embodiment of all the worst and most barbaric characteristics of a primitive Arab despotism'[3]—'a satire on the assumption of the English Protectorate'.[4] The filthy conditions in Ngambo,[5] the corruption of the officials, the venality of the judges, the lack of public works, the lavish life led by the court, and the absence of any distinction between the public and private revenues of the Sultan revolted him.

In October 1891, a little more than two months after his arrival, Portal undertook what can only be described as a *coup d'état*. He seized control of the Sultan's finances and administration, appointing Europeans, removable only with British con-

---

[1] *Hansard*, H. of C. cccxlvii, 744–52, July 1890; Hollingsworth, op. cit., p. 47.
[2] Ibid., pp. 52–54.
[3] Portal to Salisbury, 9 Sept. 1891, F.O. 84/2149, quoted by Hollingsworth, op. cit., p. 57.
[4] Ibid., p. 58, quoting Portal to Salisbury, 23 Aug. 1891, F.O. 84/2149.
[5] The African quarter of Zanzibar town.

sent, to take charge of the Treasury, army, and police, customs, post office, and public works. Lloyd Mathews[1] was made 'First Minister' to co-ordinate affairs. These officials were to be paid out of the Sultan's revenues. The Sultan lost control over public revenue, and was granted a Civil List fixed at 250,000 rupees per annum.[2] The rent from the British East Africa Company, and the interest on the purchase money paid by Germany for her mainland territories, was henceforth to be treated as public revenue.[3]

Portal's *coup* was a severe shock to the Sultan and the court. It marked the decisive step in the gradual loss of Arab political control. Lord Salisbury, after receiving a telegram of protest from the Sultan, did urge caution on Portal, but what had been done could not be undone.[4] The Arabs were powerless to resist this and further inroads which would be made on their political position. Portal's officials went ahead with their work, beginning improvements to the harbour, starting a street-cleaning service and public lighting in Zanzibar town, and balancing the budget for 1892 at just over 2 million rupees.[5]

At the end of 1892 Portal left on his mission to Uganda,[6] and Rennell Rodd was appointed in his stead. Sayyid Ali used the change to try to persuade the new Consul-General and the British Prime Minister Gladstone to return to the old system, to dismiss Mathews and restore the Sultan's financial control.[7] But it was naïve to imagine that the issue was one of personalities; behind the Sultan was the pressure from the court,[8] and Rodd, coming like Portal from Cairo, represented the same school of administrative thought. Rodd reacted forcibly, refused to concede anything, and made the Sultan sign, under protest, a declaration that he accepted Mathews as his First Minister.

[1] For W. Lloyd Mathews's position as commander of the Sultan's forces, see vol. i of this *History*, p. 240.

[2] The Sultan still retained a private income from his estates.

[3] Hollingsworth, op. cit., pp. 61–62.

[4] G. Cecil, *Life of Robert, Marquis of Salisbury*, iv (London, 1932), 306–7.

[5] For details see Hollingsworth, op. cit., pp. 63–71.

[6] See ch. xi in vol. i of this *History*.

[7] Rodd to Rosebery, 7 Jan. 1893, F.O. 107/2; Sayyid Ali to Gladstone, 24 Jan. 1893, F.O. 107/10.

[8] Hollingsworth, op. cit., pp. 78–79, in his account of these exchanges, argues that Sayyid Ali was merely the tool of the court party in this affair, and had little individual will in the matter.

Not two months later Sayyid Ali died. Rodd seized his chance to exploit the vagueness of Zanzibar succession law to intensify the British grip on the administration. Backed by British warships and marines, and by the Zanzibari troops commanded by Mathews, Rodd had the commanding power to choose and install the new Sultan. Sayyid Khalid ibn Barghash, who had attempted in traditional style to install himself in the palace, was ejected, and Sayyid Hamid ibn Thuwain chosen as the new Sultan, for he was a man with 'some idea of the advantages of European civilization'.[1] Choice of the man was not enough; as British nominee, Hamid was completely dependent on British support, and short of refusing the succession he had to agree to any terms which Rodd wished to impose. Rodd made Sayyid Hamid accept conditions which reduced the Sultan's power to ceremonial functions and influence in customary affairs only, and undermined his financial position. The new Sultan was to take an oath on the Koran to the British Crown as suzerain, accept all advice from the Consul-General affecting internal or external affairs, or slavery and the slave trade, accept that European officials could only be dismissed by the Consul-General, and agree to the reduction of his private income to 120,000 rupees per annum. After Hamid had signed, Rodd proclaimed him Sultan 'by the decision of the Protecting Power'.[2]

It is not surprising that Sayyid Hamid began his reign as a pliant and co-operative agent of the British. He cut himself off from the court faction which was hostile to Mathews, reduced the lavish scale of living at the palace, dismissed some corrupt *kadhis*, and reduced the number of his personal troops. When Arthur Hardinge became Agent and Consul-General in May 1894 the Sultan accepted without protest the humanitarian flavour which was introduced into the administration. Legislation was passed to prevent ill-treatment of African caravan porters, and to stop their recruitment for the Congo Free State,[3] whence suspiciously few returned alive. In 1895 the appointment of a vice-consul to Pemba was the prelude to a wider enforcement of British control. In January 1896 Arab society saw the implications of the new order with the sentence

---

[1] Hollingsworth, op. cit., p. 81, quoting Portal to Rosebery, 12 Oct. 1893, F.O. 84/2233.   [2] Ibid., pp. 82–84.   [3] Decree of 11 Sept. 1891.

of Shaikh Ali ibn Abdulla of Pemba to seven years imprisonment and deportation thereafter for life for gross cruelty to one of his slaves.[1]

Yet the struggle for political control was not over; even Sayyid Hamid tried to restore some of the Sultan's lost influence. In June 1895 the British Government administered a rude shock to the Sultan, which made him thereafter bitter and distrustful. This was the decision to use the £200,000 of Zanzibar government money which the Germans had paid for their mainland possessions to pay most of the £250,000 due to the bankrupt Imperial British East Africa Company as compensation for the loss of its charter. The interest already obtainable on the sum was raised by $\frac{1}{4}$ per cent. It was a shabby trick, designed to avoid the necessity for asking for the money from the British parliament, and both Hardinge and Mathews protested, demanding that Zanzibar should either retain control of the money or should receive in return the restoration of the Company's territories which had been leased from the Sultan. They were overruled.[2] An attempt was made to sweeten the Sultan by increasing his Civil List by £3,000 a year, but Hamid understood clearly that Zanzibar had been unfairly treated.[3] It so happened that an opportunity seemed to occur almost immediately to build up his power independently of the British. During the early months of 1895 the rebellion of the Mazrui, led by Mbarak ibn Rashid, presented a serious threat to British authority on the mainland. Some of the same resentments—the decline of Arab power, interference with slavery, and hostility to Christianity—lay behind Mbarak's movement. Although traditional enmity between the sultans of Zanzibar and the Mazrui prevented any concerted action, the mainland revolt absorbed most of the time of Mathews and Hardinge. In their absence Sayyid Hamid began to build up his private bodyguard; by October 1895 he had 1,000 men, and at the end of the year he reviewed them openly in the palace grounds. It seems unlikely that the Sultan planned an open revolt; more probably he hoped to use the troops as a threat to extract concessions. The arrest of one of the bodyguard by the police

[1] Hollingsworth, op. cit., pp. 92–93, gives details of this horrible case.
[2] Ibid., pp. 94–104.
[3] A. Hardinge, *A Diplomatist in the East* (London, 1928), p. 132.

brought matters to a head. Fighting broke out on 17 December, and Hardinge brought in naval forces and threatened to land marines. This was enough to overawe the Sultan, who agreed to disband his bodyguard at the rate of twenty-five each month.[1]

One more attempt by the Arab princes to resist the extension of British political control resulted in a final and decisive demonstration of British power. In August 1896 Sayyid Hamid died. Sayyid Khalid ibn Barghash, who had tried unsuccessfully to seize power in 1893, now made a more determined attempt. With what remained of the late Sultan's bodyguard, and with his own followers, Khalid seized the palace and proclaimed his own succession. After an ultimatum, the palace was bombarded by the British Navy, about 500 of the defenders being killed or wounded. Their resistance collapsed quickly, and Khalid fled to find refuge in the German consulate.[2] The severity of this bombardment was deliberate, and its purpose political. It was to be 'a lesson' which the Arabs would 'not forget for many years', and a demonstration of power before the British proceeded to tackle the problem of slavery.[3]

The new Sultan selected by the British was Sayyid Hamoud ibn Muhammad, a man who was in no position to act as a focus for Arab discontents. No large Arab faction had supported his claim, and he was totally dependent on British support. He was not a traditionalist, but an admirer of European ways and customs, so much so that he sent his only son to Harrow School. His great ambition was that this boy should succeed him, despite the fact that by Zanzibar custom the Sultan's brother had the better claim. He looked to the British to carry this through, and was willing to pay the price of co-operation. He was thus prepared to accept the throne on the same conditions as his predecessor, with the added stipulations that all armed forces should be officered by Europeans, and that he would alienate no state property without the Consul-General's consent.[4] From this time forward the Sultan's sovereignty was to be no more than a legal fiction.

---

[1] Hollingsworth, op. cit., pp. 107–16.   [2] Ibid., pp. 119–25.
[3] The phrases quoted are from Cave to Salisbury, 29 Aug. 1896, F.O. 107/54, quoted in Hollingsworth, op. cit., pp. 126–7. R. N. Lyne, in his *An Apostle of Empire* (London, 1936), p. 145, argues that Khalid's forces could easily have been overcome without using naval guns.
[4] These conditions are set out in Cave to Salisbury, 29 Aug. 1896, F.O. 107/54.

The abolition of slavery

The British seizure of political control was the prelude to measures which struck at the root of Zanzibar's social structure. Within eight months of Sayyid Hamoud ibn Muhammad's accession the legal status of slavery had been abolished. Yet this was not, as might be imagined, a direct result of the increased power wielded by British protectorate officials. Without exception these were convinced that abolition should be delayed as long as possible, and that when it came it should be so gradual as to leave the clove industry, the source of the State's revenues, unaffected. Nor was the British Government anxious to undertake experiments in social revolution. But neither the Government nor its officials were able to go as slowly as they would have liked. British policy in East Africa had been consistently defended both by the Conservative Government of Lord Salisbury and by Lord Rosebery for the Liberal Government of 1892–5 on the ground that it was a policy directed mainly against slavery and the slave trade. These arguments had ensured support for imperial expansion from religious groups in England, where both the Anglican and the Nonconformist churches were still powerful influences upon the electorate.

As soon as the Protectorate was declared in 1890 the Anti-Slavery Society began to demand that the institution of slavery in Zanzibar should be abolished as the only practical way to end the smuggling of slaves from the mainland.[1] As time passed and abolition was not announced, these demands were transformed into a formidable agitation in Britain. Meetings were organized, and questions were asked in parliament. By March 1895 this campaign was seriously worrying the Government, and Hardinge was asked to put forward a scheme for abolition.

Hardinge and the protectorate officials now began a rearguard action in favour of the Arab slave-owners.[2] Hardinge feared that complete abolition would be politically, socially, economically, and financially disastrous. He urged that any

---

[1] *Anti-Slavery Reporter*, July 1890, p. 145.

[2] Kimberley to Hardinge (tel.), 9 Mar. 1895, F.O. 107/40. The debate in parliament had taken place on the previous day. See *Hansard*, H. of C. xxxi, 664–7, 8 Mar. 1895; Hollingsworth, op. cit., pp. 133–7 discusses the campaign in more detail.

scheme should be gradual, that it should not emancipate *suria*
(concubines), and that it should not be brought about in such
a way as to cause an acute labour shortage.[1] Matters had
progressed no further when news of the bombardments reached
England. At once the anti-slavery interests announced with
one voice that this was the chance to force through slavery
abolition whilst the Arabs were cowed and beaten. There were
protests that a new Sultan had even been appointed, instead
of the institution of the Sultanate being abolished and Zanzibar
transformed into a Crown Colony.[2]

In the autumn of 1896, whilst Hardinge was in England, the
scheme of abolition was worked out. The abolitionists won their
case in principle, the protectorate officials secured theirs in
detail. The measure was carried into law by the Decree signed
by the Sultan on 5 April 1897. The exploitation of slave labour
was not made a criminal offence, as in British colonies. Instead
the onus was placed on the slave to claim his freedom by
applying to the district courts, presided over by Arab *walis*,
with right of appeal to the Sultan. Owners were to receive
compensation for each slave who successfully achieved free
status. Concubines could claim freedom only if they could
prove cruelty, or, at the court's discretion, if childless. The
decree pointedly stated that freed slaves would expose themselves to future taxation, and would be judged vagrants if they
could not prove fixed domicile and means of self-support. Rent
might be paid for domicile in labour or produce.[3]

In these conditions emancipation was not an easy matter for
the slave. The Arab *walis* who administered the law were
identified with the slave-holding class. Very few slaves were
able to read the copies of the decree posted in public places,
and the *walis* were responsible for disseminating the news orally.
Two European slavery commissioners were appointed, but they
had no direct authority to execute the decree; they were merely

[1] Hardinge to Kimberley, 13 Mar. 1894, F.O. 107/35. Hardinge prophesied
that emancipated slaves would refuse to work for free men's wages, that the clove
industry would be ruined, and that the revenue would lose £35,000 a year.

[2] e.g. *Daily News*, 27 Aug. 1896; *Spectator*, 29 Aug. 1896; *The Friend*, 4 Sept.
1896, quoted by Hollingsworth, op. cit., p. 140. Slavery would have been illegal
had Zanzibar been made a Colony, by virtue of the Abolition Act of 1833.

[3] *Abolition of the Legal Status of Slavery in Zanzibar and Pemba*, C. 8433 (1897), P.P.
lxii, p. 707.

to watch its working and report on its effects. It seems clear that for many months the plantation slaves, particularly in Pemba, were unaware of the new law.[1] Moreover, the legal processes took time, and meanwhile the slave had to return to his owner, who could make life hard even though the law prohibited open cruelty. Nor was freedom such an attractive proposition except to the very dissatisfied, the cruelly treated, or the anti-social. There was no free land upon which to settle and few possibilities of earning wages except on the clove plantations. On the whole slaves were well treated; to exchange the security of a familiar plantation for the risk of unemployment and destitution seemed foolhardy to most. Until November 1899 the vagrancy clause was interpreted in Pemba to mean that any slave must first find alternative employment before he could be given his freedom papers.[2]

It is not surprising that only a small proportion of slaves achieved immediate emancipation; 2,735 in 1898, 3,659 in 1899, and 1,720 in 1900. Thereafter the annual figures declined until in 1907 only 85 were freed, by which time 11,071 slaves had been liberated, 5,141 in Zanzibar and 5,930 in Pemba. 487,530 rupees had been paid to owners in compensation.[3] The pace was far from satisfactory to the British anti-slavery movement, which kept up persistent attacks on the Government's policy and on the protectorate officials. The quarrel became exceedingly bitter, particularly after the establishment of a Quaker mission in Pemba.[4]

Nevertheless, in the long run the gradual policy succeeded in eradicating slavery, and may have done so with less hardship to the slaves than a sweeping measure. Its indirect effects were more important than the actual clauses of the decree. By giving

[1] This is not the view of Hollingsworth, op. cit., p. 145, who says: 'Before many weeks had elapsed there could have been no slaves in Zanzibar who had not heard. . . .' But Hardinge, reporting to Salisbury on 4 July 1897 and again on 11 Aug. 1897, stated that the full import of the decree was not realized in Pemba. *Correspondence respecting the Abolition of the Legal Status of Slavery in Zanzibar and Pemba*, C. 8858 (1898), P.P. lx, pp. 559 sqq.

[2] This interpretation was abandoned as a result of an agitation by the British anti-slavery interests. After November 1899 the vagrancy clauses operated *after* the slave was freed.

[3] *Despatch from H.M. Agent and Consul-General at Zanzibar transmitting a New Slavery Decree*, Cd. 4732 (1909), P.P. lix, p. 577.

[4] For details see Hollingsworth, op. cit., pp. 146–53.

the slave a power to free himself, it improved his status as a slave. The owner could not afford to drive his slaves so hard that they would seek freedom in the courts. Cruel practices ceased almost overnight, and a gradual process began whereby the slave population was transformed into a semi-servile tenantry owing labour services to the Arab landlord. The Sultan himself led the way by declaring on the morrow of the decree that in future his plantation slaves should work for him three days in each week in return for holdings of land which he distributed. The rest of their time could be spent working for wages or on their own plots.[1] Many plantation owners followed suit, especially in Zanzibar island. By the middle of 1898 over 2,200 slaves, without claiming legal freedom, were known to have become tenants owing three or four days' labour each week.[2]

Such legal abolition as there was, and the emergence of this slave-tenantry, served to create an acute labour shortage. This in turn further improved the position of the slaves by creating competition on the part of owners to attract labour. Owners began to look favourably on the idea of free wage-labour. In 1901 a labour bureau was established, and soon afterwards Nyamwezi began to come in from the German mainland for the clove harvest, some of them settling permanently. By 1907 the question of slave status was of little economic importance. In 1909 the Administration was able to carry through what amounted to complete and final abolition. Under a new Slavery Decree no more compensation was to be paid after 31 December 1911, concubines could claim freedom (forfeiting their rights over their children), and execution of the decrees was transferred from the district courts to slavery commissioners appointed by the First Minister.[3]

In later years the Arab plantation owners were wont to blame all their ills on the labour problems arising from slavery abolition. The evidence does little to support this contention. The indebtedness of the planters and the mortgaging of estates to Indians were common phenomena well before 1897. The quantities of cloves picked actually increased in the years

[1] Hardinge to Salisbury, 9 Apr. 1897, F.O. 107/77.
[2] Salisbury to Hardinge, 29 June 1898, C. 8858 (1898), p. 84.
[3] Cd. 4732 (1909).

immediately following the Decree of 1897.[1] Yet the emancipation had more subtle effects which statistics cannot show. The Arabs had seen political sovereignty wrested roughly from their sultans; now their social influence was being slowly eaten away. It might seem that their way of life had collapsed. Many landlords found it difficult to face the new conditions, and lost interest in running the plantations. This was not an ideal frame of mind in which to face world competition from new clove-growing areas, and the dislocation of trade which was to come in the twentieth century, particularly when many owners continued to live in the old style on declining incomes and mounting debts.

The character of British administration, 1897–1914

The manner in which slavery had been abolished illustrates very well the basic character of British rule at the time. The approach to administrative problems was fundamentally conservative, rejecting policies which might upset the existing social structure. The sympathies of British officials lay with the Arab aristocracy; they saw the country not as one society, but as separate communities. The population was labelled by race, and race denoted function; Arabs were landowners and clove-planters, Indians were traders and financiers, and Africans were labourers. The 'correctness' of this hierarchy was supported by contemporary ideas of racial superiority, for the status of the communities was in theory one of ascending order according to 'whiteness'.

This conservatism was reinforced by the Protectorate's financial difficulties. Social reform is always costly, and before 1914 territories in the British empire were expected to live on their own resources. Zanzibar had to meet the cost of compensation to slave-owners, the salaries of the slavery commissioners, and the costs of the district courts and increased police force, all made necessary by the abolition decrees. Practically all the revenue came from the Arabs in the form of the 25 per cent. duty on clove exports. After September 1899 an additional duty of 5 per cent. on all imports helped to stave off bankruptcy, and in 1901 the Imperial Government floated a loan of

[1] R. H. Crofton, *Statistics of the Zanzibar Protectorate, 1893–1930* (Zanzibar, 1930), p. 15.

£100,000 at 3 per cent. so that Zanzibar could begin urgently needed public works.

Besides being congenial and financially convenient, the policy of maintaining the Arab landed aristocracy also seemed to harmonize with British theories of 'native policy' current at the time. The policy of what was later called 'Indirect Rule' was already becoming accepted in many areas. In the north of Nigeria, where Lord Lugard was developing the classic form of Indirect Rule, the policy entailed upholding the Muslim Fulani aristocracy, and the Arabs in Zanzibar might seem to hold an analogous position. When the courts of Zanzibar were re-organized in 1897[1] and 1899, though the Sultan's *kahdis* and *walis* were known to be corrupt, there was no attempt to replace them by European judges. Hardinge argued that 'a native administrative element should, if possible, be formed and trained up out of the Arab and higher Swahilis'.[2] The Native Courts Decree of 1899 embodied this idea. The *kahdis* and *walis* continued to run the district courts, though with limited powers. A new Superior Court was established, consisting of two *kahdis*, one Sunni, and one Ibadhi, and the Sultan had power to associate a British judge with them. Final appeal lay with the Supreme Court, where there was also provision for a British judge.[3]

The emphasis on the preservation of Arab privilege was in some ways an attempt to compensate for the loss of political and social influence, and was seen in this light by Hardinge and by Mathews as the Sultan's First Minister. After 1900 came new men and new situations. In that year Hardinge left to become British Minister in Persia, Mathews died in 1901, and in 1902 Sayyid Hamoud died and was succeeded by his seventeen-year-old son Sayyid Ali, fresh from school in England. The new British officials were more concerned with efficiency than with Arab susceptibilities, and the fact that the new Sultan was under age allowed the British to consolidate their control even more. A. S. Rogers, who replaced Mathews as First Minister,

---

[1] By Order in Council of July 1897 the British Consular Court was replaced by Her Britannic Majesty's Court for Zanzibar, and subordinate courts were set up administering the Indian codes, with final appeal to the High Court in Bombay.

[2] *Report . . . on the East African Protectorates*, C. 8683 (1897), P.P. lx, p. 26.

[3] For a full discussion of the legal establishment see J. H. Vaughan, *The Dual Jurisdiction in Zanzibar* (Zanzibar, 1935).

was made regent, and exercised all the Sultan's powers. The Sultan's financial resources were again reduced, his private plantations placed under the control of the Agricultural Department,[1] and the income from them was paid into the Treasury. The Sultan received a fixed annual allowance in lieu. The Treasury also undertook to pay pensions to the royal family, hitherto paid by the Sultan directly from the Civil List. Income from the property of deceased persons without heirs was also taken out of the Sultan's control.[2]

The end of French consular jurisdiction in May 1904, foreshadowing the subsequent surrender of all other European jurisdictions,[3] paved the way for a complete reorganization of the British Administration. At the end of 1905 Edward Clarke, the head of the African Department of the Foreign Office, visited Zanzibar to frame a scheme of reorganization. The tenor of his proposals was to transform the Administration into one much more like that of a Crown Colony, though Zanzibar remained under Foreign Office control. The First Minister's position, peculiar to Zanzibar, was reduced in function and many of his duties were transferred to a secretary for finance and trade and to an attorney-general. The Consul-General was made much more like a colonial governor controlling the local administration. His salary was raised, local officials were made responsible to him, he could veto administrative and legislative decisions, and was responsible for forwarding annual accounts to the Foreign Office, audited by an official lent by the East African Protectorate.[4] Clarke's proposals were put into force in 1906, and he himself became Agent and Consul-General in February 1909. Clarke resisted arguments put forward by Barton, who became First Minister in 1908, which would have given that position some independence, and would have broadened the base of government by establishing a council of officials.[5]

[1] Formed originally as an experimental unit attempting to introduce new crops to Zanzibar, but Arab landowners refused to abandon cloves and coco-nuts. After 1902 its main function was to manage the Sultan's estates. See Annual Reports of the Zanzibar Agricultural Department from 1900.

[2] Hollingsworth, op. cit., pp. 177–8.

[3] Italy, 1905; Portugal, 1906; Germany, U.S.A., Austria, and Belgium, 1907.

[4] *Despatch from H.M. Agent and Consul-General at Zanzibar*, Cd. 4816 (1909), P.P. lix, p. 581.

[5] Hollingsworth, op. cit., pp. 188–9.

Z

Clarke came at a time when European administration was beginning to make an impact on everyday life in Zanzibar island, if not in Pemba. In 1908 the Sultan's courts had been placed under the direct control of British judges.[1] The greatest effects of European administration were seen in Zanzibar city, which had been transformed, largely by the Public Health Department, into the cleanest and healthiest in East Africa. A report of 1907 by C. E. Akers, the newly appointed Secretary for Finance and Trade, criticized this concentration on the city, and demanded policies for agriculture and the population at large. Akers wanted a road- and bridge-building programme to bring the clove crop quickly to port, and urged the establishment of an Education Department to train Arabs and Swahili so that they might break the Indian monopoly of clerical and commercial work. He argued that all this could be paid for by cutting down administrative frills and making civil servants work at a less leisurely pace.[2] Though Akers soon afterwards resigned his post, the broad lines of his proposals were gradually implemented. By 1913 Zanzibar island had 75 miles of good roads, though nothing had been done for road-building in Pemba. The two islands were linked by radio, and a telephone system operated in both islands. An Education Department had been started in 1907 after Sayyid Ali had himself organized classes for Arab boys under an Egyptian teacher in the palace. But the response to government schools was poor, partly because parents were reluctant to pay the fees, partly because Swahili was the medium of instruction, and Arabic was felt to be the hall-mark of true education. When it was decided to use the Roman script, instead of the Arabic, for writing Swahili, this deprived the schools of any prestige they had in the eyes of Muslim parents, already suspicious of Christian influences. In 1910 three district schools had to close for lack of pupils, and in 1913 there were only 348 Arab and Swahili pupils.[3]

In so far as administrative 'policy' existed at all before 1913 it may be said that from about 1907 ideas of development began to override the earlier concern for preserving Arab dominance. Development was financed out of local resources by

[1] Vaughan, op. cit., p. 28.
[2] Hollingsworth, op. cit., pp. 185–7; Cd. 4816, P.P. lix (1909).
[3] Hollingsworth, op. cit., pp. 198–202; Zanzibar Annual Reports, 1909–13.

making administration more efficient, and it was thought that efficiency could only be achieved by using European personnel. In 1891 there had been only four British officials; in 1912 there were thirty-four, and the number of departments had doubled. The drive for a European kind of efficiency and incorruptibility exposed the weaknesses of the Arab aristocracy. Edward Clarke was the first Consul-General to display a lack of sympathy towards the Arabs. He regarded their financial difficulties as in no way caused by the abolition of slavery, but entirely the result of weakness of character. He rejected all ideas of assisting the clove-growers, either by reducing the clove duties or by setting up an Agricultural Bank to provide cheap credit and a way of escape from the Indian money-lender. Clarke felt that cheaper credit would result only in greater spending and greater debt. His only hope was that education of Arab children would breed a youth of sounder stuff.[1] So great was the decline of British confidence in the Arab that officials were prepared to contemplate the disappearance of the traditional clove-plantation. The Annual Report for 1913 stated that: 'The question of [land-]ownership is in a transition stage pending the formation of a new class of owner from the natives of the islands, or, alternatively, the introduction of white capital.' The same report shows that the Agricultural Department hoped one day to sell off the government plantations to 'reliable planters', stressed the improved conditions of health of the islands, and declared that 'the policy of the Government is to give every encouragement to the genuine white settler'.[2]

It is not surprising that Clarke and Sultan Sayyid Ali did not get on well together. The Sultan's position was unenviable; disliked by his own people as a British nominee, highly educated in the European way yet deprived of all power; fêted by Islamic rulers abroad yet impotent at home, he began to spend more and more time in travelling. In 1911, whilst ill in Europe, he abdicated, and Sayyid Khalifa ibn Haroub began his long reign. In the same year Clarke had been warned by doctors to retire from Zanzibar, but he refused to do so and died in office in 1913. The British Government decided to use the occasion

[1] Hollingsworth, op. cit., p. 197.
[2] Zanzibar Annual Report, 1913, p. 12. Clarke had died by the time this report was published, but his ideas clearly influenced it.

to transfer Zanzibar to Colonial Office administration.[1] The
change was more than a mere formality, and seemed to mark
a further step in the integration of Zanzibar with British
colonial territories. The system of dual administration, with the
First Minister theoretically at the head of the Sultan's Government, separate from the protectorate officials, was now completely abolished. A new post of British Resident was created,
which combined the functions of Consul-General and First
Minister. The British Resident was to be under the 'general
supervision' of the Governor of the East Africa Protectorate.[2]
Appeals from Zanzibar would in future be heard at the East
African Court of Appeal in Mombasa, not at Bombay.

It was this theoretical subordination to the mainland which
alarmed Sultan Khalifa. From the evidence which is available
it seems clear that the Colonial Office did intend to bring the
administration of Zanzibar into conformity with that of East
Africa. Khalifa's protests, supported perhaps by those of local
officials, succeeded in staying the drift towards amalgamation
with the mainland. The Colonial Office took the Sultan's
protests seriously, and devised machinery which was intended
to reassure him. This machinery was the first step, albeit slight,
towards allowing Zanzibar a share in its own government. The
new constitution, it was claimed, was *inter alia* designed to
gratify the Sultan's 'desire to participate in the administration
of his dominions'. In future there was to be a Protectorate
Council, presided over by the Sultan, with the Resident as Vice-
President. The Chief Secretary, Treasurer, and Attorney-
General were also members, with three unofficials 'selected from
gentlemen who are representative of different classes of the community'. The functions of this council were extremely vague; it was
neither an executive nor a legislative council of the normal pattern,
but was to 'consult with and advise His Highness the Sultan
on all questions which may be brought up for consideration'.[3]

---

[1] The Niger Coast Protectorate had been so transferred in 1898, Northern
Nigeria in 1900, and British East Africa, Uganda, and British Somaliland in 1905.

[2] The Governor exercised his supervision under the title of High Commissioner
for Zanzibar. The exact nature of this supervision was never very clearly defined.
In High Commissioner Sir H. C. Belfield's speech in Zanzibar on 20 Apr. 1914
he referred to 'general supervision by the High Commissioner and the Secretary of
State', which implies that the authority was to be real. See Zanzibar Annual
Report for 1914, Cd. 7622–34 (1915).

[3] Ibid., pp. 28–30; Zanzibar Protectorate Council Decree, 1914.

Between the wars, 1918–39

The first world war did not affect Zanzibar directly, as it did the mainland.[1] The withdrawal of German firms caused some dislocation, but trade soon recovered under the stimulus of an assured market. Prices rocketed,[2] and although labour was short the plantation owners were helped by government control of labour and by increased recruitment of mainlanders.[3] Zanzibar emerged from the war apparently unscathed and unchanged. For ten more years cloves and copra enjoyed high prices.[4] In some ways this was unfortunate, for prosperity bred complacency in the Administration and among Arab landowners. During the next twenty years Zanzibar was experiencing social change of a twofold kind. The Arab community was suffering a fate comparable to that of many planter aristocracies, its property and economic power dwindling whilst mounting debts maintained an accustomed standard of living. This enriched the Indian money-lenders. But more important was the way in which the African population, Pemba, Hadimu, or 'Swahili', slowly began to gather up land from needy Arabs.[5]

[1] On 20 Sept. 1914 the German cruiser *Königsberg* disabled the British H.M.S. *Pegasus* in Zanzibar harbour, but this was the only example of actual fighting in Zanzibar during the war.

[2] Copra fetched an average of £25 per ton between 1910–15; from 1916 to 1919 its average price was between £45 and £95 per ton. In 1913 Zanzibar sold 159,000 cwt. of cloves for £413,000; in 1919 192,000 cwt. sold for £759,000. See *Report of the Commission on Agriculture* (Zanzibar, 1923), pp. 61, 63.

[3] By the Native Labour Control Decree of 1917 and the Regulation of Adult Male Persons Decree of the same year the Labour Control Board was empowered to determine the amount of work to be done, where it should be done, and the rate of pay of registered 'natives'.

[4] The average price of cloves between 1904 and 1912 was 11 rupees per *frasila* (35 lb.); between 1913 and 1921 the average price was 16 rupees. C. A. Bartlett (ed.), *Statistics of the Zanzibar Protectorate, 1895–1935*, 8th edn. (Zanzibar, 1936).

[5] The Administrative Report for 1922 gave the following distribution of estates:

	Zanzibar	Pemba
Arabs	1,218	2,973
Swahili	4,840	8,717
Indian	165	158
Official trustee	53	264
Misc.	27	5

Of 1,074,905 bearing clove trees on Zanzibar island, 735,554 (69 per cent.) were in Arab hands, 236,758 (22 per cent.) in 'Swahili' hands. In Pemba of 1,926,048 bearing trees 'natives' owned 896,439; Arabs 888,259, thus in Pemba each group owned about 50 per cent. of the trees (G. D. Kirsopp, *Memorandum on Certain Aspects of the Zanzibar Clove Industry* (London, 1926), p. 6). It is an interesting

The Government was much worried at the decline of the Arabs' position, but was less aware of the rising African peasantry. British policy was wedded to a communal and racialist attitude. The Educational Commission of 1920 upheld the concept of racial separation in the professions,[1] and rejected any idea of establishing integrated schools.[2] The commission's report was alarmed by the drift of Arab youth to the towns, by their loss of interest in 'their hereditary vocation', and by their desire to become clerks. The basic problem was to recall the Arab to his estates, and thus a report on education could conclude with a demand for the 'complete transformation' of the clove industry.[3]

Changes in British policy elsewhere in Africa began to affect Zanzibar in the 1920's. In several territories these years saw the broadening of governors' councils to include representatives of local interests. In Nigeria the demand to establish palm plantations was refused on the ground that this would interfere with African rights to land. In Kenya the struggle between Indians and Europeans led in 1923 to the declaration that African interests were 'paramount'. All these developments seemed to make administration a matter primarily concerned with benefiting the African populations. Echoes were soon heard in Zanzibar. The Agricultural Report of 1923 firmly

indication of the Government's lack of information on the all-important question of landownership to note that these figures were repeated unchanged as the current figures until 1929. Yet increasingly, as time passed, government reports stressed the growth of African ownership at the expense of the Arabs.

[1] *Report of the Educational Commission* (Zanzibar, 1920), which stated (p. 9) that the purpose of education should be 'for the Arab agriculture, for the Indian commerce, and for the African industries'.

[2] All teaching was to be in the vernacular appropriate to race, in separate schools, with no higher levels of training than the vocational or functional. The commission did favour the setting up of a teachers' training college, which was in fact opened in 1923 and became the focal point of educational expansion. Many of the commission's recommendations were put into effect, and the 1920's saw the framework of primary and elementary education established. In 1923 a commercial school, mainly for Indians, was established, and in 1924 an industrial school, mainly for Africans, was set up. Rural schools were begun after 1925.

[3] A minority report by Y. E. Jivanjee, the only Indian member, and President of the Indian National Association, made a bold stand for liberal educational policies. Jivanjee demanded a secondary school open to all races which would teach to university entrance standard and which would produce not 'mere automatons' but 'men of an independent calibre' who would be 'an ornament to the State and Community' and 'serve to raise the general intellectual level'. (Ibid., pp. 21–22.)

rejected the previous support given to the idea of establishing white settlers.[1] In 1924 the Ormsby-Gore Commission visited Zanzibar as part of a wider East African investigation.[2] Local interests[3] were unanimous in pressing for the separation of the country from Kenya by abolishing the high commissionership. Ormsby-Gore agreed that the arrangement produced only expense and delay. He also criticized the lack of any effective consultation between Government and people. The Protectorate Council set up in 1913 was weak and ineffective. He therefore, with the Sultan's agreement, recommended the establishment of Executive and Legislative Councils.[4]

These recommendations were put into effect by the Colonial Office. In September 1925 the Governor of Kenya was deprived of his position as High Commissioner for Zanzibar, and the British Resident became the direct link with London. In 1926 Executive and Legislative Councils were established, the former composed of the Sultan and officials. The Legislative Council, besides 5 *ex officio* and 5 nominated officials, contained 6 nominated unofficial members appointed after consultation with local organizations.[5] At its first meeting the Sultan prophesied that future historians would regard the event 'as one of the most important that has occurred in the history of Zanzibar'. Jivanjee, replying, went further, hoping 'that before long we shall be found worthy of a still greater measure of self-government and that the principle of nomination will give way to the more popular principle of election and that, in course of time, the Council will become a full-fledged Parliament in the true sense of the word'.

British policies in West Africa, particularly the able defence of peasant proprietorship by Governor Clifford of Nigeria, also

[1] *Agricultural Commission Report* (1923), p. 17. The report stated that it was 'notorious that this Protectorate can never be a white man's country', and urged the Government to take 'great care' before allowing Europeans to obtain land.

[2] See Chapters VI and X above.

[3] i.e. the Sultan, the Chamber of Commerce, the Arab and Indian associations, and probably the British officials.

[4] *Report of the East Africa Commission* (Ormsby-Gore Report), Cmd. 2387 (1925); R. H. Crofton, *Zanzibar Affairs 1914–33* (London, 1953), pp. 75–77.

[5] Zanzibar Councils Decree, 1926. The first unofficial members seem to have been appointed on a communal basis, representing Europeans, Indians, and Arabs, but not Africans. They were Shaikh Sulaiman ibn Nasr al-Lemki, O.B.E.; Sayyid Salim ibn Kindeh Al-Busaidi; Yusufali Esmailjee Jivanjee; Kimji K. Suali; Homius Lascari; and William Grazebrook, M.C.

had influence in Zanzibar. In 1926 G. D. Kirsopp, the Chief of Customs, published a memorandum which demanded revolutionary changes in policy in Zanzibar. He argued that a social revolution was taking place, that the plantation system was disintegrating, that the Arab was becoming depressed to peasant status whilst the African was moving into the same status, rising from his former helotry.[1] It was futile for government policy to deplore the facts; they had to be recognized, and policy must fall into step with them. The idea of regenerating the plantation system must be abandoned. In conditions of free competition the peasant would inevitably destroy the planter, for the peasant was unencumbered by debt, lived modestly within his means, and had no labour problem, being able to rely on his family. The Government should accelerate the process by dividing the estates administered by the Agricultural Department into smallholdings, by controlling marketing, and by encouraging a co-operative peasant movement to fight the big European buyers and the Indian middlemen.

It was hardly to be expected that the Government would go so far. But in 1927 a tentative attempt was made to organize growers, large and small, along co-operative lines with the formation of the Clove Growers' Association (C.G.A.). The idea was to unite owners to reduce labourers' wages, to provide marketing and storage facilities, and to give harvesting loans to reduce interest rates. During 1927 9,000 joined the C.G.A., but this was mainly because the Government made membership a condition of payment for the bonus on young clove trees which had been operated since 1923. When the clove duty was reduced and the bonus abolished shortly afterwards, membership fell sharply.[2] The enthusiasm of the Agricultural Department ensured that the Association survived; it continued to lend money and store cloves, and the hard core of its members dreamed of the day when it would monopolize

---

[1] Kirsopp had odd beliefs as to the causes of this change, arguing that the Arab character had 'declined due to permanent settlement in the tropics', and that 'Arab blood has suffered from admixture with that of the native races'. He saw within the Arab community an 'inevitable tendency to racial deterioration' (Kirsopp, op. cit., p. 3.)

[2] C. F. Strickland, *Report on Co-operation and Certain Aspects of the Economic Condition of Agriculture in Zanzibar* (London, 1932), p. 10; B. H. Binder, *Report on the Zanzibar Clove Industry* (Zanzibar, 1936), pp. 22 sqq.

the industry. In 1929 the C.G.A. demanded a levy on all cloves sold, the proceeds of which it would use to take over members' debts, operate a land bank, and set up stores. It would sell cloves only at favourable times, and control the quantities released for sale to prevent price fluctuation.[1] The scheme raised opposition from Indian and European merchants, but Arab support was noticeable.[2] A committee of officials—Europeans, Indians, and Arabs—which met to discuss the proposals, whilst rejecting them, agreed that the C.G.A. should develop 'along conservative lines', and pressed for a limitation on the number of dealers, registration of labour, a land bank, and measures to control exports and stabilize prices.[3]

The season 1928–9 was the last of the post-war seasons of high prices. In 1929 came the catastrophic slump in the American share market, and in the years which followed the tentacles of depression and deflation spread over the world, Zanzibar included. Its effects were more on clove prices than quantities exported.[4] In 1928–9 the average price per *frasila* of cloves was 24 rupees, unusually high. In 1929–30 it fell to 15 rupees, remained at that level in the next season, fell to 7 rupees in 1931–2, and down to 6 rupees in 1932–3. Slight recovery began in 1933–4 at 7·5 rupees, rising to 8·5 rupees in the following year. But even at this late date prices were lower than pre-war averages.[5] Already burdened with heavy debts, the plantation owners were now faced with ruin. These prices hardly covered harvesting costs, let alone interest payments on past debts. The result was that many owners became involved in galloping debts, borrowing more and more to preserve the appearance of credit-worthiness and to pay off interest. The total of debts rose to staggering proportions.[6]

[1] *Report of the Committee appointed to discuss the Rationalisation of the Clove Industry* (Zanzibar, 1929), Proposals of the President of the C.G.A., pp. 9–10.

[2] Ibid., memorandum by Sayyid Salim ibn Kindeh, p. 14; memorandum by Shaikh Muhsin ibn Ali, p. 23.

[3] Ibid., pp. 11 sqq.

[4] Quantities exported, in '000 cwt. (from Bartlett, op. cit.):

1928	158	1932	162
1929	175	1933	215
1930	146	1934	218
1931	217	1935	190

[5] Binder's *Report*, p. 4.

[6] For full details see *Report on the Indebtedness of the Agricultural Classes* by C. A. Bartlett and J. S. Last (Zanzibar, 1935). Bartlett and Last calculated that half the

Until 1934 government policy gave the debtor no succour. The Administration, like governments the world over, floundered in indecision, stunned by the weight of the depression. Indeed, there was little to do, for until the countries to which Zanzibar exported recovered, clove prices would remain depressed.[1]

Meanwhile revenue was falling and economy became the watchword. In 1932 the Colonial Office sent Sir Alan Pim to Zanzibar to suggest how revenue might be increased and expenditure reduced without loss of efficiency. Pim's axe was wielded vigorously against the number and salaries of the European and Indian officials. He felt that it was absurd for Zanzibar to have an administration modelled on those of the large mainland territories.[2] Pim advocated the reduction of the number of European officials to sixteen, and suggested some minor ways of increasing revenue. However, his criticisms were not merely technical. He felt that the Administration was pervaded by false values and lack of purpose, and was surprisingly little influenced by British policies elsewhere. In education, 'racial, class, and caste distinctions have crystallised into stagnation'.[3] Pim argued that the arid nature of Zanzibar

trees in the Protectorate were mortgaged, and that indebted proprietors owed an average of 710 rupees per head. Ostentatious living was chiefly responsible; of 2,703 debtors analysed, 1,206 gave 'domestic expenses' as their reason for debt, and 596 ascribed it to 'social and ceremonial' reasons. In Zanzibar city indebted persons owed an average of 6,931 rupees, almost ten times the Protectorate average. Nearly all these debts were contracted after 1926, the majority in 1931 and 1932. These figures were necessarily based on samples, but in view of the natural reluctance of debtors to reveal their position, they may well be underestimates rather than exaggerations.

[1] The C.G.A. argued that because Zanzibar held a monopoly position in world markets, it should be possible to fix clove prices by controlling the quantity released for export. But this ignored the competition from Madagascar and Dutch East Indies cloves which might have been stimulated by a higher Zanzibar price. On the other hand, the experience of exporting cloves to the Dutch East Indies supported the C.G.A. view. The market here was peculiar, due to the preference of the local population for a type of cigar called *kreteh strootje*, whose distinctive flavour was obtained by mixing shredded cloves with tobacco. It was found that smokers would not buy *kreteh* which included non-Zanzibar cloves. Thus clove exports to the Dutch East Indies continued to rise, despite a general decline in the territories' trade, as the *kreteh* habit spread. See G. D. Kirsopp and C. A. Bartlett, *Report of a Mission to investigate the Clove Trade* . . . (London, Crown Agents, 1933).

[2] Unofficials in the Legislative Council had long criticized the Administration on this score, and attacked the large salaries of European officials.

[3] *Report of the Commission appointed by the Secretary of State . . . to consider and report on the Financial Position and Policy of the Zanzibar Government in relation to its Economic Resources* (London, 1932), p. 42.

administration lay in the fact that it had 'never developed a consistent policy with reference either to the all-important question of land or to any other question of native development'.[1]

Pim's desire to economize naturally made him wish to use local people in administration. But the principle was taken further, and made into an argument for introducing 'native administration', giving practice and experience to 'natives' in local government. Pim was here much influenced by the spread of techniques of using 'native authorities' in West Africa and Tanganyika. Almost the sole aspect of Zanzibar administration which Pim praised was the use of *mudirs* in local courts and government. He wanted their pay and responsibilities progressively increased, and wished Africans to be appointed as *mudirs*. He also upheld the *shehas* (magistrates), supporting the system whereby they were chosen by *wazee* (elders), and commented that some of the best *shehas* were illiterate.[2] Pim wanted this improvised system to be given life and purpose by the appointment of a 'Secretary for Native Affairs', who would be 'versed in native customs'. Pim also supported ideas put forward by the Zanzibar Government, after study of Tanganyika administration, that local councils should be established. These were to include *mudirs* and elders chosen by the villages, with power to spend revenue from hut taxation, the aim being to establish a system of 'local self-government'. He also demanded a Municipal Board for Zanzibar city, which would later develop an unofficial majority and include Africans from Ngambo.[3] Several reforms along these lines were initiated in 1934, when local government was completely reorganized into districts, divided into *mudirias*, which in turn were divided into *shehias*. At the same time Zanzibar obtained a Town Board with unofficial representation.

The year 1934 also saw the inauguration of policies to try to alleviate agricultural debt and distress. The C.G.A. had continuously demanded government control to organize clove-growing along co-operative lines. A report of 1932 by an outside adviser[4] had asked for the appointment of a Registrar to stimulate co-operation, and demanded the rapid reorganization

---

[1] Ibid., p. 21.   [2] Ibid., p. 23.   [3] Ibid., pp. 77–80.
[4] *Report on . . . Agriculture in Zanzibar*, by C. F. Strickland (London, 1932).

of the C.G.A. with either subsidization from the Government or power to levy compulsory brokerage charges. But still nothing was done. A government report on indebtedness, compiled during the clove-harvest of 1933, spoke the language of desperation. Prices did not now cover harvesting costs, 'the agricultural industry of the Protectorate is bankrupt', and 'immediate action' was necessary to preserve the economic structure of the country.[1] The report stated plainly that debtors would never be able to pay their creditors, and that conciliation boards with arbitration powers would have to be set up. With partial repudiation, the Government must ensure that debt would not re-emerge by expanding C.G.A. credit, controlling marketing by excluding all money-lenders, and making mortgaging illegal in the meantime except through the C.G.A.[2] In addition the commission proposed that the Government should establish a legal racial segregation of professions by stipulating that only 'a person of Arab or African origin' could practise agriculture.[3]

These words warned the Indian community of what to expect.[4] Soon after their publication the Government inaugurated a programme of legislation forcing the Indian creditor to take a greater share of the burden of economic depression. This legislation forbade the transfer of Arab or African land to any non-Arab or non-African without the consent of the British Resident, restricted mortgages on such land, and applied a moratorium on all debts owed by Arabs and Africans to persons of other race.[5] It established the C.G.A. as a privileged corporation, authorized it to levy a compulsory contribution on all clove exports, and gave a government guarantee to its funds.[6] The C.G.A. obtained virtual monopoly powers by a decree which insisted that all clove exporters must be licensed, gave the Resident power to limit the number of licences, and made the C.G.A. the 'licensing authority'.[7]

[1] Bartlett and Last, *Indebtedness of the Agricultural Classes*.
[2] Ibid., pp. 10-12.　　　　　　　　[3] Ibid., pp. 19-20, Appendix B.
[4] The tendency to blame the ills of the clove industry on Indians was already well established. The Agricultural Commission of 1923 recommended a ban on Indian acquisition of land and advocated extended government credit to undermine the Indian financier (*Report*, pp. 17, 24, 29-30, 51).
[5] Alienation of Land Decree, 1934.
[6] Clove Growers' Association Decree, 1934.
[7] Clove Exporters Decree, 1934.

These measures touched off an acute and bitter controversy, the first in Zanzibar's history to assume the form of open racial politics. The Arab and Swahili population strongly supported the Government. Indians, supported by British merchants, regarded it as a frontal attack on their position. In September 1934 the Indian National Association accused the Government of deliberately trying to drive Indians away from Zanzibar.[1] The Government of India sent K. P. S. Menon to investigate, and his Report substantiated the Indian charges.[2] Indians seized on the racial definition of 'agriculturalist' as an issue of principle on which to centre their case.[3]

With its new powers the C.G.A. appeared by mid-1935 to be stabilizing the situation; it had made a profit, limited the number of dealers to six including itself, and, most important of all, the price of cloves had begun to rise, though Indians argued that this was due to world recovery. A report of 1936[4] by a British chartered accountant not only upheld the Government's policy, but suggested that the C.G.A. should eliminate all other dealers completely. A decree of 1937 finally granted this complete monopoly.[5] The very success of the C.G.A. served to inflame Indian opinion, and this last measure provoked action. In August 1937 Indians in Zanzibar and India organized a boycott of the clove trade. Overseas, Indians were a key factor in channelling cloves to Asia and the Indies, and within months the government revenue was seriously depleted. By the end of 1937 the clove export duty was down by £30,000. Indians had successfully displayed the power they could wield over the Protectorate's economic life.

---

[1] *Memorandum by the Indian National Association* (Zanzibar, 1934).

[2] Report by Mr. K. P. S. Menon, 10 Sept. 1934.

[3] e.g., *Representation by Sir P. Thakurdas . . . to the Government of Bombay* (Bombay, 1935). The racial issue was essentially one of principle, rather than practice, for the British Resident did in fact grant permission for Indians to become landowners. In 1935, of sixty applications by Indians for Arab and African land to be transferred to them, only four were refused on the ground that the Indians in question had no intention to operate the land for agriculture. Forty-eight applications were accepted, and the other eight deferred (Leg. Co. *Debates*, 1935–6, p. 12). On the other hand, one practical effect of the decree which hurt Indians was that Arabs and Africans often refused to pay interest, even when they could afford to, feeling secure in the fact that their land was difficult to foreclose upon (ibid., 1934–5, p. 22).

[4] *Report on the Zanzibar Clove Industry*, by B. H. Binder, F.C.A. (Zanzibar, 1936).

[5] Clove (Purchase and Exportation) Decree, 1937.

In October 1937 Sir J. H. Hall replaced the previous Resident, Sir Richard Rankine, who had come to be regarded by Indians as dedicated to opposing them. The new Resident determined to break with the old policy, and began almost at once to resume contact with Indian opinion. By February 1938 he reached agreement with the Indian leaders, who called off the boycott. Indians were re-admitted to a share in the clove trade, and the power of the C.G.A. was reduced. In future the C.G.A. was not to employ its own buyers, nor to sell directly overseas, except in abnormal conditions. In collecting cloves the C.G.A. promised to employ sub-contractors. The Indians agreed to purchase a minimum percentage of cloves through the C.G.A.—50 per cent. in the first year. Two Indians were appointed to the C.G.A. Board, and two to the Advisory Committee which fixed prices.[1]

At the same time the Government announced its plans to deal with the problem of debt. This problem had been referred to London, and had gone before the Government of India.[2] Special courts were now established to fix the amount of disputed debts, and to value land under mortgage. The Government would then pay off the creditor to the value of the land mortgaged, and the debtor was then responsible to the Government for this sum, to be repaid in instalments, according to means. This again was a settlement which satisfied moderate Indian opinion: the usurer was cut down to size, but a place was left for legitimate financial operations and the principle of the debtor's obligation was maintained. War-time prosperity was soon to result in widespread repayments and the elimination of many debts.

The second world war and its aftermath, 1939–50

The two decades after 1939 were characterized by rapid and accelerating development. The historian writing in the 1960's is tempted to weave the story around the thread of emerging nationalism, but in Zanzibar these years were remarkable more for economic and social changes than for political advance or agitation. However, these changes may well have created

[1] Sessional Paper no. 6 of 1938, Legislative Council, Zanzibar.
[2] Revealed in Leg. Co. *Debates*, 1935–6, p. 12.

the conditions out of which the political developments of recent times have emerged.

For Zanzibar the war which began in 1939 proved almost an unmixed blessing. It galvanized the Administration into decisive and forceful policies, it stimulated the economy, and it smoothed away the racial bitterness of the immediate pre-war years.[1] By the early 1940's concepts of state control in Britain born of war-time conditions, together with the liberal trend of her colonial policy, had already begun to inaugurate far-reaching changes in the government of the Protectorate.

The initial impact of the war caused some dislocation of trade, particularly by reducing imports. This was no bad thing, for it reduced consumption, and for the first time agriculturalists began to accumulate funds and liquidate their debts. Clove exports were maintained until the Japanese entered the war. For Zanzibar this was a turning-point. When Japan over-ran the East Indies she deprived the Allies of the major source of their spices and of many other tropical products. Demand soared for Zanzibar cloves and for copra, which was now vital for vegetable-oil needs. In conditions of such scarcity it was possible to plan and control the economy under the umbrella of assured markets. In 1941 the Zanzibar Government set up the Economic Control Board with power to control prices and the distribution of necessities and to operate a licensing system for both imports and exports. The board put into effect the ideas for so long advocated by the C.G.A., but on a grand and complete scale which the C.G.A. would never have dared to demand. The British Government played its part in creating stability; in 1942 the British Ministry of Food agreed to purchase all Zanzibar's copra at specified prices, giving producers a guaranteed sale and a fair return.

The new prosperity showed itself in the wiping out of what was once thought to be the impossible burden of debt, and in

[1] Zanzibar's contribution to the war effort, in view of the smallness of her population, could hardly have been achieved without substantial unity of purpose among the population. The administration was carried on much more effectively than before the war, despite the fact that one-fifth of the European staff left for active service. Large numbers of local people served in medical, signals, transport, docks, and education units of the armed forces. £12,000 was raised for war charities, and £15,383 subscribed by the public for fighter aircraft for Britain. Zanzibar also raised a local naval force, a volunteer local defence force, and turned the police into a military body. See Annual Report for 1946.

mounting government revenue and expenditure.[1] Government policies increasingly reflected the trend towards social equality in British legislation; Zanzibar introduced income tax,[2] which had often in the past been dismissed as impracticable and inappropriate. An excess profits tax[3] was soon to follow in 1941. Zanzibar also obtained factory legislation[4] and rent restriction.[5]

In 1943 the Government submitted a general memorandum to the Colonial Office setting out its plans for economic and social development in the Protectorate. After general approval the departments then began to co-ordinate their ideas and plan in detail, and in 1945 a comprehensive plan went before the Colonial Office which granted £750,000 from Colonial Development and Welfare Act funds. Many of the details of this plan were extensions of work already begun. During the war medical services had been expanded, the pay and conditions of nurses improved, and a midwives training scheme begun. New schools had been built, village libraries had been established, and a domestic science centre set up. It was planned to bring 40 per cent. of children into schools by 1955. A town planning board, reconstituted in 1943, had begun to tackle the dreadful problem of slums in Ngambo, and the board's scheme for slum clearance and a civic centre eventually obtained £23,000 from Colonial Development and Welfare funds.

The development plans were the product of war-time enthusiasm and idealism, and the immediate post-war years saw many of the plans cut in scope. This was partly the result of post-war trade difficulties. In the 1947–8 season the clove crop failed almost completely, and the people of Zanzibar could

---

[1] Revenue and expenditure, 1938–45:

	£'000	£'000
1938	464	462
1939	497	451
1940	465	522
1941	564	480
1942	548	483
1943	533	496
1944	637	560
1945	614	631

[2] Income Tax Decree, no. 1 of 1940.
[3] Excess Profits Tax Decree, no. 12 of 1941.
[4] Factories (Supervision and Safety) Decree, no. 8 of 1943.
[5] Rent Restriction Decree, no. 3 of 1944.

indeed be grateful that policies pursued since the 'plant more food' campaign of 1941 allowed them to maintain subsistence without running back into crippling debt. The 1948–9 season also produced a very small clove crop. In 1950 the development plan was partially curtailed. Nevertheless, much had been done, especially to provide medical services, teacher-training facilities essential to future educational development, and slum clearance in Ngambo. Moreover, unknown to the Government, Zanzibar was on the verge of a tremendous increase in prosperity in the years which immediately followed. The year 1950 saw a huge clove harvest, and record prices; from 79 sh. per 100 lb. in January, prices soared to the fantastic figure of 230·25 sh. by December 1950. The pilgrimage to Mecca became a common-place in that year! The next four years saw a continuation of large harvests and good prices. The effect was to stimulate the private sector of the economy much as the development plan had expanded public services.

In view of these remarkable economic developments the quietness of Zanzibar's political life in the decade of the 1940's is noticeable, and contrasts with events in other parts of British Africa at this time. Such political progress as there was came from British reforms granted as part of British policies, and was not wrested from the Government by the threat of mass agitation, of which there was no sign before 1948. In 1944 town councils were established for the stone town of Zanzibar and for Ngambo, each with representation of local interests.[1] In 1946 a village council was established at Chwaka in Pemba, with revenues from land rentals and a share in certain export duties, which could be spent locally. In 1947 this experiment was generalized by the establishment of local government councils, upon which tribal elders and local figures were represented, and which had power to raise revenue, make by-laws, and spend money on improvements, but for several years the councils showed little initiative.[2] The British clearly thought in terms of training the population in local government, and in the administration, as a prelude to a very gradual transfer of authority. In 1947 a new branch of government service, called His Highness's Zanzibar Service, was established to train an administrative

[1] Townships Decree, no. 6 of 1944.
[2] District Administration and Rural Local Government Decree, no. 15 of 1947.

corps of Zanzibaris who might gradually replace European officials.

British policy stressed that any such transition would be slow and cautious. This emphasis is revealed by the British attitude to the Legislative Council, which in other African territories acted as the thermometer of political advance. It was not until 1945 that an African, Mr. Ameri Tajo, was appointed as an unofficial member.[1] Mr. Tajo, from the time of his maiden speech,[2] demanded additional African representation for Pemba, and this was conceded in 1947 by the appointment of Mr. Ali Sharif Musa.[3] The unofficial members now consisted of 1 European, 3 Arabs, 2 Indians, and 2 Africans, all of them nominated. Neither of the Africans was a politician commanding a party organization, whilst the other members each represented communal organizations.

The first sign of mass agitation showed itself in 1948, when a strike of wharfage workers in Zanzibar harbour developed into a general strike which for a time paralysed the island and forced the Government to take emergency powers.[4] But this movement was, on the whole, organized by mainland Africans, and much of its effectiveness may have been due to intimidation.[5] The unofficial members of the Legislative Council gave the strike no support.

The demand for rapid political advance came not from Africans, but from the Arab community, and particularly from Saif ibn Hamoud ibn Faisal, an unofficial member of the Legislative Council. In the session of 1949 he demanded that Arab and Indian members should at once become elected; that they should comprise, with nominated African members, a majority in the Legislative Council, and that they should be given representation on the Executive Council. At the same time he stated 'self-government within the Commonwealth' to be his aim, and warned the Government of the danger that

[1] The Council Amendment Decree of 1946 provided that an unofficial African should normally be nominated to the Council.

[2] Leg. Co. Debates, 1945–6, p. 148.

[3] Council (Amendment) Decree, no. 15 of 1947.

[4] Emergency Powers Decree, no. 18 of 1948.

[5] See Address by the British Resident to the Legislative Council, 6 September 1948 (Zanzibar, 1948). The Resident's view, very hostile to the strikers, was perhaps exaggerated, but his analysis clearly shows that mainlanders led the movement, and that some intimidation, at the least, did take place.

Zanzibar might begin to envy Muslim African countries like Italian Somaliland, already well on the road to self-government.[1] Such ambitions might look to African members like a move to establish an Arab hegemony to forestall eventual African self-government. Certainly they were not enthusiastic. On this occasion Mr. Ali Sharif Musa took the opportunity of insisting that Africans were not yet ready to elect their representatives. In general the African members wanted more progress towards social equality, and more places for Africans in the Sultan's Administration, before supporting demands for rapid self-government. Mr. Ameri Tajo constantly drew attention to instances of discrimination against Africans in hospitals, government services, and even in prison.[2] African members also laid great stress on the need for African education as the essential prerequisite for political advance. The organization of a popular mass-movement of Africans for self-government was still, in 1950, a thing of the future.

[1] Leg. Co. *Debates*, 1949–50, p. 36.
[2] He pointed out that African prisoners were given shorts to wear, while other races wore trousers in prison. Tajo also made vigorous protests at the lower quality of food given to Africans in hospitals (ibid., 1950–1, p. 32).

APPENDIX I

LAND POLICY IN KENYA
1895–1945[1]

M. P. K. SORRENSON

ONCE Britain had declared a protectorate over Uganda in 1894 she was similarly obliged, by the collapse of the Imperial British East Africa Company and the need to protect communication lines, to declare a second protectorate over the remaining territory between Uganda and the coast. The East Africa Protectorate, as the new Protectorate became known, was declared in 1895, but in 1920 the interior of the Protectorate was annexed as Kenya Colony, while the coastal strip remained a Protectorate under the nominal sovereignty of the Sultan of Zanzibar.

Despite its initial reputation as a barren wilderness hampering the vital communication with Uganda, the East Africa Protectorate became, within eight years, the scene of the last important attempt to found a British overseas settlement. Two factors were responsible for this remarkable change of fortune: the construction of the 'Uganda' railway from Mombasa to Kisumu on Lake Victoria, virtually completed by the end of 1901; and the transfer of Uganda's Eastern Province, including much of the fertile highlands to the west of the Rift Valley, to the East Africa Protectorate in April 1902. The latter thus came to include all the land suitable for 'temperate zone' farming. The railway passed through the highlands which were, in appearance at least, but sparsely occupied by nomadic pastoralists or shifting agricultural tribes.[2] There seemed to be ample vacant land for white settlement. The Foreign Office, prompted by a Treasury already burdened with the costs of the railway and an increasing grant-in-aid, encouraged a policy of white settlement as a solution of the Protectorate's financial problems. In the Protectorate the Commissioner, Sir Charles Eliot, took the initiative in both formulating and executing a policy which had as its ideal the

---

[1] This appendix is intended simply to summarize the main policy decisions and legislation concerning land in Kenya; it is not an attempt to explain the reasons for the decisions or to analyse the results of the settlement they were intended to promote and regulate.

[2] The facts behind this apparent underpopulation are discussed in Chapters I and V above.

foundation of a 'white man's country'. Thereafter until 1923, white settlement received paramount consideration as far as land policy was concerned. Then African interests, which, in contrast to the situation in Uganda, had so far received secondary consideration, were in turn declared paramount. And if African interests did not always in fact receive paramount consideration they could no longer be ignored. Land policy after 1923 became largely a matter of arbitrating between the rights and interests of white settlers and those of native Africans, and in particular of defining their respective rights to 'reserves' in the highlands area.

The definition of Crown land

Before the Foreign Office could encourage a policy of white settlement it had to settle the legal doubts then considered as preventing the assumption of a Crown title to land in protectorates. The Foreign Jurisdiction Act, 1890, made provision for judicial proceedings in 'divers foreign countries' which included protectorates, but there was considerable doubt whether this enabled the Crown to exercise rights over natives or their land. Elsewhere such rights had been secured by way of treaty with the existing sovereign authority, but in the East Africa Protectorate, apart from the Sultan of Zanzibar's coastal strip, it did not prove possible to secure valid treaties from the interior tribes, which had no recognized sovereign authorities, often not even acknowledged chiefs. The Imperial British East Africa Company's ninety-seven treaties were transferred to the Protectorate Government when the Company's charter was revoked, but these conveyed no rights to land; and the Company assets in the interior, which also passed to the Government, did not include more than the limited area of land formerly occupied by the Company stations. In 1896, when the Foreign Office was considering issuing land regulations, the Colonial Office was asked for an opinion on Crown rights to land. The reply was not reassuring although it did suggest an administrative expedient.

As regards Land Regulations, the Secretary of State's view is that the acquisition of partial sovereignty in a Protectorate does not carry with it any title to soil. The land is foreign soil, and does not become vested in Her Majesty, as is the case in territory which is actually annexed to the British dominions. It is therefore advisable to avoid making grants or leases or other dispositions purporting to be an alienation of land by the British authorities, to whom in fact it does not belong. Where native owners exist, it is not, of course, desired to interfere with them; but, where there are no such owners, and the land can be regarded as vacant, the object desired may be attained by other methods. In such cases the British authorities . . . may . . . permit a . . . person to take possession of . . . land, and may undertake

to secure him in that possession, subject to any such conditions as the Protecting Power may think fit to impose. The granting of such permission is
an Administrative Act, not a transfer of title; for practical purposes it will
give to the occupier all that he requires; and a land certificate authorizing
him to occupy the land, . . . will be a sufficient document of title and one
which the courts would enforce.[1]

The Foreign Office acted on this advice and in 1897 issued land
regulations authorizing the Commissioner to issue land certificates
for a term of twenty-one years but renewable for a further twenty-
one years if all conditions had been fulfilled. Occupation and
improvement conditions were to be stated in each certificate. A year
later the term of certificates was extended to ninety-nine years, but
even this concession failed to satisfy European applicants, who
pressed for freehold grants.

By this time some progress had been made in asserting the Crown's
title to the land required for the railway, and to the mile zone on
each side of the line which the Foreign Office hoped to sell or lease
at high rates to recover some of the expenditure of construction.
The land was obtained by proclamation under the Indian Land
Acquisition Act, 1894, which provided for the acquisition by the
Crown of land needed for railways, applied to the Protectorate
by the East Africa Order in Council, 1897. However, the Indian
Act did not provide for the resale of land so acquired and, it was
necessary to make provision for this right by the East Africa (Acquisition of Lands) Order in Council, 1898. This vested the railway
land in the Commissioner in trust for the Crown and enabled him
to sell or lease it. But there was still the unsolved problem of the
Crown's right to land outside the railway zone.

In 1899 the Foreign Office appealed to the Law Officers of the
Crown for an authoritative opinion on the Crown's rights to land in
protectorates, and particularly to 'waste land' in the interior of the
East Africa Protectorate. Here it was said that

sovereignty, if it can be said to exist at all in regard to territory, is held by
many small Chiefs, or Elders, who are practically savages, and who exercise a precarious rule over tribes which have not as yet developed either an
administrative or a legislative system; even the idea of tribal ownership in
land is unknown, except in so far as certain tribes usually live in a particular
region and resist the intrusion of weaker tribes, especially if the intruders
belong to another race. The occupation of ground in which a season's crops
have been sown, or where cattle are for the moment grazing, furnishes the
nearest approach to private ownership in land; but in this case, the idea of

---

[1] Colonial Office to Foreign Office, 4 Sept. 1896, Foreign Office Confidential
Print (hereinafter 'F.O.C.P.') 6861, p. 212.

ownership is probably connected rather with the crops and the cattle than with the land temporarily occupied by them.

The appeal went on to assert that, despite previous decisions limiting the Crown's rights to land, 'an important change . . . has of recent years come over the juridical conception of a Protectorate'. In some of the more advanced protectorates under the Colonial Office, such as that adjacent to the Gold Coast Colony, natives were brought under the same jurisdiction as British subjects, even in cases without a treaty granting jurisdiction. It had been assumed that 'the existence of a Protectorate in an uncivilized country implies the right to assume whatever jurisdiction, over all persons, may be needed for the effective exercise of the Protectorate'. As it had already been assumed in the East Africa Protectorate that the Crown had the power to grant a freehold title in the case of land obtained compulsorily from natives for the railway zone, it seemed that 'power could all the more properly be assumed for giving a similar title to land lying waste and not claimed by anyone'. Besides, other Orders and Regulations had already been applied in practice, though not strictly applicable in theory, without producing any evil effects.

It seems therefore proper to consider whether . . . in order that the Protectorate may produce its due effect in regard to the good government and the development of the country, the Protecting Power should not assume jurisdiction over waste and uncultivated land in places where the native Ruler is incompetent, whether from ignorance or otherwise, to exercise that jurisdiction.[1]

The Law Officers replied in the affirmative:

We are of the opinion that in such regions the right of dealing with waste and unoccupied land accrues to Her Majesty by virtue of her right to the Protectorate. These Protectorates over territories occupied by savage tribes have little in common with Protectorates over states such as Zanzibar, which enjoy some form of settled government, and in which the land has been appropriated either to the Sovereign or to individuals. Protectorates such as those now under consideration really involve the assumption of control over all lands unappropriated. Her Majesty might, if she pleased, declare them to be Crown lands, or make grants of them to individuals in fee simple or for any term.
The question of the system to be pursued is really one of policy. . . .[2]

The Law Officers' opinion was given legal effect by the East

---

[1] Foreign Office to Law Officers of the Crown, 18 Nov. 1899, F.O.C.P. 7403, pp. 78–82.
[2] Law Officers to Foreign Office, 13 Dec. 1899, ibid., p. 113.

Africa (Lands) Order in Council, 1901. This defined Crown lands as

All public lands within the East Africa Protectorate which for the time being are subject to control of His Majesty by virtue of any Treaty, Convention or Agreement, or of His Majesty's Protectorate, and all lands which have been or may hereafter be acquired by His Majesty under The Lands Acquisition Act, 1894, or otherwise howsoever.

Admittedly this did not define 'public lands', but these were assumed to be all 'waste lands', i.e. all lands not used by natives for occupation, cultivation or grazing, and land vacated by them. It was left to the Commissioner, or more frequently to the provincial commissioner and his staff, to determine what in fact were to be considered public (hence Crown) and native lands.

The problem of deciding the terms for settlement was considered more important, and this, as the Law Officers had suggested, was mainly a matter of policy. However, in 1901 the Foreign Office had no clearly defined policy for future settlement, largely because it lacked information on the potentialities of the Protectorate. Land policy thus became a matter of trial and error, and this enabled Eliot and the European settlers to take the initiative. The 1901 Order in Council permitted the Commissioner to 'make grants or leases of any Crown lands on such terms and conditions as he may think fit, subject to any directions of the Secretary of State'. In April 1902 Eliot, without waiting for any such directions, issued a notice permitting the sale of land at 2 rupees per acre and leases, for ninety-nine years, at a rental of 15 rupees per 100 acres. The notice was approved by the Foreign Office on condition that no more than 1,000 acres were to be sold in any one lot. Later in the year the Crown Lands Ordinance was passed.

Land policy and legislation, 1902–15

The 1902 Crown Lands Ordinance, drafted in the Foreign Office, was felt by the European settlers to be restrictive on their settlement. While it repealed the 1897 regulations and provided for sales, leases, and temporary occupation licences of Crown land, the terms were unacceptable to them. Sales to any single applicant were not to exceed 1,000 acres in one lot without the consent of the Foreign Secretary; and the Commissioner was given power to declare any land forfeited if the purchaser failed to occupy and develop it to 'a reasonable extent'. Leases were not to exceed ninety-nine years. Covenants written into the ordinance and implied in each lease included a prohibition of transfer without the Commissioner's consent, and an obligation to pay rents and taxes when due, to

provide access for roads, to maintain the repair of buildings, to 'use
and develop the natural resources of the land leased with all
reasonable speed, having regard to the circumstances of the case',
and not to interfere with native settlements on the land. Temporary
occupation licences were not to be for more than one year's duration
or for more than 5 acres of land. Licensees were obliged to 'keep
the land in reasonably clean condition'. Such licences might be
issued to natives and 'such other persons, not being Europeans or
Americans, as he [the Commissioner] may think fit'. This seemed to
imply that freehold grants and leases were to be for Europeans and
temporary occupation licences for Africans and Indians. The
Administration turned this provision into actual discrimination by
refusing to grant Indians agricultural land in the Highlands, except
on the basis of temporary occupation licences.[1]

The ordinance empowered the Commissioner to pass rules to
ensure the more effective working of its provisions, and Eliot took
advantage of this to promote the various white settlement schemes
he considered desirable for the Highlands. In December 1902 he
introduced Homestead Rules providing for the sale of a homestead
block of 160 acres with payments spread over sixteen years (at 2
annas per acre per annum). A further area of 480 acres was pre-
empted for each homestead and, provided certain development
conditions on the homestead block were fulfilled within three years,
this additional area could be purchased, again by deferred payments.
Then in February 1904 Eliot was allowed to offer homestead grants
within the railway zone between Nairobi and Kijabe stations. He
had already been granted permission, in May 1903, to sell and lease
land in the railway zone. This land was to be cut up into alternating
lots of 160 and 480 acres, the former for sale, the latter for lease.
In July he announced that this land was to be sold at prices varying
from 1 rupee to 6 rupees per acre, according to locality; and that
leases were to be at the rates prevailing for land outside the zone.
Earlier, in May 1903, Eliot had issued rules providing for free grants
of agricultural land, in an effort to stimulate European settlement
in less popular localities. The free grants were not to exceed 640
acres and were offered between Mazeras and Machakos Road and
Elburgon and Fort Ternan. They were to be outside but parallel to
the railway zone. Grazing leases were offered in the same localities
at a nominal rent for the first ten years. Finally, in July 1903, Eliot
issued rules for leases of pastoral land in blocks of 1,000–10,000 acres
at a rental of $\frac{1}{2}$ anna ($\frac{1}{2}d.$) per acre. These rules also permitted the

[1] See Chapter VI, p. 78, above. They could and did, however, acquire urban
land, although at times restrictions were imposed to prevent non-Europeans from
bidding at government auctions of urban land.

lessee to purchase the whole of his holding by deferred payments, but this provision was disallowed by the Foreign Office. However, lessees were subsequently allowed to purchase 1,000 acres of their holdings although neither the rules, as amended, nor the 1902 Ordinance made any express provision for this.

Eliot's rules, rather than the ordinance itself, provided the main basis for alienation of land to European settlers in the Highlands until 1915, and by then most of the available land in the Highlands had been alienated. From 1908 there were several amendments of the rules, reducing the area of grants and introducing revaluation of rents, pending the amendment of the 1902 Ordinance, but these were largely a dead letter. In addition much of the land was alienated as large concessions—including Delamere's 100,000 acres of leasehold and the East Africa Syndicate's 500 square miles (ultimately granted in freehold)—negotiated directly through the Foreign Office and, after March 1905, the Colonial Office.

Pressure from the white settlers had already been an important influence behind Eliot's rules. After he resigned in June 1904 his successor, Sir Donald Stewart, appointed a committee to examine the working of the 1902 Ordinance. Since Lord Delamere, the settlers' main spokesman, gained control of the committee, the report reflected settler criticism of existing legislation and made proposals for its amendment. It argued the settlers' case in the strongest terms.

The Government has, in fact, adopted the rôle of a strict landlord insisting on the development of his property by his tenants, and endeavouring, as far as may be, to create and maintain a personal and almost feudal relationship between itself and the holders of land. . . . The existing system is no doubt largely due to a desire to check anything in the nature of speculation. . . . Speculation and particularly over-speculation is not good for any country, but . . . the evils that it may cause are far outweighed by the impetus given to genuine business and the attraction held out to capital where the greatest possible security is given to title, and the greatest possible freedom to transfer of interests in land.[1]

By the time the committee had reported, the Colonial Office had taken over the administration of the Protectorate. Under the direction of successive Liberal Secretaries of State the Colonial Office sought to tighten up rather than to relax the existing conditions. Lord Elgin gave his first indication of this policy in March 1906.

The evils of unrestricted speculation in land [are] much more serious than the Committee appear to regard them. . . . The evils of allowing land

[1] *Papers relating to British East Africa*, H.L. 158 (1907), No. 1, p. 7.

in a new country to be transferred freely without any regard to the intention of the transferee to utilize within a reasonable time the resources of the land, are not confined to the period of depression and stagnation which inevitably follows a time of inflated speculation, but have a wider scope. . . . [He then cited examples of speculation in the Australasian Colonies following the abolition of restrictions in the 1850's.] With these examples before me, I fear that, in the interests of the future prosperity of the Protectorate, I shall be unable to assent to any legislation which facilitates the holding of land in large areas for speculative purposes. . . .[1]

A Commissioner of Lands, Colonel Montgomery, was appointed to inquire into the situation and report on the committee's findings. After receiving his report Elgin issued instructions for a new ordinance which would retain most of the existing restrictions against transfers, reduce the areas of homestead grants, reduce the term of leases to twenty-one years (with a right of renewal at an enhanced rent) and introduce provisions against 'dummying'—applying in the name of dependants for land in excess of the permitted maximum.

When the settlers protested, Elgin defended these proposals by appealing to the theory of the land tax reformer, Henry George.

It is clear, looking at the experience of other Colonies, that steps must be taken to prevent the accumulation of enormous quantities of land in the hands of individuals through the operation of free transfer, and also that conditions of tenure must be such that the Government may be able from time to time to obtain its share of the unearned increment in the value of the land—that is the portion of its value which is due to the growth around it of an organised economic and political system.[2]

Elgin agreed to modify his leasehold proposals but made no significant concession to settler demands. Leases were to be for ninety-nine years with a revision of rents in the 33rd and 66th years at the rate of 5 per cent. of the unimproved value of land up to maxima of 9d. and 2s. 3d. per acre respectively. A graduated land tax was to be incorporated in the new ordinance.

The attempt to force these proposals on to the settlers was unsuccessful, largely because the successive governors, Sadler, Girouard, and Belfield, were unwilling to use their official majority to push the ordinance through the Legislative Council. In 1912 Lewis Harcourt, who had become Colonial Secretary, began to give way. In March he dropped the land tax and later in the year, on Belfield's advice, he agreed to modify the revaluation scheme for rentals and drop the anti-dummying provisions. The new ordinance was finally passed in 1915, and by this time the Colonial Office had

---

[1] Elgin to Sadler, 23 Mar. 1906, ibid., No. 4, p. 37.
[2] Elgin to Sadler, 19 Mar. 1908, in *Correspondence relating to the Tenure of Land in the East Africa Protectorate*, Cd. 4117 (1908), No. 9, p. 30.

accepted the settler demand for a 999-year instead of the 99-year lease for agricultural land.

The Crown Lands Ordinance, 1915, allowed those holding land under the 1897 Land Regulations and the 1902 Ordinance to exchange their grants for leases under the new ordinance. Two types of lease were provided for: a 99 years' lease for town lots and a 999 years' lease for agricultural lands. Leases were to be disposed of by public auction and the conditions for each lot (upset price, rental, term, and any special covenants) were to be stated in the terms of auction. The 999-year leases were to have an initial rent of 20 cents per acre with revaluation every 30 years at a rate of 1 per cent. of the unimproved value of the land at the first revaluation, 2 per cent. at the second revaluation, and 3 per cent. at the third and subsequent revaluations. Minimum development conditions were laid down, based on the capital value of permanent and non-permanent improvements. Leases were not to be subdivided, assigned, or sub-let without the consent of the Governor in Council. A comprehensive registration scheme was introduced, not merely for original deeds but also for transfers, sub-leases, mortgages and powers of attorney. The ordinance made no specific provision for sales in freehold although the Governor could, subject to special instructions from the Secretary of State, alienate Crown land on any terms he thought fit.

The European settlers, though still dissatisfied with the rent revision conditions, regarded the 1915 Ordinance as a moral victory: it was not substantially altered before 1945, except in such special cases as the ex-soldiers' settlement scheme of 1919. Thereafter up to the outbreak of the second world war, the main controversial issues were the Indian claim for equal rights in the acquisition and tenure of land, and later the more fundamental problem raised by the expansion of the African population and by the more articulate expression of its sense of grievance.

The Indian controversy

White settler opposition to Indian landholding in the Highlands was influential from the beginning. In August 1902 Jackson, the Acting Commissioner, issued a circular stating that the country between Kiu and Fort Ternan was not to be open for Indian settlement. Eliot instructed his Land Office to the same effect in 1903.[1] The Foreign Office was not informed of these measures, but when the 1905 Land Committee, supported by Eliot's successor Stewart, advocated the continuation of the policy, Elgin had to pronounce

[1] See Chapter VI, pp. 271–2, above.

on it. Instead of resisting the settlers' demands—as he did with their proposals for the liberalization of the land laws—he gave way, and wrote to the Governor (Sir James Hayes Sadler):

... that it would not be in accordance with the policy of His Majesty's Government to exclude any class of his subjects from holding land in any part of a British Protectorate, but that, in view of the comparatively limited area in the Protectorate suitable for European colonization, a reasonable discretion will be exercised in dealing with applications for land on the part of natives of India and other non-Europeans. ... I approve of your adhering to the principle acted on by your predecessors, viz. that land outside municipal limits, roughly between Kiu and Fort Ternan, should be granted only to European settlers.[1]

The settlers then tried to get discriminatory provisions inserted in the new Land Ordinance, but Elgin, in March 1908, resisted this, without, however, attempting to reverse the existing policy.

With regard to the question of granting land to Indians, it is not consonant with the views of His Majesty's Government to impose *legal* restriction on any particular section of the community, but as a matter of administrative convenience grants in the upland area should not be made to Indians.[2]

Yet when the ordinance was finally passed in 1915 it did allow legal restrictions to be imposed on 'non-Europeans', who included Indians. Notices of auctions were to specify 'whether persons other than Europeans will be permitted to bid for leases of the farms'. European lessees could not, without the permission of the Governor in Council, allow non-Europeans to manage or otherwise control their land. All sales, transfers, mortgages, assignments, leases, and sub-leases of land held under the ordinance (or the 1897 Regulations or the 1902 Ordinance) from one race to another were to be reported to the Commissioner of Lands and could be vetoed by the Governor in Council, as long as the veto was exercised within three months.

Indians in the Protectorate persistently but unsuccessfully opposed the land restrictions and other discriminatory practices. Even in their campaign after the first world war—which was also an agitation for elected political representation based on a common voters' roll[3]—they were forestalled when the Devonshire White Paper of 1923 pronounced the 'paramountcy' of African interests whenever they clashed with those of immigrant communities, Indian or European. The important qualifications following the

---

[1] Elgin to Sadler, 17 July 1906, H.L. 158 (1907), No. 7, p. 43. Sadler had succeeded Sir Donald Stewart on the latter's death in 1905.
[2] Elgin to Sadler, 19 Mar. 1906, Cd. 4117 (1908), No. 9, p. 33.
[3] See Chapter VI, pp. 291-7, above.

paramountcy declaration even strengthened the white settler claim
to exclude Indians from the Highlands.

After reviewing the history of . . . [the exclusion of Indians from the High-
lands] and taking into consideration the facts that during the last fifteen
[*sic*] years European British have been encouraged to develop the Highlands
and that during this period settlers have taken up land in the Highlands on
this understanding, His Majesty's Government have decided that the existing practice must be maintained as regards both initial grants and transfers.[1]

It was suggested that Indians should be offered land elsewhere, as
had been the case in the past but, when an offer of land in the lowlands was finally made, the Indians considered it unsuitable.

The Kenya Land Commission of 1932–3 was required, *inter alia*,

to define the area, generally known as the Highlands, within which persons
of European descent are to have a privileged position in accordance with
the White Paper of 1923.[2]

It recommended definite boundaries for the 'White Highlands'
and these were proclaimed by the Highlands Order in Council,
1939. By this time, however, the Indian question had been overshadowed by the question of African rights to land in the Highlands
and elsewhere.

African rights in land

The assumption behind the Law Officers' opinion of 1899 and
the East Africa (Lands) Order in Council, 1901, giving legal effect
to it, was that native rights in regard to land were confined to
occupation, cultivation, and grazing, and did not amount to a title
in the land itself. Hence it was assumed that once land was deserted
by the African occupants it could be considered waste and thus
Crown land. The 1902 Crown Lands Ordinance was drafted on
these assumptions. The Commissioner, in dealing with Crown land,
was to regard the 'rights and requirements' of natives and could
not sell or lease any land actually occupied by them. He could,
however, lease land containing African settlements, 'without
specifically excluding such villages or settlements'. These were
'deemed to be excluded from the lease' as long as they remained
occupied. Once the natives ceased to occupy the land it was to pass
to the lessee. Alternatively the Commissioner could allot a portion
of the leased land to natives but again, as soon as they ceased to
occupy, the land passed to the lessee. Even these slender rights were
not protected adequately when the ordinance came into operation:

[1] *Indians in Kenya*, Cmd. 1922 (1923), p. 17.
[2] *Report of the Kenya Land Commission* (Carter Commission), Cmd. 4556 (1934),
p. 2.

the administrative officials allowed European lessees to pay Africans compensation for cultivation and huts, and then exclude them from the land.

No attempt was made to set aside native reserves before the first settlers arrived, or indeed for some time afterwards. This was a result of indecision and differences of policy as much as of shortage of funds and survey staff. Eliot was anxious to avoid a system of native reserves and favoured a policy of 'inter-penetration': of allowing settlers to take up land amongst Africans, allegedly to speed the process of 'civilization'. It seemed, however, when the Foreign Office instructed Stewart to set aside reserves for the Masai, that a definite reserves policy was going to be introduced, and some tentative steps were taken to set aside reserves for other tribes. Girouard's monumental report of 1909 recommended a system of defined, inalienable reserves but, although the Colonial Office accepted his recommendation, little more was done. Admittedly some districts had already been set aside as African areas, as in the case of the Nandi and the Kikuyu, and in the Sultan's coastal strip an attempt was made under the Land Titles Ordinance of 1908 to adjudicate and record titles before declaring the remaining land available for settlement. Under Montgomery's direction the Land Office took more care to exclude native land before allowing alienation, but there was no formal guarantee that the boundaries would be respected. The 1915 Crown Land Ordinance empowered the Governor to proclaim reserves but, except in two instances, the reserves were not proclaimed formally until 1926.

One tribe, the Masai, did receive exceptional treatment. In August 1904 Stewart signed a special treaty with them providing for their removal from the Rift Valley pastoral land along the railway, then required for European settlement. According to the treaty the Masai

of our own free will, decided that it is for our best interests to remove our people, flocks, and herds into definite reservations away from the railway line, and away from any land that may be thrown open to European settlement . . . our removal to definite and final reserves are [sic] for the undoubted good of our race.

One reserve was to be to the south of the railway line, the other at Laikipia, some distance to the north. There was to be a special connecting passage between the two. The treaty concluded with a statement that it was to be

enduring so long as the Masai as a race shall exist, and that European or other settlers shall not be allowed to take up land in the [Masai] settlements.[1]

[1] Ibid., Appendix viii, pp. 572–4.

The treaty endured for less than seven years. Laikipia was found
to be too small for the rapidly expanding northern Masai herds,
despite several extensions of the original reserve. White settlers
urged the removal of the northern Masai to the south and the opening of Laikipia for European settlement. The Government eventually
agreed, and in April 1911 a second Masai treaty was negotiated.
This stated that the Laikipia Masai,

being satisfied that it is to the best interests of the tribe that the Masai people
should inhabit one area . . . enter of our own free will with [sic] the following
agreement . . . to vacate . . . the Northern Masai Reserve . . . and to remove
. . . our people, herds and flocks to such an area on the South side of the
Uganda Railway as the Governor may locate to us.[1]

The new move caused a storm of controversy, leading ultimately to
Girouard's resignation, and Harcourt, the Secretary of State, did
not allow the move to be completed until he was assured that the
extensions promised to the southern reserve were adequate. It was
not completed until March 1913.

In the meantime a section of the northern Masai, led by Legalishu,
had taken legal action against the Government. They claimed that
not having signed the 1911 treaty they were not bound by it and
were thus still entitled to Laikipia under the 1904 treaty. The decision of the High Court, when the case was heard in 1913, was that
the issue was purely one of jurisdiction—whether the Masai claims
were cognizable in the High Court. Mr. Justice Hamilton held that
the Masai plaintiffs were not

subjects of the Crown, nor is East Africa British territory. But East Africa
being a Protectorate in which the Crown has jurisdiction is in relation to
the Crown a foreign country under its protection, and its native inhabitants
are not subjects owing allegiance to the Crown but protected foreigners,
who, in return for that protection, owe obedience. . . . In my opinion there
is here no legal contract as alleged between the Protectorate Government
and the Masai signatories of the agreements, but the agreements are in
fact treaties between the Crown and the representatives of the Masai, a
foreign tribe living under its protection.[2]

The treaties were 'Acts of State' and not cognizable in a municipal
court. Hamilton's judgement was upheld by the Court of Appeal
and an attempt to appeal to the Privy Council was not pursued
through lack of funds.

---

[1] Carter Commission *Report*, pp. 575–8.
[2] Civil Case No. 91 of 1912, enclosure in Bowring to Harcourt, 27 June 1913,
*Judgement of the High Court in the Case brought by the Masai Tribe against the Attorney-
General of the East African Protectorate and others*, Cd. 6939 (1913), pp. 5–6. The
judgement was dated 26 May 1913.

This judgement was an indication of the insecurity of African rights in land. There were soon other indications. The 1915 Crown Lands Ordinance redefined Crown lands as including

all lands occupied by the native tribes of the Protectorate and all lands reserved for the use of any members of any native tribe.

The reserves, even if proclaimed by the Governor, were not necessarily secure as the Governor could subsequently offer land in them for sale if he was satisfied it was no longer required by the natives, and if the Secretary of State had given his assent. When a portion of the Nandi reserve was excised for the ex-soldiers' settlement scheme in 1919 the insecurity of native reserves became apparent.

In 1921 there was another illustration of the fragility of African land rights, when a Kikuyu land case was heard by the High Court. Barth C. J.'s judgement in this case held that

the effect of the Crown Lands Ordinance, 1915, and the Kenya (Annexation) Order in Council, 1920, by which no native rights were reserved, and the Kenya Colony Order in Council, 1921 . . . is clearly, inter alia, to vest land reserved for the use of the native tribe in the Crown. If that be so, then all native rights in such reserved land, whatever they were under the Gathaka [sic] system, disappeared, and the natives in occupation of Crown land became tenants at will of the Crown of the land actually occupied.[1]

When the Ormsby-Gore parliamentary commissioners visited Kenya in 1924 they were impressed by the widespread feeling of insecurity among the Africans. The Commission recommended the immediate proclamation of native reserves—only two had been proclaimed in the nine years since the passing of the 1915 Ordinance. In 1926 the remaining reserves were proclaimed. An important step had been taken in dividing Kenya between the European and African communities. But neither community yet felt secure and both were anxious to expand into the remaining undemarcated areas. By 1926, however, Kenya was in the midst of another controversy, this time over 'paramountcy', which had a definite influence on land policy.

The implications of the 'paramountcy' controversy

The historic wrangle over 'paramountcy', traced at length earlier in this volume,[2] was reflected in the delays over the Native Lands Trust Bill, the major piece of land legislation following the declaration of native reserves in 1926. The Governor, Sir Edward Grigg, introduced the Bill in 1928 after obtaining the approval of

[1] Colony and Protectorate of Kenya Law Reports, vol. ix, part ii, 1923, p. 104.
[2] See Chapter VI above.

A a

Leopold Amery, the Colonial Secretary. He also secured the co-operation of European settler representatives in the Legislative Council, an example of how they were being associated in trusteeship. The object of the Bill was to declare a trust over land in the reserves, exercised by the Governor, who was to be advised by a Central Board. This was to have some unofficial (in practice European settler) but no African representatives. The Bill also provided for the alienation of land in the reserves if the Governor was satisfied that this was in the Africans' interests. At the request of the Hilton Young Commission, appointed in 1927 to consider the question of union in East and Central Africa, the Bill was shelved to be reconsidered along with their report. This advocated more stringent restrictions on alienation of land in the reserves:

Adequate areas of land should be reserved in perpetuity for native use . . . [and] no substantial alienation of land within them to non-natives must be permitted until the whole body of natives has so advanced in education as to be able to express a responsible corporate opinion. The only exceptions to this rule should be when the Secretary of State (or the central authority acting on his behalf), has after proper inquiry satisfied himself that the alienation of land is to the clear and undoubted advantage of the natives.[1]

The report also recommended that adequate land should be set aside outside reserves for 'detribalized' Africans and granted to them as individual holdings. There was further delay when Lord Passfield, the Labour Government's Colonial Secretary, insisted that the Bill must be amended to provide, *inter alia*, compensation in Crown land equal in value to any land taken from the reserves for public purposes (except where the land was required for roads, railways or buildings, when monetary compensation was sufficient). This amendment was unpopular with the settlers' representatives and Grigg had to use his official majority to pass the Bill.

This eventually became law as the Native Lands Trust Ordinance, 1930. The ordinance stated that reserves were to be 'for the use and benefit of the native tribes . . . for ever'. They were to be administered by a Central Trust Board, presided over by the Governor and consisting of five other officials, four nominated unofficials and an African member if one was found to be fitted for the task. Local Land Boards were to consist of the provincial commissioner as chairman, one other official, one non-official European, and one African. The ordinance allowed non-natives to obtain 33-year (or in exceptional cases 99-year) leases or one year licences of land in the reserves if it was not occupied or required by the natives. But

[1] *Report of the Commission on Closer Union of the Dependencies in Eastern and Central Africa* (Hilton Young Commission), Cmd. 3234 (1929), p. 55.

if the Local Native Council or the African representative on the Local Land Board objected, the lease or licence could only be granted with the approval of the Secretary of State.

In 1932 the ordinance was given its first real test. Gold was discovered in paying quantities near Kakamega, a densely populated part of the Kavirondo reserve. Although the ordinance reserved mineral rights to the Crown it was considered desirable to cut out the gold-bearing area, paying the African occupants compensation for disturbance but not providing land elsewhere as the ordinance required. The ordinance was amended accordingly with the approval of Cunliffe Lister, the Secretary of State; but the amendment was bitterly attacked in England by Passfield, Lugard, and other influential figures as a breach of the very trust the original ordinance was supposed to fulfil. It was left to the Carter Commission, which had already approved the amendment, to inquire into the working of the ordinance.

The Carter Land Commission, 1932–4

The Kenya Land Commission was appointed in April 1932, under the chairmanship of Sir Morris Carter, to investigate the whole Kenya land situation, and to carry out the inquiries requested by the Joint Select Parliamentary Committee.[3] It was required to examine African grievances resulting from past alienations of land to non-natives and recommend the best way to settle them; to study existing African requirements in land and consider what land could be set aside to satisfy them on a tribal or individual basis; to consider the working of the Native Lands Trust Ordinance of 1930; and, on the European side, to define the Highlands, 'within which persons of European descent are to have a privileged position in accordance with the White Paper of 1923'; and to consider whether better ways could be adopted for dealing with land protected under Section 86 of the Crown Lands Ordinance of 1915 (which guaranteed the rights of natives to land they occupied within European leases). Thus the terms of reference reflected the contradictions that had been apparent ever since the paramountcy declaration of 1923.

The recommendations of the Commission conformed strictly to the terms of reference. As far as the African claims to alienated land were concerned the Commission worked out an elaborate 'profit and loss' account, subtracting the area given to native tribes after

---

[1] The Joint Select Committee of both Houses of Parliament was set up in 1930 to consider the issues arising from the report of the Hilton Young Commission on closer union and native policy in East Africa. See Chapter VI, pp. 314–18, above.

1902 from that which they had lost by way of alienation which proved to have infringed existing rights. It concluded from this that the Africans had a claim 'as of right' to an additional 1,474 square miles and recommended that this area be added to the reserves from Crown land outside the European Highlands. On the grounds of 'economic needs' it recommended adding 896 square miles to the reserves and another 259 square miles as temporary reserves, terminable by the Government. A further area of 939 square miles was to be set aside as 'Native Leasehold Areas' in which individuals could obtain leases. Crown land outside the European Highlands, the native reserves, and the areas promised to the Africans by the Commission (and apart from the northern Turkana area) was to be available to all races without special privileges regarding initial rights or transfers.

On the questions of providing greater security for native reserves and of the working of the Lands Trust Ordinance the Commission recommended that land in reserves be termed 'Native' not 'Crown' land, and that it should be vested in a Trust Board independent of the Government with protective but not administrative powers. This should be provided for by order in council, not by an ordinance of the local legislature. Finally, provision was to be made for leases of land for social services, trade and industry, but any lease of over 10 acres should be approved by the Trust Board after consulting Local Land Boards.

The Commission recommended boundaries for the European Highlands, enclosing an area of 16,700 square miles (including 3,950 square miles of forest reserve). Apart from minor modifications the boundaries were those proposed by a 1928 sub-committee of the Kenya Executive Council.[1] It was considered that the boundaries should be proclaimed by order in council 'so that the European community may have the same measure of security . . . as we have recommended for the natives'.[2] African rights to land within European farms in the Highlands, guaranteed by Section 31 of the 1902 Ordinance and Section 86 of the 1915 Ordinance, were to be extinguished on payment of compensation where it was found to be due. The recommendation that 'the slate be cleansed by expunging these nebulous rights'[3] can be contrasted with the Commissioners' other recommendation for two islands of European settlement—the Kipkarren and Kaimosi blocks—surrounded by native reserves. These were to remain in European hands, although

[1] Carter Commission *Report*, p. 486. The committee consisted of the Chief Native Commissioner, G. V. Maxwell, and C. Harvey, a settler representative.
[2] Ibid., p. 493.
[3] Ibid., p. 534.

outside the European Highlands, with the Africans getting the rents and the reversionary interest in the land after the 999 years' leases had expired.

In a White Paper accompanying the publication of the report the Secretary of State indicated the Government's acceptance of the main proposals of the Commission, proposed giving legislative effect to them, and promised a gift of £50,000 towards carrying out the recommendations.[1] However, the legislation was not passed until 1938–9. The Native Lands Trust Ordinance, 1938, and the Kenya (Native Areas) Order in Council, 1939, dealt with the reserves and the areas added to them according to the Commission's recommendations. The existing reserves were divided into nine lands units and allocated to the major tribes. The Trust Ordinance provided for a Trust Board although, contrary to the Commission's recommendations, unofficials were given representation under the chairmanship of the Chief Native Commissioner. In addition the ordinance repealed Section 86 of the 1915 Ordinance, thus paving the way for the exclusion of Africans from European-leased land. The Crown Lands (Amendment) Ordinance, 1938, defined the various categories of land: 'Native' instead of 'Crown' land in the case of the original reserves, Temporary Native Reserves and Native Leasehold Areas, the position of the Northern Frontier and Turkana Districts, and the European Highlands. The boundaries for each category were set out in schedules to the ordinance. Finally, there was the Kenya (Highlands) Order in Council, 1939, which, in addition to proclaiming the boundaries of the European Highlands, provided for a Highlands Land Board composed mainly of settlers to advise the Governor in matters relating to land in the Highlands. The Board was finally constituted in 1944 by the Land Control Ordinance, which gave it power to control transfers.

[1] *Kenya Land Commission Report: Summary of Conclusions reached by His Majesty's Government*, Cmd. 4580 (1934).

APPENDIX II

BRITISH MANDATE FOR EAST AFRICA

The Council of the League of Nations:

Whereas by Article 119 of the Treaty of Peace with Germany signed at Versailles on 28th June, 1919, Germany renounced in favour of the Principal Allied and Associated Powers all her rights over her oversea possessions, including therein German East Africa; and

Whereas in accordance with the treaty of 11th June, 1891, between Her Britannic Majesty and His Majesty the King of Portugal, the River Rovuma is recognized as forming the northern boundary of the Portuguese possessions in East Africa from its mouth up to the confluence of the River M'Sinje; and

Whereas the Principal Allied and Associated Powers agreed that, in accordance with Article 22, Part 1 (Covenant of the League of Nations), of the said treaty, a mandate should be conferred upon His Britannic Majesty to administer part of the former colony of German East Africa, and have proposed that the mandate should be formulated in the following terms; and

Whereas His Britannic Majesty has agreed to accept the mandate in respect of the said territory, and has undertaken to exercise it on behalf of the League of Nations in accordance with the following provisions; and

Whereas by the afore-mentioned Article 22, paragraph 8, it is provided that the degree of authority, control or administration to be exercised by the Mandatory, not having been previously agreed upon by the Members of the League, shall be explicitly defined by the Council of the League of Nations;

Confirming the said mandate, defines its terms as follows;

ARTICLE I

The territory over which a mandate is conferred upon His Britannic Majesty (hereinafter called the Mandatory) comprises that part of the territory of the former colony of German East Africa situated to the east of the following line;

From the point where the frontier between the Uganda Protectorate and German East Africa cuts the River Mavumba, a straight line in a south-easterly direction to point 1640, about 15 kilometres south-south-west of Mount Gabiro;

Thence a straight line in a southerly direction to the north shore of Lake Mohazi, where it terminates at the confluence of a river situated about 2½ kilometres west of the confluence of the River Msilala;

If the trace of the railway on the west of the River Kagera between Bugufi and Uganda approaches within 16 kilometres of the line defined above, the boundary will be carried to the west, following a minimum distance of 16 kilometres from the trace, without, however, passing to the west of the straight line joining the terminal point on Lake Mohazi and the top of Mount Kivisa, point 2100, situated on the Uganda–German East Africa frontier about 5 kilometres south-west of the point where the River Mavumba cuts this frontier;

Thence a line south-eastwards to meet the southern shore of Lake Mohazi;

Thence the watershed between the Taruka and the Mkarange and continuing southwards to the north-eastern end of Lake Mugesera;

Thence the median line of this lake and continuing southwards across Lake Ssake to meet the Kagera;

Thence the course of the Kagera downstream to meet the western boundary of Bugufi;

Thence this boundary to its junction with the eastern boundary of Urundi;

Thence the eastern and southern boundary of Urundi to Lake Tanganyika.

This line described above is shown on the attached [not printed] British 1:1,000,000 map. G.S.G.S. 2932, sheet Ruanda and Urundi. The boundaries of Bugufi and Urundi are drawn as shown in the *Deutscher Kolonialatlas* (Dietrich-Reimer), scale 1:1,000,000, dated 1906.

ARTICLE 2

Boundary Commissioners shall be appointed by His Britannic Majesty and His Majesty the King of the Belgians to trace on the spot the line described in Article 1 above.

In case any dispute should arise in connection with the work of these commissioners, the question shall be referred to the Council of the League of Nations, whose decision shall be final.

The final report by the Boundary Commission shall give the precise description of this boundary as actually demarcated on the ground; the necessary maps shall be annexed thereto and signed by the commissioners. The report, with the annexes, shall be made in triplicate; one copy shall be deposited in the archives of the League of Nations, one shall be kept by the Government of His Majesty the

King of the Belgians and one by the Government of His Britannic Majesty.

ARTICLE 3

The Mandatory shall be responsible for the peace, order and good government of the territory, and shall undertake to promote to the utmost the material and moral well-being and the social progress of its inhabitants. The Mandatory shall have full powers of legislation and administration.

ARTICLE 4

The Mandatory shall not establish any military or naval bases, nor erect any fortifications, nor organize any native military force in the territory except for local police purposes and for the defence of the territory.

ARTICLE 5

The Mandatory:

(1) Shall provide for the eventual emancipation of all slaves and for as speedy an elimination of domestic and other slavery as social conditions will allow;

(2) Shall suppress all forms of slave trade;

(3) Shall prohibit all forms of forced or compulsory labour, except for essential public works and services, and then only in return for adequate remuneration;

(4) Shall protect the natives from abuse and measures of fraud and force by the careful supervision of labour contracts and the recruiting of labour;

(5) Shall exercise a strict control over the traffic in arms and ammunition and the sale of spirituous liquors.

ARTICLE 6

In the framing of laws relating to the holding or transfer of land, the Mandatory shall take into consideration native laws and customs, and shall respect the rights and safeguard the interests of the native population.

No native land may be transferred, except between natives, without the previous consent of the public authorities, and no real rights over native land in favour of non-natives may be created except with the same consent.

The Mandatory will promulgate strict regulations against usury.

ARTICLE 7

The Mandatory shall secure to all nationals of States Members of the League of Nations the same rights as are enjoyed in the territory by his own nationals in respect of entry into and residence in the territory, the protection afforded to their person and property, the acquisition of property movable and immovable, and the exercise of their profession or trade, subject only to the requirements of public order, and on condition of compliance with the local law.

Further, the Mandatory shall ensure to all nationals of States Members of the League of Nations, on the same footing as to his own nationals, freedom of transit and navigation, and complete economic, commercial and industrial equality; provided that the Mandatory shall be free to organize essential public works and services on such terms and conditions as he thinks just.

Concessions for the development of the natural resources of the territory shall be granted by the Mandatory without distinction on grounds of nationality between the nationals of all States Members, of the League of Nations, but on such conditions as will maintain intact the authority of the local Government.

Concessions having the character of a general monopoly shall not be granted. This provision does not affect the right of the Mandatory to create monopolies of a purely fiscal character in the interest of the territory under mandate, and in order to provide the territory with fiscal resources which seem best suited to the local requirements; or, in certain cases, to carry out the development of natural resources either directly by the State or by a controlled agency, provided that there shall result therefrom no monopoly of the natural resources for the benefit of the Mandatory or his nationals, directly or indirectly, nor any preferential advantage which shall be inconsistent with the economic, commercial and industrial equality hereinbefore guaranteed.

The rights conferred by this article extend equally to companies and associations organized in accordance with the law of any of the Members of the League of Nations, subject only to the requirements of public order, and on condition of compliance with the local law.

ARTICLE 8

The Mandatory shall ensure in the territory complete freedom of conscience and the free exercise of all forms of worship which are consonant with public order and morality; missionaries who are nationals of States Members of the League of Nations shall be free to enter the territory and to travel and reside therein, to acquire and possess property, to erect religious buildings and to open schools throughout the territory; it being understood however, that the Mandatory shall have the right to exercise such control as may be necessary for the maintenance of public order and good government, and to take all measures required for such control.

ARTICLE 9

The Mandatory shall apply to the territory any general international conventions already existing, or which may be concluded hereafter, with the approval of the League of Nations, respecting the slave trade, the traffic in arms and ammunition, the liquor traffic and the traffic in drugs, or relating to commercial equality, freedom of transit and navigation, aerial navigation, railways, postal, telegraphic and wireless communication and industrial, literary and artistic property.

The Mandatory shall co-operate in the execution of any common policy adopted by the League of Nations for preventing and combating disease, including diseases of plants and animals.

ARTICLE 10

The Mandatory shall be authorized to constitute the territory into a customs, fiscal and administrative union or federation with the adjacent territories under his own sovereignty or control, provided always that the measures adopted to that end do not infringe the provisions of this mandate.

ARTICLE 11

The Mandatory shall make to the Council of the League of Nations an annual report to the satisfaction of the Council, containing full information concerning the measures taken to apply the provisions of this mandate.

A copy of all laws and regulations made in the course of the year and affecting property, commerce, navigation or the moral and material well-being of the natives shall be annexed to this report.

ARTICLE 12

The consent of the Council of the League of Nations is required for any modification of the terms of this mandate.

ARTICLE 13

The Mandatory agrees that if any dispute whatever should arise between the Mandatory and another Member of the League of Nations relating to the interpretation or the application of the provisions of the mandate, such dispute, if it cannot be settled by negotiation, shall be submitted to the Permanent Court of International Justice provided for by Article 14 of the Covenant of the League of Nations.

States Members of the League of Nations may likewise bring any claims on behalf of their nationals for infractions of their rights under this mandate before the said Court for decision.

The present instrument shall be deposited in original in the archives of the League of Nations. Certified copies shall be forwarded by the Secretary-General of the League of Nations to all Members of the League.

Done at London, the twentieth day of July one thousand nine hundred and twenty-two.

Certified true copy:

For the Secretary-General, League of Nations,

RAPPARD,

Director of the Mandates Section.

APPENDIX III

A NOTE ON EAST AFRICAN CURRENCY EQUIVALENTS

AT the beginning of our period, because of the influence of Indian trade and settlement, the rupee was the principal unit of currency throughout East Africa. In Zanzibar, Uganda, and the East Africa Protectorate, accounts were kept in rupees, annas, and pice. R.1 = 16 annas = 64 pice.) Cowries (*kauris*) were also extensively used (R.1 = approximately 800 cowries) but were demonetized in 1901. In 1905 annas and pice were replaced by cents. (R.1. = 100 cents.)

In German East Africa, the once ubiquitous Maria Theresa dollar (*taler* or *real*) was withdrawn in 1896, and was replaced by a similar large silver 2-rupee coin. The rupee was divided into 64 pesa, but these too were withdrawn in 1910 and replaced by the heller. (R.1 = 100 heller.) The approximate foreign exchange rate was £1 = 20 marks = Rs. 15. During the first world war several emergency coins were issued, including the Tabora gold sovereign, worth 15 rupees, and various private tokens called *marken* issued by plantations and other employers of labour.

In 1919 the East Africa Currency Board was established and issued a new coin, the florin (= 2 shillings) divided into 100 cents. Because of depreciation of the rupee in India, and ensuing difficulties[1] the Board withdrew the florin and substituted the East African shilling as a standard unit (again divided into 100 cents). In Tanganyika, German rupees and hellers were also withdrawn and shillings and cents issued in their place.

REFERENCES

P. EINZIG, *Primitive Money*, London (1951).

I. GREAVES, *Colonial Monetary Conditions*, Colonial Research Studies No. 10, London (1953).

W. McGREGOR ROSS, *Kenya from within*, Ch. XII, 'The Collapse of the Great Shilling Swindle', London (1927).

W. T. NEWLYN and D. C. ROWAN, *Money and Banking in Colonial Africa*, London (1954).

Monetary Systems of the Colonies—eight articles reprinted from the *Banker*, London (1950).

Handbook of Tanganyika, Government Printer, Dar es Salaam (1958).

[1] See Chapter V, pp. 234–5, and Chapter VIII, pp. 430–1, above.

APPENDIX IV

MINISTERS AND PRINCIPAL OFFICIALS RESPONSIBLE FOR EAST AFRICAN AFFAIRS
1895–1945

SECRETARIES OF STATE FOR FOREIGN AFFAIRS

(responsible for the East Africa Protectorate and Uganda up to 1905, for Zanzibar up to 1914)

Jan.	1895	The Marquess of Salisbury
Oct.	1900	Lord Lansdowne
Dec.	1905	Sir Edward Grey (later Lord Grey)

SECRETARIES OF STATE FOR THE COLONIES

Oct.	1903	Alfred Lyttelton
Dec.	1905	The Earl of Elgin and Kincardine
Apr.	1908	The Earl (later Marquess) of Crewe
Nov.	1910	Lewis Harcourt (later Viscount Harcourt)
May	1915	A. Bonar Law
Dec.	1916	W. H. Long (later Viscount Long)
Jan.	1919	Viscount Milner
Feb.	1921	W. S. Churchill (later Sir Winston Churchill)
Oct.	1922	The Duke of Devonshire
Jan.	1924	J. H. Thomas
Nov.	1924	L. C. M. S. Amery
June	1929	Lord Passfield (Sidney Webb)
Aug.	1931	Sir Philip Cunliffe-Lister (later Viscount Swinton)
June	1935	Malcolm Macdonald
Nov.	1935	J. H. Thomas
May	1936	W. G. A. Ormsby-Gore (later Lord Harlech)
May	1938	Malcolm Macdonald
May	1940	Lord Lloyd
Feb.	1941	Lord Moyne
Feb.	1942	G. H. Hall (later Viscount Hall)
Nov.	1942	O. F. G. Stanley

COMMISSIONERS AND GOVERNORS OF THE EAST AFRICA PROTECTORATE / KENYA COLONY

COMMISSIONERS

1895–1900 Sir Arthur Hardinge (*responsible as Consul-General in Zanzibar up to 1896*)

| 1900–4 | Sir Charles Eliot |
| 1904–5 | Sir Donald Stewart |

GOVERNORS

1905–9	Sir James Hayes Sadler (*Commissioner 1905–6*)
1909–12	Sir Percy Girouard
1912–19	Sir Henry Belfield
1919–22	Maj.-Gen. Sir Edward Northey
1922–5	Sir Robert Coryndon
1925–31	Sir Edward Grigg (later Lord Altrincham)
1931–7	Sir Joseph Byrne
1937–40	Air Chief Marshal Sir Robert Brooke-Popham
1940–4	Sir Henry Monck-Mason Moore
1944–52	Sir Philip Mitchell

COMMISSIONERS AND GOVERNORS OF THE UGANDA PROTECTORATE

COMMISSIONERS

1893	Sir Gerald Portal
1893–5	Col. H. Colvile
1895–9	E. J. L. Berkeley
1899–1902	Sir Harry Johnston
1902–5	Col. Sir James Hayes Sadler

GOVERNORS

1905–10	Sir Hesketh Bell (*Commissioner 1905–7*)
1910–11	Maj. Sir Harry Cordeaux (*never took office*)
1911–18	Sir Frederick Jackson
1918–22	Sir Robert Coryndon
1922–5	Sir Geoffrey Archer
1925–32	Sir William Gowers
1932–5	Sir Bernard Bourdillon
1935–40	Sir Philip Mitchell
1940–4	Sir Charles Dundas
1944–52	Sir John Hathorn Hall

GOVERNORS OF GERMAN EAST AFRICA / TANGANYIKA TERRITORY

German Period

1891–2	J. von Soden
1893–5	J. von Schele
1895–6	Gen. H. von Wissmann
1896–1901	Gen. E. von Liebert

1901–6   Count A. von Götzen
1906–12   Baron F. von Rechenberg
1912–16   H. Schnee

British Period

1916–25   Sir Horace Byatt ('*Administrator*' *1916–20*)
1925–31   Sir Donald Cameron
1931–4   Sir Stewart Symes
1934–8   Sir Harold MacMichael
1938–42   Sir Mark Young
1942–5   Sir Wilfrid Jackson
1945–9   Sir William Battershill

CONSULS-GENERAL AND RESIDENTS IN ZANZIBAR

CONSULS-GENERAL

1891–2   Sir Gerald Portal
1892–4   Sir Rennell Rodd
1894–1900   Sir Arthur Hardinge
1900–4   Sir Charles Eliot
1904–8   Basil (later Sir Basil) Cave
1906–13   Edward Clarke

RESIDENTS

1914–22   Maj. F. B. Pearce
1922–4   J. H. Sinclair
1924–30   Sir Claud Hollis
1930–7   Sir Richard Rankine
1937–41   Sir John Hathorn Hall
1941–6   Sir Guy Pilling
1946–52   Sir Vincent Glenday

SELECT BIBLIOGRAPHY

Compiled[1] *by* ALISON SMITH

A. UNPUBLISHED SOURCES
>   IN THE UNITED KINGDOM
>   IN GERMANY
>   IN EAST AFRICA

B. UNPUBLISHED THESES

C. BIBLIOGRAPHIES AND GUIDES

D. PARLIAMENTARY DEBATES

E. OTHER PUBLISHED MATERIALS

A. UNPUBLISHED SOURCES

IN THE UNITED KINGDOM

For a fuller guide to the use of material in U.K. archives, reference should be made to the Bibliography of Volume III of the *Cambridge History of the British Empire*, pp. 769–907. This gives a broad survey of the historical source material for the Commonwealth during the period 1870–1919, and is particularly valuable as an introduction to the official records and to parliamentary papers. The selection given below—both in this section and on official publications in subsequent sections—while extending in time beyond the period covered by the *C.H.B.E.*, is intended only to indicate the main series, &c., which directly concern this area and period. Apart

---

[1] This bibliography is based upon material supplied by the contributors to the volume, while a number of libraries and individuals have made valuable additions and comments. The aim has been to make the bibliography as full as space permits, and not all the items listed were necessarily available to the authors when they wrote. Especial thanks for their help are due to Miss Anne Brewin, Mrs. Colin Newbury, and Mr. George Bennett.

from two or three basic collections, it does not include the many general
series which cover a much wider field than East Africa.

I. *Public Record Office, London*
(*a*) *Foreign Office Records*

Series F.O. 2   (Africa) General. The whole series comprises 983 volumes.
Series F.O. 107   (Zanzibar) 131 volumes. Correspondence 1893–8.
                   [Zanzibar correspondence from 1898 to 1905 is in F.O.
                   2/188.]
Series F.O. 367   (Africa) 361 volumes. New Series, 1906–13.
Series F.O. 403   (Africa) Confidential Prints. This is a printed selection
                   of Foreign Office correspondence, not comprehensive in
                   subject-matter, but often invaluable as a guide to impor-
                   tant political topics. Other sets of the relevant volumes of
                   these prints, although less complete, are available in
                   the Institute of Commonwealth Studies (London Univer-
                   sity), Rhodes House (Oxford) and the Entebbe Secreta-
                   riat Archives.

(*b*) *Colonial Office Records*

Series C.O. 519   1 volume. Original correspondence on the hand-over of
                   the Protectorates from the Foreign Office to the Colonial
                   Office 1904–5.
Series C.O. 533   515 volumes. Original correspondence, East Africa
                   Protectorate/Kenya, from 1903.
Series C.O. 534   57 volumes. K.A.R. files.
Series C.O. 536   204 volumes. Correspondence, Uganda, from 1905.
Series C.O. 544   58 volumes. Sessional Papers, East Africa Protectorate/
                   Kenya, from 1905.
Series C.O. 628   17 volumes. Register of correspondence, East Africa
                   Protectorate/Kenya, 1904–26.
Series C.O. 630   14 volumes. Acts, East Africa Protectorate/Kenya, 1901–40.
Series C.O. 684   4 volumes. Acts, Uganda, 1901–39.
Series C.O. 685   26 volumes. Sessional Papers, Uganda, 1907–40. Vol.
                   18 is a mimeographed summary of the Proceedings of the
                   Uganda Legislative Council from 1921 to 1934.
Series C.O. 735   6 volumes. Acts, Tanganyika, 1919–39.
Series C.O. 842   2 volumes. Acts, Zanzibar, 1926–36.
Series C.O. 879   Colonial Office Confidential Prints, Africa.
Series C.O. 885   Colonial Office Confidential Prints, Miscellaneous.

II. *Colonial Office, London*
Mimeographs of evidence submitted to the Hilton Young Commission
(*see under* Published/Materials).

III. *London University*
At the London School of Economics:
    The papers of Sidney and Beatrice Webb.

At the School of Oriental and African Studies:

The papers of William Mackinnon, Chairman of the British East Africa Company.

IV. *Oxford*

Of the manuscript collections held at Rhodes House Library, the following are specially relevant:

The papers of the British Anti-Slavery Society (especially for Zanzibar), 1820–1951.

The papers of Lord Lugard (correspondence on African affairs), 1858–1919.

The papers of Francis Hall (an administrative officer of the I.B.E.A. Company and subsequently East Africa Protectorate), 1880–1901.

The papers of Lord Portal (Zanzibar and Uganda), 1881–95.

The diaries of E. J. H. Russell (an administrator in the East Africa Protectorate), 1895–9, 1900.

The diaries, &c., of John Ainsworth (an administrator in the East Africa Protectorate), 1895–1902.

'Enquiry into Native Land Tenure in the Uganda Protectorate' (J. Roscoe and Sir Apolo Kagwa).

The commonplace books of E. C. Baker (Tanganyika papers, tribal histories), 1918–50 [microfilm].

Two other important general collections in Oxford are the Salisbury papers, deposited at Christ Church, and the Milner papers, deposited at New College.

V. *Cambridge*

At the University Library:

The Zanzibar collection.

VI. *Birmingham*

The papers of Joseph Chamberlain.

VII. *Other collections*

The most important collections of missionary material for the history of East Africa are those held by the Church Missionary Society (6 Salisbury Square, Fleet Street, London E.C. 4); the London Missionary Society (Livingstone House, Westminster, S.W. 1); the Universities Mission to Central Africa (Great Peter Street, London S.W. 1); the Church of Scotland Mission, held by the National Library of Scotland. These are generally accessible to accredited students.

The personal papers of many prominent individuals are still in private hands: among these, contributors to this volume have had access to (and would like to express their thanks for the privilege) those of Dr. Arthur, pioneer C.S.M. missionary in Kenya, Lord Altrincham (Sir Edward Grigg), Governor of Kenya, and Dr. J. H. Oldham.

IN GERMANY

The archives of the *Kolonial-Abteilung* of the German Foreign Office (1890–1907) and of the *Reichskolonialamt* (1907–19) are held in the German Central Archives, Potsdam (DZAP), German Democratic Republic, and have been listed in Helmut Lötzke, *Übersicht über die Bestände des deutschen Zentralarchivs Potsdam* (Berlin, 1957). The holdings include series dating from 1884. Access is not automatically granted to foreign scholars. The files of the Political Department of the German Foreign Office for the period 1867–1920 were captured during the second world war and many were microfilmed by the German War Documents Project of the American, British, and French Governments; these were microfilmed by a combined State Department and Foreign Office unit and are listed in *A Catalogue of Films and Microfilms of the German Foreign Ministry Archives 1867–1920*, American Historical Association, Committee for the study of War Documents, 1959, which indicates where microfilms may be obtained. The captured archives were returned to the Federal German Foreign Ministry at Bonn between 1950 and 1958, and are being transferred to the Federal Archives at Koblenz. The holdings in the German Federal Republic include papers dealing with international colonial issues.

The commercial papers of Wm. O'swald and Company, and of A. J. Hertz, are held in the Staatsarchiv at Hamburg; and the Bundesarchiv Koblenz holds the papers of a number of 'colonial pioneers', including Dr. Carl Peters.

IN EAST AFRICA

(For a general description of the East African archives, see P. D. Curtin, 'The Archives of Tropical Africa', in the *Journal of African History*, i. 1 (1960), 129–47.)

1. *Kenya*

Nairobi Secretariat Records. The Nairobi Secretariat records for the E.A.P. Administration were destroyed by a fire in 1939. The Secretariat Library today contains no more than a very few miscellaneous notes and memoranda concerning the East Africa Protectorate, although other Kenya government departments, especially the Attorney-General's Office and the Lands Office, preserve records of considerable value. Some of the records of the Commissioner of the E.A.P. for 1895–1900 are in Zanzibar, partly in the Residency Archives and to a lesser extent in the Museum and Secretariat Archives.

Attempts are being made to preserve and classify the surviving records held in the local Administration Offices in the Regions. There are valuable collections of papers in the P.C.'s office at Mombasa; in the P.C.'s and D.C.'s offices at Kisumu; in the P.C.'s office at Isiolo; and in the D.C.s' offices at Kiambu and Machakos. There are also smaller collections, which in the absence of Secretariat Records are also of great value, in the D.C.s' offices at Eldoret, Embu, Kakamega, Kapsabet, Kericho, Kisii, Kitu, Meru, Ngong, Nyeri, Tambach, Thomson's Falls, and Wundanyi.

Non-official collections include the private papers (in Mombasa) of the late Mr. P. D. Masters, who was for long the Secretary of the East African Indian National Congress, and who was collecting material for its history, and (in Nairobi) the Archives of the Christian Council of Kenya.

2. *Uganda*

Entebbe Secretariat Archives. These contain the records of the Uganda Protectorate from its inception. Up to 1906 the records are mainly in boxes or box files which have each been given a catalogue number. After 1906 the records are still kept in the main as Secretariat Minute Papers. The Secretariat Archives contain in particular fairly full collections of Provincial and District Annual and Monthly Reports. There are also records to be found in some of the headquarters of the African Kingdom and District Governments of Uganda.

Much material on agriculture, and especially on the cotton industry, is available in the records of the Department of Agriculture at Entebbe, and some also at Jinja.

At Makerere College, Kampala, a number of private collections have been deposited, among them:

> The archives of the Uganda Company. These include the Company's prospectus (1905); various letter books between 1908 and 1912; Minutes of the meetings of the Board of Directors, 1910–12, 1916–45; and Reports to shareholders, 1923–45.
> The archives of the Uganda Chamber of Commerce.
> The papers of Sir Apolo Kagwa.

There are also several typescripts held by the East African Institute of Social Research, e.g.:

> MUKWAYA, A. B.: 'Economic Causes of the 1949 Disturbances.'
> PRATT, R. C.: 'The British and the Basoga.'
> TAMUKEDDE, W. P.: 'The Great Lukiko.'

Valuable collections of papers are held by some of the mission centres in Kampala, notably at the Bishop's House at Namirembe; and the diaries, from 1895, of the Mill Hill Mission at Nsambya.

3. *Tanganyika*

Of particular value for local developments are the District Books, compiled under the direction of the Administration from 1923 to 1929 and containing, besides historical sections of varying quality, much useful statistical, fiscal, and political material. Copies of most of these are in the Makerere College Library, at the School of Oriental and African Studies, London, and in microfilm at Rhodes House, Oxford.

Lands and Survey Department, Dar es Salaam. Here are deposited the bulk of what survive of the local records of the period (1884–1916) of German administration, a very large proportion of which in fact consist of land records (some 4,000 files), and surveys (2,000 files). There are also about 40 Agricultural Department files and between 1,000 and 2,000 other files of which no satisfactory record exists. A number of German judicial records have recently been transferred from the High Court, and have been listed.

Certain other Departments (Customs, Education, Labour, Medical, Public Works, Railway, Veterinary and Game, Water) hold the few surviving German files—less than 150 in all—which concern them.

Treasury. In the Treasury Building at Dar es Salaam have been collected the records of the British period. At the time of compilation, these still await checking for completeness and cataloguing.

University Library. The Library of the University College at Dar es Salaam has acquired some series of government official publications, both German and British. It also holds the papers of Dr. Hans Cory.

4. *Zanzibar*

The Secretariat Archives. These contain, besides the correspondence with the Foreign Office on Zanzibar affairs from 1840 to 1905 (duplicated in the P.R.O.), some material on the East Africa Protectorate up to 1900. There are also a number of German consular files, running up to 1914.

Residency and Museum Archives. These contain the greater part of the records of the East Africa Protectorate from 1895 to 1900, in addition to material concerning Zanzibar and East Africa generally.

There is a full list of the contents of the Zanzibar Archives, of which a mimeographed copy is kept in the Colonial Office Library.

B. UNPUBLISHED THESES

London University (Senate House Library)

EHRLICH, C.: 'The Marketing of Cotton in Uganda, 1900–50.' Ph.D., 1958.

FEARN, H.: 'The Economic Development of the Nyanza Province of Kenya Colony, 1903–53.' Ph.D., 1953. (Since published.)

HOLLINGSWORTH, L. W.: 'Zanzibar under the Foreign Office, 1890–1913.' Ph.D., 1951. (Since published.)

HOOD, C.: 'The Agriculture of the White Highlands of Kenya.' M.A., 1958.

DE KIEWIET, M. J.: 'History of the Imperial British East Africa Company, 1876–1895.' Ph.D., 1955.

MORRIS, H. S.: 'Immigrant Indian Communities in Uganda.' Ph.D., 1963.

PARKER, M.: 'Political and Social Aspects of the Development of Municipal Government in Kenya with special reference to Nairobi.' Ph.D., 1949.

DE SOUZA, F. R. S.: 'Indians in Kenya.' M.A., 1959.

Oxford University (Rhodes House Library)

BATES, M. L.: 'Tanganyika under British Administration, 1920–1955.' D.Phil., 1957.

BEATTIE, J. H. M.: 'The Banyoro, a Social Study of an Interlacustrine Bantu People.' D.Phil., 1956.

KNOWLES, O. S.: 'Agricultural Marketing in Kenya.' B.Litt., 1955.

LOW, D. A.: 'The British and Uganda, 1862–1900.' D.Phil., 1957.

McWILLIAM, M. D.: 'The East African Tea Industry, 1920–1956.' B.Litt., 1957.

POCOCK, D. F.: 'Indians in East Africa.' D.Phil., 1955.

SORRENSON, M. P. K.: 'Land Policy, Legislation and Settlement in the East Africa Protectorate.' D.Phil., 1962.

VON CLEMM, M. F. M.: 'People of the White Mountain; the interdependence of political and economic activity amongst the Chagga in Tanganyika.' D.Phil., 1962.

Cambridge University

LONSDALE, J. M.: 'European Penetration into the Nyanza Province of Kenya, 1890–1914.' D.Phil., 1964.

Harvard University

REMOLE, R. A.: 'White Settlers, or the Foundation of European Agricultural Settlement in Kenya.' Ph.D., 1959. [Microfilm in Rhodes House Library, Oxford.]

Northwestern University

LIEBENOW, J. G.: 'Chieftainship and Local Government in Tanganyika; a study in institutional adaptation.' Ph.D., 1955.

C. BIBLIOGRAPHIES AND GUIDES

The main readily accessible bibliographies dealing specifically with East Africa are:

JONES, R. (ed.): *East Africa*, London (1961) in the *Africa Bibliography* Series published by the International African Institute. While very comprehensive in its own field, this is primarily ethnographic rather than historical.

The relevant volumes of the Ethnographic Survey published by the Institute (and listed in the appropriate sections below) also have excellent ethnographic bibliographies.

LIBRARY OF CONGRESS: *Official Publications of British East Africa*, 4 parts, Washington (1960–63).

Other compilations which will be found useful are:

ROYAL EMPIRE SOCIETY: *Subject Catalogue of the Library of the Royal Empire Society*, 4 vols., London (1930–7).

While this is no longer an accurate catalogue to the Library, which was heavily damaged during the second world war, it is still of great bibliographical value, especially for published works up to 1937.

SCHNEE, H. (ed.): *Deutsches Kolonial-Lexikon*, 3 vols., Leipzig (1920).

Apart from these published works, the current catalogues of the Colonial Office and Royal Commonwealth (formerly Empire) Society libraries in London, and of Rhodes House Library in Oxford, are invaluable.

TAYLOR MILNE, A.: Bibliography of the *Cambridge History of the British Empire*, Vol. III, *Empire and Commonwealth, 1870–1919*, pp. 769–907, Cambridge (1959).
This is particularly valuable as a guide to unpublished material.

D. PARLIAMENTARY DEBATES

References to East African affairs are widely scattered in U.K. parliamentary debates throughout the period. The main occasions on which fuller discussion regularly took place were the annual debates on the Colonial Office Vote, and sometimes on Supplementary Votes. A few of the most important of these 'Supply' debates, together with others in which specific issues of East African interest were discussed, are noted below:

Commons

13 June 1895	(Supply) Grant to the British East Africa Company on its retirement.
1 July–1 Aug. 1896	Debates on Uganda Railway Bill, &c.
3 Mar. 1898 27 Feb. 1899 10 Mar. 1899	(Supply) Sudanese mutiny; Uganda administration.
22 Mar. 1899	Debate on slavery in East Africa.
10 Apr. 1899	(Supply) Administration in Uganda or the East Africa Protectorate.
22 Feb. 1900	(Supply) Attack on Uganda administration.
19 July 1901	(Supply) Zanzibar, Uganda, East Africa Protectorate Administration.
9–11 Dec. 1902	Uganda Railway.
9–20 June 1904	(Supply) Jewish settlement in East Africa; Eliot's resignation.
28 May 1908 27 July 1909 20 July 1911	(Supply) East Africa Protectorate administration; relations with Masai.
28 July 1912	(Supply) Uganda Railway and cotton.
16 Mar.–5 Aug. 1914	East Africa Protectorate (Loans) Bill.
26 Apr. 1920	(Supply) East African currency; Kenya labour policies.
25 July 1923	(Supply) East African customs union; Voi–Taveta railway.
25 Feb.–3 Mar. 1924	(Supply) Uganda Railway; general discussion of colonial development finance.
8 Apr. 1924	Debate on proposal to send commission to report on Closer Union.
27 July 1925	(Supply) Land; labour; taxation; Uganda Railway.
29 July 1926	Debate on Dominion and Colonial Affairs; East African economic development policies.
1 Dec. 1926	Debate on Palestine and East African Loans Bill.

19 July 1927	(Supply) Closer Union.
20 Feb. 1928	(Supply) Closer Union; debate on composition of Hilton Young Commission.
11 Dec. 1929	Debate on colonial policy towards coloured races; female circumcision in Kenya.
14–22 Mar. 1932	Debate on Tanganyika and British Honduras Loans (Guarantee) Bill.
22 Apr. 1932	(Supply) Economic policy; appointment of Kenya Land Commission.
1 July 1932	(Supply) Moyne Commission's report on Kenya finance; composition of Carter Land Commission.
8 Feb. 1933	Debate on land issues raised by Kavirondo gold-mining.
14 July 1933	(Supply) Kavirondo gold-mining; Kenya income tax.
12 July 1934	(Supply) Report of Carter Land Commission in Kenya.
25 July 1935	(Supply) General government policy in Kenya.
21 Apr. 1936	Debate on future of mandated territories.
9 July 1936	(Supply) Kenya land policy.
2 June 1937	(Supply) Discussion of Kenya and Tanganyika.
7 Dec. 1938	Debate on future of mandated territories.
7 June 1939	(Supply) General discussion of colonial administration.
26 Mar. 1942	Debate on African labour in Kenya.
17 Dec. 1943	Debate on East Africa, especially Kenya.

Lords

14 Feb. ⎫ 1895 24 May ⎭	Administration, communications, development of Uganda Protectorate.
27 June 1907	1905 Land Commission Report, East Africa Protectorate.
14 July 1920	Status of Indian and Native Labour in East Africa.
20 May 1925	Report of the East Africa (Ormsby-Gore) Commission.
17 Feb. 1927	Kenya Legislative Council.
7 Dec. 1927	East African policy.
13 Mar. 1929	Report of Commission (Hilton Young) on Closer Union.
3 July ⎫ 1930 12 Nov. ⎭	Motion to appoint Joint Parliamentary Committee on Closer Union.
16 Feb. 1932	Lord Moyne's Mission (Financial) to Kenya.
4 May 1932	Kenya (Carter) Land Commission.
8 Feb. 1933	Native rights in Kenya; Kavirondo goldfields.
1 Feb. 1944	White settlement in East Africa.

E. OTHER PUBLISHED MATERIALS

I. GENERAL, AND EAST AFRICA AS A WHOLE

(a) *Official and Periodical Publications, Newspapers*

(i) U.K. Government publications

1921 Report on the Railway Systems of Kenya, Uganda and Tanganyika (F. D. Hammond).

1926 Summary of Proceedings of the Conference of Governors of the East African Dependencies.

Parliamentary Papers

[The list of Parliamentary Papers, both here and in the sections dealing with individual territories below, cannot be exhaustive. For material relating to British colonial territories in general, for instance, such as Statistical Abstracts, reference should be made to the Bibliography of Vol. III of the *Cambridge History of the British Empire*.]

1895 C. 7646 Correspondence respecting the Retirement of the Imperial British East Africa Company.

1903 Cd. 1635 Memorandum showing the Position of the Four African Protectorates under the Foreign Office.

1904 Cd. 2163   Memoranda on the State of the African Protectorates
1905 Cd. 2408   under the Foreign Office.

1910 Cd. 5192–4 Report of the Committee on Emigration from India to the Crown Colonies and Protectorates.

1916 Cd. 7875 Further Correspondence regarding Gifts of Foodstuffs and Other Supplies to His Majesty's Government from Overseas Dominions and Colonies.

1925 Cmd. 2374 Education Policy in British Tropical Africa.
      Cmd. 2387 Report of the East Africa (Ormsby-Gore) Commission.
      Cmd. 2463 Memorandum on Transport Development and Cotton-growing in East Africa.

1927 Cmd. 2904 Future Policy in regard to Eastern Africa.

1929 Cmd. 3234 Report of the (Hilton Young) Commission on Closer Union of the Dependencies in Eastern and Central Africa.

      Cmd. 3378 Report of Sir Samuel Wilson on his Visit to East Africa.

1930 Cmd. 3573 Memorandum on Native Policy in East Africa.

      Cmd. 3574 Statement of the Conclusions of His Majesty's Government in the United Kingdom as regards Closer Union in East Africa.

1931 H.C. Joint Parliamentary Committee on Closer Union in
     No. 156 East Africa. Report and Minutes of Evidence.

1932 Cmd. 4141 Correspondence arising from the Report of the Joint Committee on Closer Union in East Africa.

1933 Cmd. 4235 Report by Mr. Roger Gibb on Railway Rates and Finance in Kenya, Uganda and Tanganyika Territory, September 1932.

1934 Cmd. 4623   Report of the (Bushe) Commission of Enquiry into the Administration of Justice in Kenya, Uganda and the Tanganyika Territory.
1955 Cmd. 9475   Report of the (Dow) East Africa Royal Commission.

Colonial Reports

1931 Col. 57   Papers relating to the Question of the Closer Union of Kenya, Uganda and the Tanganyika Territory.
1937 Col. 142   Report of the Commission on Higher Education in East Africa.
1945 Col. 191   Inter-territorial Organisation in East Africa.
1946 Col. 193   Labour Conditions in East Africa (G. St. J. Orde-Browne).

Department of Overseas Trade

Reports on the Trade and Commerce of East Africa, 1923–45.

(ii) Publications in East Africa

Report of the Conference of Advisers on Native Affairs. Nairobi (1933).
East African Population Census. Nairobi (1948).
African Population of Kenya: Geographical and Tribal Studies 1948. Nairobi (1950).
African Population of Tanganyika: Geographical and Tribal Studies 1948. Nairobi (1950).

(iii) Relevant periodical publications

[This includes a selection of the main German non-official periodicals — other than missionary — dealing with colonies and with Africa. For German official periodical publications, see Tanganyika section below.]

Africa, from 1928.
African Affairs, from 1944 (formerly *Journal of the Royal African Society*).
African Standard, 1903–5 (thereafter *East African Standard*).
African Studies, from 1942 (formerly *Bantu Studies*).
African World, from 1902.
Annual Reports of the East African Board, 1924–30.
Anthropos, from 1908.
Bantu Studies, 1921–42 (thereafter *African Studies*).
Central Africa, 1883–1914 (journal of the U.M.C.A.).
Church Missionary Intelligencer, 1849–1907, thereafter—
Church Missionary Review, 1907–27.
Corona, 1949–62.
Der Tropenpflanzer, and supplements (organ of the Economic Committee of the *Deutsche Kolonialgesellschaft*), Berlin, 1897–1914.
Die Koloniale Zeitschrift, from 1913.
East Africa, 1924–35, thereafter—
East Africa and Rhodesia, from 1935.
East African Journal.

East African Standard, from 1905 (formerly *African Standard*), daily and weekly editions.

International Review of Missions, from 1912.

Journal of African Administration, 1949–61 (thereafter *Journal of Local Administration Overseas*).

Journal of the [*Royal*] *African Society,* 1901–44 (thereafter *African Affairs*).

Journal of African History, from 1960.

Journal of the [*Royal*] *Anthropological Institute,* from 1872.

Journal, and *Proceedings, of the Royal Colonial Institute,* 1869–1909 (thereafter *United Empire*).

Koloniale Rundschau.

Kolonie und Heimat (organ of the Women's Section of the *Deutsche Kolonialgesellschaft*), from 1908.

Mitteilungen aus den deutschen Schutzgebieten, 1890–1920 (thereafter incorporated in *Koloniale Rundschau*).

Petermann's Mitteilungen, from 1855.

Round Table, from 1910.

United Empire, 1910–58.

Verhandlungen des deutschen Kolonialkongresses, 1902, 1905, 1910, 1924.

Zeitschrift für Kolonialpolitik, Kolonialrecht und Kolonialwirtschaft, 1904–12 (thereafter *Koloniale Monatsblätter*).

(b) *Other Works* [select list. This includes a number of the most useful of the general works on the German colonies.]

AMERY, L. S.: *The Empire in the New Era,* London (1928).

——*My Political Life,* Vol. II, London (1953).

ANDERSON, J. N. D.: *Islamic Law in Africa,* Colonial Research Publication No. 16, London (1954).

ANKERMANN, B.: 'Ostafrika' in Schultz-Ewerth, E., and Adam, L., *Das Eingeborenenrecht,* Vol. I, Stuttgart (1929).

ATTWATER, D.: *The White Fathers in Africa,* London (1937).

BEATTIE, J. H. M.: 'Ethnographic and Sociological Research in East Africa: a review', *Africa,* xxvi. 3 (1956), 265–95.

BENSON, W.: 'Closer Union in Africa', *Journal of the African Society,* xxx (1931), 337–44.

BOVILL, *see* MATHESON.

BUELL, R. L.: *The Native Problem in Africa,* 2 vols., New York (1928).

CAMERON, D.: *The Principles of Native Administration and their Application,* Lagos (1934).

CHÉRADAME, A.: *La Colonisation et les colonies allemandes,* Paris (1905).

CHURCHILL, W. S.: *My African Journey,* London (1908).

COUPLAND, R.: *The Exploitation of East Africa, 1856–1890,* London (1939).

DÉCHARME, P.: *Compagnies et sociétés coloniales allemandes* (1903).

DENNY, *see* ROBINSON.

DUNDAS, C.: *African Crossroads,* London (1955).

FITZGERALD, W. A. A.: *Travels in the Coastlands of British East Africa and the Islands of Zanzibar and Pemba,* London (1898).

FORD, V. C. R.: *The Trade of Lake Victoria*, East African Studies No. 3, Kampala (1955).

FRANKEL, S. H.: *Capital Investment in Africa*, London (1938).

—— *The Economic Impact on Underdeveloped Countries*, Oxford (1953).

FROBENIUS, L.: *Kulturgeschichte Afrikas*, Frankfurt (1933).

GALLAGHER, *see* ROBINSON.

GIBBONS, E. J.: *African Local Government Reform: Kenya, Uganda and Eastern Nigeria*, Lagos (1949).

GOLDTHORPE, J. E.: *Outlines of East African Society*, Kampala (1958).

GREAVES, I. C.: *Modern Production among Backward Peoples*, London (1935).

GROVES, C. P.: *The Planting of Christianity in Africa*, Vol. III, 1878–1914, London (1954); Vol. IV, 1914–54, London (1958).

HAILEY, LORD: *An African Survey*, London (1938).

—— *Native Administration and Political Development in British Tropical Africa, 1940–42*, London (1944).

—— *Native Administration in the British African Territories*, Vol. I, London (1950).

—— *An African Survey, Revised 1956*, London (1957).

HALL, H. D.: *Mandates, Dependencies and Trusteeship*, London (1948).

HANCOCK, W. K.: *Survey of British Commonwealth Affairs*, Vol. I, *Problems of Nationality, 1918–1936*, London (1937); Vol. II, *Problems of Economic Policy, 1918–1939*, 2 parts. London (1940–2).

—— *Wealth of Colonies*, Oxford (1950).

HARRIES, L. P.: *Islam in East Africa*, London (1954).

HERSKOVITS, M.: *Anthropology and Cultural Change in Africa*, Pretoria (1957).

HERTSLET, E.: *The Map of Africa by Treaty*, 2 vols., London (1894); 2nd edn. (1909); 3rd edn. (1911).

HILL, M. F.: *Permanent Way*, Vol. I, *The Story of the Kenya and Uganda Railway*, Nairobi (1950); Vol. II, *The Story of the Tanganyika Railways*, Nairobi (1958).

HOYT, E.: 'Economic Sense and the East African: impressions of a visiting American economist', *Africa*, xxii. 2 (1952), 165–9.

HUNTINGFORD, G. W. B.: *The Southern Nilo-Hamites*, London (1953).

HUXLEY, J. S.: *Africa View*, London (1931).

INGHAM, K.: *A History of East Africa*, London (1962).

JACKSON, F. J.: *Early Days in East Africa*, London (1930).

JOELSON, F. S. (ed.): *Eastern Africa Today and Tomorrow*, London (1934).

JOHNSTON, H. H.: 'The East African Problem', *The Nineteenth Century and After*, lxiv (1908), 567–87.

JONES, T. J.: *Education in East Africa*, New York (1925).

KONDAPI, C.: *Indians Overseas, 1838–1949*, New Delhi (1951).

KUCZYNSKI, R. R.: *Demographic Survey of the British Colonial Empire*, Vol. II, London (1949).

LEGGETT, E. H. M.: 'The Economic Development of British East Africa and Uganda', *Journal of the Royal Society of Arts*, lxiii (1915), 209–18.

—— 'Economics and Administration in British East Africa', *United Empire*, xix. 2 (1928), 91–97.

LEUTWEIN, P. (ed.): *Dreissig Jahre deutsche Kolonialpolitik* (1914).

LIVERSAGE, V.: *Land Tenure in the Colonies*, Cambridge (1945).

LIVIE-NOBLE, F. S.: 'Closer Union in Africa', *Journal of the African Society*, xxxi. 122 (1932), 77–79.

LUGARD, F. D.: *The Dual Mandate in British Tropical Africa*, London (1922); later edns. (1923, 1926, 1929).

MAHER, C.: 'The People and the Land; some problems', *East African Agricultural Journal*, viii (1942/3), 63–69, 146–51.

MAIR, L. P.: *Native Policies in Africa*, London (1936).

—— *Primitive Government*, London (1962).

MATHESON, J. K. and BOVILL, E. W.: *East African Agriculture*, London (1950).

MEEK, C. K.: *Land Law and Custom in the Colonies*, London (1946).

MENON, K. P. S.: 'Marketing Legislation in Tanganyika, Uganda and Kenya', *The Gazette of India* Extraordinary, 24 June 1935.

MITCHELL, P.: *African Afterthoughts*, London (1954).

MOYSE-BARTLETT, H.: *The King's African Rifles*, Aldershot (1956).

NEWLYN, W. T., and ROWAN, D. C.: *Money and Banking in British Colonial Africa*, Oxford (1954).

OLDHAM, J. H.: 'The Educational Work of Missionary Societies', *Africa*, vii. 1 (1934), 47–59.

OLIVER, R.: *The Missionary Factor in East Africa*, London (1952).

ORMSBY-GORE, W. G. A.: 'The Work of the East Africa Commission', *Journal of the African Society*, xxiv. 95 (1925), 165–7.

—— 'The Meaning of "Indirect Rule"', ibid., xxxiv. 136 (1935), 283–6.

PERHAM, M.: 'Some Problems of Indirect Rule in Africa', *Journal of the Royal Society of Arts*, lxxxii (18 May 1934), 689–701.

—— and BULL, M.: *The Diaries of Lord Lugard*, London (1959).

PIM, A. W.: *The Financial and Economic History of the African Tropical Territories*, Oxford (1940).

—— *Colonial Agricultural Production: the contribution made by native peasants and by foreign enterprise*, London (1946).

PRINS, H.: *The Coastal Tribes of the North-Eastern Bantu*, Ethnographic Survey of Africa, London (1952).

RICHARDS, A. I. (ed.): *East African Chiefs: a study of political development in some Uganda and Tanganyika tribes*, London (1960).

ROBINSON, R. E., GALLAGHER, J., and DENNY, A.: *Africa and the Victorians. The official mind of Imperialism*, London (1961).

ROWAN, *see* NEWLYN.

SCHMIDT, R.: *Deutschlands Kolonien, ihre Gestaltung, Entwicklung und Hilfsquellen*, 2 vols., Berlin (1898).

SCHNEE, H. (ed.): *Deutsches Kolonial-Lexikon*, 3 vols., Leipzig (1920).

SCHRAMM, P. E.: *Deutschland und Übersee*, Berlin (1950).

SMITH, R.: 'Education in British Africa', *Journal of the African Society*, xxxi (1932), Parts I and II, pp. 54–76; Part III, pp. 133–47; Part IV, pp. 255–81.

STAHL, K. M.: *The Metropolitan Organization of British Colonial Trade*, London (1951).

STIGAND, C. H.: *The Land of Zinj . . . an account of British East Africa*, London (1913).

STOPFORD, J. G. B.: 'What Africa can do for White Men', *Journal of the African Society*, v (1902), 50–63.

TATE, H. R.: 'The Report of the Joint Select Committee on Closer Union in East Africa', ibid. xxxi. 122 (1932), 38–53.

TOWNSEND, M. E.: *The Rise and Fall of Germany's Colonial Empire, 1884–1918*, New York (1930).

WASON, J. C.: *East Africa and Uganda: or, our last land*, London (1905).

WEIGT, E. F. M.: *Europäer in Ostafrika*, Cologne (1955).

WOOLF, L.: *Empire and Commerce in Africa*, London (1920).

ZIMMERMANN, A.: *Geschichte der deutschen Kolonialpolitik*, Berlin (1914).

2. KENYA

(a) Official and Periodical Publications, Newspapers

[See also General section, especially for publications on Closer Union.]

(i) U.K. Government Publications

Parliamentary Papers

1. Annual Reports of the East Africa Protectorate. Up to 1919 these were numbered in the Command series, as follows:

Cd. 769 (1901); Cd. 1626 (1903); Cd. 2331 (1905); Cd. 2684–21 (1905); Cd. 3285–6 (1907); Cd. 3720–31 (1908); Cd. 4448–51 (1908); Cd. 4964–9 (1910); Cd. 5467–5 (1911); Cd. 6007–5 (1912); Cd. 6007–51 (1913); Cd. 8172–7 (1916); Cd. 8434 (1917); Cmd. 1–11 (1918); Cmd. 1–36 (1919). Thereafter see under *Colonial Reports* below.

2. Returns of Land Concessions in the East Africa and Uganda Protectorates, from 1903:

Cd. 1628; Cd. 2100; Cd. 2331; Cd. 2902; Cd. 3285–6; Cd. 3720–21; Cd. 4448–1; Cd. 4964–9; Cd. 5467–5; Cd. 6007–5; Cd. 6007–51.

3. Others:

1896 C. 8274	British East Africa; correspondence relating to the recent rebellion.
1898 C. 8683	Report of Sir A. Hardinge on the Condition and Progress of the East Africa Protectorate from its Establishment to 20th January 1897, with Map.
1899 C. 1925	Report by Hardinge on British East Africa Protectorate for 1897–8.
1901 Cd. 671	Report by His Majesty's Special Commissioner.
1902 Cd. 787	Report on the Agricultural Prospects of the Plateaux of the Uganda Railway.
1904 Cd. 2099	Correspondence relating to the Resignation of Sir Charles Eliot and to the Concession to the East Africa Syndicate.
1906 Cd. 2740	Reports relating to the Administration of the East Africa Protectorate ('Ainsworth's Report').

1907 H.L. No. 158   Papers relating to British East Africa.

Cd. 3561   Report on Forests in the East Africa Protectorate.

Cd. 3562   Correspondence relating to the Flogging of Natives by Certain Europeans at Nairobi.

1908 Cd. 4117   Correspondence relating to the Tenure of Land in the East Africa Protectorate.

Cd. 4122   Correspondence relating to Affairs in East Africa.

1909 Cd. 4723   Report on Forests in the East Africa Protectorate.

1911 Cd. 5584   Correspondence relating to the Masai, July 1911.

1913 Cd. 6939   Judgment of the High Court in the Case brought by the Masai Tribe against the Attorney-General of the East Africa Protectorate and Others, dated 26th May, 1913.

1920 Cmd. 873   Despatch to the Governor of the East Africa Protectorate relating to Native Labour and Papers connected therewith.

1921 Cmd. 1311   Correspondence regarding the Position of Indians in East Africa (Kenya and Uganda).

Cmd. 1509   Despatch to the Officer administering the Government of the Kenya Colony and Protectorate relating to Native Labour.

1922 Cmd. 1691   Papers relating to Native Disturbances in Kenya, March, 1922.

1923 Cmd. 1922   Indians in Kenya.

1925 Cmd. 2464   Compulsory Labour for Government Purposes in Kenya.

Cmd. 2500   Correspondence with the Government of Kenya relating to an Exchange of Lands with Lord Delamere.

1926 Cmd. 2573   Reports of Tours in the Native Reserves, and on Native Development in Kenya.

Cmd. 2629   Correspondence with the Government of Kenya relating to Lord Delamere's Acquisition of Land in Kenya.

Cmd. 2747   Return showing Crown Grants of Land of over 5,000 Acres in extent.

1930 Cmd. 3494   Report of the East Africa Guaranteed Loan Committee, 1926–29.

1932 Cmd. 4093   Report by the Financial Commissioner (Lord Moyne) on Certain Questions in Kenya.

1934 Cmd. 4556   The Kenya Land Commission (Carter) Report.

Cmd. 4580   Kenya Land Commission: Summary of Conclusions reached by His Majesty's Government.

1960 Cmd. 1030   Historical Survey of the Origins and Growth of Mau Mau (Corfield Report).

Colonial Reports

1920–45   Annual Reports for Kenya Colony.

1934 Col. 91   Kenya Land Commission: Evidence and Memoranda.

1936 Col. 116   Report of the Commission appointed to Enquire into and Report on the Financial Position and System of Taxation of Kenya (Sir A. Pim).

(ii) Kenya Government publications

[Published in East Africa unless otherwise stated.]

Kenya Legislative Council. From 17 February 1925 there is a full Hansard record of proceedings, referred to in the text as Leg. Co. *Debates*; the previous summary is footnoted as Leg. Co. *Minutes*.

Laws, Ordinances, &c., of the East Africa Protectorate and Kenya Colony. There are a number of series, and revisions, of these, which it is impossible to list in detail here. A full set is held at the Public Record Office and is listed under C.O. 630. See under Unpublished Sources above.

The East Africa Protectorate/Kenya *Official Gazette*, 1903–45.

Blue Books for the East Africa Protectorate and Kenya Colony, 1905–46.

Annual Trade Reports, 1925–45.

Departmental Annual Reports, especially—

Native Affairs Department, Agricultural Department, Education Department, Medical Department, Police, Local Government Department.

1905   Report of the Land Committee.
1910   Memoranda for Provincial and District Commissioners.
1913   Report and Evidence of the Native Labour Commission.
1917   Jubaland and the Northern Frontier District (T. S. Thomas).
1919   Final Report of the Economic Commission.
       Report of the Commission on Land Settlement.
       An Administrative and Political History of the Masai Reserve (G. R. Sandford), London, 1919.
1922   Land and Land Conditions in the Colony and Protectorate of Kenya.
       Final Reports of the Economic and Financial (Bowring) Committee, 1922–3.
1927   Report of the Labour Commission.
       Report of the Coffee Conference, held in Nairobi in June, 1927.
       Report of the (Feetham) Commission on Local Government, 1927.
1928   Report of the Advisory Committee on Land and Settlement.
1929   Report of the Agricultural (Hall) Commission.
1932   Report of the Non-native Census Enumeration in the Colony and Protectorate of Kenya on the Night of 6th March, 1931.
1933   Report of the Expenditure Advisory Committee, 1933.
1935   Report of the Economic Development Committee, 1934.
       Report of the Select Committee on Economy.
1936   Interim Report of the Committee on Agricultural Indebtedness.
1937   Report of the Meat and Livestock Enquiry Committee.
1939   Report of the Alternative Revenue Proposals Committee, 1933.
       The Settlement Committee Report.
       Report of the Committee of Inquiry into the Disturbances in Mombasa.
1943   Report of the Committee on Post-war Employment, 1943.
       Report of the Food Shortage Commission.
1945   Report on Native Tribunals (A. Phillips).
       The Kikuyu Lands (N. Humphrey).

1946   The Housing of Africans in Urban Areas of Kenya (G. C. W. Ogilvie).
1947   The Agrarian Problem in Kenya. Note by Sir Philip Mitchell, Governor of Kenya.
       The Liguru and the Land (N. Humphrey).

(iii) Other periodical publications

Journal of the Kenya Historical Society.
Kenya Weekly News.
Leader of British East Africa.

(b) *Other Works* [select list]

AARONOVITCH, S., and AARONOVITCH, K.: *Crisis in Kenya*, London (1947).
ALTRINCHAM, LORD, *see* GRIGG.
BENNETT, G.: 'The Development of Political Organizations in Kenya', *Political Studies*, v. 2 (June 1957), 113–30.
—— 'Early Procedural Developments in the Kenya Legislative Council', *Parliamentary Affairs*, x. 3 (1957), 296–307; x. 4 (1957), pp. 469–79.
——'The Eastern Boundary of Uganda in 1902', *Uganda Journal*, xxiii. 1 (1959), 69–72.
—— 'Paramountcy to Partnership: J. H. Oldham and Africa', *Africa*, xxx. 4 (1960), 356–61.
—— *Kenya: a political history*, London (1963).
—— 'Imperial Paternalism: the representation of African interests in the Kenya Legislative Council', in *Essays in Imperial Government*, ed. K. E. Robinson and A. F. Madden, Oxford (1963).
—— and ROSBERG, C. G.: *The Kenyatta Election: Kenya 1960–61*, London (1961).
BERNARDI, B.: *The Mugwe, a Failing Prophet*, London (1959).
BLIXEN, K.: *Out of Africa*, London (1937).
BOYES, J.: *The Company of Adventurers*, London (1928).
BRADFORD, E. L.: 'African Mixed Farming Economics as applied to Bukura, Nyanza Province, Kenya', *East African Agricultural Journal*, xii (1946), 74–83.
BULPETT, C. W. L. (ed.): *John Boyes, King of the Wa-Kikuyu*, London (1911).
BUXTON, M. A.: *Kenya Days*, London (1927).
CAGNOLO, C. (trans. V. M. PICK): *The Akikuyu. Their customs, traditions and folklore*, Nyeri (1933).
CHURCH, A. G.: *East Africa: a new Dominion*, London (1927).
COLQUHOUN, A. R.: 'Our East African Empire', *Proceedings of the Royal Colonial Institute*, xxxix (1907–8), 198–228.
CRANWORTH, LORD: *A Colony in the Making . . . British East Africa*, London (1912).
—— *Profit and Sport in British East Africa* (revised edn. of *A Colony in the Making*), London (1919).
—— 'Kenya Colony—her Present Progress and Future Possibilities', *United Empire*, xvii. 5 (1926), 260–9.
—— *Kenya Chronicles*, London (1939).

CRAWFORD, E. M.: *By the Equator's Snowy Peak: a record of medical missionary work and travel in British East Africa*, London (1913).

DAVIS, A., and ROBERTSON, H. J.: *Chronicles of Kenya* [fiction], London (1928).

DELAMERE, LORD: *The Grant of Land to the Zionist Congress and Land Settlement in British East Africa*, London (1903).

DILLEY, M. R.: *British Policy in Kenya Colony*, New York (1937).

DUNDAS, C.: *African Crossroads*, London (1955).

ELIOT, C.: 'The East Africa Protectorate as a European Colony', *The Nineteenth Century and After*, lvi (1904), 370–85.

—— *The East Africa Protectorate*, London (1905).

FARSON, N.: *Last Chance in Africa*, London (1949).

FEARN, H.: 'Cotton Production in the Nyanza Province of Kenya Colony, 1908–1954', *Empire Cotton Growing Review*, xxxiii. 2 (1956).

—— 'The Gold-Mining Era in Kenya Colony', *Journal of Tropical Geography*, xi (1958), 43–58.

—— *An African Economy. A study of the economic development of the Nyanza Province of Kenya, 1903–1953*, London (1961).

FITZGERALD, W. W. A.: *Travels in the Coastlands of British East Africa and the Islands of Zanzibar and Pemba*, London (1898).

FORAN, W. R.: *A Cuckoo in Kenya*, London (1936).

GOLDSMITH, F. H.: *John Ainsworth, Pioneer Kenya Administrator, 1864–1946*, London (1955).

GRAHAM, M. D.: 'Some Notes on Soil Fertility with particular reference to African Farmers', *East African Agricultural Journal*, xi (1945), 3–11.

GREGORY, J. W.: *The Foundation of British East Africa*, London (1901).

GRIGG, E. W. M. (later LORD ALTRINCHAM): *Speeches by Sir E. W. M. Grigg, 1925–1930, as Governor of Kenya Colony and High Commissioner for Transport in Kenya and Uganda*, Nairobi (n.d.).

—— 'British Policy in Kenya', *Journal of the African Society*, xxvi. 103 (1927), 193–208.

—— *Kenya's Opportunity*, London (1955).

GULLIVER, P. H.: *The Family Herds*, London (1955).

GULLIVER, PAMELA and GULLIVER, P. H.: *The Central Nilo-Hamites*, Ethnographic Survey of Africa, London (1953).

HALL, D.: 'The Native Question in Kenya', *The Nineteenth Century and After*, cvii (1930), 70–80.

HARDINGE, A. H.: *A Diplomatist in the East*, London (1928).

HILL, M. F.: *The Dual Policy in Kenya*, Nairobi (1945).

—— *Permanent Way: Vol. I, The Story of the Kenya and Uganda Railway*, Nairobi (1950).

—— *Cream Country: the story of Kenya Co-operative Creameries Limited*, Nairobi (1956).

—— *Planters' Progress: the story of coffee in Kenya*, Nairobi (1956).

HINDLIP, LORD: *British East Africa: past, present, and future*, London (1905).

HOBLEY, C. W.: *Kenya from Chartered Company to Crown Colony*, London (1929).

HOLLIS, A. C.: *The Masai: their language and folklore*, Oxford (1905).

—— *The Nandi*, Oxford (1909).

HOTCHKISS, W. R.: *Then and Now in Kenya: forty adventurous years in East Africa*, London (1937).

HUMPHREY, N.: 'The Gede Native Settlement Scheme, Kenya', *East African Agricultural Journal*, iv (1938/9), 447–50.

—— *The Kikuyu Lands*, Nairobi (1945).

—— *The Liguru and the Land*, Nairobi (1947).

HUNTINGFORD, G. B. W.: *Nandi Work and Culture*, H.M.S.O., London (1950).

—— *The Nandi of Kenya*, London (1953).

——*The Southern Nilo-Hamites*, Ethnographic Survey of Africa, London (1953).

HUXLEY, E.: *White Man's Country: Lord Delamere and the making of Kenya*, 2 vols., London (1935).

—— *Murder in Government House* [fiction], London (1937).

—— *Red Strangers* [fiction], London (1939).

—— *Settlers of Kenya*, London (1948).

—— *No Easy Way. A history of the Kenya Farmers' Association and Unga Limited*, Nairobi (1957).

—— *The Flame Trees of Thika. Memories of an African childhood*, London (1959).

—— *The Mottled Lizard*, London (1962).

—— and PERHAM, M.: *Race and Politics in Kenya*, London (1944); 2nd edn. (1956).

INGHAM, K.: 'Uganda's old Eastern Province: the transfer to East Africa Protectorate in 1902', *Uganda Journal*, xxi. 1 (1957), 41–46.

JACKSON, F. J.: *Early Days in East Africa*, London (1930).

JOHNSTON, H. H.: *The Uganda Protectorate*, 2 vols., London (1902).

KENYATTA, J.: *Facing Mount Kenya. The tribal life of the Gikuyu*, London (1938).

KNOWLES, O. S.: 'The Development of Agricultural Marketing in Kenya', *East African Economics Review*, iii. 1 (1956), 191–7.

KOINANGE, P. M.: *The People of Kenya Speak for Themselves*, Detroit (1955).

LAMBERT, H. E.: *Kikuyu Social and Political Institutions*, London (1956).

LEAKEY, L. S. B.: 'The Kikuyu Problem of the Initiation of Girls', *Journal of the Royal Anthropological Institute*, lxi (1931), 277–85.

—— *White African*, London (1937).

—— *Mau Mau and the Kikuyu*, London (1952).

LEYS, N.: *Kenya*, London (1924); 3rd edn. (1926).

—— *A Last Chance in Kenya*, London (1931).

LINDBLOM, G.: *The Akamba in British East Africa*, 2nd edn., Uppsala (1920).

LIPSCOMB, J. F.: *White Africans*, London (1955).

—— *We Built a Country*, London (1956).

LIVERSAGE, V. L.: 'Labour and Land in Native Reserves', *East African Agricultural Journal*, iii (1938), 37–42.

—— 'Some Observations on Farming Economics in Nakuru District', ibid., iv (1938), 195–204.

—— 'What is Wrong with European Agriculture in Kenya?', ibid., xi (1945), 80–81.

MAHER, C.: 'African Labour on the Farm in Kenya Colony', ibid., vii (1942), 228–35.

MAHER, C.: 'The People and the Land: some problems', *East African Agricultural Journal*, viii (1942/3), 63–69, 146–51.

MATSON, A. T.: 'Uganda's Old Eastern Province and East Africa's Federal Capital', *Uganda Journal*, xxii. 1 (1958), 43–53.

MEINERTZHAGEN, R.: *Kenya Diary, 1902–1906*, Edinburgh (1957).

MIDDLETON, J.: *The Kikuyu and Kamba of Kenya*, Ethnographic Survey of Africa, London (1953).

MILLIGAN, *see* WARD.

MOCKERIE, P. G.: *An African Speaks for his People*, London (1934).

MORRISON, G. R.: *Mixed Farming in East Africa*, London (1935).

OGOT, B. A.: 'British Administration in the Central Nyanza District of Kenya', *Journal of African History*, iv. 2 (1963), 249–74.

PANKHURST, R. K. P.: *Kenya: the history of two nations*, London (1954).

PATTERSON, J. H.: *The Man-Eaters of Tsavo*, London (1910).

PERISTIANY, J. G.: *The Social Organization of the Kipsigis*, London (1939).

PHILLIPS, A.: *Report on Native Tribunals*, Nairobi (1945).

PHILP, H. R. A.: *A New Day in Kenya*, London (1936).

PLAYNE, S. (ed.): *East Africa (British): its history, people, commerce, industries and resources*, Woking (1908–9).

PRINS, A. H. J.: *The Coastal Tribes of the North-Eastern Bantu*, Ethnographic Survey of Africa, London (1952).

—— *The Swahili Speaking Peoples of Zanzibar and the East African Coast*, Ethnographic Survey of Africa, London (1961).

RAWCLIFFE, D. H.: *The Struggle for Kenya*, London (1954).

RICHARDS, C. G.: *Archdeacon Owen of Kavirondo*, Nairobi (1947).

ROBERTSON, *see* DAVIS.

ROSBERG, *see* BENNETT.

ROSS, W. McGREGOR: *Kenya from Within*, London (1927).

ROUTLEDGE, W. S., and ROUTLEDGE, K.: *With a Prehistoric People: the Akikuyu of British East Africa*, London (1910).

SALVADORI, M.: *La Colonisation européenne au Kenya*, Paris (1938).

SANDFORD, G. R.: *An Administrative and Political History of the Masai Reserve*, London (1919).

SMART, J.: *Jubilee History of Nairobi, 1900–1950*, Nairobi (1950).

STRANGE, N. K.: *Kenya To-day*, London (1934).

THOMAS, T. S.: *Jubaland and the Northern Frontier District*, Nairobi (1917).

WAGNER, G.: *The Bantu of North Kavirondo*, Vol. I, London (1949); Vol. II, London (1956).

WARD, H. F., and MILLIGAN, J. W.: *A Handbook of British East Africa 1912–13*, London (1912).

WEDGWOOD, J. C.: 'Land Settlement in East Africa', *Contemporary Review*, 1916.

WELBOURN, F. B.: *East African Rebels*, London (1961).

WEST, R. L.: 'An Estimated Balance of Payments for Kenya, 1923–1939', *East African Economics Review*, iii. 1 (1956), 181–90.

WYMER, N. G.: *The Man from the Cape*, London (1959).

3. UGANDA

(a) Official and Periodical Publications, Newspapers

(i) U.K. Government publications

Parliamentary Papers:

1. Annual Reports of the Uganda Protectorate. From 1901 to 1904 these were published in the Command Series, as follows:
Cd. 769 (1901); Cd. 1839, 1902–3 (1904); Cd. 2250, 1903–4 (1905). Thereafter see under *Colonial Reports* below.

2. Others:

1898	C. 8718	Papers relating to Recent Events in the Uganda Protectorate.
	C. 9027	Report by Her Majesty's Commissioner in Uganda on the Recent Mutiny of the Sudanese Troops in the Protectorate.
	C. 9123	Papers relating to Recent Events in the Uganda Protectorate.
1899	C. 9232	Papers relating to Events in the Uganda Protectorate and Lieut. Col. Macdonald's Expedition.
	C. 9503	Report by Lieut. Col. Macdonald, R.E., of his Expedition from the Uganda Protectorate.
1900	Cd. 256 Cd. 361	Preliminary Report by Her Majesty's Special Commissioner on the Protectorate of Uganda; and Maps.
1901	Cd. 571	Report by the Special Commissioner on the Protectorate of Uganda.
	Cd. 590	Despatch from His Majesty's Special Commissioner in Uganda relating to Travellers in the Protectorate.
	Cd. 671	Report by His Majesty's Special Commissioner on the Protectorate of Uganda.
1908	Cd. 4358	Correspondence relating to the Famine in the Busoga District of Uganda.
	Cd. 4524	Report by the Governor on a Tour through the Eastern Province.
1909	Cd. 4910	Report on the Introduction of the Cotton Industry in the Uganda Protectorate (H. H. Bell).
1910	Cd. 4990	Uganda. Report on the Measures adopted for the Suppression of Sleeping Sickness in Uganda.
1920	Cmd. 523	Report to the Board of Trade of the Empire Cotton-Growing Committee.
1921	Cmd. 1311	Correspondence regarding the Position of Indians in East Africa (Kenya and Uganda).
1923	Cmd. 1922	Indians in Kenya.

Colonial Reports

1905–45, Annual Reports for the Uganda Protectorate.

(ii) Uganda Government publications

[Published in East Africa unless otherwise stated.]

Uganda Legislative Council, *Proceedings*, December 1939–December 1945.
(For summary of earlier proceedings, see under Unpublished Sources above.)

Laws, Ordinances, &c., of the Uganda Protectorate.
[See note under Kenya Government publications above, and C.O. 684 under Unpublished Sources.]

The Uganda *Official Gazette*, 1903–45.

Blue Books for the Uganda Protectorate, 1907–45.

Annual Trade Reports, 1925–45.

Departmental Annual Reports, especially—

Medical and Sanitary, 1919–45; Education, 1925–45; Agricultural, 1911–45; Police, 1930–45.

Uganda Provincial Commissioners' Annual Reports on Native Administration.

1907 The System of Chieftainship in Ankole.

1910 Report on Cotton in Uganda (P. H. Lamb).

1914 Report of the Committee appointed to Consider the Question of Native Settlement in Ankole, Bunyoro, Busoga and Toro (and subsequent reports of the same committee).

1919 Report of the Civil Service Commission.

1920 Report of the Development Commission.

1923 The Baganda Land-holding Question (prepared by the Bataka community).

n.d. Notes read to the Committee assembled at Kampala on 15th January 1924 to Reconsider Future Education Policy in the Uganda Protectorate (E. R. J. Hussey).

1926 Enquiry into the Grievances of the Mukama and the People of Toro.

1927 A History of Sleeping Sickness and Reclamation in Uganda.

1929 Report of the Commission of Enquiry into the Cotton Industry of Uganda.

1930 Report of the Local Government Committee.

1931 First Report of the Finance Committee.

1932 Enquiry into Land Tenure and the Kibanja System in Bunyoro, 1931: Report of the Committee.

1934 Memorandum on Departmental Policy (Medical) (W. H. Kauntze).

1936 Report of the Cotton Committee.

1937 Report on an Investigation into . . . Unskilled Labour . . . within the Uganda Protectorate.

1938 Committee of Inquiry into the Labour Situation in the Uganda Protectorate.
A History of Uganda Land and Surveys and of the Uganda Land and Survey Department (H. B. Thomas and A. E. Spencer).
Interim Report of the Uganda Cotton Commission.
The Higher College of East Africa. Proceedings of an international conference.

1939 Uganda Protectorate: Native Administration (P. E. Mitchell).
Uganda Cotton Commission Report.

1940 Report of the African Education Committee.
Native Administration in Uganda (C. Dundas).
1941 Handbook on Native Courts for the Guidance of Administrative Officers.
1945 Report of the Commission of Inquiry into the Disturbances which occurred in Uganda during January, 1945.
1947 A Development Plan for Uganda (E. B. Worthington) [revisions, 1948 and 1949].
1957 Bibliography of Land Tenure.
1958 Report of the Commission of Inquiry into the Affairs of the Bugisu Co-operative Union Limited.

(iii) Other periodical publications

Annual Reports of the British Cotton Growing Association, Manchester, 1904–45.
Annual Reports of the Empire Cotton Growing Corporation. London, 1921–45.
Ebifa mu Buganda, from 1907 (sponsored by the C.M.S.). Monthly.
Mengo Notes, 1900–1, becoming thereafter—
Uganda Notes, 1901–8 (the journal of the C.M.S.). Monthly.
The Uganda Herald, from 1912. Daily.
The Uganda Journal, Kampala, from 1934 (the journal of the Uganda Society). Quarterly.

(b) *Other Works* [select list]

APTER, D. E.: *The Political Kingdom in Uganda*, London (1961).
ASHE, R. P.: *Chronicles of Uganda*, London (1894).
BARBER, J. P.: 'The Karamoja District of Uganda; a pastoral people under colonial administration', *Journal of African History*, iii. 1 (1963), 111–26.
BEATTIE, J. H. M.: 'The Kibanja System of Land Tenure in Bunyoro, Uganda', *Journal of African Administration*, vi. 1 (1954), 18–28.
—— 'A Further Note on the Kibanja System of Land Tenure in Bunyoro, Uganda', ibid., vi. 4 (1954), 178–85.
—— *Bunyoro: an African Kingdom*, New York (1960).
BELL, H. H. J.: *Glimpses of a Governor's Life*, London (1946),
CHWA, KABAKA DAUDI: *Lwaki Sir Apolo Kagwa Katikiro w'e Buganda Yawumula*, Kampala (1928).
COLVILE, H. E.: *The Land of the Nile Springs*, London (1895).
COOK, A. R.: *Uganda Memories*, Kampala (1945).
DRIBERG, J. H.: *The Lango*, London (1923).
DUNBAR, A. R.: 'The British and Bunyoro-Kitara, 1891–1899', *Uganda Journal*, xxiv. 2 (1960), 229–41.
DUNDAS, C.: *Native Administration in Uganda*, Entebbe (1940).
EDEL, M. M.: *The Chiga of Western Uganda*, New York (1957).
EHRLICH, C. (*see also* WALKER): *The Uganda Company Limited: the first fifty years*, Kampala (1953).
FALLERS, L. A.: *Bantu Bureaucracy*, Cambridge (1956).
GALE, H. P.: *Uganda and the Mill Hill Fathers*, London (1959).

GEE, W. T.: 'Uganda's Legislative Council between the Wars', *Uganda Journal*, xxv. 1 (1961), 54–64.

GORJU, J.: *Entre le Victoria, l'Albert et l'Edouard*, Rennes (1920).

GRAY, J. M.: 'The Uganda Staff List for 1895', *Uganda Journal*, i. 1 (1934), 61–63.

HALL, J.: 'Some Aspects of Economic Development in Uganda', *African Affairs*, ii. 203 (1952), 124–32.

HARFORD-BATTERSBY, C. F.: *Pilkington of Uganda*, London (1898).

HATTERSLEY, C. W.: *The Baganda at Home*, London (1908).

HAYDON, E. S.: *Law and Justice in Buganda*, London (1960).

HUTTON, J. A.: *The Work of the British Cotton Growing Association*, Manchester (1914).

INGHAM, K.: 'British Administration in Lango District, 1907–1935', *Uganda Journal*, xix. 2 (1955), 156–68.

—— *The Making of Modern Uganda*, London (1958).

JACKSON, F. J.: *Early Days in East Africa*, London (1930).

JOHNSTON, H. H.: *The Uganda Protectorate*, 2 vols., London (1902).

JONES, G. H.: *Uganda in Transformation, 1876–1926*, C.M.S., London (1926).

KAGWA, A.: *Basekabaka b'e Buganda, Bunyoro, Toro, Ankole ne Koki*, 3rd edn., Kampala (1927).

KATATE, A. G. and KAMUGUNGUNU, L.: *Abagabe d'Ankole*, 2 vols., Kampala (1955).

LAWRANCE, J. C. D.: *The Iteso*, London (1957).

LOW, D. A.: *Religion and Society in Buganda, 1875–1900*, East African Studies No. 8, Kampala (1956).

—— 'The British and the Baganda', *International Affairs*, xxxii. 3 (1956), 308–17.

—— and PRATT, R. C.: *Buganda and British Overrule, 1900–1955: two studies*, London (1960).

LUBOGO, Y. K.: *A History of Busoga*, East African Literature Bureau, Jinja (1960).

LUGARD, F. D.: *The Rise of our East African Empire*, 2 vols., Edinburgh (1893).

MAIR, L. P.: *An African People in the Twentieth Century*, London (1934).

MITCHELL, P.: 'Indirect Rule', *Uganda Journal*, iv (1936), 101–7.

MITI, J. K.: *Obulamu bw'Omutaka*, Kampala (n.d.)

MORRIS, H. S.: 'Communal Rivalry among Indians in Uganda', *British Journal of Sociology*, viii (Dec. 1957), 306–17.

MUKHERJEE, R.: *The Problem of Uganda: a study in acculturation*, Berlin (1956).

MUKWAYA, A. B.: *Land Tenure in Buganda: present day tendencies*, East African Studies No. 1, Kampala (1953).

MULIRA, E. M. K.: *Troubled Uganda*, Fabian Colonial Bureau Pamphlet, London (1950).

NYAKATURA, J. W.: *Abakama ba Bunyoro-Kitara*, St. Justin, Canada (1947).

OLIVER, R.: *Sir Harry Johnston and the Scramble for Africa*, London (1957).

POSTLETHWAITE, J. R. P.: *I Look Back*, London (1947).

POWESLAND, P. G.: *Economic Policy and Labour: a study in Uganda's economic history*, East African Studies No. 10, Kampala (1957).

RICHARDS, A. I. (ed.): *East African Chiefs: a study of political development in some Uganda and Tanganyika tribes*, London (1960).

—— (ed.): *Economic Development and Tribal Change: a study of immigrant labour in Buganda*, Cambridge (1954).

ROBERTS, A. D.: 'The Sub-Imperialism of the Baganda', *Journal of African History*, iii. 3 (1962), 435–50.

ROSCOE, J.: *The Baganda*, London (1911).

—— *Twenty-five years in East Africa*, Cambridge (1921).

—— *The Banyankole*, Cambridge (1923).

—— *The Bakitara*, Cambridge (1923).

—— *The Bagesu*, Cambridge (1924).

SOUTHALL, A. W.: *Alur Society*, Cambridge (1956).

TAYLOR, J. V.: *The Growth of the Church in Buganda*, London (1958).

THOMAS, H. B.: 'Capax Imperii—the Story of Semei Kakunguru', *Uganda Journal*, vi. 3 (1939), 125–36.

—— and SCOTT, R.: *Uganda*, Oxford (1935).

—— and SPENCER, A. E.: *A History of Uganda Land and Surveys*, Entebbe (1938).

TOTHILL, J. D. (ed.): *Agriculture in Uganda*, Oxford (1940).

TUCKER, A. R.: *Eighteen Years in Uganda and East Africa*, 2 vols., London (1908).

WALKER, D., and EHRLICH, C.: 'Stabilisation and Development Policy in Uganda: an appraisal', *Kyklos*, xii 3 (1959), 341–53.

WELBOURN, F. B.: 'Abamalaki in Buganda, 1914–1919', *Uganda Journal*, xxi. 2 (1957), 150–1.

—— *East African Rebels*, London (1961).

WILD, J. V.: *The Story of the Uganda Agreement*, Nairobi (1950).

—— *The Uganda Mutiny, 1897*, London (1954).

WINTER, E. H.: *Bwamba Economy*, East African Studies No. 5, Kampala (1955).

WRIGLEY, C. C.: 'Buganda, an Outline Economic History', *Economic History Review*, 2nd ser., x (1957), 60–80.

—— *Crops and Wealth in Uganda*, East African Studies No. 12, Kampala (1959).

ZIMBE, B. M.: *Kabaka ne Buganda*, Katwe (1939).

4. TANGANYIKA

(a) Official and Periodical Publications, Newspapers

(i) German Government publications. [It is impossible to give within this space a full list of the official publications relating specifically to German East Africa, but the following short list of the main relevant German official periodical publications will give some preliminary guidance.]

Amtlicher Anzeiger für den Bezirk Mische, 1908–15.

Amtlicher Anzeiger für den Bezirk Aruscha, 1914.

Amtlicher Anzeiger für Deutsch-Ostafrika, Dar es Salaam, from 1900.

Amtlicher Bericht über die Kolonialausstellung, 1896, 1904.

Anzeiger für Tanga, 1902–4.

Amtsblatt für die deutschen Schutzgebiete, vols. 1–31, Berlin, 1890–1918.
Die deutschen Schutzgebiete in Afrika und in der Südsee, Official Annual Reports and Supplements, Reichs-Kolonialamt, Berlin, 1894–1914.
Deutsches Kolonialblatt, vols. 1–32, 1890–1921.
Deutsche Kolonialzeitung, vols. 1–39, 1884–1922.
Jahresberichte über die Entwicklung der deutschen Schutzgebiete in Afrika und in der Südsee, Berlin, 1895–1913.

(ii) U.K. Government publications

Parliamentary Papers

1894 C. 7582–7   Report on German Colonies in Africa and the South Pacific.

1897 C. 8649–3   Report on East Africa (Foreign Office).

1921 Cmd. 1312   Report by Sir Benjamin Robertson, 4th August, 1920, regarding the Proposed Settlement of Indian Agriculturalists in Tanganyika Territory, and Letters from the Government of India to the Secretary of State for India.

Cmd. 1428   Report on Tanganyika Territory from the Conclusion of the Armistice to the End of 1920.

1932 Cmd. 4182   Report by Sir S. Armitage-Smith on a Financial Mission to Tanganyika.

Colonial Reports

Annual Reports on Tanganyika Territory to the League of Nations, 1924–39. These are numbered in the Colonial series.

Annual Reports of the East African Agricultural Research Station, Amani, 1930–46. These are numbered in the Colonial series.

1926 Col. 19   Report of Major G. St. J. Orde-Browne, O.B.E., upon Labour in the Tanganyika Territory.

1936 Col. 113   'A Population Map of Tanganyika Territory' (C. Gillman) in *Report to the League of Nations on Tanganyika Territory for 1935*, Appendix 6, pp. 197–215.

1939 Col. 165   Memorandum on the Closing of Land in Tanganyika Territory to Alienation.

Others

1921   *A Handbook of German East Africa*, prepared by the Admiralty, Naval Intelligence Division, Geographical Section.

1941   *Military Operations: East Africa*, Vol. I, Aug. 1914–Sept. 1916, by C. Hordern and F. M. Stacke, in *History of the Great War based on Official Documents*.

(iii) League of Nations/United Nations publications

1922   Tanganyika Territory Mandate.

1921–39   *Minutes* of the Permanent Mandates Commission.

1949   *The Population of Tanganyika*, U.N. Department of Social Affairs, Lake Success, New York.

SELECT BIBLIOGRAPHY   727

(iv) Tanganyika Government publications

[Published in East Africa unless otherwise stated.]

Tanganyika Legislative Council, *Proceedings* and Sessional Papers, 1926–45.
The Tanganyika *Official Gazette*, 1919–45.
Laws, Ordinances, Proclamations, &c., of Tanganyika territory.
[Published in London up to 1923, thereafter in Dar es Salaam. See note
under Kenya Government publications above, and C.O. 735 under
Unpublished Sources.]
Blue Books for Tanganyika Territory, 1921–48.
Annual Trade Reports, 1921–48.
Departmental Annual Reports, especially—

Agriculture, 1923–45; Education, 1923–45; Labour, 1927–31, 1939–45;
Medical, 1923–45.

Reports of Provincial Commissioners, 1929–45.

1925–30 Native Administration Memoranda.
No. I. Principles of Native Administration and their Applica-
tion (2nd revised edn., 1930).
No. II. Native Courts.
No. III. Native Treasuries, (1926); 2nd edn. (1930).
1929   Report on the Development of the Rufiji and Kilombero Valleys
(London, Crown Agents).
1929–32 Land Development Survey:
First Report,   1928/29: Iringa Province (1929).
Second Report, 1930: Iringa Province (1930).
Third Report, 1929/30: Uluguru Mountains, Eastern Province
(1931).
Fourth Report, 1930: Mbulu District (1931).
Fifth Report, 1931: Eastern Province (1932).
1930   Handbook of Tanganyika (ed. G. F. Sayers).
Report of a Committee appointed by His Excellency the Gover-
nor to Submit Proposals in connexion with Land Development
and the Provision of Financial Assistance to Settlers and Planters.
(Sessional Paper No. 3).
Report on the Railway Systems of Tanganyika Territory (F. D.
Hammond), London, 1930.
1933   Memorandum on the Recruitment, Care and Employment of
Government Labour.
1934   Report on Social and Economic Conditions in the Tanga Province
(E. C. Baker).
1936   The Tribes of Tanganyika: their districts, usual dietary, and pursuits (R. C. Jerrard).
1937   Report on the Kilimanjaro Native Co-operative Union. (Sessional
Paper No. 4).
Memorandum on the Closing of Land in Tanganyika to Alienation.
1938   Report of the Committee appointed to Consider and Advise on

Questions relating to the Supply and Welfare of Native Labour in the Tanganyika Territory.

1940   Report of the Central Development Committee (G. R. Sandford).

1943   Report of the Central Education Committee.

1944   The Welfare of the African Labourer in Tanganyika (K. C. Charron).

An Outline of Post-war Development Proposals.

1946   A Ten-Year Development and Welfare Plan for Tanganyika Territory.

1956   Atlas of Tanganyika (1952); 3rd edn. (1956)

1957   Detribalization, a Study of the Areas of Tanganyika where Detribalized Persons are Living with Recommendations as to the Administrative and Other Measures required to Meet the Problems arising therein (M. J. B. Molohan).

1958   Handbook of Tanganyika (ed. J. P. Moffett).

(v) Other periodical publications

Dar es Salaam Times, 1919–26 (thereafter *Tanganyika Times*).

Das Hochland, 1930–7.

Deutsche-ostafrikanische Rundschau, 1908–12.

Deutsche-ostafrikanische Zeitung, 1899–1916 (and supplements).

Mambo Leo, up to 1962 (main Swahili publication of the Public Relations Department).

Tanga Post and East Coast Advertiser, 1919–25.

Tanganyika Notes and Records, from 1936.

Tanganyika Standard and *Tanganyika Weekly Standard*, from 1930.

Tanganyika Times, 1926–30 (thereafter *Tanganyika Standard*).

Usambara Post, 1904–16 (and supplements).

(*b*) *Other Works* (select list. A selection of the most useful of the many works dealing with the German colonies in general has been included in the General Section above. Since it is often difficult for students in English-speaking countries to track down works on the German period, the list that follows is fuller than those given for other territories).

ADAMSON, *see* CARNOCHAN.

ADOLPHI, H. (Neubearbeitet von Missionar Joh. Schanz): *Am Fusse der Bergriesen Ostafrikas. Geschichte der Leipziger Mission am Kilimandscharo und in den Nachbargebieten*, Leipzig (1912).

ALEXANDER, G.: *Tanganyika Memories*, London (1936).

ARNING, W.: *Vier Jahre Weltkrieg in Deutsch-Ostafrika*, Hanover (1919).

—— *Deutsch-Ostafrika gestern und heute*, Berlin (1936).

BECKER, A.: *Aus Deutsch-Ostafrikas Sturm-und-Drang Periode*, Halle (1911).

BEHR, H. F. VON: *Kriegsbilder aus dem Araberaufstand in Deutsch-Ostafrika*, Leipzig (1891).

BENNETT, A. L. B.: 'Short Account of the Work of the KNCU Ltd.', *East African Journal*, September 1935.

BLÖCKER, H.: *Deutsch-Ostafrika* (Tanganyika Territory und Ruanda-Urundi) *in der Weltwirtschaft*, Berlin (1928).

BLOHM, W.: *Die Nyamwezi: Land und Wirtschaft*, 3 vols., Hamburg (1931).
BOELL, L.: *Die Operationen in Ostafrika*, Hamburg (1951).
BÖSCH, FR.: *Les Banyamwezi*, Münster (1930).
BOUNIOL, J.: *The White Fathers and their Missions*, London (1929).
BRIGGS, J. H.: 'German East Africa during the War', *Journal of the African Society*, xvi. 63 (1917), 193–9.
BROOMFIELD, G. W.: *Towards Freedom* (history of the U.M.C.A.), London (1957).
BROWN, G. G., and HUTT, A. McD. B.: *Anthropology in Action; an experiment in the Iringa Province, Tanganyika Territory*, Oxford (1935).
BRUCK, W. F.: *Die Sisalkultur in Deutsch-Ostafrika*, Berlin (1913).
BURGT, J. M. VAN DER: *Un Grand peuple de l'Afrique Équatoriale* (the Warundi), Bois le Duc, Holland (1903).
BÜTTNER, K.: *Die Anfänge der deutschen Kolonialpolitik in Ostafrika* (1959).
BYATT, H.: 'Tanganyika', *Journal of the African Society*, xxiv. 93 (1924), 1–9.
BYERN, G. VON: *Deutsch-Ostafrika und seine weissen und schwarzen Bewohner*, Berlin (1913).
CALVERT, A. F.: *German East Africa*, London (1917).
CAMERON, D.: 'Position and Prospects in Tanganyika', *Journal of the African Society*, xxvi. 104 (1927), 315–22.
—— *My Tanganyika Service, and some Nigeria*, London (1939).
CANA, F. R.: 'Frontiers of German East Africa', *Geographical Journal*, xlvii. 4 (1916), 297–303.
CARNOCHAN, F. G., and ADAMSON, H. C.: *The Empire of the Snakes*, London (n.d.).
—— —— *Out of Africa*, London (1937).
CHAMBERS, G. A.: *Tanganyika's New Day*, London (1931).
CHIDZERO, B. T. G.: *Tanganyika and International Trusteeship*, London (1961).
CORY, H.: *Sukuma Law and Custom*, London (1953).
—— *The Indigenous Political System of the Sukuma and Proposals for Political Reform*, East African Studies No. 2, Nairobi (1954).
—— and HARTNOLL, M. M.: *Customary Law of the Haya Tribe*, London (1945).
CROWE, J. H. V.: *General Smuts' Campaign in East Africa*, London (1918).
CULWICK, G. M.: 'New Ways for Old in the Treatment of Adolescent African Girls', *Africa*, xii. 4 (1939), 425–32.
—— and CULWICK, A. T.: *Ubena of the Rivers*, London (1935).
—— —— 'What the Wabena think of Indirect Rule', *Journal of the Royal African Society*, xxxvi. 143 (1937), 176–93.
DALWICK ZU LICHTENFELS, E. VON: *Dernburgs amtliche Tätigkeit . . . und seine Eingeborenenpolitik in Deutsch-Ostafrika*, Berlin (1911).
DEPPE, L.: *Mit Lettow-Vorbeck durch Afrika*, Berlin (1919).
DOLBEY, R. V.: *Sketches of the East Africa Campaign*, London (1918).
DOSSER, see PEACOCK.
DOVE, K.: *Die deutschen Kolonien*, Vol. III, Ostafrika, Leipzig (1912).
DOWNES, W. B.: *With the Nigerians in German East Africa*, London (1919).
DUDBRIDGE, B. J., and GRIFFITHS, J. E. S.: 'The Development of Local

Government in Sukumaland', *Journal of African Administration*, iii. 3 (1951), 141–6.

DUNDAS, C. C. F.: *Kilimanjaro and its People*, London (1924).

—— *Asili na Habari za Wachaga*, London (1932).

FARSON, N.: *Behind God's Back*, London (1940).

FENDALL, C. P.: *The East African Force, 1915–1919*, London (1921).

FORTIE, M.: *Black and Beautiful. A life in safari land*, London (1938).

FOSBROOKE, H. A. (*see also* YOUNG): 'An Administrative Survey of the Masai Social System', *Tanganyika Notes and Records*, xxvi (1948), 1–50.

—— 'Tanganyika's Population Problem: an historical explanation', *Human Problems of British Central Africa*, no. 23 (1958), 54–58.

FÜLLEBORN, F.: *Das deutsche Njassa- und Ruvumagebiet; Land und Leute*, Berlin (1906).

GEILINGER, W.: *Der Kilimanjaro; sein Land und seine Menschen*, Bern (1930).

GILLMAN, C.: 'South-West Tanganyika Territory', *Geographical Journal*, lix. 2 (1927), 97–126.

—— 'Dar es Salaam, 1860 to 1940: a story of growth and change', *Tanganyika Notes and Records*, xx (1945), 1–23.

GORJU, J.: *Face au royaume hamite du Ruanda*, Brussels (1938).

GÖTZEN, A. VON: A. *Deutsch-Ostafrika im Aufstand 1905–6*, Berlin (1909).

GRIFFITHS, *see* DUDBRIDGE.

GULLIVER, P. H.: 'A History of the Songea Ngoni', *Tanganyika Notes and Records*, xli (1955), 16–30.

—— *Labour Migration in a Rural Economy; a study of the Ngoni and Ndendeuli of southern Tanganyika*, Kampala (1955).

—— *Land Tenure and Social Change among the Nyakyusa*, East African Studies No. 11, Kampala (1958).

GUNZERT, TH.: 'Eingeborenenverbände und -verwaltung in Deutsch-Ostafrika', *Koloniale Rundschau*, Berlin (1929).

GUTMANN, B.: *Gemeindeaufbau aus dem Evangelium*, Leipzig (1925).

—— *Das Recht der Dschagga*, Munich (1926).

—— *Die Stammeslehren der Dschagga*, 3 vols., Munich (1932–8).

HÄFLINGER, J.: *Land und Leute von Ungoni*, (1901).

HALL, R. DE Z.: 'Local Migration in Tanganyika', *African Studies*, iv. 2 (1945), 53–69.

HÄNISCH, C., SCHMIDT, J., and WALLENBERG-PACHALY, G. VON: 'Ostafrikanische Landwirtschaft', *Arb. d. Deutschen Landwirtsch. Gesellsch.*, 230, Berlin (1912).

HARVEY, *see* TEALE.

HATCHELL, G. W.: 'The British Occupation of the South-western Area of Tanganyika Territory', *Tanganyika Notes and Records*, li (1958), 131–55.

HERMAS, Y.: *Von meiner Heimat in Ostafrika*, Bethel bei Bielefeld (1953).

HIEKE, E.: *Zur Geschichte des deutschen Handels mit Ostafrika. Das hamburgische Handelshaus, Wm. O'Swald & Co., 1831–1870*, Vol. I, Hamburg (1939).

HILL, M. F.: *Permanent Way*, Vol. II, *The Story of the Tanganyika Railways*, Nairobi (1958).

HOLLIS, A. C.: *The Masai, their Language and Folklore*, Oxford (1905).

HUTT, *see* BROWN.

INGHAM, K.: 'Tanganyika in the Twenties', *Tanganyika Notes and Records*, lii. (1959), 18–30.

JAMALIDDINI, ADBUL KARIM BIN (introduction by M. Bates): *Utenzi wa Vita vya Maji-Maji*, Arusha (1957). Supplement to the *East African Swahili Committee Journal*.

JOELSON, F. S.: *The Tanganyika Territory*, London (1920).

JOHNSON, V. E.: *The Augustana Lutheran Mission of Tanganyika Territory, East Africa*, Rock Island, Illinois (1939).

KANDT, R.: *Caput Nili, eine empfindsame Reise zu den Quellen des Nils*, Berlin (1914).

KARDORFF, W. VON: *Bebel oder Peters. (Die Amtstätigkeit des Kaiserlichen Kommissars Dr. Carl Peters am Kilimanjaro, 1891–2)*, Berlin (1907).

KARSTEDT, O.: *Beiträge zur Praxis der Eingeborenenrechtssprechung in Deutsch-Ostafrika* (1912).

KAYAMBA, H. M. TH.: *African Problems*, London (1948).

—— *An African in Europe*, London (1948).

KLAMROTH, M.: *Der Islam in Deutsch-Ostafrika*, Berlin (1912).

KOHL-LARSEN, L.: *Simbo-Jaira: Kleiner grosser schwarzer Mann* (1939).

KOOTZ-KRETSCHMER, E.: *Die Safwa, ein ostafrikanischer Volksstamm in seinem Leben und Denken*, 3 vols., Berlin (1926–9).

KURTZE, B.: *Die Deutsch-ostafrikanische Gesellschaft*, Jena (1913).

LANGHELD, W.: *Zwanzig Jahre in den deutschen Kolonien*, Berlin (1909).

—— *Die afrikanischen Helden*, Berlin (1912).

LEMKE, H.: *Die Suahelizeitungen und -zeitschriften in Deutsch-Ostafrika*, Leipzig (1929).

LETCHER, O.: 'Notes on the South-western Area of "German" East Africa', *Geographical Journal*, li. 3 (1918), 164–72.

LETTOW-VORBECK, P. VON (translated from the German): *My Reminiscences of East Africa*, London (1920).

LEUBUSCHER, C.: 'Marketing Schemes for Native-grown Produce in African Territories', *Africa*, xii. 2 (1939), 163–87.

——*Tanganyika Territory: a study of economic policy under mandate*, London (1944).

LIEBENOW, J. G.: 'Responses to Planned Political Change in a Tanganyika Tribal Group', *American Political Science Review*, l (1956), 442–61.

LINDEQUIST, F. VON: *Deutsch-Ostafrika als Siedlungsgebiet*, Berlin (1912).

LOUIS, W. R.: *Ruanda-Urundi, 1884–1919*, Oxford (1963).

MACKENZIE, D. R.: *The Spirit-Ridden Konde*, London (1925).

MAERCKER, G. VON: 'Kriegführung in Ostafrika', Supplement to the *Militär-Wochenblatt*, vi (1894), 149–77.

MALCOLM, D. W.: *Sukumaland: an African people and their country*, London (1953).

MAQUET, J. J.: *Le Système des relations sociales dans le Ruanda ancien*, Tervuren (1954). [Translated as *The Premise of Inequality in Ruanda*, London (1961).]

MAYNARD, W. J.: 'Among the Wanyamwezi', *Inland Africa*, Oct. 1925.

MERENSKY, A.: *Deutsche Arbeit am Nyassa*, Berlin (1894).

METHNER, W.: *Unter drei Gouverneuren, 16 Jahre Dienst in deutschen Tropen*, Breslau (1938).

MEYER, H. (ed.): *Das deutsche Kolonialreich*, Vol. I: *Ostafrika*, Wien, (1909–10).

MNYAMPALA, M. E.: *Historia Mila na Desturi za Wagogo wa Tanganyika*, Nairobi (1954).

MOFFETT, J. P.: 'Native Courts in Tanganyika', *Journal of African Administration*, iv. 1 (1952), 17–25.

—— (ed.): *Tanganyika: a review of its resources and their development*, Dar es Salaam (1955).

—— (ed.): *Handbook of Tanganyika*, 2nd edn., Dar es Salaam (1958).

MORRIS, see SOMERVILLE.

MOST, K.: *Die wirtschaftliche Entwicklung Deutsch-Ostafrikas, 1885–1905*, Berlin (1906).

NIGMANN, E.: *Die Wahehe*, Berlin (1908).

—— *Geschichte der Kaiserlichen Schutztruppe für Deutsch-Ostafrika*, Berlin (1911).

OHM, T.: *Stammesreligion im südlichen Tanganyika-Territorium*, Köln n. Opladen (1953).

PAASCHE, H.: *Deutsch-Ostafrika*, Berlin (1906).

PALING, see SOMERVILLE.

PAUL, C.: *Die Missionen in unseren Schutzgebieten*, Vol. II: *Deutsch-Ostafrika*, Leipzig (1900).

PEACOCK, A. T., and DOSSER, D. G. M.: *The National Income of Tanganyika, 1952–54*, Colonial Research Publication No. 26, London (1958).

PERHAM, M.: 'The System of Native Administration in Tanganyika', *Africa*, iv. 3 (1931), 302–12.

PETERS, C.: *Die Gründung von Deutsch-Ostafrika*, Berlin (1906).

—— *Lebenserinnerungen*, Hamburg (1918).

PFEIFFER, H.: *Bwana Gazetti, Als Journalist in Ostafrika*, Berlin (1933).

PFRANK, C.: *Die Landarbeiterfrage in Deutsch-Ostafrika* (1919).

PLUMON, C.: *La Colonie allemande de l'Afrique Orientale*, dissertation, Rennes, (1905).

POESCHEL, H.: *Bwana Hakimu. Richterfahrten in Deutsch-Ostafrika* (1940).

PRINCE, M. VON: *Eine deutsche Frau im Innern Deutsch-Ostafrikas*, Berlin (1903).

PRINCE, T. VON: *Gegen Araber und Wahehe, 1890–1895*, Berlin (1914).

PRÜSSE, A.: *Zwanzig Jahre Ansiedler in Deutsch-Ostafrika*, Stuttgart (1929).

RAMSDEN, see SOMERVILLE.

RATHENAU, W.: 'Erwägungen über die Erschliessung des Deutsch-Ostafrikanischen Schutzgebietes' (memorandum to Dr. Dernburg, 15 November 1907, reprinted in W. Rathenau, *Reflexionen*, 1908, pp. 143–98).

RAUM, O. F.: *Chaga Childhood*, Oxford (1940).

RAUSCHER, F.: *Die Mitarbeit der einheimischen Laien am Apostolat in den Missionen der Weissen Väter*, Münster/Westfalen (1952).

RECHE, O.: *Zur Ethnographie des abflusslosen Gebietes Deutsch-Ostafrikas*, Hamburg (1914).

REDEKER, D.: *Journalismus in Deutsch-Ostafrika*, Frankfurt a. M. (1937).

REHSE, H.: *Kiziba, Land und Leute*, Stuttgart (1910).

REICHARD, P.: *Deutsch-Ostafrika. Sein Land und seine Bewohner*, Leipzig (1892).

REID, E.: *Tanganyika without Prejudice*, London (1934).

REINING, *see* RICHARDS.

REMER, O.: *Die Agrarverfassung der Bantu* (1918).

RICHARDS, A. I., and REINING, P.: 'Report on Fertility Surveys in Buganda and Buhaya, 1952', in *Culture and Human Fertility* (ed. F. Lorimer), UNESCO, Zürich (1954).

RICHTER, C. G.: *Eine Studienfahrt nach Deutsch-Ostafrika*, Breslau (1911).

RICHTER, D. J.: *Tanganyika and its Future*, London (1934).

SAMASSA, P.: *Die Besiedlung Ostafrikas* (1909).

SAYERS, G. F. (ed.) (*see also* MOFFETT): *The Handbook of Tanganyika*, London (1930).

SCHÄPPI, F. S.: *Die katholischen Missionsschulen im ehemaligen Deutsch-Ostafrika*, Zürich (1937).

SCHLOIFER, O. (ed.): *Bana Uleia. Ein Lebenswerk in Afrika*, Berlin (1939), 2nd ed. Berlin (1941).

SCHMIDT, J., *see* HÄNISCH.

SCHMIDT, R.: *Geschichte des Araberaufstandes in Ostafrika*, Frankfurt a. M. (1892).

—— *Aus kolonialer Frühzeit*, Berlin (1922).

SCHNEE, A.: *Meine Erlebnisse in Deutsch-Ostafrika während der Kriegzeit*, Leipzig (1918).

SCHNEE, H.: *Deutsch-Ostafrika im Weltkriege. Wie wir lebten und kämpften*, Leipzig (1919).

—— *Die Kolonialschuldlüge* (1924); 9th edn. (1926) [English translation *German Colonization Past and Present*, London (1926)].

SOMERVILLE, A. A., *et al.*: 'The Parliamentary Visit to Tanganyika, 1928', *Journal of the African Society*, xxviii. 110 (1929), 122–48.

STIRLING, L.: *Bush Doctor*, Westminster (1947).

STUART-WATT, E.: *Africa's Dome of Mystery* . . . *history of the Wachagga people of Kilimanjaro*, London (1930).

STUEMER, W. VON: *Die Kaiserliche Schutztruppe für Deutsch-Ostafrika*, Berlin (1937).

STUHLMANN, F.: *Handwerk und Industrie in Ostafrika*, Hamburg (1910).

SUNDKLER, B. G. M.: 'Marriage Problems in the Church in Tanganyika', *International Review of Missions*, xxxiv. 135 (1945), 253–66.

SURRIDGE, B. J.: 'Cooperation Advances', *Corona*, ix (Feb. 1957), 65–69.

SYMES, S.: *Tour of Duty*, London (1946).

TANNER, R. E. S.: 'The Sorcerer in Northern Sukumaland, Tanganyika', *Southwestern Journal of Anthropology*, xii (1956), 437–43.

TEALE, E. O., and HARVEY, S.: 'A Physiographical Map of Tanganyika Territory', *Geographical Review*, xxiii (1933), 402–13.

THURNWALD, H.: *Die schwarze Frau im Wandel Afrikas*, Stuttgart (1935).

THURNWALD, R.: *Black and White in Africa*, London (1935).

VELTEN, C.: *Safari za Wasuaheli*, Göttingen (1901) [German translation *Reiseschilderungen der Suaheli*].

WAGNER, H.: *Falsche Propheten. Gouverneur von Liebert und seine Presse*, Charlottenburg (1900).

WAGNER, J.: *Deutsch-Ostafrika, Geschichte der Gesellschaft für Deutsche Kolonisation und der Deutsch-Ostafrikanischen Gesellschaft*, 2nd edn., Munich (1895).

WALLENBERG-PACHALY, *see* HÄNISCH.

WEHLING, F.: *Die Entwicklung der deutsch-ostafrikanischen Rupie*, Münster (1929).

WEIDNER, F.: *Die Haussklaverei in Ostafrika*, Jena (1915).

WERTH, E.: *Das deutsch-ostafrikanische Küstenland und die vorgelagerten Inseln*, 2 vols., Berlin (1915).

WESTERMANN, D.: *Afrikaner erzählen ihr Leben*, Essen (1938).

WEULE, K.: *Negerleben in Ostafrika*, Leipzig (1908).

WHITE, P. H. H.: *Doctor of Tanganyika*, Eerdmans, Grand Rapids (1955).

WILSON, M.: *Good Company; a study of Nyakyusa age-villages*, Oxford (1951).

—— *The Peoples of the Nyasa-Tanganyika Corridor*, Communications from the School of African Studies, New Series No. 29, Cape Town (1958).

WRIGHT, F. C.: *African Consumers in Nyasaland and Tanganyika*, Colonial Research Publication No. 17, London (1955).

YONGOLO, W. D.: *Maisha na Desturi ya Wanyamwezi*, London (1956).

YOUNG, F. BRETT: *Marching on Tanga; with General Smuts in East Africa*, London (1919); new edn. [1938.]

YOUNG, R., and FOSBROOKE, H. A.: *Land and Politics among the Luguru of Tanganyika*, London (1960).

ZACHE, H.: *Deutsch-Ostafrika*, Berlin (1926).

5. ZANZIBAR

(a) *Official and Periodical Publications, Newspapers*

(i) U.K. Government publications

Parliamentary Papers

1. Annual Reports on the Zanzibar Protectorate. From 1912 to 1919 these were numbered in the Command Series, as follows:

(For 1912) Cd. 6665–34; (1913) Cd. 7622–14; (1914) Cd. 7622–34; (1915) Cd. 8172–12; (1916) Cd. 8434–12; (1917) Cd. 8973–22; (1918) Cmd. 1–23; (1919) Cmd. 508–35.

From 1920 onwards see under *Colonial Reports* below.

2. Slavery and the Slave Trade in East Africa and the Islands of Zanzibar and Pemba. The most relevant papers during this period are the following:

1895, C. 7707; 1896, C. 8275; 1897, C. 8394; 1900, Cd. 96; 1901, Cd. 593; 1903, Cd. 1389; 1905, Cd. 2330.

3. The Abolition of Slavery in Zanzibar and Pemba. The most relevant papers are the following:

1897, C. 8394, C. 8433; 1898, C. 8858; 1899, C. 9502; 1909, Cd. 4732.

4. Others.

1893 C. 6955 Reports on the Zanzibar Protectorate.
1895 C. 7706 Report on the Revenue and Administration of Zanzibar in 1894.
1898 C. 8701 Report on the Island of Pemba, 1896/97 (D. R. O'Sullivan).

1906 Cd. 2685 Anglo-American Convention *re* Extra-territorial Jurisdiction in Zanzibar.
1909 Cd. 4816 Despatch from His Majesty's Agent and Consul-General furnishing a Report on the Administration, Finance, and General Condition of the Zanzibar Protectorate.

Colonial Reports

1920–45 Annual Reports on the protectorate of Zanzibar.
1890–1 ⎫ Judicial Powers in Zanzibar.
1893–4 ⎭

(ii) Zanzibar Government publications

[Published in Zanzibar unless otherwise stated.]

Debates of the Legislative Council, and Papers laid before Legislative Council, from 1926.
The Zanzibar *Official Gazette*, from 1914.
Blue Books for the Zanzibar Protectorate, from 1914 (London).
Sultan's Decrees, 1908–21.
Laws, Ordinances, &c., of Zanzibar, from 1922.
[See note under Kenya Government Publications above, and C.O. 842 under Unpublished Sources.]
Annual Trade Reports, from 1928.
Administrative Reports, 1916–32.
Estimates of Revenue and Expenditure, from 1948.
Statistics of the Zanzibar Protectorate,[1] annually 1921–35.
Departmental Annual Reports, especially—
Agricultural Department, from 1900; Education Department, from 1933; Provincial Administration, from 1938; Labour Department, from 1948.
1920 Report of the Education Commission.
1923 Report of the Commission on Agriculture.
1926 Memorandum on Certain Aspects of the Zanzibar Clove Industry (G. D. Kirsopp). London, 1926.
1929 Report of the Committee appointed to Discuss the Rationalization of the Clove Industry.
1930 Statistics of the Zanzibar Protectorate, 1893–1920 (R. H. Crofton).
1932 Report of the Commission appointed by the Secretary of State for the Colonies to Consider and Report on the Financial Position and Policy of the Zanzibar Government in relation to its Economic Resources (Sir A. Pim). London, 1932.
Report on Co-operation and Certain Aspects of the Economic Condition of Agriculture in Zanzibar (C. F. Strickland). London, 1932.
Report on Clove Cultivation in the Zanzibar Protectorate (R. S. Troup).
1933 Report of a Mission appointed to Investigate the Clove Trade . . . [of Zanzibar] (C. A. Bartlett and G. D. Kirsopp). London, 1933.

[1] Statistics for 1921 published in London, otherwise in Zanzibar.

1935 Report of the Commission on Agricultural Indebtedness and Memorandum thereon by the Government of Zanzibar.
Report of the Indebtedness of the Agricultural Classes, 1933.
1936 Report of the Commission of Enquiry concerning the Riot.
Memorandum on Settlement and Regulation of Rights to Land. (Sessional Paper No. 10 of 1936).
Report on the Zanzibar Clove Industry (B. H. Binder).
1948 Revised Statements of Estimated Development and Ordinary Expenditure of the Development Departments for 1946–55.

(iii) Other periodical publications

Annual Reports of the Clove Growers' Association, from 1935.

(*b*) *Other Works* [select list]

CROFTON, R. H.: *The Old Consulate at Zanzibar*, London (1935).
—— *Zanzibar Affairs, 1914–1933*, London (1953).
FIRMINGER, W. K.: 'Protectorate of Zanzibar', *British Empire Series*, Vol. II, London, 1899, pp. 259–78.
FITZGERALD, W. W. A.: *Travels in the Coastlands of British East Africa and the Islands of Zanzibar and Pemba*, London (1898).
HARDINGE, A. H.: *A Diplomatist in the East*, London (1928).
HOLLINGSWORTH, L. W.: *Zanzibar under the Foreign Office, 1890–1913*, London (1953).
INGRAMS, W. H.: *Chronology of Genealogies of Zanzibar Rulers*, Zanzibar (1926).
—— *Zanzibar, its History and its People*, London (1931).
KINGDON, H. E.: *The Conflict of Laws in Zanzibar*, Zanzibar (1940).
LYNE, R. N.: *Zanzibar in Contemporary Times*, London (1905).
—— *An Apostle of Empire, being the Life of Sir Lloyd William Mathews, K.C.M.G.*, London (1936).
NEWMAN, H. S.: *Banana; the transition from slavery to freedom in Zanzibar and Pemba*, London (1898).
PEARCE, F. B.: *Zanzibar*, London (1920).
RODD, J. R.: *Social and Diplomatic Memories*, London (1922).
SCHEEL, J. O.: *Tanganyika und Sansibar*, Bonn (1959).
SMITH, H. MAYNARD: *Frank, Bishop of Zanzibar*, London (1926).
VAUGHAN, J. H.: *The Dual Jurisdiction in Zanzibar*, Zanzibar (1935).
WALLER, H.: *The Case of our Zanzibar Slaves. Why not liberate them?*, Westminster (1896).
WESTON, F.: *The Black Serfs of Great Britain*, Zanzibar (1920).
YOUNGHUSBAND, E.: *Glimpses of East Africa and Zanzibar*, London (1910.)

INDEX

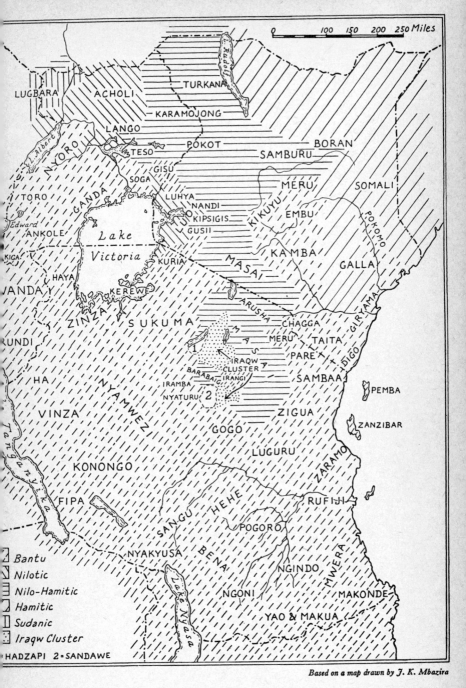

MAP 9. The main tribal groups of East Africa, showing the broad pattern of
language distribution

Based on a map drawn by J. K. Mbazira

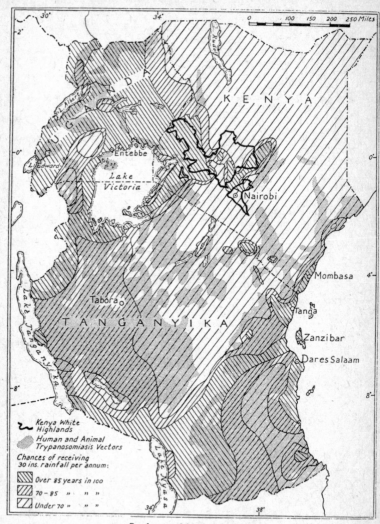

Based on material in the *East Africa Royal Commission 1953–1955 Report*

MAP 10. East Africa: tsetse fly and rainfall distribution